Closing
the Ring

★ ★ ★ ★ ★

The Second World War
★ ★ ★ ★ ★

Closing
the Ring

Winston S. Churchill

HOUGHTON MIFFLIN COMPANY BOSTON
The Riverside Press Cambridge
1951

The quotations from *Crusade in Europe*, by Dwight D. Eisenhower, copyright, 1948, by Doubleday & Company, Inc., are reprinted by courtesy of Doubleday & Company, Inc. The quotations from *Roosevelt and Hopkins* by Robert E. Sherwood are reprinted by courtesy of Harper & Brothers. The quotation from *The Struggle for Guadalcanal* by Samuel Eliot Morison is reprinted by courtesy of the Atlantic Monthly Press and Little, Brown & Company. The quotations from *I Was There* by Admiral William D. Leahy are reprinted by courtesy of the McGraw-Hill Book Company.

PRINTED IN THE UNITED STATES OF AMERICA BY
KINGSPORT PRESS, INC., KINGSPORT, TENNESSEE

★

PREFACE

IN THE *Hinge of Fate* I described the decisive change for
the better in our fortunes, which lighted the winter of 1942
and the spring of 1943. *Closing the Ring* sets forth the year of
conflict from June 1943 to June 1944. Aided by the command
of the oceans, the mastery of the U-boats, and our ever-growing
superiority in the air, the Western Allies were able to conquer
Sicily and invade Italy, with the result that Mussolini was
overthrown and the Italian nation came over to our side. Hitler
with the circle of countries he had occupied was isolated, and
with the immense onslaught of Russia from the East was completely surrounded. At the same time Japan had been forced
onto the defensive and was vainly trying to hold the vast territories she had overrun.

The danger which faced the United Nations was no longer
Defeat but Stalemate. Before them lay the formidable task of
invading the two aggressors in their home lands and liberating
from their grip the peoples they had struck down. This world-
wide problem was faced at the Conferences between Great
Britain and the United States at Quebec and Washington in
the summer, and at the Triple Meeting of the main Allies at
Teheran in November. There was between us no difference
of aim or of resolve to give all to the common cause. Grave
divergencies of method and of emphasis were inevitable be-

v

cause of the various angles from which the three partners naturally approached the decisions which were required. How agreement was reached upon all the supreme issues is the tale I now have to tell. It carries us to the liberation of Rome and to the eve of the British and American crossing of the Channel and entry into Normandy.

I have followed the method I used in earlier volumes. I do not seek to do more than make a contribution to history from the standpoint of the British Prime Minister and Minister of Defence. In this my directives, telegrams, and minutes, written at the time and not in the afterlight, are my stepping-stones. It has been suggested that the answers to many of these documents should also be included. I, on the other hand, have found it necessary in this volume to practise compression and selection in an increasing degree. A final volume is already needed to record and complete the story. I can therefore only make my excuses to any who may feel that their point of view is not fully set forth.

More than seven years have passed since the events here recorded happened. Many international relationships have changed. Deep rifts have opened between former comrades. New and perhaps darker clouds have gathered. Old foes have become friends and even allies. In this setting some of the sentiments and expressions contained in telegrams, minutes, and reports of Conferences may jar upon the readers in other countries. I can only remind them that these documents have an historical value and that we were then engaged in a fierce and terrible war. When men are fighting for their lives, they are not often disposed to be complimentary to those who are trying to kill them. On the other hand, to soften all harsh expressions about the enemy nations of those days would prevent a true picture being presented. Time and Truth are healers.

WINSTON S. CHURCHILL

CHARTWELL,
WESTERHAM, KENT,
September 1, 1951

★

ACKNOWLEDGMENTS

I MUST AGAIN ACKNOWLEDGE the assistance of those who helped
me with the previous volumes, namely, Lieutenant-General
Sir Henry Pownall, Commodore G. R. G. Allen, Colonel F. W.
Deakin, Mr. Denis Kelly, and Mr. C. C. Wood. I have also to
thank the very large number of others who have kindly read
these pages and commented upon them.

I am obliged to Air Chief Marshal Sir Guy Garrod for his
help in presenting the Air aspect.

Lord Ismay has continued to give me his aid, as have my
other friends.

I record my obligation to His Majesty's Government for
permission to reproduce the text of certain official documents
of which the Crown copyright is legally vested in the Controller
of His Majesty's Stationery Office. At the request of His
Majesty's Government, on security grounds, I have paraphrased
some of the telegrams published in this volume. These changes
have not altered in any way the sense or substance of the telegrams.

I am indebted to the Roosevelt Trust for the use they have
permitted of the President's telegrams quoted here, and also to
others who have allowed their private letters to be published.

★

Moral of the work

In War: Resolution
In Defeat: Defiance
In Victory: Magnanimity
In Peace: Good Will

★

THEME OF THE VOLUME

How
Nazi Germany was Isolated
and
Assailed on All Sides

★

CONTENTS

Book One

ITALY WON

Book Two
TEHERAN TO ROME

★

Facsimile, Maps, and Diagrams

★

Book One

ITALY WON

1

The Command of the Seas

Guadalcanal and New Guinea

EARLIER VOLUMES have led us to the point where the aggressors, both in Europe and Asia, had been driven to the defensive. Stalingrad in February 1943 marked the turn of the tide in Russia. By May all German and Italian forces in the African continent had been killed or captured. The American victories in the Coral Sea and at Midway Island a year before had stopped Japanese expansion in the Pacific Ocean. Australia and New Zealand were freed from the threat of invasion. Henceforward in Europe the Axis must expect and await the Anglo-American assault which had so long been purposed. The tremendous armies of the United States were growing in strength and quality with every month that passed. But the Western Allies could never strike home at Hitler's Europe, and thus bring the war to a decisive end, unless another major favourable change came to pass. Anglo-American "maritime power," a modern term expressing the combined strength of naval and air forces properly woven together, became supreme on and under the surface of the seas and the oceans during 1943. It was not until April and May that the

U-boats were beaten and the mastery of the life-lines across the Atlantic was finally won. Without this no amphibious operations on the enormous scale required to liberate Europe would have been possible. Soviet Russia would have been left to face Hitler's whole remaining strength while most of Europe lay in his grip.

In the Mediterranean the U-boats were also mastered. Our armies for the Sicilian and Italian campaigns were assembling and could now be launched across the sea against the under-belly of Hitler's Europe. Besides this the Mediterranean was the main artery in the communications of the British Empire. The extirpation of Axis power in North Africa opened to our convoys the direct route to Egypt, India, and Australia, pro-tected from Gibraltar to Suez by sea and air forces working from the newly won bases along the route. The long haul round the Cape, which had cost us so dear in time and effort, would soon be ended. The saving of an average of forty-five days for each convoy to the Middle East increased magnifi-cently at one stroke the fertility of our shipping.

*   *   *   *   *

The single-handed British struggle against the U-boats, the magnetic mines, and the surface raiders in the first two and a half years of the war has already been described. The long-awaited supreme event of the American Alliance which arose from the Japanese attack on Pearl Harbour seemed at first to have increased our perils at sea. In 1940 four million tons of merchant shipping were lost, and more than four million tons in 1941. In 1942, after the United States was our ally, nearly eight million tons of the augmented mass of Allied shipping had been sunk. Until the end of 1942, the U-boats sank ships faster than the Allies could build them. The foundation of all our hopes and schemes was the immense shipbuilding pro-gramme of the United States. By the beginning of 1943, the curve of new tonnage was rising sharply and losses fell. Before the end of that year, new tonnage at last surpassed losses at sea from all causes, and the second quarter saw, for the first

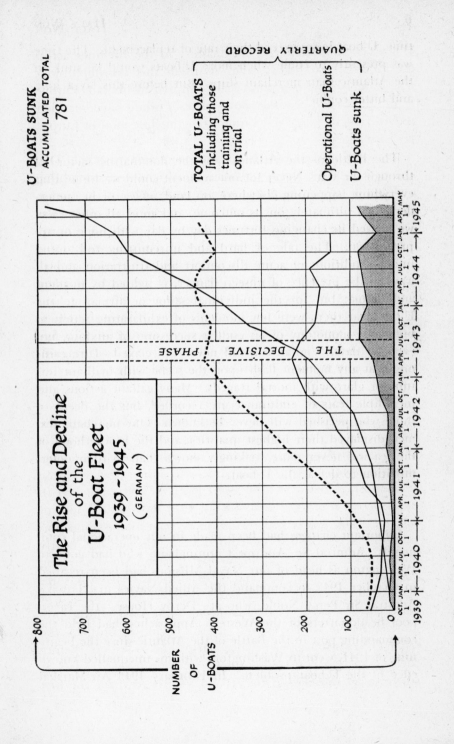

U-BOATS SUNK
ACCUMULATED TOTAL
781

QUARTERLY RECORD

TOTAL U-BOATS
Including those
training and
on trial

Operational U-Boats

U-Boats sunk

THE DECISIVE PHASE

The Rise and Decline
of the
U-Boat Fleet
1939 – 1945
(GERMAN)

NUMBER
OF
U-BOATS

800
700
600
500
400
300
200
100
0

OCT. JAN. APR. JUL. OCT. JAN. APR. JUL. OCT. JAN. APR. JUL. OCT. JAN. APR. JUL. OCT. JAN. APR. JUL. OCT. JAN. APR. MAY
1939 → | ← 1940 → | ← 1941 → | ← 1942 → | ← 1943 → | ← 1944 → | ← 1945

time, U-boat losses exceed their rate of replacement. The time was presently to come when more U-boats would be sunk in the Atlantic than merchant ships. But before this lay a long and bitter conflict.

*   *   *   *   *

The Battle of the Atlantic was the dominating factor all through the war. Never for one moment could we forget that everything happening elsewhere, on land, at sea, or in the air, depended ultimately on its outcome, and amid all other cares we viewed its changing fortunes day by day with hope or apprehension. The tale of hard and unremitting toil, often under conditions of acute discomfort and frustration and always in the presence of unseen danger, is lighted by incident and drama; but for the individual sailor or airman in the U-boat war there were few moments of exhilarating action to break the monotony of an endless succession of anxious, uneventful days. Vigilance could never be relaxed. Dire crisis might at any moment flash upon the scene with brilliant fortune or glare with mortal tragedy. Many gallant actions and incredible feats of endurance are recorded, but the deeds of those who perished will never be known. Our merchant seamen displayed their highest qualities, and the brotherhood of the sea was never more strikingly shown than in their determination to defeat the U-boat.

*   *   *   *   *

Important changes had been made in our operational commands. Admiral Sir Andrew Cunningham, who had gone to Washington as head of our Naval Mission, had been recalled in October 1942 to command the Allied Navies in "Torch." Admiral Sir Percy Noble, who at "Derby House," the Liverpool headquarters of the Western Approaches, had held the commanding post in the Battle of the Atlantic since the beginning of 1941, went to Washington, with his unequalled knowledge of the U-boat problem. In February 1943 Air-Marshal

Slessor became Chief of the Coastal Air Command. These arrangements were vindicated by the results.

The Casablanca Conference had proclaimed the defeat of the U-boats as our first objective. In March 1943 an Atlantic Convoy Conference met in Washington, under Admiral King, to pool all Allied resources in the Atlantic. This system did not amount to full unity of command. There was well-knit co-operation at all levels and complete accord at the top, but the two Allies approached the problem with differences of method. The United States had no organisation like our Coastal Command, through which on the British or reception side of the ocean air operations were controlled by a single authority. A high degree of flexibility had been attained. Formations could be rapidly switched from quiet to dangerous areas, and the command was being reinforced largely from American sources. In Washington control was exerted through a number of autonomous subordinate commands called "sea frontiers," each with its allotment of aircraft.

* * * * *

After the winter gales, which caused much damage to our escorts but also checked the U-boat attack, the month of February 1943 had shown an ugly increase in the hostile concentrations in the North Atlantic. In spite of heavy losses, the number of operational U-boats at Admiral Doenitz's disposal at the beginning of the year rose to two hundred and twelve. In March there were over a hundred of them constantly at sea, and the packs in which they hunted could no longer be evaded by skilful routeing. The issue had to be fought out by combined sea and air forces round the convoys themselves. Sinkings throughout the world rose to nearly seven hundred thousand tons in that month.

Amid these stresses a new agreement was reached in Washington whereby Britain and Canada assumed entire responsibility for convoys on the main North Atlantic route to Britain. The decisive battle with the U-boats was now fought and won. Control was vested in two joint naval and air headquarters, one at

Liverpool under a British and the other at Halifax under a Canadian admiral. Naval protection in the North Atlantic was henceforward provided by British and Canadian ships, the United States remaining responsible for their convoys to the Mediterranean and their own troop transports. In the air British, Canadian, and United States forces all complied with the day-to-day requirements of the joint commanders at Liverpool and Halifax.

The air gap in the North Atlantic southeast of Greenland was now closed by means of the very long-range (V.L.R.) Liberator squadrons based in Newfoundland and Iceland. By April a shuttle service provided daylight air-cover along the whole route. The U-boat packs were kept underwater and harried continually, while the air and surface escort of the convoys coped with the attackers. We were now strong enough to form independent flotilla groups to act like cavalry divisions, apart from all escort duties. This I had long desired to see.

*   *   *   *   *

It was at this time that the H$_2$S apparatus, described in Volume IV, page 280, of which a number had been handed over somewhat reluctantly by our Bomber Command to Coastal Command, played a notable part. The Germans had learnt how to detect the comparatively long waves used in our earlier radar, and to dive before our flyers could attack them. It was many months before they discovered how to detect the very short wave used in our new method. Hitler complained that this single invention was the ruin of the U-boat campaign. This was an exaggeration.

In the Bay of Biscay however the Anglo-American air offensive was soon to make the life of U-boats in transit almost unbearable. The rocket now fired from aircraft was so damaging that the enemy started sending the U-boats through in groups on the surface, fighting off the aircraft with gunfire in daylight. This desperate experiment was vain. In March and April 1943 twenty-seven U-boats were destroyed in the Atlantic alone, more than half by air attack.

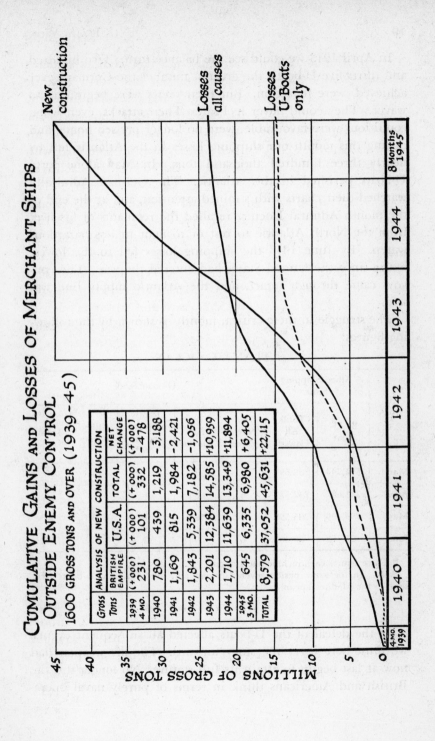

Cumulative Gains and Losses of Merchant Ships Outside Enemy Control (1939–45)
1600 Gross Tons and Over

In April 1943 we could see the balance turn. Two hundred and thirty-five U-boats, the greatest number the Germans ever achieved, were in action. But their crews were beginning to waver. They could never feel safe. Their attacks, even when conditions were favourable, were no longer pressed home, and during this month our shipping losses in the Atlantic fell by nearly three hundred thousand tons. In May alone forty U-boats perished in the Atlantic. The German Admiralty watched their charts with strained attention, and at the end of the month Admiral Doenitz recalled the remnants of his fleet from the North Atlantic to rest or to fight in less hazardous waters. By June 1943 the shipping losses fell to the lowest figure since the United States had entered the war. The convoys came through intact, and the Atlantic supply line was safe.

The struggle in these critical months is shown by the following figures:

ATLANTIC OCEAN

1943	Allied Shipping Sunk		U-boats Sunk				
	By U-boat	Total. All Causes	By Naval Forces	By Air Forces	Jointly by Naval and Air Forces	Other Causes	Total
March	514,744	538,695	4	7	—	1	12
April	241,687	252,533	6	8†	1	—	15
May	199,409	205,598	12†	18†	7	3	40
June	21,759	28,269	6	9†	2	—	17

† These figures each include one Italian.
Note. In the same period seven German and three Italian U-boats were sunk in the Mediterranean.

*   *   *   *   *

As the defeat of the U-boats affected all subsequent events, we must here carry the story forward. The air weapon had now at last begun to attain its full stature. No longer did the British and Americans think in terms of purely naval opera-

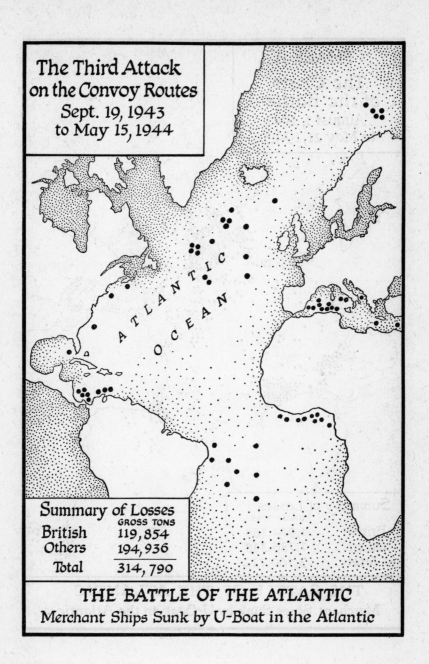

The Third Attack
on the Convoy Routes
Sept. 19, 1943
to May 15, 1944

ATLANTIC OCEAN

Summary of Losses

	GROSS TONS
British	119,854
Others	194,936
Total	314,790

THE BATTLE OF THE ATLANTIC
Merchant Ships Sunk by U-Boat in the Atlantic

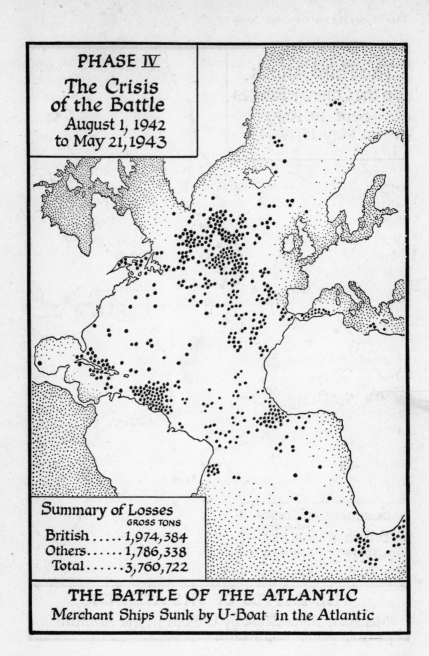

PHASE IV

The Crisis
of the Battle
August 1, 1942
to May 21, 1943

Summary of Losses
GROSS TONS
British 1,974,384
Others 1,786,338
Total 3,760,722

THE BATTLE OF THE ATLANTIC
Merchant Ships Sunk by U-Boat in the Atlantic

tions, or air operations over the sea, but only of one great
maritime organisation in which the two Services and the two
nations worked as a team, perceiving with increasing aptitude
each other's capabilities and limitations. Victory demanded
skilful and determined leadership and the highest standard of
training and technical efficiency in all ranks.

In June 1943 the beaten remnants of the U-boat fleet ceased
to attack our North Atlantic convoys, and we gained a welcome
respite. For a time the enemy's activity was dispersed over
the remote wastes of the South Atlantic and Indian Oceans,
where our defences were relatively weak but where we presented fewer targets. Our air offensive in the approaches to the
U-boat bases in the Bay of Biscay continued to gather strength.
In July, thirty-seven of them were sunk, thirty-one by air attack,
and of these nearly half were sunk in the Bay. In the last
three months of 1943, fifty-three U-boats were destroyed in
sinking only forty-seven merchant ships.

Throughout a stormy autumn the U-boats struggled vainly
to regain the ascendancy in the North Atlantic. Our combined sea and air defence was by that time so strong that they
suffered heavy losses for small results in every convoy battle.
In anti-U-boat warfare the air weapon was now an equal
partner with the surface ship. Our convoys were guarded by
more numerous and formidable surface escorts than ever
before, reinforced with escort carriers giving close and advanced
air protection. More than this, we had the means to seek out
and destroy the U-boats wherever we could find them. The
combination of support groups of carriers and escort vessels,
aided by long-range aircraft of the Coastal Command, which
now included American squadrons, proved decisive. One such
group commanded by Captain F. J. Walker, R.N., our most
outstanding U-boat killer, was responsible for the destruction
of six U-boats in a single cruise.

The so-called merchant aircraft-carrier, or M.A.C. ship,
which came out at this time, was an entirely British conception. An ordinary cargo ship or tanker was fitted with a flying-
deck for naval aircraft. While preserving its mercantile status

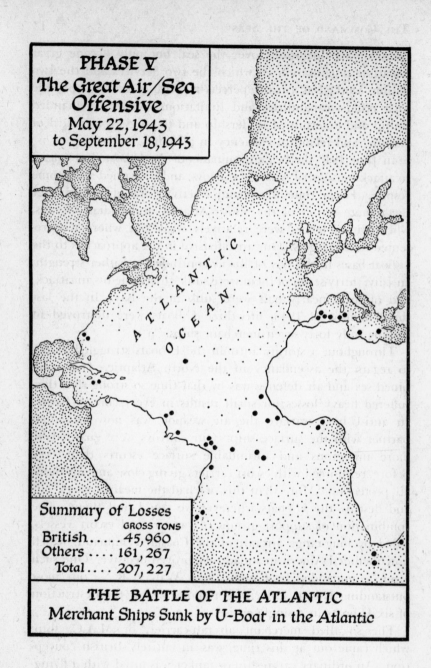

**PHASE V
The Great Air/Sea
Offensive**
May 22, 1943
to September 18, 1943

ATLANTIC OCEAN

Summary of Losses
GROSS TONS
British..... 45,960
Others 161,267
Total 207,227

THE BATTLE OF THE ATLANTIC
Merchant Ships Sunk by U-Boat in the Atlantic

and carrying cargo, it helped to defend the convoy in which it sailed. There were nineteen of these vessels in all, two wearing the Dutch flag, working in the North Atlantic. Together with the catapult-aircraft merchant ships (C.A.M.S.), which had preceded them with a rather different technique, they marked a new departure in naval warfare. The merchant ship had now taken the offensive against the enemy instead of merely defending itself when attacked. The line between the combatant and non-combatant ship, already indistinct, had almost vanished.

The immense United States war production was now reaching its peak. Long-range aircraft and ships of many types, including the escort carriers we so greatly needed, were flowing from American yards and workshops. Many of these, and much special equipment, especially radar, were placed at our disposal to help our own industry, and American naval and air forces joined in the battle everywhere.

Although in the face of the harsh facts Admiral Doenitz was forced to recoil, he continued to maintain as many U-boats at sea as ever, but their attack was blunted, and they seldom attempted to cut through our defences. He did not however despair. On January 20, 1944, he said:

The enemy has succeeded in gaining the advantage in defence. The day will come when I shall offer Churchill a first-rate submarine war. The submarine weapon has not been broken by the setbacks of 1943. On the contrary, it has become stronger. In 1944, which will be a successful but a hard year, we shall smash Britain's supply [line] with a new submarine weapon.

This confidence was not wholly unfounded. At the beginning of 1944, a gigantic effort was being made in Germany to develop a new type of U-boat which could move more quickly underwater and travel much farther. At the same time many of the older boats were withdrawn so that they could be fitted with the "Schnorkel" and work in British coastal waters. This new device enabled them to recharge their batteries while submerged with only a small tube for the intake of air remaining above the surface. Their chances of eluding detection from the air were thus improved, and it soon became evident that the Schnorkel-fitted boats were intended to dispute the passage of the English Channel whenever the Allied invasion was launched.

*   *   *   *   *

A retrospect is necessary here to remind the reader of the stirring far-flung operations which had changed the whole scene in the Far East in 1942.

While British sea-power was deployed mainly in the Atlantic and the Mediterranean, the United States was bearing almost alone the whole burden of the war against Japan. In the immense ocean spaces from India to the western coast of America itself, we could give little support except with slender Australian and New Zealand naval forces. Our depleted Eastern Fleet, now based in East Africa, could do no more for a time than protect our convoys. In the Pacific however the balance had turned. The naval superiority of the United States was re-established, and the Japanese, while trying to consolidate their gains in the East Indies, had nothing to spare for incursions into the Indian Ocean. Much had happened in the Pacific since the battles of the Coral Sea and Midway Island in the summer of 1942. Admiral Nimitz, with his headquarters at Pearl Harbour, controlled the North, Central, and South Pacific. General MacArthur, who had reached Australia from the Philippines in March 1942, commanded the Southwest Pacific, extending from the China coast to Australia, and including the Philippines, the Bismarck Archipelago, New Guinea, all the east coast of Australia, and the Solomon Islands.

The Imperial Japanese Navy, deeply conscious of defeat in the Central Pacific, turned once more to the Southwest. Here, more remote from the main sources of American power, they hoped to renew their triumphant advance. Their first thrust, towards Port Moresby, in New Guinea, having been foiled by the Battle of the Coral Sea, the enemy resolved to attack by land across the Owen Stanley Mountains. Thus began the struggle for New Guinea. Simultaneously they determined to

seize the Solomon Islands. They already held the small island
of Tulagi, and could quickly set about the construction of an
air base in the neighbouring island of Guadalcanal. With both
Port Moresby and Guadalcanal in their possession, they hoped
the Coral Sea would become a Japanese lake, bordering upon
Northeastern Australia. From Guadalcanal Japanese airmen
could reach out towards other and still more distant island
groups along the main line of sea communications between
America and New Zealand. American and Australian resistance to these two assaults form an admirable example of bold
inter-Service action resting on maritime power.

The Solomon Islands became the objective of both sides, and
Admiral King in Washington had long planned their occupation. On July 4, 1942, air reconnaissance disclosed that the
enemy were already constructing an airfield on Guadalcanal.
Admiral Ghormley, commanding the South Pacific area, without waiting to perfect his plans, struck on August 7 with the
1st Marine Division, already in New Zealand. The uncom-
pleted Japanese air base was quickly captured and the battle
for Guadalcanal began. It was to last six months.

*   *   *   *   *

From their main fleet base in the Carolines and from Raba
the Japanese could maintain greatly superior naval and
forces in these waters. The Japanese Commander in Rab
at once sent a strong force of cruisers and destroyers to Gua
canal. In the early hours of August 9, aided by heavy
squalls, the Japanese surprised the Allied naval forces gι
ing the approach to the landing-place and almost annihi
them. In about forty minutes they sank three American |
cruisers and the Australian cruiser *Canberra,* while rec(
themselves only minor damage. Had the Japanese Admiι
lowed up this remarkable success, he could have swept tʰ
the strait to the eastward and destroyed the American
ports, which were still discharging their troops and
Like other Japanese commanders before and after hiᵐ
war, he missed his opportunity and withdrew.

The American Commander could however no longer support the landing. After unloading all that he could, he retired, leaving his seventeen thousand Marines ashore alone on a hostile island without air-cover and exposed to reinforced land attack. This was indeed a grim moment. But the United States Marines were undaunted. In spite of ceaseless air attack they held and improved their position, while a supply service by sea was improvised and the captured airfield was brought into use. From this moment fighters and dive-bombers manned by the Marines worked from Guadalcanal itself and gave instant relief.

The Japanese now sought a decision at sea. On August 24, an inconclusive action was fought to the north of the Solomons. Enemy transports approaching Guadalcanal were driven off by air attack. On August 31, the *Saratoga* was damaged by a submarine, and a fortnight later the carrier *Wasp*, of Mediterranean repute, was sunk. Both sides built up their strength. Early in October, in another night engagement, a strong force of Japanese cruisers was beaten off, one being sunk; but two enemy battleships bombarded the airfield, and presently landed forty-five hundred reinforcements at a stroke. Another crisis was at hand.

* * * * *

Admiral Nimitz and General MacArthur urged, not unnaturally, that priority should be given to the Pacific theatre at the expense of European operations. They were powerfully supported at Washington by Admiral King. But the descent in Northwest Africa ("Torch") was now dominant, and major strategy prevailed. The climax of the battle on land now came. For ten days from October 19, 1942, the Marines in close jungle fighting held all their positions and beat the Japanese to a standstill. In another fleet action, mainly fought by aircraft north of the Solomons, the carrier *Hornet*, which had replaced the *Wasp*, was sunk. The carrier *Enterprise*, the battleship *South Dakota*, and two cruisers were damaged. The Japanese had two carriers disabled.

Admiral Halsey, who had succeeded Admiral Ghormley, and who found himself for the moment without any carriers, now appealed through Admiral Nimitz for one or more British carriers. Although we had little knowledge of American Pacific plans, we realised that an intense crisis had arisen in the Solomons. It was obvious that no carriers could reach the scene for many weeks. I earnestly desired to help in this heroic struggle, but with the main naval responsibility for landing the Anglo-American Army in Northwest Africa upon us we could make no immediate proposal. It was not until December that the strain and climax of "Torch" lessened. I then sent the President a full account of our carrier position and made the best offer in our power.

Former Naval Person to President Roosevelt   2 Dec. 42

Ever since we received a request for carrier reinforcement for your Pacific Fleet, we have been earnestly seeking to meet your wishes. We did not feel able to come to a decision about these very few vital units until we knew how our carriers had fared in the restricted and dangerous waters in which they had to operate for "Torch." The hazards of "Torch" are not yet ended, as our build-up of shore-based aircraft will not enable the withdrawal for some time of the two carriers now employed on "Torch." Knowing however how urgently you require a reinforcement of carriers in the Pacific, we are prepared to take a risk now and come to a decision as to what we can give you.

Our carrier strength consists of four long-endurance armoured fleet carriers. We are prepared to withdraw *Illustrious* from the Eastern Fleet, and give Admiral Somerville the *Unicorn* and an auxiliary carrier. We are also prepared to withdraw *Victorious* from the Home Fleet and to send you both *Victorious* and *Illustrious* if you can allow [your] *Ranger* [a small carrier] to join the Home Fleet. In view of the vital importance of the Atlantic communications, the necessity of supporting the North Russian convoys, the possible appearance of *Graf Zeppelin* at the end of the year, and the present condition of *Indomitable* and *Formidable*, we could not release both *Victorious* and *Illustrious* without the addition of *Ranger* to the Home Fleet.

I am much in favour of sending you two carriers rather than one

if this can be managed, as this will not only give you increased
strength, but would allow the two ships to work as a tactical unit,
which would appear to be necessary, as neither ship carries sufficient aircraft to operate singly. I would propose to send Admiral
Lyster, who is known to a good many of your officers, in command.
Both ships should proceed to Pearl Harbour, arriving about the
end of December, to adjust their complement of aircraft. If you
are in favour of this exchange, Pound will settle details with King.

Admiral King was however unwilling to spare the *Ranger,*
and in consequence we could only send the *Victorious.* She
left the Home Fleet for Pearl Harbour in December.

                    *   *   *   *   *

Meanwhile, in November a series of sea and air fights which
eventually proved decisive began around the Solomons, with
heavy losses on both sides. On the night of November 13, in
a fierce action, two United States cruisers and four destroyers
were lost, with both the American admirals engaged. On the
Japanese side a battleship and two destroyers were sunk. Eleven
Japanese transports, with strong supporting forces, were at the
same time moving towards Guadalcanal. In the thirty-six hours
of ceaseless fighting which followed, a second Japanese battleship, a cruiser, and three destroyers, and, above all, seven
transports filled with troops, were sunk, at the cost to the
Americans of only one more destroyer. The Japanese at this
point lost confidence in the venture. Ever-increasing American
reinforcements began to arrive, and the glorious Marines were
relieved by the Army. The conflict continued without pause,
but the enemy made no further bid for victory. On January 4,
1943, Imperial Headquarters in Tokyo ordered the evacuation
of Guadalcanal, which was accomplished without serious loss.
On February 9, Admiral Halsey was able at last to report that
the island had been conquered.

This episode marked the end of the Japanese offensive surge.
In six major naval engagements and many lesser encounters
two American carriers, seven cruisers, and fourteen destroyers
had been sunk, besides the Australian cruiser *Canberra.* The

Japanese losses were one carrier, two battleships, four cruisers, and eleven destroyers. The loss of life on both sides was severe, on land, at sea, and in the air. "For us who were there," writes an American eye-witness, whose moving account I have followed, "Guadalcanal is not a name but an emotion, recalling desperate fights in the air, furious night naval battles, frantic work at supply and construction, savage fighting in the sodden jungle, nights broken by screaming bombs and deafening explosions of naval shells," [1] Long may the tale be told in the great Republic.

*   *   *   *   *

The tide of war had also turned in New Guinea. The Japanese overland advance began on July 22, 1942, from the north coast towards Port Moresby, which was guarded by two brigades of the 7th Australian Division back from the Middle East. The Owen Stanley Mountains, rising to over thirteen thousand feet, form the spine of the New Guinea land mass. Through these a foot-track traverses the passes and the virgin jungle. A single Australian militia battalion fought a stubborn delaying action, and it was not until the second week of September that the five Japanese battalions employed approached Port Moresby. Here, at the Imita Ridge, the enemy advance was stayed.

While all this was in progress two thousand Japanese Marines landed from the sea and tried on August 26 to take the three air-strips being built near Milne Bay, at the southernmost tip of the great island. After a fortnight's intense fighting along the seashore, more than half of the invaders were killed and the rest dispersed. The Japanese were thenceforth thrown on the defensive in New Guinea. By trying to take both New Guinea and Guadalcanal they had lost their chance of winning either. They now had to retreat over the mountain track under close Australian ground and air pursuit. Disease and hunger took a heavy toll. The American-Australian air-power grew constantly. The United States 32d Division was

---

[1] S. E. Morison, *The Struggle for Guadalcanal.*

flown in. The Japanese convoys carrying reinforcements suffered enormous losses. Ten thousand desperate fighting men,
with their backs to the sea, held the final perimeter at Buna.
It was not till the third week of January 1943 that the last
resistance was overcome. Only a few hundred Japanese survived. More than fifteen thousand had been killed or perished
from starvation and disease. By February the southeastern end
of New Guinea, as well as Guadalcanal, was firmly in Allied
hands. A Japanese convoy of twelve transports, escorted by
ten warships, on its way to reinforce their important outpost
at Lae, was detected in the Bismarck Sea. It was attacked from
the air on March 2 and 3, and both transports and escort, carrying about fifteen thousand men, were destroyed.

*   *   *   *   *

By June 1943, when this volume opens, the prospect in the
Pacific was encouraging. The last Japanese thrusts had been
hurled back and the enemy was now everywhere on the
defensive. The Japanese were compelled to reinforce by costly
processes the positions they still held in New Guinea, especially the garrisons of Salamaua and Lae, and to build a series of
supporting airfields along the coast. The American movement
towards the Philippines began to be defined. General Mac-
Arthur was working westward along the north coast of New
Guinea, and Admiral Halsey was slowly advancing along the
island chain of the Solomons towards Rabaul. Behind all
towered up the now rapidly rising strength of the United
States. The eighteen months which had passed since Pearl
Harbour had revealed to the rulers of Japan some of the facts
and proportions they had ignored.

2

The Conquest of Sicily

July and August 1943

*Preparations for Invading Sicily — General Alexander's Final Plan
— Order of Battle — Concentration of Widespread Forces —
Hitler's Conference of May 20 — Our Seizure of Pantelleria
Island — Successful Cover Plans — The Appointed Day, July 10
— An Ugly Turn of the Weather — Serious Air Losses — Successful Seaborne Landings — Advance of the British and American Armies — Our Next Strategic Move — My Telegram to
Smuts of July 16 — Progress of the Campaign — Eisenhower
Declares for the Invasion of Italy — Discussions Between the
British and American Chiefs of Staff — General Patton's Fine
Advance — Centuripe, Catania, and Messina — Alexander's Report — Sicily Liberated in Thirty-Eight Days.*

THE CASABLANCA CONFERENCE in January decided to invade
Sicily after the capture of Tunis. This great enterprise,
known by the code-name "Husky," presented new and formidable problems. Severe resistance had not been expected in
the "Torch" landing, but now the still numerous Italian Army
might fight desperately in defence of its homeland. In any
event it would be stiffened by strong German ground and air
forces. The Italian Fleet still possessed six effective modern
battleships and might join in the battle.

General Eisenhower considered that Sicily should be attacked
only if our purpose was to clear the Mediterranean sea-route.
If our real purpose was to invade and defeat Italy, he thought
that our proper initial objectives were Sardinia and Corsica,
"since these islands lie on the flank of the long Italian boot

and would force a very much greater dispersion of enemy
strength in Italy than the mere occupation of Sicily, which lies
off the mountainous toe of the peninsula." [1] This was no doubt
a military opinion of high authority, though one I could not
share. But political forces play their part, and the capture of
Sicily and the direct invasion of Italy were to bring about
results of a far more swift and far-reaching character.

The capture of Sicily was an undertaking of the first magnitude. Although eclipsed by events in Normandy, its importance and its difficulties should not be underrated. The landing was based on the experience gained in "Torch," and those
who planned "Overlord" learned much from "Husky." In the
initial assault nearly 3000 ships and landing-craft took part, carrying between them 160,000 men, 14,000 vehicles, 600 tanks, and
1800 guns. These forces had to be collected, trained, equipped,
and eventually embarked, with all the vast impedimenta of
amphibious warfare, at widely dispersed bases in the Mediterranean, in Great Britain, and in the United States. Detailed
planning was required from subordinate commanders whose
headquarters were separated by thousands of miles. All these
plans had to be welded together by the Supreme Commander
at Algiers. Here a special Allied Staff controlled and co-ordinated all preparations. As the plan developed, many problems
arose which could only be solved by the Combined Chiefs of
Staff. Finally, the convoys had to be assembled, escorted across
the oceans and through the narrow seas, and concentrated in
the battle area at the right time.

* * * *

Planning at General Eisenhower's Headquarters had begun
in February. It now became necessary to appoint his principal
subordinates.

In all wars where allies are fighting together the control of
strategy usually rests in the main with whoever holds the
larger forces. This may be modified by political considerations or the relative war effort in other theatres, but the prin-

[1] *Crusade in Europe*, chapter IX, page 159.

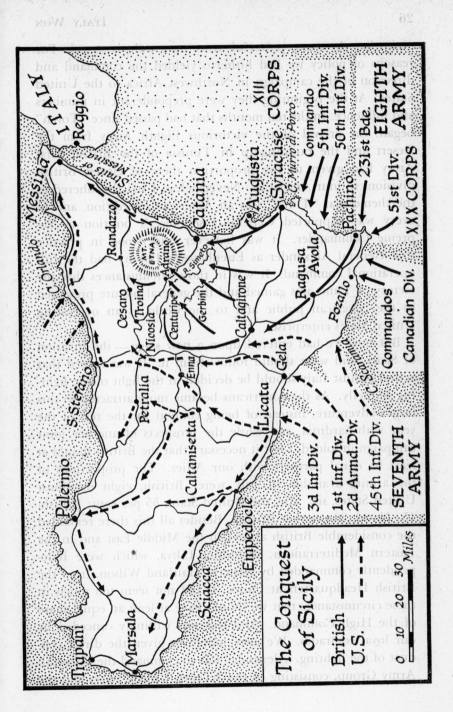

The Conquest
of Sicily

British ----
U.S. ------

0 10 20 30
Miles

ITALY

Reggio

C. Orlando

Messina

Straits of
Messina

Randazzo

MT.
ETNA

Adrano

R. Simeto

Catania

Augusta

Syracuse
C. Murro di Porco

XIII
CORPS

EIGHTH
ARMY

Commando
5th Inf. Div.
50th Inf. Div.

231st Bde.

Pachino

51st Div.
XXX CORPS

Avola

Ragusa

Canadian Div.

Commandos

C. Scaramia

Pozallo

Cesaro

Troina

Nicosia

Centuripe

Gerbini

Caltagirone

S. Stefano

Petralia

Enna

Gela

Licata

Caltanisetta

Palermo

Empedocle

Sciacca

45th Inf. Div.
2d Armd. Div.
1st Inf. Div.
3d Inf. Div.

SEVENTH
ARMY

Marsala

Trapani

ciple that the more powerful army must rule is sound. For
reasons of policy we had hitherto yielded the command and
direction of the campaign in Northwest Africa to the United
States. At the beginning they were preponderant in numbers
and influence. In the ten months that had passed since "Torch"
began, the arrival of the victorious Eighth Army from the
Desert and the building-up in Tunisia of the British First
Army had given us the proportion there of eleven British
divisions to four American. Nevertheless, I strictly adhered to
the theme that "Torch" was an American expedition, and in
every way supported General Eisenhower's position as Supreme Commander. It was however understood in practice
that General Alexander as Eisenhower's Deputy had the full
operational command. It was in those circumstances that the
victory of Tunis was gained and the general picture presented
to the American public and to the world as an overriding
United States enterprise.

But now we had entered upon a new stage — the invasion
of Sicily, and what should follow from it. It was agreed that
action against Italy should be decided in the light of the fighting in Sicily. As the Americans became more attracted to this
larger adventure, instead of being content for the rest of the
year with Sardinia, and while the prospects of another joint
campaign unfolded, I felt it necessary that the British should at
least be equal partners with our Allies. The proportions of
the armies available in July were: British, eight divisions;
United States, six. Air, the United States 55 per cent; British,
45. Naval, 80 per cent British. Besides all this there remained
the considerable British armies in the Middle East and in the
Eastern Mediterranean, including Libya, which were independently commanded by General Maitland Wilson, from the
British Headquarters at Cairo. It did not seem too much in
these circumstances that we should have at least an equal share
of the High Command. And this was willingly conceded by
our loyal comrades. We were moreover given the direct conduct of the fighting. Alexander was to command the Fifteenth
Army Group, consisting of the Seventh United States and the

Eighth British Armies. Air Chief Marshal Tedder commanded the Allied Air Force, and Admiral Cunningham the Allied naval forces. The whole was under the over-all command of General Eisenhower.

The British assault was entrusted to General Montgomery and his Eighth Army, while General Patton was nominated to command the United States Seventh Army. The naval collaborators were Admiral Ramsay, who had planned the British landings in "Torch," and Admiral Hewitt, U.S.N., who with General Patton had carried out the Casablanca landing. In the air the chief commanders under Air Chief Marshal Tedder were General Spaatz, United States Army Air Force, and Air Marshal Coningham, while the air operations in conjunction with the Eighth Army were in the hands of Air Vice-Marshal Broadhurst, who had recently added to the fame of the Western Desert Air Force.

The plan and the troops were at first considered only on a tentative basis, as the fighting in Tunisia was still absorbing the attention of commanders and staffs, and it was not until April that we could tell what troops would be fit to take part. The major need was the early capture of ports and airfields to maintain the armies after the landings. Palermo, Catania, and Syracuse were suitable, but Messina, the best port of all, was beyond our reach. There were three main groups of airfields at the southeast corner of the island, in the Catania plain, and in the western portion of the island.[2]

Air Chief Marshal Tedder argued that we must narrow the attack, capture the southeastern group of airfields, and seize Catania and Palermo later on. This meant that for some time only the small ports of Syracuse, Augusta, and Licata were likely to be available, and the armies would have to be supplied over the open beaches. This was successful, largely because of the new amphibious load-carrier, the American "D.U.K.W.," and even more the "landing-ship tank" (L.S.T.). This type of vessel had first been conceived and developed in Britain in 1940. A new design, based on British experience,

2 See map, "Conquest of Sicily," page 25.

was thereafter built in large numbers in the United States and
was first used in Sicily. It became the foundation of all our
future amphibious operations and was often their limiting
factor.

*   *   *   *   *

General Alexander's final plan prescribed a week's preliminary bombardment to neutralise the enemy's navy and air. The
British Eighth Army, under General Montgomery, was to
assault between Cape Murro di Porco and Pozzallo and capture
Syracuse and the Pachino airfield. Having established a firm
bridgehead and gained touch with the United States forces on
its left, it was to thrust northward to Augusta, Catania, and
the Gerbini airfields. The United States Seventh Army, under
General Patton, was to land between Cape Scaramia and
Licata, and to capture the latter port and a group of airfields
north and east of Gela. It was to protect the flank of the
Eighth Army at Ragusa in its forward drive. Strong British
and United States airborne troops were to be dropped by parachute or landed by glider beyond the beachheads to seize key
points and aid the landings.

The Eighth Army comprised seven divisions, with an infantry brigade from the Malta garrison, two armoured brigades, and Commandos. The United States Seventh Army had
six divisions under its command.[3] The enemy garrison in
Sicily, at first under an Italian general, consisted of two German divisions, one of them armoured, four Italian infantry
divisions, and six Italian coast-defence divisions of low quality.
The German divisions were split up into battle groups, to

[3] Order of battle:
EIGHTH ARMY, Headquarters XIIIth and XXXth Corps.
    In the first assault: 1st Canadian 5th, 50th, 51st, Divisions; part of 1st Air-
borne Division, 231st Infantry Brigade, 4th and 23d Armoured Brigades, and
three Commandos.
    In reserve in North Africa: 78th, 46th Divisions; remainder of 1st Airborne
Division.
U.S. SEVENTH ARMY, Headquarters IId Corps.
    In the first assault: 1st, 3d, 45th Divisions, 2d Armoured Division; part of
82d Airborne Division, 1st Battalion Rangers (Commando).
    In reserve in North Africa: 9th Division, remainder of 82d Airborne Division.

stiffen their allies and to counter-attack. Misreading our intentions, the enemy held the western end of the island in considerable strength. In the air our superiority was marked. Against more than 4000 operational aircraft (121 British and 146 United States squadrons) the enemy could muster in Sicily, Sardinia, Italy, and Southern France only 1850 machines.

Provided therefore that there were no mishaps in assembling and landing the troops, the prospects seemed good. The naval and military forces were however widely dispersed. The 1st Canadian Division came direct from Britain and one American division from the United States, staging only at Oran. The forces already in the Mediterranean were spread throughout North Africa. General Dempsey's XIIIth Corps was training partly in Egypt and partly in Syria, and their ships and landing-craft would have to load not only in the Canal area and Alexandria, but at various small ports between Beirut and Tripoli. General Leese's XXXth Corps, composed of the 1st Canadian Division in England, the 51st Division in Tunisia, and the independent 231st Brigade from Malta, would concentrate for the first time on the battlefield. American troops were similarly spread throughout Tunisia, Algeria, and beyond the Atlantic.

Subordinate commanders and Staff officers had to cover great distances by air to keep in touch with developments in the plan and to supervise the training of their units. Their frequent absence on such missions added to the burdens of the planners. Training exercises afloat were mounted in the United Kingdom and throughout the Mediterranean and the Red Sea. In the Middle East vital craft and equipment had as yet arrived only in token quantities, or not at all. All this material had in the preparatory stages to be taken on trust and included in the plan without trial. In the event nearly all the promises of the supply departments were fulfilled. In spite of many anxieties the plan went forward smoothly, and proved a remarkable example of joint Staff work.

*   *   *   *   *

On May 20, Hitler held a conference at which Keitel, Rommel, Neurath, the Foreign Secretary, and several others were present. The American translations of the secret records of this and other German conferences are taken from the manuscript in the University of Pennsylvania Library, annotated by Mr. Felix Gilbert. They are a valuable contribution to the story of the war.

Hitler: You were in Sicily?

Neurath: Yes, my Fuehrer, I was down there, and I spoke to General Roatta [Commander of the Italian Sixth Army in Sicily]. Among other things he told me that he did not have too much confidence in the defence of Sicily. He claimed that he is too weak, and that his troops are not properly equipped. Above all, he has only one motorised division; the rest are immobile. Every day the English do their best to shoot up the locomotives of the Sicilian railroads, for they know very well that it is almost impossible to bring up material to replace or repair them, or not possible at all. The impression I gained on the crossing from Giovanni to Messina was that almost all traffic on this short stretch is at a virtual standstill. Of the ferries there — I think there were six — only one remains. This one was being treated as a museum piece; it was said that it was being saved for better purposes.

Hitler: What are the "better purposes"?

Neurath: Well, my Fuehrer, sometimes the Italians explain, "When the war is over"; others say, "You never know what's going to happen next."

The German troops in Sicily have undoubtedly become rather unpopular. That can be explained very easily, because the Sicilians hold the view that we have brought the war to their country. First, we have eaten up everything they had, and now we are going to cause the English to come themselves, although — and I must emphasise this — the Sicilian peasant really wouldn't mind that. He thinks that this will end his suffering. The general opinion all over Southern Italy is that the war will be over when the English come, and that the presence of the Germans just delays this.

Hitler: What is the Italian Government doing to counter this attitude?

Neurath: My Fuehrer, as far as I know the prefects and officials who are still around are not doing much about it. Whenever I directed their attention to it and complained that German soldiers were being cursed in the streets, I was told that they didn't know what to do about it, since this represented the popular view. They said, "That's how the people feel; you have made yourselves unpopular; you have requisitioned things and eaten up all our chickens." But I do think that the officials could make more of an effort, and make examples of the more flagrant cases.

Hitler: They won't take action?

Neurath: It is very difficult. They just won't take action. The Sicilian temperament is different from the North Italian. But on the whole it is very unpleasant to see how they let things slide.

The threat to Sicily from the enemy air is extremely strong.

The discussion then turned on the fidelity of General Roatta and other Italian leaders, and the increasingly difficult position of Mussolini. Altogether a very disquieting picture was presented to the Fuehrer.

*　　*　　*　　*　　*

In the channel between Tunisia and Sicily lay the small island of Pantelleria, which served as an enemy base for aircraft and E-boats. In January 1941 we had planned to assault and capture it, but the opportunity passed and it remained a thorn in our side throughout the hardest period of the siege of Malta. Now it became necessary, not only to subdue it, but to use it ourselves for our fighter aircraft. Attacks by air and sea began immediately after the fall of Tunis. Bombardment continued until June 8, when unconditional surrender was demanded. This being refused, a landing from the sea was carried out on June 11, supported by heavy naval and air bombardment. Much had been made beforehand of the magnitude and perils of this enterprise. It was entirely successful, with no casualties except, according to sailors' stories, one soldier bitten by a mule. Over eleven thousand prisoners fell into our hands. During the next two days the neighbouring islands of Lampedusa and Linosa also capitulated, the former to the pilot of an aircraft who had been compelled to land by lack of fuel. No enemy outpost now remained south of Sicily.

*　　*　　*　　*　　*

Intense air attack upon Sicily began on July 3 with the bombing of airfields both there and in Sardinia, which made many unusable. The enemy fighters were thrown onto the defensive and their long-range bombers forced to withdraw their bases to the Italian mainland. Four of the five train ferries operating across the Straits of Messina were sunk. By the time our convoys were approaching the island, air superiority was firmly established, and Axis warships and aircraft made no serious effort to interfere with the seaborne assault. By our cover plans, the enemy were kept in doubt until the last moment where our stroke would fall. Our naval movements and military preparations in Egypt suggested an expedition to Greece. Since the fall of Tunis, they had sent more planes to the Mediterranean, but the additional squadrons had gone, not to Sicily, but to the Eastern Mediterranean, Northwest Italy, and Sardinia. In the critical period while the convoys were approaching their target, General Eisenhower established his Headquarters in Malta, where communications were excellent. Here he was joined by General Alexander and Admiral Cunningham. Air Chief Marshal Tedder remained near Carthage to control the combined air operations.

July 10 was the appointed day. On the morning of July 9, the great armadas from east and west were converging south of Malta, and it was time for all to steam for the beaches of Sicily. Admiral Cunningham says in his dispatch:

The only incidents which occurred to mar the precision of this remarkable concentration were the loss by U-boat attack of three ships in convoy. The passage of the convoys was covered most effectively; the majority were not sighted by enemy aircraft.

On my way to Chequers, where I was to await the result, I spent an hour in the Admiralty War Room. The map covered an entire wall and showed the enormous convoys, escorts, and supporting detachments moving towards their assault beaches. This was the greatest amphibious operation so far attempted in history. But all depended on the weather.

*   *   *   *   *

The morning of the 9th was fine, but by noon a fresh and unseasonable northwest wind sprang up. During the afternoon the wind increased, and by evening there was a heavy swell, which would make landings hazardous, particularly on the western beaches in the American sector. The landing-craft convoys, plunging northward from Malta and from many African ports between Bizerta and Benghazi, were having a rough voyage.

Arrangements had been made for postponing the landing in case of necessity, but a decision would have to be taken not later than noon. Watching anxiously from the Admiralty, the First Sea Lord inquired by signal about the weather conditions. Admiral Cunningham replied at 8 P.M., "Weather not favourable, but operation proceeding." "It was," he says, "manifestly too late for postponement, but considerable anxiety was felt, particularly for the small-craft convoys making up against the sea." They were indeed much delayed and became scattered. Many ships arrived late, but fortunately no great harm resulted. "The wind," says Cunningham, "mercifully eased during the night, and by the morning of the 10th had ceased, leaving only a tiresome swell and surf on the western beaches."

The bad weather helped to give us surprise. Admiral Cunningham continues:

The very efficient cover plan and the deceptive routeing of convoys played their part. In addition the vigilance of the enemy was undoubtedly relaxed owing to the unfavourable phase of the moon. Finally came this wind, dangerously close at the time to making some, if not all, the landings impracticable. These apparently unfavourable factors had actually the effect of making the weary Italians, who had been alert for many nights, turn thankfully in their beds, saying, "Tonight at any rate they can't come." BUT THEY CAME.

The airborne forces however met hard fortune. More than one-third of the gliders carrying our 1st Air Landing Brigade were released too early by their American towing aircraft and many of the men they carried were drowned. The rest were

scattered over southeastern Sicily, and only twelve gliders arrived at the important bridge which was their aim. Out of
eight officers and sixty-five men who seized and held it until
help came twelve hours later, only nineteen survived un-
wounded. This was a forlorn feat of arms. On the American
front the air landings were also too widely dispersed, but the
many small parties creating damage and confusion inland worried the Italian coastal divisions.

The seaborne landings, under continuous fighter protection, were everywhere highly successful. Syracuse and Pachino
on the British front, Licata and Gela on the American, were
captured. The Eighth Army took Augusta on the 12th. On
the American front very heavy counter-attacks were made on
the United States 1st Division by part of a German armoured
division. For a time the position was critical, but after a stiff
fight the enemy were beaten off and our Allies pressed on to
capture the important airfields east of Gela.

The major effort of the Eighth Army was now directed
against the airfields at Catania and Gerbini. Aided by more
airborne and seaborne landings of parachute and Commando
troops, which captured vital bridges, the army crossed the river
Simeto. But now German troops from farther west reinforced
the Italians and progress beyond the river was stopped. On
the 16th, the left flank of the Eighth Army reached Caltagirone,
in close touch with the Americans, who were also pressing
westward along the coast and had taken Porto Empedocle.

Twelve airfields were now in our hands, and by July 18
there were only twenty-five serviceable German aircraft in the
island. Eleven hundred planes, more than half of them German, were left behind destroyed or damaged. Our air forces
tried hard to stop the passage of troops from the mainland to
Messina. They were only partly successful against the heavy
anti-aircraft fire.

On July 16, General Alexander ordered the Eighth Army to
attack the western side of Mount Etna, and the Seventh Army
to seize the roads around Enna and cut the west-east highway
at Petralia. The 50th Division could make little progress, and

the Germans had brought reinforcements, including six battalions of the redoubtable 1st Parachute Division, from the
mainland. On its left we made some ground, but it was clear
that a new plan and more troops were needed. There was a
lull on the British front till the 78th Division arrived from
Tunisia.

*   *   *   *   *

Our next strategic move was still in suspense. Should we
cross the Straits of Messina and seize the toe of Italy, should we
seize the heel at Taranto, or should we land higher up the west
coast, in the Gulf of Salerno, and capture Naples? Or, again,
must we restrict ourselves to the occupation of Sardinia? In
June, General Eisenhower had been asked for his opinion.
The problem was a difficult one. At the Washington Conference in May ("Trident"), we had decided to transfer to India
about August much of the assault shipping and certain air
forces then allotted to the Sicily attack. He had also been
warned that after November 1 four American and three British
divisions would have to be withdrawn to Britain for the cross-
Channel invasion in 1944. On June 30, he proposed that when
the capture of Sicily had been completed, we should attack
either the toe of Italy, or Sardinia. If Sardinia were chosen,
he could probably be ready by October, but he did not expect
to be able to invade the mainland of Italy before November,
and by then the weather might be too bad for amphibious
landings. To justify so late a descent upon Italy there had to
be a good prospect of a speedy advance.

The progress made in Sicily clarified the scene. The contrast may be judged from the telegram in which I set the whole
position before Smuts on July 16:

Prime Minister to General Smuts   16 July 43

In our May talks at Washington we found serious American
misgivings lest we should become deeply involved in the Mediterranean, and a hankering for winding up the campaign there with
the capture of Sardinia. This we combated, and, as our forces in
the Mediterranean far outnumber the American, we were able to

have the matter left open till after the capture of Sicily. Not being satisfied with this, I requested the President to send General Marshall with me to North Africa and there upon the spot to convince Eisenhower and others that nothing less than Rome could satisfy the requirements of this year's campaign. We agreed that the decision should be taken when it was seen how the fighting in Sicily went. If it was severe and prolonged, then only Sardinia might be possible. If however our enterprise prospered and Italian resistance was seen not to be formidable, then we were immediately to invade the Italian mainland.

2. The moment is now approaching when this choice must be made, and I need not tell you I shall make it a capital issue. I believe the President is with me; Eisenhower in his heart is naturally for it. I will in no circumstances allow the powerful British and British-controlled armies in the Mediterranean to stand idle. I am bringing the very fine Polish army from Persia into Syria, where it can also participate.

3. The situation in the Balkans is also most hopeful, and I am sending you a report from the Middle East Headquarters showing the Italian forces on the verge of collapse. Not only must we take Rome and march as far north as possible in Italy, but our right hand must give succour to the Balkan patriots. In all this there is great hope, provided action is taken worthy of the opportunity. I am confident of a good result, and I shall go all lengths to procure the agreement of our Allies. If not, we have ample forces to act by ourselves.

4. When are you coming over here? You know what a warm welcome awaits you and how close is our community of ideas on war. All the above is for your eye alone and of operational secrecy.

*   *   *   *   *

Meanwhile, Allied air forces were harrying the enemy communications and airfields in Southern Italy, and the port of Naples. On July 19, a strong force of American bombers attacked the railway yards and air port at Rome. Havoc was wrought; and the shock was severe. In Sicily itself the Americans were advancing steadily under the spirited leadership of General Patton. Their 3d Infantry and 2d Armoured Divisions were given the task of reducing the western end, where only Italians now remained, while their IId Corps, comprising the 1st and 45th Divisions, was directed to gain the northern coast and then to thrust eastward along the two main roads towards Messina. Palermo was taken on July 22, and by the end of the month the Americans had reached the line Nicosia-San Stefano. Their 3d Division, its task in Western Sicily completed, had been brought in to support the coastal drive, while the 9th Division was brought over from Africa, where, like our 78th, it had been in reserve.

The field was thus disposed for the final battles. These were certain to be severe, since, apart from what remained of the Italian garrison, more than three German divisions were now in action under a well-tried German Commander, General Hube. But the speedy collapse of Italy became probable. There was a marked change of feeling in our circles in White-hall, and we decided on the bolder plan of a direct attack on the west coast of Italy to seize Naples. Washington agreed, but insisted that no more forces could be provided than those agreed upon at the "Trident" Conference. The Americans held that none of the operations elsewhere, especially "Over-lord," should be prejudiced by more vigorous action in the Mediterranean. This reservation was to cause keen anxiety during the landing at Salerno.

General Eisenhower and his principal commanders now agreed that Italy should be the next and immediate target. They still preferred to land first on the toe, because they were short of landing-craft and planes, but for the first time they too began to favour the direct attack on Naples. This was so far from our newly won air bases in Sicily that it would much reduce the fighter cover for the landing. Nonetheless, Naples soon became the centre of all thoughts. The chance of quickly crushing Italy seemed to justify delaying operations against Burma; and the Admiralty stopped the assault shipping for India from leaving the Mediterranean.

On July 22, the British Chiefs of Staff urged their Ameri-can colleagues to plan the direct attack on Naples on the as-sumption that extra shipping and aircraft carriers would be

available. The Americans took a different view. While agreeing to the attack, they adhered to their original decision that
no reinforcements from America should be sent to General
Eisenhower for this or any other purpose. He should do the
best he could with what he had. Moreover, they insisted that
three of his heavy bomber groups should be withdrawn to
Britain. Conflict thus arose. The American Chiefs of Staff did
not believe that the conquest of Italy would threaten Germany,
and they also feared that the Germans would withdraw and
that we should find ourselves hitting the air. They did not
think there was much to be gained by bombing Southern Germany from airfields in Southern Italy, and they wanted
all efforts against Germany to be concentrated on the shortest
route across the English Channel, although nothing could happen there for ten months.

The British Chiefs of Staff pointed out that the Washington
Conference had expressly stated that the elimination of Italy
from the war was one of the prime Allied objects. The attack
on Naples, now given the code-name of "Avalanche," was the
best means of accomplishing this, and the collapse of Italy
would increase enormously the chances of the cross-Channel
invasion being not only successful but decisive. Portal, Chief
of the Air Staff, emphasised that the full-scale attack on German industry, particularly on factories producing fighters,
could only be effective with the help of the Italian airfields.
Their possession would therefore be a great contribution to a
successful invasion of France. The Americans remained unmoved. However, most of the forces to be employed in
"Avalanche" were British, and we resolved to do everything in
our power to ensure its success. To overcome the weakness in
long-range fighters the Admiralty allotted four escort carriers
and a light fleet carrier to support the landing, and the Air
Ministry gave General Eisenhower three of our bomber squadrons which had been due for early withdrawal.

While these somewhat sharp discussions were in progress,
the scene was completely transformed by the fall of Mussolini
on July 25. The argument for invading Italy seemed over-

whelming. As will be seen, the Germans reacted very quickly, and our invasion, and particularly the attack on Naples, was not greatly eased. "Avalanche" only just succeeded, and it was fortunate that we had provided additional British sea- and air-power. The risks would have been further reduced if there had been the extra shipping which we considered essential to accelerate the build-up after landing. In this we could not carry American opinion with us, and before the operation began many American ships were withdrawn, and some of the British assault shipping was also released to India.

*   *   *   *   *

We must now return to the Sicilian battlefield. On August 3, Alexander telegraphed:

The offensive has opened well. . . . I have just returned from a visit to General Patton, who is in great heart. The Seventh American Army have done a grand job of work and are fighting really well. The Canadians have made a very satisfactory début and are fighting well. Progress may be slow, but the country must be seen to be believed. Only a few mountain roads, which pass through gorges and round cliffs, which are easily defended and more easily demolished.

The brilliant capture of Centuripe by our newly arrived 78th Division marked the last phase. Catania fell on the 5th, and thereafter the whole British line swung forward to the southern and western slopes of Mount Etna The United States 1st Division took Troina on August 6 after a stiff fight, and their 9th Division, passing through the 1st, entered Cesaro on the 8th. Along the north coast the United States 45h Division, followed by their 3d Division, reached Cape Orlando on August 10, with the aid of two small but skilful outflanking amphibious operations. After the capture of Randazzo on the 13th, the enemy broke contact all along the front, and, under cover of their strong anti-aircraft defences of the Messina Straits, escaped during the following nights to the mainland. Our armies raced for Messina. Enemy demolitions on the coastal road from Catania slowed up the Eighth Army, and by a narrow margin the prize fell to the Americans, who entered it on August 16.

General Alexander to Prime Minister   17 Aug. 43

The following facts are of interest.

Sicily invaded July 10. Messina entered August 16. Island taken in thirty-eight days. Sicily has coastline 600 miles and area 10,000 square miles. Island is heavily fortified with concrete pill-boxes and wire. Axis garrison: Italian 9 divisions, German 4 divisions, equalling 13 divisions; total forces: Italian 315,000, German 90,000, making total 405,000 soldiers. Our forces: Seventh Army, 6 divisions, including airborne division; Eighth Army, 7 divisions, including airborne and armoured brigades, making Allied total 13 divisions. . . .

It can be assumed that all Italian forces in island on July 10 have been destroyed, though a few battered units may have escaped to mainland. It is impossible yet to estimate booty and war material captured. Guns, tanks, rifles, and machine-guns are lying scattered about all over island.

During whole operation the air forces have maintained domination throughout, and their tactical air forces have in consequence concentrated a record proportion of their efforts on support of our armies in the field. Over one thousand enemy aircraft have been taken on airfields. The Royal Navy have kept our sea-lanes open and supplied us with everything we needed.

And later:

General Alexander to Prime Minister   17 Aug. 43

By 10 A.M. this morning, August 17, 1943, the last German soldier was flung out of Sicily and the whole island is now in our hands.

*   *   *   *   *

So ended a successful and skilful campaign of thirty-eight days. The enemy, once they had recovered from the initial surprise, had fought stubbornly. The difficulties of the ground were great. The roads were narrow, and cross-country movement was often impossible except for men on foot. On the Eighth Army front the towering mass of Mount Etna blocked the way, and enabled the enemy to watch our moves. As they lay on the low ground of the Catania plain, malaria ran riot among our men. Nevertheless, once we were safely ashore and our air forces were operating from captured airfields, the issue was never in doubt. The enemy, according to General Marshall's report, lost 167,000 men, of whom 37,000 were Germans. The Allies lost 31,158 killed, wounded, and missing.

3

The Fall of Mussolini

Mussolini in the Toils — My Agreement with Roosevelt About Our Joint Proclamation — Mussolini Confers with Hitler Near Rimini — The Fascist Grand Council Meets, July 24 — Grandi's Motion Carried — The Arrest of Mussolini, July 25 — The End of Twenty-One Years' Dictatorship — Hitler's Unwise Dispersion of Forces — He Receives the News from Italy, July 26 — My Forecast of November 25, 1942 — Correspondence with Roosevelt on Impending Italian Peace Proposals — My Thoughts on the Fall of Mussolini, July 26 — Our Anxiety About British Prisoners in Italy — Anglo-American Discussion of Armistice Terms — An Emergency Draft — Correspondence with President Roosevelt About Dealing with the House of Savoy, or Badoglio.

MUSSOLINI now had to bear the brunt of the military disasters into which he had, after so many years of rule, led his country. He had exercised almost absolute control and could not cast the burden on the Monarchy, Parliamentary institutions, the Fascist Party, or the General Staff. All fell on him. Now that the feeling that the war was lost spread throughout well-informed circles in Italy, the blame fell upon the man who had so imperiously thrust the nation onto the wrong and the losing side. These convictions formed and spread widely during the early months of 1943. The lonely Dictator sat at the summit of power, while military defeat and Italian slaughter in Russia, Tunis, and Sicily were the evident prelude to direct invasion.

In vain he made changes among the politicians and generals. In February, General Ambrosio had succeeded Cavallero as Chief of the Italian General Staff. Ambrosio, together with the Duke of Acquarone, the Minister of Court, were personal advisers of the King and had the confidence of the Royal circle. For months they had been hoping to overthrow the Duce and put an end to the Fascist régime. But Mussolini still dwelt in the European scene as if he were a principal factor. He was affronted when his new military chief proposed the immediate withdrawal of the Italian divisions from the Balkans. He regarded these forces as the counterpoise to German predominance in Europe. He did not realise that defeats abroad and internal demoralisation had robbed him of his status as Hitler's ally. He cherished the illusion of power and consequence when the reality had gone. Thus he resisted Ambrosio's formidable request. So durable however was the impression of his authority and the fear of his personal action in extremity that there was prolonged hesitation throughout all the forces of Italian society about how to oust him. Who would "bell the cat"? Thus the spring had passed, with invasion by a mighty foe, possessing superior power by land, sea, and air, drawing ever nearer.

During July the climax came. Since February the taciturn, cautious-minded, constitutional King had been in contact with Marshal Badoglio, who had been dismissed after the Greek disasters in 1940. He found in him at length a figure to whom he might entrust the conduct of the state. A definite plan was made. It was resolved that Mussolini should be arrested on July 26, and General Ambrosio agreed to find the agents and create the situation for this stroke. The General was aided unwittingly by elements in the Fascist Old Guard, who sought a new revival of the Party, by which, in many cases, they would not be the losers. They saw in the summoning of the highest Party organ, the Fascist Grand Council, which had not met since 1939, the means of confronting the Duce with an ultimatum. On July 13, they called on Mussolini and induced him to convene a formal session of the Council on July 24.

The two movements appear to have been separate and independent, but their close coincidence in date is significant.

*   *   *   *   *

We had at the time no definite knowledge of the inner
stresses of Italian politics, but reports of growing demoralisation and unrest had for some time reached Allied Headquarters. Strikes and rioting in the Northern Italian cities had followed on our bombing raids. We knew that the food situation
in Italy had worsened as rail traffic was disrupted. It seemed
that the time had come to launch an appeal to the Italian
people upon the Sicily landing. President Roosevelt had proposed a proclamation which seemed to us to assume for the
United States a position which was not fair to the British share
in the Italian war. On July 5 I cabled him as follows:

Former Naval Person to President Roosevelt   5 July 43

The War Cabinet had contemplated a joint declaration to the
Italian people in the name of both our countries. Whereas "Torch"
was by agreement planned as an American expedition with a British contingent and I have acted as your lieutenant throughout, we
consider "Husky" [Sicily] and post-"Husky" as joint undertakings
in which we are equal partners. This would certainly seem justified
by the proportion of troops, naval forces, shipping, and aircraft
involved. I fully accept your dictum that "there should be no
senior partner."

2. However, since we have been longer in quarrel or war with
Italy than you, and also since a document of this character written
by one man in its integrity is better than a joint production, we
are ready that you should speak at this juncture to the Italian
people on behalf of both our countries and in the interests of the
common cause.

3. There are a few amendments which I venture to suggest to
you in all the frankness of our friendship. They are of importance,
because without them untoward reactions might grow among the
British people and their forces that their contribution had not
received equal or sufficient recognition. In fact, they are only mentioned once, and all else is either United States or United Nations.

4. The amendments are as follows: (*a*) After the words, "against

whom on December 11, 1941, your Government declared war,"
insert, "I speak also on behalf of His Britannic Majesty's Government and in their name." (b) After the words, "under the command of General Eisenhower," insert, "and his Deputy, General
Alexander." (c) The end of the sentence, "The skies over Italy
are dominated by the vast air armadas of the United Nations,"
should read, "of the United States and Great Britain. Italy's seacoasts are threatened by the greatest accumulation of British and
Allied sea-power ever concentrated in the Mediterranean." I am
sure you will see the justice of this, as after all it is the United
States and Great Britain who are doing virtually the whole thing.
5. Finally, we think that the message to the Italian people
would seem to come better after an initial success in Sicily has been
achieved, because a repulse would make it somewhat inappropriate.
It would anyhow be lost to the world in the cannonade, and will
hardly get through to the Axis fighting troops in time to influence
the crunch.

Roosevelt recognised the justice of our case, and I sent him
a revised draft which we felt would be appropriate.

This is a message to the Italian people from the President of the
United States of America and the Prime Minister of Great Britain.
At this moment the combined armed forces of the United States
and Great Britain, under the command of General Eisenhower
and his Deputy, General Alexander, are carrying the war deep into
the territory of your country. This is the direct consequence of the
shameful leadership to which you have been subjected by Mussolini
and his Fascist régime. Mussolini carried you into this war as the
satellite of a brutal destroyer of peoples and liberties. Mussolini
plunged you into a war which he thought Hitler had already won.
In spite of Italy's great vulnerability to attack by air and sea, your
Fascist leaders sent your sons, your ships, your air forces, to distant battlefields to aid Germany in her attempt to conquer England, Russia, and the world. This association with the designs
of Nazi-controlled Germany was unworthy of Italy's ancient traditions of freedom and culture — traditions to which the people of
America and Great Britain owe so much. Your soldiers have
fought, not in the interests of Italy, but for Nazi Germany. They
have fought courageously, but they have been betrayed and aban-

doned by the Germans on the Russian Front and on every battlefield in Africa from El Alamein to Cape Bon.

Today Germany's hopes for world conquest have been blasted on
all fronts. The skies over Italy are dominated by the vast air
armadas of the United States and Great Britain. Italy's seacoasts
are threatened by the greatest accumulation of British and Allied
sea-power ever concentrated in the Mediterranean. The forces now
opposed to you are pledged to destroy the power of Nazi Germany,
which has ruthlessly been used to inflict slavery, destruction, and
death on all those who refuse to recognise the Germans as the
master race.

The sole hope for Italy's survival lies in honourable capitulation to the overwhelming power of the military forces of the United
Nations. If you continue to tolerate the Fascist régime, which
serves the evil power of the Nazis, you must suffer the consequences
of your own choice. We take no satisfaction in invading Italian
soil and bringing the tragic devastation of war home to the Italian
people; but we are determined to destroy the false leaders and
their doctrines which have brought Italy to her present position.
Every moment that you resist the combined forces of the United
Nations — every drop of blood that you sacrifice — can serve only
one purpose: to give the Fascist and Nazi leaders a little more time
to escape from the inevitable consequences of their own crimes. All
your interests and all your traditions have been betrayed by Germany and your own false and corrupt leaders; it is only by disa-
vowing both that a reconstituted Italy can hope to occupy a respected place in the family of European nations.

The time has now come for you, the Italian people, to consult
your own self-respect and your own interests and your own desire
for a restoration of national dignity, security, and peace. The time
has come for you to decide whether Italians shall die for Mussolini
and Hitler — or live for Italy, and for civilisation.

ROOSEVELT
CHURCHILL

Allied aircraft dropped leaflets of this proclamation over
Rome and other Italian cities on July 17.

*   *   *   *   *

Two days later, the Duce, accompanied by General Ambrosio, left by air to meet Hitler at the Feltre Villa, near Rimini. "There was a most beautiful cool and shady park," writes Mussolini in his *Memoirs,* "and a labyrinthine building which some people found almost uncanny. It was like a crossword puzzle frozen into a house." All preparations had been made to entertain the Fuehrer for at least two days, but he left the same afternoon. "The meeting," says Mussolini, "was, as usual, cordial, but the entourage and the attitude of the higher Air Force officers and of the troops was chilly."[1]

The Fuehrer held forth lengthily upon the need for a supreme effort. The new secret weapons, he said, would be ready for use against England by the winter. Italy must be defended, "so that Sicily may become for the enemy what Stalingrad was for us." The Italians must produce both the man-power and the organisation. Germany could not provide the reinforcements and equipment asked for by Italy owing to the pressure on the Russian Front.

Ambrosio urged his Chief to tell Hitler plainly that Italy could not continue in the war. It is not clear what advantage would have come from this, but the fact that Mussolini seemed almost dumbstruck finally decided Ambrosio and the other Italian generals present that no further leadership could be expected from him.

In the midst of Hitler's discourse on the situation, an agitated Italian officer entered the room with the news, "At this moment Rome is undergoing a violent enemy air bombardment." Apart from a promise of further German reinforcements for Sicily, Mussolini returned to Rome without anything to show. As he approached, he flew into a huge black cloud of smoke rising from hundreds of wagons on fire in the Littorio railway station. The next day he had an audience of the King, whom he found "frowning and nervous." "A tense situation," said the King. "We cannot go on much longer. Sicily has gone west now. The Germans will double-cross us. The discipline of the troops has broken down. . . ."

[1] Mussolini, *Memoirs, 1942–43* (English edition), pages 50 ff.

Mussolini answered, according to the records, that he hoped
to disengage Italy from the Axis Alliance by September 15.
The date shows how far he was out of contact with reality.

The chief actor in the final drama now appeared on the
scene. Dino Grandi, veteran Fascist, former Foreign Minister
and Ambassador to Britain, a man of strong personal determination, who had hated the Italian declaration of war upon
Britain, but had hitherto submitted to the force of events,
arrived in Rome to take the lead at the meeting of the Grand
Council. He called on his old leader on July 22, and told him
brutally that he intended to propose the formation of a
National Government and the restoration to the King of the
supreme command of the armed forces.

*   *   *   *

At 5 P.M. on the 24th, the Grand Council met. Care appears
to have been taken by the Chief of Police that they should
not be disturbed by violence. Mussolini's musketeers, his personal bodyguard, were relieved of their duty to guard the
Palazzo Venezia, which was also filled with armed police. The
Duce unfolded his case, and the Council, who were all dressed
in their black Fascist uniforms, took up the discussion. Mussolini ended:

War is always a party war — a war of the party which desires
it; it is always one man's war — the war of the man who declared
it. If today this is called Mussolini's war, the war in 1859 could
have been called Cavour's war. This is the moment to tighten the
reins and assume the necessary responsibility. I shall have no difficulty in replacing men, in turning the screw, in bringing forces to
bear not yet engaged, in the name of our country, whose territorial
integrity is today being violated.

Grandi then moved a resolution calling upon the Crown
to assume more power and upon the King to emerge from
obscurity and assume his responsibilities. He delivered what
Mussolini describes as "a violent philippic," "the speech of a
man who was at last giving vent to a long-cherished rancour."
The contacts between members of the Grand Council and the

Court became evident. Mussolini's son-in-law, Ciano, supported Grandi. Everyone present was now conscious that a political convulsion impended. The debate continued till midnight, when Scorza, Secretary of the Fascist Party, proposed adjourning till next day. But Grandi leaped to his feet, shouting, "No, I am against the proposal. We have started this business and we must finish it this very night!" It was after two o'clock in the morning when the voting took place. "The position of each member of the Grand Council," writes Mussolini, "could be discerned even before the voting. There was a group of traitors who had already negotiated with the Crown, a group of accomplices, and a group of uninformed who probably did not realise the seriousness of the vote, but they voted just the same." Nineteen replied "Yes" to Grandi's motion and seven "No." Two abstained. Mussolini rose. "You have provoked a crisis of the régime. The session is closed." The Party Secretary was about to give the salute to the Duce when Mussolini checked him with a gesture, saying, "No, you are excused." They all went away in silence. None slept at home.

Meanwhile, the arrest of Mussolini was being quietly arranged. The Duke of Acquarone, the Court Minister, sent instructions to Ambrosio whose deputies and trusted agents in the police and the carabinieri acted forthwith. The key telephone exchanges, the police headquarters, and the offices of the Ministry of the Interior were quietly and unobtrusively taken over. A small force of military police was posted out of sight near the Royal villa.

Mussolini spent the morning of Sunday, July 25, in his office, and visited some quarters in Rome which had suffered by bombing. He asked to see the King at five o'clock. "I thought the King would withdraw his delegation of authority of June 10, 1940, concerning the command of the armed forces, a command which I had for some time past been thinking of relinquishing. I entered the villa therefore with a mind completely free from any forebodings, in a state which, looking back on it, might really be called utterly unsuspecting." On reaching the Royal abode, he noticed that there were everywhere reinforcements of carabinieri. The King, in Marshal's uniform, stood in the doorway. The two men entered the drawing-room. The King said: "My dear Duce, it's no longer any good. Italy has gone to bits. Army morale is at rock-bottom. The soldiers don't want to fight any more. . . . The Grand Council's vote is terrific — nineteen votes for Grandi's motion, and among them four holders of the Order of the Annunciation! . . . At this moment you are the most hated man in Italy. You can no longer count on more than one friend. You have one friend left, and I am he. That is why I tell you that you need have no fears for your personal safety, for which I will ensure protection. I have been thinking that the man for the job now is Marshal Badoglio. . . . "

Mussolini replied: "You are taking an extremely grave decision. A crisis at this moment would mean making the people think that peace was in sight, once the man who declared war had been dismissed. The blow to the Army's morale would be serious. This crisis would be considered as a triumph for the Churchill-Stalin set-up, especially for Stalin. I realise the people's hatred. I had no difficulty in recognising it last night in the midst of the Grand Council. One can't govern for such a long time and impose so many sacrifices without provoking resentments. In any case, I wish good luck to the man who takes the situation in hand." The King accompanied Mussolini to the door. "His face," says Mussolini, "was livid, and he looked smaller than ever, almost dwarfish. He shook my hand and went in again. I descended the few steps and went towards my car. Suddenly a carabinieri captain stopped me and said, 'His Majesty has charged me with the protection of your person.' I was continuing towards my car when the captain said to me, pointing to a motor-ambulance standing near by, 'No. We must get in there.' I got into the ambulance together with my secretary. A lieutenant, three carabinieri, and two police agents in plain clothes got in as well as the captain, and placed themselves by the door armed with machine-guns. When the door was closed, the ambulance drove off at top speed. I still thought that all this was being done, as the King had said, in order to protect my person."

Later that afternoon, Badoglio was charged by the King to form a new Cabinet of service chiefs and civil servants, and in the evening the Marshal broadcast the news to the world. Two days later, the Duce was taken on Marshal Badoglio's order to be interned on the island of Ponza.

*   *   *   *   *

Thus ended Mussolini's twenty-one years' dictatorship in Italy, during which he had raised the Italian people from the Bolshevism into which they were sinking in 1919 to a position in Europe such as Italy had never held before. A new impulse had been given to the national life. The Italian Empire in North Africa was built. Many important public works in Italy were completed. In 1935 the Duce had by his will-power overcome the League of Nations — "Fifty nations led by one" — and was able to complete his conquest of Abyssinia. His régime was far too costly for the Italian people to bear, but there is no doubt that it appealed during its period of success to very great numbers of Italians. He was, as I had addressed him at the time of the fall of France, "the Italian lawgiver." The alternative to his rule might well have been a Communist Italy, which would have brought perils and misfortunes of a different character both upon the Italian people and Europe. His fatal mistake was the declaration of war on France and Great Britain following Hitler's victories in June 1940. Had he not done this, he might well have maintained Italy in a balancing position, courted and rewarded by both sides and deriving an unusual wealth and prosperity from the struggles of other countries. Even when the issue of the war became certain, Mussolini would have been welcomed by the Allies. He had much to give to shorten its course. He could have timed his moment to declare war on Hitler with art and care. Instead he took the wrong turning. He never understood the strength of Britain, nor the long-enduring qualities of Island resistance and sea-power. Thus he marched to ruin. His great roads will remain a monument to his personal power and long reign.

*   *   *   *   *

At this time Hitler made a crowning error in strategy and war direction. The defection of Italy, the victorious advance of Russia, and the evident preparations for a cross-Channel attack by Britain and the United States should have led him to concentrate and develop the most powerful German army as a central reserve. In this way only could he use the high qualities of the German Command and fighting troops, and at the same time take full advantage of the central position which he occupied, with its interior lines and remarkable communications. As General von Thoma said while a prisoner of war in our charge, "Our only chance is to create a situation where we can use the Army." Hitler, as I have pointed out in an earlier volume, had in fact made a spider's web and forgotten the spider. He tried to hold everything he had won. Enormous forces were squandered in the Balkans and in Italy which could play no part in the main decisions. A central reserve of thirty or forty divisions of the highest quality and mobility would have enabled him to strike at any one of his opponents advancing upon him and fight a major battle with good prospects of success. He could, for instance, have met the British and Americans at the fortieth or fiftieth day after their landing in Normandy a year later with fresh and greatly superior forces. He could perhaps have so disposed his forces as to lead to the decision of the war. There was no need to consume his strength in Italy and the Balkans, and the fact that he was induced to do so must be taken as the waste of his last opportunity.

Knowing that these choices were open to him, I wished also to have the options of pressing right-handed in Italy or left-handed across the Channel, or both. The wrong dispositions which he made enabled us to undertake the main direct assault, under conditions which offered good prospects and achieved success.

*   *   *   *   *

Hitler had returned from the Feltre meeting convinced that Italy could only be kept in the war by purges in the Fascist

Party and increasing pressure by the Germans on the Fascist
leaders. Mussolini's sixtieth birthday fell on July 29, and
Goering was chosen to pay him an official visit on this occasion. But during the course of July 25 alarming reports from
Rome began to come in to Hitler's Headquarters. By the evening it was clear that Mussolini had resigned or had been removed, and that Badoglio had been nominated by the King as
his successor. It was finally decided that any major operation
against the new Italian Government would require withdrawals of more divisions than could be spared from the Eastern Front in the event of the expected Russian offensive. Plans
were made to rescue Mussolini, to occupy Rome, and to support Italian Fascism wherever possible. If Badoglio signed an
armistice with the Allies, further plans were drawn up for
seizing the Italian Fleet and occupying key positions throughout Italy, and for overawing Italian garrisons in the Balkans
and in the Aegean.

"We must act," Hitler told his advisers on July 26. "Otherwise the Anglo-Saxons will steal a march on us by occupying
the air ports. The Fascist Party is at present only stunned,
and will recover behind our lines. The Fascist Party is the
only one that has the will to fight on our side. We must therefore restore it. All reasons advocating further delays are wrong;
thereby we run the danger of losing Italy to the Anglo-Saxons.
These are matters which a soldier cannot comprehend. Only
a man with political insight can see his way clear."

*   *   *   *   *

We had long pondered over the consequences of an Italian
collapse. Eight months before I had written:

POSITION OF ITALY

NOTE BY THE PRIME MINISTER

November 25, 1942

It is in my opinion premature to assume that no internal convulsion in Italy could produce a Government which would make

a separate peace. If we increase the severity of our pressure upon Italy . . . the desire, and indeed the imperative need, of getting out of the war will come home to all the Italians, including the rank and file of the Fascist Party. Should Italy feel unable to endure the continued attacks which will be made upon her from the air, and presently, I trust, by amphibious operations, the Italian people will have to choose between, on the one hand, setting up a Government under someone like Grandi to sue for a separate peace, or, on the other, submitting to a German occupation, which would merely aggravate the severity of the war.

2. I do not share the view that it is in our interest that the Germans should occupy and take over Italy. We may not be able to prevent it. It is still my hope that the Italians themselves will prevent it and we should certainly do what we can to further this move. If there were a revolution in Italy and an Armistice Government came into power, it is at least arguable that the German interests would be as well served by standing on the Brenner as by undertaking the detailed defence of Italy against the wishes of its people, and possibly of a provisional Government.

3. When a nation is thoroughly beaten in war, it does all sorts of things which no one would imagine beforehand. The sudden, sullen, universal, simultaneous way in which Bulgaria — Government, Army, and people alike — cut out in 1918 remains in my memory. Without caring to make any arrangements for their future or for their safety, the troops simply marched out of the lines and dispersed to their homes, and King Ferdinand fled. A Government headed by a peasant leader remained to await the judgment of the victors.

4. Therefore, I would not rule out the possibilities of a sudden peace demand being made by Italy, and I agree with the United States policy of trying to separate the Italian people from their Government. The fall of Mussolini, even though precautions may have been taken against it beforehand, might well have a decisive effect upon Italian opinion. The Fascist chapter would be closed. One tale would be finished and another would begin. I consider it would be well to drop leaflets over all Italian towns that are bombed, on the theme, "One man alone is the cause of your sufferings — Mussolini."

5. It is to be observed that we are under no obligations to offer any terms to the vanquished, should they sue for them. That

decision must be taken when and if we are offered their surrender, and in the meanwhile we certainly ought not to make promises, as some of the American propaganda leaflets have seemed to do.

The news from Rome now raised these issues, and prompted me to telegraph to the President:

Former Naval Person to President Roosevelt   26 July 43
Changes announced in Italy probably portend peace proposals. Let us consult together so as to take joint action. The present stage may only be transition. But anyhow Hitler will feel very lonely when Mussolini is down and out. No one can be quite sure this may not go further.

The President's message to me crossed this telegram:

President Roosevelt to Prime Minister   26 July 43
By coincidence I was again at Shangri La this afternoon when the news from Rome came, but this time it seems to be true. If any overtures come we must be certain of the use of all Italian territory and transportation against the Germans in the north *and against the whole Balkan peninsula,*[2] as well as use of airfields of all kinds. It is my thought that we should come as close as possible to unconditional surrender, followed by good treatment of the Italian populace. But I think also that the Head Devil should be surrendered, together with his chief partners in crime. In no event should our officers in the field fix on any general terms without your approval and mine. Let me have your thoughts.

*   *   *   *   *

The results of our joint action would dominate the future course of the war. I spent part of the same day in setting down on paper my reactions to the Italian drama. In the afternoon the War Cabinet met to discuss the new situation, and to consider the draft which I had composed. That evening I sent a copy to the President for his comments.

Former Naval Person to President Roosevelt   26 July 43
I send you my thoughts in the form in which I submitted them to the War Cabinet, obtaining their full approval.

2 Author's italics.

2. I don't think myself that we should be too particular in deal-ing with any non-Fascist Government, even if it is not all we should like. Now Mussolini is gone, I would deal with any non-Fascist Italian Government which can deliver the goods. The goods are set out in my memo herewith. My colleagues also agreed with this.

THOUGHTS ON THE FALL OF MUSSOLINI

By the Prime Minister

It seems highly probable that the fall of Mussolini will involve the overthrow of the Fascist régime, and that the new Government of the King and Badoglio will seek to negotiate a separate arrange-ment with the Allies for an armistice. Should this prove to be the case, it will be necessary for us to make up our minds first of all upon what we want, and secondly, upon the measures and condi-tions required to gain it for us.

2. At this moment above all others our thoughts must be con-centrated upon the supreme aim, namely, the destruction of Hitler, Hitlerism, and Nazi Germany. Every military advantage arising out of the surrender of Italy, should that occur, must be sought for this purpose.

3. The first of these is, in the President's words, "the use of all Italian territory and transportation against the Germans in the north and against the whole Balkan peninsula, as well as use of airfields of all kinds." This must include the surrender to our garrisons of Sardinia, the Dodecanese, and Corfu, as well as of all the naval and air bases on the Italian mainland as soon as they can be taken over.

4. Secondly, and of equal importance, the immediate surrender to the Allies of the Italian Fleet, or at least its effective demobilisa-tion and paralysis, and the disarmament of the Italian air and ground forces to whatever extent we find needful and useful. The surrender of the Fleet will liberate powerful British naval forces for service in the Indian Ocean against Japan, and will be most agreeable to the United States.

5. Also, of equal consequence, the immediate withdrawal from, or surrender of, all Italian forces in Corsica, the Riviera, including Toulon, and the Balkan peninsula — to wit, in Yugoslavia, Albania, and Greece.

6. Another objective of the highest importance, about which

there will be passionate feeling in this country, is the immediate liberation of all British prisoners of war in Italian hands, and the prevention, which can in the first instance only be by the Italians, of their being transported northward to Germany. I regard it as a matter of honour and humanity to get our own flesh and blood back as soon as possible and spare them the measureless horrors of incarceration in Germany during the final stages of the war.

7. The fate of the German troops in Italy, and particularly of those south of Rome, will probably lead to fighting between the Germans and the Italian Army and population. We should demand their surrender, and that any Italian Government with whom we can reach a settlement shall do their utmost to procure this. It may be however that the German divisions will cut their way northward in spite of anything that the Italian armed forces are capable of doing. We should provoke this conflict as much as possible, and should not hesitate to send troops and air support to assist the Italians in procuring the surrender of the Germans south of Rome.

8. When we see how this process goes, we can take a further view about action to be taken north of Rome. We should however try to get possession of points on both the west coast and east coast railways of Italy as far north as we dare. And this is a time to dare.

9. In our struggle with Hitler and the German Army we cannot afford to deny ourselves any assistance that will kill Germans. The fury of the Italian population will now be turned against the German intruders, who have, as they will feel, brought all these miseries upon Italy and then have come so scantily and grudgingly to her aid. We should stimulate this process in order that the new, liberated, anti-Fascist Italy shall afford us at the earliest moment a safe and friendly area on which we can base the whole forward air attack upon South and Central Germany.

10. This air attack is a new advantage of the first order, as it brings the whole of the Mediterranean air forces into action from a direction which turns the entire line of air defences in the West, and which furthermore exposes all those centres of war production which have been increasingly developed so as to escape air attack from Great Britain. It will become urgent in the highest degree to get agents, Commandos, and supplies by sea across the Adriatic into Greece, Albania, and Yugoslavia. It must be remembered that

there are fifteen German divisions in the Balkan peninsula, of which ten are mobile. Nevertheless, once we have control of the Italian peninsula and of the Adriatic, and the Italian armies in the Balkans withdraw or lay down their arms, it is by no means unlikely that the Germans will be forced to withdraw northward to the line of the Save and Danube, thus liberating Greece and other tortured countries.

11. We cannot yet measure the effects of Mussolini's fall and of an Italian capitulation upon Bulgaria, Rumania, and Hungary. They may be profound. In connection with this situation the collapse of Italy should fix the moment for putting the strongest pressure on Turkey to act in accordance with the spirit of the Alliance, and in this Britain and the United States, acting jointly or severally, should if possible be joined or at least supported by Russia.

12. The surrender of, to quote the President, "the Head Devil, together with his chief partners in crime," must be considered an eminent object, and one for which we should strive by all means in our power short of wrecking the immense prospects which have been outlined in earlier paragraphs. It may be however that these criminals will flee into Germany or escape into Switzerland. On the other hand, they may surrender themselves or be surrendered by the Italian Government. Should they fall into our hands, we ought now to decide, in consultation with the United States, and, after agreement with them, with the U.S.S.R., what treatment should be meted out to them. Some may prefer prompt execution without trial except for identification purposes. Others may prefer that they be kept in confinement till the end of the war in Europe and their fate decided together with that of other war criminals. Personally I am fairly indifferent on this matter, provided always that no solid military advantages are sacrificed for the sake of immediate vengeance.

"Your message," replied the President to me on July 30, "expresses generally my thoughts of today on the prospects and methods of handling the Italian situation, with which we are now confronted." He suggested certain minor changes. These in no way altered the substance of the document, and were readily adjusted. "I have not had time to consult my colleagues," I replied on the 31st, "but I have no doubt what-

ever that our joint draft as amended expresses in perfect harmony the minds of our two Governments on the broad policy
to be pursued. It seems to be a case of 'two hearts that beat
as one.' "

My paper in a slightly amended form was placed before the
War Cabinet on August 2, and approved by them as a draft
joint directive from both Governments to the Combined
Chiefs of Staff. I took it with me when I went to Quebec for
a final discussion with the President. Its main interest however lies in showing our joint reactions to the news of Mussolini's fall.

*   *   *   *   *

Complex problems now lay before us. We had to consider
how to treat the new Italian Government. We had to expect
the imminent collapse of Italy as an Axis partner, and to draft
in detail the terms of surrender, bearing in mind not only the
reactions in Italy itself, but also in Germany. We had to take
into account the strategic implications of these events, to plan
what to do in areas outside Italy, in the Aegean and in the
Balkans, which were still held by Italian forces.

On July 27, the President sent me the draft of a broadcast
for General Eisenhower to make to the Italian people. This
had been approved by the Joint United States Chiefs of Staff,
and contained the following sentence: "Your men will return
to their normal life and their productive avocations, and hundreds of thousands of Italian prisoners now in our hands will
return to the countless Italian homes who long for them. The
ancient liberties and traditions of your country will be restored."

I was not only concerned about the draft of this joint
message, but about the fate of our prisoners of war in Italian
hands.

Former Naval Person to President Roosevelt   28 July 43
There are 74,000 British prisoners in Italy, and there are also
about 30,000 Yugoslavs and Greeks. We cannot agree to any
promise to release "hundreds of thousands of Italian prisoners now

in our hands" unless our men and Allied men are saved from the horrors of German captivity and restored to us.

2. Moreover, apart from Italian prisoners taken in Tunis and Sicily, we have at least a quarter of a million Italians captured by Wavell two years ago and parked about the world. We think it is too much to offer the return of such a large plurality of prisoners arising from earlier phases of the war, nor do we think it necessary. We are ready however to agree to all Italian prisoners taken in Tunis and taken or to be taken in Sicily being traded against the British and Allied prisoners mentioned above.

3. Accordingly we suggest that Eisenhower's message at this point should read as follows: "Your men will return to their normal life and to their productive avocations, and, provided all British and Allied prisoners now in your hands are restored safely to us and not taken away to Germany, the hundreds of thousands of Italian prisoners captured by us in Tunisia and Sicily will return to the countless Italian homes who long for them," etc.

The following day I telegraphed to General Eisenhower:

Prime Minister to General Eisenhower (Algiers)   29 July 43

There are obvious dangers in trying to state armistice terms in an attractive, popular form to the enemy nation. It is far better that all should be cut and dried and that their Government should know our full demands and their maximum expectations. We are sending our alternative draft to your Government, and will no doubt reach agreement with them in plenty of time for any negotiations which you may have to conduct or which we shall be handling.

All our thoughts are now concentrated upon the great battle which Alexander is about to begin under your supreme direction in Eastern Sicily. The destruction of the three German divisions now facing the Fifteenth Army Group, happening at this time of all others, may well produce decisive effects in every quarter.

And to the President:

Former Naval Person to President Roosevelt   29 July 43

I was so glad to hear your voice again [on the telephone] and that you were in such good spirits.

2. I have told Eisenhower that we fully agree to his releasing the proclamation with our amendment inserted about British and Allied prisoners.

3. Discarding etiquette, I have sent a direct message to the King of Italy through Switzerland emphasising our vehement and savage interest in this matter. I am most grateful for your promise to put the screw on through the Pope or any other convenient channel. If the King and Badoglio allow our prisoners and key men to be carried off by the Huns without doing their utmost to stop it, by which I mean using physical force, the feeling here would be such that no negotiations with that Government would stand a chance in public opinion.

4. *Armistice Terms.* The War Cabinet are quite clear that we ought not to broadcast armistice terms to the enemy. It is for their responsible Government to ask formally for an armistice on the basis of our principle of unconditional surrender. Then I suppose envoys would be appointed and a rendezvous fixed. Our version is already in your hands. As you will see, it follows the main lines of Eisenhower's draft, but is more precise and is cast in a form suited to discussion between plenipotentiaries rather than a popular appeal. There are great dangers in trying to dish this sort of dose up with jam for the patient.

5. We also think that the terms should cover civil as well as military requirements, and that it would be much better for them to be settled by envoys appointed by our two Governments than by the general commanding in the field. He can of course deal with any proposals coming from the troops on his immediate front for a local surrender.

6. Finally, all our thoughts are concentrated upon the great battle about to be fought by the British Eighth and United States Seventh Armies against the sixty-five thousand Germans cornered in the Eastern Sicilian tip. The destruction of these men could not come at a better time to influence events, not only in Italy but throughout the world. It is grand to think of our soldiers advancing side by side like brothers and with good prospects of victory ahead.

The President agreed with us that Eisenhower should not broadcast terms for an armistice with the enemy, but urged that in order to avoid unnecessary and possibly costly military action against Italy he should be authorised to state conditions when and if the Italian Government asked him for them. I did not see why such a proposal should necessarily be made to Eisenhower, none of whose forces were in contact with the enemy except in Sicily, and then only with the Germans. It seemed to me more likely that the Italian Government would negotiate through the Vatican, the Turks, or the Swiss. I agreed however that if Eisenhower were suddenly approached by an envoy he should have precise terms, embodying the principle of unconditional surrender, which he could immediately use as the basis for granting an armistice, and after much discussion the following articles were agreed:

Immediate cessation of all hostile activity by the Italian armed forces.

2. Italy will use its best endeavours to deny to the Germans facilities that might be used against the United Nations.

3. All prisoners or internees of the United Nations to be immediately turned over to the Allied Commander-in-Chief, and none of these may from the beginning of these negotiations be evacuated to Germany.

4. Immediate transfer of the Italian Fleet and Italian aircraft to such points as may be designated by the Allied Commander-in-Chief, with details of disarmament to be prescribed by him.

5. Agreement that Italian merchant shipping may be requisitioned by the Allied Commander-in-Chief to meet the needs of his military-naval programme.

6. Immediate surrender of Corsica and of all Italian territory, both islands and mainland, to the Allies, for such use as operational bases and other purposes as the Allies may see fit.

7. Immediate guarantee of the free use by the Allies of all airfields and naval ports in Italian territory, regardless of the rate of evacuation of the Italian territory by the German forces. These ports and fields to be protected by Italian armed forces until this function is taken over by the Allies.

8. Immediate withdrawal to Italy of Italian armed forces from all participation in the current war, from whatever areas in which they may now be engaged.

9. Guarantee by the Italian Government that if necessary it will employ all its available armed forces to ensure prompt and exact compliance with all the provisions of this armistice.

10. The Commander-in-Chief of the Allied Forces reserves to himself the right to take any measure which in his opinion may be necessary for the protection of the interests of the Allied forces or for the prosecution of the war, and the Italian Government binds itself to take such administrative or other action as the Commander-in-Chief may require, and in particular the Commander-in-Chief will establish Allied military government over such parts of Italian territory as he may deem necessary to the military interests of the Allied nations.

11. The Commander-in-Chief of the Allied forces will have a full right to impose measures of disarmament, demobilisation, and demilitarisation.

On July 31 I telegraphed to the President:

Former Naval Person to President Roosevelt   31 July 43

. . . So much for the immediate emergency. We hope however that you will also urgently have our Instrument of Surrender [3] examined, so that we reach full agreement on it. There are several points in this not dealt with in the emergency terms, and it is couched in a precise, formal, and legal vein, on which much thought has been bestowed here. We are rather puzzled to know why you never refer to this document, as it seems to us to be in fact only a more careful and comprehensive version of the emergency armistice terms. We should be very grateful if you would let us know how you feel about it. We ought certainly to have it, or something like it, ready as soon as possible.

The President agreed, but said that he needed further advice from the American Chiefs of Staff and the State Department. We thought it was essential that any statement made to the Italian people should be agreed formally both by the Americans and ourselves and not merely put out by Allied Headquarters at Algiers, and anyhow it was very much better for the generals to go on with the military operations and to keep the armistice terms till they were asked for.

*   *   *   *   *

Upon our attitude to the new Italian Government of

3 Not printed.

Badoglio depended the speed with which the Italians would probably approach us for peace terms.

We gave much thought to this matter, which was already being observed in the press on both sides of the Atlantic.

President Roosevelt to Prime Minister 30 July 43

There are some contentious people here who are getting ready to make a row if we seem to recognize the House of Savoy or Badoglio. They are the same element which made such a fuss over North Africa.

I told the press today that we have to treat with any person or persons in Italy who can best give us, first, disarmament, and, second, assurance against chaos, and I think also that you and I after an armistice comes could say something about self-determination in Italy at the proper time.

Former Naval Person to President Roosevelt 31 July 43

My position is that once Mussolini and the Fascists are gone, I will deal with any Italian authority which can deliver the goods. I am not in the least afraid for this purpose of seeming to recognise the House of Savoy or Badoglio, provided they are the ones who can make the Italians do what we need for our war purposes. Those purposes would certainly be hindered by chaos, Bolshevisation, or civil war. We have no right to lay undue burdens on our troops. It may well be that after the armistice terms have been accepted both the King and Badoglio will sink under the odium of surrender and that the Crown Prince and a new Prime Minister may be chosen.

I should deprecate any pronouncement about self-determination at the present time, beyond what is implicit in the Atlantic Charter. I agree with you that we must be very careful not to throw everything into the melting-pot.

Prime Minister to Foreign Secretary 31 July 43

Many things in life are settled by the two-stage method. For instance, a man is not prevented from saying, "Will you marry me, darling?" because he has not got the marriage contract, drawn up by the family solicitors, in his pocket. Personally I think the terms which Eisenhower may now offer are much more likely to be understood by an envoy, and thus be capable of immediate acceptance, than the legal verbiage of the Instrument of Surrender, and they will look much better if published. If we get emergency terms it means that the Italians will have given themselves up to us, lock, stock, and barrel. There would be nothing improper in our requiring them to hand over the pull-through and other cleaning materials afterwards.

President Roosevelt to Prime Minister   3 Aug. 43

I have read Instrument of Surrender, and while the language seems on the whole good I seriously doubt advisability of using it at all. After all, the terms of surrender already approved and sent to Eisenhower ought to be all that is necessary. Why tie his hands by an instrument that may be oversufficient or insufficient? Why not let him act to meet situations as they arise?

All this awaited our impending Conference at Quebec.

4

Westward Ho!

Synthetic Harbours

On Board the "Queen Mary" — Brigadier Wingate — The Plan for "Overlord" — A Retrospect — The Work of "Cossac" — Where to Strike? — The Need of Harbours and Piers — The Birth of the "Mulberries" — The Plan Is Unfolded — A Majestic Project — Floating Breakwaters — Vision of a Floating Island — Three Dominating Assumptions — The Supreme Command in Burma — My Note of August 7.

PROSPECTS OF VICTORY IN SICILY, the Italian situation, and the progress of the war made me feel the need early in July for a new meeting with the President and for another Anglo-American Conference. It was Roosevelt who suggested that Quebec should be the scene. Mr. Mackenzie King welcomed the proposal, and nothing could have been more agreeable to us. No more fitting or splendid setting for a meeting of those who guided the war policy of the Western world could have been chosen at this cardinal moment than the ancient citadel of Quebec, at the gateway of Canada, overlooking the mighty St. Lawrence River. The President, while gladly accepting Canadian hospitality, did not feel it possible that Canada should be formally a member of the Conference, as he apprehended similar demands by Brazil and other American partners in the United Nations. We also had to think of the claims of Australia and the other Dominions. This delicate question was solved and surmounted by the broadminded outlook of the Canadian Prime Minister and Government. I for my part was determined that we and the United States should have the Conference to ourselves, in view of all the vital business we had in common. A triple meeting of the heads of the three major Powers was a main object of the future; now it must be for Britain and the United States alone. We assigned to it the name "Quadrant."

I left London for the Clyde, where the *Queen Mary* awaited us, on the night of August 4, in a train which carried the very heavy staffs which we needed. We were, I suppose, over two hundred, besides about fifty Royal Marine orderlies. The scope of the Conference comprised not only the Mediterranean campaign, now at its first climax, but even more the preparations for the cross-Channel design of 1944, the whole conduct of the war in the Indian theatre, and our share in the struggle against Japan. For the Channel crossing we took with us three officers sent by Lieutenant-General F. E. Morgan, Chief of Staff to the Supreme Allied Commander, yet to be finally chosen, who with his combined Anglo-American staff had been working for nearly five months upon our joint plan. As the whole of our affairs in the Indian and Far Eastern theatres were under examination, I brought with me General Wavell's Director of Military Operations, who had flown specially from India.

I took also with me a young Brigadier named Wingate, who had already made his mark as a leader of irregulars in Abyssinia, and had greatly distinguished himself in the jungle fighting in Burma. These new brilliant exploits won him in some circles of the Army in which he served the title of "the Clive of Burma." I had heard much of all this, and knew also how the Zionists had sought him as a future Commander-in-Chief of any Israelite army that might be formed. I had him summoned home in order that I might have a look at him before I left for Quebec. I was about to dine alone on the night of August 4 at Downing Street when the news that he had arrived by air and was actually in the house was brought me. I immediately asked him to join me at dinner. We had not talked for half an hour before I felt myself in the presence of a man of the highest quality. He plunged at once into his theme of how the Japanese could be mastered in jungle warfare by long-range penetration groups landed by air behind the enemy lines.

This interested me greatly. I wished to hear much more about it, and also to let him tell his tale to the Chiefs of Staff.

I decided at once to take him with me on the voyage. I told him our train would leave at ten. It was then nearly nine. Wingate had arrived just as he was after three days' flight from the actual front, and with no clothes but what he stood up in. He was of course quite ready to go, but expressed regret that he would not be able to see his wife, who was in Scotland and had not even heard of his arrival. However, the resources of my Private Office were equal to the occasion. Mrs. Wingate was aroused at her home by the police and taken to Edinburgh in order to join our train on its way through and to go with us to Quebec. She had no idea of what it was all about until, in the early hours of the morning, she actually met her husband on a platform at Waverley Station. They had a very happy voyage together.

As I knew how much President Roosevelt liked meeting young, heroic figures, I had also invited Wing-Commander Guy Gibson, fresh from leading the attack which had destroyed the Mohne and Eder Dams. These supplied the industries of the Ruhr, and fed a wide area of fields, rivers, and canals. A special type of mine had been invented for their destruction, but it had to be dropped at night from a height of no more than sixty feet. After months of continuous and concentrated practice, sixteen Lancasters of the 617th Squadron of the Royal Air Force attacked on the night of May 16. Half were lost, but Gibson had stayed to the end, circling under fierce fire over the target to direct his squadron. He now wore a remarkable set of decorations — the Victoria Cross, a Distinguished Service Order and bar, and a Distinguished Flying Cross and bar — but no other ribbons. This was unique.

My wife came with me, and my daughter Mary, now a sub-altern in an anti-aircraft battery, was my aide-de-camp. We sailed on August 5, this time for Halifax, in Nova Scotia, instead of New York.

*   *   *   *   *

The *Queen Mary* drove on through the waves, and we lived in the utmost comfort on board her, with a diet of pre-war times. As usual on these voyages, we worked all day long. Our large cipher staff, with attendant cruisers to dispatch outgoing messages, kept us in touch with events from hour to hour. Each day I studied with the Chiefs of Staff the various aspects of the problems we were to discuss with our American friends. The most important of these was of course "Overlord."

I had reserved the interlude which a five days' voyage presented for the consideration of our long-wrought plans for this supreme operation of crossing the Channel. Study on an ever-expanding scale had gone forward since the struggles on the coasts of Norway and France in 1940, and we had learned much about amphibious war. The Combined Operations Organisation which I had then set up under my friend Admiral of the Fleet Sir Roger Keyes had played an all-important part and created a new technique. Small-scale raids by the Commandos paved the way for greater things, and not only gave us confidence and experience, but showed the world that although beset on all sides we were not content with passive defence. The Americans, still neutral, had observed this new trend, and later developed it in their own way on a vast scale.

In October 1941, Admiral Keyes was succeeded by Captain Lord Louis Mountbatten. We were still hard-pressed, and our only ally, Russia, seemed near to defeat. Nevertheless, I had resolved to prepare for an invasion of the Continent when the tide should turn. First, we had to increase the intensity and scope of our raids, and then translate all this experience into something much more massive. To mount a successful invasion from the United Kingdom, new engines of war must be contrived and developed, the three fighting services must be trained to plan and fight as one team, supported by the industry of the nation, and the whole island converted into an armed camp for launching the greatest seaborne assault of all time.

When Mountbatten visited me at Chequers before taking up his new duties, I told him, according to his account, "You are to plan for the offensive. In your Headquarters you will never think defensively." This governed his actions. To provide him with the necessary authority for his task, he had been made a member of the Chiefs of Staff Committee, with the acting rank of Vice-Admiral and equivalent honorary rank in the other Services. As Minister of Defence I retained personal responsibility for his Headquarters, and thus he reported direct to me whenever necessary. At Vaagso in Norway, at Bruneval, at St. Nazaire and elsewhere, the Commandos played a steadily increasing part in our affairs. Our raids culminated in the costly attack on Dieppe in August 1942. When thereafter we passed to major Anglo-American offensives, we applied our lessons to the North African landings and to our amphibious descents in the Mediterranean. In all these Mountbatten's organisation played a prominent and indispensable part.

In May 1942 a body known as "the Combined Commanders" had been appointed to grip the problem. It included the Commanders-in-Chief at home, Mountbatten, and later General Eisenhower, commanding the United States forces in Britain. At the Casablanca Conference in January 1943, it was decided to set up an Allied Inter-Service Staff under a British officer to prepare a definite plan for "Overlord." This group began its task in London, under Lieutenant-General F. E. Morgan, with the short title of "Cossac." [1]

The first question was where a landing in force could best be made. There were several options: the Dutch or Belgian coast; the Pas de Calais; between the mouths of the Somme and the Seine; Normandy; Brittany. Each of these had its own advantages and disadvantages, which had to be weighed up under a whole set of different headings and varying, sometimes uncertain, factors. Of these the principal were beaches; weather and tides; sites for constructing airfields; length of voyage; near-by ports that could be captured; the nature of the hinterland for subsequent operations; provision of cover by home-based aircraft; enemy dispositions, their minefields and defences.

[1] Chief of Staff, Supreme Allied Commander.

The choice easily narrowed to the Pas de Calais or Normandy. The former gave us the shorter sea passage and the best air cover, but here the defences were the most formidable. General Morgan and his advisers recommended the Normandy coast, which from the first had been advocated by Mountbatten. There can be no doubt now that this decision was sound. Normandy gave us the greatest hope. The defences were not so strong as in the Pas de Calais. The seas and the beaches were on the whole suitable, and were to some extent sheltered from the westerly gales by the Cotentin peninsula. The hinterland favoured the rapid deployment of large forces, and was sufficiently remote from the main strength of the enemy. The port of Cherbourg could be isolated and captured early in the operation. Brest could be outflanked and taken later.

All the coast between Havre and Cherbourg was of course defended with concrete forts and pill-boxes, but, as there was no harbour capable of sustaining a large army in this fifty-mile half-moon of sandy beaches, it was thought that the Germans would not assemble large forces in immediate support of the sea-front. Their High Command had no doubt said to themselves, "This is a good sector for raids up to ten or twenty thousand men, but unless Cherbourg is taken in working order no army in any way equal to the task of an invasion can be landed or nourished. It is a coast for a raid, but not for wider operations." If only there were harbours which could nourish great armies, here was the front on which to strike.

* * * * *

Of course, as the reader will have seen, I was well abreast of all the thought about landing-craft and tank landing-craft. I had also long been a partisan of piers with their heads floating out in the sea. Much work had since been done on them following a minute which in the course of our discussions I had issued as long ago as May 30, 1942.[2]

Prime Minister to Chief of Combined Operations
They must float up and down with the tide. The anchor prob-

2 See facsimile, page 73.

lem must be mastered. The ships must have a side-flap in them, and a drawbridge long enough to overreach the moorings of the piers. Let me have the best solution worked out. Don't argue the matter. The difficulties will argue for themselves.

Thought moved to the creation of a large area of sheltered water protected by a breakwater based on blockships brought to the scene by their own power and then sunk in a prearranged position. Mountbatten's reports in 1942 concentrated upon this idea, suggested directly by an officer on his staff, Captain J. Hughes-Hallett. Imagination, contrivance, and experiment had been ceaseless, and now in August 1943 there was a complete design for making two full-scale temporary harbours which could be towed over and brought into action within a few days of the original landing. These synthetic harbours were called "Mulberries," a code-name which certainly did not reveal their character or purpose.

*   *   *   *   *

One morning on our voyage, at my request, Brigadier K. G. McLean, with two other officers from General Morgan's Staff, came to me as I lay in my bed in the spacious cabin, and, after they had set up a large-scale map, explained in a tense and cogent tale the plan which had been prepared for the cross-Channel descent upon France. The reader is perhaps familiar with all the arguments of 1941 and 1942 upon this burning question in all its variants, but this was the first time that I had heard the whole coherent plan presented in precise detail, both of numbers and tonnage, as the result of prolonged study by the officers of both nations.

Further discussions on succeeding days led into more technical detail. The Channel tides have a play of more than twenty feet, with corresponding scours along the beaches. The weather is always uncertain, and winds and gales may whip up in a few hours irresistible forces against frail human structures. The fools or knaves who had chalked "Second Front Now" on our walls for the past two years had not had their minds burdened by such problems. I had long pondered upon them.

Piers for Use on Beaches

CONDITIONS OF BEACH

Average gradient is 1 in 200 and beaches are open to the south west.

CONDITIONS OF TIDE

2.   Range of spring tides is 30 feet and the strength of the tide parallel to the beach is 4 knots at springs.

SCAFFOLDING PIERS

3.   A pier to be of use for unloading ships of 20 foot draught would have to be 1 mile in length and 40 foot in height at the seaward end.   The present type of scaffolding pier does not exceed 20 foot in height.   It is doubtful whether a pier of these large dimensions could be made with scaffolding, but in any case tha amount of material required would be prohibitive.

PONTOON PIERS

4.   A pontoon pier would have to be similar in length. All floating piers suffer from the disadvantage of having to be securely moored with heavy anchors.   Even then they are most vulnerable and will not stand up to a gale of wind.   The strength of the tide is so great that the moorings will have to be very large.   If large pontoons were moored, 20 yards apart, at least 200 anchors would be required.   The sea-ward end of a floating pier must be particularly well moored and the mooring chains form an obstacle to ships coming alongside.   Owing to the poor ratio between the weight of a floating pontoons and the weight they can carry, and to their vulnerability to sea wind and tide, they are not favoured in comparison with scaffolding piers on open beaches.

[handwritten note:]

C.C.O.
or deputy

They must float up & down w the tide.
The anchor problem must be mastered. The ships must
have a silo-flap cut in them and a drawbridge
long enough to overreach the moorings of the pier.
Let me see the best solution worked out. Don't argue the matter.
The difficulties will argue for themselves   WSC 30.7.42

It must be remembered that in the "Mulberry" harbours we had a multiple problem to face. The whole project involved the construction in Britain of great masses of special equipment, amounting in the aggregate to over a million tons of steel and concrete. This work, undertaken with the highest priority, would impinge heavily on our already hard-pressed engineering and ship-repairing industries. All this equipment would have to be transported by sea to the scene of action, and there erected with the utmost expedition in the face of enemy attack and the vagaries of the weather.

The whole project was majestic. On the beaches themselves would be the great piers, with their seaward ends afloat and sheltered. At these piers coasters and landing-craft would be able to discharge at all states of the tide. To protect them against the wanton winds and waves breakwaters would be spread in a great arc to seaward, enclosing a large area of sheltered water. Thus sheltered, deep-draught ships could lie at anchor and discharge, and all types of landing-craft could ply freely to and from the beaches. These breakwaters would be composed of sunken concrete structures known as "Phoenix" and blockships known as "Gooseberries." In my second volume I have described the similar structures which I thought might in the First World War have been used to create artificial harbours in the Heligoland Bight.[3] Now they were to form a principal part of the great plan.

*   *   *   *   *

This was the scheme of the "Mulberry" harbour, but even so it was not enough. There would not be room for all the ships we needed. Many would have to discharge outside. To shield these and the very numerous naval vessels engaged, an additional scheme of *floating* breakwaters was proposed. For this purpose several devices were being considered, among them one to create a barrier to wave action by means of a continuous screen of air bubbles discharged from pipes laid on the sea-bed. It was hoped this screen would break up and

[3] See Volume II, *Their Finest Hour*, Chapter 12, pages 252–54.

absorb the rhythm of the waves. Another device known as a "Lilo" consisted of partially inflated air bags carrying submerged curtains of concrete. These would be moored in line to seaward of the "Phoenix" and enclose a considerable additional area of water. Neither of these ideas reached fruition, but eventually a device called the "Bombardon" was adopted, embodying some of the features of the "Lilo." It was a cruciform steel structure about two hundred feet long and twenty-five feet high, with all but the top arm of the cross submerged. In the event this device was of doubtful value, as we shall see in due course.

I was very well satisfied with the prospect of having the whole of this story presented to President Roosevelt with my full support. At least it would convince the American authorities that we were not insincere about "Overlord" and had not grudged thought or time in preparation. I arranged to assemble in Quebec the best experts in such matters from London and Washington. Together they could pool resources and find the best answers to the many technical problems.

I was now convinced of the enormous advantages of attacking the Havre-Cherbourg sector, provided these unexpected harbours could be brought into being from the first and thus render possible the landing and sustained advance of armies of a million rising to two million men, with all their immense modern equipment and impedimenta. This would mean being able to unload at least twelve thousand tons a day.

*   *   *   *   *

There was another associated problem on which my mind dwelt, namely, the maintenance of fighting air superiority over the battle area. If we could create a floating airfield, we could refuel our fighter aircraft within striking distance of the landing-points, and thus multiply our air-power on the spot at the decisive moment. Among the numerous devices discussed during this busy voyage was one called "Habakkuk." This project was conceived by a Mr. Pyke on Mountbatten's Staff. His idea was to form a structure of ice, large enough to serve as a runway for aircraft. It would be of ship-like construction, displacing a million tons, self-propelled at slow speed, with its own anti-aircraft defence, with workshops and repair facilities, and with a surprisingly small refrigerating plant for preserving its own existence. It had been found that by adding a proportion of wood pulp in various forms to ordinary sea ice the mixture lost the brittle qualities associated with ice and became extremely tough. This substance, called "Pykrete," after its inventor, seemed to offer great possibilities not only for our needs in Northwest Europe, but also elsewhere. It was found that as the ice melted the fibrous content quickly formed a furry outer surface which acted as an insulator and greatly retarded the melting process. Much development work was eventually done on this side, particularly in Canada, but for various reasons it never had any success.

I set forth my ideas about this in a minute to the Chiefs of Staff.

Prime Minister to General Ismay, for C.O.S. Committee   9 Aug. 43

Few technical devices or constructions could exercise more important strategic effects than those which would give us the power to have a number of floating Air Force refuelling stations, movable at will for particular operations. In the "Habakkuk" discussions it is stated that a timber structure can be made, and obviously steel pontoons could be fastened together. But all these when subject to the movement of the waves are liable to break up, and anyhow they are subject to intense strain and do not give that smooth run which aircraft require.

2. If however the Bubble story works, there is no reason why a pipe should not be lowered from two or three suitable ships and dangled from them at the right depth, and thus immunity from waves would be secured within an area in which the raft or pontoon runway could be stationed. The runway could always be kept head to wind, and no moorings would be necessary in deep water, as the whole of the vessels and the raft would drift together a few miles this way or that in the course of the day. This matter therefore deserves very keen examination.

3. One can imagine the use of two or three such refuelling bases for an attack on "Jupiter" [Norway]. But what about two or three

stepping-stones of this kind across the Bay of Bengal for "Culverin" [Sumatra]? This would leave the carriers free to protect the vessels and the landing, and also the nearest of the stepping-stones concerned. The *fighter* aircraft could therefore do two or three hops across the bay and come into action in much larger numbers than would be possible if they were used from ships. This apparatus seems at first sight to be far less costly and quicker to make than aircraft-carriers. Naturally, you choose good weather conditions for the operation. I am most anxious that this subject should be pursued theoretically at once, and thereafter, if all is well, on a large scale. Pray let me have your opinion.

Three dominating assumptions were made both by the framers of the plan and the British Chiefs of Staff. With these I was in entire agreement, and, as will be seen later, they were approved by the Americans and accepted by the Russians.

That there must be a substantial reduction in the strength of the German fighter aircraft in Northwest Europe before the assault took place.

2. That there should be not more than twelve mobile German divisions in Northern France at the time the operation was launched, and that it must not be possible for the Germans to build up more than fifteen divisions in the succeeding two months.

3. That the problem of beach maintenance of large forces in the tidal waters of the English Channel over a prolonged period must be overcome. To ensure this it was essential that we should be able to construct at least two effective synthetic harbours.

*   *   *   *   *

I also had many discussions with the Chiefs of Staff on our affairs in the Indian and Far Eastern theatres. We had none too good a tale to tell. A division had advanced at the end of 1942 down the Arakan coast of Burma to recapture the port of Akyab. Though strengthened until a complete corps was engaged, under the command of General Irwin, the operation had failed, and our troops were forced back over the Indian frontier.

Although there was much to be said in explanation, I felt that the whole question of the British High Command against Japan must come under review. New methods and new men were needed. I had long felt that it was a bad arrangement for the Commander-in-Chief India to command the operations in Burma in addition to his other far-reaching responsibilities. It seemed to me that the vigorous prosecution of large-scale operations against the Japanese in Southeast Asia necessitated the creation of a separate Supreme Allied Command. The Chiefs of Staff were in complete agreement, and prepared a memorandum on these lines for discussion with their American colleagues in Quebec. There remained the question of the commander of this new theatre, and we were in no doubt that he should be British. Of the various names that were put forward, I was sure in my own mind that Admiral Mountbatten had superior qualifications for this great command, and I determined to make this proposal to President Roosevelt at the first opportunity. The appointment of an officer of the substantive rank of Captain R.N. to the Supreme Command of one of the main theatres of the war was an unusual step. But, having carefully prepared the ground beforehand, I was not surprised when the President cordially agreed.

*   *   *   *   *

I produced for the Chiefs of Staff Committee a note on plans and policies, from which the following is an extract:

7 Aug. 43

Before we meet the Americans we must settle upon: (a) The general plan for the Southeast Asia Command and the Supreme Commander, and (b) positive proposals for attacking the enemy, and proving our zeal in this theatre of war, which by its failures and sluggishness is in a measure under reasonable reproach.

I feel that we ought to let Brigadier Wingate tell his story and furnish the United States Chiefs of Staff with copies of his report, and thus convince them that we mean business in this sector of the Southeast Asia Front. Obviously the Arakan force should lie up against the enemy and engage him. But the advance upon Akyab ought to be stopped now, not only in the interests of the Mediterranean campaign, which should be paramount, but also because it is in itself a faulty and unsound operation. It seeks to strike the enemy where he is best prepared. It lays itself open to serious counter-measures by him. It achieves no major strategic purpose.

$$* \quad * \quad * \quad * \quad *$$

It is astonishing how quickly a voyage can pass if one has enough to do to occupy every waking minute. I had looked forward to an interval of rest and a change from the perpetual clatter of the war. But as we approached our destination, the holiday seemed to be over before it had begun.

5

The Quebec Conference

"Quadrant"

*The Citadel — My Telegram to The King, August 11 — Visit to
Hyde Park — My Memorandum of August 17 About Italy —
The "Quadrant" Conference Opens, August 19 — The Chiefs of
Staff Report upon "Overlord" — I Propose an American Commander — Strategy in Italy — Mountbatten for Supreme Commander in Southeast Asia — Major Strategy Against Japan —
Proposed British Contribution Against Sumatra — My Telegram
to Mr. Attlee, August 22 — British Claims to Share in the Main
Attack on Japan — A Comical Incident — "Habakkuk" Dismissed — Mountbatten Appointed — My Telegram to Mr. Attlee
of August 25 — My Liaison Officers with General MacArthur
and Generalissimo Chiang Kai-shek — Eisenhower Presses for the
Invasion of Italy — Need to Take Naples — Disquieting Estimates of British Reinforcements — I Give Instructions for a
Large Increase.*

HALIFAX was reached on August 9. The great ship drew
in to the landing jetty and we went straight to our train.
In spite of all precautions about secrecy, large crowds were assembled. As my wife and I sat in our saloon at the end of the
train, the people gathered round and gave us welcome. Before
we started, I made them sing "The Maple Leaf" and "O Canada!" I feared they did not know "Rule, Britannia," though I
am sure they would have enjoyed it if we had had a band.
After about twenty minutes of handshakings, photographs, and
autographs, we left for Quebec.

Two days later I telegraphed to the King:

11 Aug. 43

Prime Minister to His Majesty the King, with humble duty

The Citadel is in every way delightful and ideally suited to the purpose. Arrangements for the President are perfect. He has the upper floor and ramps are fitted everywhere for his convenience. I am most grateful to Your Majesty for arranging this. I have telegraphed to the Governor-General thanking him for the trouble he has taken and for his kindly welcome.

2. The holding of this conference in Canada, and especially at Quebec, is most timely, as there is a lot of fretfulness here which I believe will soon be removed. I meet the Canadian Cabinet this morning and the Quebec Cabinet this afternoon, and start thereafter for Hyde Park.

3. I presume Your Majesty will already have seen the question that I put to the Deputy Prime Minister and Foreign Secretary about Dickie.[1] I have not yet heard from them, but I am increasingly inclined to suggest this solution to the President. Brigadier Wingate made a deep impression on all during the voyage, and I look for a new turn being given to the campaign in Upper Burma.

4. Your Majesty will also have noticed that I have heard from the Great Bear and that we are on speaking, or at least growling, terms again.

I also telegraphed to the President:

Former Naval Person to President Roosevelt   11 Aug. 43

I have just arrived, after a most swift and agreeable journey, on which it has been possible to work continuously. The Warden family [2] are looking forward keenly to their visit to Hyde Park, where we propose to arrive the afternoon of the 12th. Are we right in thinking we should all bring our thinnest clothes?

My wife was forced to rest in the Citadel, but next day Mary and I travelled to Hyde Park. We visited the Niagara Falls on the way. The reporters asked me what I thought of them, and gave the following account of our talk: " 'I saw them before you were born. I came here first in 1900.' 'Do they look the same?' 'Well,' he replied, 'the principle seems the same. The

1 Admiral Lord Louis Mountbatten.
2 My code-name was "Colonel Warden."

water still keeps falling over.' " We were the President's guests
till August 14. It was indeed so hot that I got up one night
because I was unable to sleep and hardly able to breathe, and
went outside to sit on a bluff overlooking the Hudson River.
Here I watched the dawn.

Harry Hopkins came to Hyde Park. He was obviously invited to please me. He explained to me his altered position.
He had declined in the favour of the President. There was
a curious incident at luncheon, when he arrived a few minutes
late and the President did not even greet him. It was remarkable how definitely my contacts with the President improved,
and our affairs moved quicker as Hopkins appeared to regain
his influence. In two days it seemed to be like old times. He
said to me, "You must know I am not what I was." He had
tried too much at once. Even his greatness of spirit broke under
his variegated activities.

*   *   *   *   *

In these same August days I prepared a general statement
upon the whole of our war policy. The greater part of it
concerned operations in Burma and the Indian Ocean and
their reactions upon the war against Japan. These will be
described later. The paper is dated August 17. The immediate
point on which my mind was focused was to procure the
invasion of Italy as the natural consequence and exploitation
of our victory in Sicily and Mussolini's fall.

Should Naples be captured [Operation "Avalanche"] in the near
future, we shall have a first-rate port in Italy, and other harbours,
like Brindisi and Taranto, will fall into our possession thereafter.
If by November our front can be established as far north as the
Leghorn-Ancona line, the landing-craft in the Mediterranean will
have played their part. A detachment would be required from the
landing fleet for amphibious turning movements such as we have
seen in Sicily, for minor descents across the Adriatic, and for operations such as "Accolade" [the capture of Rhodes and other islands
in the Aegean]. The disappearance of the Italian Fleet as a factor
should enable a great diminution in naval strength in the Mediter-

ranean to be made, just as the use of first-class harbours supersedes
the need of landing-craft. There should therefore be during the
late autumn the power to move landing-craft and assault ships back
for "Overlord," and also to send a sufficient detachment through
the Suez Canal to the Indian theatre. I repeat however that the
maximum number for which landing-craft should be supplied in
a single flight is thirty thousand men.

Although I have frequently spoken of the line of the Po or of
the Alps as being desirable objectives for us this year in Italy, it is
not possible to see so far at present. A very great advantage will
have been gained if we stop at the Leghorn-Ancona line. We
should thus avoid the danger which General Wilson has pointed
out of the immense broadening of the front which will take place
as soon as that line has been passed. The estimate which has been
given me of twenty-two divisions was presumably formed for this
broad front. What is the estimate needed to hold the Leghorn-
Ancona line? If we cannot have the best, there are very good
second-bests. From such a position we could by air supply a
fomented rising in Savoy and the French Alps, to which the young
men of France would be able to rally, and at the same time with
our right hand we could act across the Adriatic to stimulate the
Patriot activities in the Balkan peninsula. It may be necessary for
us to accept these limitations in order that the integrity of Operation "Overlord" shall not be marred.

*   *   *   *   *

On August 17, the President and Harry Hopkins reached
Quebec, and Eden and Brendan Bracken flew in from England. As the delegations gathered, further news of Italian peace
moves came out to us, and it was under the impression of
Italy's approaching surrender that our talks were held. The
Chiefs of Staff had been at work with their American colleagues in the Citadel since August 14, and had drafted a comprehensive progress report on the future strategy of the war
for 1943/44. In fact "Quadrant" was a series of technical Staff
conferences, the results of which were surveyed in two meetings between the President and myself and our Service chiefs.

The first plenary session was held on August 19. Highest
strategic priority "as a prerequisite to 'Overlord' " was given

to the combined bomber offensive against Germany. The lengthy discussions upon Operation "Overlord" were then summarised in the light of the combined planning in London by General Morgan. The Chiefs of Staff now reported as follows:

OPERATION "OVERLORD"

(a) This operation will be the primary United States-British ground and air effort against the Axis in Europe. (Target date, May 1, 1944.) After securing adequate Channel ports, exploitation will be directed towards securing areas that will facilitate both ground and air operations against the enemy. Following the establishment of strong Allied forces in France, operations designed to strike at the heart of Germany and to destroy her military forces will be undertaken.

(b) Balanced ground and air force to be built up for "Overlord," and there will be continuous planning for and maintenance of those forces available in the United Kingdom in readiness to take advantage of any situation permitting an opportunistic cross-Channel move into France.

(c) As between Operation "Overlord" and operations in the Mediterranean, where there is a shortage of resources available, resources will be distributed and employed with the main object of ensuring the success of "Overlord." Operations in the Mediterranean theatre will be carried out with the forces allotted at "Trident" [the previous conference at Washington in May], except in so far as these may be varied by decision of the Combined Chiefs of Staff.

We have approved the outline plan of General Morgan for Operation "Overlord," and have authorised him to proceed with the detailed planning and with full preparations.

These paragraphs produced some discussion at our meeting. I pointed out that the success of "Overlord" depended on certain conditions being fulfilled in regard to relative strength. I emphasised that I strongly favoured "Overlord" in 1944, though I had not been in favour of "Sledgehammer" in 1942 or "Round-up" in 1943. The objections which I had to the cross-Channel operation were however now removed. I thought that every effort should be made to add at least twenty-five per cent to the first assault. This would mean finding more landing-craft. There were still nine months to go, and much could be done in that time. The beaches selected were good, and it would be better if at the same time a landing were to be made on the inside beaches of the Cotentin peninsula. "Above all," I said, "the initial lodgment must be strong."

As the United States had the African command, it had been agreed between the President and me that the commander of "Overlord" should be British, and I proposed for this purpose, with the President's agreement, General Brooke, the Chief of the Imperial General Staff, who, it may be remembered, had commanded a corps in the decisive battle on the road to Dunkirk, with both Alexander and Montgomery as his subordinates. I had informed General Brooke of this intention *early in* 1943. This operation was to begin with equal British and American forces, and as it was to be based on Great Britain, it seemed right to make such an arrangement. However, as the year advanced and the immense plan of the invasion began to take shape, I became increasingly impressed with the very great preponderance of American troops that would be employed after the original landing with equal numbers had been successful, and now at Quebec, I myself took the initiative of proposing to the President that an American commander should be appointed for the expedition to France. He was gratified at this suggestion, and I dare say his mind had been moving that way. We therefore agreed that an American officer should command "Overlord" and that the Mediterranean should be entrusted to a British commander, the actual date of the change being dependent upon the progress of the war. In August 1943 I informed General Brooke, who had my entire confidence, of this change, and of the reasons for it. He bore the great disappointment with soldierly dignity.

* * * * *

As to Italy, the Chiefs of Staff proposed that there should be three phases in our future operations. First, we should drive Italy out of the war and establish airfields near Rome, and if possible farther north. I pointed out that I wanted it definitely understood that I was not committed to an advance beyond the Ancona-Pisa line. Second, we should seize Sardinia and Corsica, and then press hard against the Germans in the north of the peninsula to stop them joining in the fight against "Overlord." There was also "Anvil," a projected landing in Southern France in the neighbourhood of Toulon and Marseilles and an advance northward up the Rhone Valley. This was to lead to much controversy later on. Recommendations were made about supplying Balkan and French guerrillas by air, intensifying the war against the U-boats, and making more use of the Azores as a naval and air base.

*   *   *   *   *

On the major question of the Southeast Asia Command, the original proposals of the British Chiefs of Staff had been considered. The plan of a Supreme Commander found favour, and the following recommendations were made:

(a) That the Combined Chiefs of Staff will exercise a general jurisdiction over strategy for the Southeast Asia theatre and the allocation of American and British resources of all kinds between the China theatre and the Southeast Asia Command.

(b) That the British Chiefs of Staff will exercise jurisdiction over all matters pertaining to operations, and will be the channel through which all instructions to the Supreme Commander are passed.

*   *   *   *   *

There was a spirited argument at our first plenary meeting on the whole question of Far Eastern strategy, on which the work of the Chiefs of Staff was to centre in the following days. Japan's island empire must be crushed mainly by the application of maritime power. No army could be engaged without first winning control of Japanese waters. How could the air weapon be used? Opinions diverged sharply. There were some close to President Roosevelt who advocated making the main

assault through Burma into China. They argued that ports'
and air bases in China would be indispensable for intensive
and sustained air attacks against the mainland of Japan. Although politically attractive in American eyes, this idea
ignored the impossibility of deploying large armies, most of
which would have to be found by Britain, in the jungles of
Burma, and also the presence of very strong Japanese forces in
China operating on interior lines of communication, and above
all the relatively minor contribution which could be made to
such an undertaking by the expanding seapower of the United
States.

Alternatively we could make a direct attack by sea against
Japan's island barrier in the Central and South Pacific. The
burden of this would fall mainly on the Navy and the maritime
air forces. Such a thrust would be aimed first at the Philippines, which to all Americans offered an attractive goal. With
the Philippines once more in American hands, Japan would be
isolated from many of its chief sources of supply and the garrisons in the outlying islands of the Dutch East Indies would
be cut off from all hope of rescue. They would eventually
wither and die without the need for costly fighting.

From the Philippines the encirclement of the Japanese
homeland could begin. New bases on the China coast, in Formosa, and in the small islands south of Japan might all be
necessary, but once these were obtained the full-scale invasion
of Japan became practicable. The bold sweep of this conception was the more attractive in that it rested squarely on the
might of American sea-power. Very large naval forces would
be needed, but only in the final phase would great armies be
required, and by then Hitler would be overthrown and the
main strength of Britain and the United States could be hurled
against Japan.

I was anxious to state my views on this occasion before the
remaining meetings of the Chiefs of Staff. The British planners were proposing in the coming winter to extend the operations of Wingate's forces into Northern Burma, and I was
convinced that this should be supplemented by the seizure of

the tip of Sumatra. I said at the meeting that I was convinced that "the attack on Sumatra was a great strategic blow which should be struck in 1944. This operation, 'Culverin,' would be the 'Torch' of the Indian Ocean. In my opinion it would not be beyond the compass of our resources. We should be striking and seizing a point of our own against which the Japanese would have to beat themselves if they wished to end the severe drain which would be imposed on their shipping by our air action from Sumatra." The President seemed to think that such an operation would be heading away from the main direction of our advance towards Japan. I pointed out that the alternative would be to waste the entire year with nothing to show for it but Akyab and the future right to toil through the swamps and jungles of Burma, about the suggested reconquest of which I was very dubious. I emphasised the value of the Sumatra project, which I compared, in its promise of decisive consequences, with the Dardanelles operation of 1915. The idea of trying to tie up all our amphibious resources in the Indian Ocean in 1943/44 in order to retake Akyab seemed to me not to be right.

The next day I minuted:

20 Aug. 43

Prime Minister to General Ismay, for C.O.S. Committee

We are not yet agreed among ourselves about the policy to be pursued in Akyab, "Culverin," etc., and in my opinion the whole matter has been insufficiently studied. I am still studying it myself. In the meanwhile it is not possible to come to any decision with the Americans in the matter. I hope the Chiefs of Staff will beware of creating a situation where I shall certainly have to refuse to bear any responsibility for a decision which is taken on their level. This would entail the whole matter being referred to the War Cabinet at home after our return. I remain absolutely where I was at the last Conference, and where we all were, that a campaign through Rangoon up the Irrawaddy to Mandalay and beyond would be most detrimental and disadvantageous to us. The capture of Akyab without such a campaign is only an act of waste and folly. . . .

The situation I wish to have at this time next year is that we are masters of "Culverin," that Wingate is in touch with the Chinese in Yunnan, that the communications in Upper Burma have been improved as far as possible, and that we have a free option where to strike next amphibiously, having regard to the reactions from the enemy, which by then will have been apparent.

Two days later I telegraphed home:

Prime Minister (Quebec) to Deputy Prime Minister   22 Aug. 43

The President and General Marshall are very keen on Mountbatten's appointment, which it is certain the United States Government will cordially accept. Our Chiefs of Staff concur. There is no doubt of the need of a young and vigorous mind in this lethargic and stagnant Indian scene. I have no doubts whatsoever that it is my duty to make this proposal formally and to submit Mountbatten's name to the King. Mountbatten and Wingate working together have thrown a great deal of new light upon future plans. It is essential that following upon this conference an announcement should be made in a few days. I hope my colleagues will feel this is the best course to take.

2. We have also cleared up to our satisfaction the difficulties about the Southeast Asia Command. Broad strategic plans and major assignments of forces and supplies will be decided by the Combined Chiefs of Staff subject to the approval of their respective Governments. But all operational control will be vested in the British Chiefs of Staff acting under His Majesty's Government, and all orders will go through them.

3. We have not been able to reach a final conclusion about the extent to which the floods will have delayed the proposed operations in North Burma, nor have we yet given sufficient detailed study to the first stage of Operation "Culverin" to decide whether that should be given priority in amphibious operations during 1944. At least another month's intense study is required. The discussions however have been most friendly, and there is no doubt that the United States Chiefs of Staff are gratified at the constructive interest which we have shown in war plans against Japan in 1944. Soong arrives on Monday, but will in principle be told no more than what is contained in my immediately following.

4. General Marshall has consented to my being represented on

General MacArthur's staff by a British liaison officer of General's rank. This will enable us to follow much more closely than hitherto what is happening in that theatre. I discussed this matter with Dr. Evatt when he was in London. He said he was all for it, and I am now telegraphing to Curtin about it, pointing out that this will bring us more closely into touch with the war in the Pacific.

5. Eden and Hull are locked in lengthy discussions. Hull remains completely obdurate about not using the word "recognition" in respect of the French Committee. We have therefore agreed that they shall publish their document, and we ours, and the Canadians theirs, after communicating with Russia and others concerned. Eden has this matter in hand. I have pointed out in the plainest terms to the President that they will certainly have a bad press, but he says he would rather have a sheet anchor out against the machinations of de Gaulle. Our position is of course different, for we are doing no more for the Committee by our formula than we did for de Gaulle when he was alone and quite uncontrolled by others.

*   *   *   *   *

The Staff discussion upon the share we were to have in the major assault upon Japan became heated and led to an amusing incident. Each of the joint Staffs had behind them a considerable group of twelve to twenty high Staff officers, a quivering audience, silent, with gleaming eyes. Presently the Chairman said, "I think we had better discuss this without our Staffs being present," upon which the group of high Staff officers filed out into a waiting-room. The quarrel was duly settled, as usual, and Mountbatten, whose position as Chief of Combined Operations gave him a seat on the British Chiefs of Staff Committee, seized this opportunity to ask the Chairman if he might give a demonstration of the special mixture of ice which his scientists had found. This was called Pykrete.[2] On receiving permission, one of his Staff wheeled in on a large dumb-waiter two blocks of ice about three feet high, one common or garden ice, the other Pykrete. He invited the strongest

[2] The special substance for use in the Habakkuk project and named after its inventor, Mr. Pyke.

man present to chop each block of ice in half with a special chopper he had brought. All present voted General Arnold into the job of "strong man." He took off his coat, rolled up his sleeves, and swung the chopper, splitting the ordinary ice with one blow. He turned round, smiling, and, clasping his hands, seized the chopper again, and advanced upon the block of Pykrete. He swung the chopper, and as he brought it down let go with a cry of pain, for the Pykrete had suffered little damage and his elbows had been badly jarred.

Mountbatten then capped matters by drawing a pistol from his pocket to demonstrate the strength of Pykrete against gunfire. He first fired at the ordinary ice, which was shattered. He then fired at the Pykrete, which was so strong that the bullet ricocheted, narrowly missing Portal.

The waiting officers outside, who had been worried enough by the sound of the blows and the scream of pain from General Arnold, were horrified at the revolver shots, one of them crying out, "My God! They've now started shooting!"

But who in war will not have his laugh amid the skulls? — and here was one.

*   *   *   *   *

Actually the dispute between the British and American Chiefs of Staff was on the issue that Britain demanded a full and fair place in the war against Japan from the moment when Germany was beaten. She demanded a share of the airfields, a share of the bases for the Royal Navy, a proper assignment of duties to whatever divisions she could transport to the Far East after the Hitler business was finished. In the end the Americans gave way. My friends on the Chiefs of Staff Committee had been pressed by me to fight this point, not indeed to pistols, but to the utmost limit, because at this stage in the war what I most feared was that American critics would say, "England, having taken all she could from us to help her beat Hitler, stands out of the war against Japan and will leave us in the lurch." However, at the Quebec Conference this impression was effectively removed.

*   *   *   *   *

On the late afternoon of August 23, we had our second plenary meeting to discuss the draft of the final report of the Combined Chiefs of Staff. This document reiterated the points raised in their first report as amended after our discussion on them, and in addition set out in detail proposed operational arrangements in the Far East. No decision was reached in the report on the actual operations to be undertaken, though it was decided that the main effort should be put into offensive operations with the object of "establishing land communications with China and improving and securing the air route." In the "over-all strategic concept" of the Japan war, plans were to be made to bring about the defeat of Japan within twelve months after the collapse of Germany. I said I was glad to see that this was to be our target rather than planning on the basis of a prolonged war of attrition.

Finally, the general principle of a separate Southeast Asia Command, which I had proposed to the President before the Conference, was accepted. I said that I was anxious to make a public announcement about this as soon as possible. This would also help to show how much of the discussions at "Quadrant" had been concerned with the war against Japan, and thus set forth sufficient reasons why Russia had not been included in the deliberations. It was generally agreed by those present that we should do this.

*   *   *   *   *

I now told the Viceroy of the decision to set up a Southeast Asia Command, with Mountbatten as Supreme Commander.

Prime Minister to Viceroy of India   24 Aug. 43

We have now formed and set up the Southeast Asia Command, separate from the command in India, which was foreshadowed by me at the time of Field-Marshal Wavell's appointment to the Viceroyalty. There are great advantages in having under a British commander a combined command similar to that which exists in North Africa. We have had some discussions with the Americans in the weeks that have passed upon the person of the commander. After a great deal of consideration, I decided to propose Lord Louis

Mountbatten, now Chief of Combined Operations, for this very important post. Mountbatten has unique qualifications, in that he is intimately acquainted with all three branches of the Services, and also with amphibious operations. He has served for nearly a year and a half on the Chiefs of Staff Committee, and thus knows the whole of our war story from the centre. I regard this as of great importance on account of the extremely varied character of the Southeast Asia front by land and sea. Mountbatten is a fine organiser and a man of great energy and daring. His appointment has been cordially welcomed by the President and by the American Chiefs of Staff, and was hailed with delight by Soong on behalf of the Generalissimo. I am therefore, with the approval of the Cabinet, making the necessary submissions to the King, and send this message to you for your information, as it is important that the announcement should emerge out of the present Conference. It will be made public tomorrow, August 25.

Next day I sent the following telegram to my colleagues at home:

Prime Minister to Deputy Prime Minister and   25 Aug. 43
War Cabinet only

Everything here has gone off well. We have secured a settlement of a number of hitherto untractable questions, e.g., the Southeast Asia Command, "Tube Alloys," and French Committee recognition. On this last we all had an awful time with Hull, who has at last gone off in a pretty sulky mood, especially with the Foreign Secretary who bore the brunt. Unanimous agreement is expressed in a masterly report by the Combined Chiefs of Staff which the President and I have both approved. All differences have been smoothed away except that the question of the exact form of our amphibious activities in the Bay of Bengal has been left over for further study. I think however it is settling itself as I wished. There is no doubt that Mackenzie King and the Canadian Government are delighted and feel themselves thoroughly "on the map."

2. The black spot at the present time is the increasing bearishness of Soviet Russia. You will have seen the telegram received from Stalin about the Italian overtures. He has absolutely no ground for complaint, as we have done no more than to hand

the Italian representative the severe directions expressing unconditional surrender which had already received the cordial approval
of the Soviet Government and have immediately reported all these
matters to him.

3. The President was very much offended at the tone of this
message. He gave directions to the effect that the new Soviet
Chargé d'Affaires was to be told he was away in the country and
would not be back for some days. Stalin has of course studiously
ignored our offer to make a further long and hazardous journey in
order to bring about a tripartite meeting. In spite of all this, I
do not think his manifestations of ill temper and bad manners are
preparatory to a separate peace with Germany, as the hatreds
between the two races have now become a sanitary cordon in
themselves. It is disheartening to make so little progress with these
people, but I am sure my colleagues will not feel that I myself or
our Government as a whole have been wanting in any way in
patience and in loyalty.

4. I am feeling rather tired, as the work at the Conference has
been very heavy and many large and difficult questions have
weighed upon us. I hope my colleagues will think it proper for
me to take two or three days' rest at one of these mountain camps
before I broadcast on Sunday and proceed to Washington. I am
also planning to broadcast when taking a degree at Harvard University on September 3, and to return home immediately thereafter. It is only in the event of some unexpected development in
Italy or elsewhere which would make it desirable for me and the
President to be close together that I should prolong my stay. In
any case, I shall be back in good time before the meeting of Parliament. The Foreign Secretary returns by air on Saturday and is
sending Cadogan with me to Washington.

I decided to have two liaison officers, one with MacArthur
and the other with Chiang Kai-shek. When I got home, I sent
for Generals Lumsden and Carton de Wiart to come to
Chequers, and offered them these appointments, to the great
delight of both. Lumsden was one of our most distinguished
and accomplished officers, who at the very beginning of the
war, in the first contact with the enemy, had brought the
armoured car back into popularity. He soon gained General
MacArthur's confidence and proved a valuable liaison officer.

He was killed in January 1945. A Japanese suicide bomber attacked the battleship *New Mexico* during the bombardment of Lingayen Gulf. On the bridge stood Admiral Fraser, the British Commander, and General Lumsden. By pure chance the first two moved to the opposite side to get a better view. A minute later the suicide bomber struck. All at Lumden's end of the bridge were killed. His death was a loss to his country and to me personally.

*   *   *   *   *

We must now return to the Italian scene. Contrary to our earlier hopes, the bulk of the Germans successfully withdrew across the Straits of Messina. On August 16, General Eisenhower had held a meeting of his commanders to select from a variety of proposals the means by which the campaign should be carried into Italy. He had to take special account of the enemy dispositions of that time. Eight of the sixteen German divisions in Italy were in the north under Rommel, two were near Rome, and six were farther south under Kesselring. These powerful forces might be reinforced from twenty German divisions which had been withdrawn from the Russian Front to refit in France. Nothing we might gather for a long time could equal the strength which the Germans could put in the field, but the British and Americans had command of sea and air, and also the initiative. The assault upon which all minds were now set was a daring enterprise. It was hoped to gain the ports of Naples and Taranto, whose combined facilities were proportioned to the scale of the armies we must use. The early capture of airfields was a prime aim. Those near Rome were as yet beyond our reach, but there was an important group at Foggia adaptable for heavy bombers, and our tactical air forces sought others in the heel of Italy and at Montecorvino, near Salerno.

General Eisenhower decided to begin the assault in early September by an attack across the Straits of Messina, with subsidiary descents on the Calabrian coast. This would be the prelude to the capture of Naples (Operation "Avalanche") by a British and an American army corps landing on the good beaches in the Gulf of Salerno. This was at the extreme range of fighter cover from the captured Sicilian airfields. As soon as possible after the landings, the Allied forces would drive north to capture Naples.

The Combined Chiefs of Staff advised the President and me to accept this plan and to authorise the seizure of Sardinia and Corsica in second priority. We did so with alacrity; indeed, it was exactly what I had hoped and striven for. As part of the plan, it was intended to land an airborne division to capture the airfields south of Rome. This also we accepted. The circumstances in which this feature was cancelled are recounted in a later chapter.

*   *   *   *   *

What I regarded as highly satisfactory decisions had thus been obtained and all was moving forward. But towards the end of August, a British officer arrived at Quebec from General Eisenhower's headquarters with very disconcerting news. He stated that by December 1 six divisions would have crossed the Straits of Messina and passed through Calabria, and another six would have landed at Salerno. I at once protested against this alarming underestimate of our resources.

Prime Minister to General Alexander   26 Aug. 43

General Whiteley, who has been here, has told us the dates and scales of "Baytown" and "Avalanche" 3 respectively. This has filled me with the greatest concern, and I hope you will be able to reassure me. Assuming that our landings are successful and that we are not defeated in the subsequent battles, I cannot understand why two and a half months or more will be required to get ashore, or why it would be necessary, once we have obtained an effective port and bridgehead at "Avalanche," to march all the "Baytown" divisions through Calabria instead of sending some at least of them round by sea.

2. Moreover, the rate of build-up to twelve divisions on the mainland by December 1 seems to me to open dangers of the

3 "Baytown": the attack across the Straits of Messina. "Avalanche": the attack on Naples (Salerno).

gravest kind. First, no effective help can come to enable the Italians in Rome to turn against the Germans, and the dangers of a German Quisling Government being installed, or alternatively sheer anarchy supervening, will be aggravated and prolonged. Secondly, if your rate of build-up is no more than twelve divisions by December 1, and these only in the Naples area, what is to prevent the Germans in the same time from bringing far larger forces against them? They are at present said to have sixteen divisions in the Italian peninsula. I am not myself convinced that these are in fact complete divisions. On the contrary, it would seem likely that they are the leading elements and headquarters in several cases. But if the liberation of Rome and the gaining of the important political and military advantages following therefrom are to be delayed for more than three months from now, no one can measure the consequences.

3. I am most anxious to hear from you before I leave America, as the President was also much distressed by the date mentioned, and if it is really the kind of time-table that is being worked to, it would be better for us to face the worst in consultation. I hope however that you will chase these clouds away.

I addressed myself to this administrative failure as soon as I got home. The measures to re-form our armoured divisions which I had asked for on August 2, and which had been pursued by General Brooke, were already producing results, and the pessimistic estimates of which General Whiteley had been the bearer were soon overcome. The British 1st Armoured Division was re-equipped and became again a magnificent fighting force. Two Polish divisions, the New Zealand Division, and the 4th British-Indian Division were brought to the highest pitch and transported to Italy. The extraordinary prowess of the United States engineers transformed the port of Naples from ruin into a first-class harbour. In the early days of October a hundred thousand men were added to General Alexander's army. Had this not been achieved, a disaster might easily have occurred, for the Germans were arriving in strength.

6

Italy: The Armistice

Detailed plans had already been made between the British and United States Governments about the probable
surrender by Italy. The drafting of armistice terms was begun
before the end of July, and on August 3, I circulated the docu-

ments to the War Cabinet "in case of an approach being made
to us by Italy." We wished to have time to deal by political
or diplomatic channels rather than through Allied Military
Headquarters. On this same day, the first peace overtures from
Rome were made. Our Ambassador in Lisbon informed the
Foreign Office that the new Counsellor of the Italian Legation
there, who had just arrived from Rome, wished to see him,
and hinted that he bore a message from the Badoglio Government. This Italian diplomat was Ciano's former *chef de cabinet*, the Marquis D'Ayeta. He had American relations, and
was an acquaintance of Sumner Welles. His mission to Lisbon
had been planned under Badoglio's instructions by the new
Italian Foreign Secretary, Guariglia. On the following day,
D'Ayeta was invited to the British Embassy. He made no reference to an armistice, but explained that, although the King
and Badoglio wanted peace, they had to make the pretence of
continuing the fight in order to avoid a German *coup d'état* in
Italy. It was clear from what he said that Guariglia was particularly concerned to explain away to the Allies a meeting in
Northern Italy with Ribbentrop which he was about to fulfil in
order to soften German suspicions.

I immediately informed the President of this Italian approach.

Former Naval Person to President Roosevelt   5 Aug. 43

The following story has been told to British Ambassador Campbell at Lisbon by a newly arrived Italian Counsellor. . . . I send
it to you for what it is worth, which is substantial. Ambassador
Campbell was instructed to make no comment. It certainly seems
to give inside information. Though I am starting now for Quebec,
Anthony will be here, and you can communicate both with him
and me.

The King and the Army leaders had been preparing a *coup
d'état,* but this was precipitated, probably by a few days only, by
the action of the Grand Fascist Council. Fascism in Italy is extinct.
Every vestige has been swept away. Italy turned Red overnight.
In Turin and Milan there were Communist demonstrations which
had to be put down by armed force. Twenty years of Fascism has

obliterated the middle class. There is nothing between the King, with the patriots who have rallied round him, who have complete control, and rampant Bolshevism. The Germans have an armoured division just outside Rome, and will march in if there is any sign of Italian weakening. There are ten thousand scattered about inside Rome, mostly with machine-guns. If we bomb Rome again there will be a popular rising, and the Germans will then march in and slaughter everybody. They have actually threatened the use of gas. As many Italian troops as possible have been concentrated round Rome, but they have no stomach for fighting. They have practically no weapons, and are no match for even one well-equipped German division.

In these circumstances the King and Badoglio, whose first thought was to make peace, have no alternative but to put up a show of going on with the fight. Guariglia is to meet Ribbentrop, perhaps tomorrow, as a result of which there will be a communiqué stating in plainer terms than hitherto that Italy is still the active ally of Germany. But this will be only pretence. The whole country is only longing for peace, and above all to be rid of the Germans, who are universally execrated.

If we cannot attack Germany immediately through the Balkans, thus causing German withdrawal from Italy, the sooner we land in Italy the better. The Germans however are resolved to defend it line by line. When we land in Italy we shall find little opposition, and perhaps even active co-operation, on the part of the Italians.

D'Ayeta never from start to finish made any mention of peace terms, and his whole story, as you will have observed, was no more than a plea that we should save Italy from the Germans as well as from herself, and do it as quickly as possible.

He expressed the hope that we would not heap abuse on the King and Badoglio, which would precipitate the blood-bath, although a little of this would help them to keep up the pretence *vis-à-vis* the Germans.

*   *   *   *   *

The desire of all the Italian personalities involved was for peace with the Allies, and the Italian High Command were already eager to fight against the Germans. Guariglia and the Italian Foreign Office hoped by time and caution to achieve the turnover without incurring German wrath and revenge.

Thus, although we could not measure the forces at work, we came in contact with two Italian representatives. So did the Germans. On August 6, Guariglia and General Ambrosio met Ribbentrop and Keitel on the frontier. The military discussions were acrimonious. Ambrosio requested the return home of the Italian divisions in France and the Balkans. Keitel, on the contrary, during the meeting ordered the German units poised at the border posts to enter Italy. Meanwhile, Foreign Secretary Guariglia conducted a bland and meaningless conversation with Ribbentrop in the hope of postponing a German onslaught.

*   *   *   *   *

On August 6 another Italian diplomat, Signor Berio, approached our diplomatic representative in Tangier. His instructions were direct from Badoglio. Again a plea for time was made, but on this occasion a genuine desire to treat was expressed, and Berio was authorised to open negotiations.

I was on my way by sea to the Quebec Conference when this news reached me, together with Mr. Eden's comments. The Foreign Secretary wrote:

We are entitled to regard it as an offer by the Badoglio Government to negotiate on terms. . . . Should we not then reply that, as is well known, we insist on unconditional surrender, and the Badoglio Government must as a first step notify us that Italy surrenders unconditionally? Subsequently, at a later stage, if the Badoglio Government were to do this, we should then inform them of the terms on which we should be prepared to cease hostilities against Italy.

On receiving this message I minuted in red ink in the margin, "Don't miss the bus"; and again, "If they surrender immediately we should be prepared to accord conditions as acts of grace and not as a bargain." I then sent the following reply, dated August 7, to the Foreign Secretary:

Prime Minister to Foreign Secretary   7 Aug. 43

We agree with the course you have taken. Badoglio admits he

is going to double-cross someone, but his interests and the mood of the Italian people make it more likely Hitler will be the one to be tricked. Allowance should be made for the difficulties of his position. Meanwhile, the war should be carried forward against Italy in every way that the Americans will allow.

And again, on the day of my arrival in Canada:

Prime Minister to Foreign Secretary   9 Aug. 43

Badoglio must state that he is prepared to place himself unreservedly in the hands of the Allied Governments, who have already made it plain that they desire Italy to have a respectable place in the New Europe.

Reference should also be made to General Eisenhower's offer of the return of Italian prisoners of war taken in Tunisia and Sicily, provided Allied prisoners are speedily set free.

2. The object of the above is to convey to the Italian Government the feeling that, while they have to make the formal act of submission, our desire is to treat them with consideration, so far as military exigencies allow. Merely harping on "unconditional surrender," with no prospect of mercy held out even as an act of grace, may well lead to no surrender at all. The expression "honourable capitulation" has also been officially used by the President, and I do not think it should be omitted from the language we are now to use.

3. We have just arrived [at Halifax], after a most pleasant voyage filled with fruitful discussions.

I passed to the President Mr. Eden's reply.

Former Naval Person (Quebec) to President Roosevelt   12 Aug. 43

Eden suggests that our Tangier representative reply to Badoglio's emissary Berio as follows:

Badoglio must understand that we cannot negotiate, but require unconditional surrender, which means that Italian Government should place themselves in hands of Allied Governments, who will then state their terms. These will provide for an honourable capitulation.

The instructions will continue:

Badoglio's emissary should be reminded at the same time that the Prime Minister and President have already stated that we desire that in due course Italy should occupy a respected place in New Europe, when peace has been re-established, and that General Eisenhower has announced that Italian prisoners taken in Tunisia and Sicily will be released, provided all British and Allied prisoners now in Italian hands are released.

2. This is simply made up of our existing declarations. If you approve it in principle, please cable at once direct to Eden at the Foreign Office, as I shall be on the move. If text does not meet your view, we can discuss it on arrival. I think the Italian envoy ought to have an answer as soon as possible.

The President telegraphed to Mr. Eden approving this language, and the Italian envoy at Tangier was so informed.

These tentative approaches by the Italian Government were now superseded by the appearance in Spain of a plenipotentiary from the Italian High Command. On August 15 General Castellano, Chief of Staff to General Ambrosio, called on Sir Samuel Hoare at the British Embassy in Madrid. Castellano said that he was instructed by Marshal Badoglio to say that as soon as the Allies landed on the Italian mainland the Italian Government was prepared to join them against Germany. If the Allies accepted the proposal, Castellano would immediately give detailed information about German troop dispositions. I at once passed this new information to the President.

Former Naval Person (Quebec) to President Roosevelt 16 Aug. 43

I send you herewith four telegrams I have received from London about a renewed approach by Badoglio. The following is the kind of answer which I suggest should be made:

We note the statement of Italian envoy: "We are not in a position to make any terms. We will accept unconditional surrender, provided we can join as allies in fighting the Germans." We, the Allies, for our part cannot make any bargain about Italy changing sides, nor can we make plans in common at this stage. If however serious fighting breaks out between the Italian Army and German intruders, a new situation would be created. The Italians know quite well that British and United States Governments do not seek to deny Italy her respected place in Europe. The Italian Government should therefore resist the Germans to the best of their ability as soon as possible, pending arrival of Anglo-American armies. In particular they should stop further invasion of Italy by German troops by blowing up bridges and tunnels and tearing up railway lines and roads in north of Italy, and thus cutting communications of German troops in south of Italy. Effective action of this kind would be regarded by victorious Allies as valuable service, and would render further co-operation possible against the common foe. There is no doubt of the ability of Italian Government and people to destroy and paralyse the German communications, and action of this kind would be proof of their sincerity. Another proof would be the safeguarding of British and Allied prisoners from being taken away to Germany. In any case where this is attempted by Germans, and Italian Government have not the power to resist, the prisoners should be set free and succoured by Italian people. A further vital service which Italian Government certainly has in its power to render to the Allies is to sail Italian warships to any ports in Allied occupation.

Fourthly, the furnishing by the Italian Government of any information of German dispositions, and by any assistance given by Italian troops and people to the disembarkations of Allies when they take place, especially if accompanied by fighting between Italians and Germans, would be favourably recognised. Fifthly, any co-operation between Italian troops in the Balkan peninsula and the various Patriot forces in the field, taking the form of resistance to the Germans and leading to bloodshed, would be favourably viewed.

Thus, by taking action against the common enemy, the Italian Government, Army, and people could without any bargain facilitate a more friendly relationship with United Nations. In particular we state that if Allied troops arrive at any point where they find Italians fighting Germans, we shall aid Italians to our utmost.

Eden should be here tomorrow, and we can discuss the whole position together. I send you this budget in order that you may see the way my mind is working.

The Chiefs of Staff are considering the practical steps and timings required to make an Italian turnover effective.

*   *   *   *   *

The President and I agreed that Eisenhower should send

General Bedell Smith and the British General Strong, head of his Intelligence Staff, to Lisbon to open negotiations there with the Italian emissary. They took with them the final military terms of surrender, which had now been thrashed out in our "Quadrant" Conference at Quebec.

18 Aug. 43

The President and Prime Minister to General Eisenhower

The President and the Prime Minister having approved, the Combined Chiefs of Staff direct you to send at once to Lisbon two Staff officers, one United States and one British. They should report upon arrival to the British Ambassador. They should take with them the agreed armistice terms which have already been sent to you. Acting on instructions, the British Ambassador in Lisbon will have arranged a meeting with General Castellano. Your Staff officers will be present at this meeting.

2. At this meeting a communication to General Castellano will be made on the following lines:

The unconditional surrender of Italy is accepted on the terms stated in the document to be handed to him. (He should then be given the armistice terms for Italy already agreed and previously sent to you. He should be told that these do *not* include political, economic, or financial terms, which will be communicated later by other means.)

These terms do *not* visualise the active assistance of Italy in fighting the Germans. The extent to which the terms will be modified in favour of Italy will depend on how far the Italian Government and people do in fact aid the United Nations against Germany during the remainder of the war. The United Nations however state without reservation that wherever Italian forces or Italians fight Germans or destroy German property or hamper German movement they will be given all possible support by the forces of the United Nations. Meanwhile, provided information about the enemy is immediately and regularly supplied, Allied bombing will so far as possible be directed upon targets which affect the movements and operations of German forces.

The cessation of hostilities between the United Nations and Italy will take effect from a date and hour to be notified by General Eisenhower.

Italian Government must undertake to proclaim the armistice

immediately it is announced by General Eisenhower, and to order their forces and people from that hour to collaborate with the Allies and to resist the Germans.

The Italian Government must, at the hour of the armistice, order that all United Nations prisoners in danger of capture by the Germans shall be immediately released.

The Italian Government must, at the hour of the armistice, order the Italian Fleet and as much of their merchant shipping as possible to put to sea for Allied ports. As many military aircraft as possible shall fly to Allied bases. Any ships or aircraft in danger of capture by the Germans must be destroyed.

3. General Castellano should be told that meanwhile there is a good deal that Badoglio can do without the Germans becoming aware of what is afoot. The precise character and extent of his action must be left to his judgment, but the following are the general lines which should be suggested to him:

General passive resistance throughout the country, if this order can be conveyed to local authorities without the Germans knowing. . . .

Germans must not be allowed to take over Italian coast defences.

Make arrangements to be put in force at the proper time for Italian formations in the Balkans to march to the coast, with a view to their being taken off to Italy by United Nations.

On August 19, the parties met at the British Embassy in the Portuguese capital. Castellano was told that General Eisenhower would accept the Italian Government's unconditional surrender on the terms now handed to him. It is difficult to make hard-cut military negotiations fit in with flexible diplomacy. The Italian envoy general at Lisbon was placed in a hopeless position. The purpose of his visit, as he emphasised, was to discuss how Italy could take the field against Germany. Bedell Smith had to reply that he could only discuss unconditional surrender.

These talks coincided with the final conquest of Sicily. On the same day I telegraphed to General Alexander:

19 Aug. 43

Prime Minister (Quebec) to General Alexander (Middle East)

I am overjoyed at this new, brilliantly executed achievement. I

congratulate you most heartily upon all you have done. I will
shortly send you a telegram for publication to your troops of the
Fifteenth Army Group, but I think it better that President Roosevelt and the King should send their compliments to Eisenhower
first, and I am so advising.

2. You are no doubt informed of General Castellano's approaches to us and the answer we have sent from here. Our greatest
danger is that the Germans should enter Rome and set up a
Quisling-Fascist Government under, say, Farinacci. Scarcely less
unpleasant would be the whole of Italy sliding into anarchy. I
doubt if the Badoglio Government can hold their double-faced
position until the present date fixed for "Avalanche," so that anything that can be done to shorten this period without endangering
military success will be most helpful.

General Alexander to Prime Minister (Quebec)   20 Aug. 43
Many thanks for your kind message, which I value very highly.
Everything possible is being done to put on "Avalanche" at the
earliest possible date. We realise here very clearly that every hour
gives enemy more time to prepare and organise against us.

*   *   *   *   *

The discussions in Lisbon with General Castellano continued throughout the night of August 19. The Italian general
drew out on a map the dispositions of both the German and
Italian forces in Italy after he had realised that there would
be no yielding by Bedell Smith upon the question of terms.
After a suitable delay in order to cover up his visit to Portugal,
Castellano returned to Rome bearing the military terms of
surrender and also a wireless set and Allied codes in order
to remain in contact with Allied Force Headquarters in Algiers.

Yet another Italian emissary, General Zanussi, appeared on
August 26 in Lisbon. He was the principal assistant to the
chief of the Italian General Staff, and was accompanied by
General Carton de Wiart, V.C., who had been released from a
British prisoner-of-war camp to act as intermediary to this
mission. The purpose of this latest visitor was far from clear.
Perhaps Badoglio feared that Castellano had given too much

away and wanted to be clear as to what he was doing. Carton
de Wiart had been told that "one dove had been sent out, but
as it had not returned another was being dispatched." Zanussi
had instructions from Badoglio to try to reach London and
press for an Allied landing north of Rome.

As discussions had already begun with Castellano, it was
decided to send Zanussi to General Eisenhower's Headquarters. Before he left however an incident of chivalry took place.
The Italian general wished to return to Rome to report on
the failure of his mission. He discussed the matter with his
English companion, who quietly said that he was of course prepared to accompany him. Zanussi describes in his own words
Carton de Wiart's remarks: "I am a prisoner-of-war. I have
been released to accompany you on a mission to London. Since
the mission has not taken place and you are returning to Italy,
I shall take my place again at the side of my comrades." The
Italian replied that he would not hear of such a plan. He
knew that all had been done that was possible to get him to
England, and he would go and see General Eisenhower as
suggested. Carton de Wiart should therefore consider himself
free. It was an Anglo-Italian episode which may well be remembered by both nations.

The latest Italian emissary was therefore sent to Algiers,
where he gave further information about the movements of
the Germans in Italy.

On August 31, General Bedell Smith, accompanied by General Zanussi, met Castellano in Sicily, as had been arranged.
Castellano explained that if the Italian Government were a
free agent they would accept and announce the armistice terms
as the Allies desired. They were however under the control
of the Germans. Since the Lisbon meeting the Germans had
sent more troops into Italy, and the whole country was virtually under German occupation. It was therefore impossible
for the armistice to be announced at the time required by the
Allies — i.e., before the main Allied landing in Italy, details
of which Castellano was most anxious to learn. The Italians
wanted to be quite sure that these landings would be strong

enough to guarantee the security of the King and Government in Rome.

It was clear that the Italian Government were particularly anxious that we should make a landing north of Rome to protect them against the German divisions near the city. Castellano talked in terms of fifteen Allied divisions taking part in such an operation. General Bedell Smith made it clear that he was not prepared to continue the talks on the basis that the armistice should be announced *after* the main Allied landings, and refused to give him any information on the strength of the impending Allied operations. Castellano thereupon asked to be allowed to consult his Government again. He was told that the terms were final and the time-limit had already expired, but that in view of the present discussion the Allies were willing to wait until midnight of September 1/2, by which time a firm acceptance or refusal must be given. That evening Castellano returned to Rome.

The Allied High Command perceived that the Italian Government was rapidly losing its nerve and would not have the courage to sign an armistice unless convinced of the overwhelming strength of the Anglo-American attack upon the mainland of Italy. General Eisenhower therefore decided to inform General Castellano of his plan to land an airborne force near Rome. This would depend upon a guarantee by Badoglio's Government that "the armistice is signed and announced as desired by the Allies; that the Italians should seize and hold the necessary airfields and stop all anti-aircraft fire; that the Italian divisions in the Rome area would take action against the Germans."

The President and I, now together in the White House, sent the following telegram to Eisenhower: "We highly approve your decision to go on with 'Avalanche' and to land an airborne division near Rome on the conditions indicated. We fully recognise military considerations must be dominant at this juncture." The War Cabinet met in London on the same day and endorsed this view.

*   *   *   *   *

We reported to Stalin the development of the Italian situation.

2 Sept. 43

Prime Minister and President Roosevelt to Premier Stalin

We have received from General Castellano statement that the Italians accept and that he is coming to sign, but we do not know for certain whether this refers to short military terms, which you have already seen, or to more comprehensive and complete terms in regard to which your readiness to sign was specifically indicated.

2. The military situation there is at once critical and hopeful. Our invasion of the mainland is beginning almost immediately, and the heavy blow called "Avalanche" will be struck in the next week or so. The difficulty of the Italian Government and people in extricating themselves from Hitler's clutches may make a still more daring enterprise necessary, for General Eisenhower will need as much Italian help as he can get. The Italian acceptance of the terms is largely based on the fact that we shall send an airborne division to Rome to enable them to hold off the Germans, who have gathered Panzer strength in that vicinity, and who may replace the Badoglio Government with a Quisling Administration, probably under Farinacci. Matters are moving so fast there that we think General Eisenhower should have discretion not to delay settlement with the Italians for the sake of the difference between the short and long terms. It is clear that short terms are included in long terms, that they proceed on basis of unconditional surrender, placing the interpretation in hands of Allied Commander-in-Chief.

3. We are therefore assuming that you expect General Eisenhower to sign short terms on your behalf if that be necessary to avoid the further journeying of General Castellano to Rome and consequent delay and uncertainty affecting military operations. We are of course anxious that Italian unconditional surrender be to Soviet as well as to Great Britain and United States. The date of surrender announcement must of course be fitted in with the military stroke.

*   *   *   *   *

General Castellano returned to Sicily, formally authorised by his Government to sign the military terms of surrender.

On September 3, in an olive grove near Syracuse, the act was performed. I received this news in a telegram from General Alexander.

General Alexander to Prime Minister   3 Sept. 43

The short armistice terms were signed this afternoon, on the fourth anniversary of the war, between General Bedell Smith, representing General Eisenhower, and General Castellano, representing Marshal Badoglio, duly authorised to do so.

Castellano is remaining here near my Headquarters, and we are starting military talks this evening to arrange best assistance which Italian forces can contribute to our operations.

Before dawn on September 3, the British Eighth Army had crossed the Straits of Messina to enter the Italian mainland.

Prime Minister to Premier Stalin   5 Sept. 43

General Castellano, after a long struggle, signed the short terms on September 3, and he is now working out with Generals Eisenhower and Alexander the best way to bring them into force. This will certainly lead to immediate fighting between Italian and German forces, and we are going to help the Italians at every possible point as effectively and speedily as we can. The next week will show a startling development. The invasion of the toe has been successful and is being pressed, and Operation "Avalanche" and the airborne venture are both imminent. Though I believe we shall get ashore at "Avalanche" in strong force, I cannot foresee what will happen in Rome or throughout Italy. The dominant aim should be to kill Germans and make Italians kill Germans on the largest scale possible in this theatre.

I am staying over this side of the Atlantic till this business clears itself. Meanwhile, accept my warmest congratulations on your new set of victories and penetrations on your main front.

It now remained to co-ordinate the terms of the Italian surrender with our military strategy. The American General Taylor, of the 82d Airborne Division, was sent to Rome on September 7. His secret mission was to arrange with the Italian General Staff for the airfields around the capital to be seized during the night of the 9th. But the situation had radically changed since Castellano had asked for Allied protection. The Germans had powerful forces at hand, and appeared to be in possession of the airfields. The Italian army was demoralised and short of ammunition. Divided counsels seethed round Badoglio. Taylor demanded to see him. Everything hung in the balance. The Italian leaders now feared that any announcement of the surrender, which had already been signed, would lead to the immediate German occupation of Rome and the end of the Badoglio Government. At two o'clock on the morning of September 8, General Taylor saw Badoglio, who, since the airfields were lost, begged for delay in broadcasting the armistice terms. He had in fact already telegraphed to Algiers that the security of the Rome airfields could not be guaranteed. The air descent was therefore cancelled.

Eisenhower now had to make a quick decision. The attack on Salerno was due to be launched within less than twenty-four hours. He therefore telegraphed to the Combined Chiefs of Staff:

8 Sept. 43

I have just completed a conference with the principal commanders, and have determined *not* to accept the Italian change of attitude. We intend to proceed in accordance with plan for the announcement of the armistice, and with subsequent propaganda and other measures. Marshal Badoglio is being informed through our direct link that this instrument entered into by his accredited representative with presumed good faith on both sides is considered valid and binding, and that we will *not* recognise any deviation from our original agreement.

After consultation, the President and I sent the following reply:

8 Sept. 43

It is the view of the President and the Prime Minister that the agreement having been signed, you should make such public announcement regarding it as would facilitate your military operations.

Accordingly, at 6.00 P.M. General Eisenhower broadcast the announcement of the armistice, followed by the text of the declaration which Marshal Badoglio himself announced about an hour later from Rome. The surrender of Italy had been completed.

*   *   *   *   *

During the night of September 8/9, German forces began the encirclement of Rome. Badoglio and the Royal Family installed themselves in a state of siege in the building of the Ministry of War. There were hasty discussions in an atmosphere of mounting tension and panic. In the small hours a convoy of five vehicles passed through the eastern gates of Rome on the road to the Adriatic port of Pescara. Here two corvettes took on board the party, which contained the Italian Royal Family, together with Badoglio and his Government and senior officials. They reached Brindisi in the early morning of September 10, when the essential services of an anti-Fascist Italian Government were rapidly set up on territory occupied by Allied forces.

After the departure of the fugitives, the veteran Marshal Caviglia, the victor of Vittorio Veneto in the First World War, arrived in Rome to take upon himself the responsibility of negotiating with the German forces closing in round the city. Scattered fighting was already taking place at the gates. Certain regular units of the Italian Army and Partisan bands of Roman citizens engaged the Germans on the outskirts.

On September 11, opposition ceased with the signature of a military truce, and the Nazi divisions were free to move through the city.

*   *   *   *   *

The surrender had been pressed on Marshal Badoglio in order not to upset the timing of the Allied landings in the heel and in the Rome area. The essential steps were completed in the formal signature of the armistice terms, but there were other fruits to be gathered in this dread harvest: the

Italian Fleet must be safely transferred to Allied ports; there were many Italian divisions in Southeastern Europe whose equipment would be valuable to the Allies in the continued struggle against Nazi Germany; there were still more important Italian bases in the Eastern Mediterranean. It was essential that these islands should not fall into hostile hands.

I was acutely aware of this particular danger.

Prime Minister to General Wilson (Middle East)   13 Sept. 43

The capture of Rhodes by you at this time with Italian aid would be a fine contribution to the general war. Let me know what are your plans for this. Can you not improvise the necessary garrison out of the forces in the Middle East? What is your total ration strength?

This is a time to think of Clive and Peterborough and of Rooke's men taking Gibraltar.

Lest it should be thought that I pressed this mood unduly, I cite the final summary of the Combined Chiefs of Staff of our decisions recorded at Washington:

EASTERN MEDITERRANEAN

The Combined Chiefs of Staff have taken note of the action which the Commander-in-Chief Middle East is taking in respect of Rhodes and other islands in the Dodecanese. They approve this action, and are considering what further can be done.

I was soon to revert to these matters.

*   *   *   *   *

Meanwhile, after dark on September 8, in accordance with Allied instructions, the main body of the Italian Fleet left Genoa and Spezia on a daring voyage of surrender to Malta, unprotected either by Allied or Italian aircraft. Next morning, when steaming down the west coast of Sardinia, it was attacked by German aircraft from bases in France. The flagship *Roma* was hit, and blew up with heavy loss of life, including the Commander-in-Chief, Admiral Bergamini. The battleship *Italia* was also damaged. Leaving some light craft to rescue survivors, the rest of the fleet continued its painful journey. On the morning of the 10th, they were met at sea by British forces, including the *Warspite* and *Valiant*, which had so often sought them before under different circumstances, and were escorted to Malta. A squadron from Taranto, including two battleships, had also sailed on the 9th, and, after passing at sea the British force on its way to occupy that port, reached Malta the following day without incident.

On the morning of the 11th, Admiral Cunningham informed the Admiralty that "the Italian battle fleet now lies at anchor under the guns of the fortress of Malta."

*   *   *   *   *

I was anxious that we should treat the Italian Navy well. To Cunningham I cabled on September 10:

Prime Minister to Admiral Cunningham (Algiers)   10 Sept. 43
Should the Italian Fleet arrive in our ports after having scrupulously fulfilled armistice conditions and sustained the revengeful attack of German bombers, I hope you will consult General Eisenhower in order that they shall be received in kindly and generous manner. I feel sure this will be in accordance with your sentiments.

And later in the day:

Films should be taken if possible of surrender of Italian Fleet, their courteous reception by the British, and kindly treatment of wounded, etc.

The splendid prize of the whole fleet of what had been a victorious Power of the first rank thus fell into our hands. It must be made to play its part on our side.

Prime Minister to Admiral Cunningham (Algiers)   12 Sept. 43
At the earliest possible moment you should report on the ammunition of all natures of guns and torpedoes in the Italian Fleet, beginning with the most important units, showing how much on board, any taken at Taranto, etc., and estimates of quantities and exact specifications for manufacture. Without waiting for the whole story to be complete, send at once to Admiralty for trans-

mission to United States through proper channels requirements
for the principal and most modern units. I can probably arrange
for speedy manufacture here.

With the collapse of the Fascist régime every region of Italy
was in a ferment of political speculation. The organisation of
resistance to the Germans fell by default into the hands of an
underground Committee of Liberation in Rome, and linked
with the mounting activity of partisan bands which now began
activities throughout the peninsula. The members of this Committee were politicians driven from power by Mussolini in
the early nineteen-twenties or representatives of groups hostile
to Fascist rule. Over all hung the menace of a recrudescence
of the hard core of Fascism in the hour of defeat. The Germans certainly did their best to promote it.

*   *   *   *   *

Mussolini had been interned after July 26 on the island of
Ponza, and later at La Maddalena, off the coast of Sardinia.
Fearing a German *coup de main,* Badoglio had at the end of
August moved his former master to a small mountain resort
high in the Abruzzi, in Central Italy. In the haste of the flight
from Rome no precise instructions were given to the police
agents and carabinieri guarding the fallen Dictator. On the
morning of Sunday, September 12, ninety German parachutists
landed by glider near the hotel where Mussolini was confined.
He was removed, without casualties, in a light German aircraft,
and carried to yet another meeting in Munich with Hitler.

The rescue of Mussolini enabled the Germans to set up in
the North a rival Government to Badoglio's. A skeleton Fascist régime was established on the shores of Lake Como, and
it was here that was played out the drama of Mussolini's Hundred Days. The Germans clamped down their military occupation upon the regions lying north of Rome; a skeleton administration of uncertain allegiance sat in Rome, now open
to the movements of the German Army; at Brindisi the King
and Badoglio set up a rump Government under the eyes of an
Allied Commission and with no effective authority beyond the

boundaries of the administrative building of the town. As our armies advanced from the toe of the peninsula Allied military government took over the task of controlling the liberated regions.

Italy was now to pass through the most tragic time in her history and to become the battle-ground of some of the fiercest fighting in the war.

7

At the White House Again

THE QUEBEC CONFERENCE ended on August 24, and our
notable colleagues departed and dispersed. They flew off
in every direction like the fragments of a shell. After all the
study and argument there was a general desire for a few days'
rest. One of my Canadian friends, Colonel Clarke, who had
been attached to me by the Dominion Government during the
proceedings, owned a ranch about seventy-five miles away amid
the mountains and pine forests from which the newspapers get
their pulp to guide us on life's journey. Here lay the Lake of
the Snows, an enormous dammed-up expanse of water reported

to be full of the largest trout. Brooke and Portal were ardent and expert anglers, and a plan had been made, among other plans at the Conference, for them to see what they could do. I promised to join them later if I could, but I had undertaken to deliver a broadcast on the 31st, and this hung overhead like a vulture in the sky. I remained for a few days in the Citadel, pacing the ramparts for an hour each afternoon, and brooding over the glorious panorama of the St. Lawrence and all the tales of Wolfe and Quebec. I had promised to drive through the city, and I had a lovely welcome from all its people. I attended a meeting of the Canadian Cabinet, and told them all that they did not already know about the Conference and the war. I had the honour to be sworn a Privy Counsellor of the Dominion Cabinet. This compliment was paid me at the instance of my old friend of forty years' standing and trusted colleague, Mr. Mackenzie King.

There was so much to say and not to say in the broadcast that I could not think of anything, so my mind turned constantly to the Lake of the Snows, of which glittering reports had already come in from those who were there. I thought I might combine fishing by day with preparing the broadcast after dark. I resolved to take Colonel Clarke at his word, and set out with my wife by car. I had noticed that Admiral Pound had not gone with the other two Chiefs of Staff to the lake, and I suggested that he should come with us now. His Staff officer said that he had a lot of cleaning up to do after the Conference. I had been surprised by the subdued part he had taken in the far-ranging naval discussions, but when he said he could not come fishing, I had a fear that all was not well. We had worked together in the closest comradeship from the first days of the war. I knew his worth and courage. I also knew that at home he would get up at four or five in the morning for a few hours' fishing before returning to the Admiralty whenever he saw the slightest chance. However, he kept to his quarters and I did not see him before starting.

We had a wonderful all-day drive up the river valley, and after sleeping at a rest-house on the way my wife and I reached the spacious log cabin on the lake. Brooke and Portal were leaving the next day. It was just as well. They had caught a hundred fish apiece each day, and had only to continue at this rate to lower the level of the lake appreciably. My wife and I sallied forth in separate boats for several hours each day, and though we are neither of us experts we certainly caught a lot of fine fish. We were sometimes given rods with three separate hooks, and once I caught three fish at the same time. I do not know whether this was fair. We did not run at all short of fresh trout at the excellent meals. The President had wanted to come himself, but other duties claimed him. My aide-de-camp, Mary, had been invited to address an important gathering of American W.A.C.s at Oglethorpe, and was flown off accordingly. The President sent me the following:

President to Colonel Warden   27 Aug. 43

Wednesday the first is all right in every way [for Washington]. If Subaltern [Mary] wants to go to Oglethorpe, it would give her more time in Washington if she were to come down a day or two ahead. I hope Lady Warden is getting a real rest, and that you are also. Also I hope you have gone to One Lake.[1] Be sure to have big ones weighed and verified by Mackenzie King.

I sent the biggest fish I caught to him at Hyde Park. The broadcast made progress, but original composition is more exhausting than either arguing or fishing.

*   *   *   *   *

We returned to Quebec for the night of the 29th. I attended another meeting of the Canadian Cabinet, and at the right time on the 31st, before leaving for Washington, I spoke to the Canadian people and to the Allied world. A few quotations are pertinent to this account.

The contribution which Canada has made to the combined effort of the British Commonwealth and Empire in these tremen-

[1] During the Quebec Conference the President invited me to come for an afternoon's fishing with him in a lake to which he had been recommended. We had a very pleasant luncheon, but I caught only one small fish and he none. He therefore called the lake "One Lake."

dous times has deeply touched the heart of the Mother Country
and of all the other members of our widespread family of states
and races.

From the darkest days the Canadian Army, growing stronger year
by year, has played an indispensable part in guarding our British
homeland from invasion. Now it is fighting with distinction in
wider and ever-widening fields. The Empire Air Training Organisation, which has been a wonderful success, has found its seat in
Canada, and has welcomed the flower of the manhood of Great
Britain, of Australia, and New Zealand to her spacious flying-fields
and to comradeship with her own gallant sons.

Canada has become in the course of this war an important sea-
faring nation, building many scores of warships and merchant
ships, some of them thousands of miles from salt water, and sending them forth manned by hardy Canadian seamen to guard the
Atlantic convoys and our vital life-line across the ocean. The
munitions industries of Canada have played a most important part
in our war economy. Last, but not least, Canada has relieved
Great Britain of what would otherwise have been a debt for these
munitions of no less than two thousand million dollars.

All this of course was dictated by no law. It came from no treaty
or formal obligation. It sprang in perfect freedom from sentiment and tradition and a generous resolve to serve the future of
mankind. I am glad to pay my tribute on behalf of the people of
Great Britain to the great Dominion, and to pay it from Canadian
soil. I only wish indeed that my other duties, which are exacting,
allowed me to travel still farther afield and tell Australians, New
Zealanders, and South Africans to their faces how we feel towards
them for all they have done, and are resolved to do. . . .

We have heard a lot of talk in the last two years about establishing what is called a Second Front in Northern France against Germany. Anyone can see how desirable that immense operation of
war would be. It is quite natural that the Russians, bearing the
main weight of the German armies on their front, should urge us
ceaselessly to undertake this task, and should in no way conceal
their complaints, and even reproaches, that we have not done it
before. I do not blame them at all for what they say. They fight
so well, and they have inflicted such enormous injury upon the
military strength of Germany, that nothing they could say in
honest criticism of our strategy or the part we have so far been able

to take in the war would be taken amiss by us, or weaken our
admiration for their own martial prowess and achievement. We
once had a fine front in France, but it was torn to pieces by the
concentrated might of Hitler; and it is easier to have a front pulled
down than it is to build it up again. I look forward to the day
when British and American liberating armies will cross the Channel in full force and come to close quarters with the German invaders of France. . . . Personally, I always think of the Third Front
as well as the Second Front. I have always thought that the
Western democracies should be like a boxer who fights with two
hands and not one.

I believe that the great flanking movement into North Africa,
made under the authority of President Roosevelt and of His
Majesty's Government, for whom I am a principal agent, will be
regarded in the after-time as quite a good thing to do in all the
circumstances. Certainly it has reaped rich and substantial results.
Africa is cleared. All German and Italian armies in Africa have
been annihilated, and at least half a million prisoners are in our
hands. In a brilliant campaign of thirty-eight days Sicily, which
was defended by over four hundred thousand Axis troops, has been
conquered. Mussolini has been overthrown. The war impulse of
Italy has been destroyed, and that unhappy country is paying a terrible penalty for allowing itself to be misled by false and criminal
guides. How much easier it is to join bad companions than to
shake them off! A large number of German troops have lately
been drawn away from France in order to hold down the Italian
people, in order to make Italy a battle-ground, and to keep the war
as distant and as long as possible from German soil. By far the
greater part of the German Air Force has been drawn off from the
Russian Front, and indeed is being engaged and worn down with
ever-growing intensity, by night and day, by British and American
and Canadian airmen. More than all this, we have established a
strategic initiative and potential, both from the Atlantic and from
the Mediterranean, of which the enemy can neither measure the
weight nor foresee the hour of application.

To judge by the latest news from the Russian battle-fronts,
Marshal Stalin is certainly not wasting his time. The entire British
Empire sends him our salutes in this brilliant summer campaign,
and on the victories of Orel, Kharkov, and Taganrog, by which so
much Russian soil has been redeemed and so many hundreds of
thousands of its invaders wiped out.

I gave the fullest prominence to Mountbatten's appointment.

A Supreme Commander of the Southeast Asia front has been chosen, and his name has been acclaimed by British, American, and Chinese opinion. He will act in constant association with Generalissimo Chiang Kai-shek. It is true that Lord Louis Mountbatten is only forty-three. It is not often under modern conditions and in established military professions that a man gets so great a chance so early. But if an officer, having devoted his life to the military art, does not know about war at forty-three, he is not likely to learn much more about it later on. As Chief of Combined Operations Lord Louis has shown rare powers of organisation and resourcefulness. He is what — pedants notwithstanding — I will venture to call a "complete triphibian" — that is to say, a creature equally at home in three elements, earth, air, and water, and also well accustomed to fire. We all wish the new command and its commander full success in their novel, varied, and certainly most difficult task.

*   *   *   *   *

I left Quebec by train, and arrived at the White House on September 1. Throughout the talks at Quebec, events had been marching forward in Italy. The President and I, as has been recorded elsewhere, had directed during these critical days the course of the secret Armistice talks with the Badoglio Government, and had also been following anxiously and closely the military arrangement for a landing on Italian soil. I deliberately prolonged my stay in the United States in order to be in close contact with our American friends at the critical moment in Italian affairs. On the day of my arrival in Washington, the first definite and official news was received that Badoglio had agreed to accept the surrender terms proposed by the Allies. The strategic arrangements debated at Quebec had of course been considered in the light of the possible Italian collapse, and this aspect was our main concern in these days.

While in Washington I attended several American Cabinets or their equivalent and was in close touch with leading American personalities. Poor Hopkins at this time was very ill and had to retire for a complete rest to the Naval Hospital. The President was very anxious for me to keep a longstanding ap-

pointment and receive an honorary degree at Harvard. It was
to be an occasion for a public declaration to the world of
Anglo-American unity and amity. On September 6, I delivered my speech. The following extract may be printed here.

To the youth of America, as to the youth of Britain, I say, "You
cannot stop." There is no halting-place at this point. We have
now reached a stage in the journey where there can be no pause.
We must go on. It must be world anarchy or world order. Throughout all this ordeal and struggle which is characteristic of our age
you will find in the British Commonwealth and Empire good
comrades to whom you are united by other ties besides those of
state policy and public need. To a large extent they are the ties
of blood and history. Naturally I, a child of both worlds, am conscious of these.

Law, language, literature — these are considerable factors. Common conceptions of what is right and decent, a marked regard for
fair play, especially to the weak and poor, a stern sentiment of im-
partial justice, and above all the love of personal freedom, or, as
Kipling put it, "Leave to live by no man's leave underneath the
law" — these are common conceptions on both sides of the ocean
among the English-speaking peoples. We hold to these conceptions as strongly as you do.

We do not war primarily with races as such. Tyranny is our foe.
Whatever trapping or disguise it wears, whatever language it
speaks, be it external or internal, we must for ever be on our
guard, ever mobilised, ever vigilant, always ready to spring at its
throat. In all this we march together. Not only do we march and
strive shoulder to shoulder at this moment, under the fire of the
enemy on the fields of war or in the air, but also in those realms
of thought which are consecrated to the rights and the dignity of
man.

I spoke about our Combined Staffs.

At the present time we have in continual vigorous action the
British and United States Combined Chiefs of Staff Committee,
which works immediately under the President and myself as representative of the British War Cabinet. This Committee, with its
elaborate organisation of Staff officers of every grade, disposes of all
our resources, and in practice uses British and American troops,

ships, aircraft, and munitions just as if they were the resources of a single state or nation. I would not say there are never divergences of view among these high professional authorities. It would be unnatural if there were not. That is why it is necessary to have plenary meetings of principals every two or three months. All these men now know each other. They trust each other. They like each other, and most of them have been at work together for a long time. When they meet, they thrash things out with great candour and plain, blunt speech, but after a few days the President and I find ourselves furnished with sincere and united advice.

This is a wonderful system. There was nothing like it in the last war. There never has been anything like it between two allies. It is reproduced in an even more tightly knit form at General Eisenhower's Headquarters in the Mediterranean, where everything is completely intermingled and soldiers are ordered into battle by the Supreme Commander or his Deputy, General Alexander, without the slightest regard as to whether they are British, American, or Canadian, but simply in accordance with the fighting need.

Now in my opinion it would be a most foolish and improvident act on the part of our two Governments, or either of them, to break up this smooth-running and immensely powerful machinery the moment the war is over. For our own safety, as well as for the security of the rest of the world, we are bound to keep it working and in running order after the war — probably for a good many years, not only until we have set up some world arrangement to keep the peace, but until we know that it is an arrangement which will really give us that protection we must have from danger and aggression, a protection we have already had to seek across two vast world wars.

Alas, unwisdom has already prevailed.

*   *   *   *   *

I had, as usual, had an official summary of the Conference sent to the Dominion Prime Ministers. Field-Marshal Smuts was disappointed by the scale on which our plans were based, and also by their apparent leisurely time-table. I always, as the reader knows, found great comfort in feeling that our minds were in step. The cables that passed between us throw

a true and intimate light upon the main issues of the war at
this milestone. It was no burden to me but a relief to dictate
from my general body of knowledge acquired at the summit
full explanations to one I knew so well.

General Smuts to Prime Minister   31 Aug. 43

For your private ear I should like to voice my personal misgivings about the progress of the war. If you don't agree with me,
please forget my grouse. But if in any way you share my feeling,
you will take your own initiative in the matter.

While our Middle East campaign was conducted with conspicuous vigour from El Alamein to the end in Tunisia, I sense a slackening and tardiness in operations since then. It took us several
months between Tunisia and the Sicilian landing, and there is now
another strange pause after Sicily at a stage in our affairs when
the urgency is very great. To compare the Anglo-American effort,
with all our vast resources, with that of Russia during the same
period is to raise uncomfortable questions which must occur to
many others. Our comparative performance on land is insignificant
and its speed very unsatisfactory. There is much and constant
boasting of our production effort, especially of the colossal American production. And after almost two years of war the American
fighting forces must be enormous. But still, the Russians account
for the vast bulk of the German Army on land. Shipping and other
troubles account for this difference in part, but that is not the
whole story. I have the uncomfortable feeling that the scale and
speed of our land operations leave much to be desired. Our Navy
is acting up to its usual high standard, and our Air Force is magnificent. But almost all the honours on land go to the Russians, and
deservedly so, considering the scale and speed of their fighting and
the magnificence of their strategy on a vast front.

Surely our performance can be bettered and the comparison with
Russia rendered less unflattering to us. To the ordinary man it
must appear that it is Russia who is winning the war. If this impression continues, what will be our post-war world position compared with that of Russia? A tremendous shift in our world status
may follow, and will leave Russia the diplomatic master of the
world. This is both unnecessary and undesirable, and would have
especially bad reactions for the British Commonwealth. Unless
we emerge from the war on terms of equality, our position will be

both uncomfortable and dangerous. . . . I do not yet know what was being planned at Quebec, and assume the best programmes have been worked out and approved. But what about the rate of their execution? There is grave danger in delay, in tardiness of performance on our part.

General Smuts to Prime Minister   3 Sept. 43

After sending my previous message criticising our war progress, I must frankly express my disappointment with this Quebec plan as being an inadequate programme for the fifth year of the war, and especially after the enormous change that has taken place in our war fortunes recently. This plan has only added to my misgivings and fears for the future. It does no justice to the real strength of our position, and may gravely affect public morale as well as future relations with Russia. We are capable of a much greater effort, and should face the position with greater boldness.

In effect, the plan merely proposes to continue and increase the present bombing and anti-U-boat campaigns, to take Sardinia and Corsica and the South of Italy and bomb northward from there. We are then to fight our way northward through Italy over difficult mountainous terrain in a campaign which may take much time before we reach Northern Italy and the main German defence position. Next spring we shall cross the Channel in force if the air and military situation in France is favourable, and we may invade France from the south if only as a diversion. We leave the Balkans to the guerrillas, with air encouragement from us.

So much for the West. In the East we do some island-hopping which may bring us up against the enemy's main base in the Carolines some time towards the end of next year. The resources of the Dutch East Indies we leave meanwhile to the enemy while we make efforts to open the Burma route and assist China as much as possible by air. Some undefined amphibious operations against Burma are also indicated.

Bombing appears to me the only serious part of this plan. All the rest is still on a small scale, similar to what we have been doing for the last couple of years. Surely this would not be a serious effort for this stage of the war nor a proper use of our greatly improved war position. If by the end of 1944 we have done no better than merely nibble at the enemy's main positions, we may experience a dangerous revulsion of opinion, and rightly so. It would compare most unfavourably with the grand effort and achievement of Russia, who may conclude that her suspicions of us are justified.

In the absence of inner Staff information, it is difficult for me to suggest alternative plans, but I feel convinced that we can and should do much more and better than the Quebec plan, which would unduly drag out and prolong the war, with all the attendant risks and possibilities I have indicated in my former message. The bombing policy, the anti-U-boat campaign, and the large-scale attack across the Channel I approve. But in the Mediterranean we should take Sardinia and Corsica and immediately attack in North Italy without fighting our way all up the peninsula. We should immediately take Southern Italy and move on to the Adriatic, and from a suitable point there launch a real attack on the Balkans and set its resurgent forces going. This will bring Turkey into the picture and carry our Fleet into the Black Sea, where we shall join hands with Russia, supply her, and enable her to attack Hitler's fortress itself from the east and southeast. With the vast change in the war situation on the Russian Front, I do not think this too ambitious a programme to work to. . . .

After consideration, I replied to Smuts:

Prime Minister to Field-Marshal Smuts   5 Sept. 43
    Your two telegrams.
    The invasion of the toe of Italy now begun is of course only the prelude to a far heavier attack which is imminent, and will, if successful, produce consequences of a far-reaching character. We hope presently to open a heavy front across Italy as far north as we can get. Such a front will absorb about twenty divisions from the Mediterranean, and may require reinforcement if selected for counter-attack by the enemy.
    2. I have always been most anxious to come into the Balkans, which are already doing so well.[2] We shall have to see how the fighting in Italy develops before committing ourselves beyond Commandos, agents, and supplies, but the whole place is aflame, and with the defection of the twenty-four Italian divisions scattered

    [2] This sentence appears inconsistent with my general policy as so often expressed in these volumes. I did not mean "come into the Balkans" with an army.

in the Balkans, who have ceased to fight and now only try to get home, it may well be that the Germans will be forced to retire to the line of the Save and the Danube. . . .

3. I think it better not to demand entry into the war by Turkey at this present time, as the forces with which we should have to fight are more usefully employed in the Central Mediterranean. The question may be put to Turkey later in the year.

4. In spite of these serious needs and projects in the Mediterranean, which strain our resources to the full, we have to find seven divisions from that theatre from November on for the build-up of Operation "Overlord" in the spring of 1944. For this purpose every personnel ship which can be gathered, apart from those used by the United States in the Pacific, is being employed in the ceaseless transportation of American troops and air forces. None of our ships have been idle this year, and yet there are so far only two American divisions in England. It is not physically possible to make a larger concentration by the date mentioned. We shall be able to match the American expedition with a nearly equal force of British divisions, but after the initial assault the build-up must be entirely American, as I am completely at the end of man-power resources, and even now have to ask the Americans to interrupt the movement of field troops in order to send over some thousands of engineers to help make the installations and establishments required for the gathering of their trans-Atlantic army.

5. These projects in Europe, together with the air offensive and the sea war, completely absorb all our resources of man-power and of ship-power. This fact must be faced. There is no comparison with our conditions and those prevailing in Russia, where the whole strength of a nation of nearly two hundred million, less war losses, long-organised into a vast national army, is deployed on a two-thousand-miles land front. This again is a fact which must be faced.

6. I think it inevitable that Russia will be the greatest land Power in the world after this war, which will have rid her of the two military Powers, Japan and Germany, who in our lifetime have inflicted upon her such heavy defeats. I hope however that the "fraternal association" of the British Commonwealth and the United States, together with sea- and air-power, may put us on good terms and in a friendly balance with Russia at least for the period of rebuilding. Further than that I cannot see with mortal

eye, and I am not as yet fully informed about the celestial tele-
scopes.

7. In the East we British have no shortage of forces, but have
the same difficulty of coming into action as the United States in the
Atlantic and also in the Pacific. The shipping stringency rules all
oversea and amphibious action, and for the rest, in Burma there
are the jungles, the mountains, and the fact that more than half
the year is swamped by the monsoon. However, a vigorous campaign has been set on foot. I brought young Wingate to Quebec,
and he is being raised from a Brigadier to a Corps Commander,
with powerful jungle forces adapted to the purpose being formed
with the utmost speed for an attack in the first month of next year.
The appointment of Mountbatten heralds an amphibious operation of novelty and far-reaching scope which I am pressing with
all possible energy, the details of which I will unfold to you when
we meet.

8. Believe me, my dear friend, I am not at all vexed at your two
telegrams of criticism. I am confident that if we were together for
two or three days, I could remove such of your anxieties as are
not inherent inexorable facts. Night and day I press for greater
speed in action and less cumbrousness in organisation. I am
waiting this side of the Atlantic pending the Italian *coup* and its
repercussions, but I expect to be home when Parliament meets, and
hope to find you at least approaching our shores.

Smuts was to some extent reassured by this full statement.
"Your telegram," he said, "has come as a great relief. It makes
clear that the Italian expedition of twenty divisions would
cover the whole peninsula and constitute another real front."
But he added a day later:

Field-Marshal Smuts to Prime Minister   9 Sept. 43

I suggest that our victories in the Mediterranean should be followed up in Italy and the Balkans instead of our now adopting a
cross-Channel plan, which means switching onto a new theatre
requiring very large forces and involving grave risks unless much
more air softening has taken place. Preparations for the Channel
plan should be slowed down or put into temporary cold storage
while the bombing campaign is intensified to prepare for eventual
military knock-out.

This last suggestion required immediate correction from me if our two minds were to continue to work harmoniously on the problem from independent angles. Smuts alone, and far from Washington, could not know the atmosphere and proportions which governed our collective thought.

Prime Minister to Field-Marshal Smuts   11 Sept. 43

There can be no question whatever of breaking arrangements we have made with United States for "Overlord." The extra shipping available in consequence of U-boat warfare slackening and of Italian windfalls will probably enable us to increase build-up of "Avalanche" [the expedition to Italy]. I hope you will realise that British loyalty to "Overlord" is keystone of arch of Anglo-American co-operation. Personally I think enough forces exist for both hands to be played, and I believe this to be the right strategy.

*   *   *   *   *

Meanwhile, the invasion of Italy had begun. At dawn on September 3, the 5th British and 1st Canadian Divisions of the Eighth Army crossed the Straits of Messina.[3] Practically no opposition was encountered. Reggio was speedily taken, and the advance began along the narrow and hilly roads of Calabria.

The Germans [cabled Alexander on September 6] are fighting their rearguard action more by demolitions than by fire. . . . While in Reggio this morning there was not a warning sound to be heard or a hostile plane to be seen. On the contrary, on this lovely summer day naval craft of all types were plying backward and forward between Sicily and the mainland, carrying men, stores, and munitions. In its lively setting it was more like a regatta in peace-time than a serious operation of war.

In a few days the divisions of the Eighth Army had reached Locri and Rosarno, while an infantry brigade, landed by sea at Pizzo, found only the tail of the retreating Germans. There was little fighting, but the advance was severely delayed by the physical difficulties of the country, demolitions carried out by the enemy, and his small but skilfully handled rearguards.

[3] See map, "Southern Italy Operations September—December 1943," page 303.

Prime Minister to General Alexander   7 Sept. 43

Many thanks for your telegrams about operations in the toe of Italy. Please tell me exactly what the move of airborne division to seize Rome involves, and where it fits into your programme. We are all fully in favour of the bold policy proposed, although we have to take details on trust.

2. I am also deeply interested in your mention of Taranto. About when do you propose doing this?

3. I am still very much concerned about build-up after "Avalanche." Surely, if you can get the port of Naples into working order, you should be able to push in two divisions a week. Let me know the order in which you propose to bring our army into Italy. When do the New Zealanders, Poles, 4th Indian, and 1st Armoured, and other really high-class divisions come into action? It seems you will have to hold a front at least as large as that in final stages of Tunis — i.e., about a hundred and seventy miles — and one never can tell if, given time, Germans may not bring a real punch to bear upon that front.

4. I am waiting here with the President to judge results of "Avalanche," and thereafter returning home. I hope however to come out to you in the first half of October, and General Marshall will come from America. I shall have some important things to tell you then.

Alexander replied that the Italian Government, being unable to announce the Armistice, had forced him to make certain changes. The 82d United States Airborne Division could not be flown in to the Rome area as no arrangement for its reception had been made by the Italians, and the Germans were thought to be in occupation of the airfields. "Avalanche" would go in as planned, except that no airborne forces would take part. About three thousand soldiers of the 1st Airborne Division had sailed in naval ships for Taranto, and should arrive there on September 9. It was impossible to say what reception they would receive. By opening the port of Taranto early, he hoped to increase the build-up into Italy.

At the same time our efforts to seize Rhodes and other islands in the Aegean began. Later chapters will tell the tale.

*   *   *   *   *

In the White House the President and I sat talking after dinner in his study, and Admiral Pound came to see us upon a
naval point. The President asked him several questions about
the general aspects of the war, and I was pained to see that
my trusted naval friend had lost the outstanding matter-of-
fact precision which characterised him. Both the President and
I were sure he was very ill. Next morning, Pound came to see
me in my big bed-sitting-room and said abruptly, "Prime Minister, I have come to resign. I have had a stroke and my right
side is largely paralysed. I thought it would pass off, but it
gets worse every day and I am no longer fit for duty." I at once
accepted the First Sea Lord's resignation, and expressed my
profound sympathy for his breakdown in health. I told him
he was relieved at that moment from all responsibility, and
urged him to rest for a few days and then come home with me
in the *Renown*. He was completely master of himself, and
his whole manner was instinct with dignity. As soon as he left
the room, I cabled to the Admiralty placing Admiral Syfret in
responsible charge from that moment pending the appointment of a new First Sea Lord.

*   *   *   *   *

On September 9, we held a formal conference with the
President at the White House. The Chief of the Imperial
General Staff and the Chief of the Air Staff had flown back to
London some days before, and I was accompanied by Field-
Marshal Dill, Ismay, and the three representatives of the British
Chiefs of Staff in Washington. The President brought with
him Leahy, Marshall, King, and Arnold. A number of telegrams about the Italian Fleet coming over to us made an agreeable introduction. I expressed the hope that the Italian Fleet
would be treated with respect by the Allies wherever it might
arrive.

In preparation for this meeting, I had prepared a memorandum to the President, which I had submitted to him earlier in
the day. He asked me to read it out, and thought it would
make a basis for our discussion.

9 Sept. 43

It would surely be convenient before we separate to have a plenary meeting of the Combined Chiefs of Staff in order to take stock of the new world situation which will arise on the assumption that the present battle for Naples and Rome is successful and that the Germans retreat to the line of the Apennines or the Po.

2. Assuming we get the Italian Fleet, we gain not only that fleet, but the British Fleet, which has hitherto contained it. This very heavy addition to our naval power should be used at the earliest possible moment to intensify the war against Japan. I have asked the First Sea Lord to discuss with Admiral King the movement of a powerful British battle squadron, with cruisers and ancillaries, to the Indian Ocean via the Panama Canal and the Pacific. We need a strong Eastern Fleet based on Colombo during the amphibious operations next year. I should be very glad if it were found possible for this fleet to serve under the American Pacific Command and put in at least four months of useful fighting in the Pacific before taking up its Indian Ocean station. We cannot afford to have idle ships. I do not know however how the arrival of such reinforcements would enable the various tasks assigned to United States forces in the Pacific to be augmented. Apart from strategy, from the standpoint of high policy His Majesty's Government would desire to participate in the Pacific war in order to give such measure of assistance as is in their power, not only to their American Allies, but on account of the obligations to Australia and New Zealand. Such a movement of our ships to and through the Pacific would undoubtedly exercise a demoralising effect upon Japan, who must now be conscious of the very great addition of naval weight thrust against her, and besides this it would surely give satisfaction in the United States as being a proof positive of British resolve to take an active and vigorous part to the end in the war against Japan.

3. The public must be gradually led to realise what we and our Combined Staffs have so fully in mind, namely, the conversion of Italy into an active agent against Germany. Although we could not recognise Italy as an ally in the full sense, we have agreed she is to be allowed to work her passage, and that useful service against the enemy will not only be aided but recompensed. Should fighting break out between Italians and Germans, the public prejudices will very rapidly depart, and in a fortnight or so matters

may be ripe, if we can so direct events, for an Italian declaration
of war against Germany. The question of the Italian flag flying
from Italian ships, and even some arrangement of Italians manning those vessels under British or American control, requires consideration. The whole problem of handling and getting the utmost
use out of the Italian Navy requires review now on a high level.

4. On the over-all assumption of a decisive victory in the Naples
area, we are, I presume, agreed to march northward up the Italian
peninsula until we come up against the main German positions.
If the Italians are everywhere favourable and their Army comes
over to help, the deployment of at least a dozen Italian divisions
will be of great advantage in holding the front across Italy and
in permitting relief of Allied forces. If, after the battle of Naples
is over, we are not seriously resisted south of the main German
line, we ought not to be long getting up against it with light forces,
and I should hope that by the end of the year at the latest we
should be confronting it in full strength. If sooner, then better.
There can be no question of whittling down "Overlord." We
must not forget at this juncture our agreement to begin moving
the seven divisions away in succession from the beginning of
November. All the more important is it to bring Italian divisions
into the line, and our State policy should be adapted to procure
this end.

5. I have been contemplating the 1944 campaign in the light
of these new possibilities, and I remain strongly convinced that
we should be very chary of advancing northward beyond the narrow part of the Italian peninsula. Of course, if the Germans retreat
to the Alps another situation is presented, but, failing that, it
would seem beyond our strength, having regard to the requirements of "Overlord," to broaden out into the plains of Lombardy.
We have also to consider that the Germans, working on interior
lines, may perhaps bring a heavier force to bear upon our front in
Italy than we shall have there at the end of the year. The possibility of a strong German counter-attack cannot be excluded. I
should like it to be considered whether we should not, when we
come up against the main German position, construct a strong
fortified line of our own, properly sited in depth. Italian military
labour could be used on a large scale for this purpose. Italian
troops could naturally take part in defending the line. Thus by
the spring we should be able in this theatre either to make an

offensive if the enemy were weak, and anyhow to threaten one, or, on the other hand, stand on the defensive, using our air-power, which will in the meanwhile have been built up, from behind our fortified line, and divert a portion of our troops for action elsewhere, either to the west or to the east. I hope this may be studied.

6. We are both of us acutely conscious of the great importance of the Balkan situation. We should make sure that the Mediterranean High Command, absorbed in its present battle, does not overlook the needs of the patriot forces there. The problem of the Italian forces requires immediate study. The orders of the Commander-in-Chief Middle East, General Wilson, published today, are well conceived for the moment, but we require to see more clearly exactly what is intended. On the assumption that the Italians can be drawn into the war against Germany, far-reaching possibilities seem to be open. There is surely no need for us to work from the bottom of the Balkans upwards. If we can get an agreement between the patriots and the Italian troops, it should be possible to open quite soon one or more good ports on the Dalmatian coast, enabling munitions and supplies to be sent in by ship and all forces that will obey our orders to be raised to good fighting condition. The German situation in all this theatre will become most precarious, especially from the point of view of supplies. When the defensive line across Northern Italy has been completed, it may be possible to spare some of our own forces assigned to the Mediterranean theatre to emphasise a movement north and northeastward from the Dalmatian ports. For the moment the utmost efforts should be put forth to organise the attack upon the Germans throughout the Balkan peninsula and to supply agents, arms, and good direction.

7. Lastly, the question of islands is now ripe for consideration. Sardinia, I imagine, will come over immediately, though we may have to send some help to the Italians in procuring the disarmament of any German units there. In Corsica the Germans have perhaps already been overcome, but surely here is the place for a French expedition. Even if only one division could be sent by the French National Committee, the island could probably be quickly liberated, and there is little doubt that its manhood would enable at least another division or two to be raised locally. General Wilson's telegram about the operations against Rhodes and other islands in the Dodecanese is all right so far as it goes, but I am

not satisfied that sufficient use is being made under the present conditions of the forces in the Middle East. I am making an immediate inquiry into the exact location of all troops above battalion strength, hoping that improvised expeditionary forces and garrisons may be provided for various minor ventures.

8. We must expect far-reaching reactions in Bulgaria, Rumania, and Hungary, and these again may produce a movement from the Turk without our having to make any request or incur any obligation. All this again requires military and political consideration on the high level, and I feel that we should do well to take a preliminary survey this afternoon if you are agreeable.

There was wide agreement in principle between us all along the lines set forth in the above note, and the Staffs concerted the necessary action in the days that followed.

*   *   *   *   *

The next day the President left Washington for his home at Hyde Park. He asked me to use the White House not only as a residence but for any conference I might wish to hold, either with the British Empire representatives who had gathered in Washington or with the United States war chiefs, and not to hesitate to call another plenary meeting should I deem it necessary. I availed myself fully of these generous facilities. Accordingly, as there was a general desire to take stock of the rapid movement of events in Italy and of the progress of the fierce and critical battle for Naples, I convened another meeting at the White House on September 11, at which I presided myself. The United States were represented by Admiral Leahy, General Marshall, Admiral King, General Arnold, Harry Hopkins, Averell Harriman, and Lew Douglas. I brought with me Dill and Ismay, and our three representatives on the Combined Chiefs of Staff.

All current matters were discussed. General Marshall reported the conditions in the Naples area, and the rapid reinforcement of the German divisions. General Arnold mentioned that we had now nearly three thousand operative aircraft engaged over Italy, which, he said, was more than the

whole German Air Force on all fronts. I directed attention
to the lamentable proposals for building up our forces on the
mainland. I had been, I said, horrified to see the figure of only
twelve divisions to be achieved by December 1. It was vitally
important to accelerate the growth of the army in Italy by
every possible division. Even the arrival of one division a fortnight earlier might make a serious difference. General Marshall
entirely agreed and said that everything should be done.

He then told us about the brilliantly successful air landings
by the United States Air Force in the South Pacific theatre.
As a result of their descent in the Markham Valley, combined
with seaborne attack, the garrison of eight to ten thousand
Japanese had been virtually isolated. American troops were
pounding Salamaua and were close to Lae. Airfields should
soon be in our possession from which the enemy airfields could
be made untenable. This in turn would change the whole sea
situation. The Japanese position in New Britain might soon
be desperate. There were also signs of Japanese evacuation
from the Solomons.

It was an honour to me to preside over this conference of
the Combined Chiefs of Staff and of American and British
authorities in the Council Room of the White House, and it
seemed to be an event in Anglo-American history.

8

The Battle of Salerno

A Homeward Voyage

Anglo-American Descent upon Salerno — Stubborn German Resistance — Taranto Seized — We Embark on the "Renown" — Alexander on the Spot — Contacts with Stalin and Eisenhower — Progress of the Battle — Alexander's Reports — The Victory Gained — Mary and the Wave — Naples Taken — My Telegram to Eisenhower of September 15 — Interchanges with the Commanders — A Pause to Consolidate.

ON THE NIGHT OF SEPTEMBER 8, Alexander sent me his "Zip" message. As the Allied armada approached the Salerno beaches that evening, they heard the announcement from the British broadcast of the Italian surrender. To men keyed up for battle the news came as a shock, which for the moment relaxed the tension and had an unfortunate psychological effect. Many thought that on the morrow their task would be a walkover. Officers at once strove to correct any such impression, pointing out that whatever the Italians might do there would certainly be strong resistance from German forces. There was a sense of anticlimax. Nevertheless, as Admiral Cunningham remarked, to have withheld the existence of the Armistice would have been a breach of faith with the Italian people.

Covered by a strong British fleet the assault convoys entered the Gulf of Salerno with only minor air attack. The enemy was aware of their approach, but he could not tell, until the last moment, where the blow would fall.

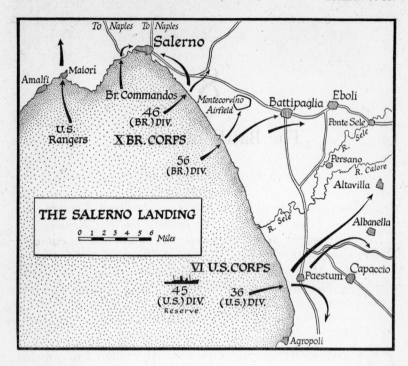

THE SALERNO LANDING

0 1 2 3 4 5 6 Miles

   The landing of the Fifth Army, commanded by General
Clark, began before dawn. The assault was delivered by the
VIth United States Corps, and the British Xth Corps, with
British Commandos and United States Rangers on the northern flank. The convoys had been sighted at sea, and General
Eisenhower's broadcast of the previous evening caused the German troops in the neighbourhood to act immediately. Disarming the Italians, they took over the whole defence themselves,
and made good use of the advantage which modern weapons
give to the defence in the early stages of a landing. Our men
were met by well-aimed fire as they waded ashore, and they
suffered heavily. It was difficult to provide proper air-cover
for them, as many of our fighters were operating at extreme
range from Sicily, but these were reinforced by carrier-borne
aircraft.
   Once across the beaches, the VIth United States Corps made

good progress, and by the night of the 11th had advanced as
much as ten miles, with their right flank bent back to the sea.
The British corps met stiffer opposition. They succeeded in
taking Salerno and Battipaglia. The Montecorvino airfield also
fell into our hands, but, as it remained under enemy fire, it
could not provide the sorely needed refuelling ground for our
fighters. The Germans reacted very quickly. Their troops
opposing the Eighth Army, which was toiling its way up the
toe of Italy, were brought at all speed to the new battle. From
the north came the greater part of three divisions, from the
east a regiment of parachutists.[1] Our own reinforcement was
much slower, as shipping, especially small craft, was scarce.
The German Air Force, though weakened by their losses in
Sicily, made an intense effort, and their new radio-controlled
and glider bombs caused losses to our shipping. All the resources of the Allied Air were turned on to hamper the approach of enemy reinforcements and blast their concentrations.
Warships steamed into Salerno Bay to give the support of their
heaviest guns. The Eighth Army was spurred on by Montgomery to gain contact with the hard-pressed Fifth. All this
helped, and in the opinion of a highly placed German officer
the eclipse of the Luftwaffe and the lack of any defence against
naval bombardment were decisive.

*　　*　　*　　*　　*

While the Salerno battle was raging, a remarkable stroke
was made upon Taranto, for which not only Alexander, but
Admiral Cunningham, on whom fell the brunt of execution,
deserve the highest credit for well-run risks. This first-class
port was capable of serving a whole army. The Italian surrender which now broke upon us seemed to Alexander to
justify daring. There were no transport aircraft to lift the
British 1st Airborne Division, nor any ordinary shipping to
carry it by sea. Six thousand of these picked men were embarked on British warships, and on September 9, the day of
the landing on Salerno beaches, the Royal Navy steamed boldly

---

[1] The order of battle of the German and Italian divisions on September 8 is
set out in Appendix F, Book One.

into Taranto Harbour and deposited the troops ashore, unopposed. One of our cruisers, which struck a mine and sank, was our only naval loss.[2]

*   *   *   *   *

It had been planned that I and those of our party who had not already flown to England should go home by sea, and the *Renown* awaited us at Halifax. I broke the train journey to say good-bye to President Roosevelt, and was thus with him at Hyde Park when the Battle of Salerno began. I resumed my train journey on the night of the 12th, to reach Halifax on the morning of the 14th. The various reports which reached me on the journey, as well as the newspapers, made me deeply anxious. Evidently a most critical and protracted struggle was in progress. My concern was all the greater because I had always strongly pressed for this seaborne landing, and felt a special responsibility for its success. Surprise, violence, and speed are the essence of all amphibious landings. After the first twenty-four hours the advantage of sea-power in striking where you will may well have vanished. Where there were ten men there are soon ten thousand. My mind travelled back over the years. I thought of General Stopford waiting nearly three days on the beach at Suvla Bay in 1915 while Mustafa Kemal marched two Turkish divisions from the lines at Bulair to the hitherto undefended battlefield. I had had a more recent experience when General Auchinleck had remained at his Headquarters in Cairo surveying orthodoxly from the summit and centre the wide and varied sphere of his command, while the battle, on which everything turned, was being decided against him in the Desert. I had the greatest confidence in Alexander, but all the same I passed a painful day while our train rumbled forward through the pleasant lands of Nova Scotia. At length I wrote out the following message for Alexander, feeling sure he would not resent it. It was not sent till after I had sailed.

2 I have in my home the Union Jack, the gift of General Alexander, that was hoisted at Taranto, and was the first Allied flag to be flown in Europe since our expulsion from France.

Prime Minister to General Alexander   14 Sept. 43

I hope you are watching above all the battle of "Avalanche," which dominates everything. None of the commanders engaged has fought a large-scale battle before. The Battle of Suvla Bay was lost because Ian Hamilton was advised by his C.G.S. to remain at a remote central point where he would know everything. Had he been on the spot he could have saved the show. At this distance and with time-lags I cannot pretend to judge, but I feel it my duty to set before you this experience of mine from the past.

2. *Nothing* should be denied which will nourish the decisive battle for Naples.

3. Ask for anything you want, and I will make allocation of necessary supplies with highest priority irrespective of every other consideration.

His answer was prompt and comforting.

General Alexander (Salerno) to Prime Minister (at sea)   15 Sept. 43

I feel sure you will be glad to know that I have already anticipated your wise advice and am now here with the Fifth Army. Many thanks for your offer of help. Everything possible is being done to make "Avalanche" a success. Its fate will be decided in the next few days.

I was also relieved to learn that Admiral Cunningham had not hesitated to hazard his battleships close inshore in support of the Army. On the 14th, he sent up the *Warspite* and *Valiant,* which had just arrived at Malta conducting to surrender the main body of the Italian Fleet. Next day they were in action, and their accurate air-directed bombardment with heavy guns impressed both friend and foe and greatly contributed to the defeat of the enemy. Unhappily, on the afternoon of the 16th the *Warspite* was disabled by a new type of glider bomb, about which we had heard something, and were to learn more.

                                                        15 Sept. 43
Prime Minister (at sea) to Admiral Cunningham (Algiers)

I am very glad you have put in the *Warspite* and *Valiant,* as importance of battle fully justifies exceptional action.

Please give them my best wishes.

The following also came in:

Premier Stalin to President Franklin D. Roosevelt   14 Sept. 43
and to Prime Minister Churchill

I have received your message of September 10. I congratulate
you with new successes, and especially with the landing at Naples.
There is no doubt that the successful landing at Naples and break
between Italy and Germany will deal one more blow upon
Hitlerite Germany and will considerably facilitate the actions of
the Soviet armies at the Soviet-German front. For the time being
the offensive of the Soviet troops is successfully developing. I think
that we shall be in a position to achieve more successes within the
next two-three weeks. It is possible that we shall have recaptured
Novorossisk within the next few days.

*   *   *   *   *

It was a relief to board the *Renown*. The splendid ship lay
alongside the quay. Admiral Pound was already on board, having come through direct from Washington. He bore himself
as erect as ever, and no one looking at him would have
dreamed that he was stricken. I invited him to join us at my
table on the homeward voyage, but he said he would prefer
to take his meals in his cabin with his Staff officer. Within half
an hour we sailed, and for the next six days we zigzagged our
way across the ocean.

*   *   *   *   *

All the time the battle at Salerno went on. The telegrams
flowed in. Alexander was kind enough to keep me fully informed, and his vivid messages can be read in their relation to
the whole event.

General Alexander to Prime Minister (at sea)   16 Sept. 43

I have just returned from an extensive tour of the Fifth Army
front. I saw both corps commanders, all division commanders, and
several front-line brigades. Although I am not entirely happy
about the situation, I am happier than I was twenty-four hours
ago, for the following reasons:

The Germans have not put in a serious attack since night of 13th. This has given us time to improve our position somewhat, rest for very exhausted troops, and get some reinforcements of men and material in. Eighth Army are also drawing nearer. I have also been able to cheer them up and issue certain directions, of which the following are most important. Hold what we have gained; at all cost consolidating key positions by digging, wiring, and mining. Reorganise scattered and mixed units and formations. Form local reserves and as strong a mobile reserve as possible. Inform troops of rapid approach of Eighth Army and flow of reinforcements now arriving day and night. Present weakness is [due to] following. Germans have been able to concentrate strong forces quicker than we have been able to build up sufficient forces to hold what had been gained in first rush. Germans hold most of the dominating features and overlook us onto the beach. Our troops are tired. There is very little depth anywhere; we have temporarily lost the initiative. Last night our Air dropped a parachute battalion behind enemy lines in Avellino area. Air flew in 1600 men of the 82d Division last night. I have arranged with the Navy to bring 1500 British infantry reinforcements from Philippeville in cruisers; these should be here in under forty-eight hours. I have speeded up arrival of 3d United States Division, which will start landing on 18th.

First elements of 7th Armoured Division arrive tonight, but will take few days to disembark and concentrate. One infantry brigade also arrives tonight. We have just completed three landing-strips, and Spitfires are now operating from Salerno and neighbourhood.

The whole of the air forces are concentrated on this battle area. We shall regain the initiative and start to gain key points as soon as we are strong enough to do so. God's blessing on our enterprise and a little luck will ensure success to our arms.

Prime Minister (at sea) to General Alexander   16 Sept. 43

My feeling about "Avalanche" is expressed in Foch's maxim, *Cramponnez partout.* The Navy are quite right to throw their heavy ships in, for this is a battle of far-reaching significance. My feeling is you are going to win.

Prime Minister to General Alexander   17 Sept. 43

I am very glad to feel you have taken a personal grip of "Ava-

lanche" position. I had, as you know, been worried about rate of
"Avalanche" build-up. It is great news that Montgomery expects
to bring Eighth Army into action on 17th.

2. It is right to use the battleships in the inshore squadron in
view of favourable naval balances.

3. Every good wish. Please continue to keep me informed. I am
in mid-ocean, but can receive fully at all hours.

For three critical days the issue hung in the balance.
Battipaglia was lost, but the 56th Division, though weakened
by heavy losses, succeeded in stopping a further drive thence
to the sea. On the front of the VIth United States Corps the
enemy, taking advantage of the thinly held gap between that
corps and the British, turned in from the north, crossed the
river Sele, and threatened to reach the landing-beaches behind
the Americans. They were stopped only just in time by the
defence of the American batteries. The Allied line was held by
the narrowest of margins. The 45th United States Division,
which had been held in reserve on board their ships, was now
in full action on the VIth Corps front. Reinforcements were
beginning to arrive. Our 7th Armoured Division and the 82d
United States Airborne Division came in by sea and air. After
six days of bitter fighting, in which we suffered moments of
grave hazard, the Germans failed to throw us back into the
sea. On the 15th, Kesselring realised he could not succeed.
Pivoting his right on the high ground above Salerno, he began
to swing his whole line back. On the 18th, the Fifth and
Eighth Armies joined hands. We had won.

General Alexander to Prime Minister (at sea)   18 Sept. 43

The general situation continues to improve, and the initiative
is passing to us. There have been several strongish attacks against
Xth British Corps in north, but all these have been repulsed. On
VIth Corps front Americans are on offensive, and fighting is still
going on in Altavilla. As you know, Fifth Army and Eighth Army
patrols have joined hands. The 7th Armoured Division are getting
ashore well; 1500 infantry reinforcements for Xth Corps arrived
last night. American reinforcement of about 1600 due to arrive
in a day or two. The 3d United States Division starts disembark-
ing tomorrow evening. The build-up of ammunition and supplies

is satisfactory. Eighth Army are advancing on Aluetta and Potenza, but up to writing I have not received [any] report as to the location of their spearheads. The 1st British Airborne Division, in Taranto area, are active, and have joined hands with the Canadians, but are too weak to do more than harass the Germans. The 78th Infantry Division is due to start unloading at Taranto on September 22, and the 8th Indian Division at Brindisi on September 23. My immediate aim is to build up three strong fighting groups: Fifth United States Army in Salerno area, Eighth Army in centre, British Vth Corps under Eighth Army in Taranto area. From these firm bases we shall advance northward, and I have issued a directive to the following effect: Fifth Army to pivot on hills northwest of Salerno and secure the heights about Avellino. Eighth Army to secure Potenza area. Next objectives will be Fifth Army to secure port of Naples, Eighth Army the airfields in Foggia area. I do not wish to mislead you by being overoptimistic, but I am satisfied that we now have the situation in hand, and will be able to carry out our future operations according to plan.

As we reached the Clyde, decisive news arrived from Alexander.

General Alexander to Prime Minister   19 Sept. 43

I can say with full confidence that the whole situation has changed in our favour and that the initiative has passed to us. . . . I am rejoining my main Headquarters at Syracuse tomorrow.

On September 21 I sent my congratulations to General Eisenhower, and asked him to convey my compliments to General Clark.

Prime Minister to General Eisenhower (Algiers)   21 Sept. 43

I congratulate you on the victorious landing and deployment northward of our armies. As the Duke of Wellington said of the Battle of Waterloo, "It was a damned close-run thing," but your policy of running risks has been vindicated. If you think fit, send a message from me on to Clark, who from all I hear has done wonders. We certainly do work together in a way never before seen among allies.

2. It does seem to me most desirable, if you could manage it, to push more French troops into Corsica and to put a substantial

detachment of British or American troops into Sardinia. As we now have good harbours for disembarkation, they need not be combat-loaded, but their presence will animate the Italian troops and the French and local patriots.

3. We are backing you up all we can about working with the Italian Government, and I am pretty sure all will go as you wish it.

4. Field-Marshal Smuts will be in Cairo Monday, September 27, staying with Casey, and will be in your theatre about four days later on his way here. He possesses my entire confidence, and everything can be discussed with him with the utmost freedom. He will stay some months in London, taking up his full duties as a member of the British War Cabinet. He will carry great weight here with public opinion. I shall be grateful if he is treated with the utmost consideration. He is a magnificent man and one of my most cherished friends.

*   *   *   *   *

Our six-day voyage would have been less pleasant if I had known what was happening to some of my children. Randolph had been in Malta on a few days' leave from his Commando in the early days of September. Here he met Brigadier Laycock, who was a great friend of his and mine. Laycock, who knew what was going to happen, said, "There is going to be a show for the Commandos. Would you like to come?" So Randolph went with him, and was closely engaged throughout the battle.

Mary had an adventure of a different kind. The *Renown* was slanting across a fairly rough sea when one of the officers suggested a walk on the quarterdeck. This, as he should have known, was forbidden on account of the zigzags, which made it impossible to calculate how waves would come aboard. Mary was leaning over the taffrail with her companion when the ship changed course. "Oh, look," she said, "there's a lovely wave coming towards us!" "Cling on!" cried the officer, who realised the danger. In one second the deluge swept them both head over heels across the deck to the starboard scuppers, and but for the fact that Mary came against an upright of the rails she would have gone overboard. The commander saw what had happened from behind the after-turret, and was about to order a "Man overboard" buoy to be dropped, when the recovery heel of the ship sent most of the water that had come on board pouring back the other way, and Mary on the return journey managed to clutch the anchor cables. The poor officer went to and fro in the same excursion. They were dragged, dripping, into safety. The officer was much scolded. Mary changed her clothes, and all this was concealed from me until we landed.

Another event of a more agreeable character also occurred in my personal circle. Among the party of a dozen Wrens who had come with us was a most beautiful girl. Leslie Rowan, my private secretary, wooed and won her in these few days at sea. But this was kept hidden from all by the parties concerned. They are now happily married.

On our arrival I received the following:

President Roosevelt to Prime Minister

Delighted you are all safely home, and I hope you had a smooth run. All is quiet here. Congress has been here for a week, and it is still quiet. My best to all three of you.

*   *   *   *   *

Once the Battle of Salerno had been won, Naples and the Foggia airfields lay before us. The British Xth Corps, with the United States VIth Corps on their right, drove back the enemy's rearguards around Vesuvius, marched past the ruins of Pompeii and Herculaneum, and entered Naples. An immense effort was now concentrated upon opening the harbour, which had been subjected to every form of destruction at experienced hands. Nevertheless, this work in which the Americans excelled was so effective that within a fortnight five thousand tons of supplies a day could be handled. The two airfields near the city were soon brought into use, and gave welcome relief to our fighter squadrons, hitherto acting from improvised landing-strips. Meanwhile, on the east coast the 1st Airborne Division had patrolled as far as Gioia and Bari by September 15. The 78th Division and an armoured brigade landed behind them, and, with the Vth Corps Headquarters, joined the Eighth Army. Six Royal Air Force squadrons began to act from the Gioia airfield at the same time. The enemy evacuated the Foggia airfields on September 25. Termoli was taken by Commandos landed from the sea, who, with the help of reinforcements, held out against fierce counter-attacks.

*   *   *   *   *

A few days after my return I sent General Eisenhower a telegram which should be borne in mind in reading all my messages and memoranda of the autumn and winter. The second paragraph sought to establish the proportion of effort, especially where bottlenecks were concerned, which should be devoted to our various enterprises. These proportions should not be overlooked by those who wish to understand the controversies with which a later chapter deals. War presents the problem of the correct employment of available means, and cannot often be epitomised as "One thing at a time."

Prime Minister to General Eisenhower (Algiers)   25 Sept. 43

As I have been pressing for action in several directions, I feel I ought to place before you the priorities which I assign in my own mind to these several desirable objectives.

2. Four-fifths of our effort should be the build-up of Italy. One-tenth should be our making sure of Corsica (which will soon finish) and in the Adriatic. The remaining tenth should be concentrated on Rhodes. This of course applies to the limiting factors only. These, I presume, are mainly landing-craft and assault shipping, with light naval craft.

3. I send this as a rough guide to my thought only because I do not want you to feel I am pressing for everything in all directions without understanding how grim are your limitations.

General Eisenhower to Prime Minister   26 Sept. 43

We are examining resources carefully to give Mid-East necessary support in this project, and feel sure that we can meet minimum requirements of Mid-East.

When Montgomery can get the bulk of his forces forward to support the right of the Fifth Army, things will begin to move more rapidly on the Naples front. As is always the case following the early stages of a combined operation, we have been badly stretched both tactically and administratively. We are working hard to improve the situation and you will have good news before long.

Eisenhower's answer did not refer as specifically as I had hoped to what I deemed the all-important part of my message, namely, the small proportion of troops required for subsidiary enterprises.

*   *   *   *   *

I continued my interchanges with Alexander and Montgomery.

Prime Minister to General Alexander   25 Sept. 43
I quite understand that the Eighth Army has to pull up its tail.
2. I like the idea of an advance on a broad front which the enemy will have difficulty in stemming, but I suppose you will also help yourself forward with minor amphibious scoops.
3. You will see that I have announced in Parliament that the Italian campaign is the "Third Front." The Second Front is here in Great Britain, in potential but not yet engaged. This form of statement should be adhered to, as it is less disagreeable to the Russians and avoids arguing with them as to whether the Italian campaign is the Second Front or not.

Naples was entered by the Anglo-American Fifth Army on October 1.

Prime Minister to General Eisenhower (Algiers)   2 Oct. 43
I rejoice with you at the brilliant turn our affairs in the Mediterranean have taken, and that Sardinia and Corsica have fallen as mere incidents in the campaign. Every good wish for the future.

Prime Minister to General Alexander (Italy)   2 Oct. 43
I consider that the advance of the Eighth Army on the eastern flank is of enormous value.
I note that Montgomery will soon have to halt to bring up supplies, but I trust this does not mean that his patrols and light

forces will not keep in touch with the enemy's rearguards. Everything in our Intelligence goes to show that the enemy's object is
to gain time and retire northward without serious losses. He has
not in any case the strength to make a front against the forces
you are now deploying. I consider that this favourable position
is due to your master-stroke in seizing Taranto, with its unequalled
harbour facilities, and beg you to accept my most sincere compliments upon it.

I have studied the plan you have sent home by your officer, and
note that you have already accomplished the first and second
phases of it. I hope the third phase will be accomplished by the
end of the month or thereabouts, and that we shall meet in Rome.

General Alexander to Prime Minister   3 Oct. 43
I am most grateful for your kind message, and I appreciate your
praise so much. . . . Once I can get the Royal Air Force properly
established and our administrative set-up working as it should,
then all will be straight sailing.

I have now established my Headquarters at Bari, where I am
near the battle-front and within easy reach of my two Army Commanders and my main bases. Air Marshal Coningham is of course
with me.

To sum up, all will be well, and the Germans will be harassed
and continuous pressure applied to his rearguards all the time by
light mobile forces and air forces when we cannot reach him with
our main bodies.

Prime Minister to General Montgomery (Italy)   2 Oct. 43
I am delighted to see the Eighth Army striding on so splendidly.
Many congratulations on all you have done. I dare say you remember what I said to you that day in Tripoli about where we might
meet.

General Montgomery to Prime Minister   5 Oct. 43
Thank you for your kind message. We have advanced a long
way and very quickly. It had to be done in order to come to the
help of Fifth Army, but it has been a very great strain on my
administration, which had to be switched from the toe to the heel
during the operations and which is now stretched to the limit.
When I have got the lateral Termoli-Campobasso I will have to

halt my main bodies for a short period and operate in advance of
that lateral only with light forces while I get my administration
on a sound basis during the period of the halt. But light forces
directed in sensitive areas can be very effective, and by this means
I will retain the initiative and gain ground. After the halt I will
advance with my whole strength on Pescara and Ancona. I shall
look forward to meeting you in Rome.

* * * * *

A pause was now enforced upon both our armies. North
of Naples the Fifth Army met strong resistance along the
river Volturno, which needed time and supplies to overcome.
In the Eighth Army's advance up the toe of Italy, General
Montgomery had deliberately taken every administrative risk
in order to reach the Salerno battlefield. His base had now
to be moved from the toe at Reggio to the heel at Taranto
and Bari. Until this was accomplished, the Eighth Army had
reached the end of its tether. Moreover, the capture of Foggia
enabled a start to be made in occupying its airfields with heavy
bombers. This was a massive task requiring the carriage of
many thousand tons of stores and could be effected only by
degrees. In mid-October the Germans had nineteen divisions
in Italy, and the Allies the equivalent of eleven. Large reinforcements and much consolidation were required to hold our
rapid and brilliant conquests. All this put a strain on our
shipping.

September had been indeed a fruitful month. Anglo-American inter-Service co-operation by land, sea, and air had reached
a new record. The Commander of the German Tenth Army in
Italy has since stated that the harmonious co-operation between our army, air, and naval forces under one supreme command was regarded by the Germans with envy. The Italian
Fleet was in our hands; their Air Force and Army, though prevented by the Germans from joining us in useful numbers,
were no longer ranged against us. The enemy had been
defeated in pitched battle and our armies had bitten three
hundred miles off Italy's boot. Behind them lay captured air-

fields and ports, ample, when developed, for our needs. Sardinia, so long thrust forward in Staff argument as the alternative to the assault on Italy, fell into our hands for nothing, as a mere bonus, on September 19, and Corsica was taken by French troops a fortnight later. The Italian enterprise, to launch which we had struggled so hard, had been vindicated beyond the hopes even of its most ardent and persistent advocates.

Great credit is due to General Eisenhower for his support of this brief and spirited campaign. Although the execution fell to Alexander, the Supreme Commander had really taken the British view of the strategy, and had been prepared to accept the ultimate responsibility for an enterprise the risks of which had been needlessly sharpened by his own military chiefs in their rigid adherence to the plans for Burma, and by their stern and strict priorities for "Overlord," which were carried in the secondary ranks to a veritable pedantry. There can be no doubt at all that Italy was the greatest prize open to us at this stage, and that a more generous provision for it could have been made without causing any delay to the main cross-Channel plan of 1944.

9

A Spell at Home

DURING THE HOMEWARD VOYAGE I prepared a speech for
Parliament upon my return. I was well aware of the
criticism I should have to meet, and that the increasing success
of the war would only make the disaffected elements in the
House and in the press feel more free to speak their minds.

On September 21, two days after landing, I accordingly
made a report to the House of Commons, which occupied no
less than two and a half hours. To avoid the Members tailing
off for luncheon, I asked for an hour's adjournment, which
was accorded.

* * * * *

The first complaint was that much time had been lost in

making the attack upon Naples by futile negotiations with the
Italian Government. To this I could see I had a good answer.

I have seen it said that forty days of precious time were lost in
these negotiations, and that in consequence British and American
blood was needlessly shed around Salerno. This criticism is as
ill-founded in fact as it is wounding to those who are bereaved.
The time of our main attack upon Italy was fixed without the
slightest reference to the attitude of the Italian Government, and
the actual provisional date of the operation was settled long before
any negotiations with them had taken place, and even before the
fall of Mussolini. That date depended upon the time necessary
to disengage our landing-craft from the beaches of Southern Sicily,
across which up to the first week in August the major part of our
armies actually engaged there had to be supplied from day to day.
These landing-craft had then to be taken back to Africa. Those
that had been damaged — and they were many — had to be repaired, and then reloaded with all their ammunition, etc., in the
most exact and complex order before there could be any question
of carrying out another amphibious operation.

I suppose it is realised that these matters have to be arranged
in the most extraordinary detail. Every landing-vessel or combat
ship is packed in the exact order in which the troops landing from
it will require the supplies when they land, so far as can be foreseen. Every lorry indeed is packed with precisely the articles which
each unit will require when that lorry comes. Some of the lorries
swim out to the ships and swim back. They are all packed exactly
in series, with the things which have priority at the top and so on,
so that nothing is left to chance that can be helped. Only in this
way can these extraordinary operations be carried out in the face
of the vast modern fire-power which a few men can bring to bear.
The condition and preparation of the landing-craft were the sole
but decisive limiting factors. It had nothing to do with "wasting
time over the negotiations," nothing to do with the Foreign Office
holding back the generals while they worried about this clause or
that clause and so forth. There was never one moment's pause in
the process of carrying out the military operations, and everything
else had to fit in with that main-line traffic.

When I hear people talking in an airy way of throwing modern
armies ashore here and there as if they were bales of goods to be

dumped on a beach and forgotten, I really marvel at the lack of knowledge which still prevails of the conditions of modern war.

．　．　．　．　．　．　．　．　．　．

I must say, if I may make a momentary digression, that this class of criticism which I read in the newspapers when I arrived on Sunday morning reminds me of the simple tale about the sailor who jumped into a dock, I think it was at Plymouth, to rescue a small boy from drowning. About a week later this sailor was accosted by a woman, who asked, "Are you the man who picked my son out of the dock the other night?" The sailor replied modestly, "That is true, ma'am." "Ah," said the woman, "you are the man I am looking for. Where is his cap?"

*　　*　　*　　*　　*

The second complaint was about the Second Front, for which the Communist elements and some others were steadily pressing.

I now tried to speak to the German High Command as well as the House of Commons, and at the same time to mislead the first and instruct the second.

I call this front we have opened, first in Africa, next in Sicily, and now in Italy, the Third Front. The Second Front, which already exists potentially and which is rapidly gathering weight, has not yet been engaged, but it is here, holding forces on its line. No one can tell — and certainly I am not going to hint — the moment when it will be engaged. But the Second Front exists, and is a main preoccupation already of the enemy. It has not yet opened or been thrown into play, but the time will come. At the right time this front will be thrown open, and the mass invasion from the West, in combination with the invasion from the South, will begin.

It is quite impossible for those who do not know the facts and figures of the American assembly in Britain, or of our own powerful expeditionary armies now preparing here, who do not know the dispositions of the enemy on the various fronts, who cannot measure his reserves and resources and his power to transfer large forces from one front to another over the vast railway system of Europe, who do not know the state and dimensions of our Fleet

and landing-craft of all kinds . . . to pronounce a useful opinion
upon this operation.

[Here one of our two Communist Members interjected: "Does
that apply to Marshal Stalin?"]

We should not in a matter of this kind take advice from British
Communists, because we know that they stood aside and cared
nothing for our fortunes in our time of mortal peril. Any advice
that we take will be from friends and Allies who are all joined
together in the common cause of winning the victory. The House
may be absolutely certain that His Majesty's present Government
will never be swayed or overborne by any uninstructed agitation,
however natural, or any pressure, however well-meant, in matters
of this kind. We shall not be forced or cajoled into undertaking
vast operations of war against our better judgment in order to gain
political unanimity or a cheer from any quarter. The bloodiest
portion — make no mistake about it — of this war for Great
Britain and the United States lies ahead of us. Neither the House
nor the Government will shrink from that ordeal. We shall not
grudge any sacrifice for the common cause.

*   *   *   *   *

The most difficult issue was the decision President Roosevelt
and I had taken, of which I was, as the reader has seen, a strong
partisan, to deal with the King and Marshal Badoglio and
recognise and treat them as co-belligerents. The same passions
were aroused on this occasion in the same kind of people as
on the Admiral Darlan affair the year before. I felt however
on even stronger ground in this case.

We may pause for a moment to survey and appraise the act of
the Italian Government, endorsed and acclaimed as it was by the
Italian nation. Herr Hitler has left us in no doubt that he con-
siders the conduct of Italy treacherous and base in the extreme —
and he is a good judge in such matters. Others may hold that the
act of treachery and ingratitude took place when the Fascist Con-
federacy — headed by Mussolini — used its arbitrary power to strike
for material gain at falling France and so became the enemy of the
British Empire, which had for so many years cherished the cause of
Italian liberty. There was the crime. Though it cannot be un-
done, and though nations which allow their rights and liberties to

be subverted by tyrants must suffer heavy penalties for those
tyrants' crimes, yet I cannot view the Italian action at this juncture
as other than natural and human. May it prove to be the first of
a series of acts of self-redemption.

The Italian people have already suffered terribly. Their manhood has been cast away in Africa and Russia, their soldiers have
been deserted in the field — their wealth has been squandered,
their empire has been irretrievably lost. Now their own beautiful
homeland must become a battlefield for German rearguards. Even
more suffering lies ahead. They are to be pillaged and terrorised
in Hitler's fury and revenge. Nevertheless, as the armies of the
British Empire and the United States march forward in Italy, the
Italian people will be rescued from their state of servitude and
degradation, and be enabled in due course to regain their rightful
place among the free democracies of the modern world.

*   *   *   *   *

I cannot touch upon this matter of Italy without exposing myself to the question, which I shall be most properly asked, "Would
you apply this line of argument to the German people?" I say,
"The case is different." Twice within our lifetime, and three times
counting that of our fathers, they have plunged the world into
their wars of expansion and aggression. They combine in the most
deadly manner the qualities of the warrior and the slave. They do
not value freedom themselves, and the spectacle of it in others is
hateful to them. Whenever they become strong, they seek their
prey, and they will follow with an iron discipline anyone who will
lead them to it. The core of Germany is Prussia. There is the
source of the recurring pestilence. But we do not war with races
as such. We war against tyranny, and we seek to preserve ourselves from destruction. I am convinced that the British, American,
and Russian peoples, who have suffered measureless waste, peril,
and bloodshed twice in a quarter of a century through the
Teutonic urge for domination, will this time take steps to put it
beyond the power of Prussia or of all Germany to come at them
again with pent-up vengeance and long-nurtured plans. Nazi
tyranny and Prussian militarism are the two main elements in
German life which must be absolutely destroyed. They must be
rooted out if Europe and the world are to be spared a third and
still more frightful conflict.

The controversies about whether Burke was right or wrong when he said, "I do not know the method of drawing up an indictment against a whole people," seem to me to be sterile and academic. Here are two obvious and practical targets for us to fire at — Nazi tyranny and Prussian militarism. Let us aim every gun, and let us set every man who will march in motion against them. We must not add needlessly to the weight of our task or the burden that our soldiers bear. Satellite states, suborned or overawed, may perhaps, if they can help to shorten the war, be allowed to work their passage home. But the twin roots of all our evils, Nazi tyranny and Prussian militarism, must be extirpated. Until this is achieved, there are no sacrifices that we will not make and no lengths in violence to which we will not go. I will add this: Having, at the end of my life, acquired some influence on affairs, I wish to make it clear that I would not needlessly prolong this war for a single day; and my hope is that if and when British people are called by victory to share in the august responsibilities of shaping the future, we shall show the same poise and temper as we did in the hour of our mortal peril.

*   *   *   *   *

I had thought it right in the course of my speech to give at this time a serious and precise warning about the attack which was impending upon us by pilotless aircraft or rockets. It is always prudent to be on record publicly as having given warning long before the event. This is more particularly true when its scale and gravity cannot be measured.

We must not in any circumstances allow these favourable tendencies to weaken our efforts or lead us to suppose that our dangers are past or that the war is coming to an end. On the contrary, we must expect that the terrible foe we are smiting so heavily will make frenzied efforts to retaliate. The speeches of the German leaders, from Hitler downward, contain mysterious allusions to new methods and new weapons which will presently be tried against us. It would of course be natural for the enemy to spread such rumours in order to encourage his own people, but there is probably more in it than that. For example, we now have experience of a new type of aerial bomb which the enemy has begun to use in attacks on our shipping, when at close quarters with the coast. This bomb, which may be described as a sort of rocket-assisted glider, is released from a considerable height, and is then apparently guided towards its target by the parent aircraft. It may be that the Germans are developing other weapons on novel lines with which they may hope to do us damage, and to compensate to some extent for the injury which they are daily receiving from us. I can only assure the House that unceasing vigilance and the most intense study of which we are capable are given to the possibilities.

*   *   *   *   *

I also outlined my thought upon the political state of Italy, and upon the now cruel reality of civil war spreading in that unhappy country.

The escape of Mussolini to Germany, his rescue by paratroops, and his attempts to form a Quisling Government which, with German bayonets, will try to refix the Fascist yoke on the necks of the Italian people, raise of course the issue of Italian civil war. It is necessary in the general interest, as well as in that of Italy, that all surviving forces of Italian national life should be rallied together around their lawful Government, and that the King and Marshal Badoglio should be supported by whatever Liberal and Left-Wing elements are capable of making head against the Fascist-Quisling combination, and thus of creating conditions which will help to drive this villainous combination from Italian soil, or, better still, annihilate it on the spot. We are coming to the rescue and liberation of Italy. [A Member interjected: "You will not get the Italian people to rise behind the banner of turncoats."] I think the honourable gentleman may be not thinking quite sufficiently of the importance of diminishing the burden which our soldiers have to bear. . . . The Government certainly intend to pursue a policy of engaging all the forces they can to make head against the Germans and drive them out of Italy. We are not going to be put off that action by any fear that perhaps we should not have complete unanimity on the subject. Parliament does not rest on unanimity; democratic assemblies do not act on unanimity. They act by majorities. That is the way they act. I wish to make it perfectly clear that we are endeavouring to rally the strongest forces together in Italy to make head against the Germans and the Mussolini-Quisling-Fascist combination.

My final words were somewhat unceremonious — but true.

The best method of acquiring flexibility is to have three or four plans for all the probable contingencies, all worked out with the utmost detail. Then it is much easier to switch from one to the other as and where the cat jumps.

These arguments convinced the House and there was no effective challenge.

*   *   *   *   *

On the same day that I finished this lengthy speech, I and my colleagues suffered a very heavy and unexpected loss in the sudden death of the Chancellor of the Exchequer. I did not hear the news till I awoke on the morning of the 22d. Kingsley Wood had become in later years a close personal friend of mine. After he went to the Air Ministry in 1938, we worked for the same objects. I gave him my full support, and undoubtedly he made an invaluable contribution to the readiness of the Royal Air Force to meet the mortal trial of 1940. He had been Chancellor of the Exchequer from the time I was called upon to form the National Government, and his record was a very fine one. His third Budget, balanced at five and three-quarter thousand millions, conformed to all the soundest principles of war-time finance. Half was raised by taxation. Our rate of borrowing was incredibly low. Instead of the slogan "Security and six per cent" of the First World War, we succeeded in borrowing enormous sums in the fifth year of this war at an average rate of two per cent. The cost of living had not risen by more than thirty per cent over the pre-war level. The "Pay as you earn" principle had occupied the closing weeks of Kingsley Wood's life, and on the very day that he died he was looking forward to making a statement to the House on the subject. He had given effect, with high efficiency, to the request I made to him in 1940 to provide compensation for those whose homes and businesses were destroyed in the Blitz, by the elaborate insurance scheme which he devised. I spent the few hours that remained before the House met in preparing a tribute to him, which is on record.

In Sir John Anderson, at this time Lord President of the

Council and Chairman of our most important Cabinet Committee, and our chief representative on "Tube Alloys," I
found a worthy successor. John Anderson had been Chairman of the Board of Inland Revenue, and also Head of the
Home Office for ten years, but he had a far wider outlook
than can be gained from any department. In the Irish troubles
he had risked his life continually with the utmost composure,
and this bearing was repeated when as Governor of Bengal an
attempt was made to assassinate him. He had an acute and
powerful mind, a firm spirit, and long experience of widely
varied responsibilities. His appointment was announced on
September 24.

*   *   *   *   *

Except for a few chats on the deck, I had seen little of Sir
Dudley Pound on our homeward voyage, as he kept to his
cabin. On the train journey to London he sent me a letter
formally resigning his office of First Sea Lord, of the burden
of which I had relieved him when his illness became pronounced in Washington. The question of his successor
required careful consideration. Admiral Sir Andrew Cunningham was an obvious choice, proposed by the First Lord, Mr.
Alexander, on account of the reputation which he had won in
all the fighting in the Mediterranean. Could he, on the other
hand, be spared from this scene at a time when so much was
going forward and all operations expanding? In Admiral
Fraser, then commanding the Home Fleet, we had an officer
of the highest seagoing reputation, who had also long experience of Admiralty administration and Staff work. It was to him
I first offered the post. The Admiral said that of course he
would serve wherever he was sent, but that he thought Andrew
Cunningham was the right man. "I believe I have the confidence of my own fleet," he said. "Cunningham has that of
the whole Navy." He asked me to weigh the matter longer.
I replied that his attitude was most becoming, and after
further thought and consultation I took him at his word and
decided to face the serious change in the Mediterranean fighting command. Admiral Andrew Cunningham was therefore

chosen. His second-in-command, Admiral John Cunningham, took his place. The changes were announced to the public and the Service, who knew nothing of Pound's illness, on October 4, when I published the following letter to Sir Dudley Pound:

I am sorry indeed that you have felt it necessary to lay down your charge on account of your health, and that our four years' work together in this war must come to an end. No one knows better than I the quality of your contribution, at the Admiralty and on the Chiefs of Staff Committee, to the safety of the country and the success of our arms. Your vast and precise knowledge of the sea war in all its aspects, your fortitude in times of anxiety and misfortune, your resourcefulness and readiness to run the risks without which victory can never be won, have combined to make your tenure as First Sea Lord memorable in the records of the Royal Navy.

You leave us at a moment when the control of the Mediterranean is virtually within our grasp, when the Italian Fleet has made its surrender in Malta Harbour, and when, above all, the U-boat peril has been broken in a degree never before seen in this war. These results have been of measureless value to your country, and your notable share in them sheds lustre on your name.

Pound lived for barely a fortnight. He became completely paralysed by another more severe stroke. The last time I saw him, though his mind was as good as ever, he could neither speak nor move the greater part of his body. When I shook his left hand on parting, he gripped me with a most surprising strength. He had been a true comrade to me, both at the Admiralty and on the Chiefs of Staff Committee. He died on October 21, Trafalgar Day.

Admiral Fraser went back to his fleet at Scapa. At the end of the year he had the distinction of fighting in his own flagship and sinking the *Scharnhorst* in a direct encounter. This was a naval episode of high honour and importance. When I next saw him in London, I reminded him of the famous lines:

> Not once or twice in our rough island-story
> The path of duty was the way to glory.

The Admiral seemed all the more pleased because, as I judged, he had never heard the quotation before. I hoped he thought I had made it up myself on purpose.

*   *   *   *   *

I have not burdened this account with the lengthy correspondence with the United States and Portugal which led to our agreement about the use by British and American flotillas and air forces of the extremely important key islands of the Azores. Everything was settled in a satisfactory manner, so that on October 12 I could report our conclusions to Parliament. "I have an announcement," I said, "to make to the House arising out of the treaty signed between this country and Portugal in the year 1373 between His Majesty King Edward III and King Ferdinand and Queen Eleanor of Portugal." I spoke in a level voice, and made a pause to allow the House to take in the date, 1373. As this soaked in, there was something like a gasp. I do not suppose any such continuity of relations between two Powers has ever been, or will ever be, set forth in the ordinary day-to-day work of British diplomacy.

This treaty [I went on] was reinforced in various forms by treaties of 1386, 1643, 1654, 1660, 1661, 1703, and 1815, and in a secret declaration of 1899. In more modern times the validity of the Old Treaties was recognised in the Treaties of Arbitration concluded with Portugal in 1904 and 1914. Article I of the Treaty of 1373 runs as follows:
"In the first place we settle and covenant that there shall be from this day forward . . . true, faithful, constant, mutual, and perpetual friendships, unions, alliances, and needs of sincere affection, and that as true and faithful friends we shall henceforth, reciprocally, be friends to friends and enemies to enemies, and shall assist, maintain, and uphold each other mutually, by sea and by land, against all men that may live or die."
This engagement has lasted now for nearly six hundred years, and is without parallel in world history. I have now to announce its latest application. At the outset of the war, the Portuguese Government, in full agreement with His Majesty's Government in the United Kingdom, adopted a policy of neutrality with a view to

preventing the war spreading into the Iberian Peninsula. The Portuguese Government have repeatedly stated, most recently in Dr. Salazar's speech of April 27, that the above policy is in no way inconsistent with the Anglo-Portuguese Alliance, which was re-affirmed by the Portuguese Government in the early days of the war.

His Majesty's Government in the United Kingdom, basing them-selves upon this ancient alliance, have now requested the Portu-guese Government to accord them certain facilities in the Azores which will enable better protection to be provided for merchant shipping in the Atlantic. The Portuguese Government have agreed to grant this request, and arrangements, which enter into force immediately, have been concluded between the two Governments regarding (1) the conditions governing the use of the above facilities by His Majesty's Government in the United Kingdom and (2) British assistance in furnishing essential material and sup-plies to the Portuguese armed forces and the maintenance of the Portuguese national economy. The agreement concerning the use of facilities in the Azores is of a temporary nature only, and in no way prejudices the maintenance of Portuguese sovereignty over Portuguese territory.

*   *   *   *   *

The next day I had to make a long speech to the House on the coal-mining situation, which was affected by the vital need of coal and the claims of the fighting forces for man-power, and also by the underlying threat of the nationalisation of the coal-mines, which was a suspended issue between the parties. There had been a lot of rumblings on this point, and I was concerned only with the maintenance of national unity.

I thought it might help if I reminded the House at the outset of this discussion of the general foundations upon which we stand at the present time. We have a National Coalition Government, which came together to try to pull the nation out of the forlorn and sombre plight into which the action, or inaction, of all politi-cal parties over a long period of years had landed it. I stand very well placed in that matter, having been out for eleven years. What holds us together is the prosecution of the war. No Socialist or Liberal or Labour man has been in any way asked to give up his convictions. That would be indecent and improper. We are held together by something outside, which rivets all our attention. The principle that we work on is, "Everything for the war, whether controversial or not, and nothing controversial that is not *bona fide* needed for the war." That is our position.

We must also be careful that a pretext is not made of war needs to introduce far-reaching social or political changes by a side-wind. Take the question of nationalising the coal-mines. Those words do not terrify me at all. I advocated nationalisation of the railways after the last war, but I am bound to say that I was a bit affected by the experience of the national control of the railways after the war, which led to the public getting a very bad service, to the shareholders having very unsatisfactory returns, and to one of the most vicious and hazardous strikes with which I have ever been concerned. However, as I say, the principle of nationalisation is accepted by all, provided proper compensation is paid. The argument proceeds not on moral grounds, but on whether in fact we could make a more fertile business for the nation as a whole by nationalisation than by relying on private enterprise and competition. It would raise a lot of difference of opinion and be a tremendous business to nationalise the coal-mines, and unless it could be proved to the conviction of the House and of the country and to the satisfaction of the responsible Ministers that that was the only way in which we could win the war, we should not be justified in embarking upon it without a General Election. It would be very difficult to have a General Election at the present time. . . .

I am told and can well realise that anxiety exists among the miners about what is to happen to them and their industry after the war. They had a very grim experience after the last war, which went on biting away at them for a long period, and greatly affected the whole conception that they had of mining as a means of getting their living. I know that there is anxiety. We can all lie awake thinking of the nightmares that we are going to suffer after the war is over, and everyone has his perplexities and anxieties about that time. But I for one, being an optimist, do not think peace is going to be so bad as war, and I hope we shall not try to make it as bad. After the last war, which I lived through in a responsible position, nearly everyone behaved as badly as he could, and the country was at times almost uncontrollable. We have profited a great deal in this war by the experience of the last. We make war much better than we did, owing to previous experience. We are also going to try to profit to the full by the hard experience of what happened in the last peace. I am casting no reflection on the Government of that day when I say that, armed with their dear-bought experience, we shall make the transition from war to peace in a more orderly and disciplined fashion than we did last time.

But the miners are worried about their future. His Majesty's Government give the assurance to them that the present system of control, plus any improvements that may be made to it, will be continued after the war until Parliament shall decide upon the future structure of the industry. That means either that there will be a settlement by agreement between the great parties, or that there will be a General Election at which the people will be free to choose between political doctrines and political leaders. But anyhow, until all that is over there will be no decisive change in the present structure of the coal industry, or any removal of the many guarantees for the continuity of employment and wages and limitation of profits which are embodied in it. I am so anxious that we should all be together in this.

This statement eased the tension which existed, and I am glad today to read it over again.

*   *   *   *   *

Finally, on October 28, there was the rebuilding of the House of Commons to consider. One unlucky bomb had blown to fragments the Chamber in which I had passed so much of my life. I was determined to have it rebuilt at the earliest moment that our struggle would allow. I had the power at this moment to shape things in a way that would last. Supported by my colleagues, mostly old Parliamentarians, and with Mr. Attlee's cordial aid, I sought to re-establish for what may well be a long period the two great principles on which the British House of Commons stands in its physical aspect. The first is that it must be oblong, and not semicircular, and the second that it must only be big enough to give seats to about two-thirds of its Members. As this argument has long surprised foreigners, I record it here.

There are two main characteristics of the House of Commons which will command the approval and the support of reflective and experienced Members. The first is that its shape should be oblong and not semicircular. Here is a very potent factor in our political life. The semicircular assembly, which appeals to political theorists, enables every individual or every group to move round the centre, adopting various shades of pink according as the weather changes. I am a convinced supporter of the party system in preference to the group system. I have seen many earnest and ardent Parliaments destroyed by the group system. The party system is much favoured by the oblong form of chamber. It is easy for an individual to move through those insensible gradations from Left to Right, but the act of crossing the Floor is one which requires serious consideration. I am well informed on this matter, for I have accomplished that difficult process, not only once, but twice. Logic is a poor guide compared with custom. Logic, which has created in so many countries semicircular assemblies with buildings that give to every member not only a seat to sit in, but often a desk to write at, with a lid to bang, has proved fatal to Parliamentary government as we know it here in its home and in the land of its birth.

The second characteristic of a chamber formed on the lines of the House of Commons is that it should *not* be big enough to contain all its Members at once without overcrowding, and that there should be no question of every Member having a separate seat reserved for him. The reason for this has long been a puzzle to uninstructed outsiders, and has frequently excited the curiosity and even the criticism of new Members. Yet it is not so difficult to understand if you look at it from a practical point of view. If the House is big enough to contain all its Members, nine-tenths of its debates will be conducted in the depressing atmosphere of an almost empty or half-empty chamber. The essence of good House of Commons speaking is the conversational style, the facility for quick, informal interruptions and interchanges. Harangues from a rostrum would be a bad substitute for the conversational style in which so much of our business is done. But the conversational style requires a fairly small space, and there should be on great occasions a sense of crowd and urgency. There should be a sense of the importance of much that is said, and a sense that great matters are being decided, there and then, by the House.

This anyhow was settled as I wished.

*   *   *   *   *

During these busy days I thought it right, now that our ultimate victory appeared certain, to dwell upon what would descend upon us at the same time as victory. This chapter may well close with the two notes I wrote to my colleagues upon these problems, already looming ahead.

WAR — TRANSITION — PEACE

MEMORANDUM BY THE PRIME MINISTER AND MINISTER OF DEFENCE

19 Oct. 43

It is the duty of His Majesty's Government to prepare for the tasks which will fall upon us at the end of the war. The urgent needs are: (*a*) A sound scheme of demobilisation, having regard to the undoubted need of our keeping considerable garrisons in enemy-occupied territory. (*b*) The provision of food for our island on a scale better than the war-time rations. (*c*) The resumption of the export trade and the restoration of our mercantile marine. (*d*) The general turnover of industry from war to peace. And, above all, (*e*) The provision during a transition period of employment for all able-bodied persons seeking it, and especially for the ex-Servicemen.

Any decisions which are needed for the supreme objects of *food* and *employment* in the years immediately after the war must be taken now, whether they involve legislation and whether they are controversial or not.

2. Much work has already been done on these lines by the departments and committees concerned. We must be careful not to have these urgent practical duties confused and overlain by party politics or held up by endless discussions about long-term schemes for building a new world order, etc.

3. There are in fact three stages, namely, (i) War, (ii) Transition, and (iii) Peace and freedom. The present Government and Parliament are fully entitled to make all necessary preparations for the transition period, and we should be held severely accountable if found in default. As early as possible in the transition period

(for which all preparations will have been made) a General Election must be held, in order that the electors may express their will upon the form that is to be given to our post-war and post-transition society.

4. We do not know whether this election will be fought on an agreed programme by the parties now composing the Coalition Government or whether the leader of the majority in the present House of Commons will be forced to place his own programme before the electors. In either case it is probable that a Four-Years Plan will be announced, which, apart from carrying out the enormous administrative measures required in the transition period, will also comprise a series of large decisions on progress and reform which will, from one angle or the other, shape the post-war and post-transition period. There will therefore be no lack of work for the new Parliament.

5. In the meanwhile there are a number of important policies, such as education, social insurance, the rebuilding of our shattered dwellings and cities, on which there is or may be found a wide measure of general agreement. These steps must be brought to a high degree of preparation now during the war, any necessary preliminary legislation being passed, so that they are ready to come into force in the early days of the transition period.

6. It is impossible to tell how long the war against Japan will outlast the war against Germany. It would perhaps be safe, as a working basis, to make the transition period last for two years after the defeat of Germany, or four years from January 1, 1944, whichever period shall end the sooner.

When this had been largely approved by the War Cabinet, I wrote a precise directive which is printed in the Appendix.[1]

A month later, I decided upon the appointment of a Minister of Reconstruction, whose office would be the focal point for all plans for the transitional period. Lord Woolton's conduct of the Food Ministry had gained widespread satisfaction and general confidence. He seemed in every way equipped with the qualities and experience to concert and stimulate the activities of the many departments concerned. He took up his duties on November 12.

[1] See Appendix D, Book One.

10

Tensions with General de Gaulle

De Gaulle Arrives in Algiers, May 30 — My Telegram to President Roosevelt of June 6 — Conflict Between de Gaulle and Giraud — The Question of Recognition of the French National Committee — President Roosevelt's Strong Opposition — Correspondence with Him — My Memorandum of July 13 — I Try to Persuade the President to Limited Recognition — He Suggests Instead a Formula of Co-operation — We Debate the Whole Position at Quebec in August — Qualified Recognition Is Accorded — The Struggle for Power Between de Gaulle and Giraud Continues — Corsica Liberated, October 3 — Formation of a Free French Consultative Assembly — Giraud Restricted to the Military Command — De Gaulle Becomes Sole President of the French National Committee — Violent Action in Syria — A Year of Disappointing Relationships with the Free French.

DURING THE SUMMER OF 1943, the relations of the British Government with de Gaulle deteriorated. We had made great efforts to bring together Frenchmen of all parties at Algiers, and I had constantly pressed the Americans to accept General de Gaulle as a leading figure in the political arrangements which we were both trying to facilitate. In the strained atmosphere which pervaded French affairs after the signature of the Clark-Darlan agreements and the appearance of Giraud, de Gaulle became more than ever intractable. His position had strengthened in recent weeks. He had many supporters in Tunisia, which was now in Allied hands. News from Metropolitan France, together with the creation of the clandestine

Central Committee there, showed the extent of his prestige and an upsurge of the Gaullist movement. It was in these circumstances that Giraud agreed to meet his rival in North Africa.

On May 30, de Gaulle arrived in Algiers, and sharp and sulky negotiations were begun with the object of setting up a united Provisional Committee to administer the affairs of Fighting France. Wrangling centred round three main issues: Giraud's assumption of supreme civil and military authority; de Gaulle's determination to affirm formally the sovereignty of Fighting France — a step which would violate the letter of the agreements which Darlan had made with General Mark Clark in November 1942; and the question of the former Vichy administrators now in key offices in North Africa, particularly Noguès, Peyrouton, and Boisson. The latter was a special target. De Gaulle had never forgiven him for the events of 1940 at Dakar.

Tension mounted in Algiers as these bitter discussions were prolonged. On the afternoon of June 3, however, agreement was reached, and a French Committee of National Liberation was set up, which included Giraud and de Gaulle, Generals Catroux and Georges, and certain members of the Gaullist Committee from London, which had been dissolved when de Gaulle left for North Africa. The former Vichy governors were excluded from the new body, which was now to be the central provisional administration of Fighting France and her Empire until the end of the war.

*   *   *   *   *

The reader will recall that I was in North Africa with General Marshall for conferences with General Eisenhower during these talks on the future of France, and just before my departure I had invited the new Committee to luncheon. When I got back to London, I received a telegram from President Roosevelt voicing his anxiety. "I want to give you," he said on June 5, "the thought that North Africa is in last analysis under British-American military rule, and that for this

reason Eisenhower can be used on what you and I want. The
bride evidently forgets that there is still a war in progress over
here. We receive only the bride's publicity. What is the matter with our British-American information services? Best of
luck in getting rid of our mutual headache."

I sent to the President in reply my impressions of Algiers:

Former Naval Person to President Roosevelt   6 June 43

We had the whole French Committee to luncheon on Friday
(June 4), and everybody seemed most friendly. General Georges,
whom I got out of France a month ago, and who is a personal
friend of mine, is a great support to Giraud. If de Gaulle should
prove violent or unreasonable, he will be in a minority of five to
two, and possibly completely isolated. The Committee is therefore
a body with collective authority with which in my opinion we can
safely work.

2. I consider that the formation of this Committee brings to an
end my official connection with de Gaulle as leader of the Fighting
French, which was set out in the letters exchanged with him in
1940 and certain other documents of later date, and I propose, in
so far as is necessary, to transfer these relationships, financial and
otherwise, to the Committee as a whole. While I consider the Committee is a safe repository for arms and supplies, I feel that we
should see how they conduct their business and themselves before
deciding what degree of recognition we should give them as representing France. Macmillan and Murphy are working in the closest
accord, and will keep Eisenhower, with whom the supreme and
ultimate power rests, fully informed.

3. I should be strongly opposed to Boisson being dismissed from
his post.

*   *   *   *   *

But the wrangling did not cease. De Gaulle would not
accept Giraud as Supreme Commander of the French forces.
Giraud was anxious to keep the French Army of North Africa
intact and clear of Free French influences. This attitude of
de Gaulle on the question of military command exacerbated
American dislike and distrust of him.

The President again telegraphed to me:

President Roosevelt to the Prime Minister 10 June 43

I have just received the following message from Murphy:

"I was told this afternoon by Giraud that de Gaulle during this morning's session of the French Committee finally brought into the open his wish to act as Commissioner for National Defence, having the attributes of a Minister of War in the ordinary Cabinet set-up. He also demanded the command of French forces not actively engaged in operations, which is contrary to what he has told Eisenhower, Macmillan, and me with respect to his intentions. Giraud absolutely refused to yield command of French forces. He insisted that General Georges be appointed Commissioner of National Defence. A compromise proposal submitted by Catroux very much favoured de Gaulle's proposition. Giraud told me of his determination to retire if the Committee outvoted him on this question, and to inform the British and American Governments and the French people of the injustice caused by de Gaulle's ambition. I have asked Giraud to delay any such action until there has been an opportunity to discuss this question with several members of the Committee."

Macmillan had reported to me in the same sense. I was only anxious that a straightforward agreement should be reached.

Prime Minister to Mr. Harold Macmillan (Algiers) 11 June 43

There can be no question of our giving recognition until we know what it is we have to recognise. See St. Matthew, chapter vii, verse 16: "Ye shall know them by their fruits. Do men gather grapes of thorns, or figs of thistles?" Indeed, the whole chapter is instructive.

You are quite right to play for time and let de Gaulle have every chance to come to his senses and realise the forces around him. We play fair with him if he plays fair with us and with France.

The President was less patient.

President Roosevelt to Prime Minister 17 June 43

The following is a paraphrase of a cable I have today sent to General Eisenhower:

"The position of this Government is that during our military occupation of North Africa we will not tolerate the control of the French Army by any agency which is not subject to the Allied Supreme Commander's direction. We must have someone whom we completely and wholly trust. We would under no circumstances continue the arming of a force without being completely confident in their willingness to co-operate in our military operations; we are not interested moreover in the formation of any Government or Committee which presumes in any way to indicate that, until such time as the French people select a Government for themselves, it will govern in France. When we get into France, the Allies will have a civil Government plan that is completely in consonance with French sovereignty. Lastly, it must be absolutely clear that in North and West Africa we have a military occupation, and therefore without your full approval no independent civil decision can be made. . . . "

*   *   *   *   *

These telegrams from the President revealed such a mounting hostility to de Gaulle's actions in Algiers that I feared for the whole future of Allied relations with the Free French. The Americans reached the point where they might refuse to recognise any provisional administrative body if they thought that de Gaulle would be the dominating influence which would affect the future of France after the war. It was essential to allay American fears on the military question and at the same time to keep in being the new Provisional Committee.

Former Naval Person to President Roosevelt   18 June 43

. . . I am not in favour at this moment of breaking up the Committee of Seven or forbidding it to meet. I should prefer that General Eisenhower should take your instructions as his directive, and that Murphy and Macmillan should work towards its fulfilment by whatever means they find most appropriate. His Majesty's Government will associate themselves with this policy.

The Committee will then be confronted with a choice of either accepting our decision by a majority or placing themselves in definite opposition to the two rescuing Powers. If, as seems probable, they accept the decision by a majority, it will be for de Gaulle to decide whether he and other dissentients will submit or resign. If de Gaulle resigns, he will put himself in the wrong with public opinion, and the necessary measures must be taken to prevent him from creating a disturbance. If he submits, we shall probably have further trouble in the future, but this will be better than our sweeping away a Committee on which many hopes are founded among the United Nations as well as in France. We should prescribe the conditions essential for the safety of our forces and place the onus on de Gaulle. At any rate, it would be wise to try this first.

*   *   *   *   *

The American attitude to the French political scene in North Africa was in part dominated by military necessity. The background to the dispute over de Gaulle was the preparation of the Sicily landings. The quarrels over the French High Command, provoked by de Gaulle, had come at the critical moment. Whatever past arrangements had existed between the British Government and de Gaulle, they could not be allowed to impair our relations with the United States.

On July 13, I had written a paper for my colleagues summarising these developments in American policy towards France, in which I stated:

It has for a good many months past been our object to bring about a union between the French elements cultivated by the Americans in Northwest Africa and the French National Committee in London, and particularly between Generals Giraud and de Gaulle. I could, I think, have made a good arrangement at Casablanca, but, as my colleagues know, this was frustrated by the preposterous conduct of General de Gaulle. Since then the President has armed General Giraud's troops in North Africa on a very considerable scale and he is now much concerned about the demeanour and control of this army. Meanwhile, the de Gaullist organs in London and at Brazzaville, with their backers in the British and American press, have ceaselessly criticised American policy, and there is no doubt that not only Mr. Hull but the President have become bitterly antagonised thereby.

For all these reasons we have hoped that the personality of de Gaulle should be merged first in the National Committee in London, and, now that juncture has been effected with the Algiers.

elements, in the Committee of National Liberation. After some crises and spasms, this Committee is gradually acquiring a collective character, especially now that the civilian elements are increasing and asserting themselves. The lines of cleavage are no longer defined by the partisans of Giraud or of de Gaulle. These healthy tendencies should be allowed to develop, and if it should become clear in the course of the next few months that de Gaulle and his faction are not the masters of the Liberation Committee, and that he himself has settled down to honest teamwork within its ranks, it might be possible to procure from the President some kind of recognition of the Committee. This result will not however be easily or swiftly obtained, and we have to consider what our course should be in the meanwhile.

When the Liberation Committee was formed, I made haste to transfer to it the engagements previously made with General de Gaulle. This process must continue, as otherwise we should have no one to deal with about finance, propaganda, Syria and other French possessions, and the control of the French armed forces. The Foreign Secretary has pointed out to me that we passed an Act of Parliament investing de Gaulle with powers of discipline over the Free French forces in British territory, and certainly these powers must now be vested in the new Committee. There is no objection to dealing with the Committee in its collective capacity as the *de facto* authority. Transacting necessary business with them can only do them good, and, if they are worthy of their responsibilities, will add to their strength.

In a certain sense this implies recognition of the Committee, but it will only be making unnecessary trouble with the United States to emphasise this point or do anything of a *de jure* character at the present stage. We should avoid the use of the word "recognition," and avoid also anything in the nature of a splash or a gesture, while at the same time working with them, for what they are worth, from day to day. It is the duty of the Committee and also in their interest to regain or build up the wounded confidence of the rescuing Powers, and in particular the estranged United States Government. If we were to take any step of formally recognising the Committee at this juncture, this would give the very greatest offence in Washington. It would draw upon the Administration there the hostile criticism of all who are attempting to oust the President at next year's election. The whole course of the war depends upon our cordial relations with the American Government and President, and we owe it to our troops in the field not to make their task harder by taking any step which would lead to a serious decline in the present very remarkable co-operation. Even if Soviet Russia recognises de Gaulle on account of his recent flirtations with Communist elements, we should still be wise to measure our course by that of the United States. Indeed, in this case it would be still more important not to leave them isolated and give the appearance of working with Russia against them. . . .

I have repeatedly stated that it is in the major interests of Great Britain to have a strong France after the war, and I should not hesitate to sustain this view. I am afraid lest the anti-de Gaullism of the Washington Government may harden into a definite anti-France feeling. If however de Gaulle is gradually merged and submerged into the Committee, and the Committee comports itself in a reasonable and loyal manner, this dangerous tendency on the part of the United States may be deflected and assuaged.

There is no harm in the French Committee coming to feel that we would like to put them into better relations with the United States. It may still be possible to gain for France and the French Empire a recognised place in the councils of the Allies, if the healthy and helpful processes I have noted are allowed to take their course, and if we act with patience, and above all with a sense of proportion, in these vexatious matters.

*   *   *   *   *

Opinion in our Cabinet circle moved steadily towards some form of recognition, and I sent a further telegram to the President.

Former Naval Person to President Roosevelt   21 July 43

I am under considerable pressure from the Foreign Office, from my Cabinet colleagues, and also from the force of circumstances, to "recognise" the National Committee of Liberation in Algiers. What does recognition mean? One can recognise a man as an Emperor or as a grocer. Recognition is meaningless, without a defining formula. Until de Gaulle went to Northwest Africa and the new Committee was formed, all our relations were with him and his Committee. I stated to Parliament on June 8 that "The formation of this Committee with its collective responsibility supersedes the situation created by the correspondence between General de Gaulle and myself in 1940. Our dealings, financial and otherwise, will henceforward be with the Committee as a whole." I was glad to do this because I would rather deal with the Committee collectively than with de Gaulle alone. I had in fact for many months been working to induce or compel de Gaulle to "put himself in commission." This seemed to be largely achieved by the new arrangement. Macmillan tells us repeatedly that the Committee is acquiring a collective authority and that de Gaulle is by no means its master. He tells us further that if the Committee breaks down, as it may do if left utterly without support, de Gaulle will become once again the sole personality in control of everything except the powers exercised by Giraud under the armed force of the United States in Northwest Africa and Dakar. He strongly recommends a measure of recognition. He reports that Eisenhower and Murphy both agree with this. . . .

I am therefore reaching the point where it may be necessary for me to take this step so far as Great Britain and the Anglo-French interests set out above are concerned. If I do, Russia will certainly recognise (them), and I fear lest this might be embarrassing to you.

I do hope therefore that you will let me know (a) whether you could subscribe to our formula or something like it, or (b) whether you would mind if His Majesty's Government took that step separately themselves. There is no doubt whatever in my mind that the former would be far the better. There are a lot of good men on the Committee — Catroux, Massigli, Monnet, Georges, and of course Giraud, who arrived here yesterday. He will certainly raise all this and bring it to a head.

But it was clear that the Americans were not prepared to recognise the Algiers Committee as now constituted. Giraud had been in the United States negotiating for the supply of arms and equipment for the French army in North Africa. His presence there did not smooth the temper of the de Gaullists.

On July 22, I received a long and important telegram from the President setting forth the considered view of his Government on French affairs.

President Roosevelt to Prime Minister 22 July 43

Various sources continue, though with less pressure, to ask recognition of the existing French Committee of National Liberation. Some people want to recognise it as the organisation acting for French interests in all French territory, including France. Other people want to recognise it as acting for French interests only in former French Empire. Most, not all, are willing to accept the Committee's authority, subject to the military requirements of the British and American forces.

We have been saying, first, that the military requirements are and will be paramount to all civil matters; second, that the French Committee of National Liberation has only begun to function, and should give further and more satisfactory evidence of the complete and genuine unity of the Committee. This unity must eliminate hitherto French political or factional controversies designed to promote either group antagonisms or individual aspirations, and demonstrate a real purpose to unify itself and, behind it, all Frenchmen in support of the co-operative efforts of the United Nations in the prosecution of the war against the Axis Powers, having in mind its single cause of the liberation of France and the success of the United Nations.

The French Committee was supposedly conceived on the principle of collective responsibility of individual Frenchmen for the prosecution of the war, and our relations with it should be kept on this basis, it being understood that as to matters of a military character the two Governments will deal directly with the French Commander-in-Chief of the French forces. French political questions must be left to solution by the people of France when they have been freed from the present domination of the enemy. . . .

This Government is most anxious to join with you and the other United Nations to move along the line of limited acceptance of the Committee, subject always to military requirements, but we should make it clear that the plain conditions of French unity must be properly met.

I do not think we should at any time use the word "recognition," because this would be distorted to imply that we recognise the Committee as the Government of France as soon as we land on French soil. Perhaps the word "acceptance" of the Committee's local civil authority in various colonies on a temporary basis comes nearer to expressing my thought. We must however retain the

right and continue the present practice of dealing directly with
local French officials in the colonies whenever military advantage
to the Allied cause so dictates. Martinique is an illustrative example.

Giraud's visit here was very successful. We kept it on a purely
military basis, and we are starting immediately to send additional
equipment for his army with every North African convoy. . . .

Roosevelt ended by suggesting a joint formula based on "co-
operation with" instead of "recognition of" the French Committee.

I replied to the President's telegram of July 22:

Former Naval Person to President Roosevelt   3 Aug. 43

I thought first that your proposed formula was rather chilling
and would not end the agitation there is for recognition in both
our countries. Meanwhile, events have moved in our favour. The
Committee have felt acutely being ignored while the whole Italian
problem is open. De Gaulle, I feel, is now more enclosed in the
general body of the Committee. The arrangements for command
also seem more satisfactory to us than the previous deadlock.

2. I have therefore asked the Foreign Office to suggest a certain
modification in your formula designed to bring our two views into
harmony. . . . If we cannot agree, we will talk it over.

The Quebec Conference already described was now imminent. Meanwhile, we had reached a deadlock.

President Roosevelt to Prime Minister   4 Aug. 43

I earnestly hope that nothing will be done in the matter of
recognition of the Committee of National Liberation until we have
an opportunity to talk it over together.

*   *   *   *   *

It was only after stubborn talks that I was able to persuade
the Americans to make a declaration in general terms supporting the political arrangements which had already taken
shape in North Africa.

Prime Minister (Quebec) to Mr. Macmillan (Algiers)   25 Aug. 43

After prolonged discussions of a laborious character, we reached what I trust will be considered a series of satisfactory solutions about recognition. We thought it better that we should all express our thought in our own words rather than persevere in a joint declaration by the United States and United Kingdom.

2. In my opinion the President and Mr. Hull have gone a long way to meet our desires. You should tell my friends on the Committee that I am sure the right course for them is to welcome the American declaration in most cordial terms, and not to draw invidious distinction between any of the forms in which recognition is accorded. On the contrary, the more pleasure they show at the American declaration the more value it will have for them. This is a moment when a friendly attitude towards the United States would be singularly helpful to the interests of France. If, on the other hand, newspapers or radio polemics and reproaches are indulged in, the only effect will be to rouse new flames of resentment in the State Department.

*   *   *   *   *

The announcement of the recognition of the French National Committee on the following day marked the end of a period, and though the French leaders were not brought into the armistice negotiations with Italy, nor into the Mediterranean Commission which was subsequently set up to deal with Italian affairs, they were now on formal terms with the Allies as the representatives of France.

*   *   *   *   *

The struggle for power between de Gaulle and Giraud went on unabated as the weeks passed, and frequent clashes took place over both civil and military appointments. The fault did not lie always with de Gaulle, and there were unnecessary incidents over the liberation of Corsica, where Free French elements on the island had occupied Ajaccio on the night of September 13/14. Giraud ordered a French expedition to Corsica three days later, and the unfortunate disputes between his military commander and the de Gaullist leaders on the spot still further worsened relations. The liberation of the island, from the military point of view, was slowly but successfully accomplished.

Prime Minister to Mr. Harold Macmillan (Algiers)   3 Oct. 43

If you think well, you should give the following message from me to Generals Giraud and de Gaulle:

"Many congratulations on the successful progress of your troops in Corsica. I look forward intensely to this famous island soon being liberated and restored to France."

The occupation of the island by French forces was completed on the following day.

*   *   *   *   *

Plans for summoning a provisional Consultative Assembly to broaden the basis of French administration advanced during the month of October. Giraud's position steadily weakened. The only support he possessed lay in certain Army circles who valued American good will, and in his rôle of co-President of the National Committee this was fast disappearing. De Gaulle showed himself incomparably the more powerful personality. On November 3, the Assembly met for the first time in Algiers. French political life was crystallising into an embryo Government for the future. On November 8, one year exactly after the North African landings, Giraud resigned from the National Committee, but remained Commander-in-Chief of the French forces. I was disturbed at the possible consequences of these events. It was essential for the future unity of France that some balance of power between these divergent elements should be reached.

I therefore telegraphed to the President:

Prime Minister to President Roosevelt   10 Nov. 43

I am not at all content with the changes in the French National Committee which leave de Gaulle sole President. The body we recognised was of a totally different character, the essence being the co-Presidency of Giraud and de Gaulle. I suggest we maintain an attitude of complete reserve until we can discuss the position together.

I hoped, on my way through to Cairo to the Teheran Conference, to bring the rival Generals together myself at a review of the new French Army.

Prime Minister to Mr. Macmillan (Algiers)   2 Nov. 43

In case I am able to find a few days in Africa between now and Christmas, I should like to see something of the new French Army. You might ascertain discreetly from both Generals de Gaulle and Giraud whether this would be agreeable to them. We might have an afternoon parade, spend the night somewhere, and see some exercises in the morning. In these circumstances I should like to be the guest of the French National Committee. It occurred to me they might take this as a compliment, which it is intended to be. I cannot fix dates at the present time, for many obvious reasons.

*   *   *   *   *

My intention was frustrated by the rough and tragic behaviour of the Free French Administration in Syria. The formal independence of Syria and the Lebanon had been proclaimed by the Free French at the end of 1941. We had recognised these republics, and Sir Edward Spears had been sent as British Minister in February 1942. Throughout the year however no progress was made. Changes of Ministry took place in both countries, but no elections were held. Anti-French antagonisms grew. Provisional Governments were appointed in March 1943. The elections in July and August resulted in an overwhelming Nationalist expression in both republics. The majorities demanded the complete revision of the mandatory constitution. The weakness of the Free French Administration led the local politicians, who had little faith in French promises of after-war independence, to strike. On October 7, the Lebanese Government proposed to abolish the French position in the republic. A month later, the Free French Committee in Algiers challenged the right of the Lebanese to act in this one-sided manner. M. Helleu, General Catroux's deputy, returned from Algiers to give orders for the arrest of the Lebanese President and most of the Ministers, thereby provoking disturbances, which led to bloodshed, particularly at Beirut. The British Cabinet was disturbed by these events.

The action taken by the French stultified the agreements we had made with the French, and also with the Syrians and Lebanese. It was contrary to the Atlantic Charter and much else that we had declared. It seemed that the situation would be distorted throughout the whole of the Middle East and the Arab world, and also everywhere people would say, "What kind of France is this which, while itself subjugated by the enemy, seeks to subjugate others?"

Accordingly, I felt that the British and United States Governments should react strongly together. Already the character of the body we had recognised at Quebec had been totally altered by de Gaulle's complete assumption of power. But the outbreaks in the Levant were of a different character, and afforded full justification, with the support of world public opinion, for bringing the issue with de Gaulle to a head. I thought that the kidnapped Lebanese President and Ministers should be set at liberty and permitted to resume their full function, and that the Lebanon Assembly should meet again as soon as conditions of law and order could be guaranteed. If de Gaulle refused to do this at once, we should withdraw our recognition from the French National Committee and stop the process of arming the French troops in North Africa.

I was forced to give instructions to General Wilson to be prepared if necessary to take over control of the Lebanon and to re-establish order with British troops. Happily this was not necessary. General Catroux had arrived from Algiers on November 16 to act as mediator, and on November 22 the French authorities released the politicians under arrest, and protracted negotiations began for the ultimate independence of Syria and the Lebanon.

These incidents left their mark upon our relations with the Free French Committee and with General de Gaulle. The result of our year of effort to bring about a united policy founded upon a true sense of comradeship between the United States, Britain, and the Free French leaders had been disappointing.

11

The Broken Axis

Autumn 1943

Civil War in Italy — Need to Sustain the King and Badoglio Government — My Telegram to President Roosevelt of September 21 — Our Agreement — Mussolini Meets Hitler, September 14 — He Sets up the Republic of Salo — Fate of the Italian Forces in the Balkans and Aegean — I Explain the Situation to Stalin — He Favours Backing the Badoglio-King Government — Marshal Badoglio Signs the Surrender Agreement at Malta — Triple Declaration About Italian Co-belligerency by the President, Stalin, and Me — Count Sforza's Changeable Attitude — Arrangements About Italian Prisoners and Shipping — Italy Declares War on Germany, October 13 — A Fragile Situation.

MUSSOLINI's bid for a Fascist revival plunged Italy into the horrors of civil war. In the weeks following the September Armistice, officers and men of the Italian Army stationed in German-occupied Northern Italy and patriots from the towns and countryside began to form partisan units and to operate against the Germans and against their compatriots who still adhered to the Duce. Contacts were made with the Allied armies south of Rome and with the Badoglio Government. In these months the network of Italian resistance to the German occupation was created in a cruel atmosphere of civil strife, assassinations, and executions. The insurgent movement in Central and Northern Italy here as elsewhere in occupied Europe convulsed all classes of the people. Not the least of their achievements was the succour and support given to our prisoners of war trapped by the Armistice in camps in Northern Italy. Out of about eighty thousand of these men, conspicuously clothed in battle dress, and in the main with little knowledge of the language or geography of the country, at least ten thousand, mostly succoured by the local population with civilian clothes, were guided to safety thanks to the risks taken by members of the Italian Resistance and the simple people of the countryside.

*   *   *   *   *

From the moment when the Armistice was signed and when the Italian Fleet loyally and courageously joined the Allies, I felt myself bound to work with the King of Italy and Marshal Badoglio, at least until Rome should be occupied by the Allies and we could construct a really broad-based Italian Government for the prosecution of the war jointly with us. I was sure that King Victor Emmanuel and Badoglio would be able to do more for what had now become the common cause than any Italian Government formed from the exiles or opponents of the Fascist régime. The surrender of the Italian Fleet was solid proof of their authority. On the other hand, there were the usual arguments against having anything to do with those who had worked with or helped Mussolini, and immediately there grew an endless series of intrigues among the six or seven Leftish parties in Rome to get rid of the King and Badoglio and take the power themselves. Considering the critical nature of the battle and the supreme importance of getting Italy to fight with a good heart on our side, I resisted these movements whenever they came to my notice. In this I was supported by Marshal Stalin, who followed the Russian maxim, "You may always walk with the Devil till you get to the end of the bridge."

*   *   *   *   *

After considering proposals from Macmillan at Algiers, and from General Eisenhower, I telegraphed to the President asking for his comments.

Prime Minister to President Roosevelt   21 Sept. 43

. . . I and my colleagues in the War Cabinet have come to the following conclusions:

It is vital to build up the authority of the King and the Brindisi Administration as a Government and have unity of command throughout Italy. . . . Despite Badoglio's broadcast tonight we still feel it is essential that the King should go to the microphone at Bari, tell the Italian people he is there, and proclaim that Badoglio is carrying on the legitimate Government of Italy under his authority. This is needed, not only for the Italian people, but for the Italian representatives and garrisons abroad.

The King and Badoglio should be told that they must build up the broadest-based anti-Fascist coalition Government possible. Any healthy elements that can deliver some goods should be rallied in this crisis. These points should be made plain in the King's broadcast. It would be very useful if Count Sforza and the professors who claim to represent the six parties were willing to join in the common effort. It must however be clearly understood that none of these provisional arrangements, dictated by war needs, will stand in the way of the free choice by the Italian people of the form of democratic government which they prefer.

The question of giving the Badoglio Government an Allied status does not come into our immediate programme. Co-belligerency is good enough. On this footing we should work for the gradual conversion of Italy into an effective national force against Germany, but, as we have said, she must work her passage. Useful service against the enemy will be recognised by us in the adjustment and working of the Armistice terms. In return we expect Badoglio to continue to work for the Allies on the basis of the Armistice. Our principle will be payment by results. Badoglio should be free to declare war on Germany, and by so doing he would at once become, though not an ally, a co-belligerent.

Badoglio can be told that it is no part of our plan to install Allied military government everywhere. If he will co-operate, we are ready to hand over territory to his Government as quickly as it is free from the enemy. This offer applies to the historic mainland of Italy, Sicily, and Sardinia. The dealings of the United Nations with the Italian Government in territories which they are allowed to administer will be carried out through a Control Commission.

It would make it much easier for us if the full instrument of surrender, even though somewhat superseded, could now be signed. It is true that many of the clauses could not be operated by the Brindisi Administration in their present situation. But as we go up the peninsula and turn over territory to the Italian Government, these questions will become real. We do not want to put ourselves in the position of having to haggle over every requirement with the Government. The longer we leave it the more difficult it becomes to get the instrument signed, so I hope Eisenhower will get Badoglio's signature to it as soon as possible on the basis suggested in the Foreign Secretary's telegrams.

This programme should be put to the King and Badoglio at once. The first essential is that the King should make the public announcement suggested. This should not surely await final refinements of policy.

This crossed the following telegram from the President:

President Roosevelt to Prime Minister   21 Sept. 43

I will send the following message to General Eisenhower immediately upon your concurrence:

In view of the existing situation in Italy the earliest practicable action is important.

You will withhold long-term Armistice provisions pending further instructions.

2. On the basis of military necessity, you are empowered to make recommendations from time to time to lighten the provisions of the military armistice in order to enable the Italians, within the limit of their capacities, to wage war against Germany.

3. On condition that it declares war on Germany, the present Government of Italy should be permitted, subject to the provisions of paragraph 4 hereunder, to carry on as the Government of Italy, and as such should be treated as a co-belligerent in the war against Germany; such relationship to be based on the clear understanding that it is not in any way to prejudice the untrammelled right of the people of Italy to decide on the form of government they will eventually have, and that no final form of government of Italy will be decided upon until the Germans are evicted from Italian territory.

4. The Allied Military Government and the appropriate functions contemplated for the Armistice Control Commission will be merged as promptly as practicable into an Allied Commission under the Allied Commander-in-Chief, which shall be empowered to furnish guidance and instructions from time to time to the Badoglio Government on military, political, and administrative matters.

5. You will encourage in all practicable ways the vigorous use, under your direction, of the Italian armed forces against Germany.

Our two messages did not seem to me to conflict on any important point, except the question of withholding the long terms of surrender. On this I deferred to the President, and we agreed that his telegram should be sent to General Eisenhower as a directive from both of us.

*   *   *   *   *

On September 14, Mussolini met Hitler for the first time since his "liberation." During the succeeding days the two men debated how to extend the life of Italian Fascism in those parts of Italy still occupied by the German troops. On the 15th, the Duce announced that he had reassumed the leadership of Fascism and that a new Republican-Fascist Party, purged and uplifted from traitorous elements, would rebuild a faithful Government in the North. For a moment it seemed that the old system, now dressed up in a pseudo-revolutionary garb, might flare again into life. But the results disappointed the Germans. Goebbels's comment at this time is revealing:

The Duce has not drawn the moral conclusions from Italy's catastrophe which the Fuehrer had expected. He was naturally overjoyed to see the Fuehrer and to be fully at liberty again. But the Fuehrer expected that the first thing the Duce would do would be to wreak full vengeance on his betrayers. That he gave no such indication showed his real limitations. He is not a revolutionary like the Fuehrer or Stalin. He is so bound to his own Italian people that he lacks the broad qualities of a world-wide revolutionary and insurrectionist.[1]

[1] *The Goebbels Diaries*, page 378.

But there was to be no turning back. Mussolini's half-hearted "Hundred Days" began. At the end of September he set up his headquarters on the shores of Lake Garda. This pitiful shadow Government is known as the "Republic of Salo." Here the squalid tragedy was played out. The dictator and lawgiver of Italy for more than twenty years dwelt with his mistress in the hands of his German masters, ruled by their will, and cut from the outside world by carefully chosen German guards and doctors.

The Italian surrender caught their armies in the Balkans completely unawares, and many troops were trapped in desperate positions between local guerrilla forces and the vengeful Germans. There were savage reprisals. The Italian garrison of Corfu, over seven thousand strong, was almost annihilated by their former allies. The Italian troops of the island of Cephalonia held out until September 22. Many of the survivors were shot and the rest deported. Some of the garrisons of the Aegean islands managed to escape in small parties to Egypt. In Albania, on the Dalmatian coast, and inside Yugoslavia, a number of detachments joined the partisans. More often they were taken off to forced labour and their officers shot. In Montenegro, the greater part of two Italian divisions were formed by Tito into the "Garibaldi Division," which suffered heavy losses by the end of the war.   In the Balkans and Aegean, the Italian armies lost after the Armistice of September 8 nearly forty thousand men, not including those who died in deportation camps.

* * * * *

I explained the situation and our policy to Stalin.

Prime Minister to Premier Stalin   21 Sept. 43

Now that Mussolini has been set up by the Germans as the head of a so-called Republican-Fascist Government, it is essential to counter this move by doing all we can to strengthen the authority of the King and Badoglio, who signed the Armistice with us, and have since faithfully carried it out to the best of their ability and surrendered the bulk of their Fleet. Besides, for military reasons we must mobilise and concentrate all the forces in Italy which are anxious to fight or at least obstruct the Germans. These are already active.

I propose therefore to advise the King to appeal on the wireless to the Italian people to rally round the Badoglio Government, and to announce his intention to build up a broad-based, anti-Fascist coalition Government, it being understood that nothing shall be done to prevent the Italian people from settling what form of democratic Government they will have after the war.

It should also be said that useful service by the Italian Government, Army, and people against the enemy will be recognised in the adjustment and working of the Armistice; but that, while the Italian Government is free to declare war on Germany, this will not make Italy an ally, but only a co-belligerent.

I want at the same time to insist on the signing of the comprehensive Armistice terms, which are still outstanding, even though some of those terms cannot be enforced at the present time. Against this Badoglio would be told that the Allied Governments intend to hand over the historic mainland of Italy, Sicily, and Sardinia to the administration of the Italian Government under the Allied Control Commission as it is freed from the enemy.

I am putting these proposals also to President Roosevelt, and I hope that I may count on your approval. As you will readily understand, the matter is vitally urgent for military reasons. For instance, the Italians have already driven the Germans out of Sardinia, and there are many islands and key points which they still hold and which we may get.

He replied as follows:

Premier Stalin to Premier Churchill   22 Sept. 43
I received your message of September 21.

I agree with your proposal concerning the appeal by radio of the Italian King to the Italian people; but I consider it entirely necessary that in the appeal of the King it should be clearly stated that Italy, which capitulated to Great Britain, the United States, and the Soviet Union, will fight against Germany together with Great Britain, the United States, and the Soviet Union.

2. I also agree with your proposal about the necessity of signing comprehensive Armistice terms. In regard to your reservation that certain of these terms cannot be put into force at the present moment, I understand this reservation only in the sense that these

terms cannot be realised now on the territory which so far is held
by the Germans. In any case, I should like to receive confirmation
or the necessary explanation from you on that point.

I asked the President what he thought of this, and said that
I considered that the long term provisions of surrender might
well be dealt with by the Armistice Commission which we
were setting up in Italy. I later sent him the following:

Former Naval Person to President Roosevelt   24 Sept. 43
Macmillan now tells me that he is confident that Badoglio's
signature can be obtained to the whole set of terms within the
next few days, and that the longer we leave it the more haggling
there will be. It may be some time before the new Commission
can give their views, and I should myself feel happier if we
clinched the matter now. This might save us a good deal of trouble
later on.

At Eisenhower's suggestion we have made the preamble less
harsh. We also provided that the Armistice of September 3 will
remain operative.

Prime Minister to President Roosevelt   25 Sept. 43
I have not answered Uncle Joe's [2] telegram in favour of backing
up the King of Italy, and also his remarks about the comprehensive
terms, because I do not know what line you are taking with him.
You will no doubt have received my telegram. Macmillan reports
that there will be no difficulty in getting Badoglio to sign.

The President replied:

President Roosevelt to Prime Minister   25 Sept. 43
I go along with your thought about the long set of terms if
signature can be obtained quickly, and I am so advising Eisenhower.

*   *   *   *   *

Other political complications occurred.

2 President Roosevelt and Mr. Churchill, in their messages to each other,
often used "Uncle Joe," "U.J.," and "Uncle J.," in referring to Stalin.

Prime Minister to Mr. Macmillan (Algiers)   25 Sept. 43

Astonishment was caused here at a broadcast from the Bari radio in the name of "the King of Italy and Albania and Emperor of Ethiopia." I need scarcely say that any repetition of follies like that will bring our whole policy into discredit here. How would the King like to be sent back to his Empire in Ethiopia to be crowned?

. . . I presume we are going to see the King's speech before he lets it off, or if there is no time for this that you will anyhow vet it. The reference to the Soviet is of capital importance, as Stalin's support for our policy of using the Italian Government is invaluable.

On September 28, Marshal Badoglio left Brindisi in an Italian cruiser to sign the long-term surrender at Malta. He was received with ceremony on board the battleship *Nelson* by General Eisenhower, and his Chief of Staff, General Bedell Smith, Lord Gort, and General Alexander. Badoglio hoped to be spared the clause on unconditional surrender, but the Allied commanders insisted that this was a formal meeting to sign documents presented by the Allied Governments which would admit of no discussion.

After the signatures had been appended, Badoglio had a short discussion with General Eisenhower about declaring war on Germany, which the Italian Marshal wished to do. The day ended with a visit to the units of the Italian Fleet anchored in Malta Harbour.

Prime Minister to President Roosevelt   28 Sept. 43

We agree that the long-term surrender document should be kept secret for the present. I have no doubt U.J. will concur, but it would be well if you told him our views, speaking for both of us.

We think it would be a mistake to talk about making Rome an open city, as it may hamper our forward movement, and will anyway not bind the enemy.

*   *   *   *   *

The situation was at first bewildering for our troops on the spot. The Italians had been their enemies for more than three

years. By joining the United Nations they had in the space of
a few weeks acquired a new status, and some of them assumed
a new attitude. Requisitioning was no longer possible. Accommodation was denied to British troops, and food refused to
officers without Italian ration cards. British military currency
was treated with suspicion. Senior officers who had held the
rank of Military Governor now became mere liaison officers
with the Italians, from whom they could request but no longer
compel the facilities which they needed. Much of this was the
growing pains of the new régime in Italy, and was presently
rectified by high authority, but some Italian civilians were
ready to take the fullest advantage of the changes which had
occurred. The President and General Eisenhower felt that a
public declaration was needed in order to explain "co-belligerent" status to the Italians, and indeed to the world. I welcomed this.

Prime Minister to President Roosevelt   30 Sept. 43

I agree that we should make a joint announcement, but would
it not be a good chance of getting U.J. in too? It is clear now that
he does accept the Italians as co-belligerents. It is true that we
may lose a few days in communicating with Moscow, but this delay
seems relatively unimportant compared with the value of Russian
participation.

If you agree, would you put it to Stalin in the form that we
wish an announcement of the kind made; will he join with us in
making it, or would he prefer us to go ahead without him? Of
course, we should consider any drafting alterations he might wish
to propose.

I myself would like to see several changes, and my immediately
following telegram embodies these. If you see no objection to
them, would you, if you agree to approach Stalin, put the text to
him in this form?

The text of the declaration which I drafted read as follows:

The Governments of Great Britain, the United States, and the
Soviet Union acknowledge the position of the Royal Italian Government as stated by Marshal Badoglio, and accept the active co-

operation of the Italian nation and armed forces as a co-belligerent in the war against Germany. The military events since September 8 and the brutal maltreatment by the Germans of the Italian population, culminating in the Italian declaration of war against Germany, have in fact made Italy a co-belligerent, and the American, British, and Soviet Governments will continue to work with the Italian Government on that basis. The three Governments acknowledge the Italian Government's pledge to submit to the will of the Italian people after the Germans have been driven from Italy, and it is understood that nothing can detract from the absolute and untrammelled right of the people of Italy by constitutional means to decide on the democratic form of government they will eventually have.

The relationship of co-belligerency between the Government of Italy and the United Nations Governments cannot of itself affect the terms recently signed, which retain their full force and can only be adjusted by agreement between the Allied Governments in the light of the assistance which the Italian Government may be able to afford to the United Nations' cause.

This was approved by both President Roosevelt and Stalin.

*   *   *   *   *

Count Sforza now entered the Italian scene. Before the Fascist Revolution he had been Foreign Minister and Ambassador in Paris. During Mussolini's régime he had been an exile. He had become an outstanding figure among Italians in America. He had declared himself in favour of bringing Italy into the war on the side of the Allies, and had, in a letter which he had recently written to a high State Department official, expressed his willingness to work with Badoglio. As the situation sharpened, he saw his opportunity to gain the chief power in Italy, and was convinced of his right to it. He commanded a good deal of American support, and some of the American-Italian vote. The President hoped it might be possible to bring him into the new system of government without upsetting the King and Badoglio, upon whom our military thought about the Italian campaign was based.

President Roosevelt to Prime Minister   30 Sept. 43

Referring to your telegram in regard to Sforza playing with the team, his public speech was, to say the least, not complimentary to the King of Italy. I find however in a recording of his September 26 speech the following extracts, which indicate that he may be useful to our war effort:

"With the present leaders of Italy, if they behave well, if they wage war well, our duty is to go to war, all of us, and to oust the Germans out of Italy.

"I say so out of my only main desire to do a thing which helps victory. We may rally round any Government which enjoys the confidence of the Allies if this Government for the time being proves that it is able to wage a war and to oust the Germans out of Italy.

"If I had to proclaim a republic to-morrow I would say, 'No. First of all we must oust the Germans out of Italy. This is what the Italians want; but when Italy is free the Italians will decide.' "

Former Naval Person to President Roosevelt   1 Oct. 43

Your telegram about Sforza. He seems to be saying all sorts of things, many very different to what he wrote in his letter. He really should make up his mind whether he is going to try to help the Royal Badoglio Government or try to discredit it. We ought to know where we are before we build him up. Would it not be a good thing for you to route him to Italy via the United Kingdom and let us give him further friendly treatment here? I don't see much use in having him go to Italy merely to undermine whatever small fighting head against Fascism and the Germans Eisenhower has been able to produce out of the Italians.

President Roosevelt to Prime Minister   2 Oct. 43

Your telegram in regard to Sforza. I am informed that he, with his son, expects to arrive by airplane at Prestwick, October 3, en route to Marrakesh.

I hope you can effectively indoctrinate him during his stop in United Kingdom.

I am this date sending the following to Eisenhower:

"Inform Badoglio that it is the view of this Government that Grandi's presence in Badoglio Government at this time would not be acceptable. Even though Grandi was perhaps the chief figure in deposition of Mussolini, he had been so closely associated with Fascism that to place him now in Brindisi Government would cause much adverse comment and misinterpretation. First accretions to Badoglio Government should be men of unequivocal liberal and democratic principle. It is only through the use of such men in responsible positions that this Government can feel justified in supporting the present Italian Government.

"Germany has already taken active belligerent steps against Italy, and the chief strength of Badoglio's Government is its announced determination to rid Italy by force of the German invader. An immediate declaration of war by the Italian Government on Germany is necessary if Italy is to be given the status of a cobelligerent."

I had a long conversation with Count Sforza on his way through London, and believed we had reached an agreement whereby he was to work loyally with the King and Badoglio until we were in a position, following on the capture of Rome at the earliest moment, to form a broad-based non-Fascist Government. I thus steadily held to our charted course. We intended to sustain the Monarchy until the liberation of Italy, to bring an Italian Government in on our side in the struggle against Germany, to strengthen that Government by adding representative and resisting elements, and to associate the Russians with our immediate arrangements about Italian affairs.

*   *   *   *   *

While these exchanges went on, I pressed for the fullest use of Italian man-power and shipping.

Prime Minister to Foreign Secretary   26 Sept. 43

Ought we not to make a convention with the Italian Government in respect of the use of Italian prisoners of war and man-power? We cannot allow these large numbers of Italians to be freed from discipline and control and left at large in Britain or North Africa. There is no means of repatriating them without straining our shipping. Meanwhile we need their man-power. We cannot have the operations in Africa cumbered up with heavy masses of prisoners to guard. Our 1st Armoured Division has been virtually destroyed by being used as mere guards to prisoners.

There is empty shipping coming back from Africa to the United Kingdom. We should ask that the process of shipping prisoners to the United Kingdom should continue pending some new arrangement with the Italian Government. I am quite prepared to consider a change of status for the Italians, provided they continue to do the same work as now and that the discipline is effective.

Prime Minister to First Lord, V.C.N.S.,   2 Oct. 43
and Admiral Cunningham

We cannot afford to allow units of the Italian Navy to remain idle, whether at Alexandria or elsewhere. My present idea is that we suggest to the Americans that the *Littorios* go to the United States to be fitted for the Pacific warfare and to be used there by them. I would also suggest to the President that after the war these ships be ceded to us, because, first, we have had the main part of the war against them; secondly, we have had heavy losses in capital units; and, thirdly, we have discontinued building capital units in order to further current short-term operations. I am sure such proposals will be received in a most friendly spirit. I should like your advice about all this, and also of course about the structure and value of these ships.

2. With regard to cruisers and other vessels, they must all be put to the highest use. We cannot have valuable ships lolling about in the Mediterranean harbours. The most valuable and modern should be brought into service and our older ones laid up. The older Italian battleships may also have a part to play in the inshore bombarding squadrons, which will certainly be required, though only for short periods during 1944, both in the Channel and the Indian Ocean.

*   *   *   *   *

Former Naval Person to President Roosevelt   4 Oct. 43

Now that Uncle Joe has come in with us about the Italian declaration, it appears of the highest importance to compel the King to declare war as soon as possible. This is, as I know, your view. I suggest that instructions be given to Eisenhower to put the fullest pressure upon him. There should be no nonsense about waiting until Rome is taken. It seems to us high time that the Italians began to work their passage. If you are in agreement, pray give the necessary orders without further reference to us.

The President acted promptly.

President Roosevelt to Prime Minister   8 Oct. 43
On October 5, I informed Eisenhower as follows:
"The President and Prime Minister are in agreement that the King of Italy declare war on Germany as soon as possible. There appears to be no necessity for waiting until Rome is occupied. You will therefore put pressure on the Italian Government for an early declaration of war without waiting for further successes."

Accordingly on October 13, the Royal Italian Government declared war on Germany.

*   *   *   *   *

Prime Minister to Mr. Macmillan (*Algiers*)   23 Oct. 43
. . . Our policy is to abandon the base and increase the Leftward emphasis of the Italian Government. We have very little information here about the personalities who are already available. You will be watching all this and should keep me fully informed.
I am clear that any reconstruction of the Italian Government had better wait until we are in Rome. In Rome lie the title-deeds of Italy and of the Roman Catholic Church. Badoglio and the King reinstated there will have a far better chance of rallying such elements of Italian strength as exist. There is the place for us to make our deal and for them to issue their prospectus.
In the meanwhile, be careful that nothing is done to make the King and Badoglio weaker than they are. On the contrary, we must hold them up and carry them forward with our armies. Meanwhile, all search for strengthening elements can continue.

Prime Minister to President Roosevelt   6 Nov. 43
All my information goes to show that we should lose a lot in breaking up the present King-Badoglio show. Victor Emmanuel is nothing to us, but his combination with Badoglio did in fact deliver the Italian Fleet, which is rendering very useful service now, and this same combination is at this moment holding the loyalties of a very large part of the unhappy Italian Army and people, and

of course of Italian diplomatic representatives everywhere. Why should we add to the burden of our British and United States soldier on the march to Rome by weakening any of those aids? We ought not, in my personal opinion, to countenance a change in the Badoglio-King régime till we are seated in Rome and a really broad-based Italian Government can be formed.

I understand Eisenhower in the main inclines to this view. Surely we should stick to what we have got till we are sure we can get something better, and this can only be ascertained when we have Rome in our possession.

Such was the fragile state of Italian affairs when I set out for Cairo and Teheran.

12

Island Prizes Lost

Rhodes and Leros

Rhodes, Key of the Eastern Mediterranean — General Wilson's Plans — Seizure of Rhodes, Leros, and Cos Approved by the Combined Chiefs of Staff, September 10 — The German Grip on Rhodes — Hitler's Concern About the Aegean — The Germans Retake Cos — Imperative Need to Attack Rhodes — My Telegram to President Roosevelt of October 7 — His Disappointing Reply — My Further Appeal, October 8 — Washington Obdurate — My Wish to Attend Conference at Algiers Denied — News of Hitler's Decision to Fight South of Rome — Wilson's Report of October 10 — I Submit with Grief — The Fate of Our Leros Garrison — The Germans Attack, November 12 — A Bitter Blow.

T HE SURRENDER OF ITALY gave us the chance of gaining important prizes in the Aegean at very small cost and effort. The Italian garrisons obeyed the orders of the King and Marshal Badoglio, and would come over to our side if we could reach them before they were overawed and disarmed by the Germans in the islands. These were much inferior in numbers, but it is probable that for some time past they had been suspicious of their allies' fidelity and had their plans laid. Rhodes, Leros, and Cos were island fortresses which had long been for us strategic objectives of a high order in the secondary sphere. Rhodes was the key to the group, because it had good airfields from which our own air forces could operate in defence of any other islands we might occupy and complete our naval control of these waters. Moreover, the British air forces in Egypt and Cyrenaica could defend Egypt just as well, or even better, if some of them moved forward to Rhodes. It seemed to me a rebuff of fortune not to pick up these treasures. The command of the Aegean by air and by sea was within our reach. The effect of this might be decisive upon Turkey, at that time deeply moved by the Italian collapse. If we could use the Aegean and the Dardanelles, the naval short-cut to Russia was established. There would be no more need for the perilous and costly Arctic convoys, or the long and wearisome supply line through the Persian Gulf.

I felt from the beginning we must be ready to take advantage of any Italian landslide or German round-up.

Prime Minister to General Ismay, for C.O.S. Committee   2 Aug. 43

Here is a business of great consequence, to be thrust forward by every means. Should the Italian troops in Crete and Rhodes resist the Germans and a deadlock ensue, we must help the Italians at the earliest moment, engaging thereby also the support of the populations.

2. The Middle East should be informed today that all supplies to Turkey may be stopped for the emergency, and that they should prepare expeditionary forces, not necessarily in divisional formations, to profit by the chances that may offer.

3. This is no time for conventional establishments, but rather for using whatever fighting elements there are. Can anything be done to find at least a modicum of assault shipping without compromising the main operation against Italy? It does not follow that troops can only be landed from armoured landing-craft. Provided they are to be helped by friends on shore, a different situation arises. Surely caiques and ships' boats can be used between ship and shore?

I hope the Staffs will be able to stimulate action, which may gain immense prizes at little cost, though not at little risk.

Plans and preparations for the capture of Rhodes had been perfected in the Middle East Command over several months. In August, the 8th Indian Division had been trained and rehearsed in the operation, and was made ready to sail on September 1. But on August 26, in pursuance of a minor decision at the Washington Conference in the previous May, the Command received the orders of the Combined Chiefs of Staff to dispatch to India, for an operation against the coast of Burma, the shipping that could have taken the 8th Indian Division to Rhodes. The division itself was put under orders to join the Allied forces in the Central Mediterranean.

*   *   *   *   *

When the tremendous events of the Italian surrender occurred, my mind turned to the Aegean islands, so long the object of strategic desire. On September 9, I had cabled from Washington to General Wilson, Commander-in-Chief of the Middle East, "This is the time to play high. Improvise and dare." General Wilson was eager for swift action, but his command had been stripped. He had only available the 234th Brigade, formerly part of the hard-tried garrison of Malta, and no shipping other than what could be scraped up from local

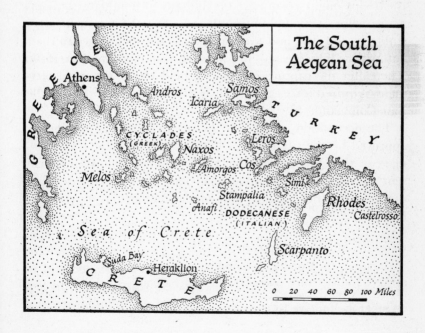

The South Aegean Sea

resources. The trained assault shipping recently taken from him was not beyond superior control, but the American pressure to disperse our shipping from the Mediterranean, either westward for the preparations for a still remote "Overlord" or to the Indian theatre, was very strong. Agreements made before the Italian collapse and appropriate to a totally different situation were rigorously invoked, at least at the secondary level. Thus Wilson's well-conceived plans for rapid action in the Dodecanese were harshly upset. Thereafter we were condemned to try our best with insufficient forces to occupy and hold islands of invaluable strategic and political importance.

The "Long-Range Desert Group," composed of soldiers of the highest quality, had been transformed into an amphibious unit, intending to reproduce on the sea the fame they had won in the sand. On the night of September 9, Major Lord Jellicoe, son of the Admiral, who was a leading figure in this daring unit, landed by parachute in Rhodes with a small mission to try to procure the surrender of the island. If we could gain a port and an airfield, the quick dispatch of a handful of British troops might encourage the Italians to dominate the Germans, whom they far outnumbered. But the Germans were stubborn and stiff, and the Italians yielded themselves to their authority. Jellicoe and his mission had to leave hurriedly. Thereafter the capture of Rhodes, held by six thousand Germans, required forces greater than were available to the Middle East Command.

The occupation of Rhodes, Leros, and Cos was specifically approved by the Combined Chiefs of Staff in their final summary of the Quebec decisions on September 10.[1] Wilson had sent with great promptitude small parties by sea and air to a number of other islands, and on September 14 reported as follows:

General Maitland Wilson to C.I.G.S.   14 Sept. 43
Situation in Rhodes deteriorated too rapidly for us to take action. Italians surrendered town and harbour (to the Germans)

[1] See Chapter 6, page 114.

after light bombing. Only an assault landing was thereafter practicable, but unfortunately 8th Indian Division, which had been trained and rehearsed for this operation, is now diverted to the Central Mediterranean and its ships and craft are dispersed by order of the Admiralty. Italian morale in Rhodes is below zero, and indicates little intention of ever resisting Germans in spite of asseverations to the contrary. We have occupied Castelrosso island, and have missions in Cos, Leros, and Samos. A flight of Spitfires will be established in Cos today, and an infantry garrison tonight by parachute. An infantry detachment is also proceeding to Leros. Thereafter I propose to carry out piratical war on enemy communications in the Aegean and to occupy Greek islands with Hellenic forces as opportunity offers. Since the New Zealand Division is also to proceed to Central Mediterranean, the 10th Indian Division, partially equipped, is the only formation immediately available.

As all Middle East resources have been put at disposal of General Eisenhower, we have no means of mounting an assault landing on Rhodes, but I hope to reduce the island by the methods adopted by the Turks in 1522, though in less time.

Once Rhodes was denied to us, our gains throughout the Aegean became precarious. Only a powerful use of air forces could give us what we needed. It would have taken very little of their time had there been accord. General Eisenhower and his Staff seemed unaware of what lay at our finger-tips, although we had voluntarily placed all our considerable resources entirely in their hands.

We now know how deeply the Germans were alarmed at the deadly threat which they expected us to develop on their southeastern flank. At a conference at the Fuehrer's Headquarters on September 25, both the Army and the Navy representatives strongly urged the evacuation of Crete and other islands in the Aegean while there was still time. They pointed out that these advanced bases had been seized for offensive operations in the Eastern Mediterranean, but that now the situation was entirely changed. They stressed the need to avoid the loss of troops and material which would be of decisive importance for the defence of the Continent. Hitler overruled them. He insisted that he could not order evacuation, particularly of Crete and the Dodecanese, because of the political repercussions which would follow. He said, "The attitude of our allies in the southeast and Turkey's attitude is determined solely by their confidence in our strength. Abandonment of the islands would create a most unfavourable impression." In this decision to fight for the Aegean islands he was justified by events. He gained large profits in a subsidiary theatre at small cost to the main strategic position. In the Balkans he was wrong. In the Aegean he was right.

*   *   *   *   *

We rightly made no attempt to occupy Crete, where the considerable German garrison rapidly disarmed the Italians and took charge, but for a time our affairs prospered in the outlying small islands. Troop movements by sea and air began on September 15. The Royal Navy lent a helping hand with destroyers and submarines. For the rest, small coasting vessels, sailing ships, launches, were all pressed into service, and by the end of the month Cos, Leros, and Samos were occupied by a battalion each, and small parties were landed on a number of other islands. Italian garrisons, where encountered, were friendly enough, but their vaunted coast and anti-aircraft defences were found to be in poor shape, and the transport of our own heavier weapons and vehicles was hardly possible with the shipping at our disposal.

Apart from Rhodes, the island of Cos was strategically the most important. This alone had an airfield from which our fighter aircraft could operate. It was rapidly brought into use and twenty-four Bofors guns landed for its defence. Naturally it became the objective of the first enemy counter-attack, and from September 18 onward the target of increasing air raids. Our reconnaissance reported an enemy convoy approaching, and at dawn on October 3, German parachutists descended on the central airfield and overwhelmed the solitary company defending it. The rest of the battalion, in the north of the island, where the enemy landed, was cut off. Clearly a single battalion

— all we could spare — could do little on an island thirty miles long to ward off such a double blow. The island fell. The Navy had done their best, without success, to intercept the convoy on its way to Cos, but owing to an unlucky event all but three destroyers had been for the moment drawn away. As part of the main naval concentration at Malta, which was not especially urgent, two of our battleships had been ordered thither at this moment, and needed all the remainder to escort them.

*   *   *   *   *

On September 22, Wilson reported his minimum and modest needs for an attack on Rhodes about October 20. Using the 10th Indian Division and part of an armoured brigade, he required only naval escorts and bombarding forces, three L.S.T.s, a few M.T. ships, a hospital ship, and enough transport aircraft to lift one parachute battalion. I was greatly troubled at our inability to support the Aegean operations, and on September 25, I cabled to General Eisenhower:

Prime Minister to General Eisenhower   25 Sept. 43
You will have seen the telegrams from the Commander-in-Chief Middle East about Rhodes. Rhodes is the key both to the Eastern Mediterranean and the Aegean. It will be a great disaster if the Germans are able to consolidate there. The requirements which the Middle East ask for are small. I should be most grateful if you would let me know how the matter stands. I have not yet raised it with Washington.[2]

The small aids needed seemed very little to ask from our American friends in order to gain the prize of Rhodes and thus retain Leros and retake Cos. The concessions which they had made to my unceasing pressure during the last three months had been rewarded by astounding success. Surely I was entitled to the very small aid which I required to supplement the British forces which were available for action in the Aegean, or had, with the approval of the Combined Chiefs of Staff, already been sent to dangerous positions. The land-

[2] See also my telegram to him of the same date, Chapter 8, page 150.

ing-craft for a single division, a few days' assistance from the
main Allied Air Force, and Rhodes would be ours. The Germans, who had now regripped the situation, had moved many
of their planes to the Aegean to frustrate the very purpose
which I had in mind.

*   *   *   *   *

I laid the issue before the President in its full scope.

Former Naval Person to President Roosevelt   7 Oct. 43

I am much concerned about the situation developing in the
Eastern Mediterranean. On the collapse of Italy, we pushed small
detachments from Egypt into several of the Greek islands, especially
Cos, which has a landing-ground, and Leros, which is a fortified
Italian naval base with powerful permanent batteries. We ran
this risk in the hope that the Italian garrisons which welcomed us
would take part in the defence. This hope appears vain, and Cos
has already fallen except for some of our troops fighting in the
mountains. Leros may well share its fate. Our enterprises against
Rhodes have not yet succeeded.

2. I believe it will be found that the Italian and Balkan penin-
sulas are militarily and politically united, and that really it is one
theatre with which we have to deal. It may indeed not be possible
to conduct a successful Italian campaign ignoring what happens
in the Aegean. The Germans evidently attach the utmost importance to this Eastern sphere, and have not hesitated to divert a
large part of their straitened air force to maintain themselves
there. They have to apprehend desertion by Hungary and Rumania and a violent schism in Bulgaria. At any moment Turkey
may lean her weight against them. We can all see how adverse to
the enemy are the conditions in Greece and Yugoslavia. When we
remember what brilliant results have followed from the political
reactions in Italy induced by our military efforts, should we not
be shortsighted to ignore the possibility of a similar and even
greater landslide in some or all of the countries I have mentioned?
If we were able to provoke such reactions and profit by them, our
joint task in Italy would be greatly lightened.

3. I have never wished to send an army into the Balkans, but
only by agents, supplies, and Commandos to stimulate the intense

guerrilla prevailing there. This may yield results measureless in their consequence at very small cost to main operations. What I ask for is the capture of Rhodes and the other islands of the Dodecanese; the movement northward of our Middle Eastern air forces and their establishment in these islands and possibly on the Turkish shore, which last might well be obtained, thus forcing a diversion on the enemy far greater than that required of us. It would also offer the opportunity of engaging the enemy's waning air-power and wearing it down in a new region. This air-power is all one, and the more continually it can be fought the better.

4. Rhodes is the key to all this. I do not feel the present plan of taking it is good enough. It will require and is worth at least up to a first-class division, which can of course be replaced by static troops once the place is ours. Leros, which for the moment we hold so precariously, is an important naval fortress, and, once we are ensconced in this area, air and light naval forces would have a most fruitful part to play. The policy should certainly not be pursued unless done with vigour and celerity requiring the best troops and adequate means. In this way the diversion from the main theatre would only be temporary, while the results may well be of profound and lasting importance.

5. I beg you to consider this and not let it be brushed aside and all these possibilities lost to us in the critical months that lie ahead. Even if landing-craft and assault ships on the scale of a division were withheld from the build-up of "Overlord" for a few weeks without altering the zero date, it would be worth while. I feel we may easily throw away an immense but fleeting opportunity. If you think well, would you very kindly let General Marshall see this telegram before any decision is taken by the Combined Chiefs of Staff.

I was pained to receive from the President a telegram which he had sent to Eisenhower which practically amounted to the refusal of all help, and left me, already committed, with his and the American Chiefs of Staff approval, to face the impending blow. The negative forces which hitherto had been so narrowly overcome had indeed resumed their control.

President Roosevelt to Prime Minister   8 Oct. 43

I do not want to force on Eisenhower diversions which limit

the prospects for the early successful development of the Italian operations to a secure line north of Rome.

I am opposed to any diversion which will in Eisenhower's opinion jeopardise the security of his current situation in Italy, the build-up of which is exceedingly slow, considering the well-known characteristics of his opponent, who enjoys a marked superiority in ground troops and Panzer divisions.

It is my opinion that no diversion of forces or equipment should prejudice "Overlord" as planned.

The American Chiefs of Staff agree.

I am transmitting a copy of this message to Eisenhower.

I noticed in particular the sentence "It is my opinion that no diversion of forces or equipment should prejudice 'Overlord' as planned." To pretend that the delay of six weeks in the return of nine landing-craft for "Overlord" out of over five hundred involved, which would in any case have had six months in hand, would compromise the main operation of May 1944 was to reject all sense of proportion. I therefore resolved to make a further earnest appeal to the President. Looking back upon the far-reaching favourable results which had followed from my journey with General Marshall to Algiers in June, from which the whole of our good fortune had sprung, I thought I might ask for the same procedure, and I made all preparations to fly at once to Tunis.

Prime Minister to President Roosevelt   8 Oct. 43

I earnestly pray that my views may receive some consideration from you at this critical juncture, remembering how fruitful our concerted action has been in the past and how important it is for the future.

2. I am sure that the omission to take Rhodes at this stage and the ignoring of the whole position in the Eastern Mediterranean would constitute a cardinal error in strategy. I am convinced also that if we were round the table together this operation could be fitted into our plan without detriment either to the advance in Italy, of which, as you know, I have always been an advocate, or to the build-up of "Overlord," which I am prepared faithfully to support.

3. May I remind you of my anxiety at Quebec when we were informed that the build-up in Italy could not exceed twelve divisions ashore by December 1? There are now by October 9, over fifteen divisions ashore, of which about twelve are in action. We know that the enemy is withdrawing to the north, fighting rearguard actions and carrying off booty; we cannot yet tell whether it is in October or November that we can occupy Rome; but it is certain that we shall not come in contact with the main German forces at the top of the leg till December, or even later, and we certainly have control of the rate of advance.

4. There is therefore plenty of time to provide a division for the conquest of Rhodes and restore it to the battle-front in Italy before we reach the German fortified line.

5. We must find some means of resolving these difficulties and making sure of what is the right thing to do. I am willing to proceed to Eisenhower's Headquarters with the British Chiefs of Staff immediately, if you will send General Marshall, or your personal representative, to meet me there, and we can then submit the results of a searching discussion to you and your Chiefs of Staff. We can be there Sunday afternoon [October 10].

And later in the day:

I should have added that my estimate of the effect on "Overlord" to which I referred is limited to a delay of about six weeks in sending home nine landing-craft which were to have started from the Mediterranean this month, nearly six months before they would actually be needed for "Overlord." There ought, I think, to be some elasticity and a reasonable latitude in the handling of our joint affairs.

2. The Quebec decision to send four landing-ships with the craft they carry from the Eastern Mediterranean to the Bay of Bengal also for training purposes has turned out ill. This decision should have been reviewed in the light of the new circumstances opened by the surrender of Italy. Unhappily this was not done, and in consequence the Middle East was stripped bare [of landing craft] at a moment when great prizes could be cheaply secured.

It is important to note the date of these two telegrams, October 8. On that day our information fully justified the belief that the enemy were withdrawing under cover of rearguards towards or beyond Rome. It was not till a day or two afterwards that we began to apprehend that their intention was to stand and fight south of the city. Though that produced a new situation, it did not in itself involve any immediate peril to our forces in Italy.

President Roosevelt to the Prime Minister   9 Oct. 43

I have received your [telegrams of October 8] and given careful personal consideration to the points you make. I have given careful thought to them, and so has the Staff. I am concerned about the possibility of our armies suffering a reverse by the action of an enemy with superior forces except by air, under a commander of proved audacity and resourcefulness. This applies especially to the absolute safety of the line we hope to gain in Italy.

With a full understanding of your difficulties in the Eastern Mediterranean, my thought in sending [my previous telegram] was that no diversion of force from Italy should be made that would jeopardise the security of the Allied armies in Italy, and that no action toward any minor objective should prejudice the success of "Overlord."

We have almost all the facts now at our disposal on which to judge the commitments probably involved in the Rhodes operation. As I see it, it is not merely the capture of Rhodes, but it must mean of necessity, and it must be apparent to the Germans, that we intend to go further. Otherwise Rhodes will be under the guns of both Cos and Crete.

I was in accord with obtaining whatever hold we could in the Dodecanese without heavy commitments, but the present picture involves not only a well-organised, determined operation, but a necessary follow-through. This in turn involves the necessity of drawing for the means, largely shipping and air, not ground troops, from some other source, which inevitably must be Italy, "Overlord," or possibly Mountbatten's amphibious operation. The problem then is, are we to enter into a Balkan campaign, starting with the southern tip, or is there more to be gained, and with security, by pushing rapidly to the agreed upon position north of Rome? It appears to me that a greater Allied threat against the Balkans is implied in this than by a necessarily precarious amphibious operation against Rhodes, with a lack evident to the enemy of the neces-

sary means for the follow-through. Strategically, if we get the
Aegean islands, I ask myself, where do we go from there? and vice
versa, where would the Germans go if for some time they retain
possession of the islands?

As to the meeting you propose for Sunday [10th] in Africa, this
would be in effect another meeting of the Combined Chiefs of
Staff, necessarily involving only a partial representation and in
which I cannot participate. Frankly, I am not in sympathy with
this procedure under the circumstances. It seems to me the issue
under discussion can best be adjusted by us through our Chiefs of
Staff set-up in better perspective than by the method you propose.
We have most of the facts, and will soon have the results of the
conference scheduled for tomorrow in Tunis.

*   *   *   *   *

Mr. Roosevelt's reply quenched my last hopes. All I could
now do was to ask that the President's original negative message
should not prevent a free discussion of the issue at the conference of Commanders-in-Chief. This was accorded for what it
was worth.

Prime Minister to General Wilson   9 Oct. 43
You should press most strongly at the Conference for further
support for "Accolade" [Rhodes]. I do not believe the forces at
present assigned to it are sufficient, and if you are left to take a
setback it would be bad. It is clear that the key to the strategic
situation in the next month in the Mediterranean is expressed
in the two words, "Storm Rhodes." Do not therefore undertake
this on the cheap. Demand what is necessary, and consult with
Alexander. I am doing all I can.

Prime Minister to President Roosevelt   9 Oct. 43
Thank you very much for your kindness in giving so much of
your time and thought to the views which I ventured to set before
you. At your wish, and as you cannot send General Marshall, I
have cancelled my journey, which I told Harry on the telephone I
would never undertake without your blessing.

2. I agree with the end of your telegram of today, namely, that
we should await the result of the conference scheduled for today

in Tunis, which can then be considered and adjusted by us through the Combined Chiefs of Staff Committee.

3. I am afraid however that your telegram of October 8 to me, a copy of which was sent to Eisenhower, will be taken as an order from you and as closing the subject finally. This I should find it very hard to accept. I hope therefore that you will make it clear that the Conference is free to examine the whole question in all its bearings, and should report their conclusions to you and me through Combined Chiefs of Staff. I ask that the Conference shall give full, free, patient, and unprejudiced consideration to the whole question after they have heard the Middle East point of view put forward by its representatives.

4. At the present time General Wilson is preparing to attack Rhodes on the 23d, with forces from his own command, or which have been assigned to him by General Eisenhower. He thinks these forces are sufficient, but I am doubtful whether they are not cut too fine.

The question, to my mind, therefore is whether he should have this modest reinforcement or whether the operation should be cancelled.

5. Cancellation will involve loss of Leros, even if they can hold out so long, and the complete abandonment by us of any foothold in the Aegean, which will become a frozen area, with most unfortunate political and psychological reactions in that part of the world instead of great advantages.

6. I fully agree with all you say about the paramount importance of the build-up in Italy, and I have given every proof of my zeal in this matter by stripping the British Middle Eastern Command of everything which can facilitate General Eisenhower's operations, in which we also have so great a stake.

To this the President replied:

President Roosevelt to Prime Minister   9 Oct. 43

The following message has been sent to Eisenhower:

"The Prime Minister in a message to the President expresses the fear that the repetition to you of the President's message of October 8 to the Prime Minister would be taken as an order from the President and as closing the subject finally. The Prime Minister desires that it be made clear to you that the Conference scheduled

for today in Tunis is free to examine the whole question in all its
bearings and should report their (your and General Wilson's) conclusions to the President and the Prime Minister through the Combined Chiefs of Staff. The Prime Minister asks that the Conference
shall give full, free, patient, and unprejudiced consideration to the
whole question after having heard the Middle East point of view
put forward by its representatives.

"The President directs that the foregoing desire expressed by
the Prime Minister be accepted for your guidance."

At this critical moment of the Conference, information was
received that Hitler had decided to reinforce his army in
Italy and fight a main battle south of Rome. This tipped the
scales against the small reinforcement required for the attack
on Rhodes. Wilson reported:

General Wilson to Prime Minister   10 Oct. 43

I received your message before Conference at Tunis yesterday.
I also had a talk with Cunningham and Alexander. I agree that
our Rhodes plan as it stood was on such a scale as to incur risk of
failure. It might have been worked at the moment of the Armistice,
but unfortunately some days earlier our shipping resources had
been removed and the fleeting opportunity found us powerless to
act.

2. Since then conditions have changed to the extent that an
assault of a single brigade group followed up by one other brigade
four days later would risk having both flights defeated in detail if
bad weather intervened. If the forces which at yesterday's Conference we all agreed are now necessary were to be made available,
this would be at the expense of "Overlord" in landing-craft and
of Alexander's offensive in ships, landing-craft, and aircraft. The
conditions in Italy also having changed materially according to
latest information received yesterday, I could but agree that Alexander's operations ought to have the whole of the available resources.

3. This morning John Cunningham, Linnell, and I reviewed the
situation in the Aegean on the assumption that Rhodes would not
take place till a later date. We came to the conclusion that the
holding of Leros and Samos is not impossible, although their maintenance is going to be difficult, and will depend on continued

Turkish co-operation. I am going to talk to Eden about this when he arrives on Tuesday. In any case, the problem of evacuation of the garrison would be one of extreme difficulty, and we hope it may never arise. Our tenancy in the Aegean has hitherto caused the enemy to divert considerable forces in attempts to turn us out.

I replied at once:

Prime Minister to General Wilson   10 Oct. 43

Cling on if you possibly can. It will be a splendid achievement. Talk it all over with Eden and see what help you can get from the Turk. If after everything has been done you are forced to quit, I will support you, but victory is the prize.

Although I could understand how, in the altered situation, the opinion of the generals engaged in our Italian campaign had been affected, I remained — and remain — in my heart unconvinced that the capture of Rhodes could not have been fitted in. Nevertheless, with one of the sharpest pangs I suffered in the war I submitted. If one has to submit, it is wasteful not to do so with the best grace possible. When so many grave issues were pending, I could not risk any jar in my personal relations with the President. I therefore took advantage of the news from Italy to accept what I thought — and think — to have been an improvident decision, and sent him the following telegram, which, although the first paragraph is also recorded elsewhere, I now give in full:

Former Naval Person to President Roosevelt   10 Oct. 43

I have now read General Eisenhower's report of the meeting. The German intention to reinforce immediately the south of Italy and to fight a battle before Rome is what General Eisenhower rightly calls "a drastic change within the last forty-eight hours." I agree that we must now look forward to very heavy fighting before Rome is reached instead of merely pushing back rearguards. I therefore agree with the conclusions of the Conference that we cannot count on any comparative lull in which Rhodes might be taken, and that we must concentrate all important forces available on the battle, leaving the question of Rhodes, etc., to be reconsidered, as General Eisenhower suggests, after the winter line north of Rome has been successfully occupied.

2. I have now to face the situation in the Aegean. Even if we had decided to attack Rhodes on the 23d, Leros might well have fallen before that date. I have asked Eden to examine with General Wilson and Admiral Cunningham whether with resources still belonging to the Middle East anything can be done to regain Cos, on the basis that Turkey lets us use the landing-grounds close by. If nothing can be worked out on these lines, and unless we have luck tonight or tomorrow night in destroying one of the assaulting convoys, the fate of Leros is sealed.

3. I propose therefore to tell General Wilson that he is free, if he judges the position hopeless, to order the garrison to evacuate by night, taking with them all Italian officers and as many other Italians as possible and destroying the guns and defences. The Italians cannot be relied upon to fight, and we have only twelve hundred men, quite insufficient to man even a small portion of the necessary batteries, let alone the perimeter. Internment in Turkey is not strict, and may not last long; or they may get out along the Turkish coast.

4. I will not waste words in explaining how painful this decision is to me.

*   *   *   *   *

To Alexander I said:

Prime Minister to General Alexander   **10 Oct. 43**

You should now try to save what we can from the wreck. . . . If there is no hope and nothing can be done, you should consider with General Wilson whether the garrison of Leros should not be evacuated to Turkey or perhaps wangled along the coast after blowing up the batteries: efforts must also be made to withdraw the Long Range Desert Groups who are on other islands. This would be much better than their being taken prisoners of war and the Italian officers executed.

And to General Wilson:

Prime Minister to General Wilson   **14 Oct. 43**

I am very pleased with the way in which you used such poor bits and pieces as were left you. *Nil desperandum.*

*   *   *   *   *

Nothing was gained by all the overcaution. The capture of Rome proved to be eight months distant. Twenty times the quantity of shipping that would have helped to take Rhodes in a fortnight were employed throughout the autumn and winter to move the Anglo-American heavy bomber bases from Africa to Italy. Rhodes remained a thorn in our side. Turkey, witnessing the extraordinary inertia of the Allies near her shores, became much less forthcoming, and denied us her airfields.

The American Staff had enforced their view; the price had now to be paid by the British. Although we strove to maintain our position in Leros, the fate of our small force there was virtually sealed. Having voluntarily placed at Eisenhower's disposal all our best fighting forces, ground and air, far beyond anything agreed at Washington in May or Quebec in August, and having by strenuous exertions strengthened the army in Italy beyond the plans and expectations of its Supreme Headquarters, we had now to see what could be done with what remained. Severe bombing attacks on Leros and Samos were clearly the prelude to a German enterprise. The Leros garrison was brought up to the strength of a brigade — three fine battalions of British infantry who had undergone the whole siege and famine of Malta [3] and were still regaining their physical weight and strength.

On the day that Cos fell, the Admiralty had ordered strong naval reinforcements, including five cruisers, to the Aegean from Malta. General Eisenhower also dispatched two groups of long-range fighters to the Middle East as a temporary measure. There they soon made their presence felt. On October 7, an enemy convoy carrying reinforcements to Cos was destroyed by naval and air action. Some days later, the Navy sank two more transports. However, on the 11th the long-range fighters were withdrawn. Thereafter the Navy once more faced conditions similar to those which had existed in the battle for Crete two years before. The enemy had air mastery, and it

---

[3] 4th Battalion, the Buffs, 2d Battalion, Royal Irish Fusiliers, 1st Battalion, King's Own.

was only by night that our ships could operate without
crippling loss.

*　　*　　*　　*　　*

The withdrawal of the fighters sealed the fate of Leros. The
enemy could continue to build up his forces without serious
interference, using dispersed groups of small craft. We now
know that the enemy faced a critical situation in shipping.
The delay in attacking Leros was due mainly to his fears about
an Allied attack in the Adriatic. On October 27, we heard
that four thousand German Alpine troops and many landing-
craft had reached the Piraeus, apparently destined for Leros,
and early in November reports of landing-craft movements
portended an attack. Concealed from our destroyers at night
amid the islands, moving in small groups by day, under their
strong fighter protection, the German troops and aircraft gathered. Our own naval and air forces were unable to interfere
with their stealthy approach.

The garrison was alert, but too few. The island of Leros

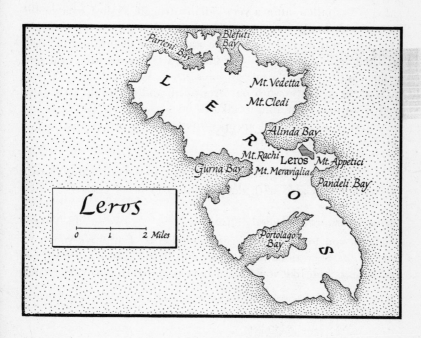

is divided by two narrow necks of land into three hilly sectors, to each of which one of our battalions was allotted.[4] Early on November 12, German troops came ashore at the extreme northeast of the island, and also in the bay southeast of Leros town. The attack on the town was at first repulsed, but that afternoon six hundred parachutists dropped on the neck between Alinda and Gurna Bays, and cut the defence in two. Previous reports had stated that the island was unsuited for paratroop landings, and the descent was a surprise. Very strong efforts were made to recapture the neck. In the last stages the garrison of Samos, the 2d Royal West Kents, had been dispatched to Leros, but all was over. They fell themselves a prey. With little air support of their own and heavily attacked by enemy aircraft, the battalions fought on till the evening of November 16, when, exhausted, they could fight no more. Thus this fine brigade of troops, who had so long defended Malta, fell into enemy power. General Wilson reported:

General Wilson to Prime Minister   17 Nov. 43

Leros has fallen, after a very gallant struggle against overwhelming air attack. It was a near thing between success and failure. Very little was needed to turn the scale in our favour and to bring off a triumph. Instead we have suffered a reverse of which the consequences are only too easy to foresee. . . . When we took the risk in September, it was with our eyes open, and all would have been well if we had been able to take Rhodes. Some day I trust it will be our turn to carry out an operation with the scales weighted in our favour from the start.

I had read the telegrams as they came in day after day during my voyage to Cairo with deep feelings. I now replied:

Prime Minister to General Wilson   18 Nov. 43

Thank you for your messages about Leros. I approve your conduct of the operations there. Like you, I feel this is a serious loss and reverse, and like you I feel I have been fighting with my hands

4 See Map, "Leros."

tied behind my back. I hope to have better arrangements made as a result of our next Conference.

*   *   *   *   *

With the loss of Leros all our hopes in the Aegean were for the time being ended. We tried at once to evacuate the small garrisons in Samos and other islands, and to rescue survivors from Leros. Over a thousand British and Greek troops were brought off, as well as many friendly Italians and German prisoners, but our naval losses were again severe. Six destroyers and two submarines were sunk by aircraft or mine and four cruisers and four destroyers damaged. These trials were shared by the Greek Navy, which played a gallant part throughout.

*   *   *   *   *

To Anthony Eden, who had now returned home, I telegraphed:

Prime Minister (at sea) to Foreign Secretary   21 Nov. 43

Leros is a bitter blow to me. Should it be raised in Parliament, I recommend the following line:

One may ask, should such operation ever have been undertaken without the assurance of air superiority. Have we not failed to learn the lessons of Crete, etc.? Have we not restored the Stukas to a fleeting moment of their old triumphs? The answer is that these are very proper questions to ask, but it would not be advisable to answer them in detail. All that can be said at the moment is that there is none of these arguments which was not foreseen before the occupation of these islands was attempted, and if they were disregarded it was because other reasons and other hopes were held to predominate over them. If we are never going to proceed on anything but certainties, we must certainly face the prospect of a prolonged war.

No attempts should be made to minimise the poignancy of the loss of the Dodecanese, which we had a chance of getting so easily and at so little cost and which we have now lost after heavy expenditure. You should also stress the tremendous effort made by the Germans, their withdrawal of almost half their air forces from

Italy, where they were already outmatched, and the assistance given to our troops thereby.

3. Don't forget that we probably drowned the best part of two thousand Germans on the way, which, together with those killed in action, is at any rate an offset to our three thousand prisoners. It may well be that the Germans have paid much more than life for life, including prisoners, in this struggle. Nonetheless, it is just to say that it is our first really grievous reverse since Tobruk, 1942. I hope however that there will be no need to make heavy weather over this at all.

*   *   *   *   *

I have recounted the painful episodes of Rhodes and Leros in all their details. They constitute, happily on a small scale, the most acute difference I ever had with General Eisenhower. For many months, in the face of endless resistances, I had cleared the way for his successful campaign in Italy. Instead of only gaining Sardinia, we had established a large group of armies on the Italian mainland. Corsica was a bonus in our hands. We had drawn an important part of the German reserves away from other theatres. The Italian people and Government had come over to our side. Italy had declared war on Germany. Their Fleet was added to our own. Mussolini was a fugitive. The liberation of Rome seemed not far distant. Nineteen German divisions, abandoned by their Italian comrades, lay scattered throughout the Balkans, in which we had not used a thousand officers and men. The date for "Overlord" had not been decisively affected.

I had been instrumental in finding from the British and Imperial forces in Egypt four first-class divisions over and above those which, according to General Whiteley's report, the Northwest African Supreme Headquarters had deemed possible. Not only had we aided General Eisenhower's Anglo-American Staff upon their victorious career, but we had furnished them with substantial unexpected resources, without which disaster might well have occurred. I was grieved that the small requests I had made for strategic purposes almost as high as those already achieved should have been so obdurately resisted and rejected. Of course, when you are winning a war, almost everything that happens can be claimed to be right and wise. It would however have been easy, but for pedantic denials in the minor sphere, to have added the control of the Aegean, and very likely the accession of Turkey, to all the fruits of the Italian campaign.

13

Hitler's Secret Weapon

*General Ismay's Minute of April 15, 1943 — Mr. Sandys' Appoint-
ment — Reports on Peenemünde — Decision of the Defence
Committee to Attack Peenemünde, June 29 — Hitler's Sanguine
Hopes — Warning of Rockets and Pilotless Aircraft — Difference
of Opinion About Their Relative Importance — Successful Attack on Peenemünde, August 17 — Prolonged Delay Caused to
the Germans Thereby — Far-reaching Consequences — Report
by Dr. R. V. Jones, September 25 — My Telegram to President
Roosevelt, October 25 — His Reply, November 9 — Our Timely
Measures of Defence.*

SEVERAL YEARS BEFORE THE WAR, the Germans had begun the
development of rockets and pilotless aircraft, and had built
an experimental station to carry out this work on the Baltic
coast at Peenemünde. This activity was of course a closely
guarded secret. Nevertheless, they were not able entirely to
conceal what was going on, and already in the autumn of 1939
references to long-range weapons of various kinds began to
appear in our Intelligence reports. During the early years of
the war, rumours on this subject and scraps of information,
often contradictory, reached us from various quarters. In the
spring of 1943, the position was reviewed by the Chiefs of
Staff, as a result of which on April 15 General Ismay sent me
the following minute:

Prime Minister   15 April 43
    The Chiefs of Staff feel that you should be made aware of reports
of German experiments with long-range rockets. The fact that five

reports have been received since the end of 1942 indicates a foundation of fact even if details are inaccurate.

The Chiefs of Staff are of the opinion that no time should be
lost in establishing the facts, and, if the evidence proves reliable,
in devising counter-measures. They feel this is a case where investigation directed by one man who could call on such scientific and
Intelligence advisers as may be appropriate would give the best
and quickest results. They therefore suggest that you should appoint an individual who should be charged with the task forthwith.
They suggest for your consideration the name of Mr. Duncan
Sandys, who, they think, would be very suitable if he could be
made available.

In addition, the Chiefs of Staff propose to warn the Minister of
Home Security of the possibility of such an attack, and of what is
proposed. It is not considered desirable to inform the public at
this stage, when the evidence is so intangible.

The Chiefs of Staff ask for your approval to the proposals above.

Mr. Sandys had served in an anti-aircraft unit in Norway
in the early days of the war. Later he had suffered crippling
disablement to both his feet in a motor accident when commanding the first experimental rocket regiment. He had
joined the Government in July 1941 as Financial Secretary at
the War Office, and afterwards as Under-Secretary at the Ministry of Supply. In both these offices he had had considerable
responsibility for the general direction of weapon development, and had consequently been brought into close contact
with the Chiefs of Staff Committee. As he was my son-in-law,
I was naturally glad that the Chiefs of Staff should wish to give
him this important work, though I had in no way suggested it.

A month later he presented his first report, which was circulated to the War Cabinet. The following extract gives the
main points:

I have reviewed the evidence regarding German long-range
rocket development. In order to supplement this, I asked that an
air reconnaissance should be undertaken of the area around
Peenemünde, on the Baltic coast of Germany, where, judging from
the reports, it seemed probable that rocket development was pro-

ceeding. This flight has been made, and the photographs obtained
have provided further important information.

It would appear that the Germans have for some time past been
trying to develop a heavy rocket capable of bombarding an area
from a very long range. This work has probably been proceeding
side by side with the development of jet-propelled aircraft and
airborne rocket torpedoes. Very little information is available
about the progress of this development. However, such scanty
evidence as exists suggests that it may be far advanced. London,
in view of its size, is much the most likely target.

An intensive effort should be made to obtain further information on this subject from agents on the Continent, from prisoners
of war, and by air reconnaissance.

The experimental establishments and factories which appear
most likely to be connected with the development and production
of this weapon in Germany and German-occupied territory, together with any suspicious works in the coastal region of Northwest
France, should be subjected to bombing attack. A preliminary list
of suggested targets is being sent to the Air Staff.

On June 4, Air Marshal Evill, Vice-Chief of the Air Staff,
issued instructions enabling Sandys to deal directly with the
Intelligence branches concerned about obtaining further information from agents and prisoners of war, and requested
him to make recommendations for air reconnaissance and to
notify the Air Staff of the conclusions drawn therefrom. All
possible methods of tracing the trajectory of such projectiles
and of locating the firing-point were examined. Civil Defence
and security measures were set on foot.

On June 11, Mr. Sandys sent a minute to the Air Staff asking that reconnaissance flights should be made at regular intervals over the Peenemünde area and that air photographs should
be obtained of all territory in Northern France within a hundred and thirty miles of London. He also recommended that
the experimental station at Peenemünde should be bombed.
In his next report he stressed the importance of making the
attack without delay.

The latest reconnaissance photographs provide evidence that the
Germans are pressing on as quickly as possible with the develop-

ment of the long-range rocket at the experimental establishment at Peenemünde, and that frequent firings are taking place. There are also signs that the light anti-aircraft defences at Peenemünde are being further strengthened.

In these circumstances it is desirable that the projected bombing attack upon this establishment should be proceeded with as soon as possible.

On June 28, Sandys reported that aerial photographs of Peenemünde showed large rockets alongside the firing-point. They might have a range of about ninety to a hundred and thirty miles.

In spite of all efforts to prevent them, the Germans may, without being detected, succeed in emplacing a number of projectors in Northern France, and in launching a rocket attack upon London. In that event it would be necessary to locate with the utmost speed the sites from which the rockets were being fired, in order that these might be put out of action by immediate bombing attack.

With the equipment already available at existing radar stations, it should be possible to observe the rockets during flight and to determine the points from which they have been fired, to within a circle of ten miles radius. This performance can be considerably improved by fitting certain ancillary apparatus. The construction of this ancillary apparatus has already been put in hand. The first equipment is now in process of being installed at Rye. The remainder will be completed within two to three months. Special instructions have been issued to the five most suitable stations (Swingate, Rye, Pevensey, Poling, and Ventnor), and the necessary training of operators has begun.

On June 29, the Defence Committee, having been kept fully informed since April, decided:

That the most searching and rigorous examination of the area in Northern France within a radius of one hundred and thirty miles of London should be organised and maintained, no step being neglected to make this as efficient and thorough as possible.

That the attack on the experimental station at Peenemünde should take the form of the heaviest possible night attack by

Bomber Command on the first occasion when conditions are suitable.

That as far as possible plans should be prepared for immediate air attack on rocket firing-points in Northern France as soon as these are located.

*   *   *   *   *

Hitler was meanwhile intent upon the plan. Accompanied by some of his principal adherents of Cabinet level, he inspected Peenemünde about the beginning of June 1943. We were at this time better informed about rocket missiles than about pilotless aircraft. Both methods were in full preparation on a large scale, and Peenemünde was the summit of all research and experiment. No decisive progress had been made by the Germans towards the atomic bomb. "Heavy water" gave little encouragement, but in pilotless aircraft and the rockets Hitler and his advisers saw a means of delivering a new and possibly decisive attack upon England and the rupturing of the Anglo-American plans for a major cross-Channel return to the Continent. The Fuehrer was comforted by all he learned at Peenemünde, and he hurled the utmost German effort into this new and perhaps last hope.

About June 10, he told his assembled military leaders that the Germans had only to hold out. By the end of 1943, London would be levelled to the ground and Britain forced to capitulate. October 20 was fixed as zero day for rocket attacks to begin. It is said that Hitler personally ordered the construction of 30,000 rockets for that day. This, if true, shows the absurd ideas on which he lived. The German Minister of Munitions, Dr. Speer, said that each V2 [1] required about as many man-hours to make as six fighters. Hitler's demand was therefore for the equivalent of 180,000 fighters to be made in four months. This was ridiculous, but the production of both weapons was given first priority and 1500 skilled workers were transferred from anti-aircraft and artillery production to the task.

On July 9, Mr. Sandys reported that, in addition to their plans for a rocket attack on London, there was also evidence

[1] Our name for the rocket. Pilotless aircraft were called V1.

that the Germans intended to use pilotless aircraft and very
long-range guns. Two excavations of a suspicious character
had been detected — at Watten, near St. Omer, and at Bruneval, near Fécamp. Special instructions were therefore issued
to the selected radar stations in Southeast England to watch
for rocket-firing. Plans were also made by the Home Office,
not for any wholesale evacuation of London, but for the
removal when the time came of a hundred thousand persons
in priority classes, such as school-children and pregnant
mothers, at the rate of ten thousand a day. Thirty thousand
Morrison table shelters were moved into London, bringing
the reserve in the Metropolis up to about fifty thousand.

On July 19, our reports stated:

Work of an unexplained nature, including railway sidings, turn-
tables, buildings, and concrete erections, is proceeding in Northwest France. At most of these places construction is going ahead
at a considerable pace, particularly in the case of Watten, where
great activity is developing. Some attempt is being made to camou-
flage this work, and in one case the arrival of anti-aircraft guns
has been observed.

When all these facts and reports were brought before the
Defence Committee, many differences of opinion arose concerning them. Among the scientists and technical officers
opinions varied deeply and sharply on the question whether
the new form of attack on the island would be by rocket bombs
or by pilotless aircraft. At first the rocket was favourite, but
its backers weakened their case by what turned out to be vastly
exaggerated estimates of the size and destructive power of the
missile. Confronted with these, those responsible for home
security faced the possibility not only of evacuating children,
expectant mothers, and other selected persons from London,
but even a wholesale evacuation of the capital itself.

The Minister for Home Security was profoundly disquieted
by the reports he studied, and always presented the danger in
its most serious aspect. It was certainly his special duty to
make sure that the danger was not underrated. Lord Cherwell,

on the other hand, did not believe that even if giant rockets could be made, it would pay the Germans to make them. As he had maintained from the very beginning, he insisted that they would get far better results at much smaller cost by using pilotless aircraft. Even if they used rockets with war-heads of ten or twenty tons, as had been forecast, but which he did not believe was possible, he did not think the destruction in Britain would approach the figures which were produced. Listening to the discussions, which were frequent over many months, between him and Mr. Herbert Morrison, it might have seemed at times that the two protagonists were divided as to whether the attack by self-propelled weapons would be annihilating or comparatively unimportant. Actually the issue, as is usual, was not in the realm of "Yes or No," but in that of "More or Less."

Lord Cherwell's minutes show very clearly that his views on the possible scale of attack were on the whole right and that the most alarmist estimates were wrong.

*   *   *   *   *

These discussions caused no delay or indecision in our actions. An attack on Peenemünde was difficult, but imperative, and on the night of August 17, Air Marshal Harris, Chief of Bomber Command, struck with 571 heavy bombers. The buildings were scattered along a narrow strip of coast and protected by a smoke-screen. They could neither be reached by radio-navigation beams from the United Kingdom nor sufficiently identified by the apparatus carried in our planes. It was therefore necessary to bomb by moonlight, although the German night-fighters were close at hand and it was too far to send our own. The crews were ordered to bomb from eight thousand feet, much below their usual height, and were told by Air Marshal Harris that if the operations failed on the first night, it would have to be repeated on the next night, and on all suitable nights thereafter, regardless of casualties and regardless of the fact that the enemy would obviously do everything possible to increase his defences after the first attack. At the same time, everything was done to guide our airmen and deceive the foe. Pathfinders flew ahead to mark the route and the straggling installations, and a master bomber circled the target, assessing results and instructing our planes by radio-telephone. The route taken was almost the same as in previous raids on Berlin, and a small force of Mosquitoes was sent over the capital to mislead the enemy.

The weather was worse than expected and landmarks were difficult to find, but it cleared towards Rügen Island and many crews punctually started their time and distance runs. There was more cloud over the target and the smoke-screen was working, but, says Harris, "the very careful planning of the attack ensured a good concentration of bombs on all the aim-ing points." The enemy was at first deceived by the feint on Berlin, but not for long enough. Most of our force got away, but the German fighters caught them during their return, and in the bright moonlight forty of our bombers were shot down.

*   *   *   *   *

The results were of capital importance. Although the physical damage was much less than we supposed, the raid had a far-reaching influence on events. All the constructional draw-ings just completed for issue to the workshops were burned, and the start of large-scale manufacture was considerably delayed. The parent factory at Peenemünde was hit, and the fear of attacks on factories producing the rocket elsewhere led the Germans to concentrate manufacture in underground works in the Hartz Mountains. All these changes caused serious delays in perfecting and producing the weapon. It was also decided to shift their experimental activities to an estab-lishment in Poland beyond the range of our bombers. There our Polish agents kept vigilant watch, and in the middle of January 1944 the new weapon was tried. They soon discovered its range and line of fire, but of course the rockets came down many miles apart from each other. German patrols always raced to where they fell and collected the fragments, but one day a rocket fell on the bank of the river Bug and did not explode. The Poles got there first, rolled it into the river, waited till the Germans had given up the search, and then salvaged and dismantled it under cover of darkness. This dangerous task accomplished, a Polish engineer was picked up by a Royal Air Force Dakota on the night of July 25, 1944, and flown to England with many technical documents and more than one hundred pounds of essential parts of the new weapon. The gallant man, Mr. A. Kocjan, returned to Poland, and was later caught by the Gestapo and executed in Warsaw on August 13, 1944.

*   *   *   *   *

The attack on Peenemünde, for which such sacrifices were made, therefore played an important and definite part in the general progress of the war. But for this raid and the subsequent attacks on the launching points in France, Hitler's bombardment of London by rockets might well have started early in 1944. In fact it was delayed until September. By that time the prepared launching sites in Northern France had been overrun by General Montgomery's forces. In consequence the projectiles had to be fired from improvised positions in Holland, nearly twice as far from the target of London, and with much less accuracy. By the autumn, German communications became so congested by battle needs that the transport of rockets to the firing-point could no longer secure high priority.

In his book, *Crusade in Europe,* General Eisenhower expressed his opinion that the development and employment of the "V" weapons were greatly delayed by the bombing of the experimental plants at Peenemünde and other places where they were being manufactured. He goes so far as to say (page 260):

It seemed likely that if the German had succeeded in perfecting and using these new weapons six months earlier than he did, our invasion of Europe would have proved exceedingly difficult, perhaps impossible. I feel sure that if they had succeeded in using these weapons over a six-month period, and particularly if they had made the Portsmouth-Southampton area one of their principal targets, "Overlord" might have been written off.

This is an overstatement. The average error of both these weapons was over ten miles. Even if the Germans had been able to maintain a rate of fire of a hundred and twenty a day and if none whatever had been shot down, the effect would have been the equivalent of only two or three one-ton bombs to a square mile per week. However, it shows that the military commanders considered it necessary to eliminate the menace of the "V" weapons, not only to protect civilian life and property, but equally to prevent interference with our offensive operations.

*　　*　　*　　*　　*

In the early autumn, it became clear that the Germans were planning to attack us, not only with rockets, but also with pilotless aircraft. On September 13, 1943, Mr. Sandys reported:

There is evidence that the enemy is considering using pilotless aircraft as a means of delivering bombs on London. Unless the aircraft used are abnormally small or are capable of flying at an exceptional height or speed, it should be possible to deal with them by means of the fighter and anti-aircraft defences of this country. If these pilotless aircraft should be capable of flying at such heights and speeds as to render their interception impossible by air-defence methods, they should for all practical purposes be regarded as projectiles.

The counter-measures should be the same as for the long-range rocket, namely, the destruction by bombing of the sources of manufacture and of the sites or airfields from which they are launched.

The state of our knowledge at that time was summed up in a report, dated September 25, by Dr. R. V. Jones, the head of the Air Ministry's Scientific Intelligence Branch:

Much information has been collected. Allowing for the inaccuracies which often occur in individual accounts, they form a coherent picture which despite the bewildering effect of propaganda has but one explanation: the Germans have been conducting an extensive research into long-range rockets at Peenemünde. Their experiments have naturally encountered difficulties, which may still be holding up production. Although Hitler would press the rockets into service at the earliest possible moment, that moment is probably still some months ahead.

It is probable that the German Air Force has also been developing a pilotless aircraft for long-range bombardment in competition with the rocket, and it is very possible that the aircraft will arrive first.

Meanwhile, it was observed that in Northern France a large number of groups of curiously shaped structures were being erected. All were laid out after the same fashion, and most of them appeared to be directed on London. Each included one or more buildings shaped rather like a ski. We later discovered from air photographs that there were structures similar to these in the neighbourhood of Peenemünde, and one of the photographs revealed a minute aircraft close to an inclined ramp. From this it was deduced that the so-called "ski-sites" in Northern France were probably designed to store, fill, and launch small unmanned aircraft or flying bombs.

*   *   *   *   *

It was not until late in the autumn that I burdened President Roosevelt with our grave and prolonged preoccupations. The United States Staffs were kept constantly informed on the technical level; but at the end of October, I cabled by our special personal contact:

Former Naval Person to President Roosevelt   25 Oct. 43

I ought to let you know that during the last six months evidence has continued to accumulate from many sources that the Germans are preparing an attack on England, particularly London, by means of very long-range rockets which may conceivably weigh sixty tons and carry an explosive charge of ten to twenty tons. For this reason we raided Peenemünde, which was their main experimental station. We also demolished Watten, near St. Omer, which was where a construction work was proceeding the purpose of which we could not define. There are at least seven such points in the Pas de Calais and the Cherbourg peninsula, and there may be a good many others which we have not detected.

2. Scientific opinion is divided as to the practicability of making rockets of this kind, but I am personally as yet unconvinced that they cannot be made. We are in close touch with your people, who are ahead of us in rocket impulsion, which they have studied to give airplanes a send-off, and all possible work is being done. The expert committee which is following this business thinks it possible that a heavy though premature and short-lived attack might be made in the middle of November, and that the main attack would be attempted in the New Year. It naturally pays the Germans to spread talk of new weapons to encourage their troops, their satellites, and neutrals, and it may well be that their bite will be found less bad than their bark.

3. Hitherto we have watched the unexplained constructions proceeding in the Pas de Calais area without (except Watten) attacking them in the hope of learning more about them. But now we have decided to demolish those we know of, which should be easy, as overwhelming fighter protection can be given to bombers. Your airmen are of course in every way ready to help. This may not however end the menace, as the country is full of woods and quarries, and slanting tunnels can easily be constructed in hillsides.

4. The case of Watten is interesting. We damaged it so severely that the Germans, after a meeting two days later, decided to abandon it altogether. There were six thousand French workers upon it as forced labour. When they panicked at the attack, a body of uniformed young Frenchmen who are used by the Germans to supervise them fired upon their countrymen with such brutality that a German officer actually shot one of these young swine. A week later, the Germans seem to have reversed their previous decision and resumed the work. Three thousand more workmen have been brought back. The rest have gone to some of those other suspected places, thus confirming our views. We have an excellent system of Intelligence in this part of Northern France, and it is from these sources as well as from photographs and examination of prisoners that this story has been built up.

5. I am sending you by air courier the latest report upon the subject, as I thought you would like to know about it.

He replied after an interval:

President Roosevelt to Prime Minister   9 Nov. 43

We too have received many reports of the German rocket activity. The only information recently coming to me which might be of value to you is a statement that factories manufacturing the rocket bomb are situated in Kaniafried, Richshafen, Mitzgennerth, Berlin, Kugellagerwerke Schweinfurt, Wiener Neustadt, and at an isolated factory on the left side of the road going from Vienna to Baden, just south of Vienna. Production is said to have been delayed, owing to the death, in the bombing of the experimental station at Peenemünde, of Lieutenant-General Shemiergembeinski, who was in charge. This came from an informer via Turkey.

* * * * *

The evidence and conflicting views both among the scientists and my colleagues on the Defence Committee continued to be so evenly balanced and confusing that I asked Sir Stafford Cripps, the Minister of Aircraft Production, with his special knowledge and judicial mind, to review all the information about the German long-range weapons and present a conclusion. On November 17, he made his report.

It would seem that the order of probability from the purely experimental point of view is: (1) Large glider bombs. (2) Pilotless aircraft. (3) Small long-range rockets. (4) Large long-range rockets.

The R.A.F. raid on Peenemünde was undoubtedly of the greatest value, and has set back the developments, whatever they may be, for the long-range offensive weapon.

There is no doubt that the Germans are doing their utmost to perfect some long-range weapon, and the new unexplained structures in Northern France are certainly most suspicious, unless we can assign some other use to them. Under these circumstances I feel we should make all reasonable preparations to cope with the consequences if and when the attack materialises, though there is no evidence of its materialisation before the New Year at the earliest.

We should at the same time maintain photographic cover, and destroy the sites whenever we get the opportunity to do so.

This certainly left much in doubt. On December 14, Air Marshal Bottomley, the Deputy Chief of the Air Staff, reported:

> The "Large Sites" in Northern France (including three which have been attacked) are suspected to be connected with long-range rocket attack. One of these sites is protected by as many as fifty-six heavy and seventy-six light anti-aircraft guns.
>
> Evidence is accumulating that the "ski sites" are designed to launch pilotless aircraft. The existence of sixty-nine "ski sites" has been confirmed by photographic reconnaissance, and it is expected that the number will eventually total approximately a hundred. If present rates of construction are maintained, the work on some twenty sites should be completed by early January 1944, and the remainder by February. The launching points on the sites in the Pas de Calais and Somme-Seine areas are oriented on London, and those on some of the sites in the Cherbourg area on Bristol.

On December 18, Lord Cherwell, who had been in close touch with Dr. Jones throughout, sent me a report giving his ideas about the date and intensity of the attack which might be expected from the flying bombs. In his view the bombardment would not begin before April, and not more than a hundred a day would be dispatched after the first day or two; of these about twenty-five would get within ten miles of the aiming point. As this would only correspond to fifty to a hundred fatal casualties a day, he deprecated large-scale panic measures of evacuation. He still discounted the probability of the use of large rockets. Even if they could be made, which seemed impossible with any existing technique, they would cost twenty or thirty times as many man-hours to produce as the flying bombs, without, in his view, being more efficient.

During the early months of 1944, we developed our plans for meeting the flying-bomb attack. It was decided that the defences should be laid out in three zones — a balloon barrage on the outskirts of London, beyond that a gun belt, and beyond that again, an area in which the fighter aircraft would operate. Steps were also taken to hasten the supply from

America of the electronic predictors and radio proximity fuses, which, when the bombardment eventually started, made it possible for the gunners to take a heavy toll of the flying bombs.

Meanwhile, the British and American Air Forces continued to bomb the hundred or so "ski-sites" in Northern France. This was so effective that at the end of April aerial reconnaissance indicated that the enemy was giving up work on them. But our satisfaction was short-lived, for it was discovered that he was building instead modified sites which were much less elaborate and more carefully camouflaged and therefore harder to find and to hit. Wherever found these new sites were bombed. Many were destroyed, but about forty escaped damage or detection. It was from these that the attack was ultimately launched in June.

*   *   *   *   *

Nearly fifteen months passed between the minute which the Chiefs of Staff sent me in April 1943 and the actual attack in June 1944. Not a day was wasted. No care was lacking. Preparations involving many months to perfect were set on foot on a large and costly scale in good time. When at length the blow fell upon us, we were able, as the next volume will describe, to ward it off, albeit with heavy loss in life and much damage to property, but without any effective hindrance to our war-making capacity or to the operations in France. The whole story may stand as an example of the efficiency of our governing machine, and of the foresight and vigilance of all connected with it.

14

Deadlock on the Third Front

Hitler Resolves to Stand South of Rome — The German Winter Line — Alexander's Army Weakened — My Telegram to Alexander of October 24 — General Eisenhower's Conference of Commanders — He Endorses Alexander's Review of the Battle Situation in Italy — The Withdrawal of Landing-Craft Deprives Our Armies of Flexibility — Fall in the Rate of Build-up — Survey of the Changed Situation — My Telegrams to General Marshall and President Roosevelt — I Appeal for the Retention of More Landing-Craft in the Mediterranean — Eisenhower Authorised to Retain an Extra Sixty-Eight until December 15 — My Telegram to Our Ambassador in Moscow, November 9 — Need for the Polish Corps — Undue Demands of the Allied Strategic Air Force for Transport to Italy — The Eighth Army Crosses the Sangro River — The United States Fifth Army Approaches the German Main Positions at Cassino — Air Fighting — Reduction of German Air Force in Italy — Diversionary Value of the Third Front.

EARLY IN OCTOBER, on Kesselring's advice, Hitler changed his mind about his Italian strategy. Till then he had meant to withdraw his forces behind Rome and hold only Northern Italy. Now he ordered them to fight as far south as possible. The line selected, the so-called "Winterstellung," ran behind the river Sangro, on the Adriatic side, across the mountainous spine of Italy, to the mouth of the Garigliano on the west. The natural features of the country, its steep mountains and swift rivers, made this position, several miles in depth, immensely strong. After a year of almost continuous retreat in Africa, Sicily, and Italy, the German troops were glad to turn about and fight.

Although the approach of winter would seriously impede our actions, the main strategic decisions taken at Quebec were helped by the Germans committing themselves so deeply. The primacy accorded to our cross-Channel invasion made Italy henceforward a secondary theatre. That Hitler felt impelled to use so many troops to resist our advance favoured our major objective, but did not justify our making a failure of the Italian campaign.

The Fifth Army resumed their attacks on October 12, and after a ten days' struggle both its corps, the Xth British and VIth American, were well established across the river Volturno and ready to engage the enemy's next delaying position, a series of heights lying south of the river Garigliano. Another week of fighting was needed to eject the enemy from these, but in the first fortnight in November the Army came to grips with the forward defences of the "Winterstellung." On this front the Fifth Army, of six divisions, was faced by an equal number of Germans, who were fighting with their usual stubbornness. The first probing efforts at the German line met with little success. Our men had been fighting hard for two months, the weather was shocking, and troops needed rest and regrouping. Nevertheless, the plans made at Quebec for a different situation were rigidly enforced, and the Mediterranean was to be largely stripped of landing-craft.

Thus the position in Italy was changed greatly to our disadvantage. The Germans were strongly reinforced and ordered to resist instead of to withdraw. The Allies, on the contrary, were sending seven of their best divisions from Italy and the Mediterranean back to England for the cross-Channel attack in 1944. The four extra divisions I was gathering or had sent did not repair the loss. A deadlock supervened and was not relieved for eight months of severe fighting, which will presently be recounted.

*   *   *   *   *

With these facts on my mind, I telegraphed to General Alexander on October 24:

Prime Minister to General Alexander   24 Oct. 43

Naturally I am made anxious by the departure while your battle is on of our two fine divisions, 50th and 51st, in pursuance of Quebec decisions. I should like to have your feelings about the strength of your army for the tasks which lie immediately ahead. Has the Eighth Army yet pulled its tail up? You mentioned 24th as the date.

2. I am asking for a Combined Staffs Conference somewhere in Africa about November 15. Anyhow, I shall be along your way about that time. I have much to tell you. Every good wish.

Alexander replied that the number of German divisions in Italy was naturally causing him some anxiety. Their effect would depend on how far the enemy could maintain strong forces south of Rome. Everything was being done to paralyse the German lines of communication by air action, and he was keen to build up our air forces in Italy. All this took time, labour, and material. The Eighth Army had wound up their tail and started their offensive, which was making satisfactory progress in its early stages. "I consider," he said, "that the situation requires very careful watching. I am glad to hear you are visiting us shortly, and will be very glad to see you."

*   *   *   *   *

On the same day, General Eisenhower held a Commanders' Conference. He called upon Alexander to review the situation. His report was so serious that Eisenhower transmitted the entire text to President Roosevelt and to me. He endorsed all that Alexander had said and described his statement as giving a clear and accurate picture.

PART I

1(*a*) On September 9, the date of the launching of "Avalanche" and the announcement of the Italian Armistice, the estimate of the general enemy situation was that two divisions were opposing the advance of the Eighth Army in Calabria: one division was in the heel of Italy; three divisions were in a position south of Rome and available to take action against the Allied landing in Salerno Bay; more than two divisions were in the neighbourhood of Rome and nine in the north of Italy. The Germans therefore had a total of some eighteen divisions at their disposal on the mainland. Of these it was considered that some would be engaged in Northern Italy to deal with the internal situation which was expected to cause them considerable embarrassment.

(b) It was of course realised that our assaults near Salerno would prove hazardous in the face of German opposition, but it was thought that the Italian situation, coupled with the opportunity of landing light forces in the heel and our overwhelming air superiority, weighted the scales sufficiently in our favour, and the risks quite rightly were taken. Further, landing-craft were available in large numbers and gave us liberty of manoeuvre and flexibility in both build-up and maintenance by sea. They also afforded the possibility of further amphibious operations to assist the advance by land. This flexibility proved invaluable and was utilised fully by the Eighth Army in its operations along the coast of Calabria and by the Seventh Army in reinforcing the Salerno area with one division from Sicily in the critical early days of the battle.

(c) Although at that time it was known that craft were to be withdrawn during the winter, the number to be withdrawn and the dates of withdrawal were not established. Our plans then envisaged an estimated build-up of thirteen hundred vehicles a day from all Mediterranean ports. Such a figure meant that a total of twenty Allied divisions, together with the Tactical Air Forces, could factually have been put into Italy by the end of the year, provided that they could be equipped and their maintenance assured. At the same time, the estimates of craft available for the future allowed sufficient elasticity to assist maintenance and to provide for amphibious operations in conjunction with the land advance to Rome, should such steps be necessary.

PART II

2 (a) Today the situation has changed greatly. In the south, 11 Allied divisions oppose 9 German, while farther north there are some 15 more, a known total of 24 divisions, and perhaps as high as

28 divisions. On the basis that there are no unforeseen causes of a still lower rate of build-up, the optimum number of formations at our disposal on the mainland will be: end of November, 13 divisions; end of December, 14/15 divisions; end of January, 16/17 divisions. Our rate of build-up has fallen from the previous estimate of thirteen hundred vehicles a day to an estimated 2000 a week with a consequent delay in the calling forward of air forces and army formations. The reduction in the build-up of ground forces has also been influenced by the decision to move the strategic air force into the Foggia area as rapidly as possible rather than to wait for the capture of bases in the Rome area. The demands of the air forces should be met by the end of the year.

(b) The reduction in craft, already decreased by wear and tear, has been so serious as to preclude us from taking advantage, other than with minor forces, of the enemy's inherent weakness, which is the exposure of his two flanks to turning movements from the sea. The majority of such craft as are available are required for build-up and for coastwise maintenance on account of demolitions to road and rail facilities, and traffic in the ports, owing to the shortage of lighters and tugs and enemy sabotage to berthing facilities, which will take time to repair.

3 (a) An examination of the enemy position has shown that his lines of communication enable him to build up in Italy, mainly in the north, to the order of sixty divisions, should they be available, and maintain them there in the winter months, despite our air superiority. The Germans clearly are trying to form a reserve by shortening their lines round the Fortress of Europe. Such a reserve could be employed in reinforcing further their armies in Italy.

(b) In comparison, the Allied position is less favourable. With the resources available, no increase in rate of build-up can be made. A stabilised front south of Rome cannot be accepted, for the capital has a significance far greater than its strategic location, and sufficient depth must be gained before the Foggia airfields and the port of Naples can be regarded as secure. This being so, the seizure of a firm defensive base north of Rome becomes imperative. Moreover, we cannot afford to adopt a purely defensive rôle, for this would entail the surrender of the initiative to the Germans.

PART III

4. The obvious present German intention is to hold a line south of Rome, where the country favours defence and allows no scope to the deployment of our superiority in armour or artillery. Coming bad weather will limit the employment of our air forces, as indeed it has done already. Enemy troops may be tired, but they can be relieved by formations from the north. There are indications that this is being done now. We have neither the formations nor the shipping to enable us to do so. It would therefore appear that we are committed to a long and costly advance to Rome, a "slogging match" with our present slight superiority in formations on the battlefront offset by the enemy opportunity for relief: for, without sufficient resources in craft, no outflanking amphibious operation of a size sufficient to speed up our rate of advance is possible. There is a danger that a successful conclusion of this "slogging match" might leave us north of Rome in such a state of exhaustion and weakness as not to be able to hold what we have gained, if the Germans bring down from the north fresh divisions for a counter-offensive. An enemy strike of this nature may not be fully neutralised by our air forces during the winter months; otherwise, I should feel no concern. The German reinforcement of Italy appears greater than warranted by the internal situation or by purely defensive requirements. If the opportunity for an easy success occurs, there is little doubt that it will be seized upon to counter the effects of a year of defeats on all fronts and to raise German morale prior to the campaigns of 1944. The effect in the Balkans and in France might be particularly to our disadvantage.

5 (a) In conclusion, the picture in September looked rosy, provided the initial assault at Salerno was successful. The German Divisions in the north were about to become involved in difficult internal security problems. In the south the rate of build-up was believed to be such that, given no reinforcement by reserve German formations, we should have had twenty divisions opposed to probably his eighteen by the end of December, and our full air force requirements have been on the mainland. It was believed that sufficient craft would be available to turn his sea flanks and maintain forces over the beaches, as might be necessary.

(b) To sum up: Today the situation is that eleven Allied divisions are fighting a frontal battle in country favouring the defence against an immediate strength of nine German divisions, which can be reinforced at any moment. Our build-up has dwindled to a maximum of 16/17 divisions by the end of January against a present enemy strength of a certain twenty-four divisions, and our resources are not available for amphibious operations of much more than of local character. We may be delayed south of Rome sufficiently long to enable the Germans to clear up the situation in Northern Italy and then reinforce their southern front. In this case, the initiative might well pass to them.

This was indeed a masterly document which touched all the gravest issues of our strategy.

* * * * *

I had already raised some of these issues with General Marshall.

Prime Minister to General Marshall (Washington)   24 Oct. 43

I hope the President will show you my long telegram to him about our much-needed meeting in Africa. Naturally I feel in my marrow the withdrawal of our 50th and 51st Divisions, our best, from the very edge of the Battle of Rome in the interests of distant "Overlord." We are carrying out our contract, but I pray God it does not cost us dear.

And I now telegraphed the President:

Former Naval Person to President Roosevelt   26 Oct. 43

You will have seen by now Eisenhower's [report] setting forth the condition into which we are sinking in Italy. We must not let this great Italian battle degenerate into a deadlock. At all costs we must win Rome and the airfields to the north of it. The fact that the enemy have diverted such powerful forces to this theatre vindicates our strategy. No one can doubt that by knocking out Italy we have enormously helped the Russian advance in the only way in which it could have been helped at this time. I feel that Eisenhower and Alexander must have what they need to win the battle in Italy, no matter what effect is produced on subsequent operations.

I am so grieved to worry you with these matters while you are still suffering from influenza.

General Marshall replied on October 27 that he believed Eisenhower had adequate troops to fight in Italy without taking undue risks. His immediate problem was landing-craft, which would be examined. It seemed to him that in estimating the Italian situation the tremendous advantage of our overwhelming superiority in aircraft was almost ignored. Bad weather could not blot out for certain or for a long period the inevitable result of massed attack on enemy communications.

*   *   *   *   *

I now appealed to the President about the landing-craft in the Mediterranean.

Prime Minister to President Roosevelt   4 Nov. 43

It is with very great regret that I must bring to your notice the increasing anxiety of His Majesty's Government about the withdrawal of landing-craft from the Mediterranean at this critical juncture. We now have before us General Eisenhower's forecast that he will not be able to occupy the line necessary to protect the Rome airfields before the end of January, or even February, if the present programme of withdrawals of landing-craft is rigidly adhered to. He further explains the costly and prolonged frontal attacks that will be necessary in order to achieve this disappointing result. We feel entitled to ask our American Allies to attach weight to our earnest representations in view of the very great preponderance of British troops deployed against the enemy in Italy, with proportionate losses, and also in view of the clear opinions of the United States Commander-in-Chief, under whom we serve.

2. Accordingly, the War Cabinet have formally desired me to ask that consideration shall be given by the United States Chiefs of Staff to the requests put forward by the British Chiefs of Staff. We very much regret that the urgency of the matter does not permit us to wait another three weeks until the next Staff Conference can be convened, as this would entail the departure or immobilisation meanwhile of the landing-craft, with grave injury to the Italian campaign.

3. I may mention that by various intense efforts we have every hope that an additional seventy-five tank landing-craft can be produced in the United Kingdom by the date fixed for "Overlord."

I was relieved to receive his reply.

President Roosevelt to Prime Minister   6 Nov. 43

The Combined Chiefs of Staff today authorised Eisenhower to retain until December 15 sixty-eight L.S.T.s now scheduled for an early departure for the United Kingdom.

It seems to me that this action ought to meet his essential requirements.

I told Alexander at once. He answered:

General Alexander to Prime Minister   9 Nov. 43

The retention of L.S.T.s will do a great deal to help my plans, and am most grateful for them. December 15 will not however allow me to carry out the whole of my plan, and I have explained this in telegram to C.I.G.S.

Prime Minister to General Alexander   9 Nov. 43

You should make alternative campaign plans on the basis that the L.S.T.s stay on till January 15. I am pretty certain this will be agreed to at our Conference.

I also sent the following to our Ambassador in Moscow:

Prime Minister to Sir A. Clark Kerr   9 Nov. 43

.... The exceptionally good weather on the Russian Front has carried with it heavy rains in Italy, and the frontal attacks we have had to make with forces which, though not very much stronger than those of the enemy, have been continuously active, have necessarily yielded slow progress. . . .

My wish has always been to sustain and press to the utmost the campaign in Italy and to attract to that front and hold upon it as many divisions as possible. I am glad to say that agreement has been reached by the Combined Staffs that no more landing-craft shall be withdrawn until December 15. This will enable greater power to be put into the whole of our Italian operations. By new intense exertions at home I hope to make up by additional building of landing-craft for the delay in sending home the others.

Half the German strength is in Northern Italy and Istria, separated from our front by some three hundred miles. It is from that half that the withdrawals back to South Russia have been made. They have been rendered possible, not by any inactivity on our fighting front, but by a diminution of the risks to internal security due to the passive attitude of the Italians in Northern Italy. We are in no doubt of the correctness of the estimate of German strength given by General Ismay. When he spoke there were six Panzer divisions there, half of them fighting on our front. Deployed south of Rome there are now ten German divisions identified in action, against which we have twelve or thirteen of rather greater strength. This is not much of a preponderance for a continuous frontal attack in mountainous country.

To General Brooke I wrote:

Prime Minister to C.I.G.S.   16 Nov. 43

It has now become urgent that Poles should enter the line. They have not done all these years, although an immense amount of preparation and material has been employed. Reinforcements also are urgently needed in Italy, and the Poles are scheduled to go next after the New Zealanders. This is not the time to make changes in their organisation. It is better to take the chance of two divisions becoming under strength. They would still be called the Polish Corps, and we must endeavour to find drafts from other quarters. . . .

Sooner than break up these organisations so laboriously formed in Persia, I would make an inroad on the Polish Armoured Division in Great Britain, which will not be engaged for some time to come. However, I believe that if Polish troops enter the line and are seen to be fighting the Germans it may be possible to obtain a further draft of Poles from Stalin, and I propose to try for this when we meet. The Soviet Government is inclined to be sceptical about this Polish Corps, and suspect that it is being held back and nursed so as to be employed against the Russians in defence of Polish rights. If however the Polish Corps enters line against the Germans and begins to fight, this view will be dissipated. Meanwhile, I cannot approve any alteration in the existing unit.

*   *   *   *   *

I was increasingly disturbed by the great strain thrown on our limited shipping by the demands of the Allied Heavy

Bomber Force, which was being built up on the Foggia air-fields in order to attack industrial targets in Eastern Germany beyond the range of our home-based squadrons. It seemed to me that these demands were disproportionate and unrelated to the general situation at that time.

Prime Minister to General Ismay, for C.O.S. Committee 17 Nov. 43

It is surely altogether wrong to build up the Strategic Air Force in Italy at the expense of the battle for Rome. The strategic bombing of Germany, however important, cannot take precedence over the battle, which must ever rank first in our thoughts. Major tactical needs must always have priority over strategic policy. I was not aware until recently that the build-up of the Army had been obstructed by the forward move of a mass of strategic air not connected with the battle. This is in fact a departure from all orthodox military doctrine, as well as seeming wrong from the point of view of common sense.

And a week later:

The monstrous block of Air, in its eagerness to get ahead, has definitely hampered the operations of the Army.

*   *   *   *   *

The Eighth Army meanwhile had moved forward, and after a series of actions closed up to the river Sangro. Here four German divisions were installed. In order to retain the initia-tive, it was General Alexander's intention that the Eighth Army should cross the river, break through the "Winter-stellung" on this front, and then advance as far as the road Pescara-Avezzano, whence they would threaten Rome and endanger the communications of the enemy on the western coast. Bridgeheads were thrown across the river, but the main enemy defences lay on high ground beyond. Bad weather, with rain, mud, and swollen rivers, postponed the attack until November 28, but then the 78th, 8th Indian, and New Zealand Divisions, the last recently arrived, attacked and made good progress. After a week of heavy fighting, they were established ten miles beyond the Sangro. By December 20, the Canadians had reached the outskirts of Ortona, but it was not until three days after Christmas, after very severe fighting, that the town was cleared of the enemy. This was the first big street-fighting battle, and from it many lessons were learned. But the enemy still held firm, and more reinforcements came to them from Northern Italy. Some more ground was gained during December by the Eighth Army, but no vital objectives were taken, and winter weather brought active operations to a close.

The United States Fifth Army, under General Clark, struggled on up the road towards Cassino, and attacked the foremost defences of the German main positions. The enemy were strongly posted on mountains overlooking the road on either side. The formidable Monte Cassino massif to the west was attacked by the Xth British and IId United States Corps on December 2, and finally cleared a week later after a tough struggle. East of the road equally severe operations were carried out by the IId and VIth United States Corps, the latter now including the 2d Moroccan Division. It was not till the beginning of the New Year that the enemy were ejected and the Fifth Army fully aligned along the river Garigliano and its tributary, the Rapido, where it faced the heights of Cassino and the famous monastery.

In all these land operations the armies had been fully supported by our Tactical Air Forces, while our Strategical Air Force had carried out a number of useful raids behind the enemy lines, notably on Turin, where an important ball-bearing plant was destroyed by American Fortresses. The German Air Force, on the other hand, put forth relatively little effort. By day fighter and fighter-bomber sorties were few. Half a dozen raids by their long-range heavy bombers on Naples had little effect, but a very damaging surprise attack on our crowded harbour of Bari on December 2 blew up an ammunition ship with a chance hit and caused the sinking of sixteen other ships and the loss of thirty thousand tons of cargo.

The Germans hardly troubled to contest the mastery of the air that winter over Italy, and greatly reduced their air strength, as the following table shows:

GERMAN AIR FORCE STRENGTHS

	July 1, 1943	*Oct.* 1, 1943	*Jan.* 1, 1944
Central Mediterranean	975	430	370

Our growing air offensive from England made the enemy withdraw all that could be spared from the Mediterranean and Russia. Every long-range bomber in Italy was taken away for "reprisals" against England, the "Little Blitz" of the following spring.

For reasons which have been explained, I had called the Italian campaign the Third Front. It had attracted to itself twenty good German divisions. If the garrisons kept in the Balkans for fear of attack there are added, nearly forty divisions were retained facing the Allies in the Mediterranean. Our Second Front, Northwest Europe, had not yet flared into battle, but its existence was real. About thirty enemy divisions was the least number ever opposite it, and this rose to sixty as the invasion loomed closer. Our strategic bombing from Britain forced the enemy to divert great numbers of men and masses of material to defend their homeland. These were not negligible contributions to the Russians on what they had every right to call the First Front.

*　*　*　*　*

I must end this chapter with a summary.

In this period in the war all the great strategic combinations of the Western Powers were restricted and distorted by the shortage of tank landing-craft for the transport, not so much of tanks, but of vehicles of all kinds. The letters "L.S.T." (Landing Ship, Tanks) are burnt in upon the minds of all those who dealt with military affairs in this period. We had invaded Italy in strong force. We had an army there which, if not supported, might be entirely cast away, giving Hitler the greatest triumph he had had since the fall of France. On the other hand, there could be no question of our not making the "Overlord" attack in 1944. The utmost I asked for was an easement, if necessary, of two months — i.e., from some time in

May 1944 to some time in July. This would meet the problem of the landing-craft. Instead of their having to return to England in the late autumn of 1943 before the winter gales, they could go in the early spring of 1944. If however the May date were insisted upon pedantically, and interpreted as May 1, the peril to the Allied Army in Italy seemed beyond remedy. If some of the landing-craft earmarked for "Overlord" were allowed to stay in the Mediterranean over the winter, there would be no difficulty in making a success of the Italian campaign. There were masses of troops standing idle in Africa: three or four French divisions, two or three American divisions, at least four (including the Poles) British or British-controlled divisions, were ready for action. The one thing that stood between these and effective operation in Italy was the L.S.T.s, and the main thing that stood between us and the L.S.T.s was the insistence upon an early date for their return to Britain.

The reader of the telegrams printed in this chapter must not be misled by a chance phrase here and there into thinking (*a*) that I wanted to abandon "Overlord"; (*b*) that I wanted to deprive "Overlord" of vital forces; or (*c*) that I contemplated a campaign by armies operating in the Balkan peninsula. These are legends. Never had such a wish entered my mind. Give me the easement of six weeks or two months from May 1 in the date of "Overlord" and I could for several months use the landing-craft in the Mediterranean in order to bring really effective forces to bear in Italy, and thus not only take Rome, but draw off German divisions from either or both the Russian and Normandy fronts. All these matters had been discussed in Washington without regard to the limited character of the issues with which my argument was concerned.

As we shall see presently, in the end everything that I asked for was done. The landing-craft not only were made available for upkeep in the Mediterranean; they were even allowed a further latitude for the sake of the Anzio operation in January. This in no way prevented the successful launching of "Overlord" on June 6 with adequate forces. What happened however was that the long fight about trying to get these small easements and to prevent the wholesale scrapping of one vast front in order to conform to a rigid date upon the other led to prolonged, unsatisfactory operations in Italy. Months were wasted, with grievous outflow in blood and resources, and in the end, though too late, I was actually given more than I asked.

15

Arctic Convoys Again

THE YEAR 1942 had closed in Arctic waters with the spirited action by British destroyers escorting a convoy to North Russia. As recorded in a previous volume, this had led to a crisis in the German High Command and the dismissal of Admiral Raeder from control of naval affairs. Between January and March, in the remaining months of almost perpetual darkness, two more convoys, of forty-two ships and six ships sailing independently, set out on this hazardous voyage. Forty arrived. During the same period thirty-six ships were safely brought back from Russian ports and five were lost. The return of daylight made it easier for the enemy to attack

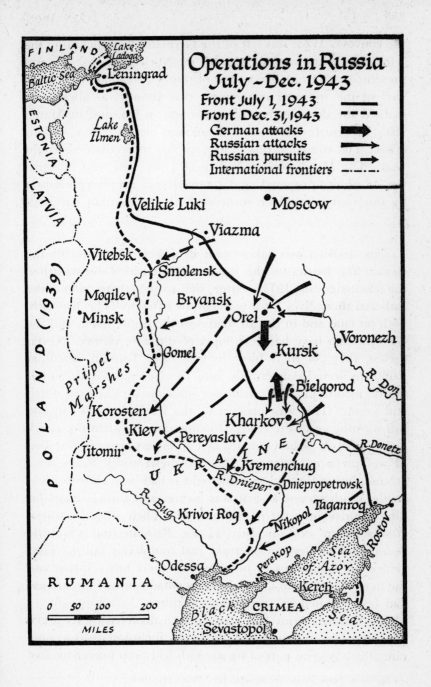

Operations in Russia
July ~ Dec. 1943

Front July 1, 1943
Front Dec. 31, 1943
German attacks
Russian attacks
Russian pursuits
International frontiers

FINLAND
Lake Ladoga
Baltic Sea
Leningrad
ESTONIA
Lake Ilmen
LATVIA
Velikie Luki
Moscow
Viazma
Vitebsk
Smolensk
POLAND (1939)
Mogilev
Bryansk
Minsk
Orel
Voronezh
Gomel
Kursk
R. Don
Pripet Marshes
Bielgorod
Korosten
Kharkov
Kiev
Pereyaslav
R. Donetz
Jitomir
U K R A I N E
Kremenchug
R. Dnieper
Dniepropetrovsk
R. Bug
Krivoi Rog
Nikopol
Taganrog
Rostov
Odessa
Perekop
Sea of Azov
RUMANIA
Kerch
0   50 100   200
Black
CRIMEA
Sea
MILES
Sevastopol

the convoys. What was left of the German Fleet, including the *Tirpitz,* was now concentrated in Norwegian waters, and presented a formidable and continuing threat along a large part of the route. Furthermore, the Atlantic, as always, remained the decisive theatre in the war at sea, and in March 1943 the battle with the U-boats was moving to a violent crisis. The strain on our destroyers was more than we could bear. The March convoy had to be postponed, and in April the Admiralty proposed, and I agreed, that supplies to Russia by this route should be suspended till the autumn darkness.

*   *   *   *   *

This decision was taken with deep regret because of the tremendous battles on the Russian Front which distinguished the campaign of 1943. After the spring thaw both sides gathered themselves for a momentous struggle. The Russians, both on land and in the air, had now the upper hand, and the Germans can have had few hopes of ultimate victory. Nevertheless, they got their blow in first. The Russian salient at Kursk projected dangerously into the German Front, and it was decided to pinch it out by simultaneous attacks from north and south.[1] This was foreseen by the Russians, who had had full warning and were ready. In consequence, when the attack started on July 5 the Germans met an enemy strongly installed in well-prepared defences. The northern attack made some ground, but at the end of a fortnight it had been thrown back. In the south success at first was greater and the Germans bit fifteen miles into the Russian lines. Then major counterattacks began, and by July 23 the Russian line was fully restored. The German offensive had completely failed. They gained no advantages to make up for their heavy losses, and the new "Tiger" tanks, on which they had counted for success, had been mauled by the Russian artillery.

The German Army had already been depleted by its previous campaigns in Russia and diluted by inclusion of its second-rate allies. A great part of its strength had been massed against

[1] See map, "Operations in Russia, July–December 1941."

Kursk at the expense of other sectors of the thousand-mile
active front. Now, when the Russian blows began to fall, it was
unable to parry them. While the Kursk battle was still raging
and the German reserves had been deeply committed, the first
blow came on July 12 against the German salient around Orel.
After intense artillery preparation the main Russian attack fell
on the northern face of the salient, with subsidiary onslaughts
in the east. Deep penetrations were soon made, and although
the defenders fought stoutly their strong-points were in succession outflanked, surrounded, and reduced. Their counter-
attacks were repulsed, and under the weight of superior numbers and material they were overborne. Orel fell on August 5,
and by the 18th the whole salient to a depth of fifty miles had
been cut out.

The second major Russian offensive opened on August 3,
while the Orel attack was still at its height. This time it was
the German salient around Kharkov that suffered. Kharkov
was an important centre of communications, and barred the
way to the Ukraine and the Donetz industrial basin. Its
defences had been prepared with more than usual thorough-
ness. Again the major attacks fell on the northern face of the
salient, one being directed due south against Kharkov itself,
another thrusting southwestward so as to threaten the whole
German rear. Within forty-eight hours both of these had bitten
deep, in places up to thirty miles, and Bielgorod had been
taken. By August 11, Kharkov was threatened on three sides,
a further attack from the east having been launched, while
fifty miles to the northwest the Russians were advancing fast.
On that day Hitler ordered that Kharkov was to be held at
all costs. The German garrison stood to fight it out, and it was
not till the 23d that the whole town was in Russian hands.

These three immense battles of Kursk, Orel, and Kharkov,
all within a space of two months, marked the ruin of the
German army on the Eastern Front. Everywhere they had
been outfought and overwhelmed. The Russian plan, vast
though it was, never outran their resources. It was not only
on land that the Russians proved their new superiority. In

the air about twenty-five hundred German aircraft were opposed by at least twice as many Russian planes, whose efficiency
had been much improved. The German Air Force at this
period of the war was at the peak of its strength, numbering
about six thousand aircraft in all. That less than half could
be spared to support this crucial campaign is proof enough of
the value to Russia of our operations in the Mediterranean
and of the growing Allied bomber effort based on Britain. In
fighter aircraft especially the Germans felt the pinch. Although inferior on the Eastern Front, yet in September they
had to weaken it still more in order to defend themselves in
the West, where by the winter nearly three-quarters of the
total German fighter strength was deployed. The swift and
overlapping Russian blows gave the Germans no opportunity
to make the best use of their air resources. Air units were
frequently moved from one battle area to another in order to
meet a fresh crisis, and wherever they went, leaving a gap behind them, they found the Russian planes in overmastering
strength.

In September, the Germans were in retreat along the whole
of their southern front, from opposite Moscow to the Black
Sea. The Russians swung forward in full pursuit. At the
northern hinge a Russian thrust from Viazma took Smolensk
on September 25. No doubt the Germans hoped to stand on
the Dnieper, the next great river line, but by early October
the Russians were across it north of Kiev, and to the south at
Pereyaslav and Kremenchug. Farther south again Dniepropetrovsk was taken on October 25. Only near the mouth of
the river were the Germans still on the western bank of the
Dnieper; all the rest had gone. The land approach to the
Crimea, at Perekop, was captured by the Red Army, and the
retreat of the strong German garrison in the Crimea was cut
off. Kiev, outflanked on either side, fell on November 6, with
many prisoners, and the Russians, driving forward, reached
Korosten and Jitomir. But a strong armoured counter-attack
on their flank drove them back, and the Germans recaptured
the two towns. Here the front stabilised for the time being.

In the north, Gomel was taken at the end of November, and the upper reaches of the Dnieper crossed on each side of Mogilev.

By December, after a three months' pursuit, the German armies in Central and South Russia had been thrust back more than two hundred miles, and, failing to hold the Dnieper River line, lay open and vulnerable to a winter campaign in which, as they knew from bitter experience, their opponents excelled. Such was the grand Russian story of 1943.

*   *   *   *   *

It was natural that the Soviet Government should look reproachfully at the suspension of the convoys, for which their armies hungered. On the evening of September 21, M. Molotov sent for our Ambassador in Moscow and asked for the sailings to be resumed. He pointed out that the Italian Fleet had been eliminated and that the U-boats had abandoned the North Atlantic for the southern route. The Persian railway could not carry enough. For three months the Soviet Union had been undertaking a wide and most strenuous offensive, yet in 1943 they had received less than a third of the previous year's supplies. The Soviet Government therefore "insisted" upon the urgent resumption of the convoys, and expected His Majesty's Government to take all necessary measures within the next few days.

Though there was much to be said in answer to all this I raised the matter with the Admiralty and others on September 25.

Prime Minister to Foreign Secretary, Minister of   25 Sept. 43
Production, Minister of War Transport, General Ismay,
for C.O.S. Committee, and Acting First Sea Lord

It is our duty if humanly possible to reopen these Arctic convoys, beginning in the latter part of November in accordance with the moon phase. We should try to run November, December, January, February, and March convoys — total five. Plans should be prepared by the Admiralty and the Ministry of War Transport. I understand that this is feasible.

Now that the Russians have asked for the reopening of these convoys, we are entitled to make a very plain request to them for the better treatment of our personnel in North Russia.

The first reply from the Admiralty about the convoys was disappointing to me.

CONVOYS TO NORTH RUSSIA

Prime Minister to Foreign Secretary, First Lord,   27 Sept. 43
General Ismay, for C.O.S. Committee, and others concerned

This is not satisfactory. Why cannot the November convoy be a full one? This also applies to the December 8 convoy. We must try to run at least five full convoys before "Overlord" operations start. I do not agree that the situation in the Atlantic or in the Mediterranean will be as strained as it was when we were running these convoys before. Naturally I am not going to make a solemn contract with Marshal Stalin, and we must safeguard ourselves against unforeseeable contingencies, but I consider that November, December, January, February, and March should each see a full-sized convoy dispatched.

I will have a Staff meeting on this subject at 10 P.M. on Tuesday night.

When we met on the night of the 29th to discuss the problem, an agreeable new fact was before us. The *Tirpitz* had been disabled by the audacious and heroic attack of our midget submarines. Of six craft which took part two penetrated all the elaborate defences. Their commanding officers, Lieutenant Cameron, R.N.R., and Lieutenant Place, R.N., rescued by the Germans, survived as prisoners of war, and received the Victoria Cross. Later air reconnaissance showed that the battleship was heavily damaged and would require refit in a dockyard before she could again be ready for action. The *Lützow* had already gone to the Baltic. Thus we had an easement, probably of some months, in the Arctic waters, and I was able to minute to the Foreign Secretary:

The resumption of the convoys question is practically settled in a favourable sense. Before I send my telegram to Stalin about it, let me see your list of grievances about the treatment of our people in North Russia, so that I can combine the two to the best advantage.

I should like to do the telegram tonight.

Mr. Eden's complaints were serious, and I accordingly sent the following telegram to Stalin:

Prime Minister to Premier Stalin   1 Oct. 43

I have received your request for the reopening of the convoys to North Russia. I and all my colleagues are most anxious to help you and the valiant armies you lead to the utmost of our ability. I do not therefore reply to the various controversial points made in M. Molotov's communication. Since June 22, 1941, we have always done our best in spite of our own heavy burdens to help you defend your own country against the cruel invasion of the Hitlerite gang, and we have never ceased to acknowledge and proclaim the great advantages that have come to us from the splendid victories you have won and from the deadly blows you have dealt the German armies.

2. For the last four days I have been working with the Admiralty to make a plan for sending a new series of convoys to North Russia. This entails very great difficulties. First, the Battle of the Atlantic has begun again. The U-boats have set about us with a new kind of acoustic torpedo, which has proved effective against the escorting vessels when hunting U-boats. Secondly, we are at very full stretch in the Mediterranean, building up an army in Italy of about 600,000 men by the end of November, and also trying to take full advantage of the Italian collapse in the Aegean islands and the Balkan peninsula. Thirdly, we have to provide for our share of the war against Japan, in which the United States are greatly interested, and whose people would be offended if we were lukewarm.

3. Notwithstanding the above, it is a very great pleasure to me to tell you that we are planning to sail a series of four convoys to North Russia in November, December, January, and February, each of which will consist of approximately thirty-five ships, British and American. Convoys may be sailed in two halves to meet operational requirements. The first convoy will leave the United Kingdom about November 12, arriving North Russia ten days later;

subsequent convoys at about twenty-eight-day intervals. We intend to withdraw as many as possible of the merchant vessels now in North Russia towards the end of October, and the remainder with returning convoy escorts.

To avoid new charges of breach of faith from the Soviet, if our efforts to help them proved vain, I inserted a safeguarding paragraph:

4. However, I must put it on record that this is no contract or bargain, but rather a declaration of our solemn and earnest resolve. On this basis I have ordered the necessary measures to be taken for the sending of these four convoys of thirty-five ships.

I then proceeded with our list of grievances about the treatment of our men in North Russia:

5. The Foreign Office and the Admiralty however request me to put before you for your personal attention, hoping indeed that your own eye may look at it, the following representations about the difficulties we have experienced in North Russia.

6. If we are to resume the convoys we shall have to reinforce our establishments in North Russia, which have been reduced in numbers since last March. The present numbers of naval personnel are below what is necessary, even for our present requirements, owing to men having to be sent home without relief. Your civil authorities have refused us all visas for men to go to North Russia, even to relieve those who are seriously overdue for relief. M. Molotov has pressed His Majesty's Government to agree that the number of British Service personnel in North Russia should not exceed that of the Soviet Service personnel and trade delegation in this country. We have been unable to accept this proposal, since their work is quite dissimilar and the number of men needed for war operations cannot be determined in such an unpractical way. Secondly, as we have already informed the Soviet Government, we must ask to be the judges of the personnel required to carry out operations for which we are responsible. Mr. Eden has already given his assurance that the greatest care will be taken to limit the numbers strictly to the minimum.

7. I must therefore ask you to agree to the immediate grant

of visas for the additional personnel now required, and for your assurance that you will not in future withhold visas when we find it necessary to ask for them in connection with the assistance that we are giving you in North Russia. I emphasise that of about one hundred and seventy naval personnel at present in the North, over one hundred and fifty should have been relieved some months ago, but Soviet visas have been withheld. The state of health of these men, who are unaccustomed to the climatic and other conditions, makes it very necessary to relieve them without further delay.

8. We should also wish to send the small medical unit for Archangel to which your authorities agreed, but for which the necessary visas have not been granted. Please remember that we may have heavy casualties.

9. I must also ask your help in remedying the conditions under which our Service personnel and seamen at present find themselves in North Russia. These men are of course engaged in operations against the enemy in our joint interest, and chiefly to bring Allied supplies to your country. They are, I am sure you will admit, in a wholly different position from ordinary individuals proceeding to Russian territory. Yet they are subjected by your authorities to the following restrictions, which seem to me inappropriate for men sent by an ally to carry out operations of the greatest interest to the Soviet Union: (a) No one may land from one of His Majesty's ships or from a British merchant ship except by a Soviet boat in the presence of a Soviet official and after examination of documents on each occasion. (b) No one from a British warship is allowed to proceed alongside a British merchantman without the Soviet authorities being informed beforehand. This even applies to the British Admiral in charge. (c) British officers and men are required to obtain special passes before they can go from ship to shore or between two British shore stations. These passes are often much delayed, with consequent dislocation of the work in hand. (d) No stores, luggage, or mail for this operational force may be landed except in the presence of a Soviet official, and numerous formalities are required for the shipment of all stores and mail. (e) Private Service mail is subjected to censorship, although for an operational force of this kind censorship should, in our view, be left in the hands of British Service authorities.

10. The imposition of these restrictions makes an impression

upon officers and men alike which is bad for Anglo-Soviet relations, and would be deeply injurious if Parliament got to hear of
it. The cumulative effect of these formalities has been most
hampering to the efficient performance of the men's duties, and on
more than one occasion to urgent and important operations. No
such restrictions are placed upon Soviet personnel here.

11. We have already proposed to M. Molotov that as regards
offences against Soviet law committed by personnel of the Services
and of the ships of the convoys, they should be handed over to the
British Service authorities to be dealt with. There have been a few
such cases, no doubt, partially at any rate due to the rigorous conditions of service in the North.

12. I trust indeed, M. Stalin, that you will find it possible to
have these difficulties smoothed out in a friendly spirit, so that we
may help each other, and the common cause, to the utmost of our
strength.

These were modest requests considering the efforts we were
now to make. No answer was received for nearly a fortnight.

*   *   *   *   *

As will be described in the next chapter the Conference of
the Foreign Secretaries of the three major Allies, long planned,
was now due in Moscow. On October 9, Mr. Eden set out by
air. His journey lay through Cairo and Teheran, where he had
much business, and he did not reach Moscow till the morning
of October 18. During his absence I took charge of the Foreign
Office.

Prime Minister to Sir A. Clark Kerr (*Moscow*)   12 Oct. 43

I have received no answer to my long telegram of October 1
about resuming the Arctic convoys. If the cycle of convoys is to
begin on November 12, we must have an early reply to our requests
about personnel. Several dozens of wireless operators and signals
personnel, on whose work the safety of the convoys may well
depend, are to leave the United Kingdom, together with about one
hundred and fifty reliefs for men due to return home, by destroyers
sailing from the United Kingdom on October 21. Pray therefore
press for an answer. Meanwhile we are preparing the convoys in
the hope that the Soviets still desire them.

Next day I received Stalin's answer.

Premier Stalin to Prime Minister   13 Oct. 43

I received your message of October 1 informing me of the intention to send four convoys to the Soviet Union by the Northern
route in November, December, January, and February. However,
this communication loses its value by your statement that this
intention to send Northern convoys to the U.S.S.R. is neither an
obligation nor an agreement, but only a statement, which, as it
may be understood, is one the British side can at any moment re-
nounce regardless of any influence it may have on the Soviet armies
at the front. I must say that I cannot agree with such a posing of
the question. Supplies from the British Government to the
U.S.S.R., armaments and other military goods, cannot be considered otherwise than as an obligation, which, by special agreement between our countries, the British Government undertook in
respect of the U.S.S.R., which bears on its shoulders, already for
the third year, the enormous burden of struggle with the common
enemy of the Allies — Hitlerite Germany.

It is also impossible to disregard the fact that the Northern
route is the shortest way which permits delivery of armaments
supplied by the Allies within the shortest period to the Soviet-
German Front, and the realisation of the plan of supplies to the
U.S.S.R. in appropriate volume is impossible without an adequate
use of this way. As I already wrote to you earlier, and as experience
has shown, delivery of armaments and military supplies to the
U.S.S.R. through Persian ports cannot compensate in any way for
those supplies which were not delivered by the Northern route.

By the way, for some reason or other there was a very considerable decrease in the delivery of military goods sent by the Northern
route this year in comparison with those received last year; and
this makes it impossible to fulfil the established [Soviet] plan of
military supplies [to the armies] and is in contradiction to the
corresponding Anglo-Soviet protocol for military supplies. Therefore, at the present time, when the forces of the Soviet Union are
strained to the utmost to secure the needs of the front in the
interests of success of the struggle against the main forces of our
common enemy, it would be inadmissible to have the supplies of
the Soviet armies depend on the arbitrary judgment of the British
side. It is impossible to consider this posing of the question to

be other than a refusal of the British Government to fulfil the obligations it undertook, and as a kind of threat addressed to the U.S.S.R.

2. Concerning your mention of controversial points allegedly contained in the statement of M. Molotov, I have to say that I do not find any foundation for such a remark. I consider the principle of reciprocity and equality proposed by the Soviet side for settlement of the visa question in respect of personnel of the military missions to be a correct and indeed a just one. The reference to the difference in the functions of the British and Soviet military missions, and that the numbers of the staff of the British military mission must be determined by the British Government only, I consider to be unconvincing. It has already been made clear in detail in the previous *aide-mémoires* of the People's Commissariat for Foreign Affairs on this question.

3. I do not see the necessity for increasing the number of British Service-men in the North of the U.S.S.R., since the great majority of British Service-men who are already there are not adequately employed, and for many months have been doomed to idleness, as has already been pointed out several times by the Soviet side. For example, it can be mentioned that, owing to its non-necessity, the question of the liquidation of the British port base in Archangel was put forward several times, and only now the British side have agreed to liquidate it. There are also regrettable facts of the inadmissible behaviour of individual British Service-men who attempted, in several cases, to recruit, by bribery, certain Soviet citizens for Intelligence purposes. Such instances, offensive to Soviet citizens, naturally gave rise to incidents which led to undesirable complications.

4. Concerning your mention of formalities and certain restrictions existing in Northern ports, it is necessary to have in view that such formalities and restrictions are unavoidable in zones near and at the front, if one does not forget the war situation which exists in the U.S.S.R. I may add that this applies equally to the British and other foreigners as well as to Soviet citizens. Nevertheless, the Soviet authorities granted many privileges in this respect to the British Service-men and seamen, about which the British Embassy was informed as long ago as last March. Thus your mention of many formalities and restrictions is based on inaccurate information.

Concerning the question of censorship and prosecution of British Service-men, I have no objection if the censorship of private mail for British personnel in Northern ports would be made by the British authorities themselves, on condition of reciprocity, and also if cases of small violations committed by British Service-men which did not involve court procedure would be given to the consideration of the appropriate military authorities.

*   *   *   *   *

Mr. Eden had now left Cairo for Teheran on his way to Moscow, so I sent him the following:

Prime Minister to Foreign Secretary (Teheran)   15 Oct. 43

This offensive reply has been received to our telegram about convoys. I send you the reply which I have drafted. As you will be on the spot, I leave it to you to handle as you see fit. I do not think we should give way about the naval reliefs and signalmen. It would be a great relief to be freed from the burden of these convoys and to bring our men home from North Russia. If this is what they really mean and want we ought to oblige them.

Here was my draft:

Prime Minister to Foreign Secretary   15 Oct. 43

It is impossible for His Majesty's Government to guarantee that the four convoys mentioned can be run irrespective of the military situation on the seas. Every effort and heavy loss and sacrifice would however be made to do so if the Soviet Government attaches importance to the receipt of their cargoes. I cannot undertake to do more than my best, and His Majesty's Government must remain the judge of whether any particular operation of war to be carried out by their forces is in fact practicable or not.

2. The running of these four convoys would be a very great burden to the Royal Navy, and involves the diversion of much-needed flotillas from the anti-U-boat war and from the escorting of troops and other important convoys. It also exposes the main units of the Fleet to serious risks. His Majesty's Government would be very glad to be relieved of the task of running the convoys if the Soviet Government do not attach importance to them.

3. In particular the refusal of the request of the British Government in respect of the reliefs and small increases in the few hundreds of British Service-men in the North of the U.S.S.R., and in particular the signals personnel, on which the safety of these convoys to some extent depends, raises an insuperable obstacle. His Majesty's Government would be very glad to withdraw the handfuls of Service personnel from North Russia, and will do so as soon as they are assured that it is not the desire of the Soviet Government to receive the convoys under the modest and reasonable conditions which the British Government consider necessary.

I commented to the President:

Former Naval Person to President Roosevelt   16 Oct. 43

About Russian convoys. I have now received a telegram from Uncle Joe which I think you will feel is not exactly all one might hope for from a gentleman for whose sake we are to make an inconvenient, extreme, and costly exertion. I have sent a suggested answer to Anthony for him to handle as he thinks best.

2. I think, or at least I hope, this message came from the machine rather than from Stalin, as it took twelve days to prepare. The Soviet machine is quite convinced it can get everything by bullying, and I am sure it is a matter of some importance to show that this is not necessarily always true.

Mr. Eden had now reached Moscow.

Prime Minister to Foreign Secretary   18 Oct. 43

It is a very good thing you are on the spot to deal with the convoy question. I am seeing the Soviet Ambassador at 3 P.M. today, and propose to hand him back the offensive message from Stalin, saying that I do not wish to receive it, as the matter will be settled by you at Moscow. You should not hand in my suggested reply, or take it as anything more than a guide.

Further, the first convoy is assembling and leaves on November 12. The ships are being loaded, and I have not thought it right to interfere with this process, especially as it would involve the United States, who have sent their ships at our suggestion. I hope however that in personal contact with Stalin you may point out: first, the importance of these four convoys, with the hundred and forty cargoes, and the efforts I have had to make to secure the necessary escorts; secondly, the small, petty mitigations we ask in the treatment of our men in North Russia; thirdly, our natural desire to be relieved of the burden of these convoys and to bring our people home from North Russia; fourthly, you could also disabuse his mind of the idea that any threat was intended by my declining to make an absolute contract or bargain; all I wished to do was to reserve the final right of judging whether the operation was militarily practicable or could be attempted, having regard to the general situation in the Atlantic, without being accused, as usual, of a breach of faith, and I must maintain this reservation. . . .

I feel so much for you in the bleak Conference, and wish I were with you. You may have full confidence in the strength of the British position on all these questions, and I have every hope that you will make them feel at once our desire for their friendship and our will-power on essentials. All good luck.

*   *   *   *   *

On the same day I asked the Soviet Ambassador to come to see me. As this was the first occasion on which I had met M. Gousev, who had succeeded Maisky, he gave me the greeting of Marshal Stalin and M. Molotov, and I told him of the good reputation he had made for himself with us in Canada. After these compliments we had a short discussion about the Moscow Conference and the Second Front. I explained to him that this kind of operation could not be undertaken on impulse, and that I was always ready to arrange for a meeting between British and Russian military experts, who would go into the facts and figures, upon which everything depended, and without which discussion was futile. I spoke to him earnestly about the great desire we had to work with Russia and to be friends with her, how we saw that she should have a great place in the world after the war, that we should welcome this, and that we would do our best also to make good relations between her and the United States. I further said how much I was looking forward to a meeting with Marshal Stalin if it could be arranged, and how important this meeting of the heads of the British, American, and Soviet Governments was to the future of the world.

I then turned to Stalin's telegram about the convoys. I said very briefly that I did not think this message would help the situation, that it had caused me a good deal of pain, that I feared any reply which I could send would only make things worse, that the Foreign Secretary was in Moscow and I had left it to him to settle the matter on the spot, and that therefore I did not wish to receive the message. I then handed back to the Ambassador an envelope. Gousev opened the envelope to see what was inside it, and, recognising the message, said he had been instructed to deliver it to me. I then said, "I am not prepared to receive it," and got up to indicate in a friendly manner that our conversation was at an end. I moved to the door and opened it. We had a little talk in the doorway about his coming to luncheon in the near future and discussing with Mrs. Churchill some questions connected with her Russian fund, which I told him had now reached four million pounds. I did not give M. Gousev a chance of recurring to the question of the convoys or of trying to hand me back the envelope, and bowed him out.

The War Cabinet endorsed my refusal to receive Stalin's telegram. It was certainly an unusual diplomatic incident, and, as I learnt later, it impressed the Soviet Government. In fact, Molotov referred to it several times in conversation. Even before it could be reported to Moscow, there were misgivings in Soviet circles. On October 19, Mr. Eden telegraphed that Molotov had called on him at the Embassy and said that his Government greatly valued the convoys, and had sadly missed them. The Northern route was the shortest and quickest way of getting supplies to the front, where the Russians were going through a difficult time. The German winter defence line had to be broken. Molotov promised to speak to Stalin about it all and arrange a meeting. Mr. Eden continued:

Foreign Secretary to Prime Minister   19 Oct. 43

My attention has been drawn to the fate of two British merchant seamen recently given severe sentences for an assault in North Russia upon a local Communist leader. I am most reluctant, and the Ambassador agrees with me, to promise resumption of convoys unless these unfortunate British seamen are released and handed over to our naval authorities for removal. . . . I am convinced it would be utterly repugnant to you, as it is to me, to allow these men to languish in a Soviet gaol while we are accepting those risks to British seamen in future convoys. I shall try what I can do by personal appeal to Stalin or Molotov.

The important discussion took place on the 21st. Meanwhile, in order to strengthen Eden's hands, and at his suggestion, I suspended the sailing of the British destroyers, which was the first move in the resumption of the convoys.

Foreign Secretary to Prime Minister   22 Oct. 43

I saw Stalin and Molotov last evening. His Majesty's Ambassador was with me, and the conversation, which roamed over a large variety of topics, lasted two and a quarter hours.

2. After some preliminary exchanges of greetings, I raised the question of convoys. I said that I must explain how great a strain these convoys placed on the Royal Navy. The passage of each one was a major naval operation, which might require four cruisers and twelve destroyers for its immediate protection, in addition to which the entire Home Fleet would also have to come out to provide cover. To make available the necessary escorts, we must reduce our naval strength in the Atlantic. Though it was true that anti-U-boat warfare was going better for us, this struggle was still a closely run thing. At this point I showed Stalin a chart of the number of U-boats in service over the past three years. This proved that the number was now still near its peak. The reason why we were not prepared to promise that we would carry out four convoys was because we did not wish to expose ourselves to reproach if, owing to some sudden development of the war, we could not in fact send all four. But it was our earnest desire to make these convoys available, and I told Stalin that you, who had yourself laboured hard to make the necessary arrangements, had now telegraphed me that you calculated that we should be able to send 130 to 140 cargoes in all, with about 860,000 tons of supplies. If the convoys were to be run, we were anxious to start at once. We

had made our naval dispositions on this basis, and we wished to
avail ourselves of the period during which the *Tirpitz* was out of
action. Our requirements in naval personnel had been reduced
to what we considered the absolute minimum, and we must insist
on that minimum. There were also certain minor requirements
which, if general agreement were reached, I wished to put to
Molotov.

3. Stalin, who had nodded agreement at my description of the
U-boat warfare, said that his difference with you was not about
the difficulties of the operation, but as to whether we were bound
to do it. You had implied that if we sailed any one of these convoys, it would be as a gift. Stalin did not feel this was a true
description of the position. On his understanding of it, we were
under an obligation to seek to deliver these goods. When he had
sent his reply to you however you had been very much offended
and would not accept his reply. I replied that we had never suggested that to send these convoys was an act of favour or charity.
You had at all times been determined to make every effort to
deliver these goods to our Ally, but for the reasons I had explained
you could not pledge yourself to a series of operations which you
might not be able to carry out. Stalin himself surely must have
confidence in the good faith of his Ally, and therefore it was not
surprising that you should have been hurt by the message. The
Marshal said that this had not been intended.

4. After some further discussion, Stalin said that he could not
agree to increase the number of men. There were already many of
our sailors in North Russian ports with nothing to do, and then
they got into trouble with Russian sailors. The Russians might
undertake such convoys themselves. I replied that this was not
possible. He said that if only our people in North Russia had
treated his people as equals, none of these difficulties would have
arisen, and that if our people would treat his people as equals, we
could have as much personnel as we liked. After some further
argument, it was decided that Molotov and I would meet tomorrow,
when I would give him a list of our requirements and we would
see whether we could reach agreement.

*   *   *   *   *

Thus it was arranged that the convoys should be resumed.
The first started in November, and a second followed it in

December. Between them they comprised seventy-two ships. All arrived safely, and at the same time return convoys of empty ships were successfully brought out.

The December outward-bound convoy was to bring about a gratifying naval engagement. The disablement of the *Tirpitz* had left the *Scharnhorst* the only heavy enemy ship in Northern Norway. She sallied forth from Alten Fiord with five destroyers on the evening of Christmas Day 1943, to attack the convoy about fifty miles south of Bear Island. The reinforced convoy escort comprised fourteen destroyers, with a covering force of three cruisers. The Commander-in-Chief, Admiral Fraser, lay to the southwestward in his flagship, the *Duke of York*, with the cruiser *Jamaica* and four destroyers.

Twice the *Scharnhorst* tried to strike at the convoy. Each time she was intercepted and engaged by the escort cruisers and destroyers, and after indecisive fighting, in which both the *Scharnhorst* and the British cruiser *Norfolk* were hit, the Germans broke off the action and withdrew to the southward, shadowed and reported by our cruisers. The German destroyers were never seen and took no part. Meanwhile, the Commander-in-Chief was approaching at his utmost speed through heavy seas. At 4.17 P.M., when the last of the Arctic twilight had long since gone, the *Duke of York* detected the enemy by radar at about twenty-three miles. The *Scharnhorst* remained unaware of her approaching doom, until, at 4.50 P.M., the *Duke of York* opened fire at twelve thousand yards with the aid of star-shell. At the same time Admiral Fraser sent his four destroyers in to attack when opportunity offered. One of these, the *Stord*, was manned by the Royal Norwegian Navy. The *Scharnhorst* was surprised, and turned away to the eastward. In a running fight she suffered several hits, but was able with her superior speed gradually to draw ahead. However, by 6.20 P.M. it became apparent that her speed was beginning to fall and our destroyers were able to close in on either flank. At about 7 P.M. they all pressed home their attacks. Four torpedoes struck. Only one destroyer was hit.

The *Scharnhorst* turned to drive off the destroyers, and thus the *Duke of York* was able to close rapidly to about ten thousand yards and reopen fire with crushing effect. In half an hour the unequal battle between a battleship and a wounded battle-cruiser was over, and the *Duke of York* left the cruisers and destroyers to complete the task. The *Scharnhorst* soon sank, and of her company of 1970 officers and men, including Rear-Admiral Bey, we could only save thirty-six men.

Although the fate of the crippled *Tirpitz* was delayed for nearly a year, the sinking of the *Scharnhorst* not only removed the worst menace to our Arctic convoys, but gave new freedom to our Home Fleet. We no longer had to be prepared at our average moment against German heavy ships breaking out into the Atlantic at their selected moment. This was an important relief.

* * * * *

When in April 1944 there were signs that the *Tirpitz* had been repaired sufficiently to move for refit to a Baltic port, aircraft from the carriers *Victorious* and *Furious* attacked her with heavy bombs, and she was once more immobilised. The Royal Air Force now took up the attack from a base in North Russia. They succeeded in causing further damage, which led to the *Tirpitz* being removed to Tromsö Fiord, which was two hundred miles nearer to Britain and within the extreme range of our home-based heavy bombers. The Germans had now abandoned hope of getting the ship home for repair and had written her off as a seagoing fighting unit. On November 12 twenty-nine specially fitted Lancasters of the Royal Air Force, including those of 617 Squadron, famous for the Moehne Dam exploit, struck the decisive blow, with bombs of twelve thousand pounds weight. They had to fly over two thousand miles from their bases in Scotland, but the weather was clear and three bombs hit their target. The *Tirpitz* capsized at her moorings, more than half of her crew of 1900 men being killed, at the cost of one bomber, whose crew survived.

All British heavy ships were now free to move to the Far East.

16

Foreign Secretaries' Conference in Moscow

Back to the Quebec Conference — Need of a Meeting of the Three Heads of Governments — My Correspondence with Stalin — A Preliminary Conference of Foreign Ministers — My Note for Mr. Eden at This Conference, October 11 — The Meeting in Moscow, October 19 — The Soviet Proposals — My Private Note to Mr. Eden, October 20 — Stalin Concentrates on the Cross-Channel Invasion — The Question of Turkey, Finland, and Sweden Being Pressed to Join Us — Eisenhower and Alexander Report Gravely About Italy — Further Discussions at the Kremlin — A Friendly Atmosphere — Mr. Eden's Account — A Russian Share in the Italian Fleet — My Telegrams of October 29 — My Proposed Triple Declaration on German War Criminals Accepted — The Important Achievements of the Conference.

RETROSPECT is now necessary to bring the course of diplomatic events into accord with the narrative. Ever since the Quebec Conference we had been making suggestions to Stalin for a triple meeting of the heads of Governments. Already at Quebec I had received the following reply from him:

Premier Stalin to Prime Minister (Quebec)   10 Aug. 43

I have just returned from the front, and already had time to become familiar with the message of the British Government dated August 7.

I agree that a meeting of the heads of three Governments is absolutely desirable. Such a meeting must be realised at the first

opportunity, having arranged with the President the place and the
time of this meeting.

At the same time I ought to say that in the existing situation
on the Soviet-German Front, I, to my regret, have no opportunity
to absent myself and to leave the front even for one week. Although recently we have had several successes on the front, an
extreme strain on the strength and exceptional watchfulness are
required in regard to the new possible actions of the enemy from
the Soviet troops and from the Soviet Command just now. In connection with this I have to visit the troops on that or other parts
of our front more often than usual. In the circumstances at the
present time I am not able to visit Scapa Flow or any other distant
point for a meeting with you and the President.

Nevertheless, in order not to postpone an examination of the
questions which interest our countries, it would be expedient to
organise a meeting of the responsible representatives of our states,
and we might come to an understanding in the nearest future
concerning the place and date of such a meeting.

Moreover, it is necessary beforehand to agree on the scope of
the questions to be discussed and the drafts of the proposals which
have to be accepted. The meeting will hardly give any tangible
result without that.

2. Taking this opportunity, I congratulate the British Government and the Anglo-American troops on the occasion of their
most successful operations in Sicily, which have already caused
the downfall of Mussolini and the break-up of his gang.

This was the first favourable mention from the Russian side
of a meeting between the three Allies at any level. In passing
this message to Mr. Eden for transmission to Moscow, I said,
"I was very glad to hear again from Bruin in the first person.
Please forward him my reply, which is in the sense you desire."

After a discussion with President Roosevelt, we framed a
joint message to Stalin.

Prime Minister and President Roosevelt (Quebec) to   19 Aug. 43
Premier Stalin

We have both arrived here with our Staffs, and will probably
remain in conference for about ten days. We fully understand

strong reasons which lead you to remain on battle-fronts, where your presence has been so fruitful of victory. Nevertheless, we wish to emphasise once more importance of a meeting between all three of us. We do not feel that either Archangel or Astrakhan is suitable, but we are prepared ourselves, accompanied by suitable officers, to proceed to Fairbanks [in Alaska] in order to survey whole scene in common with you. The present seems to be a unique opportunity for making a rendezvous, and also a crucial point in the war. We earnestly hope that you will give this matter once more your consideration. The Prime Minister will remain on this side of Atlantic for as long as may be necessary.

2. Should it prove impossible to arrange the much-needed meeting of three heads of Governments we agree with you that a meeting on the Foreign Office level should take place in the near future. This meeting would be exploratory in character, as of course final decisions must be reserved to our respective Governments.

Stalin replied:

25 Aug. 43

I have received your joint message of August 19.

I entirely share your opinion and that of Mr. Roosevelt about the importance of a meeting between the three of us. In this connection I beg you most earnestly to understand my position at this moment, when our armies are carrying on the struggle against the main forces of Hitler with the utmost strain, and when Hitler not only does not withdraw a single division from our front, but, on the contrary, has already succeeded in transporting, and continues to transport, fresh divisions to the Soviet-German Front. At such a moment, in the opinion of all my colleagues, I cannot, without detriment to our military operations, leave the front for so distant a point as Fairbanks, although if the situation on our front were different Fairbanks undoubtedly would be very convenient as a place for our meeting, as I said before.

As regards a meeting of representatives of our States, and in particular of representatives in charge of foreign affairs, I share your opinion about the expediency of such a meeting in the near future. This meeting however ought not to have a purely exploratory character, but a practicable and preparatory character, in order that after that meeting has taken place our Governments are able to take definite decisions, on urgent questions. Therefore I consider it indispensable to revert to my proposal that it is necessary in advance to define the scope of the questions for discussion by the representatives of the three Powers, and to draft the proposals which ought to be discussed by them and presented to our Governments for final decision.

Prime Minister to Premier Stalin   5 Sept. 43

The Conference of Foreign Ministers. I was glad to get your message of August 25, in which you agree to an early meeting of Soviet, United States, and British representatives in charge of foreign affairs. If Monsieur Molotov comes, we will send Mr. Eden.

2. The Conference even thus constituted could not of course supersede the authority of all Governments concerned. We are most anxious to know what your wishes are about the future, and will tell you our views so far as they are formed. After that the Governments will have to decide, and I hope that we may be able to meet personally somewhere. I would, if necessary, go to Moscow.

3. The political representatives might require to be assisted by military advisers. I would provide a general officer, Sir Hastings Ismay, who is my personal representative on the Chiefs of Staff Committee, and conducts the Secretariat of the Ministry of Defence. He could supply the arguments and facts and figures on the military questions involved. I believe the United States would send an officer similarly qualified. This, I think, would be sufficient at this stage for the meeting of Foreign Ministers.

4. If however you wish to go in technical detail into the question of why we have not yet invaded France across the Channel, and why we cannot do it sooner or in greater strength than is now proposed, I should welcome a separate technical mission of your generals and admirals coming to London or Washington, or both, when the fullest possible exposition of our thought, resources, and intentions could be laid before them and thrashed out. Indeed, I should be very glad that you should have this explanation, to which you have every right.

5. We are disposed to think that Britain, being a midway point, would be the most convenient place for the meeting, though it might be preferable to hold it outside of London. I have made this proposal to the President, but he has not given me a final decision

upon it. If England were agreeable to you, I should be glad of your support in the proposal.

6. I hope we can aim at assembling the Conference early in October.

Premier Stalin to Prime Minister   8 Sept. 43

The time suggested by you for the meeting of the representatives of the three Governments — the beginning of October — is acceptable. As the meeting-place I propose Moscow. It is important to agree in advance on the agenda, and on the proposals concerning the decisions to be taken on the various questions of the agenda in which our Governments are interested. Now as before I believe that this is necessary for the success of the Conference, which ought to prepare the way for the subsequent agreed decisions of the Governments. I do not foresee any difficulty in coming to terms on other questions concerning the organisation of the meeting.

On the question of the personal meeting between the heads of the three Governments, I have written to the President that I have decided to bring about this meeting as soon as possible, that the time of the meeting suggested by the President — November, December — seems acceptable to me, but that the meeting-place should be selected in a country where all three states have their representatives — for example, in Persia. I made only one reservation — i.e., that the exact moment of the meeting should be fixed in the light of the situation on the Soviet-German Front, where more than five hundred divisions [1] on both sides are involved in the struggle. This necessitates practically everyday control on the part of the High Command of the U.S.S.R.

On September 10, I answered Premier Stalin's proposal.

Prime Minister to Premier Stalin   10 Sept. 43

With regard to the meeting of Foreign Office representatives, we defer to your wishes that Moscow should be the scene. Accordingly, our Foreign Secretary, Mr. Eden, will proceed thither at an early date in October. He will be attended by a suitable staff.

Agenda. His Majesty's Government declares itself willing to discuss any and every subject with its Russian and United States

[1] A Soviet division was equivalent to about a third or a quarter of a British or United States Division.

Allies. We will in a few days furnish you with our ideas. But we should particularly like to know what are the main points you have in mind.

This meeting of Foreign Office representatives seems to me a most important and necessary preliminary to the meeting of the three heads of Governments. I am pleased and relieved to feel that there is a good prospect of this taking place between November 15 and December 15. I have for months past informed you that I will come anywhere, at any time, at any risk, for such a meeting. I am therefore prepared to go to Teheran unless you can think of a better place in Persia. I should have preferred Cyprus or Khartoum, but I defer to your wishes. Marshal Stalin, I wish to tell you that on this meeting of the three of us, so greatly desired by all the United Nations, may depend not only the best and shortest method of finishing the war, but also those good arrangements for the future of the world which will enable the British, American, and Russian nations to render a lasting service to humanity.

*   *   *   *   *

Later, after my return from Quebec to London, I drafted for my colleagues a note upon the general points to be considered at the forthcoming Conference of Foreign Ministers, which had now been arranged.

NOTES BY THE PRIME MINISTER FOR FOREIGN SECRETARY AT THE FORTHCOMING MEETING

11 Oct. 43

Great Britain seeks no territory or special advantage for herself as the outcome of the war, which she entered in pursuance of her obligations and in defence of public law.

2. We hold strongly to a system of a League of Nations, *which will include a Council of Europe, with an International Court and an armed power capable of enforcing its decisions.*[2] During the Armistice period, which may be prolonged, we hold that the three Great Powers, the British Commonwealth and Empire, the United States, and the Union of Soviet Socialist Republics, with the addition of China, should remain united, well armed, and capable of

2 Author's subsequent italics.

enforcing the Armistice terms and of building up the permanent structure of peace throughout the globe.

3. We consider that states and nations that have been subjugated by Nazi or Fascist violence during the war should emerge at the Peace Conference with their full sovereign rights, and that all questions of final territorial transference must be settled at the peace table, due regard being paid to the interests of the populations affected.

4. We reaffirm the principles of the Atlantic Charter, noting that Russia's accession thereto is based upon the frontiers of June 22, 1941. We also take note of the historic frontiers of Russia before the two wars of aggression waged by Germany in 1914 and 1939.

5. We should welcome any agreement between Poland and Russia which, while securing a strong and independent Poland, afforded to Russia the security necessary for her western frontier.

6. We are resolved that Nazism and Fascism shall be extirpated in the aggressor countries where they have taken root, and that democratic Governments based upon the free expression of the people's will, obtained under conditions of reasonable tranquillity, shall be set up. This should not exclude measures of military diplomacy or relations with interim Governments which may come into being, so that our main objects may be achieved with the minimum of slaughter, especially to the forces of the Allies.

7. We repudiate all territorial expansion achieved by Germany or Italy during the Nazi or Fascist régimes, and further we consider that the future structure of Germany and the position of Prussia as a unit of the German State should be subject to an agreed policy among the three Great Powers of the West.

8. We are resolved to take all measures necessary to prevent the guilty Powers from becoming an armed menace to the peace of Europe, not only by disarmament, but by prolonged control of every form of warlike apparatus or organisation within their bounds.

9. We have no desire to keep any branch of the European family of nations in a condition of subjection or restriction, except as may be required by the general needs and safety of the world.

10. We proclaim our inflexible resolve to use the authority which victory will confer upon the three Great Powers in order to serve the general good and the cause of human progress.

*   *   *   *   *

The conference of the three Foreign Ministers in Moscow now played an invaluable part in our complicated affairs. The President had hoped Mr. Hull, at his advanced age, could be spared the full journey to Moscow, and had asked for a rendezvous in London, but Stalin had refused this change. Mr. Hull however would not be deterred. It was a gallant enterprise for this veteran in his frail health to undertake this, his first journey by air.

Before the Conference met in Moscow, there had been a considerable interchange of telegrams between the three Foreign Secretaries about the agenda. The Americans put forward four suggestions, including a four-Power declaration, upon the treatment of Germany and other enemy countries in Europe during the Armistice period, and so forth. We, for our part, put forward no less than twelve suggestions, including a common policy towards Turkey, a common policy in Persia, relations between the U.S.S.R. and Poland, and policy in relation to Poland generally. The Russians made one suggestion, and one suggestion only — "the consideration of measures to shorten the duration of the war against Germany and her allies in Europe." Although this was obviously a military rather than a political question, it was clear from the outset that they were not prepared to discuss anything else until it had been fully thrashed out. It was therefore thought advisable to include General Ismay in our delegation.

*   *   *   *   *

The first formal meeting of the Conference took place on the afternoon of October 19. M. Molotov, after a show of resistance, such as is put up by the Speaker of the House of Commons when he is escorted to the chair, was elected chairman, to the obvious satisfaction of himself and his delegation. The agenda was then settled. These preliminaries concluded, Molotov handed round the following note of Soviet proposals:

That the Governments of Great Britain and the United States take in 1943 such urgent measures as will ensure the invasion of

Northern France by Anglo-American armies, and, coupled with powerful blows of Soviet troops on the main German forces on the Soviet-German Front, will radically undermine the military-strategical situation of Germany and bring about a decisive shortening of the duration of the war.

In this connection the Soviet Government deem it necessary to ascertain whether the statement made in early June 1943 by Mr. Churchill and Mr. Roosevelt, to the effect that Anglo-American forces will undertake the invasion of Northern France in the spring of 1944, remains valid.

2. That the three Powers suggest to the Turkish Government that Turkey should immediately enter the war.

3. That the three Powers suggest to Sweden to place at the disposal of the Allies air bases for the struggle against Germany.

Molotov asked whether Mr. Hull and Mr. Eden would be prepared to discuss these proposals in a closely restricted meeting, after they had had time to study them. This was readily agreed.

Mr. Eden sent me an account of what had passed, and I sent him my views at once.

Prime Minister to Mr. Eden (Moscow)   **20 Oct. 43**

Our present plans for 1944 seem open to very grave defects. We are to put fifteen American and twelve British divisions into France in May, and will have about six American and sixteen British or British-controlled divisions on the Italian Front. Unless there is a German collapse, Hitler, lying in the centre of the best communications in the world, can concentrate at least forty to fifty divisions against either of these forces while holding the other. He could obtain all the necessary forces by cutting his losses in the Balkans and withdrawing to the Save and the Danube without necessarily weakening his Russian Front. This is one of the most elementary war propositions. The disposition of our forces between the Italian and the Channel theatres has not been settled by strategic needs, but by the march of events, by shipping possibilities, and by arbitrary compromises between the British and Americans. Neither the force built up in Italy nor that which will be ready in May to cross the Channel is adequate for what is

required, and only transferences of the order of seven or eight
divisions can physically be made between them. I am determined
that this situation shall be reviewed.

2. If it lay with me to decide, I would not withdraw any troops
from the Mediterranean and would not debouch from the narrow
leg of Italy into the valley of the Po, and would engage the enemy
strongly on the narrower front while at the same time fomenting
Balkan and Southern France disturbances. In the absence of a
German collapse, I do not think we should cross the Channel with
less than forty divisions available by the sixtieth day, and then
only if the Italian Front were in strong action with the enemy. I
do not accept the American argument that our Metropolitan Air
Forces can flatten everything out in the battle zone or on its
approaches. This has not been our present experience. All this is
for your internal consumption, and not for deployment at this
stage. It may show you however the dangers of our being committed to a lawyer's bargain for "Overlord" in May, for the sake
of which we may have to ruin the Italian Front and Balkan possibilities and yet have insufficient forces to maintain ourselves after
the thirtieth or fortieth day.

3. You should try to find out what the Russians really feel about
the Balkans. Would they be attracted by the idea of our acting
through the Aegean, involving Turkey in the war, and opening
the Dardanelles and Bosphorus so that British naval forces and
shipping could aid the Russian advance and so that we could
ultimately give them our right hand along the Danube? How great
an interest would they feel in our opening the Black Sea to Allied
warships, supplies, and Allied military forces, including Turkish?
Have they any interest in this right-handed evolution, or are they
still set only on our attacking France? — observing that of course
in any circumstances the steady building-up of forces in England
will hold large German forces in the West. It may be that for
political reasons the Russians would not want us to develop a large-
scale Balkan strategy. On the other hand, their desire that Turkey
should enter the war shows their interest in the Southeastern
theatre.

4. I remain convinced of the great importance of our getting a
foothold in the Aegean by taking Rhodes, retaking Cos, and holding Leros, and building up an effective air and naval superiority
in these waters. Do the Russians view with sympathy our effort

to hold Leros and desire to take Rhodes? Do they understand the effect this has upon Turkey, and how it opens the possibility of a naval advance into the Black Sea? Again, all the above is simply for your inner thoughts.

*   *   *   *   *

On October 21, there was a session in Moscow to consider the Soviet proposals. Mr. Eden, Ambassador Sir Archibald Clark Kerr, Mr. Strang, and General Ismay represented the British; Mr. Hull, Ambassador Harriman, and Major-General Deane the Americans; Monsieur Molotov, Marshal Voroshilov, Monsieur Vyshinsky, and Monsieur Litvinov the Russians. Ismay opened the meeting by a statement on behalf of both the British and American delegations, based on the Quebec decisions, in the course of which he emphasised the limiting conditions which governed the launching of the Cross-Channel invasion.

In the discussion that followed, our representatives made it absolutely clear that there had in fact been no change of plan on our part and that we intended to go ahead, provided the conditions which we had laid down could be fulfilled. With this the Russians seemed content for the moment. Molotov said that the Soviet Government would study Ismay's statement in detail, and would wish to have a further discussion on it later in the Conference.

Mr. Eden then turned to the question of Turkey, and pointed out that we could not at present give the necessary effective support. The question of a joint approach to Turkey was deferred until later. The Russian proposal about Sweden was also mentioned. Sweden would clearly demand guarantees about Finland, a matter which the Russians were reluctant to discuss.

*   *   *   *   *

In the evening, Eden called upon Stalin and for over two hours discussed a large variety of topics. First in importance, as we have seen, was the question of the Arctic convoys. The conversation then turned to the proposed meeting of the three heads of the Allied Governments. Stalin was insistent that this should take place at Teheran.

On the whole, the conversation seemed to go well.

*   *   *   *   *

Mr. Eden had now received my telegram of October 20, and sent his comments. He said that the Russians were completely and blindly set on our invasion of Northern France. It was the one decision in which they took an absorbing interest. They asked again and again whether there had been any change in the understanding given to Stalin by the President and myself after the Washington Conference in May, that we would invade in the early spring of 1944, and when would the operation start.

On the first point he had assured them that there had been no change, but had emphasised the three conditions [3] which must be present to allow the expedition to be launched with any chance of success. On the second point it was thought better not to give the actual date, but Mr. Eden assured them that all preparations were going forward to attack in the spring after the weather became favourable.

I replied by return:

Prime Minister to Foreign Secretary (Moscow)   23 Oct. 43

If we force Turkey to enter the war, she will insist on air support, etc., which could not be provided without detriment to our main operations in Italy. If however Turkey enters on her own initiative, perhaps moving through a phase of non-belligerency, we should not have the same obligation, and yet great advantages might be reaped. Obviously timing is vital, and dependent upon what is the aggressive strength of the enemy in Bulgaria and Thrace. *The prize would be to get into the Black Sea with supplies for Russia, warships, and other forces. This is what I call "giving Russia the right hand."* [4] Such a movement by Turkey is not impossible, especially if the Germans should begin to cut their

3 See Chapter 4, page 114.
4 Author's subsequent italics.

losses in the Balkans and withdraw towards the Danube and the Save.

2. *Finland and Sweden.* It would be a great advantage to bring Sweden into the war. We do not think the Germans have the strength to undertake a heavy invasion of Sweden. We should gain a new country and a small but good army. Our gains in Norway would be far-reaching. Valuable facilities would be afforded to Russian air forces. For ourselves, we can do far better bombing of Germany from East Anglia, where we are mounted on a vast scale, than from Sweden, where everything would have to be improvised and imported by air. Our range from England over Germany is just as good as from Sweden. In fact, with present British facilities plus those we hope to acquire north of Rome, there is no part of Germany we cannot reach with great weight.

3. Personally I would like to see Turkey come in on her own, and also Sweden. I do not think either of them would be overrun, and every new enemy helps Hitler's ruin. I suggest however that the first step is to find out what we and the Russians want and what will help both of us most in both quarters, and then as a second step go into ways and means immediately thereafter. Try this and let me know.

And two days later, I added:

Prime Minister to Foreign Secretary   25 Oct. 43

Further reflection confirms my view that we should not discourage the Russian desire that Turkey and Sweden should of their own volition become co-belligerents or actual allies. The Russians should not be put in the position of arguing for this and we of simply making difficulties. We should agree in principle and let the difficulties manifest themselves, as they will certainly do, in the discussion of ways and means. They may well be overcome or put in their proper place and proportion. Anyhow, we ought not to begin by crabbing everything.

*   *   *   *   *

The serious telegram, recorded in an earlier chapter, from General Eisenhower reporting General Alexander's appreciation of the battle in Italy, had now reached me.[5] I repeated it to Eden and asked him to show it to Stalin. I added:

[5] See Chapter 14, pages 243–47.

Prime Minister to Foreign Secretary   26 Oct. 43

The reason why we are getting into this jeopardy is because we are moving some of our best divisions and a large proportion of vital landing-craft from the Mediterranean in order to build up for "Overlord," seven months hence. This is what happens when battles are governed by lawyers' agreements made in all good faith months before, and persisted in without regard to the ever-changing fortunes of war. You should let him know, if you think fit, that I will not allow, while I am responsible, the great and fruitful campaign in Italy, which has already drawn heavy German reserves into action, to be cast away and end in a frightful disaster, for the sake of crossing the Channel ["Overlord"] in May. The battle must be nourished and fought out until it is won. We will do our very best for "Overlord," but it is no use planning for defeat in the field in order to give temporary political satisfaction.

2. It will therefore be necessary for you to make it clear that the assurances you have given about May "Overlord," subject to the specified conditions, must be modified by the exigencies of the battle in Italy. I am taking the matter up with President Roosevelt, but nothing will alter my determination not to throw away the battle in Italy at this juncture, so far as the King's armies are concerned. Eisenhower and Alexander must have what they need to win the battle, no matter what effect is produced on subsequent operations. This may certainly affect the date of "Overlord."

I concluded my comments on this subject three days later:

Prime Minister to Mr. Eden (*Moscow*)   29 Oct. 43

There is of course no question of abandoning "Overlord," which will remain our principal operation for 1944. The retention of landing-craft in the Mediterranean in order not to lose the Battle of Rome may cause a slight delay, perhaps till July, as the smaller class of landing-craft cannot cross the Bay of Biscay in the winter months and would have to make the passage in the spring. The delay would however mean that the blow when struck would be with somewhat heavier forces, and also that the full bombing effort on Germany would not be damped down so soon. We are also ready at any time to push across and profit by a German collapse. These arguments may be of use to you in discussion.

*   *   *   *   *

In the evening our Ambassador and Ismay accompanied Mr. Eden to the Kremlin. Molotov was with Stalin. Eden opened the proceedings by handing Stalin the Russian text of Eisenhower's telegram about the situation in Italy. Stalin read it aloud to Molotov. When he had finished, he showed no trace of disappointment, but said that according to Russian Intelligence there were twelve Anglo-American divisions fighting six German divisions south of Rome, and that there were a further six German divisions on the river Po. He admitted however that General Alexander was likely to have the better information. Mr. Eden said I was anxious that Stalin should have the latest account of the situation in Italy, and should know not only that I was anxious about it, but also that I was insistent that the battle in Italy should be nourished and fought out to victory whatever the implications on "Overlord." He added that the vitally important decisions now confronting the Allies made it all the more necessary that the three heads of Governments should meet as soon as possible.

Stalin observed with a smile that if there were not enough divisions a meeting of the heads of Governments could not create them. He then asked point-blank whether the telegram which he had just read meant a postponement of "Overlord." Eden replied that until it had been fully examined by the Combined Chiefs of Staff and decisions made about improving the position, it was impossible to say, but the possibility must be faced. He quoted the passage in my telegram, that we were determined to "do our very best for 'Overlord,'" but that it was "no use planning for defeat in the field in order to give temporary political satisfaction." There were two difficulties: first, landing-craft, and, secondly, moving seven battle-tried divisions to the United Kingdom at the beginning of November for the spearhead of the "Overlord" assault. Perhaps the moving of some or all of them would now have to be postponed, but whether or not this would affect the date of "Overlord," and if so to what extent, it was impossible to say.

Stalin then turned to questions of general strategy. As he saw it, there were two courses open to us: to take up a defen-

sive position north of Rome and use all the rest of our forces
for "Overlord," or to push through Italy into Germany.

Mr. Eden said that the first alternative was what we had in
mind. There was no intention, so far as he knew, to go beyond
the Pisa-Rimini line. This would give us depth north of Rome
and air bases for bombing Southern Germany. Stalin clearly
thought we were right, and said that it would be very difficult
to get through the Alps, and that it would suit the Germans
well to fight us there. After the capture of Rome, British prestige would certainly be high enough to permit us to pass over
to the defensive in Italy.

The discussion then turned to the other point of attack.
Mr. Eden said that we might be able to stage a diversionary
attack against Southern France synchronising with "Overlord." If we could secure a bridgehead with a couple of divisions it might be possible to use the French divisions which
were trained and equipped in North Africa. Stalin thought
that this was a good idea, since the more we made Hitler
disperse the better. These were the tactics he was employing
on the Russian Front. But would there be enough landing-
craft?

He then put the question, "Will the postponement of
'Overlord' be one month or two months?" Mr. Eden said
that he could not possibly give an answer. All that he could
state definitely was that we would do our very best to launch
"Overlord" at the earliest possible moment at which it had a
reasonable prospect of success, and that it was most desirable
that the three heads of Governments should meet as soon as
possible. Stalin entirely agreed, but said that there was some
hesitation on the part of the President about going to Teheran.
When Eden suggested Habbaniya, both he and Molotov firmly
refused. Stalin said that he himself could not go far away so
long as there was an opportunity of continuing to damage
Hitler's armies. The Germans had recently moved some tank
divisions from France and Belgium to the Soviet Front, but
they were short of equipment and raw materials. It was
essential to give Hitler no rest, and he volunteered that the

Soviet armies would not have had the success that they had won if the Germans had been able to move from the West the forty divisions which were pinned there by the mere threat of our invasion. The Soviet fully understood this contribution to the cause.

Mr. Eden said that the Marshal well knew that the Prime Minister was just as keen on hurting Hitler as he was. Stalin fully acknowledged this, but added with a gust of laughter that I had a tendency to take the easy road for myself and leave the difficult jobs to the Russians. Eden refused to agree, and mentioned the difficulties of naval operations and our recent heavy losses in destroyers. Stalin became serious again, and said that his people spoke little about naval operations, but realised how difficult they were.

The whole talk [cabled Mr. Eden] went off surprisingly well. Stalin seemed in excellent humour, and at no point in the evening was there any recrimination about the past or any disposition to ignore real difficulties that face us. This may only have been a first reaction and second thoughts may not be so good, but it is significant that he should have gone out of his way to acknowledge the contribution we were making by merely pinning forty German divisions in the West, and his sympathetic references to the difficulties of naval operations and to the necessity for landing-craft, etc., seemed to show that he no longer regards an overseas operation as a simple matter. It is clear however that he expects us to make every effort to stage "Overlord" at the earliest possible moment, and the confidence he is placing in our word is to me most striking.

There had been many signs during the Conference that the Soviet Government sincerely desired permanent friendship with Britain and the United States. They had met us on a number of points, both large and small, about which we foresaw difficulties. Stalin had shown understanding of our problems, and so far there had been no unsatisfactory afterthoughts.

Molotov [said Mr. Eden] has shown that spirit on many occasions, notably as chairman of our Conference today, when we had our final session on military matters. Though he was obviously disappointed at the outcome of what I had told him and Stalin last night, and at our failure wholly to endorse in a manner satisfactory to him Soviet proposals about Turkey and Sweden, he conducted our business with an evident desire to avoid embarrassment to either country. As an indication of good will I received a message from him tonight that our two imprisoned sailors had been pardoned.

Russian representatives have given many other signs of an intention to open a new chapter. Your gesture in respect of convoys has made a deep impression. For the first time for many years Molotov and a number of his colleagues came to dinner at this Embassy tonight. Mikoyan, whose task it is to keep these people informed, was especially eloquent in his tributes to your personal share in the sailing of these convoys.

In this atmosphere I would give much to be able to close the Conference with some tangible evidence of our good will. I am quite sure that if I could give them some encouraging message about their desire to have a small share of the Italian Fleet the psychological effect would be out of all proportion to the value of the ships, whatever that may be. The Ambassador and Harriman fully endorse this view. If it is impossible to give a specific reply before I leave it will be greatest help to me if I can at least tell Monsieur Molotov that in principle we agree that the Soviet Government shall have a share of the captured Italian ships and that the proportion for which they ask is reasonable. Details can be worked out subsequently, including dates of delivery. If you can do this to help me, I feel sure that the return will more than justify your gesture. I beg your aid.

On October 29, I sent him the Cabinet view about the Italian Fleet.

Prime Minister to Foreign Secretary   29 Oct. 43

. . . In principle we willingly admit the Russians' right to a share in the Italian Fleet. We had however thought that this fleet would play its part against Japan, and we had been planning to tropicalise the *Littorios* and some other units for this later phase of the war. If Russia would like to have a squadron in being in the Pacific, that would be a very considerable event, and we should like to discuss this project when we meet. . . .

5. At present the only place where Italian ships could be handed over to the Russians would be Archangel and Murmansk. The Italian warships are quite unsuited for working in Arctic waters, and would need several months of dockyard work first. We should also have to be careful lest the immediate transfer to the Russians would have an ill-effect on Italian co-operation. It is important for Italy to have her flag on the sea against Germany. We do not want to provoke a refusal by the Italians to carry on the important work they are doing for us in Taranto dockyard. One cannot be absolutely sure that they would not scuttle some of the ships they brought out from the German clutches if they thought they were to be handed over to foreign crews. They are doing a good deal for us at the present time. Italian submarines are carrying supplies to Leros. Italian destroyers, of which there are only seven good ones, are escorting local convoys. Their cruisers are transporting troops and supplies. We should therefore in any case have to ensure against publicity until we could take steps to counter these ill-effects. Once distribution of the Italian Fleet begins, the French, the Yugoslavs, and the Greeks would put in their claims, which are pretty good.

6. For all these reasons it would be better to put off this question till "Eureka" [Teheran].

7. It is quite true that we have gained some Italian merchant tonnage, but the amount is actually less than what we have to provide for the minimum requirements of conquered and Italian territory, so that we are actually down on the balance, especially as most of these Italian ships are not fit for anything more than local traffic.

8. Has Mr. Hull referred this request to his Government? It would be essential that we should be agreed. I should like best of all to talk over all this at "Eureka," if that ever comes off.

And later the same day:

Provided the Americans agree, you may tell Molotov that in principle we agree that the Soviet Government shall have a share of the captured Italian ships and that the proportion for which they ask is reasonable. I am presuming the battleship for which they ask is not a *Littorio*. Details and dates of delivery must be settled with regard to operations and not losing Italian aid by precipitate publicity. This is very important. Of course, we are looking forward to using the very newest vessels of this fleet in the war against Japan, and the Russians will surely understand that we ought not to prejudice that. We also feel we [the British] ought to have the two *Littorios* after the war, first, because of the overwhelming share we have had in the whole war against Italy, secondly, because of our heavy naval losses in capital units, and, thirdly, because we have suspended the long-term building of battleships already sanctioned by Parliament in order to concentrate on the current needs of the war.

2. Most especially secret and for your own thought and perhaps fly-throwing: If it were decided that on the defeat of Hitler Russia would play her part against Japan, a great design might come into being, as a part of which the fitting out under the Soviet flag and manning with Russian sailors of a substantial naval force at some Pacific base in our possession and the participation of this force of surface ships in the final phase of the war might come into view. However, I hope that the consent I have sent you in the first lines of this telegram will meet your difficulties.

*　　*　　*　　*　　*

I had drafted a proposed declaration on German war criminals as a basis of discussion at the forthcoming meeting of the three heads of Governments.

12 Oct. 43

Prime Minister to President Roosevelt and Premier Stalin

Would you very kindly consider whether something like the following might not be issued over our three signatures:

Great Britain, the United States, and the Soviet Union [in whatever order is thought convenient, we being quite ready to be last] have received from many quarters evidence of the atrocities, massacres, and cold-blooded mass-executions which are being perpetrated by the Hitlerite forces in the many countries they have overrun and from which they are now being steadily expelled. The brutalities of the Nazi domination are no new thing, and all peoples or territories in their grip have suffered from the worst forms of government by terror. What is new is that many of these territories are now being redeemed by the advancing armies of the liberating Powers, and that in their desperation the recoiling Hitlerites and Huns are redoubling their ruthless cruelties.

Accordingly the aforesaid three Allied Powers, speaking in the interest of the thirty-two United Nations, hereby solemnly declare, and give full warning of their declaration, as follows:

At the time of the granting of any armistice to any Government which may be set up in Germany those German officers and men and members of the Nazi Party who have been responsible for or have taken a consenting part in the above atrocities, massacres, and executions will be sent back to the countries in which their abominable deeds were done, in order that they may be judged and punished according to the laws of these liberated countries and the free Governments which will be erected therein. Lists will be compiled in all possible detail from all these countries, having regard especially to the invaded parts of Russia, to Poland and Czechoslovakia, to Yugoslavia, Greece, including Crete and other islands, to Norway, Denmark, the Netherlands, Belgium, Luxemburg, France, and Italy. Thus Germans who take part in the wholesale shootings of Italian officers or in the execution of French, Dutch, Belgian, or Norwegian hostages, or of Cretan peasants, or who have shared in the slaughters inflicted on the people of Poland or in the territories of the Soviet Republic, which are now being swept clear of the enemy, will know that they will be brought back, regardless of expense, to the scene of their crimes and judged on the spot by the peoples whom they have outraged. Let those who have hitherto not imbrued their hands with innocent blood beware lest they join the ranks of the guilty, for most assuredly the three Allied Powers will pursue them to the uttermost ends of the earth, and will deliver them to their accusers in order that justice may be done.

The above declaration is without prejudice to the case of the major criminals, whose offenses have no particular geographical localisation.

ROOSEVELT
STALIN
CHURCHILL

If this, or something like this (and I am not particular about the wording), were put over our three signatures, it would, I believe, make some of these villains shy of being mixed up in butcheries now that they know they are going to be beaten. We know, for instance, that our threats of reprisals about Poland have brought about a mitigation of the severities being inflicted on the people there. There is no doubt that the use of the terror-weapon by the enemy imposes an additional burden on our armies. Lots of Germans may develop moral scruples if they know they are going to be brought back and judged in the country, and perhaps the very place, where their cruel deeds were done. I strongly commend to you the principle of the localisation of judgment as likely to exert a deterrent effect on enemy terrorism. The British Cabinet endorses this principle and policy.

This was accepted and endorsed, with a few verbal changes.

*　　*　　*　　*　　*

The three Foreign Ministers had met regularly every day, and covered an immense amount of ground. Their agreements were recorded in a secret protocol, drawn up on November 3. The importance of these lay in the additional machinery of co-operation which was now to be set up. It was agreed to establish a European Advisory Committee in London to begin work on the problems which would arise in Germany and on the Continent when the Hitler régime neared collapse. It was this body which drew up the initial plans for dividing Germany into zones of occupation, an arrangement which caused grave problems later. Of this more in due course. For Italian affairs another Advisory Council was to be constituted, to include a Russian representative. There was to be an exchange of information on any peace feelers put out by the Axis satellites. The Americans were anxious that a Four-Power Declaration, to include China, pledging themselves to a united conduct of the war "against those Axis Powers with which they are respectively at war," should be signed at this Moscow meeting. This was achieved on October 30. Finally, a protocol agreeing on joint action between Russia and Great Britain in regard to Turkey was drafted by Mr. Eden and signed on November 2.

We had every reason to be content with these results. There

had been a smoothing of many points of friction, practical steps for further co-operation had been taken, the way had been prepared for an early meeting of the heads of the three major Allied Governments, and the mounting deadlock in our working with the Soviet Union had in part been removed.

Those who took part in the Conference sensed a far more friendly atmosphere, both on and off duty, than had ever existed before. One of the best-known Russian painters was commissioned by his Government to do a conversation piece of the Conference, and he had made preliminary sketches of various members of the British and American delegations. It is not known whether the picture was ever completed, but it has not yet seen the light of day.

17

Advent of the Triple Meeting

The High Commands

Urgency of Choosing a Commander for "Overlord" — We Favour the Choice of Marshall — Speculation in the American Press — My Correspondence with President Roosevelt, October 1 and 5 — The President's Delay in Deciding — His Desire For a Supreme Commander to Control Both Western Theatres — My Telegram to Field Marshal Dill of November 8 — Need to Arrange for a Meeting of the Three Powers — My Telegram to Stalin of September 25, and His Reply, October 3 — Difficulties of Agreement upon a Suitable Place — Roosevelt's Suggestions — Stalin Will Come Only to Teheran — Roosevelt's Disappointment — Constitutional Difficulties Invoked — I Seek a Preliminary Anglo-American Discussion — My Telegram to the President of October 23 — His Proposal to Invite Generalissimo Chiang Kai-shek — His Suggestion of Including the Russians in the Preliminary Meeting — I Argue Against This — Agreement for a Meeting — Proposals for a Rendezvous at Cairo — Or at Oran — The Russians Decline to Confer with the Chinese Government at This Stage — A Great Relief to Me — The President Agrees to Meet at Teheran after Cairo.

THE SELECTION OF A SUPREME COMMANDER for "Overlord," our cross-Channel entry into Europe in 1944, was urgent. This of course affected in the most direct manner the military conduct of the war, and raised a number of personal issues of importance and delicacy. At the Quebec Conference I had agreed with the President that "Overlord" should fall to an American officer, and had so informed General Brooke, to

whom I had previously offered the task. I understood from
the President that he would choose General Marshall, and this
was entirely satisfactory to us. However, in the interval between Quebec and our meeting in Cairo I became conscious
that the President had not finally made up his mind about
Marshall. None of the other arrangements could of course be
made before the main decision had been taken. Meanwhile,
rumour became rife in the American press and there was the
prospect of Parliamentary reactions in London. Admiral Leahy
in his book [1] mentions some of the American cross-currents.

The public [he writes] assumed that Roosevelt would name Marshall as Supreme Commander. There was vehement objection to
such a move in the press. Opponents charged that Marshall was
being given "Dutch promotion"; that Roosevelt planned to take
him out of a big job and put him into a small job; that it was a
plot against Marshall. At the other extreme there were reports that
the American Joint Chiefs considered the post of Supreme Command promotion, and were jealous of Marshall.

This question was discussed between us at some length. I
was anxious to emphasise the status of General Marshall in
every way, provided that the authority of the Joint and Combined Chiefs of Staff was not impaired. I cabled Hopkins in
this sense at the end of September.

Prime Minister to Mr. Harry Hopkins   26 Sept. 43
There is a lot of talk in the papers about Marshall becoming
Supreme Commander-in-Chief over all the forces in the West.
What I understood from our talks was that he would command the
Operation "Overlord." He would not however be only a theatre
commander. He might have the same sort of general outlook with
us on the whole war against Germany, in addition to his specific
command, as Dill has on the Combined Chiefs of Staff Committee
in Washington over the whole field. We should be very glad for
him to sit with our Chiefs of Staff frequently, and to have the
whole scene laid before him. But I made it clear that our Chiefs
of Staff would more often have to sit together to consider our posi-

[1] *I Was There* (Gollancz), page 227.

tion from the British point of view, just as your Chiefs of Staff sit together in Washington. It would not fall to him to give decisions outside the sphere of "Overlord." The control of all our combined operations and world strategy must rest with the Combined Chiefs of Staff in Washington under the final direction of the Heads of Governments. Please let me know whether there is anything wrong with this.

A few days later, I addressed myself to the President.

Former Naval Person to President Roosevelt   1 Oct. 43

I am somewhat worried by the way in which our great changes in the High Commands are being broken to the public. So far nothing has been said here, but almost every day some statement is made in the United States about Marshall, and I shall certainly be asked questions when Parliament meets on Tuesday, the 12th. Moreover, it would be difficult for me if Marshall's appointment to the Chief Command in Britain were to be announced apart from Alexander's succession in the Mediterranean. Rumour runs riot, and is fed by carefully balanced and guarded statements, such as that made by Stimson reported in today's papers. An impression of mystery and of something to be concealed is given. This is a fine field for malicious people. All this would be blown away by publication of the clear-cut decisions to which we have come. In all the circumstances I hope you will see your way to a simultaneous announcement by us both of the changes, coupled with a statement that they will be brought into effect as soon as convenient to the military situation.

2. Will you also consider my difficulties in the consequential appointments. For instance, I understood that Marshall would like Montgomery for Deputy, or, alternatively, to command under him the British expeditionary armies in "Overlord." This would entail my clearing the Home Command here, now held by General Paget. An opportunity is now open for this, as General Pownall, who was formerly Commander-in-Chief Iraq and Persia, goes with Mountbatten to India as Chief of Staff, and I can post Paget to Iraq and Persia. It is difficult and also harmful to leave these commands vacant for long.

3. Some of the United States papers seem to have begun attacking Mountbatten bitterly, and he has been affected by accounts

telegraphed here describing him as "the British princeling and glamour boy who has ousted the proved veteran MacArthur from his rightful sphere," or words to that effect. The prominence given to the Indian Front Command by these controversies is of course leading the Japanese to reinforce in that quarter, and intelligence to this effect has already been received. We are told that a large number of correspondents are proceeding or trying to proceed from the United States to Delhi, and that expectation is rife of an early beginning of the campaign. On the other hand, the floods and the monsoon rains will of course prevent any decisive action till the New Year. But this cannot be stated publicly without relieving any anxieties of the Japanese. The prospects of having a formidable band of correspondents champing their bits in Delhi is not a pleasant one, and it would help our fighting chances if everything possible could be done to damp down controversy and publicity in this area.

4. In these circumstances a plain statement of what we have settled for all theatres, including Commanders, their Chiefs of Staff, and one or two of the principal officers, all brought out together, would in my opinion be a great advantage. I could, if you desire, draft such a statement and submit it to you.

The President replied:

President Roosevelt to Prime Minister   5 Oct. 43

The newspapers here, beginning with the Hearst-McCormick crowd, had a field day over General Marshall's duties. The drums were beaten rather loudly by the rest of the press for a few days, but it is pretty much of a dead cat now. It seems to me that if we are forced into making public statements about our military commands we will find ourselves with the newspapers running the war. I therefore hope that nothing will be said about the business until it is actually accomplished. It may be that the situation, other than newspaper criticism by our political enemies, will warrant a joint announcement sooner than I have anticipated, but at the moment I earnestly urge that we say nothing. I agree with you that at the appropriate time we must make an over-all statement relative to commands, and I fully appreciate your position at home, but I do not think that the difficulties about secondary commands throughout the world are adequate reasons for making the major announcement in regard to Marshall.

I will do what I can about Mountbatten, because I realise that some of our press have been treating him very badly, although, on the whole, he has come out of it very well. Certainly American public opinion thoroughly approves of his appointment. I agree with you that we should not permit any undue optimism about this [Burma] campaign either at home or abroad. Nevertheless, there is a very proper feeling that Mountbatten will prosecute vigorously anything he is assigned to do.

I hope very much that you will agree that statement about Marshall need not be made at present.

I found the delay in the American decision embarrassing, and on October 17, I cabled to the President:

Former Naval Person to President Roosevelt   17 Oct. 43

It seems to me that it is becoming very necessary to have a decision about the High Commands. Unless there is a German collapse, the campaign of 1944 will be far the most dangerous we have undertaken, and personally I am more anxious about its success than I was about 1941, 1942, or 1943.

Nearly a fortnight passed before I received an answer, and then it was indeterminate.

President Roosevelt to Prime Minister   30 Oct. 43

Preparations for "Overlord" seem to have reached a stage from which progress is difficult unless and until the Commander is appointed. As you know, I cannot make Marshall available immediately. I am none the less anxious that preparations proceed on schedule agreed at "Quadrant," with target date May 1. I suggest you may care to consider the early appointment of British Deputy Supreme Commander for "Overlord," who, in receipt of precisely the same measure of support as will eventually be accorded to Marshall, could well carry the work forward. If I may make proposal, I suggest appointment of Dill, Portal, or Brooke.

*   *   *   *   *

By the beginning of November, we became aware that the President himself and his advisers desired that the Supreme Commander of "Overlord" should also command the Mediterranean, and that the President's idea was that Marshall should command both theatres, and play them in one with another. I presumed that this would be from a headquarters at Gibraltar. I thought it necessary to make the British position clear without delay. As the matter was not suited at this stage for a direct interchange between me and the President, I thought it better to tell Field-Marshal Sir John Dill to talk about it to Admiral Leahy, the Chairman of the American Chiefs of Staff Committee at Washington.

Prime Minister to Field-Marshal Dill (Washington)   8 Nov. 43

You should leave Admiral Leahy in no doubt that we should never be able to agree to the proposal of putting the "Overlord" and Mediterranean Commands under an American Commander-in-Chief. Such an arrangement would not be conformable to the principle of equal status which must be maintained among the great Allies. I cannot accept a combination of the two Commands under one Commander-in-Chief. This would place him above the Combined Chiefs of Staff, and would also affect the constitutional control of the movements of forces by the President as United States Commander-in-Chief and by the Prime Minister acting on behalf of the War Cabinet. I should certainly never be able to accept responsibility for such an arrangement. Hitherto we have successfully prevented any carping here at the fact that we have been fighting and sustaining casualties in Tunis, Sicily, and Italy on something like a two-and-a-half-to-one basis, although we are serving loyally under a United States General. If I were to attempt to propose anything such as is suggested above there would be an explosion. However, this will not occur while I hold my present office. You may at your discretion impart the above to Mr. Hopkins.

The next day Dill saw Leahy, and made my attitude towards the unification of the "Overlord" and Mediterranean Commands quite clear. Leahy, though personally disappointed, accepted the position, saying, "If that is the opinion of the Prime Minister there is nothing more to be said about it." Dill also saw Hopkins, whom he reported as similarly "disappointed." "At any rate," said Dill, "Hopkins and Leahy know how useless it would be to return to the charge, and I hope they won't."

*   *   *   *   *

I had hardly got home after my visits to the Citadel, the White House, and Hyde Park during the Quebec Conference, already described, when I turned again to the theme of a meeting of the three heads of Governments which logically followed the Anglo-American conversations. In principle there was general agreement that this was urgent and imperative; but no one who did not live through it can measure the worries and complications which attended the fixing of the time, place, and conditions of this, the first conference of what were then called the Big Three. I give a full account here, because the tale is at least a diplomatic curiosity.

I addressed myself first to Stalin, who I knew favoured the idea of a rendezvous at Teheran.

Prime Minister to Premier Stalin   25 Sept. 43

I have been pondering about our meeting of heads of Governments at Teheran. Good arrangements must be made for security in this somewhat loosely controlled area. Accordingly I suggest for your consideration that I make preparations at Cairo in regard to accommodation, security, etc., which are bound to be noticed in spite of all praiseworthy efforts to keep them secret. Then perhaps only two or three days before our meeting we should throw a British and a Russian brigade around a suitable area in Teheran, including the airfield, and keep an absolute cordon till we have finished our talks. . . . Thus we shall have an effective blind for the world Press, and also for any unpleasant people who might not be as fond of us as they ought.

2. I suggest also that we use the expression "Cairo Three" instead of Teheran, which should be buried, and also that the codename for the operation should be "Eureka," which I believe is Ancient Greek. If you have other ideas let me know, and we can then put them to the President. I have not said anything to him about this aspect yet.

Stalin's reply was direct and positive.

Premier Stalin to Premier Churchill   3 Oct. 43

I have no objection to the diversionary preparations which you intend to carry out in Cairo. Regarding your proposal to throw British and Russian brigades into the region of "Cairo Three" several days before our meeting in that city, I find this measure inexpedient, as it would cause an unnecessary sensation and would decamouflage the preparations. I suggest that each of us should take with him a sufficient police guard. In my opinion this would be enough to secure our safety. . . .

In fact, a complete cordon was established and the military and police forces used, especially by the Russians, were numbered by thousands.

*   *   *   *   *

As I could not be sure whether the President would be allowed by his security advisers to go to Teheran, I suggested alternatives. One of these was a desert encampment around the Air Force Training School at Habbaniya, which had made so brilliant a defence in 1941. Here we should have been absolutely by ourselves and in perfect security, and the President would have had no difficulty in flying thither in a few hours from Cairo. I therefore telegraphed this proposal to him.

Former Naval Person to President Roosevelt   14 Oct. 43

I have a new idea about "Eureka," which I have asked Anthony [at that time in Moscow] to try on Uncle Joe for subsequent submission to you if U.J. agrees. There is a place in the Desert which I now call "Cyprus," but whose real name is Habbaniya. This would be a much easier journey for you from Cairo than "Cairo Three," and very little longer for U.J. We could put up three encampments and live comfortably in perfect seclusion and security. I am going into details on the chance of agreement in the trinity. See also, meanwhile, St. Matthew, chapter 17, verse 4.

President Roosevelt to the Prime Minister   15 Oct. 43

I have finally sent the following telegram to Uncle Joe, and I think your idea is an excellent one. St. Peter sometimes had real inspirations. I like the idea of three tabernacles. We can add one later for your old friend Chiang.

"The problem of my going to Teheran is becoming so acute that I feel I should tell you frankly that, for constitutional reasons, I cannot take the risk. The Congress will be in session. New laws and resolutions must be acted on by me after their receipt, and must be returned to the Congress physically before ten days have elapsed. None of this can be done by radio or cable. Teheran is too far to be sure that the requirements are fulfilled. The possibility of delay in getting over the mountains — first east-bound and then west-bound — is insurmountable. We know from experience that planes in either direction are often held up for three or four days. . . .

"In many ways Cairo is attractive, and I understand there is a hotel and some villas out near the Pyramids which could be completely segregated.

"Asmara, the former Italian capital of Eritrea, is said to have excellent buildings, and a landing-field good at all times.

"Then there is the possibility of meeting at some port in the Eastern Mediterranean, each one of us to have a ship. . . . Another suggestion is in the neighborhood of Baghdad. . . .

"In any event, I think the Press should be entirely banished, and the whole place surrounded by a cordon so that we would not be disturbed in any way.

"I am placing a very great importance on the personal and intimate conversations which you and Churchill and I will have, for on them the hope of the future world will greatly depend.

"Your continuing initiative along your whole front heartens all of us."

Prime Minister to President Roosevelt   16 Oct. 43

I entirely agree with the telegram you have sent to Uncle Joe about "Eureka." Let me know what he replies.

Stalin was however adamant on Teheran.

President Roosevelt to Prime Minister   21 Oct. 43

Last night I received the following from U.J.:

" . . . Unfortunately, not one of the places proposed instead of Teheran by you for the meeting is suitable to me. It became clear during the operations of the Soviet forces in the summer and fall of this year that the summer campaign may overgrow into a winter one and that our troops can continue their offensive operations against the German Army. It is considered by all my colleagues that these operations demand my personal contact with the Command and daily guidance on the part of the Supreme Command. Conditions are better in Teheran, because wire telegraph and telephone communications with Moscow exist there. This cannot be said about the other locations. My colleagues insist on Teheran as the place of the meeting for this reason.

"I accept your suggestion of November 20 or 25 as a possible date for the Conference, and I also agree that representatives of the Press should be excluded from the meeting. I hope that a great deal of good will be accomplished by the direct participation in Moscow meeting of Mr. Hull, who has arrived safely in Moscow."

The President had replied:

President Roosevelt to Premier Stalin

I am deeply disappointed in your message received today in regard to our meeting. I fully understand your reason for requiring daily guidance on the part of the Supreme Command, and your personal contact with the command, which is bringing such outstanding results. . . .

I wish you would realise that there are other vital matters which, in this constitutional American Government, represent fixed obligations on my part which I cannot change. Our Constitution calls for action by the President on legislation within ten days of the passage of such legislation. That means that the President must receive and return to the Congress with his written approval or his veto physical documents in that period. I cannot act by cable or radio, as I have told you before. The trouble with Teheran is the simple fact that the approaches to that city over the mountains often make flying an impossibility for several days at a time. This is a double risk — first, for the plane delivering documents from Washington, and, second, for the plane returning these documents to the Congress. I regret to say that, as head of the nation, it is impossible for me to go to a place where I cannot fulfil my constitutional obligations. I can assume the flying risks for docu-

ments up to and including the low country as far as the Persian
Gulf, through a relay system of planes, but I cannot assume the
delays attending flights in both directions into the saucer over the
mountains in which Teheran lies. Therefore, with much regret I
must tell you that I cannot go to Teheran, and in this my Cabinet
members and the legislative leaders are in complete agreement.

The President suggested Basra.

I am not in any way considering the fact that from United
States territory I would have to travel six thousand miles, and you
would only have to travel six hundred miles from Russian territory.
I would gladly go ten times the distance to meet you were it not for
the fact that I must carry on a constitutional Government more
than one hundred and fifty years old. . . . I am begging you to remember that I also have a great obligation to the American Government and to maintain the full American war effort.

As I have said to you before, I regard the meeting of the three
of us as of the greatest possible importance, not only to our peoples
as of today, but also to our peoples in relation to a peaceful world
for generations to come. It would be regarded as a tragedy by
future generations if you and I and Mr. Churchill failed today because of a few hundred miles. . . .

Mr. Eden was still in Moscow, and was doing all he could to
extract from Stalin an agreed place and time of meeting which
would satisfy the President. It was clear that Stalin would insist on Teheran as the place of meeting, and, although it was
yet by no means certain that the President would be induced
to go there, I began to consider the planning of such a meeting.

*   *   *   *   *

Several serious aspects of the impending Conference absorbed my mind. I thought it most important that the British
and American Staffs, and above them the President and I,
should reach a general agreement on the policy of "Overlord"
and its impingement on the Mediterranean. The whole armed
strength overseas of our two countries was involved, and the

British forces were to be equal at the outset of "Overlord," twice as strong as the Americans in Italy, and three times as numerous in the rest of the Mediterranean. Surely we ought to reach some solid understanding before inviting the Soviet representatives, either political or military, to join us.

I therefore suggested such a plan to the President.

President Roosevelt to Prime Minister   22 Oct. 43

. . . There should be sufficient time allowed to analyse the results of the current Moscow Conference, and also I think the subsequent Conference we have in mind. For us to stage a meeting while the Moscow Conference is in progress, or at least before its results can be carefully considered, probably would have unfavourable results in Russia.

2. Combined planning teams are now planning an over-all plan for the defeat of Japan. It is important that this work be completed and that the respective Chiefs of Staff have an opportunity to study it before a general meeting.

3. Certain outline plans from Eisenhower and commanders in the Pacific covering operations approved at Quebec are to be submitted on November 1, and these should receive some consideration before we arrive at the moment for a combined meeting. . . .

The President thus appeared to favour the idea, but not the timing. There was emerging a strong current of opinion in American Government circles, which seemed to wish to win Russian confidence even at the expense of co-ordinating the Anglo-American war effort. I therefore returned to the charge. I felt it of the utmost importance that we should meet the Russians with a clear and united view both on the outstanding problems of "Overlord" and upon the question of the High Commands.

Former Naval Person to President Roosevelt   23 Oct. 43

The Russians ought not to be vexed if the Americans and British closely concert the very great operations they have in hand for 1944 on fronts where no Russian troops will be present. Nor do I think we ought to meet Stalin, if ever the meeting can be arranged, without being agreed about Anglo-American operations as such.

2. I would be content with November 15 if this is the earliest date for your Staffs. I thought the Staffs would work together for a few days before you and I arrive, say 18th or 19th, and we could then go on together to "Eureka." I do not yet know whether it is to be November 20 or 25. I had not imagined that "Eureka" would take more than three or four days or that large technical staffs would take part in it.

3. November 15 would be ninety days from the beginning of our Conference at Quebec. In these ninety days events of first magnitude have occurred. Mussolini has fallen; Italy has surrendered; her Fleet has come over; we have successfully invaded Italy, and are marching on Rome with good prospects of success. The Germans are gathering up to twenty-five or more divisions in Italy and the Po Valley. All these are new facts.

4. . . . The date of "Overlord" itself was fixed by splitting the difference between the American and British views. It is arguable that neither the forces building up in Italy nor those available for a May "Overlord" are strong enough for the tasks set them.

5. The British Staffs and my colleagues and I all think this position requires to be reviewed, and that the commanders for both our fronts should be named and should be present. In pursuance of the Quebec decisions, we have already prepared two of our best divisions, the 50th and the 51st, now in Sicily, for transfer to England. Thus they can play no part in the Italian battle to which they stood so near, but will not come into action again for seven months, and then only if certain hypothetical conditions are fulfilled. Early in November a decision must be taken about moving landing-craft from the Mediterranean to "Overlord." This will cripple Mediterranean operations without the said craft influencing events elsewhere for many months. We stand by what was agreed at Quebec, but we do not feel that such agreement should be interpreted rigidly and without review in the swiftly changing situations of war.

6. Personally I feel that if we make serious mistakes in the campaign of 1944, we might give Hitler the chance of a startling come-back. Prisoner German General von Thoma was overheard saying, "Our only hope is that they come where we can use the Army upon them." All this shows the need for the greatest care

and foresight in our arrangements, the most accurate timing between the two theatres, and the need to gather the greatest possible forces for both operations, particularly "Overlord." I do not doubt our ability in the conditions laid down to get ashore and deploy. I am however deeply concerned with the build-up and with the situation which may arise between the thirtieth and sixtieth days. I feel sure that the vast movement of American personnel into the United Kingdom and the fighting composition of the units requires to be searchingly examined by the commander who will execute "Overlord."

I wish to have both the High Commands settled in a manner agreeable to our two countries, and then the secondary commands, which are of very high importance, can be decided. I repeat I have the greatest confidence in General Marshall, and that if he is in charge of "Overlord," we British will aid him with every scrap of life and strength we have. My dear friend, this is much the greatest thing we have ever attempted, and I am not satisfied that we have yet taken the measures necessary to give it the best chance of success. I feel very much in the dark at present, and unable to think or act in the forward manner which is needed. For these reasons I desire an early conference.

7. All that you say about the plans for Eisenhower and the commanders in the Pacific which are due to be submitted on November 1 would harmonise with a meeting on November 15 at latest. I do not know how long you consider is required for the long-term over-all plan for the defeat of Japan to be completed by the combined planners and studied by our respective Chiefs of Staff. I do not consider that the more urgent decisions to which I have referred above ought to be held up for this long-term view of the war against Japan, which nevertheless should be pressed forward with all energy.

8. I hope you will consider that these reasons for [an Anglo-American] meeting are solid. We cannot decide finally until an answer is received from Uncle Joe. Should the Teheran meeting not be possible, it makes all the more necessary that we should meet in the light of the information now being received from the Moscow Conference [of Foreign Secretaries]. I am expecting Anthony to start home before the end of the month, and am ready myself to move any day after the first week in November.

9. You will, I am sure, share my relief that Leros has so far

managed to hold out. "The dogs eat of the crumbs which fall from
their master's table."

*   *   *   *   *

Before the President replied to this proposal, he sent me the
following message, which showed that he was not yet decided
to accept the idea of going to Teheran:

President Roosevelt to Prime Minister   25 Oct. 43

It is a nuisenza to have the influenza. McIntire says I need a
sea voyage.

No word from Uncle J. yet.

If he is adamant, what would you think of you and me meeting
with small staffs in North Africa, or even at the Pyramids, and
toward the close of our talks getting the Generalissimo [Chiang
Kai-shek] to join us for two or three days? At the same time we
could ask Uncle J. to send Molotov to the meeting with you and
me. Our people propose November 20.

Two days later he sent me his comments on my idea of a
preliminary meeting of the Combined Chiefs of Staff.

President Roosevelt to Prime Minister   27 Oct. 43

The present Moscow Conference appears to be a genuine beginning of British-Russian-United States collaboration, which should
lead to the early defeat of Hitler. . . .

He suggested sending Stalin the following:

Heretofore we have informed you of the results of our combined
British-American military Staff Conferences. You may feel that
it would be better to have a Russian military representative sit in
at such meetings to listen to the discussions regarding British-
American operations and take note of the decisions. He would be
free to make such comments and proposals as you might desire.
This arrangement would afford you and your Staff an intimate
and prompt report of these meetings. . . .

The suggestion of including the Russians in such a meeting
filled me with alarm.

Former Naval Person to President Roosevelt 27 Oct. 43

Like you I rejoice in the good progress made at Moscow, and I greatly hope we may arrange "Eureka."

2. I deprecate the idea of inviting a Russian military representative to sit in at the meetings of our Joint Staffs. Unless he understood and spoke English the delays would be intolerable. I do not know of any really high officer of the Russian Army who can speak English. Such a representative would have no authority or power to speak except as instructed. He would simply bay for an earlier Second Front and block all other discussions. Considering they tell us nothing of their own movements, I do not think we should open this door to them, as it would probably mean that they would want to have observers at all future meetings and all discussions between us would be paralysed. We shall very soon have six or seven hundred thousand British and American troops and airmen in Italy, and we are planning the great operation of "Overlord." There will not be a Russian soldier in any of these. On the other hand, all our fortunes depend upon them.

I regard our right to sit together on the movements of our own two forces as fundamental and vital. Hitherto we have prospered wonderfully, but I now feel that the year 1944 is loaded with danger. Great differences may develop between us and we may take the wrong turning. Or, again, we may make compromises and fall between two stools. The only hope is the intimacy and friendship which has been established between us and between our High Staffs. If that were broken, I should despair of the immediate future. . . . I need scarcely say the British Chiefs of Staff fully share these views. I must add that I am more anxious about the campaign of 1944 than about any other in which I have been involved.

* * * * *

The President was still unsure about going to Teheran, and strong pressure was being brought to bear on him in American political circles and his position under the United States Constitution was invoked. I fully appreciated his difficulties.

Prime Minister to President Roosevelt 30 Oct. 43

I will meet you in Cairo on the 20th as you suggest, and will, if you will allow me, assume responsibility for making all arrangements for your general security and comfort which would fall upon us as the Occupying Power. Casey has been lent a beautiful villa, which I have seen myself, and am sure would be in every way suitable for you. It is a mile or two from the Pyramids, and surrounded by woods affording complete seclusion. It can be reached from the airfield in twenty minutes without going through any towns. The whole area can be easily cordoned off by British troops. There are some very interesting excursions into the desert which we could make together. I have no doubt Casey would be delighted to place the villa at your disposal. I should probably myself stay at the British Embassy in Cairo, which is perhaps twenty minutes away, but it may be that arrangements could be made for us both to be in the Pyramids area. I believe your Mr. Kirk also has a very fine house. Every facility exists in Cairo for the full Staffs to be accommodated and to meet for business, and they can easily come out to your villa whenever desired. If you like this plan, which, knowing the lay-out, I consider far the best, I will immediately make all preparations, and perhaps you would send an officer to make sure everything is arranged to your liking. . . .

Our plans now began to take shape.

President Roosevelt to Prime Minister   31 Oct. 43

Hull's departure from Moscow has meant two days' delay in his getting home. It is essential I see him before I myself leave, as you can readily understand. I had hoped to get three days in North Africa before reaching Cairo. I can however do some of the North African and Italian business on the way back. Therefore I still hope to arrive Cairo by the 20th by flying there directly I reach the harbour. But if wind and weather are bad, I might not make Cairo until the 22d. I think my ship will take me to Oran.

Ever so many thanks for offering to make arrangements at Cairo, which we accept with pleasure. If any hitch develops there, we can of course meet in Alexandria, the Staff living ashore and we on our respective ships.

I am wiring Generalissimo [Chiang Kai-shek] to prepare to meet us in the general neighborhood of Cairo about November 25.

Prime Minister to President   31 Oct. 43

Everything will be ready for Operation "Sextant" [2] from 20th

___
[2] Our code-name for the Conference between Britain, the United States, and China.

onward, and Colonel Warden will await Admiral Q and also Celestes [3] at rendezvous. No difficulty about accommodation for Staffs.

Eden told me that there was no question of being able to move Stalin from the Teheran proposal. I made therefore every effort to smooth the way.

Prime Minister to General Ismay (Moscow) 1 Nov. 43

Reason which prevents triple meeting at "Cairo Three" [Teheran] is said to be possible interruptions of flying over the mountains between Cairo and "Cairo Three," thus putting Admiral Q [President Roosevelt] constitutionally out of touch for transmission of documents. Pray probe the weather facts on the spot, and also let me know whether there is a road from Teheran into Syria, and how long a motor-car would take to travel it with dispatches, which could be brought on by air once south of the mountains. If I could convince Admiral Q that there would be no interruption in the movement of dispatches, our original plan might again be valid.

I now tried a last expedient, namely, that the President and I should meet at Oran in our respective battleships, and that the two Staffs should have a preliminary consultation of four days at Malta. This failed, but the President decided to start in his battleship. He now proposed that the Combined Chiefs of Staff should meet in Cairo before any contact was made with the Russians or the Chinese, whose presence in Cairo had been so strongly urged by him. But the first possible date for a meeting of the Combined Chiefs of Staff would be November 22. The Americans were proposing that the Chinese delegation should arrive on that day, and their presence would inevitably lead to their being drawn into our discussions. I further learned indirectly that the President was simultaneously inviting Molotov to Cairo. I therefore sent the following messages to the President:

Prime Minister to President Roosevelt 11 Nov. 43

There seems to have been a most unfortunate misunderstanding.

[3] "Your humble servant, yourself, and the Generalissimo respectively."

I thought from your telegram that the British and American Staffs
would have "many meetings" before being joined by the Russians
or Chinese. But now I hear from Ambassador Clark Kerr that on
November 9 the United States Ambassador at Moscow delivered a
message from you to Stalin inviting Monsieur Molotov to go to
Cairo on November 22 with a military representative. November
22 is however the first day on which the Staffs can meet. I ask
therefore that the date of the arrival of Molotov and his military
representative shall be postponed till November 25 at the earliest.

2. I am very glad to hear also from Ambassador Clark Kerr that
you contemplate going on November 26 to Teheran. I rather wish
you had been able to let me know direct.

I wished the proceedings to take three stages: first, a broad
Anglo-American agreement at Cairo; secondly, a Supreme
Conference between the three heads of the Governments of
the three major Powers at Teheran; and, thirdly, on returning
to Cairo, the discussion of what was purely Anglo-American
business about the war in the Indian theatre and the Indian
Ocean, which was certainly urgent. I did not want the short
time we had at our disposal to be absorbed in what were after
all comparatively minor matters, when the decision involving
the course of the whole war demanded at least provisional
settlement. It seemed also unsuitable that the Soviet should
be formally brought into conference with the Chinese Government when they had not declared war against Japan.

"It is very difficult," I wrote to Stalin on the 11th, "to settle
things by triangular correspondence, especially when people
are moving by sea and air." Some of the difficulties, happily,
cancelled each other out.

President Roosevelt to Prime Minister   12 Nov. 43
I have just heard that Uncle J. will come to Teheran. . . . I wired
him at once that I had arranged the constitutional matter here,
and therefore that I could go to Teheran for a short meeting with
him, and told him I was very happy. Even then I was in doubt
as to whether he would go through with his former offer to go
to Teheran. His latest message has clinched the matter, and I
think that now there is no question that you and I can meet him

there between the 27th and the 30th. Thus endeth a very difficult situation, and I think we can be happy.

In regard to Cairo, I have held all along, as I know you have, that it would be a terrible mistake if Uncle J. thought we had ganged up on him on military action. During the preliminary meetings in Cairo, the Combined Staffs will, as you know, be in the planning stage. That is all. It will not hurt you or me if Molotov and a Russian military representative are in Cairo too. They will not feel that they are being given the "run around." They will have no Staff and no planners. Let us take them in on the high spots.

It is only five hours ago that I received Uncle J.'s telegram confirming Teheran. Undoubtedly Molotov and the military representative will return there with us between the 27th and the 30th, and when and after we have completed our talk with Uncle J. they will return with us to Cairo, possibly adding other military staff to the one representative accompanying Molotov on the first trip.

I think it essential that this schedule be carried out. I can assure you there will be no difficulties.

I am just off. Happy landing to us both.

Prime Minister to President Roosevelt   12 Nov. 43

I am very pleased that you have managed to arrange the constitutional matter and that our meeting is now definitely arranged. That is a great step forward.

2. The Chiefs of Staff are however very apprehensive about the arrangements which you have settled for military conversations, and I share their misgivings. I thought from your message that the British and American Staffs would have "many meetings" before being joined by the Russians or Chinese. I still regard this as absolutely essential in view of the serious questions which have to be settled. There is no objection to you and me seeing Molotov before our meeting with U.J., but the presence of a Soviet military observer so early in the Conference may cause grave embarrassment. His Majesty's Government cannot abandon their rights to full and frank discussions with you and your officers about the vital business of our intermingled armies. A Soviet observer cannot possibly be admitted to the intimate conversations which our own Chiefs of Staff must have, and his exclusion may easily cause

offence. None of these objections would have applied to the formal Triple Staff Conference which I suggested should take place in due course.

In the end this danger was removed by the President's invitation to Chiang Kai-shek. Nothing would induce Stalin to compromise his relations with the Japanese by entering a four-Power conference with their three enemies. All question of Soviet representatives coming to Cairo was thus negatived. This was in itself a great relief. It was obtained however at a serious inconvenience and a subsequent cost.

Premier Stalin to Premier Churchill   12 Nov. 43

Although I wrote to the President that Monsieur Molotov would come to Cairo on November 22, now I must say however that for certain reasons of serious character Monsieur Molotov, to my regret, cannot come to Cairo. He will be able to come to Teheran at the end of November, and will arrive there together with me. Several military men will also accompany me.

It stands to reason that a meeting of the heads of only three Governments must take place at Teheran as it had been agreed. There should be absolutely excluded the participation of the representatives of any other Powers.

I wish success to your meeting with the Chinese concerning the Far Eastern affairs.

It was in this manner that our arrangements took final shape, and we started on our journeys.

END OF BOOK ONE

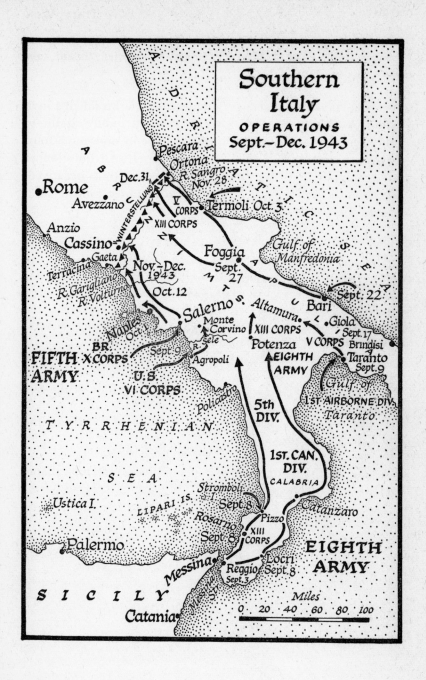

Southern Italy
OPERATIONS
Sept.–Dec. 1943

Rome
Avezzano
Anzio
Cassino
Gaeta
Terracina
R. Garigliano
R. Volturno
Naples
Oct.
FIFTH
ARMY
BR.
X CORPS
U.S.
VI CORPS

Pescara
Ortona
Dec. 31
R. Sangro
Nov. 28
V
CORPS
XIII CORPS
Termoli Oct. 3
WINTERSTELLUNG
Nov.–Dec.
1943
Oct. 12
Foggia
Sept.
27
Salerno
Monte
Corvino
R. Sele
Sept. 9
Agropoli
Policastro

Gulf of
Manfredonia
Bari
Sept. 22
Altamura
Giola
XIII CORPS
Sept. 17
Potenza
V CORPS
Brindisi
EIGHTH
ARMY
Taranto
Sept. 9
Gulf of
Taranto
1ST AIRBORNE DIV.

5th
DIV.

1ST. CAN.
DIV.
CALABRIA

T Y R R H E N I A N

S E A

Ustica I.
LIPARI IS.
Stromboli
I.
Sept. 8
Rosarno
Sept. 8
Palermo
XIII
CORPS
Messina
Reggio
Sept. 3
Locri
Sept. 8
Pizzo
Catanzaro
EIGHTH
ARMY

S I C I L Y

Catania

Miles
0 20 40 60 80 100

★

Book Two

Teheran to Rome

1

Cairo

ON THE AFTERNOON of November 12, I sailed in the *Renown* from Plymouth with my personal staff on a journey which was to keep me from England for nearly three months. With me came Mr. Winant, the American Ambassador, Admiral Cunningham, First Sea Lord, and General Ismay and other members of the Defence Office. I was feeling far from well, as a heavy cold and sore throat were reinforced by the consequences of inoculations against typhoid and malaria. I stayed in bed for several days. My Cabinet colleagues had expressed the kindly wish that my daughter Sarah should come with me, and it gave me pleasure to defer to their request. She was serving in the Air Force, and became my aide-de-camp.

We had an uneventful voyage across the Bay of Biscay, and I was able to go on deck as we passed the Straits of Gibraltar. While we stopped for a few hours at Algiers on the 15th, I had a long talk with General Georges about the French situation in Africa. As darkness fell, we resumed our course for Malta, which we reached on the 17th.

Here I found Generals Eisenhower and Alexander, and other important personages. After the conclusion of the Tunisian campaign, I had suggested to the King that General Alexander should receive the distinction of the North Africa ribbon, with the numerals 1 and 8 upon it, representing the two victorious British armies of the campaign. I felt that as Eisenhower had been the Supreme Commander this was also his by right, and I sought and obtained the King's approval. I had the honour of investing these two Commanders with this unique decoration. They were both taken by surprise, and seemed highly gratified when I pinned the ribbons on their coats. I arrived in Malta quite ill with a new cold and temperature, but I had sufficient strength to attend the dinner at the Governor's war-time palace, the real one being uninhabitable from bombardment.

Although I continued to conduct business without cessation, I had to remain in bed all the time I was in Malta, except for a Staff conference and a final tour of the frightfully battered dockyard, where the whole of the people and workmen gathered with great enthusiasm. At midnight on November 19, we sailed again on our voyage to Alexandria.

A telegram had reached me from the President saying that his security advisers thought that Cairo was too dangerous for the Conference. They feared a German air attack from Greece or Rhodes, and suggested Khartoum instead. Roosevelt of course had nothing to do with this himself, as he was entirely indifferent to his personal safety. Khartoum would have been quite unequal to handling the great staffs we were bringing, amounting altogether to nearly five hundred. I therefore asked Ismay to examine the resources of Malta. He reported that owing to air damage the accommodation was not only inadequate for

our considerable gathering, but also extremely primitive. I
therefore decided that we had better stick to Cairo, where all
arrangements had been perfected. The eight squadrons of
British aircraft based on Alexandria would certainly intercept
and destroy any German attack. The enclave near the Pyramids which we were to occupy was to be guarded by more
than a brigade of infantry, and there were upwards of five
hundred anti-aircraft guns hard by. Accordingly I wirelessed
the *Iowa,* which was bringing the President across the ocean:

Prime Minister to President Roosevelt   21 Nov. 43
   See St. John, chapter xiv, verses 1 to 4.

On reading this through more carefully after it had gone I
was a little concerned lest, apart from a shadow of unintended
profanity, it should be thought I was taking too much upon
myself and thus giving offence. However, the President
brushed all objections aside and our plans continued unchanged. In the event no German airplanes ever came within
several hundred miles of the Pyramids.

*   *   *   *   *

The *Renown* reached Alexandria on the morning of November 21, and I flew at once to the desert landing-ground near
the Pyramids. Here Mr. Casey had placed at my disposal the
agreeable villa he was using. We lay in a broad expanse of
Kasserine woods thickly dotted with the luxurious abodes
and gardens of the cosmopolitan Cairo magnates. Generalissimo Chiang Kai-shek and Madame had already been ensconced half a mile away. The President was to occupy the
spacious villa of the American Ambassador Kirk, about three
miles down the road to Cairo. I went to the desert airfield to
welcome him when he arrived in the "Sacred Cow" from Oran
the next afternoon, and we drove to his villa together.
   The Staffs congregated rapidly. The headquarters of the
Conference and the venue of all the British and American
Chiefs of Staff was at the Mena House Hotel, opposite the
Pyramids, and I was but half a mile away. The whole place

bristled with troops and anti-aircraft guns, and the strictest cordons guarded all approaches. Everyone set to work at once at the various levels upon the immense mass of business which had to be decided or adjusted.

What we had apprehended from Chiang Kai-shek's presence now in fact occurred. The talks of the British and American Staffs were sadly distracted by the Chinese story, which was lengthy, complicated, and minor. Moreover, as will be seen, the President, who took an exaggerated view of the Indian-Chinese sphere, was soon closeted in long conferences with the Generalissimo. All hope of persuading Chiang and his wife to go and see the Pyramids and enjoy themselves till we returned from Teheran fell to the ground, with the result that Chinese business occupied first instead of last place at Cairo. The President, in spite of my arguments, gave the Chinese the promise of a considerable amphibious operation across the Bay of Bengal within the next few months. This would have cramped "Overlord" for landing- and tank-landing-craft, which had now become the bottleneck, far more than any of my Turkey and Aegean projects. It would also have hampered grievously the immense operations we were carrying out in Italy. On November 29, I wrote to the Chiefs of Staff: "The Prime Minister wishes to put on record the fact that he specifically refused the Generalissimo's request that we should undertake an amphibious operation simultaneously with the land operations in Burma." It was not until we returned from Teheran to Cairo that I at length prevailed upon the President to retract his promise. Even so, many complications arose. Of this more anon.

I of course took occasion to visit the Generalissimo at his villa, where he and his wife were suitably installed. This was the first time I had met Chiang Kai-shek. I was impressed by his calm, reserved, and efficient personality. At this moment he stood at the height of his power and fame. To American eyes he was one of the dominant forces in the world. He was the champion of "the New Asia." He was certainly a steadfast defender of China against Japanese invasion. He was a strong anti-Communist. The accepted belief in American circles was that he would be the head of the great Fourth Power in the world after the victory had been won. All these views and values have since been cast aside by many of those who held them. I, who did not in those days share the excessive estimates of Chiang Kai-shek's power or of the future helpfulness of China, may record the fact that the Generalissimo is still serving the same causes which at this time had gained him such wide renown. He has however since been beaten by the Communists in his own country, which is a very bad thing to be.

I had a very pleasant conversation with Madame Chiang Kai-shek, and found her a most remarkable and charming personality. I told her how much I had regretted that we could not find an occasion for a meeting at the time when we had both been in America together, and we agreed that no undue formalities should stand in the way of our talks in the future. The President had us all photographed together at one of our meetings at his villa, and although both the Generalissimo and his wife are now regarded as wicked and corrupt reactionaries by many of their former admirers, I am glad to keep this as a souvenir.

*   *   *   *   *

During the outward voyage I had prepared what was in effect an indictment of our mismanagement of operations in the Mediterranean during the two months which had passed since our victory at Salerno. I gave this to the Chiefs of Staff, and they, while agreeing in principle, made a number of comments in detail upon it. The final version read as follows:

For a year from Alamein and the landings in Northwest Africa the British and Americans have had virtually unbroken success in every theatre, and there is no doubt that our methods of war direction, through the Combined Chiefs of Staff working under the heads of the two Governments, have enabled our commanders in the field to gain resounding victories and achieve solid results. In all the history of alliances there never has been such harmony and mutual comprehension, not only in the high direction of the war, but among the commanders and troops in the field. Our combined operations from the beginning of the Battle of Alamein to the end of the Battle of Naples and the deployment of the Army in Italy may well be regarded as an extremely well-managed and prosperous affair.

2. However, since then there has been a change. We have been overtaken and in a sense outrun by our own successes. Certain divergences of view, of emphasis rather than principle, have opened between the British and American Staffs. We must not allow ourselves to be prevented by victories already gained from subjecting ourselves severally and jointly to searching self-examination with a view to improving our methods and giving an increasingly high standard of service.

3. Since the successful landing and deployment of the Army in Italy in September, the war in the Mediterranean has taken an unsatisfactory course. Both the build-up and advance of the Army in Italy, making allowance for bad weather, must be considered extremely slow. There is not a sufficient preponderance over the enemy in the front line. Many of the divisions have been continuously in action since the landing without any spell of relief. At the same time, two of the best British divisions, the 50th and 51st, which stood in Sicily close to the battlefield, were first stripped of their equipment and have since been withdrawn to the United Kingdom. It has not been found possible to assist the forward movement of the Army to the extent that might have been hoped by making amphibious scoops along either coast. Some of the vitally needed landing-craft have been sent home, losing heavily from the weather on the way. A large number of others have been withdrawn and assembled in preparation for their homeward journey. These orders have now been arrested till December 15, but this is a useless date for Mediterranean purposes. The landing-craft have done nothing in October and November except assist in bringing vehicles ashore. At the same time the build-up of the Strategic Air Force in Italy has hampered the reinforcement of the fighting front. Thus the whole campaign on land has flagged. There is no prospect of Rome being taken in 1943. . . .

5. Side by side with this we have failed to give any real measure of support to the partisans and patriots in Yugoslavia and Albania. These guerrilla forces are containing as many [German] divisions as are the British and American armies put together. Hitherto

they have been nourished only by droppings from the air. It is now more than two months since we have had air and naval superiority in the mouth of the Adriatic, yet no ships with supplies have entered the ports taken by the partisans. On the contrary, the Germans are systematically driving them from these ports and acquiring mastery of the whole Dalmatian coast. It was not possible to prevent the Germans obtaining Corfu and Argostoli, and they actually hold these islands at the moment. Thus the Germans have weathered the difficulties caused by the Italian collapse and desertion, and with great severity are mopping up many of the patriot forces and cutting them off from the sea.

6. How has it happened? An imaginary line has been drawn down the Mediterranean which relieves General Eisenhower's armies of all responsibility for the Dalmatian coast and the Balkans. These are assigned to General Wilson of the Middle East Command, but he does not possess the necessary forces. One Command has the forces but not the responsibilities, the other the responsibilities but not the forces. This can hardly be considered an ideal arrangement.

7. Most unfortunate of all has been the Dodecanese and the Aegean. Immediately after the fall of Italy a number of islands held by the Italians were occupied by us with Italian consent. Of these the two most important were Cos and Leros. We did not succeed in getting Rhodes, which is of course the master key to the Aegean. Hitler was not slow to recognise the naval and political importance of the fortress of Leros, which had fallen so cheaply into our hands, and with great stubbornness and tenacity he personally set himself to restore the situation in the Aegean. A very large proportion of the German air forces which would have been available to fight in Italy was moved into the Aegean theatre, and sea transport was improvised.[1] It was evident early in October that attacks on Leros and Cos were imminent, and on October 4, Cos, where we had only one battalion, was retaken by the Germans. In spite of unexpectedly prolonged defence, Leros fell on November 16, the British losses in the whole business being about 5,000 and the enemy scoring his first success since Alamein. All this of course is outside the parish of the High North African Command. . . .

[1] German records show that during this period their Aegean air forces were increased by nearly three hundred aircraft, while those in Italy were reduced by about two hundred.

332 TEHERAN TO ROME

9. The Germans are now complete masters of the Eastern Aegean. Although already outmatched in the air in Italy, they have not hesitated to reduce their air-power there; and have transferred to the Aegean forces sufficient to dominate this theatre. Although the United States and British air forces in the Mediterranean have a first-line strength of over four thousand — i.e., practically equal to the whole of the German Air Force — the Germans have been able to reproduce in the Aegean theatre all the old technique of the days of our air nakedness, and with their Stuka dive-bombers have broken down the resistance of our best troops and sunk or damaged our ships. . . .

11. There are two causes for these misfortunes. The first has been mentioned — the artificial line of division between East and West in the Mediterranean, absolving the Western Commanders, who have the forces, of all responsibility for the vital interests at stake in the East. The second cause of course is the shadow of "Overlord." The decisions at Quebec were taken before the consequences of the collapse of Italy were apparent and before the surrender of the Italian Fleet and the successful invasion of the mainland of Europe. Nevertheless, they have been maintained until a fortnight ago with inflexible rigidity. It has not been found possible to meet together earlier. We are now faced with the prospect that a fixed target date for "Overlord" will continue to hamper and enfeeble the Mediterranean campaign, that our affairs will deteriorate in the Balkans, and that the Aegean will remain firmly in German hands. All this is to be accepted for the sake of an operation fixed for May upon hypotheses that in all probability will not be realised at that date, and certainly not if the Mediterranean pressure is relaxed.

12. Nor must we overlook the discouraging and enfeebling effect upon the whole of the operations in the Mediterranean of the fact that it is now common knowledge in the armies that the theatre is to be bled as much as necessary for the sake of an operation elsewhere in the spring. The fact of troops and landing-craft being withdrawn from the very battlefield and of units being put under orders for home is in itself injurious. The intense desire to concentrate upon the enemy which carried us from Alamein and sustained us in Tunisia has been impaired. Yet in the Mediterranean alone are we in contact with the enemy and able to bring superior numbers to bear upon him now. It is certainly an odd

way of helping the Russians, to slow down the fight in the only
theatre where anything can be done for some months.

*   *   *   *   *

The first plenary meeting of the Cairo Conference (which
was given the code name "Sextant") was held at the President's villa on Tuesday, November 23. Its purpose was to outline formally to Chiang Kai-shek and the Chinese delegation
the proposed operations in Southeast Asia, as drawn up by the
Combined Chiefs of Staff at Quebec. Admiral Mountbatten,
with his officers, had flown from India, and he first gave a description of the military plans he had been given and was exe-
cuting for 1944 in that theatre. To this I added the general
naval picture. Owing to the surrender of the Italian Fleet
and other naval events of a favourable character a British
fleet would be established soon in the Indian Ocean. There
would be ultimately no fewer than five modernised capital
ships, four heavy armoured cruisers, and up to twelve auxiliary
carriers. Chiang Kai-shek intervened to say that he thought
that the success of operations in Burma depended not only
on the strength of our naval forces in the Indian Ocean, but on
the simultaneous coordination of naval action with land operations. I pointed out that there was no necessary connection
between the land campaign and fleet action in the Bay of Bengal. Our main fleet base would be able to exercise its influence
in sea-power from areas two thousand to three thousand miles
away from the scene where the armies were operating. There
was therefore no comparison between these operations and
those carried out in Sicily, where the Fleet had been able to
work in close support of the Army.

This meeting was brief, and it was agreed that Chiang Kai-
shek should discuss further details with the Combined Chiefs
of Staff.

*   *   *   *   *

On the following day, a second meeting of our Combined
Chiefs of Staff was held by the President, without the presence

of the Chinese delegation, to discuss operations in Europe
and the Mediterranean. We sought to survey the relations of
the two theatres and to exchange our views before going on to
Teheran. The President opened upon the effect on "Overlord" of any possible action we could take in the meantime in
the Mediterranean, including the problem of Turkey's entry
into the war.

When I spoke, I said "Overlord" remained top of the bill,
but this operation should not be such a tyrant as to rule out
every other activity in the Mediterranean; for example, a little
flexibility in the employment of landing-craft ought to be
conceded. General Alexander had asked that the date of their
leaving for "Overlord" should be deferred from mid-December
to mid-January. Eighty additional L.S.T.s had been ordered to
be built in Britain and Canada. We should try to do even
better than this. The points which were at issue between the
American and British Staffs would probably be found to affect
no more than a tenth of our common resources, apart from
the Pacific. Surely some degree of elasticity could be arranged.
Nevertheless, I wished to remove any idea that we had weakened, cooled, or were trying to get out of "Overlord." We
were in it up to the hilt. To sum up, I said that the programme
I advocated was to try to take Rome in January and Rhodes in
February; to renew suppplies to the Yugoslavs, settle the Command arrangements, and to open the Aegean, subject to the
outcome of an approach to Turkey; all preparations for "Overlord" to go ahead full steam within the framework of the foregoing policy for the Mediterranean.

This is a faithful record of my position on the eve of
Teheran.

*   *   *   *   *

Mr. Eden had now joined us from England, whither he had
flown after his discussions in Moscow. His arrival was a great
help to me. On the way back from the Moscow Conference,
he and General Ismay had met the Turkish Foreign Minister

and other Turks at Cairo. At these talks Mr. Eden pointed
out that we had urgent need of air bases in the southwest of
Anatolia. He explained that our military situation at Leros
and Samos was precarious, owing to German air superiority.
Both places had since been lost. Mr. Eden also dwelt on the
advantages that would be derived from Turkey's entry into
the war. In the first place, it would oblige the Bulgarians to
concentrate their forces on the frontier, and thus would compel the Germans to replace Bulgarian troops in Greece and
Yugoslavia to the extent of some ten divisions. Secondly, it
would be possible to attack the one target which might be
decisive — Ploesti. Thirdly, Turkish chrome would be cut off
from Germany. Finally, there was the moral advantage. Turkey's entry into the war might well hasten the process of disintegration in Germany and among her satellites. By all this
argument the Turkish delegation were unmoved. They said,
in effect, that the granting of bases in Anatolia would amount
to intervention in the war, and that if they intervened in the
war there was nothing to prevent a German retaliation on Constantinople, Angora, and Smyrna. They refused to be comforted by the assurances that we would give them sufficient
fighters to deal with any air attack that the Germans could
launch and that the Germans were so stretched everywhere
that they had no divisions available to attack Turkey. The
only result of the discussions was that the Turkish delegation
promised to report to their Government. Considering what
had been happening under their eyes in the Aegean, the Turks
can hardly be blamed for their caution.

*   *   *   *   *

As I had heard no more about the plans for the Combined
Command of "Overlord" and the Mediterranean, I assumed
that the British view had been accepted. But on November 25,
during our stay in Cairo, the proposal for one over-all Supreme
Command was presented to us by the American Chiefs of Staff
in a formal memorandum. From this it was apparent that the

President and the American High Command felt strongly that a Supreme Commander should be appointed to command all the United Nations operations against Germany, both from the Mediterranean and the Atlantic. They still wished to see a commander for Northwest European operations, a commander of the Allied forces in the Mediterranean, and above both a supreme figure who would not only plan and conduct the war in both theatres, but move the forces from one to the other as he might think best. It must be remembered that we not only had at that time, and were bound to have for many months to come, a very large superiority in all the forces, Army, Navy, and Air, but also that with Alexander's and Montgomery's victories in Tunis and the Desert our reputation stood high. The American memorandum immediately encountered strong opposition from the British Chiefs of Staff. Both they and I recorded our views in writing. The rejoinder of the British Chiefs of Staff was as follows:

COMMAND OF BRITISH AND UNITED STATES FORCES OPERATING AGAINST GERMANY

MEMORANDUM BY THE BRITISH CHIEFS OF STAFF

25 Nov. 43

The British Chiefs of Staff have given careful consideration to the proposal put forward by the United States Chiefs of Staff that "a Supreme Commander be designated at once to command all United Nations operations against Germany from the Mediterranean and the Atlantic." This proposal has immense political implications, and is clearly a matter for the most earnest consideration of the United States and British Governments. Nevertheless the British Chiefs of Staff must say at once that, from the military point of view, they profoundly disagree with the proposal. Their reasons are set out in the paragraphs that follow.

Total war is not an affair of military forces alone, using the word "military" in the widest sense of the term. There are political, economic, industrial, and domestic implications in almost every big war problem. Thus it seems clear that the Supreme Commander for the war against Germany will have to consult both the United States and the British Governments on almost every important question. In fact, it boils down to this, that he will only be able to make a decision without reference to high authority on comparatively minor and strictly military questions, such as the transfer of one or two divisions, or a few squadrons of aircraft, or a few scores of landing-craft, from one of his many fronts to another. He will thus be an extra and unnecessary link in the chain of command.

There is no real analogy between the position of Marshal Foch in the last war and the position now contemplated for the Supreme Commander against Germany. Marshal Foch was responsible only for the Western Front and the Italian Front. His authority did not extend to the Salonika Front, the Palestine Front, or the Mesopotamia Front. Under the arrangements now contemplated the Supreme Commander will have not only "Overlord" and the Italian Front under his authority, but also the Balkan Front and the Turkish Front (if this is opened). There must be some limit to the responsibilities which Allied Governments can delegate to a single soldier, and the sphere now proposed seems to exceed these limits considerably.

The United States Chiefs of Staff propose that the decisions of the Supreme Commander should be "subject to reversal by the Combined Chiefs of Staff." If the main object of this new arrangement is to ensure rapid decisions, it looks as though the above proviso will lead to deplorable consequences. Instances will occur in which the Supreme Commander has issued orders and the troops have marched in accordance with these orders, only to be followed by a reversal of the order by the Combined Chiefs of Staff and consequent confusion. Again, it may happen that the British Chiefs of Staff agree with a decision taken by the Supreme Commander, while the United States Chiefs of Staff totally disagree with it. What happens then? Or, again, the Combined Chiefs of Staff may wholeheartedly support, on military grounds, a decision taken by the Supreme Commander, only to find that one or other of the Governments concerned is not prepared to ratify it. Then what happens?

If the Supreme Commander is going to exercise real control, he will need to assemble the whole paraphernalia of Intelligence, Planning, and Administration on an unprecedented scale. This staff will merely be a great pad between the theatre commanders and the Combined Chiefs of Staff. . . .

If the well-tried machinery that has led us safely through the last two years has failed in the smaller problems, it would be better to examine that machinery and see how it could be speeded up and adjusted, rather than to embark upon an entirely novel experiment, which merely makes a cumbrous and unnecessary link in the chain of command, and which will surely lead to disillusionment and disappointment.

*   *   *   *   *

I warmly approved of the Chiefs of Staff paper, and developed the argument still further in a note which I wrote the same day.

SUPREME COMMANDER OF ALL OPERATIONS AGAINST GERMANY

NOTE BY THE PRIME MINISTER AND MINISTER OF DEFENCE

25 Nov. 43

The difficulties and shortcomings in our conduct of the war since the Battle of Salerno have arisen from divergences of view between our two Staffs and Governments. It is not seen how these divergences would be removed by the appointment of a Supreme Commander working under the Combined Chiefs of the Staff and liable to have his decisions reversed by them. The divergences, which are political as much as military, would still have to be adjusted by the present methods of consultation between the Combined Staffs and the heads of the two Governments. Thus the Supreme Commander, after being acclaimed as the World-War-winner, would in practice find his functions restricted to the narrow ground between the main decisions of policy and strategy, which can only be dealt with by the present methods, and the spheres of the two chief regional commanders.

2. This would certainly not be sufficient to justify arousing all the expectations and setting up all the apparatus inseparable from

the announcement of a "Supreme Commander for the defeat of Germany."

3. On the other hand, if the power of decision is in fact accorded to the Supreme Commander, the work of the Combined Chiefs of Staff would be virtually superseded, and very great stresses would immediately arise between the Governments and the Supreme Commander. Without going into personalities, it is greatly to be doubted whether any single officer exists who would be capable of giving decisions over the vast range of problems now dealt with by the heads of Governments assisted by the Combined Chiefs of Staff.

4. The principle which should be followed as far as possible between allies of equal status is that the command in any theatre should go to the ally who has the largest forces deployed or about to be deployed there. On this it would be natural that the command in the Mediterranean should be British and that the command of "Overlord" should be American.

5. If the two commands are merged under a Supreme Commander, the British would have available against Germany in May [1944] decidedly larger forces than the United States. It would therefore appear that the Supreme Command should go to a British officer. I should be very reluctant, as head of His Majesty's Government, to place such an invidious responsibility upon a British officer. If, on the other hand, disregarding the preponderance of forces involved, the Supreme Command were given to a United States officer and he pronounced in favour of concentrating on "Overlord" irrespective of the injury done to our affairs in the Mediterranean, His Majesty's Government could not possibly agree. The Supreme Commander, British or American, would therefore be placed in an impossible position. Having assumed before the whole world the responsibility of pronouncing and being overruled by one Government or the other, he would have little choice but to resign. This might bring about a most serious crisis in the harmonious and happy relations hitherto maintained between our two Governments.

6. It is not seen why the present arrangement should not continue, subject to any minor improvements that can be suggested. Under this arrangement an American commander would conduct the immense Cross-Channel Operation and a British commander

would conduct the war in the Mediterranean, their action being concerted and forces assigned by the Combined Chiefs of Staff, working under the heads of the two Governments. . . . More frequent meetings of the Combined Chiefs of Staff should also be arranged, and possibly monthly visits of one week's duration by the chairman of each Chiefs of Staff Committee alternately to London and Washington.

This paper I handed to the President before we left for Teheran, and I was not aware during the Conference at Teheran what his answer would be. I understood from private sources that the American Chiefs of Staff realised fully the clash of authority that might arise between our Combined Staff organisation and the new Supreme General, and that after weighing our arguments they were by no means wedded to the plan. Neither the President nor any of his immediate circle referred to the matter in any way on the occasions, formal and informal but always friendly, when we came into contact. I therefore rested under the impression that General Marshall would command "Overlord," that General Eisenhower would succeed him in Washington, and that it would fall to me, representing His Majesty's Government, to choose the Mediterranean commander, who at that time I had no doubt would be Alexander, already waging the war in Italy. Here the issue rested till we returned to Cairo.

                    *   *   *   *   *

Thanksgiving Day, the fourth Thursday in November, is a feature in American life. Every soldier in the American armies is supposed to eat turkey on that day, and most of them did in 1943. Ample supplies of turkeys for all the United States Staffs at Cairo had been brought out in the President's ship. Mr. Roosevelt invited me to join him at dinner in his villa. "Let us make it a family affair," he said. So Sarah was asked too, and also "Tommy" (Commander Thompson), to whom he had taken a great liking. The President's guests included his personal circle, his son Elliott, his son-in-law Mr. Boettiger, and Harry Hopkins and his son Robert. We had a pleasant and peaceful feast. Two enormous turkeys were brought in with all ceremony. The President, propped up high in his chair, carved for all with masterly, indefatigable skill. As we were above twenty, this took a long time, and those who were helped first had finished before the President had cut anything for himself. As I watched the huge platefuls he distributed to the company I feared that he might be left with nothing at all. But he had calculated to a nicety, and I was relieved, when at last the two skeletons were removed, to see him set about his own share. Harry, who had noted my anxiety, said, "We have ample reserves." Speeches were made of warm and intimate friendship. For a couple of hours we cast care aside. I had never seen the President more gay. After the meal was over we returned to the big room in which we had held so many conferences. Dance music — from gramophone records — began to play. Sarah was the only woman present, and she had her work cut out, so I danced with "Pa" Watson (Roosevelt's trusted old friend and aide), to the delight of his chief, who watched us from the sofa. This jolly evening and the spectacle of the President carving up the turkeys stand out in my mind among the most agreeable features of the halt at Cairo.

*   *   *   *   *

At last all the puzzles had been solved. The difficulties of the American Constitution, Roosevelt's health, and Stalin's obduracy, the complications of a journey to Basra and the Trans-Persian Railway, were all swept away by the inexorable need of a triple meeting, and the failure of every other alternative but a flight to Teheran. So we sailed off into the air from Cairo, at crack of dawn on November 27, in perfect weather for the long-sought meeting-place, and arrived safely by different routes at different times.[2]

---

[2] I have not broken the thread of the narrative to insert a domestic matter which was at this time causing me concern. The question of the release of the Mosleys will be found in Appendix A, Book Two.

2

Teheran: The Opening

Security Arrangements Wise and Unwise — Recapitulation of My Views — The First Plenary Meeting, November 28 — President Roosevelt Opens — Stalin's Account of the Fighting on the Soviet Front — He Urges the Allied Cross-Channel Attack in Preference to Any Invasion of Germany from Italy — I State the British View — The Position of Turkey — The Crucial Point: Thirty-Five Divisions for "Overlord" — Stalin Favours the Invasion of Southern France as the Secondary Objective — I Insist upon the Capture of Rome — More About Turkey.

I COULD NOT ADMIRE the arrangements which had been made for my reception after landing in Teheran. The British Minister met me in his car, and we drove from the airfield to our Legation. As we approached the city, the road was lined with Persian cavalrymen every fifty yards, for at least three miles. It was clearly shown to any evil people that somebody of consequence was coming, and which way. The men on horseback advertised the route, but could provide no protection at all. A police car driving a hundred yards in advance gave warning of our approach. The pace was slow. Presently large crowds stood in the spaces between the Persian cavalry, and as far as I could see there were few, if any, foot police. Towards the centre of Teheran these crowds were four or five deep. The people were friendly but noncommittal. They pressed to within a few feet of the car. There was no kind of defence at all against two or three determined men with pistols or a bomb. As we reached the turning which led to the Lega-

342

tion there was a traffic block, and we remained for three or four minutes stationary amid the crowded throng of gaping Persians. If it had been planned out beforehand to run the greatest risks, and have neither the security of quiet surprise arrival nor an effective escort, the problem could not have been solved more perfectly. However, nothing happened. I grinned at the crowd, and on the whole they grinned at me. In due course we arrived at the British Legation, which lay within a strong cordon of British-Indian troops.

The American Security were more clever about the President. An elaborate escort of armoured cars surrounded the Presidential vehicle on its route. Actually he alighted at an unknown landing point, and went quite unguarded to the American Legation through utterly unpredictable streets and byways.

The British Legation and its gardens lay almost adjoining the Soviet Embassy, and as the Anglo-Indian brigade entrusted with our safety was in direct contact with the still larger Russian force that encircled their own domain, both soon joined and we became an isolated area with all the precautions of war. The American Legation, which was guarded by United States forces, was more than half a mile away, and this meant that either the President or else Stalin and I would have to traverse the narrow streets of Teheran two or three times a day, back and forth, during the Conference. Meanwhile, Molotov, who had been in Teheran twenty-four hours before our arrival, produced a story that the Soviet Secret Intelligence had unearthed a plot to kill one or more of the "Big Three," as we were regarded, and the idea of one or other of us continually going to and fro through the streets filled him with deep alarm. "If anything like that were to happen," he said, "it could produce a most unfortunate impression." This could not be denied. I strongly supported Molotov in his appeals to the President to move forthwith inside the Soviet Embassy, which was three or four times as big as the others, and stood in extensive grounds, now ringed by Soviet troops and police. We prevailed upon Mr. Roosevelt to take this good advice, and

next afternoon he moved with his whole staff, including the
excellent Filipino cooks from his yacht, into the Russian domain, where ample and comfortable quarters were provided
for him. Thus we were all within a circle, and could discuss
the problems of the World War without any chance of annoy-
ance. I was made very comfortable in the British Legation,
and had only to walk a couple of hundred yards to reach the
Soviet palace, which might be said to be for the time being the
centre of the world. I continued to be far from well, and my
cold and sore throat were so vicious that for a time I could
hardly speak. However, Lord Moran with sprays and ceaseless
care enabled me to say what I had to say — which was a lot.

*   *   *   *   *

There have been many misleading accounts of the line I
took, with the full agreement of the British Chiefs of Staff, at
this Conference. It has become a legend in America that I
strove to prevent the cross-Channel enterprise called "Overlord," and that I tried vainly to lure the Allies into some mass
invasion of the Balkans, or a large-scale campaign in the Eastern Mediterranean, which would effectively kill it. Much of
this nonsense has already in previous chapters been exposed
and refuted, but it may be worth while to set forth what it
was I actually sought, and what, in a very large measure, I got.

"Overlord," now planned in great detail, should be launched
in May or June, or at the latest in the opening days of July
1944. The troops and all the ships to carry them still had first
priority. Secondly, the great Anglo-American army in action
in Italy must be nourished to achieve the capture of Rome and
advance to secure the airfields north of the capital, from which
the air attack on Southern Germany became possible. After
these were gained, there should be no advance in Italy beyond
the Pisa-Rimini line — i.e., we should not extend our front
into the broader part of the Italian peninsula. These operations, if resisted by the enemy, would attract and hold very
large German forces, would give the Italians the chance to
"work their passage," and keep the flame of war burning continually upon the hostile front.

I was not opposed at this time to a landing in the south of France, along the Riviera, with Marseilles and Toulon as objectives, and thereafter an Anglo-American advance northward up the Rhone Valley in aid of the main invasion across the Channel. Alternatively, I preferred a right-handed movement from the north of Italy, using the Istrian peninsula and the Ljubljana Gap, towards Vienna. I was delighted when the President suggested this, and tried, as will be seen, to engage him in it. If the Germans resisted, we should attract many of their divisions from the Russian or Channel fronts. If we were not resisted, we should liberate at little cost enormous and invaluable regions. I was sure we should be resisted, and thus help "Overlord" in a decisive manner.

My third request was that the Eastern Mediterranean, with all the prizes that it afforded, should not be neglected, provided no strength which could be applied across the Channel should be absorbed. In all this I adhered to the proportions which I had mentioned to General Eisenhower two months earlier — namely, six-tenths of our realisable strength across the Channel, three-tenths in Italy, and one-tenth in the Eastern Mediterranean. From this I never varied — not an inch in a year.

We were all agreed, British, Russians, and Americans, upon the first two major campaigns, involving nine-tenths of our available strength. All I had to plead was the effective use of one-tenth of our strength in the Eastern Mediterranean. Simpletons will argue, "Would it not have been much better to centre all upon the decisive operation and dismiss all other opportunities as wasteful diversions?" But this ignores the governing facts. All the available shipping in the Western Hemisphere was already committed, to the last ton, to the preparation of "Overlord" and the maintenance of our front in Italy. Even if more shipping had been found, it could not have been used, because the programmes of disembarkation filled to the utmost limit all the ports and camps involved. As for the Eastern Mediterranean, nothing was needed that could be applied elsewhere. The air force massed for the defence of Egypt could equally well or better discharge its duty if used from a forward frontier. All the troops, two or three divisions at the outside, were already in that theatre, and there were no ships, except local vessels, to carry them to the larger scenes. To get the active, vigorous use of these forces, who otherwise would be mere lookers-on, might inflict grave injury upon the enemy. If Rhodes were taken, the whole Aegean could be dominated by our air force and direct sea-contact established with Turkey. If, on the other hand, Turkey could be persuaded to enter the war, or to strain her neutrality by lending us the airfields we had built for her, we could equally dominate the Aegean and the capture of Rhodes would not be necessary. Either way it would work.

And of course the prize was Turkey. If we could gain Turkey, it would be possible, without the subtraction of a single man, ship, or aircraft from the main and decisive battles, to dominate the Black Sea with submarines and light naval forces, and to give a right hand to Russia and carry supplies to her armies by a route far less costly, far more swift, and far more abundant than either the Arctic or the Persian Gulf.

This was the triple theme which I pressed upon the President and Stalin on every occasion, not hesitating to repeat the arguments remorselessly. I could have gained Stalin, but the President was oppressed by the prejudices of his military advisers, and drifted to and fro in the argument, with the result that the whole of these subsidiary but gleaming opportunities were cast aside unused. Our American friends were comforted in their obstinacy by the reflection that "at any rate we have stopped Churchill entangling us in the Balkans." No such idea had ever crossed my mind. I regard the failure to use otherwise unemployable forces to bring Turkey into the war and dominate the Aegean as an error in war direction which cannot be excused by the fact that in spite of it victory was won.

*   *   *   *   *

Shortly after the President's move into his new quarters in the Soviet Embassy, Stalin came to greet him, and they had a friendly talk. According to the Hopkins biography the President informed Stalin of his promise to Chiang Kai-shek of ac-

tive operations in Burma. Stalin expressed a low opinion of
the fighting qualities of the Chinese troops. The President
"referred to one of his favourite topics . . . the education of the
peoples of the Far Eastern colonial areas . . . in the arts of self-
government. . . . He cautioned Stalin against bringing up the
problems of India with Churchill, and Stalin agreed that this
was undoubtedly a sore subject. Roosevelt said that reform in
India should begin from the bottom, and Stalin said that re-
form from the bottom would mean revolution." [1] I passed
the morning peacefully in bed nursing my cold and dealing
with many telegrams from London.

*   *   *   *   *

The first plenary meeting was held at the Soviet Embassy
on Sunday, November 28, at 4 P.M. The conference room was
spacious and handsome, and we seated ourselves at a large
round table. I had with me Eden, Dill, the three Chiefs of
Staff, and Ismay. The President had Harry Hopkins, Admiral
Leahy, Admiral King, and two other officers. General Marshall
and General Arnold were not present: "they had misunder-
stood the time of the meeting," says Hopkins' biographer, "and
had gone off on a sight-seeing tour round Teheran." [2] I had
my admirable interpreter of the previous year, Major Birse.
Pavlov again performed this service for the Soviets, and Mr.
Bohlen, a new figure, for the United States. Molotov and Marshal Voroshilov alone accompanied Stalin. He and I sat almost
opposite one another. We had agreed beforehand that the
President should preside at this first meeting, and Roosevelt
consented to do so. He opened our proceedings in a felicitous
speech, saying, according to our record, that the Russians, the
British, and the Americans, were sitting round the table for
the first time as members of the same family, with the single
purpose of winning the war. No fixed agenda had been drawn
up for the meeting, and it was open to anybody to discuss whatever he liked and to leave undiscussed whatever he did not

[1] Sherwood, *Roosevelt and Hopkins*, page 777.
[2] *Ibid.*, 778.

like. Everyone could speak as freely as he wished on the basis
of friendship, and nothing would be published.

In my opening remarks I also stressed the importance of the
occasion. This meeting, I said, probably represented the greatest concentration of worldly power that had ever been seen
in the history of mankind. In our hands lay perhaps the shortening of the war, almost certainly victory, and, beyond any
shadow of doubt, the happiness and fortunes of mankind.

Stalin said that he appreciated our references to the friendship of the three Powers. It was indeed true that a great opportunity had been given to them, and he hoped they would make
good use of it.

The President then began the discussion with a brief account
of the war situation from the American point of view. He first
dealt with the Pacific, which had particular importance for the
United States, since American forces there were bearing the
main load, assisted by Australia, New Zealand, and China. The
United States had concentrated in the Pacific the greater part
of their Navy and the best part of a million men. The vast
extent of that theatre could be gauged by the fact that a supply
ship could do only three trips a year. The United States were
pursuing a policy of attrition, which up to the present had
been successful. It was certain that Japanese ships, both naval
and mercantile, were being sunk more rapidly than new construction could replace them. Mr. Roosevelt then explained
the plans for the recapture of Northern Burma. Anglo-American forces would co-operate with the Chinese, and would be
under the command of Admiral Lord Louis Mountbatten.
Plans were also being discussed for an amphibious operation
against the Japanese lines of communication from Bangkok.
Considerable forces were to be employed, although every effort
had been made to keep them down to the minimum required
to achieve our essential objectives. Those objectives were to
keep China actively in the war, to open the Burma Road, and
to establish positions from which Japan could be vanquished
with the greatest possible speed, once Germany had collapsed.
It was hoped to secure bases in China which would enable
Tokyo to be attacked in the coming year.

The President then turned to Europe. There had been many Anglo-American conferences and many plans. A year and a half ago it had been decided to launch an expedition across the English Channel, but owing to transportation and other difficulties it was still impossible to decide a definite date for the operation. An adequate force must be assembled in England, not only for the actual landing, but also for marching inland. The English Channel had proved such a disagreeable body of water that it was impossible to stage an expedition before May 1, 1944. This was the date decided upon at Quebec. He explained that landing-craft were the limiting factor in all landings, and if it were decided to mount a very big expedition in the Mediterranean, we should have to give up the cross-Channel operation altogether. If a lesser operation in the Mediterranean were decided upon, the delay would amount to one, two, or perhaps three months. Consequently, both he and I wished in this military conference to hear from Marshal Stalin and Marshal Voroshilov what action would be of the greatest service to the Soviet. Many plans had been mooted — increasing the strength of our attack in Italy, the Balkans, the Aegean, Turkey, and so forth. The most important task of the Conference would be to decide which of these to adopt. The governing object would be for the Anglo-American armies to draw the greatest weight off the Soviet forces.

Stalin, speaking next, welcomed the successes of the United States in the Pacific, but said that the Soviets could not join in the struggle against Japan at the present time, since practically all their forces were required against Germany. The Soviet forces in the Far East were more or less sufficient for defence, but they would have to be at least trebled in order to attack. The moment for joining their friends in this theatre would be the moment of Germany's collapse: then they would march together.

As for Europe, Stalin said that he would like to begin with a few words about the Soviet experiences in the conduct of the war. Their attack in July had been anticipated by the Germans; but when sufficient troops and equipment had been collected, the Soviet had found it comparatively easy to pass to the offensive. He frankly admitted that they had not expected the successes which were gained in July, August, and September. The Germans had proved weaker than had been thought.

He then gave details of the latest situation on the Soviet Front. On some of the sectors they had been slowed down, on others they had stopped altogether, while in the Ukraine, west and south of Kiev, the initiative had passed to the Germans within the last three weeks. The Germans had recaptured Zhitomir, and would probably recapture Korosten. Their objective was the recapture of Kiev. Nevertheless, in the main the initiative still rested with the Soviet armies.

He had been asked, he said, how the Anglo-American forces could best help Russia. The Soviet Government had always felt that the Italian campaign had been of great value to the Allied cause in that it opened the Mediterranean. But Italy was not a suitable jumping-off ground for the invasion of Germany. The Alps stood between. Therefore, nothing was to be gained by concentrating large numbers of troops in Italy for the invasion of Germany. Turkey would be a better point of entry than Italy; but it was a long way from the heart of Germany. He believed that North or Northwest France was the place for Anglo-American forces to attack, though it was of course true that the Germans there would resist desperately.

*   *   *   *   *

Though invited to speak earlier, I had hitherto said nothing. I now stated the British position.

It had long been agreed, I said, with the United States that we should invade North or Northwest France across the Channel. The enterprise was absorbing most of our preparations and resources. A long dissertation on facts and figures would be necessary to show why it had been impossible to carry out this operation in 1943, but we were resolved to do it in 1944. Instead of the cross-Channel invasion of 1943, a series of operations had been launched in the Mediterranean. This had been done with full recognition that they were of a secondary character; but we had felt that they were the best contribution we could make in 1943, having regard to our resources and to transportation. The British and American Governments had now set themselves the task of carrying out a cross-Channel invasion in the late spring or summer of 1944. The forces which could be accumulated by that time amounted to about sixteen British and nineteen United States divisions — a total of thirty-five divisions. These divisions were much stronger both in numbers and equipment than the German divisions.

Stalin here observed that he never regarded the operations in the Mediterranean as being of a secondary character. They were of the first importance, but not from the point of view of invading Germany.

I replied that nonetheless the President and I had both regarded them as stepping-stones to the decisive cross-Channel operation. Having regard to the British forces engaged in the Mediterranean and India, the sixteen British divisions which were being put into the cross-Channel operation were the most that could be provided by a country with a total population of forty-five millions. These divisions could be kept up to strength in the line, but the number could not be increased. It would have to be left to the United States, who had a large number of reserve divisions, to broaden the front and nourish the battle. The early spring and summer of 1944 were still six months away however, and the President and I had been asking ourselves what could be done during these six months with the resources available in the Mediterranean that would best take the weight off Russia, without postponing "Overlord" for more than perhaps a month or two. Seven of the best Anglo-American divisions and a certain number of landing-craft had already been, or were being, moved from the Mediterranean to the United Kingdom. The result had been a weakening of effort on the Italian Front. The weather had been bad, and it had not yet been possible to take Rome. But it was hoped to take it by January; and General Alexander, who, under General Eisenhower, was commanding the Fifteenth Army Group in Italy, aimed, not only at taking Rome, but at destroying or capturing ten or eleven German divisions.

I explained that we had not contemplated going into the broad part of the leg of Italy, still less invading Germany across the Alps. The general plan was first to capture Rome and seize the airfields north of it, which would enable us to bomb Southern Germany, and then to establish ourselves on a line towards Pisa-Rimini. After that, the possibility of establishing a Third Front in conformity with, but not in substitution for, the cross-Channel operation would have to be planned. One of the possibilities was to move into Southern France, and the second, suggested by the President, was to move from the head of the Adriatic northeast towards the Danube.

Meanwhile, what should be done in the next six months? There was much to be said for supporting Tito, who was holding a number of German divisions and doing much more for the Allied cause than the Chetniks under Mihailovic. There would clearly be great advantage in supporting him with supplies and guerrilla activities, but these would not contain any considerable number of enemy troops. This brought us to the biggest problem which would have to be decided after consideration by the military staffs, namely, how to bring Turkey into the war and open communications through the Aegean to the Dardanelles and thence to the Black Sea. Once Turkey was in the war and we had the use of her air bases, we could capture the islands in the Aegean with comparatively small forces, say two or three divisions, and the air forces already in that theatre. If we had access to the Black Sea ports, convoys could be run continuously. At present we had had to limit ourselves to four convoys by the Northern route, as the escorts were required for "Overlord"; but once the Dardanelles were open, the escort vessels already in the Mediterranean could keep up a ceaseless flow of supplies to the Soviet Black Sea ports.

How could we persuade Turkey to come into the war? If she came in, what should she be asked to do? Should she merely give us her bases, or should she attack Bulgaria and declare war on Germany? Should she move forward or should she stay on the Thracian frontier? What would be the effect on Bul-

garia, who owed a profound debt to Russia for rescuing her
in former days from the Turkish yoke? How would Rumania
react? They were already putting out genuine peace feelers for
unconditional surrender. Then there was Hungary. Which
way would she go? There might well be a political landslide
among the satellite states which would enable the Greeks to
revolt and hustle the Germans out of Greece. All these were
questions on which the Soviets had a special point of view and
special knowledge. It would be invaluable to know what they
thought about it all. Would these plans in the Eastern Mediterranean be of sufficient interest to the Soviet Government to
make them wish us to go ahead, even if it meant a delay of one
to two months from May 1 in launching "Overlord"? The British and American Governments had deliberately kept their
minds open on the subject until they knew what the Soviet
Government felt about these problems.

The President here reminded me of the further project of
moving up to the Northern Adriatic and then northeast to
the Danube. I agreed, and said that once we had taken Rome
and destroyed the German armies south of the Apennines in
the narrow part of Italy, the Anglo-American armies would
advance far enough to make contact with the enemy. We
could then hold the line with the minimum forces and keep
the option to strike with the remainder either in the South
of France or, in accordance with the President's idea, northeast from the head of the Adriatic. Neither of these problems
had been considered in detail, but if Stalin should look upon
them with favour a technical sub-committee could be set up
to examine ways and means and facts and figures and to report
to the Conference.

The discussion now came to a crucial point. The record
says:

Marshal Stalin addressed the following questions to the Prime
Minister:
Question: Am I right in thinking that the invasion of France
is to be undertaken by thirty-five divisions?
Answer: Yes. Particularly strong divisions.

Question: Is it intended that this operation should be carried out by the forces now in Italy?

Answer: No. Seven divisions have already been, or are in process of being, withdrawn from [Italy] and North Africa to take part in "Overlord." These seven divisions are required to make up the thirty-five divisions mentioned in your first question. After they have been withdrawn, about twenty-two divisions will be left in the Mediterranean for Italy or other objectives. Some of these could be used either for an operation against Southern France or for moving from the head of the Adriatic towards the Danube. Both these operations will be timed in conformity with "Overlord." Meanwhile, it should not be difficult to spare two or three divisions to take the islands in the Aegean.

*   *   *   *   *

I then explained that it would be quite impossible to transfer any divisions from the Mediterranean to the United Kingdom over and above the seven mentioned. Shipping would not run to it. Thirty-five Anglo-American divisions would be assembled in the United Kingdom for the initial assault. Thereafter the British could do no more than maintain in Northern France their sixteen divisions, but the United States would continue to pump in further troops until the Expeditionary Force in Northern France amounted all told to fifty or sixty divisions. Both the British and American divisions, if line of communication troops, corps troops, flak, etc., were taken into account, amounted gross to about forty thousand men each. There were already very considerable Anglo-American air forces in the United Kingdom, but even so the United States Air Force was going to be doubled, or perhaps trebled, in the next six months. Thus there would be a tremendous weight of air-power concentrated in an area from which the enemy could be easily reached. All the forces and equipment were being built up according to a prearranged schedule, which would be shown to the Soviet authorities if they so desired.

Stalin asked me about the operation against the South of France. I said it had not yet been planned in detail, but the idea was that it might be done in conformity or simultaneously with "Overlord." The assault force would consist of troops now in Italy. I added that it would also be necessary to examine the President's idea of moving northeast from the head of the Adriatic.

Stalin next asked how many Anglo-American troops would have to be allotted if Turkey came into the war.

Observing that I spoke for myself alone, I said that two or three divisions at the most would be required to take the islands in the Aegean, and that, in addition, we should probably have to give Turkey about twenty squadrons of air forces and several regiments of flak to defend herself. Both the air forces and the flak could be provided without prejudice to other operations.

Stalin thought it would be a mistake to send part of our forces to Turkey and elsewhere and part to Southern France. The best course would be to make "Overlord" the basic operation for 1944, and, once Rome had been captured, to send all available forces in Italy to Southern France. These forces could then join hands with the "Overlord" forces when the invasion was launched. France was the weakest spot on the German Front. He did not himself expect Turkey to agree to enter the war.

I asked whether the Soviet Government was not very anxious to get Turkey into the war. We had tried once and failed. But was it not intended that we should renew the effort?

"I am all in favour of trying again," said Stalin. "We ought to take them by the scruff of the neck if necessary."

I then said that I entirely agreed with Marshal Stalin's observations about the undesirability of dispersion, but all that I suggested was that a handful of divisions — say two or three — would be very well employed in making contact with Turkey, while the air forces which would come into play were those which were already defending Egypt and would merely be advancing their line. Thus there was no appreciable diversion of effort, either from the Italian Front or from "Overlord."

Stalin thought it would be well worth while to take the islands if this could be done with three or four divisions.

What I particularly dreaded, I said, was an interval of six
months' inactivity between the capture of Rome and "Overlord." We ought to be fighting the enemy all the time, and
the operations which I had suggested, although admittedly of
a secondary character, should be the subject of careful consideration.

Stalin repeated that "Overlord" was a very serious operation,
and that it was better to help it by invading the South of
France. He would even prefer to assume a defensive rôle in
Italy and forgo the capture of Rome for the present if this
would admit the invasion of Southern France by, say, ten
divisions. Two months later, "Overlord" would follow, and
the two invasions could then join hands.

I replied that we should be no stronger if we pulled out of
the advance on Rome, and once we had taken the city we
should be in a much stronger position through having
destroyed or badly mutilated ten or eleven German divisions.
Moreover, we required the airfields north of Rome for the
bombing of Germany. It would be impossible for us to forgo
the capture of Rome. To do so would be regarded on all
sides as a crushing defeat, and the British Parliament would
not tolerate the idea for a moment.

*   *   *   *   *

The President now suggested that the timing of operations
required the most careful consideration. Any operation undertaken in the Eastern Mediterranean would probably put off
"Overlord" until June or July. He himself was opposed to
such a delay if it could possibly be avoided. He therefore
suggested that the military experts should examine the possibility of operations against Southern France on the timing
put forward by Stalin — i.e., two months before "Overlord,"
the governing factor being that "Overlord" should be launched
at the prescribed time.

Stalin said that the experience gained by the Soviets during
the last two years of fighting was that a big offensive, if undertaken from only one direction, rarely yielded results. The

better course was to launch offensives from two or more directions simultaneously. This compelled the enemy to disperse his forces, and at the same time gave an opportunity for the attacks, provided they were close enough to each other, to make contact and increase the power of the offensive as a whole. He suggested that this principle might well be applied to the problem under discussion.

I did not disagree in principle with these views. The suggestions that I had made for minor help to Yugoslavia and Turkey did not, I said, conflict in any way with that general conception. At the same time, I wished it to be placed on record that I could not in any circumstances agree to sacrifice the activities of the armies in the Mediterranean, which included twenty British and British-controlled divisions, merely in order to keep the exact date of May 1 for "Overlord." If Turkey refused to come into the war, it could not be helped. I earnestly hoped that I should not be asked to agree to any such rigid timing of operations as the President had suggested. Would it not be right for the Conference to meditate over all that had been said and to continue their discussions on the following day? The President agreed, and suggested that the Staffs should set to work the following morning.

Stalin then observed that he had not expected that military questions would be discussed at the Conference, and he had not brought his military experts with him. Nevertheless, Marshal Voroshilov would do his best.

I asked how it was proposed to discuss the question of Turkey. The problem was probably as much political as military. The questions to which the Conference should address itself were as follows: (a) What do we want Turkey to do? (b) What are we prepared to offer her to bring her into the war? (c) What will be the consequences of any such offer?

Stalin agreed. Turkey was an ally of England and on terms of friendship with the United States. It was for them to persuade her to take the proper course. When I said that Turkey would be mad if she declined Russia's invitation to come in on the winning side, and at the same time lost the sympathy of

Great Britain, Stalin rejoined that a number of people preferred to be mad, and all neutrals regarded those who were waging war as fools to fight when they might be doing nothing.

I concluded the meeting by saying that, although we were all great friends, it would be idle for us to delude ourselves that we saw eye to eye on all matters. Time and patience were necessary. Here ended our first talk.

3

Conversations and Conferences

A Talk with Stalin About Germany — Poland and Her Frontiers — Roosevelt's Plan for the "Four Policemen" — I Present the Stalingrad Sword of Honour by the King's Command — Our Second Plenary Session — Stalin Asks Who Will Command "Overlord" — I State the British View About "Overlord" and Italy — Argument About the Date of Crossing the Channel — The Importance of Not Wrecking the Italian Campaign — Stalin's Direct Question to Me — Discussion at Dinner — I Declare Against Mass Executions of Germans.

THE FORMAL CONFERENCES were interspersed with what may be thought to be even more important talks between Roosevelt, Stalin, and myself at luncheons and dinners. Here there were very few things that could not be said and received in good-humour. On Sunday night the 28th, President Roosevelt was our host for dinner. We were a party of ten or eleven, including the interpreters, and conversation soon became general and serious.

After dinner on this first evening, when we were strolling about the room, I led Stalin to a sofa and suggested that we talk for a little on what was to happen after the war was won. He assented with good-humour, and we sat down. Eden joined us. "Let us," said the Marshal, "first consider the worst that might happen." He thought that Germany had every possibility of recovering from this war, and might start on a new one within a comparatively short time. He feared the revival of German nationalism. After Versailles peace had seemed assured, but Germany had recovered very quickly. We must therefore establish a strong body to prevent Germany starting a new war. He was convinced that she would recover. When I asked "How soon?" he replied, "Within fifteen to twenty years." I said that the world must be made safe for at least fifty years. If it was only for fifteen to twenty years, then we should have betrayed our soldiers.

Stalin thought we should consider restraints on Germany's manufacturing capacity. The Germans were an able people, very industrious and resourceful, and they would recover quickly. I replied that there would have to be certain measures of control. I would forbid them all aviation, civil and military, and I would forbid the General Staff system. "Would you," asked Stalin, "also forbid the existence of watchmakers' and furniture factories for making parts of shells? The Germans produced toy rifles which were used for teaching hundreds of thousands of men how to shoot."

"Nothing," I said, "is final. The world rolls on. We have now learnt something. Our duty is to make the world safe for at least fifty years by German disarmament, by preventing rearmament, by supervision of German factories, by forbidding all aviation, and by territorial changes of a far-reaching character. It all comes back to the question whether Great Britain, the United States, and the U.S.S.R. can keep a close friendship and supervise Germany in their mutual interest. We ought not to be afraid to give orders as soon as we see any danger."

"There was control after the last war," said Stalin, "but it failed."

"We were inexperienced then," I replied. "The last war was not to the same extent a national war, and Russia was not a party at the Peace Conference. It will be different this time." I had a feeling that Prussia should be isolated and reduced; that Bavaria, Austria, and Hungary might form a broad, peaceful, unaggressive confederation. I thought Prussia should be dealt with more sternly than the other parts of the Reich, which might thus be influenced against throwing in their lot with her. It must be remembered that those were war-time moods.

"All very good, but insufficient," was Stalin's comment.

Russia, I continued, would have her army, Great Britain and the United States their navies and air forces. In addition, all three Powers would have their other resources. All would be strongly armed, and must not assume any obligation to disarm. "We are the trustees for the peace of the world. If we fail, there will be perhaps a hundred years of chaos. If we are strong, we can carry out our trusteeship. There is more," I went on, "than merely keeping the peace. The three Powers should guide the future of the world. I do not want to enforce any system on other nations. I ask for freedom and for the right of all nations to develop as they like. We three must remain friends in order to ensure happy homes in all countries."

Stalin asked again what was to happen to Germany.

I replied that I was not against the toilers in Germany, but only against the leaders and against dangerous combinations. He said that there were many toilers in the German divisions who fought under orders. When he asked German prisoners who came from the labouring classes (such is the record, but he probably meant "Communist Party") why they fought for Hitler, they replied that they were carrying out orders. He shot such prisoners.

* * * * *

I suggested that we should discuss the Polish question. He agreed and invited me to begin. I said that we had declared war on account of Poland. Poland was therefore important to us. Nothing was more important than the security of the Russian western frontier. But I had given no pledges about frontiers. I wanted heart-to-heart talks with the Russians about this. When Marshal Stalin felt like telling us what he thought about it, the matter could be discussed and we could reach some agreement, and the Marshal should tell me what was necessary for the defence of the western frontiers of Russia.

After this war in Europe, which might end in 1944, the Soviet Union would be overwhelmingly strong and Russia would have a great responsibility in any decision she took with regard to Poland. Personally I thought Poland might move westward, like soldiers taking two steps "left close." If Poland trod on some German toes, that could not be helped, but there must be a strong Poland. Poland was an instrument needed in the orchestra of Europe.

Stalin said the Polish people had their culture and their language, which must exist. They could not be extirpated.

"Are we to try," I asked, "to draw frontier lines?"

"Yes."

"I have no power from Parliament, nor, I believe, has the President, to define any frontier lines. But we might now, in Teheran, see if the three heads of Governments, working in agreement, could form some sort of policy which we could recommend to the Poles and advise them to accept."

We agreed to look at the problem. Stalin asked whether it would be without Polish participation. I said "Yes," and that when this was all informally agreed between ourselves, we could go to the Poles later. Mr. Eden here remarked that he had been much struck by Stalin's statement that afternoon that the Poles could go as far west as the Oder. He saw hope in that and was much encouraged. Stalin asked whether we thought he was going to swallow Poland up. Eden said he did not know how much the Russians were going to eat. How much would they leave undigested? Stalin said the Russians did not want anything belonging to other people, although they might have a bite at Germany. Eden said that what Poland lost in the East she might gain in the West. Stalin replied that possibly she might, but he did not know. I then demonstrated with the help of three matches my idea of Poland moving westward. This pleased Stalin, and on this note our group parted for the moment.

*   *   *   *   *

The morning of the 29th was occupied by the conference of

the British, Soviet, and American military chiefs. As I knew that Stalin and Roosevelt had already had a private conversation, and were of course staying in the same building, I suggested that the President and I might lunch together before the second plenary meeting that afternoon. Roosevelt however declined, and sent Harriman to me to explain that he did not want Stalin to know that he and I were meeting privately. I was surprised at this, for I thought we all three should treat each other with equal confidence. The President after luncheon had a further interview with Stalin and Molotov, at which many important matters were discussed, including particularly Mr. Roosevelt's plan for the government of the post-war world. This should be carried out by the "Four Policemen," namely, the U.S.S.R., the United States, Great Britain, and China. Stalin did not react favourably to this. He said the Four Policemen would not be welcomed by the small nations of Europe. He did not believe that China would be very powerful when the war ended, and even if she were, European states would resent having China as an enforcement authority for themselves. In this the Soviet leader certainly showed himself more prescient and possessed of a truer sense of values than the President. When Stalin proposed as an alternative that there should be one committee for Europe and another for the Far East — the European committee to consist of Britain, Russia, the United States, and possibly one other European nation — the President replied that this was somewhat similar to my idea of regional committees, one for Europe, one for the Far East, and one for the Americas. He does not seem to have made it clear that I also contemplated a Supreme United Nations Council, of which the three regional committees would be the components. As I was not informed till much later of what had taken place, I was not able to correct this erroneous presentation.

*   *   *   *   *

Before our second plenary session began at four o'clock, I presented, by the King's command, the Sword of Honour which His Majesty had had specially designed and wrought to commemorate the glorious defence of Stalingrad. The large outer hall was filled with Russian officers and soldiers. When, after a few sentences of explanation, I handed the splendid weapon to Marshal Stalin, he raised it in a most impressive gesture to his lips and kissed the blade. He then handed it to Voroshilov, who dropped it. It was carried from the room in great solemnity, escorted by a Russian guard of honour. As this procession moved away, I saw the President sitting at the side of the room, obviously stirred by the ceremony. We then moved to the conference chamber and took our seats again at the round table, this time with all the Chiefs of Staff, who were now to report the result of their morning's labours.

The Chief of the Imperial General Staff said that they had surveyed various operations, and they realised that unless something was done in the Mediterranean between now and the launching of "Overlord," the Germans would be able to transfer troops from Italy to Russia or Northern France. They had considered carrying the advance up the leg of the Italian peninsula, strengthening the partisans in Yugoslavia so that they could hold German divisions in the Balkans, and getting Turkey into the war. They had also discussed a landing in Southern France to coincide with "Overlord." Portal had reviewed our bombing offensive and Marshall the United States build-up in Britain.

General Marshall said that the problem confronting the Western Allies in Europe was not one of troops or material, but of ships and landing-craft and getting fighter airfields close enough to the scene of operations. Landing-craft were particularly short, and the most vital need was for the L.S.T.s, which carried forty tanks apiece. So far as "Overlord" was concerned, the flow of troops and supplies was proceeding according to schedule. The variable and questionable factor in almost every one of the problems facing the Allies was landing-craft. The building programme had been accelerated both in the United Kingdom and in the United States, with two objects: first, to increase the scale of the initial assault for "Overlord," and, secondly, to enable us to undertake the operations which we thought right in the Mediterranean.

* * * * *

Stalin then put the crucial question, "Who will command 'Overlord'?" The President replied that this had not yet been decided. Stalin said bluntly that the operation would come to nought unless one man was placed in charge of all the preparation for it. Roosevelt explained that this had already been done. General Morgan, a British officer, had been given a combined Anglo-American Staff and had been planning the operation for some considerable time. Everything, in fact, had already been decided, except the name of the Supreme Commander. Stalin declared it essential that a man should be appointed at once to be responsible, not only for the planning, but also for the execution. Otherwise, although General Morgan might say that everything was ready, the Supreme Commander, when appointed, might have very different ideas and wish to alter everything.

I said that General Morgan had been appointed some months before by the Combined Chiefs of Staff, with the approval of the President and myself, to be Chief Staff Officer to the Supreme Commander (Designate). His Majesty's Government had expressed their willingness to serve under a United States Commander, since the United States would be responsible for the build-up of the invasion force and would have the preponderance in numbers. In the Mediterranean, on the other hand, practically all the naval forces were British and we had also a considerable preponderance in army forces. We therefore felt that the command of this theatre should properly go to the British. I suggested that the appointment of a Supreme Commander was more appropriate for discussion by the three heads of Governments than in a somewhat large conference. Stalin said that the Soviet Government laid no claim to a voice in the appointment. They merely wanted to know who it would be. It was vital that this appointment should be made as soon as possible and that the General chosen should be responsible, not only for the preparation of the plan, but also for carrying it out. I agreed that the decision who was to command "Overlord" was one of the most important points to be dealt with, and said it would be settled within the next fortnight at latest.

*   *   *   *   *

I then set out the British case. I said that I was somewhat concerned at the number and complexity of the problems which confronted us. The Conference represented some twelve to fourteen hundred millions of the human race, who depended upon our reaching right conclusions. It was therefore imperative that we should not separate until the great military, political, and moral problems confronting us had been firmly resolved; but I proposed to confine myself to a few specific points which might be studied by a military sub-committee.

First, what help could be given to "Overlord" by the large forces already assembled in the Mediterranean? In particular, what was the scale of operations which could be launched against Southern France by the troops in Italy? This project had been mentioned by both the President and Stalin, but it had not yet been studied in sufficient detail for anyone to express a final view. Stalin had very rightly stressed the value of pincers operations, but it was obviously useless to attack with a small force which could be annihilated before the main force came on the scene. Speaking entirely for myself, I said I thought that sufficient landing-craft to transport at least two divisions should be retained in the Mediterranean. With a landing-craft force of this size we could help forward the advance up the leg of Italy by seaborne outflanking movements, and thus avoid the slow, laborious methods of frontal attack. Secondly, these landing-craft would enable us to take Rhodes and open the Aegean simultaneously with the entry of Turkey into the war. This same force of landing-craft would enable us five or six months hence to make a descent upon Southern France in concert with "Overlord."

Clearly, all these operations would require the most careful timing and study, but there seemed to be a good hope that all those I had mentioned could be carried through. On the other hand, it was obvious that landing-craft sufficient to transport two divisions could not be kept in the Mediterranean without setting back the date of "Overlord" for perhaps six to eight weeks, or, alternatively, without recalling from the East the assault craft and ships which had been sent there for operations against the Japanese. This placed us in a dilemma. It was a case of balancing one problem against the other. I said I should be grateful to hear the views of Marshal Stalin and Marshal Voroshilov on these points, since their military record inspired their British Allies with so much admiration and respect.

The second main point was the question of Yugoslavia and the Dalmatian coast. No fewer than twenty-one German divisions were held in the Balkans by partisan forces. There were, in addition, nine Bulgarian divisions in Greece and Yugoslavia. Thus thirty enemy divisions were being contained by these gallant guerrillas. Surely therefore the Balkan theatre was one of the areas in which we could stretch the enemy to the utmost and give ourselves relief in the heavy battles which lay ahead. We ourselves had no ambitions in the Balkans. All we wanted to do was to nail down these thirty hostile divisions. Monsieur Molotov, Mr. Eden, and a representative of the President should meet together and advise the Conference on all the political points at issue. For example, did our Soviet friends and Allies see any political difficulty in the course advocated? If so, what? We were determined to work harmoniously with them. From the military point of view there was no question of using large forces in this area. All that was required was to help the partisans with supplies and equipment and Commando operations.

The third and last point was Turkey. Great Britain was Turkey's ally, and had accepted the task of trying to persuade or induce Turkey to enter the war before Christmas. If the President was prepared to come in at this point and take the

lead, the British Government would be entirely happy to leave
it to him. I said I was prepared, on behalf of His Majesty's
Government, to give an assurance that Great Britain would
go a long way towards bringing Turkey into the war. From
the military point of view, the entry of Turkey into the war
would not mean the diversion of more than two or three Allied
divisions at most.

I then asked what the Soviet Government felt about Bulgaria. Would they be prepared to tell Bulgaria that if Turkey
found herself at war with Germany and Bulgaria were to attack Turkey, the Soviets would at once regard Bulgaria as an
enemy? I suggested that Molotov and Eden and a representative of the President might meet to advise the Conference on
the best way of getting Turkey into the war. If we could only
bring this about, it would be a terrible blow to Germany. Bulgaria would be weakened, Rumania was already trying desperately hard to surrender unconditionally, and the effects on
Hungary would be considerable. The object of all the operations in the Mediterranean which I had contemplated was to
take the weight off Russia and to give the best possible chance
to "Overlord."

             *   *   *   *   *

I had spoken for about ten minutes. There was a pause.
Stalin then said: "The Soviet Government will consider themselves at war with Bulgaria if, as a result of Turkey's entry into
the war, Bulgaria threatens Turkey." I thanked him for this
assurance, and inquired whether I could inform the Turks.
Stalin said that he was quite agreeable to this. He then proceeded to give his own ideas on the Balkans. He said there
seemed to be no difference of opinion, and he was all in favour
of help being given to the partisans. But he added bluntly
that the entry of Turkey into the war, the support of Yugoslavia, and the capture of Rome were, to the Russian way of
thinking, relatively unimportant. If the Conference had been
convened to discuss military matters, "Overlord" must come
first.

If a military commission was to be set up, as had been suggested, it would clearly have to be given precise instructions as to the task it was required to perform. The Russians needed help, and urgent help, in their great struggle against the German Army. This could best be given by the early and vigorous prosecution of Operation "Overlord." There were three main matters to be decided: First, the date. This should be some time in May and no later. Secondly, it should be supported by a landing in the South of France. If this could be carried out two or three months before "Overlord," so much the better, but, if not, it might coincide with it, and, if it could not coincide, it would still help if it took place a little after it. The assault on the South of France as a supporting operation would be definitely helpful to "Overlord." The capture of Rome and other operations in the Mediterranean could only be regarded as diversions.

The third matter to be decided was the appointment of a Commander-in-Chief for "Overlord." Stalin said he would like to see this made before the Conference ended, or at least within a week thereafter. Preparations for "Overlord" could not be carried on successfully unless there was a Supreme Commander. Choosing the man was of course a matter for the British and American Governments, but the Soviet Government would be glad to know his name.

The President said we were all agreed on the importance of "Overlord," but not about its date. If "Overlord" was to be carried out during May, one at least of the Mediterranean operations would have to go by the board. If however landing-craft and other equipment were retained in the Mediterranean, then it would have to be postponed till June or July. There were obvious dangers in delaying "Overlord." If we launched expeditions in the Eastern Mediterranean, even with only two or three divisions, there was always the possibility of their developing into bigger commitments involving the dispatch of larger forces. If this happened, even the later date of "Overlord" would be prejudiced.

* * * * *

Mr. Roosevelt then referred to my point about the thirty German and Bulgarian divisions which were contained in the Balkans. He recommended that we should intensify the process of keeping them pinned down by Commando forces. It was important to hold them in this area and prevent them from doing harm elsewhere. There was clearly general agreement that Tito should be supported, but that this should be done without subtracting from the "Overlord" Operation.

Stalin said that, according to his information, the Germans had eight divisions in Yugoslavia, five in Greece, and three in Bulgaria, and twenty-five divisions in France. He was not prepared to agree to any delay in "Overlord" beyond the month of May.

I said I could not agree to give any such undertaking. Nevertheless, I did not think there was any fundamental divergence in the views so far expressed. I was willing to do everything in the power of His Majesty's Government to begin "Overlord" at the earliest possible moment, but I did not consider that the very great possibilities in the Mediterranean should be ruthlessly sacrificed and cast aside as if they were of no value, merely to save a month or so in the launching of "Overlord." There was a large British army in the Mediterranean, and I could not agree that it should stand idle for nearly six months. It should be fighting the enemy with the greatest vigour alongside its American Allies. I had every hope that, together, British and American forces would destroy a large force of Germans in Italy, and, having advanced northward of Rome, would hold a considerable German army on the Italian Front. To be quiescent in Italy and remain inert for nearly six months would be an improper use of our forces and lay us open to the reproach that the Russians were bearing almost the entire burden of the land war. Stalin said that he had never contemplated a complete cessation of all operations in Italy during the winter.

I explained that if landing-craft were taken away from the Mediterranean this would mean a definite curtailment of our operations there. I reminded Stalin of the three conditions on which the success of "Overlord" depended. First, there must be a satisfactory reduction in the strength of the German fighter force in Northwest Europe between now and the assault. Secondly, German reserves in France and the Low Countries must not be more on the day of the assault than about twelve full-strength first-quality mobile divisions. Thirdly, it must not be possible for the Germans to transfer from other fronts more than fifteen first-quality divisions during the first sixty days of the operation. To obtain these conditions we should have to hold as many Germans as possible in Italy and Yugoslavia. If Turkey entered the war, this would be an added help, but not an essential condition. The Germans now in Italy had for the most part come from France. If we slackened off our pressure in Italy, they would go back again. We must continue to engage the enemy on the only front where at present we could fight them. If we engaged them as fiercely as possible during the winter months in the Mediterranean this would make the best possible contribution towards creating the conditions needed for a successful "Overlord."

Stalin asked what would happen if there were thirteen or fourteen mobile German divisions in France and more than fifteen available from other fronts. Would this rule out "Overlord"?

I said, "No, certainly not."

* * * * *

I then turned the discussion back to Turkey. We had agreed to press her to enter the war by the end of the year. If she did, the only military operations needed would be to establish our planes on the Turkish airfields in Anatolia and capture the island of Rhodes. One assault division and some garrison troops would suffice. Once in possession of Rhodes and the Turkish air bases, we could starve out all the other Aegean islands at our leisure. These operations would not involve us in an unlimited liability, and could be regarded as a commitment of a strictly limited character. If our efforts to bring Turkey in were unsuccessful, that would be the end of the

matter. Nevertheless, failure to bring Turkey in would also
be a relief to the Germans. There was a further point about
Turkey. If she came in and we captured Rhodes, and subsequently turned the Germans out of the other Aegean islands,
our troops and air forces in Egypt could all move forward into
action to the northward instead of remaining in their present
defensive rôle.

The issue of Turkey should not be lightly turned aside. As
the President and General Marshall had stated, the scale,
nature, and timing of our operations all turned upon the availability of landing-craft and transportation of forces across the
sea. I said I was prepared to go into this question at any
time and at any length and in any detail, but if the small number of landing-craft involved could not be retained in the Mediterranean or found from some other theatre, no operations on
any scale would be possible in the Mediterranean area, and
this ban included an assault on the South of France. These
arguments should be very carefully weighed before decisions
were taken. I told Stalin that I agreed with him that a definite
reference should be given to the Technical Military Committee, and I suggested that the terms of reference should be
drawn up severally by the heads of the three Governments.

Stalin said that, on thinking it over, he did not feel that a
Military Committee was necessary. In order to take decisions
it was not necessary to go into detail. The issues at stake were
the date of "Overlord," the appointment of the Commander-
in-Chief, and whether any supporting operations could be carried out in the South of France. All this had to be decided
by the plenary Conference. Nor did he see any necessity for a
Committee of the Foreign Secretaries. The appointment of
these Committees would delay the completion of the Conference, and he, for his part, could not extend his visit to Teheran
beyond December 1, or at the latest December 2.

The President said that he had drawn up tentative terms of
reference in simple form for the Military Committee, if it was
decided that this body should get to work. The terms were in
two sentences, namely: "Paragraph 1. The Committee of three

Staffs will assume that Operation 'Overlord' is the dominating operation in 1944. Paragraph 2: The Committee will make recommendations as to subsidiary operations to be carried out, taking into most careful account any delay on Operation 'Overlord.' " This was agreed.

Stalin said that the Soviet Government was vitally concerned with the date of "Overlord," particularly because of the need for co-ordinating operations on the Russian Front. The President observed that the "Overlord" date had been fixed at the Quebec Conference, and it was only the important developments which had occurred since then that had caused any change to be contemplated.

Before we separated, Stalin looked at me across the table and said, "I wish to pose a very direct question to the Prime Minister about 'Overlord.' Do the Prime Minister and the British Staff really believe in 'Overlord'?" I replied, "Provided the conditions previously stated for 'Overlord' are established when the time comes, it will be our stern duty to hurl across the Channel against the Germans every sinew of our strength." On this we separated.

*   *   *   *   *

Stalin was our host at dinner. The company was strictly limited — Stalin and Molotov, the President, Hopkins, Harriman, Clark Kerr, myself and Eden, and our interpreters. After the labours of the Conference, there was a good deal of gaiety, and many toasts were proposed. Presently Elliott Roosevelt, who had flown out to join his father, appeared at the door, and somebody beckoned him to come in. He therefore took his seat at the table. He even intervened in the conversation, and has since given a highly coloured and extremely misleading account of what he heard. Stalin, as Hopkins recounts, indulged in a great deal of "teasing" of me, which I did not at all resent until the Marshal entered in a genial manner upon a serious and even deadly aspect of the punishment to be inflicted upon the Germans. The German General Staff, he said, must be liquidated. The whole force of Hitler's mighty armies depended upon about fifty thousand officers and technicians. If these were rounded up and shot at the end of the war, German military strength would be extirpated. On this I thought it right to say: "The British Parliament and public will never tolerate mass executions. Even if in war passion they allowed them to begin, they would turn violently against those responsible after the first butchery had taken place. The Soviets must be under no delusion on this point."

Stalin however, perhaps only in mischief, pursued the subject. "Fifty thousand," he said, "must be shot." I was deeply angered. "I would rather," I said, "be taken out into the garden here and now and be shot myself than sully my own and my country's honour by such infamy."

At this point the President intervened. He had a compromise to propose. Not fifty thousand should be shot, but only forty-nine thousand. By this he hoped, no doubt, to reduce the whole matter to ridicule. Eden also made signs and gestures intended to reassure me that it was all a joke. But now Elliott Roosevelt rose in his place at the end of the table and made a speech, saying how cordially he agreed with Marshal Stalin's plan and how sure he was that the United States Army would support it. At this intrusion I got up and left the table, walking off into the next room, which was in semi-darkness. I had not been there a minute before hands were clapped upon my shoulders from behind, and there was Stalin, with Molotov at his side, both grinning broadly, and eagerly declaring that they were only playing, and that nothing of a serious character had entered their heads. Stalin has a very captivating manner when he chooses to use it, and I never saw him do so to such an extent as at this moment. Although I was not then, and am not now, fully convinced that all was chaff and there was no serious intent lurking behind, I consented to return, and the rest of the evening passed pleasantly.

4

Teheran: The Crux

My Sixty-Ninth Birthday — I See Stalin Alone — I Explain the
Difference of View Between the British and Americans — A Nar-
row Issue — The Great Battle Impending in Italy — An Am-
phibious Landing Near the Tiber — Stalin Emphasises the Need
for "Overlord" — He Offers a Russian Offensive in May or June
— The President's Luncheon of "Three Only" — The President
and I Promise a Date in May — Russia's Claim to Warm-Water
Ports — The Third Plenary Session — The Main Decisions
Taken — The Communiqué Agreed — Dinner at the British
Legation, November 30 — Compliments All Round — Many
Speeches — General Brooke's Rejoinder to Stalin — Stalin Ad-
mires His Candour.

NOVEMBER 30 was for me a crowded and memorable day.
It was my sixty-ninth birthday, and was passed almost
entirely in transacting some of the most important business
with which I have ever been concerned. The fact that the
President was in private contact with Marshal Stalin and dwelling at the Soviet Embassy, and that he had avoided ever seeing
me alone since we left Cairo, in spite of our hitherto intimate
relations and the way in which our vital affairs were inter-
woven, led me to seek a direct personal interview with Stalin.
I felt that the Russian leader was not deriving a true impression of the British attitude. The false idea was forming in his
mind that, to put it shortly, "Churchill and the British Staffs
mean to stop 'Overlord' if they can, because they want to in-

vade the Balkans instead." It was my duty to remove this double misconception.

The exact date of "Overlord" depended upon the movements of a comparatively small number of landing-craft. These landing-craft were not required for any operation in the Balkans. The President had committed us to an operation in the Bay of Bengal. If this were cancelled there would be enough landing-craft for all I wanted, namely, the amphibious power to land against opposition two divisions at a time on the coasts of Italy or Southern France, and also to carry out "Overlord" as planned in May. I had agreed with the President that May should be the month, and he had, for his part, given up the specific date of May 1. This would give me the time I needed. If I could persuade the President to obtain relief from his promise to Chiang Kai-shek and drop the Bay of Bengal plan, which had never been mentioned in our Teheran conferences, there would be enough landing-craft both for the Mediterranean and for a punctual "Overlord." In the event the great landings began on June 6, but this date was decided much later on, not by any requirement of mine, but by the moon and the weather. I also succeeded when we returned to Cairo, as will be seen, in persuading the President to abandon the enterprise in the Bay of Bengal. I therefore consider that I got what I deemed imperative. But this was far from certain at Teheran on this November morning. I was determined that Stalin should know the main fact. I did not feel entitled to tell him that the President and I had agreed upon May for "Overlord." I knew that Roosevelt wanted to tell him this himself at our luncheon which was to follow my conversation with the Marshal.

The following is founded upon the record made by Major Birse, my trusted interpreter, of my private talk with Stalin.

*   *   *   *   *

I began by reminding the Marshal that I was half American and had a great affection for the American people. What I was going to say was not to be understood as disparaging to the

Americans and I would be perfectly loyal towards them, but there were things which it was better to say outright, between two persons.

We had a preponderance of troops over the Americans in the Mediterranean. There were two or three times more British troops than American there. That was why I was anxious that the armies in the Mediterranean should not be hamstrung if it could be avoided. I wanted to use them all the time. In Italy there were some thirteen to fourteen divisions, of which nine or ten were British. There were two armies, the Fifth Anglo-American Army, and the Eighth Army, which was entirely British. The choice had been represented as keeping to the date of "Overlord" or pressing on with the operations in the Mediterranean. But that was not the whole story. The Americans wanted me to undertake an amphibious operation in the Bay of Bengal against the Japanese in March. I was not keen about it. If we had the landing-craft needed for the Bay of Bengal in the Mediterranean, we should have enough to do all we wanted there and still be able to keep to an early date for "Overlord." It was not a choice between the Mediterranean and the date of "Overlord," but between the Bay of Bengal and the date of "Overlord." However, the Americans had pinned us down to a date for "Overlord" and operations in the Mediterranean had suffered in the last two months. Our army in Italy was somewhat disheartened by the removal of seven divisions. We had sent home our three divisions, and the Americans were sending four of theirs, all in preparation for "Overlord." That was why we had not been able to take full advantage of the Italian collapse. But it also proved the earnestness of our preparations for "Overlord."

It was vital to get an early decision on the appointment of the Commander-in-Chief. Up till August we British were to have had the Supreme Command in "Overlord," but at Quebec I had told the President that I would agree to the appointment of an American while we should have the Supreme Command in the Mediterranean. I was content with this because the Americans, although equal in numbers to the British when we landed, would soon have a preponderance, and their stake would be greater after the first few months. On the other hand, as the British had the preponderance in the Mediterranean and I had my own ideas about the war there, I considered it right that we should have the Supreme Command in that theatre. The President had accepted this arrangement, and it now rested with him to nominate the Commander-in-Chief for "Overlord." As soon as the President did so, I would nominate the Mediterranean Commander-in-Chief and other commanders. The President had delayed the appointment for domestic reasons connected with high personages, but I had urged him to decide before we all left Teheran.

Stalin said that was good.

I then turned to the question of landing-craft, and explained once again how and why they were the bottleneck. We had plenty of troops in the Mediterranean, even after the removal of the seven divisions, and there would be an adequate invading British and American army in the United Kingdom. All turned on landing-craft. When the Marshal had made his momentous announcement two days before about Russia's coming into the war against Japan after Hitler's surrender, I had immediately suggested to the Americans that they might find more landing-craft for the operations we had been asked to carry out in the Indian Ocean, or that they might send some landing-craft from the Pacific to help the first lift of "Overlord." In that case there might be enough for all. But the Americans were very touchy about the Pacific. I had pointed out to them that Japan would be beaten much sooner if Russia joined in the war against her, and that they could therefore afford to give us more help.

The issue between myself and the Americans was in fact a very narrow one. It was not that I was in any way lukewarm about "Overlord." I wanted to get what I needed for the Mediterranean and at the same time keep to the date for "Overlord." The details had to be hammered out between the Staffs, and I had hoped that this might be done in Cairo. Unfortunately, Chiang Kai-shek had been there and Chinese questions had taken up nearly all the time. But I was sure that in the end enough landing-craft would be found for all.

Now about "Overlord." The British would have ready by the date fixed in May or June nearly sixteen divisions, with their corps troops, landing-craft troops, anti-aircraft, and services, a total of slightly over half a million men. These would consist of some of our best troops, including battle-trained men from the Mediterranean. In addition, the British would have all that was needed from the Royal Navy to handle transportation and to protect the Army, and there would be the Metropolitan Air Forces of about four thousand first-line British aircraft in continuous action. The American import of troops was now beginning. Up till now they had sent mainly air troops and stores for the Army, but in the next four or five months I thought a hundred and fifty thousand men or more would come every month, making a total of seven to eight hundred thousand men by May. The defeat of the submarines in the Atlantic had made this movement possible. I was in favour of launching the operation in the South of France at about the same time as "Overlord" or at whatever moment was found correct. We would be holding enemy troops in Italy, and of the twenty-two or twenty-three divisions in the Mediterranean as many as possible would go to the South of France and the rest would remain in Italy.

A great battle was impending in Italy. General Alexander had about half a million men under him. There were thirteen or fourteen Allied divisions, against nine or ten German. The weather had been bad and bridges had been swept away. But in December we intended to push on, with General Montgomery leading the Eighth Army. The amphibious landing would be made near the Tiber. At the same time the Fifth Army would be fiercely engaged holding the enemy. It might turn into a miniature Stalingrad. We did not intend to push into the wide part of Italy, but to hold the narrow leg.

Stalin said he must warn me that the Red Army was depending on the success of our invasion of Northern France. If there were no operations in May 1944, then the Red Army would

think that there would be no operations at all that year. The
weather would be bad and there would be transport difficulties.
If the operation did not take place, he did not want the Red
Army to be disappointed. Disappointment could only create
bad feeling. If there was no big change in the European war
in 1944, it would be very difficult for the Russians to carry on.
They were war-weary. He feared that a feeling of isolation
might develop in the Red Army. That was why he had tried
to find out whether "Overlord" would be undertaken on time
as promised. If not, he would have to take steps to prevent bad
feeling in the Red Army. It was most important.

I said "Overlord" would certainly take place, provided the
enemy did not bring into France larger forces than the Americans and British could gather there. If the Germans had thirty
to forty divisions in France I did not think the force we were
going to put across the Channel would be able to hold on. I
was not afraid of going on shore, but of what would happen
on the thirtieth, fortieth, or fiftieth day. However, if the Red
Army engaged the enemy and we held them in Italy and possibly the Turks came into the war, then I thought we could
win.

Stalin said that the first steps of "Overlord" would have a
good effect on the Red Army, and if he knew that it was
going to take place in May or June, he could already
prepare blows against Germany. The spring was the best time.
March and April were months of slackness, during which he
could concentrate troops and material, and in May and June
he could attack. Germany would have no troops for France.
The transfer of German divisions to the East was continuing.
The Germans were afraid of their Eastern Front because it had
no Channel which had to be crossed and there was no France
to be entered. The Germans were afraid of the Red Army advance. The Red Army would advance if it saw that help was
coming from the Allies. He asked when "Overlord" would
begin.

I said that I could not disclose the date for "Overlord" with-

out the President's agreement, but the answer would be given
at lunch-time, and I thought he would be satisfied.

*   *   *   *   *

After a short interval, the Marshal and I separately proceeded
to the President's quarters for the luncheon of "Three Only"
(with our interpreters) to which he had invited us. Roosevelt
then told Stalin that we were both agreed that "Overlord"
should be launched during the month of May. The Marshal
was evidently greatly pleased and relieved by this solemn and
direct engagement which we both made. The conversation
turned on lighter subjects, and the only part of which I have a
record was the question of Russia's outlet upon the seas and
oceans. I had always thought it was a wrong thing, capable
of breeding disastrous quarrels, that a mighty land-mass like
the Russian Empire, with its population of nearly two hundred
millions, should be denied during the winter months all effective access to the broad waters.

When Marshal Stalin raised this question of warm-water
ports for Russia, I said there were no obstacles. He also asked
about the Dardanelles and the revision of the Treaty of Sèvres.
I said that I wanted to get Turkey into the war, and this was
an awkward moment for raising the question. Stalin replied
that the time would come later. I said I expected Russia would
sail the oceans with her Navy and merchant fleet and we would
welcome her ships. At this Stalin remarked that Lord Curzon
had had other ideas. I said that in those days we did not see
eye to eye with Russia.

The President said that the Baltic should be free to all
nations for merchant shipping. There should be free zones in
the ports, and trustees should be appointed for the Kiel Canal,
while the Dardanelles ought to be free to the commerce of the
world. Stalin asked whether this would apply to Russian commerce, and we assured him that it would.

Stalin then asked what could be done for Russia in the Far
East. I replied that Russia had Vladivostok, but he pointed

out that the port was ice-bound, and also depended on the
Straits of Tsushima. At present the only exit that the Russians
had was Murmansk. I answered that I wished to meet the
Russian grievance, because the government of the world must
be entrusted to satisfied nations, who wished nothing more for
themselves than what they had. If the world-government were
in the hands of hungry nations, there would always be danger.
But none of us had any reason to seek for anything more. The
peace would be kept by peoples who lived in their own way
and were not ambitious. Our power placed us above the rest.
We were like rich men dwelling at peace within their habita-
tions.

*   *   *   *   *

After a brief interval, the third plenary session began as before in the Russian Legation at four o'clock. There was a full
attendance and we numbered nearly thirty.

The President said he was very happy to inform the Conference that agreement had been reached on the main military
problems. Sir Alan Brooke said that, after sitting in combined
session, the United States and British Chiefs of Staff had recommended us to launch "Overlord" in May, "in conjunction
with a supporting operation against the South of France, on
the largest scale that was permitted by the landing-craft available at that time."

I then emphasised the need for the combined United States
and British Staffs to keep in closest touch with the Soviet military authorities, so that all operations on the Eastern as well
as the Western and Mediterranean fronts were concerted together. By this means the three Great Powers would close in
on the wild beast so that he was engaged on all sides at the
same moment. Very detailed Staff work would be necessary to
launch "Overlord," which was the biggest combined operation
ever planned.

Stalin said that he understood the importance of the decision
taken by the Staffs and the difficulties inherent in carrying it
out. The danger period for "Overlord" would be at the time

of deployment from the landings. At this point the Germans might transfer troops from the East in order to create the maximum difficulties for "Overlord." In order to prevent any movement from the East of any considerable German forces, he undertook to organise a large-scale Russian offensive in May.[1]

The President remarked on the importance of the timing of operations in all theatres. Now that the three Staffs had got together, he hoped they would keep together. He had already informed Marshal Stalin that the next step was to appoint the Commander for "Overlord." After consultation with his own Staffs and with me, it should be possible to make a decision within three or four days. Now that the main military decisions had been taken, it seemed right for the British and American Staffs to return to Cairo as soon as possible to work out the details. To this Stalin and I agreed.

I added that now that the supreme decisions had been taken, every effort must be bent to find the ways and means to get more landing-craft. With five months still to go before the launching of "Overlord," and with all the resources of America and Great Britain at our disposal, it should be possible to do this. If "Overlord" was to be done, it must be done with smashing force, and I hoped that the Staffs would find ways and means of increasing the initial assault forces.

I asked if there would be any difficulty in the three Staffs concerting cover plans. Stalin explained that the Russians had made considerable use of deception by means of dummy tanks, aircraft, and airfields. Radio deception had also proved effective. He was entirely agreeable to the Staffs collaborating with the object of devising joint cover and deception schemes. "In war-time," I said, "Truth is so precious that she should always be attended by a bodyguard of lies." Stalin and his comrades greatly appreciated this remark when it was translated, and upon this note our formal conference ended gaily.

I then suggested that the Staffs should draft a short communiqué to cover the military talks for submission to the President, Marshal Stalin, and myself. The note to be sounded

[1] The main Russian attack began on June 23.

was brevity, mystery, and a foretaste of impending doom for Germany. The following communiqué was therefore framed and agreed to by all:

> . . . Our Military Staffs have joined in our round-table discussions, and we have concerted our plans for the destruction of the German forces. We have reached complete agreement as to the scope and timing of the operations which will be undertaken from the east, west, and south.

*   *   *   *   *

Hitherto we had assembled for our conferences or meals in the Soviet Embassy. I had claimed however that I should be the host at the third dinner, which should be held in the British Legation. This could not well be disputed. Great Britain and I myself both came first alphabetically, and in seniority I was four or five years older than Roosevelt or Stalin. We were by centuries the longest established of the three Governments; I might have added, but did not, that we had been the longest in the war; and, finally, November 30 was my birthday. These arguments, particularly the last one, were conclusive, and all preparations were made by our Minister for a dinner of nearly forty persons, including not only the political and military chiefs but some of their higher staffs. The Soviet Political Police, the N.K.V.D., insisted on searching the British Legation from top to bottom, looking behind every door and under every cushion, before Stalin appeared; and about fifty armed Russian policemen, under their own General, posted themselves near all the doors and windows. The American Security men were also much in evidence. Everything however passed off agreeably. Stalin, arriving under heavy guard, was in the best of tempers, and the President, from his wheel chair, beamed on us all in pleasure and good will.

This was a memorable occasion in my life. On my right sat the President of the United States, on my left the master of Russia. Together we controlled practically all the naval and three-quarters of all the air forces in the world, and could direct armies of nearly twenty millions of men, engaged in the most terrible of wars that had yet occurred in human history. I could not help rejoicing at the long way we had come on the road to victory since the summer of 1940, when we had been alone, and, apart from the Navy and the Air, practically unarmed, against the triumphant and unbroken might of Germany and Italy, with almost all Europe and its resources in their grasp. Mr. Roosevelt gave me for a birthday present a beautiful Persian porcelain vase, which, although it was broken into fragments on the homeward journey, has been marvellously reconstructed and is one of my treasures.

During dinner I had a most pleasant conversation with both my august guests. Stalin repeated the question he had posed at the Conference, "Who will command 'Overlord'?" I said that the President had not yet finally made up his mind, but that I was almost certain it would be General Marshall, who sat opposite us at no great distance, and that was how it had stood hitherto. Stalin was evidently very pleased at this. He then spoke about General Brooke. He thought that he did not like the Russians. He had been very abrupt and rough with them at our first Moscow meeting in August 1942. I reassured him, remarking that military men were apt to be blunt and hardcut when dealing with war problems with their professional colleagues. Stalin said that he liked them all the better for that. He gazed at Brooke intently across the room.

When the time came, I proposed the health of our illustrious guests, and the President proposed my health and wished me many happy returns of the day. He was followed by Stalin, who spoke in a similar strain.

*   *   *   *   *

Many informal toasts were then proposed, according to the Russian custom, which is certainly very well suited to banquets of this kind. Hopkins made a speech couched in a happy vein, in the course of which he said that he had made "a very long and thorough study of the British Constitution, which is unwritten, and of the War Cabinet, whose authority and composition are not specifically defined." As the result of this study, he said, "I have learnt that the provisions of the British Constitution and the powers of the War Cabinet are just whatever Winston Churchill wants them to be at any given moment." This caused general laughter. The reader of these volumes will know how little foundation there was in this jocular assertion. It is true that I received a measure of loyal support in the direction of the war from Parliament and my Cabinet colleagues which may well be unprecedented, and that there were very few large issues upon which I was overruled; but it was with some pride that I reminded my two great comrades on more than one occasion that I was the only one of our trinity who could at any moment be dismissed from power by the vote of a House of Commons freely elected on universal franchise, or could be controlled from day to day by the opinion of a War Cabinet representing all parties in the State. The President's term of office was fixed, and his powers, not only as President, but as Commander-in-Chief, were almost absolute under the American Constitution. Stalin appeared to be, and at this moment certainly was, all-powerful in Russia. They could order; I had to convince and persuade. I was glad that this should be so. The process was laborious, but I had no reason to complain of the way it worked.

*   *   *   *   *

As the dinner proceeded, there were many speeches, and most of the principal figures, including Molotov and General Marshall, made their contribution. But the speech which stands out in my memory came from General Brooke. I quote the account he was good enough to write for me:

Halfway through the dinner [he says] the President very kindly proposed my health, referring to the time when my father had visited his father at Hyde Park. Just as he was finishing, and I was thinking what an easy time I should have replying to such kind words, Stalin got up and said he would finish the toast. He then proceeded to imply that I had failed to show real feelings of friendship towards the Red Army, that I was lacking in a true appreciation of its fine qualities, and that he hoped in future I should be able to show greater comradeship towards the soldiers of the Red Army!

I was very much surprised by these accusations, as I could not think what they were based on. I had however seen enough of Stalin by then to know that if I sat down under these insults I should lose any respect he might ever have had for me, and that he would continue such attacks in the future.

I therefore rose to thank the President most profusely for his very kind expressions, and then turned to Stalin in approximately the following words:

"Now, Marshal, may I deal with your toast. I am surprised that you should have found it necessary to raise accusations against me that are entirely unfounded. You will remember that this morning while we were discussing cover plans Mr. Churchill said that 'in war Truth must have an escort of lies.' You will also remember that you yourself told us that in all your great offensives your real intentions were always kept concealed from the outer world. You told us that all your dummy tanks and dummy aeroplanes were always massed on those fronts that were of an immediate interest, while your true intentions were covered by a cloak of complete secrecy.

"Well, Marshal, you have been misled by dummy tanks and dummy aeroplanes, and you have failed to observe those feelings of true friendship which I have for the Red Army, nor have you seen the feelings of genuine comradeship which I bear towards all its members."

As this was translated by Pavlov, sentence by sentence, to Stalin, I watched his expression carefully. It was inscrutable. But at the end he turned to me and said, with evident relish, "I like that man. He rings true. I must have a talk with him afterwards."

At length we moved into the antechamber, and here everyone moved about in changing groups. I felt that there was a greater sense of solidarity and good-comradeship than we had ever reached before in the Grand Alliance. I had not invited Randolph and Sarah to the dinner, though they came in while my birthday toast was being proposed, but now Stalin singled them out and greeted them most warmly, and of course the President knew them well.

As I moved around, I saw Stalin in a small circle face to face with "Brookie," as I call him. The General's account continues:

As we walked out of the room, the Prime Minister told me that he had felt somewhat nervous as to what I should say next when I had referred to "truth" and "lies." He comforted me however by telling me that my reply to the toast had had the right effect on Stalin. I therefore decided to return to the attack in the anteroom. I went up to Stalin and told him how surprised I was, and grieved, that he should have found it necessary to raise such accusations against me in his toast. He replied at once through Pavlov, "The best friendships are those founded on misunderstandings," and he shook me warmly by the hand.

It seemed to me that all the clouds had passed away, and in fact Stalin's confidence in my friend was established on a foundation of respect and good will which was never shaken while we all worked together.

It must have been after two in the morning when we finally separated. The Marshal resigned himself to his escort and departed, and the President was conveyed to his quarters in the Soviet Embassy. I went to bed tired out but content, feeling sure that nothing but good had been done. It certainly was a happy birthday for me.

5

Teheran: Conclusions

Conversation at Luncheon, December 1 — How to Gain Turkey — The Russian Share of Italian Ships — The Frontiers of Poland — The "Curzon Line" and the Line of the Oder — A Frank Talk — Finland — "No Annexations and No Indemnities" — Final Accord — The Question of Germany — Partition? — President Roosevelt's Suggestion — I Unfold a Personal View — Marshal Stalin's Standpoint — More About Poland — Broad Agreement on Military Policy — Political Aspects Remote and Speculative — Deep Fear of German Might at This War Climax — The Present Partition — "It Cannot Last."

S EVERAL OF OUR GRAVEST POLITICAL ISSUES stood out before and after the main decision on strategy had been reached. The Three lunched together again at the President's table in the Soviet Legation on December 1. In addition, on this occasion Molotov, Hopkins, Eden, Clark Kerr, and Harriman were present. The question of inducing Turkey to enter into the war was our first topic.

Hopkins asked what support we should have to give Turkey if she came in. Roosevelt said that Inönü would ask what we could do. Until the landing-craft situation had been studied, we should be careful in making promises. I said that we had in Egypt seventeen British squadrons not under the Anglo-American command, and Air Chief Marshal Tedder had three more squadrons which we could spare. They were chiefly fighters and could be used to protect Turkey. In addition, we had three regiments of anti-aircraft guns. This was all we had promised. We had not promised Turkey any troops. She had fifty divisions equipped, and there was no need to send any troops.

Stalin said that if Turkey entered the war, she would make part of her territory available. I agreed, and said Ploesti would be vulnerable. We British were not offering Turkey anything that was not ours to give, and we were only giving three squadrons from the Central Mediterranean to make up the number from seventeen to twenty. Perhaps the Americans could add a few bomber squadrons. We had said that we would only give air protection. We had no army available. The landing-craft required in March for taking Rhodes could be sandwiched in between Italy and "Overlord." The President hoped this could be done, but said that casualties among landing-craft were very heavy and we should want all we could get for "Overlord." I replied that I saw no difficulty. We had made no offers to Turkey, nor did I know whether Inönü would accept any. The President would be in Cairo and could see what his Staffs would have to say. We British could only offer our twenty squadrons. The Turks did not need any army; they needed air protection. In addition, Inönü might not come to Cairo.

"He might fall ill," interjected Stalin.

I said that if he refused to come and the President had to leave, I proposed to go in a cruiser and see him in Adana. Inönü would come there. . . . Landing-craft were the bottleneck for all our operations. Some might be forthcoming from the Indian Ocean or the Pacific, or more could be built. If this could not be done, we should have to give up something, but it was agreed that "Overlord" was not to suffer.

Roosevelt then said that my suggestion that landing-craft should be provided from the Pacific was impossible. Distances were too great, and every day the Americans were proceeding north in the Gilbert and Marshall Islands to attack Japanese supply lines. They needed all the landing-craft they had.

Hopkins asked how many landing-craft would be needed for taking Rhodes. I replied that there was no commitment

to Turkey about Rhodes or any other island, and there was
no commitment in landing-craft. Roosevelt said that if he
were Inönü he would ask for Crete and other islands to be
taken.

I said: "What I want is air bases in the region of Smyrna
and Badrun. Those airfields have been constructed by us.
When we get them and put in squadrons, we can drive the
Germans out of the air. It pays us anyhow to lose one aircraft for every German machine shot down. We must starve
out the German garrisons on the islands. If Turkey takes an
active part, the islands will fall of themselves. It would not
be necessary in that case to attack even Rhodes. The islands
have to be supplied by Germany, and if we have air cover
from Turkey, our destroyers can cut down German convoys,
which they cannot do at present because Germany commands the air. Turkish bases will give us continued pressure
against the Germans, and that will be a preparation for 'Overlord.' "

Stalin agreed, and the President consented to go forward on
the basis of twenty squadrons and some bombers, but no amphibious operations.

I then summed up. We were offering Turkey only limited
air protection and anti-aircraft guns, but the winter was approaching and Germany would not invade Turkey. We
would continue to supply her with arms. There was the priceless opportunity for Turkey of accepting the Soviet invitation
to sit beside us at the Peace Conference. There was the assurance that if Bulgaria attacked Turkey because the latter had
declared war on Germany, the Soviet Union would retaliate
on Bulgaria, a thing which had never happened before. Then
there was the offer of association with the victorious Powers
and our good offices and friendship.

"What measures," asked Stalin, "does Mr. Churchill expect
from the Soviet Union in case Turkey declares war on Germany, as a result of which Bulgaria attacks Turkey and the
Soviet declares war on Bulgaria?"

I said I was not asking for anything specific, but as the Soviet

armies advanced through Odessa they would create a great
effect among the population in Bulgaria. The Turkish Army
had rifles, brave infantry, fairly good artillery, but no anti-
aircraft guns, no aircraft, and very few tanks. We had established military schools, but they were not attended regularly.
The Turks were not quick to learn. Their army was brave
but not modern. Twenty-five million pounds had been spent
on weapons, mainly American, and we had shipped them.

Stalin said it was possible Turkey would not have to fight.
They would give us their air bases; that might be the course
of events, and it would be good.

The President then asked Mr. Eden to tell us what the
Turks had said in Cairo. Mr. Eden said he had asked the
Turkish Foreign Minister to give us air bases and told him
that Germany would not attack Turkey. The Foreign Minister
had refused, saying Germany would react against Turkish prov-
ocation. Turkey would rather come in by agreement than be
brought in indirectly as a result of such action as had been
suggested.

I observed that when we asked the Turks to strain their
neutrality by giving us their air bases, they replied, "Oh, no,
we cannot play a passive rôle," but if we asked them to start
war in earnest, they answered, "Oh, no, we are not sufficiently
armed." I proposed, if necessary, to try other methods. If
Turkey refused, she would forfeit her chance to sit at the Peace
Conference. She would be treated like other neutrals. We
would say that Great Britain had no further interest in her
affairs and we would stop the supply of arms.

Mr. Eden said he would like to get quite clear in his mind
the demands that were to be made on Turkey. Was it understood that Turkey should go to war with Germany and no
one else? If as a result the Germans made Bulgaria join them
in a war against Turkey, would the Soviet Government go to
war with Bulgaria? Stalin agreed on both points. I said that,
for myself, I should be satisfied with strained neutrality from
Turkey. There was thus a very great measure of agreement
on the limited steps for which I asked in order to win the

great prize of bringing Turkey into the war, and it was settled that President Inönü should be invited to come to Cairo and talk it all over with me and the President. Although I felt how deeply Turkish minds had been affected by our failure to attack Rhodes, by the loss of Cos and Leros, and the consequent German command of the air in the Aegean, I left the subject, having got all I had thought it right to ask, and with fair hopes that it would not be insufficient.

*　　*　　*　　*　　*

Molotov now asked whether the Soviet Government could not be given an answer about the Italian ships. Roosevelt's reply was very simple. A large number of merchant ships and a smaller number of warships could be used by the three nations during the war, and could then be distributed by title. It would be best until then that those should use these ships who could use them best. Molotov said that Russia would be able to make good use of them. I asked where the Soviet Government would like them delivered. Stalin said in the Black Sea, and, if this were not possible, then in the North. If Turkey did not come into the war, the Black Sea would be impossible. But use could be made of them in the North.

I said that this was a very small thing after all the efforts that Russia was making or had made. We only asked for a little time to handle the matter with the Italians. I said I should like to see the ships go to the Black Sea, and that perhaps I might at the same time send some of His Majesty's ships with them. The President and I needed time to arrange the matter with the Italians, who were already helping with some of their smaller ships in patrol work, and some Italian submarines were carrying important supplies. There must be no mutiny in the Italian Fleet and no scuttling of ships. A couple of months should be enough for me and the President to arrange with the Italians. The ships could pass under Russian orders by that date, after refitting. I went on to say that I should like to put four or five British submarines into the Black Sea. This was one of the things which might be asked

of Turkey if she accepted only "strained neutrality." But we
would abide by Marshal Stalin's wishes. We had no ambitions
in the Black Sea.

Stalin replied that he would be grateful for any help.

*   *   *   *   *

After an interval, when luncheon was over, we moved into
another room and took our seats at a conference table. Our
discussions continued all through the afternoon. Poland was
the next important subject.

The President began by saying that he hoped the Polish and
Soviet Governments would resume relations, so that any deci-
sion taken could be accepted by the Polish Government. But
he admitted there were difficulties. Stalin asked with what
Government he would have to negotiate. The Polish Govern-
ment and their friends in Poland were in contact with the
Germans. They killed the partisans. Neither the President nor
I could have any idea of what was now going on there.

I said that the Polish question was important for us in the
United Kingdom, because we had declared war on Germany
for invading Poland. Although Great Britain had been unpre-
pared, the German attack on Poland had launched us into the
war. I reverted to my illustration of the three matches — Germany, Poland, and the Soviet Union. One of the main objects
of the Allies was to achieve the security of the Soviet western
frontier, and so to prevent an attack by Germany in the future.
Here I reminded Stalin of his mention of the line of the Oder
in the West.

Stalin, interrupting, said that previously there had been no
mention of re-establishing relations with the Polish Government, but only of determining Poland's frontiers. Today the
matter had been put quite differently. Russia, even more than
other states, was interested in good relations with Poland, because for her it was a question of the security of her frontiers.
Russia was in favour of the reconstruction, development, and
expansion of Poland mainly at the expense of Germany. But

he separated Poland from the Polish Government in exile. He had broken off relations with the Polish Government in exile, not on account of caprice, but because it had joined with Hitler in slanderous propaganda against Russia. What guarantee was there that this would not happen again? He would like to have a guarantee that the Polish Government in exile would not kill partisans, but, on the contrary, would urge the Poles to fight the Germans and not concern themselves with any machinations. He would welcome any Polish Government which would take such active measures, and he would be glad to renew relations with them. But he was by no means sure that the Polish Government in exile was ever likely to become the kind of Government it ought to be.

Here I said that it would be a great help if round that very table we could learn what were the Russian ideas about the frontiers. I should then put the matter before the Poles and say frankly if I thought the conditions fair. His Majesty's Government, for whom alone I spoke, would like to be able to tell the Poles that the plan was a good one and the best that they were likely to get, and that His Majesty's Government would not argue against it at the peace table. Then we could get on with the President's idea of resuming relations. What we wanted was a strong and independent Poland, friendly to Russia.

Stalin said that that was true, but that the Poles could not be allowed to seize the Ukraine and White Russian territory. That was not fair. According to the 1939 frontier, the soil of the Ukraine and White Russia was returned to the Ukraine and to White Russia. Soviet Russia adhered to the frontiers of 1939, for they appeared to be ethnologically the right ones.

Eden asked if this meant the Ribbentrop-Molotov Line.

"Call it whatever you like," said Stalin.

Molotov remarked that it was generally called the Curzon Line.

"No," said Eden, "there are important differences."

Molotov said there were none.

I then produced a map and showed the Curzon Line and the

1939 line, and indicated also the line of the Oder. Eden said
that the south end of the Curzon Line had never been defined
in terms.

At this point the meeting broke into groups. There was a
general gathering round my map and round a map which was
produced by the Americans, and it was difficult for the interpreters to take notes.

Eden suggested that the Curzon Line was intended to pass
to the east of Lvov.

Stalin replied that the line on my map had not been drawn
correctly. Lvov should be left on the Russian side and the line
should go westward towards Przemysl. Molotov would get a
map of the Curzon Line and a description of it. He said that
he did not want any Polish population, and that if he found
any district inhabited by Poles he would gladly give it up.

I suggested that the value of the German land was much
greater than the Pripet Marshes. It was industrial and it
would make a much better Poland. We should like to be able
to say to the Poles that the Russians were right, and to tell the
Poles that they must agree that they had had a fair deal. If the
Poles did not accept, we could not help it. Here I made it clear
that I was speaking for the British alone, adding that the President had many Poles in the United States who were his fel-
low-citizens.

Stalin said again that if it were proved to him that any district were Polish, he would not claim it, and here he made
some shadowing on the map west of the Curzon Line and south
of Vilna, which he admitted to be mainly Polish.

At this point the meeting again separated into groups, and
there was a prolonged study of the Oder Line on a map. When
this came to an end, I said I liked the picture, and that I would
say to the Poles that if they did not accept it they would be
foolish, and I would remind them that but for the Red Army
they would have been utterly destroyed. I would point out to
them that they had been given a fine place to live in, more
than three hundred miles each way.

Stalin said that it would indeed be a large, industrial State. "And friendly to Russia," I interjected.

Stalin replied that Russia wanted a friendly Poland.

I then, runs the record, said to Mr. Eden, with some emphasis, that I was not going to break my heart about this cession of part of Germany to Poland or about Lvov. Eden said that if Marshal Stalin would take the Curzon and Oder Lines as a basis on which to argue, that might provide a beginning.

At this point Molotov produced the Russian version of the Curzon Line, and the text of a wireless telegram from Lord Curzon giving all the place-names. I asked whether Molotov would object to the Poles getting the Oppeln district. He said he did not think so.

I said that the Poles would be wise to take our advice. I was not prepared to make a great squawk about Lvov. Turning to Marshal Stalin, I added that I did not think we were very far apart in principle. Roosevelt asked Stalin whether he thought a transfer of population on a voluntary basis would be possible. The Marshal said that probably it would be.

On this we left the Polish discussion.

*   *   *   *   *

The President next asked Stalin whether he was ready to discuss Finland. Could the United States Government do anything to help to get Finland out of the war?

Stalin said that recently the Swedish Vice-Minister for Foreign Affairs had told Madame Kollontay (the Soviet Ambassadress) that the Finns were afraid that Russia wanted to turn Finland into a Russian province. The Soviet Government had replied that they had no wish to make Finland a Russian province unless the Finns forced them to do so. Madame Kollontay had then been instructed to tell the Finns that the Soviet Government would have no objection to receiving a Finnish delegation in Moscow. But they wished the Finns to state their views about dropping out of the war. In Teheran he had just received the gist of the Finnish reply, which was conveyed to him through M. Boheman. The reply did not make any mention of Finland's desire to dissociate herself from Germany. It raised the question of frontiers. The Finns suggested that as a basis of discussion the 1939 frontier should be adopted, with some corrections in favour of the Soviet Union. Stalin believed that the Finns were not really anxious to conduct serious negotiations. Their conditions were unacceptable and the Finns well knew it. The Finns still hoped for a German victory; and some of them at any rate had a strong belief that the Germans were going to win.

Roosevelt asked if it would help if the United States Government advised the Finns to go to Moscow. Stalin replied they were ready enough to go to Moscow, but it would not do much good if they went with their present programme.

I said that in the days of the Russo-Finnish War I had been sympathetic to Finland, but I had turned against her when she came into the war against the Soviets. Russia must have security for Leningrad and its approaches. The position of the Soviet Union as a permanent naval and air Power in the Baltic must be assured. But people in the United Kingdom would be unhappy if the Finns were incorporated in the Soviet Union against their will. I had therefore been glad to hear what Marshal Stalin had said. I did not think it useful to ask for indemnities. The Finns might cut down a few trees, but that would not do much good.

Stalin said that he did not want money, but within, say, five or eight years the Finns would be well able to make good the damage they had done to Russia by supplying her with paper, wood, and many other things. He thought the Finns should be given a lesson, and he was determined to get compensation.

I said I imagined that the harm the Finns did to Russia by their improper attack far exceeded what a poor country like Finland could supply. I added, "There is still ringing in my ears the famous slogan, 'No annexations and no indemnities.'

Perhaps Marshal Stalin will not be pleased with me for saying that."

Stalin, with a broad grin, replied, "I have told you that I am becoming a Conservative."

I then asked what it was he wanted. We had "Overlord" coming. I should like to have Sweden with us in the war and Finland out of the war by the spring. Stalin said that would be good.

The conversation then turned to territorial detail — Viborg ("Nothing doing about Viborg," said Stalin), the Karelian Isthmus, Hangö. "If the cession of Hangö presents a difficulty," said Stalin, "I am willing to take Petsamo instead." "A fair exchange," said Roosevelt.

I said the British wanted two things: first, that Russia should be satisfied with her frontiers; second, that the Finns should be free and independent and live as well as they could in those very uncomfortable regions. But we did not want to put any pressure on Russia. Stalin said that, after all, allies could squeeze each other if they wanted to from time to time. But let the Finns live. It would be all right so long as half the damage they had done was made good. Roosevelt asked whether it would be any use if the Finns were to go to Moscow without any conditions. Stalin said that if there were no assurances that an agreement would be concluded, then an expedition to Moscow would help Germany, who would make capital out of any failure. This applied also to the aggressive elements in Finland, who would say that the Russians did not really want peace.

I said that would be a lie, and that we would all say so loudly.

"All right," said Stalin, "let them come if you insist."

Roosevelt said that the present Finnish leaders were pro-German; if there were others we might get somewhere. Stalin thought it would be better to have others, but he did not object even to Ryti. Anyone, even the Devil, might come. He was not afraid of devils.

I said I hoped Marshal Stalin would handle the question of

Finland, with due regard to the possibility of Sweden coming into the war in time for our general offensive in May.

Stalin agreed, but said that he could not diverge from several conditions: (1) Restoration of the 1940 treaty. (2) Hangö or Petsamo. (Here he added that Hangö was leased to the Soviet Union, but he would propose to take Petsamo.) (3) Compensation in kind as to 50 per cent for damage. Quantities could be discussed later. (4) A breach with Germany. (5) The expulsion of all Germans. (6) Demobilisation.

I replied about compensation that it was easy enough to do damage, but very hard to repair it, and that it was bad for any one country to fall into tribute to another. Stalin said that the Finns might perhaps be given an opportunity to repay the damage they had done in, say, five to eight years. I said, "Experience shows that large indemnities do not work." Stalin proposed to occupy a region of Finland if the Finns did not pay, but if they did pay, the Russians would withdraw within the year.

"I have not yet," I said, "been elected a Soviet commissar, but if I were, I should advise against this. There are much bigger things to think about." We were behind the Russians and ready to help them at every turn, but we must think of the May battle. President Roosevelt said that he was ready to stand behind all that had been said (against large indemnities).

*   *   *   *

Stalin now asked, "Are there any other questions?" The President replied, "There is the question of Germany." Stalin said that he would like to see Germany split up. The President agreed, but Stalin suggested that I should object.

I said I did not object in principle. Roosevelt said that, so that there could be some discussion, he and his advisers had had a shot at a plan some three months before. This involved the dividing of Germany into five parts. Stalin, with a grin, suggested that I was not listening because I was not inclined to see Germany split up. I said that I considered that the root of the evil lay in Prussia, in the Prussian Army and General Staff.

Roosevelt then explained his plan for splitting Germany into five parts: (1) Prussia. (2) Hanover and the northwest part of Germany. (3) Saxony and the Leipzig area. (4) Hesse-Darmstadt, Hesse-Cassel, and the section south of the Rhine. (5) Bavaria, Baden, and Württemberg. These five sections would be self-governing, but there were two more that would be governed by the United Nations: (1) Kiel and its canal and Hamburg. (2) The Ruhr and the Saar. These would be under the control of the United Nations as trustees. He was only throwing this out as an idea which might be talked over.

"If," I said, "I might use the American idiom, I would say that the President has 'said a mouthful.' Mr. Roosevelt's plan is a new one to me. In my opinion there are two things, one destructive and the other constructive. I have two clear ideas in mind. First, the isolation of Prussia. What is to be done to Prussia after that is only secondary. Then I should like to detach Bavaria, Württemberg, the Palatinate, Saxony, and Baden. Whereas I would treat Prussia sternly, I would make things easier for the second group, which I should like to see work in with what I would call a Danubian Confederation. The people of these parts of Germany are not the most ferocious, and I should like to see them live tolerably, and in a generation they would feel differently. South Germans are not going to start another war, and we would have to make it worth their while to forget Prussia. I do not much mind whether there are one or two groups." I asked Marshal Stalin whether he would be prepared to go into action on this front.

Stalin said he would, but he preferred a plan for the partition of Germany — something like the President's plan, which was more likely to weaken Germany. When one had to deal with large masses of German troops, one found them all fighting like devils, as the British and American armies would soon learn. The Austrians by themselves were different, and he described the way they surrendered. All Germans were the same. It was the Prussian officers that provided the cement. But fundamentally there was no difference between North Germans and South Germans, for all Germans fought like fierce beasts. We should be careful not to include the Austrians in any kind of combination. Austria had existed independently, and could do so again. So also must Hungary exist independently. After breaking up Germany it would be most unwise to create new combinations, Danubian or otherwise.

President Roosevelt agreed warmly. There was no difference between Germans. The Bavarians had no officer class; otherwise they were exactly like the Prussians, as the American troops had already discovered.

I said that if Germany were divided into a number of parts as suggested by the President, and these parts were not attached to other combinations, they would reunite. It was not a question of dividing Germany so much as giving a life to the cut-off bits and making them content not to be dependent on the Greater Reich. Even if this were achieved for fifty years, that would be a lot.

Stalin said that a Danubian combination would not be able to live, and the Germans would take advantage of this by putting flesh on something that was only a skeleton and thus creating a new great state. Here he asked whether Hungary and Rumania would be members of any such combination. He then reiterated his views about the advantages which it would present to Germany in the future. It was far better to break up and scatter the German tribes. Of course, they would want to unite, no matter how much they were split up. They would always want to reunite. In this he saw great danger, which would have to be neutralised by various economic measures, and in the long run by force if necessary. That was the only way to keep the peace. But if we were to make a large combination with Germans in it trouble was bound to come. We had to see to it that they were kept separate, and that Hungary and Germany should not be coupled. There were no measures possible to exclude a movement towards reunion. Germans would always want to reunite and to take their revenge. It would be necessary to keep ourselves strong enough to beat them if they ever let loose another war.

I asked Stalin if he contemplated a Europe of little states, all disjointed, with no larger units at all.

He replied that he was speaking of Germany, not Europe. Poland and France were large states. Rumania and Bulgaria were small states. But Germany should at all costs be broken up so that she could not reunite. The President said that what he proposed was a method of doing this. I said that I must make it clear that the present was only a preliminary survey of a vast historical problem. Stalin said that it was certainly very preliminary.

* * * * *

I then brought the discussion back to Poland. I said I did not ask for any agreement, nor was I convinced on the matter myself, but I should rather like to get something down on paper. I then produced the following formula: "It is thought in principle that the home of the Polish state and nation should be between the so-called Curzon Line and the Line of the Oder,[1] including for Poland East Prussia (as defined) and Oppeln; but the actual tracing of the frontier line requires careful study, and possibly disentanglement of population at some points." Why not a formula on which I could say something like this to the Poles: "I do not know if the Russians would approve, but I think that I might get it for you. You see, you are being well looked after." I added that we should never get the Poles to say that they were satisfied. Nothing would satisfy the Poles.

Stalin then said that the Russians would like to have the warm-water port of Königsberg, and he sketched a possible line on the map. This would put Russia on the neck of Germany. If he got this, he would be ready enough to agree to my formula about Poland. I asked what about Lvov. Stalin said he would accept the Curzon Line.

* * * * *

[1] No question as to whether it should be the Eastern or Western Neisse had yet arisen.

The same evening, Roosevelt, Stalin, and I initialled the following document, which sets forth the military conclusions of our Triple Conference.

The Conference:

(1) Agreed that the partisans in Yugoslavia should be supported by supplies and equipment to the greatest possible extent, and also by Commando operations.

(2) Agreed that, from the military point of view, it was most desirable that Turkey should come into the war on the side of the Allies before the end of the year.

(3) Took note of Marshal Stalin's statement that if Turkey found herself at war with Germany, and as a result Bulgaria declared war on Turkey or attacked her, the Soviet would immediately be at war with Bulgaria. The Conference further took note that this fact would be explicitly stated in the forthcoming negotiations to bring Turkey into the war.

(4) Took note that Operation "Overlord" would be launched during May 1944, in conjunction with an operation against Southern France. The latter operation would be undertaken in as great a strength as availability of landing-craft permitted. The Conference further took note of Marshal Stalin's statement that the Soviet forces would launch an offensive at about the same time with the object of preventing the German forces from transferring from the Eastern to the Western Front.

(5) Agreed that the military Staffs of the three Powers should henceforward keep in close touch with each other in regard to the impending operations in Europe. In particular it was agreed that a cover plan to mystify and mislead the enemy as regards these operations should be concerted between the Staffs concerned.

*   *   *   *   *

Thus our long and hard discussions at Teheran reached their end. The military conclusions governed in the main the future of the war. The cross-Channel invasion was fixed for May, subject naturally to tides and the moon. It was to be aided by a renewed major Russian offensive. At first sight I liked the proposed descent upon the French Southern shore by part of the Allied Armies in Italy. The project had not been examined in detail, but the fact that both the Americans and the Russians favoured it made it easier to secure the landing-craft necessary for the success of our Italian campaign and the capture of Rome, without which it would have been a failure. I was of course more attracted by the President's alternative suggestion of a right-handed move from Italy by Istria and Trieste, with ultimate designs for reaching Vienna through the Ljubljana gap. All this lay five or six months ahead. There would be plenty of time to make a final choice as the general war shaped itself, if only the life of our armies in Italy was not paralysed by depriving them of their modest requirements in landing-craft. Many amphibious or semi-amphibious schemes were open. I expected that the seaborne operations in the Bay of Bengal would be abandoned, and this, as the next chapter will show, proved correct. I was glad to feel that several important options were still preserved. Our strong efforts were to be renewed to bring Turkey into the war with all that might accompany this in the Aegean, and follow from it in the Black Sea. In this we were to be disappointed. Surveying the whole military scene, as we separated in an atmosphere of friendship and unity of immediate purpose, I personally was well content.

* * * * *

The political aspects were at once more remote and speculative. Obviously they depended upon the results of the great battles yet to be fought, and after that upon the mood of each of the Allies when victory was gained. It would not have been right at Teheran for the Western democracies to found their plans upon suspicions of the Russian attitude in the hour of triumph and when all her dangers were removed. Stalin's promise to enter the war against Japan as soon as Hitler was overthrown and his armies defeated, was of the highest importance. The hope of the future lay in the most speedy ending of the war and the establishment of a World Instrument to prevent another war, founded upon the combined strength of the three

Great Powers whose leaders had joined hands in friendship around the table.

We had procured a mitigation for Finland, which on the whole is operative today. The frontiers of the new Poland had been broadly outlined both in the East and in the West. The Curzon Line, subject to interpretation in the East, and the line of the Oder in the West, seemed to afford a true and lasting home for the Polish nation after all its sufferings. At the time the question between the Eastern and Western Neisse, which flow together to form the Oder River, had not arisen. When in July 1945 it arose in a violent form and under totally different conditions at the Potsdam Conference, I at once declared that Great Britain adhered only to the Eastern tributary. And this is still our position.

* * * * *

The supreme question of the treatment to be accorded to Germany by the victors could at this milestone only be the subject of "a preliminary survey of a vast political problem," and, as Stalin described it, "certainly very preliminary." It must be remembered that we were in the midst of a fearful struggle with the mighty Nazi Power. All the hazards of war lay around us, and all its passions of comradeship among Allies, of retribution upon the common foe, dominated our minds. The President's tentative projects for the partition of Germany into five self-governing states and two territories of vital consequence under the United Nations were of course far more acceptable to Marshal Stalin than the proposal which I made for the isolation of Prussia and the constitution of a Danubian Confederation, or of a South Germany and also a Danubian Confederation. This was only my personal view. But I do not at all repent having put it forward in the circumstances which lay about us at Teheran.

We all deeply feared the might of a united Germany. Prussia had a great history of her own. It would be possible, I thought, to make a stern but honourable peace with her, and at the same time to re-create in modern forms what had been in general outline the Austro-Hungarian Empire, of which Bismarck is supposed to have said, "If it did not exist, it would have to be invented." Here would be a great area in which not only peace but friendship might reign at a far earlier date than in any other solution. Thus a United Europe might be formed in which all the victors and vanquished might find a sure foundation for the life and freedom of all their tormented millions.

I do not feel any break in the continuity of my thought in this immense sphere. But vast and disastrous changes have fallen upon us in the realm of fact. The Polish frontiers exist only in name, and Poland lies quivering in the Russian-Communist grip. Germany has indeed been partitioned, but only by a hideous division into zones of military occupation. About this tragedy, it can only be said, "IT CANNOT LAST."

6

Cairo Again: The High Command

Anglo-American Discussions in Cairo — Andaman Islands Plan —
No Agreement at Our First Plenary Meeting, December 4 —
The President Agrees to Abandon the Andamans Plan, December
5 — Our Joint Telegram to Premier Stalin, December 6 — Ques-
tion About the Number of Troops Required by Admiral Mount-
batten — Staff Discussion of the Strategy Against Japan — Our
Conference with the Turks at Cairo — Outline Plan for Aiding
Turkey — The Turks Will Not Commit Themselves — Presi-
dent Roosevelt Decides to Appoint General Eisenhower to Com-
mand "Overlord" — The President and I Visit the Sphinx.

ON DECEMBER 2, I got back to Cairo from Teheran, and
was once more installed in the villa near the Pyramids.
The President arrived the same evening, and we resumed our
intimate discussions on the whole scene of the war and on the
results of our talks with Stalin. Meanwhile, the Combined
Chiefs of Staff, who had refreshed themselves by a visit to
Jerusalem on their way back from Teheran, were to carry forward their discussions on all their great business the next day.
Admiral Mountbatten had returned to India, whence he had
submitted the revised plan he had been instructed to make for
an amphibious attack on the Andaman Islands (Operation
"Buccaneer"). This would absorb the vitally needed landing-
craft already sent from the Mediterranean. I wished to make
a final attempt to win the Americans to the alternative enterprise against Rhodes.

The next evening I dined again with the President. Eden

was with me. We remained at the table until after midnight, still discussing our points of difference. I shared the views of our Chiefs of Staff, who were much worried by the promise which the President had made to Generalissimo Chiang Kai-shek before Teheran to launch an early attack across the Bay of Bengal. This would have swept away my hopes and plans for taking Rhodes, on which I believed the entry of Turkey into the war largely depended. But Mr. Roosevelt's heart was set upon it. When our Chiefs of Staff raised it in the military conferences, the United States Staffs simply declined to discuss the matter. The President, they said, had taken his decision and they had no choice but to obey.

On the afternoon of December 4, we held our first plenary meeting since Teheran, but made little headway. The President began by saying that he must leave on December 6, and that all reports should be ready for the final agreement of both parties by the evening of Sunday, December 5. Apart from the question of the entry of Turkey into the war, the only outstanding point seemed to be the comparatively small one of the use to be made of a score of landing-craft and their equipment. It was unthinkable that one could be beaten by a petty item like that, and he felt bound to say that the detail *must* be disposed of.

I said that I did not wish to leave the Conference in any doubt that the British delegation viewed our early dispersal with great apprehension. There were still many questions of first-class importance to be settled. Two decisive events had taken place in the last few days. In the first place, Marshal Stalin had voluntarily proclaimed that the Soviet would declare war on Japan the moment Germany was defeated. This would give us better bases than we could ever find in China, and made it all the more important that we should concentrate on making "Overlord" a success. It would be necessary for the Staffs to examine how this new fact would affect operations in the Pacific and Southeast Asia.

The second event of first-class importance was the decision to cross the Channel during May. I myself would have preferred a July date, but I was determined nevertheless to do all in my power to make a May date a complete success. It was a task transcending all others. A million Americans were to be thrown in eventually, and five or six hundred thousand British. Terrific battles were to be expected, on a scale far greater than anything that we had experienced before. In order to give "Overlord" the greatest chance of success, it was thought necessary that the descent on the Riviera ("Anvil") should be as strong as possible. It seemed to me that the crisis for the invading armies would come at about the thirtieth day, and it was essential that every possible step should be taken by action elsewhere to prevent the Germans from concentrating a superior force against our beachheads. As soon as the "Overlord" and "Anvil" forces got into the same zone, they would come under the same commander.

The President, summing up the discussion, asked whether he was correct in thinking that there was general agreement on the following points: (*a*) Nothing should be done to hinder "Overlord." (*b*) Nothing should be done to hinder "Anvil." (*c*) By hook or by crook we should scrape up sufficient landing-craft to operate in the Eastern Mediterranean if Turkey came into the war. (*d*) Admiral Mountbatten should be told to go ahead and do his best [in the Bay of Bengal] with what had already been allocated to him.

On this last point I suggested that it might be necessary to withdraw resources from Mountbatten in order to strengthen "Overlord" and "Anvil." The President said that he could not agree with this. We had a moral obligation to do something for China, and he would not be prepared to forgo the amphibious operation except for some very good and readily apparent reason. I replied that this "very good reason" might be provided by our supreme adventure in France. At present the "Overlord" assault was only on a three-division basis, whereas we had put nine divisions ashore in Sicily on the first day. The main operation was at present on a very narrow margin.

Reverting to the Riviera attack, I expressed the view that it should be planned on the basis of an assault force of at least two divisions. This would provide enough landing-craft to do the outflanking operations in Italy, and also, if Turkey came into the war soon, to capture Rhodes. I then pointed out that operations in Southeast Asia must be judged in their relation to the predominating importance of "Overlord." I said that I was surprised at the demands for taking the Andamans which had reached me from Admiral Mountbatten. In the face of Marshal Stalin's promise that Russia would come into the war, operations in the Southeast Asia Command had lost a good deal of their value, while, on the other hand, their cost had been put up to a prohibitive extent.

The discussion continued on whether or not to persist in the Andamans project. The President resisted the British wish to drop it. No conclusion was reached, except that the Chiefs of Staff were to go into details.

*   *   *   *   *

On December 5, we met again, and the report of the Combined Staffs on operations in the European theatre was read out by the President and agreed. Everything was now narrowed down to the Far Eastern operation. Rhodes had receded in the picture, and I concentrated on getting the landing-craft for "Anvil" and the Mediterranean. A new factor had presented itself. The estimates of the Southeast Asia Command of the force needed to storm the Andamans had been startling. The President said that fourteen thousand should be sufficient. Anyhow, the fifty thousand men proposed certainly broke the back of the Andamans expedition so far as this meeting was concerned. It was agreed for the moment that Mountbatten should be asked what amphibious operations he could undertake on a smaller scale, on the assumption that most of the landing-craft and assault shipping were withdrawn from Southeast Asia during the next few weeks. Thus we parted, leaving Mr. Roosevelt much distressed.

Before anything further could be done, the deadlock in Cairo was broken. In the afternoon the President, in consultation

with his advisers, decided to abandon the Andaman Islands
plan. He sent me a laconic private message: " 'Buccaneer' is
off." General Ismay reminds me that when I told him the welcome news cryptically on the telephone that the President had
changed his mind and was so informing Chiang Kai-shek, I
said, "He is a better man that ruleth his spirit than he that
taketh a city." We all met together at 7.30 the next evening at
the Kirk Villa to go over the final report of the Conference.
The Southern France assault operation was formally approved,
and the President read out his telegram to Generalissimo
Chiang Kai-shek, informing him of the decision to abandon
the Andamans plan.

*   *   *   *   *

I now worked out with the President a joint summary of
our decisions to be sent to Stalin.

Prime Minister and President Roosevelt to   6 Dec. 43
Premier Stalin

In the Cairo Conference just concluded, we have arrived at the
following decisions as to the conduct of war in 1944 against Germany additional to the agreement reached by the three of us at
Teheran.

The bomber offensive against Germany, with the objective of
destroying German air combat strength, the German military, industrial, and economic system, and preparing the way for a cross-
Channel operation, will be given the highest strategical priority.

We have reduced the scale of operations scheduled for March in
the Bay of Bengal to permit the reinforcement of amphibious craft
for the operation against Southern France.

We have ordered the utmost endeavours to increase the production of landing-craft in U.K. and the U.S.A. for the reinforcement
of "Overlord," and further orders have been issued to divert certain landing-craft from the Pacific for the same purpose.

*   *   *   *   *

In informing the Southeast Asia Command of our decisions,
I did not conceal from Mountbatten the shock which the estimates of his advisers which he had endorsed had been to me.

Prime Minister to Admiral Mountbatten (Delhi)   9 Dec. 43

You will have seen the President's telegram to the Generalissimo about the abandonment of "Buccaneer" with which as you know I am in entire agreement. This arises from the decision at Teheran to concentrate everything on "Overlord" and a simultaneous operation against the South of France.

Everyone here has been unpleasantly affected by your request to use 50,000 British and Imperial troops of which 33,700 are combatant against 5000 Japanese. I was astounded to hear of such a requirement and I cannot feel sure you are getting competent military advice. The Americans have been taking their islands on the basis of two and a half to one and that your Generals should ask for six and a half to one has produced a very bad impression. Even the detailed figures with which I have been furnished do not remove it.

I hope that preparations will now go forward for Sumatra after the monsoon. However, while such standards as those you have accepted for the Andamans prevail, there is not much hope of making any form of amphibious war.

Mountbatten replied that the United States in their recent landings had deployed a superiority of troops varying from between three to one to over six to one. The larger figure applied when cover from shore-based aircraft was not possible. For taking the Andamans he would have carrier-borne and not shore-based aircraft, and their effort was likely to be expended after four days. It was therefore essential to capture the Andamans airfield within that time. The resources already allotted to him would enable him to carry the fifty thousand men proposed. Of these however only nine thousand could be landed by the first two waves. He did not therefore feel he was asking for an undue superiority in order to ensure quick success. He cited the American landing at Munda, where, with an even higher ratio of superiority, only very slow progress had been made.

I remained unconvinced. But the following post-war comment from the War Office should be printed in order that the point at issue may be fairly presented:

Operation "Buccaneer," an assault on the Andaman islands, involved transporting our forces one thousand miles from the nearest
base, and the force included all troops required for the development of facilities, the building of airfield and strips, and for work
in the docks. It was estimated that sixteen thousand would be non-
fighting troops, and included in the balance of "fighting" troops
were all headquarters, engineers, and anti-aircraft units. The
enemy was considered to have air superiority in the area. Admittedly the "teeth" part of the force outnumbered the estimated
Japanese garrison by about four to one, but this was not much
greater than what was at that time accepted as a desirable preponderance for an assault landing. It cannot be overlooked that
we had been uniformly unsuccessful against the Japanese for the
previous twelve months. Lord Mountbatten undoubtedly wished
to make his first assault a success, if only for the sake of theatre
morale.

*   *   *   *   *

The Combined Chiefs of Staff also discussed among themselves the British share in the strategy to be pursued against
Japan, and presented their recommendations to the President
and me in their Final Report of the Cairo Conference. In
summary, they proposed that the main effort of the Southeast
Asia Command should be in Burma. After the defeat of Germany, an army and air contingent, with air resources all based
on Australia, should be sent to co-operate with General Mac-
Arthur. The British effort by sea should be mainly in the
Pacific and not in the Bay of Bengal. The British Chiefs of
Staff, like myself, recoiled from the idea of a strenuous and
wasteful campaign in North Burma for the sake of building
a road to China of doubtful value. On the other hand, they
accepted the fact that Admiral Mountbatten could not carry
out any large-scale amphibious operations until six months
after a German collapse. The plan of reinforcing the Pacific
could be begun much sooner. They therefore endorsed the
American view. In their Final Report both Staffs stated that
they "had agreed in principle as a basis for further investigation and preparation" the over-all plan for the defeat of Japan.

This plan contemplated the dispatch of a detachment of the British Fleet which was provisionally scheduled to become active in the Pacific in June 1944. The President and I both initialled this document, but in the pressure of more urgent business and of the President's imperative need to return to the United States, no occasion was found when we could discuss the long-term schemes either with our own advisers or between ourselves. We however felt sure there would be time to review the whole position later.

* * * * *

One of the main purposes of our Cairo meeting had been to resume talks with the Turkish leaders. I had telegraphed President Inönü on December 1 from Teheran suggesting that he should join the President and myself in Cairo. It was arranged that Vyshinsky should also be present. These conversations arose out of the exchange of views between Mr. Eden and the Turkish Foreign Minister in Cairo at the beginning of November on the former's journey home from Moscow. The Turks now came again to Cairo on December 4, and the following evening I entertained the Turkish President to dinner. My guest displayed great caution, and in subsequent meetings showed to what extent his advisers were still impressed by the German military machine. I pressed the case hard. With Italy out of the war the advantages of Turkey's entry were manifestly increased and her risks lessened.

On December 6, I drafted a memorandum to the British Chiefs of Staff setting forth in detail the policy and action which would be necessary if, after all, Turkey came in on our side.

OPERATION "SATURN"

Prime Minister to General Ismay, for C.O.S. Committee   6 Dec. 43

After the Cairo Conference, the Turkish Government will state that their policy is unchanged, and use all precautionary measures to allay enemy suspicions.

2. Nevertheless, it is necessary that the preparation and protec-

tion of the Turkish airfields should proceed at full speed without a day's delay, and that all necessary personnel, in mufti, and materials should be sent in. A period of six or seven weeks should suffice for this, the British squadrons being ready to fly in to the airfields at any time after February 1, the exact date to be fixed in consultation with the Turkish Government and in relation to the moves of the enemy. A margin of a fortnight may be allowed for this, during which time further supplies and personnel will be introduced at full speed.

3. In the lull following the expected capture of Rome in January, it is desirable that three groups of medium bombers should be placed under the command of the A.O.C.-in-C. Middle East and posted in Cyrenaica for "softening" action against enemy airfields and shipping, and to cover the "fly-in" of the British fighter squadrons. The action of these bombers can begin irrespective of any decision taken about the "fly-in." But if the enemy are quiescent, it would be better to reserve their action to cover the "fly-in" and the events immediately following it. The details of the employment and timing of the movement of this force should be worked out by the Commander-in-Chief.

4. By February 15 the "fly-in" should be completed, and from that moment onward a very considerable degree of protection against air attack will have been secured to Turkey.

5. Once established in the airfields, the British squadrons, in consultation with the Turkish Government, will begin their operations in the Aegean, being supported at the same time by the medium bomber groups from Cyrenaica. Under this air cover British naval forces in the Levant, strengthened as may be necessary, will attack enemy shipping and convoys engaged in supplying the islands.

6. All preparations should meanwhile be made for Rhodes. For this purpose a first-class British division should be used for the assault, a lower category division being held ready to garrison the island, thereby setting free the British division for further operations in Italy. Rhodes of course depends upon the landing-craft being available. This operation should take place before the end of February, all landing-craft thereafter being prepared for "Anvil."

7. What action should be expected from the enemy? Evidently it is the Allied interest to delay this as long as possible. Therefore, the Turkish Government should continue to the last moment in

relations with Germany and Bulgaria, and should reply diplomatically to any protest they may make, while continuing their preparations. If Bulgaria adopts a threatening attitude to Turkey, she should be notified by the Russians that if she delivers an attack at Germany's orders, the Russian Soviet Union will immediately declare war on Bulgaria. It is for consideration whether the Bulgarians should not also be told that for every ton of bombs dropped by the Germans or by them upon Constantinople or Smyrna, two or three tons will be dropped on Sofia. Should the Russian armies be continuing their victorious advance in South Russia, and should the Anglo-American armies prosper in the Battle of Rome, it seems most unlikely that Bulgaria will attempt to invade Turkey. She may however withdraw her nine divisions from Greece and Yugoslavia and make a concentration opposite the Turkish Front in Thrace.

8. Meanwhile, it is also possible that, under the increasing pressure of events, Bulgaria will endeavour to make a separate peace with the three Great Allies. It is not suggested that Turkey should declare war at any stage; she should continue her protective re-equipment and await the enemy's actions.

9. Meanwhile, as soon as the sea passage from Egypt to Turkey has been opened by the British and naval domination of the Aegean, every effort will be made to pass supplies and support into Smyrna, and if possible through the Dardanelles, so that the further equipment of the Turkish Army and the feeding of Constantinople can proceed as fast as possible.

10. After the "fly-in" of the British squadrons has been completed, the Turkish Government should facilitate the secret passage into the Black Sea of six or eight British submarines, together with the necessary stores. As no depot ship can be made available, base facilities should, if possible, be arranged at Ismet. These submarines should suffice to take a heavy toll of any Rumanian and German evacuations from the Crimea, and also to assist any Russian descent on the Rumanian shore which the Rumanian political attitude might render possible. Such a movement would however be dependent on Russian wishes.

The Turks departed to report to their Parliament, and it was agreed that in the meantime British specialists should be

assembled to implement the first stages of Operation "Saturn."
And there the matter rested.

*   *   *   *   *

In all our many talks at Cairo, the President never referred
to the vital and urgent issue of the Command of "Overlord,"
and I was under the impression that our original arrangement
and agreement held good. But on the day before his departure
from Cairo, he told me his final decision. We were driving in
his motor-car from Cairo to the Pyramids. He then said, almost
casually, that he could not spare General Marshall, whose great
influence at the head of military affairs and of the war direction, under the President, was invaluable, and indispensable to
the successful conduct of the war. He therefore proposed to
nominate Eisenhower to "Overlord," and asked me for my
opinion. I said it was for him to decide, but that we had also
the warmest regard for General Eisenhower, and would trust
our fortunes to his direction with hearty good will.

Up till this time I had thought Eisenhower was to go to
Washington as Military Chief of Staff, while Marshall commanded "Overlord." Eisenhower had heard of this too, and
was very unhappy at the prospect of leaving the Mediterranean
for Washington. Now it was all settled: Eisenhower for "Overlord," Marshall to stay at Washington, and a British Commander for the Mediterranean.

The full story of the President's long delay and hesitations
and of his final decision is referred to by Mr. Hopkins' biographer, who says that Roosevelt made the decision on Sunday,
December 5, "against the almost impassioned advice of Hopkins and Stimson, against the known preference of both Stalin
and Churchill, against his own proclaimed inclination." Then
Mr. Sherwood quotes the following extract from a note which
he had from General Marshall after the war: "If I recall," said
Marshall, "the President stated, in completing our conversation, 'I feel I could not sleep at night with you out of the
country.' " [1] There can be little doubt that the President felt

1 Sherwood, *Roosevelt and Hopkins*, pages 802, 803.

that the command only of "Overlord" was not sufficient to justify General Marshall's departure from Washington.

*   *   *   *   *

At last our labours were finished. I gave a dinner at the villa to the Combined Chiefs of Staff, Mr. Eden, Mr. Casey, and one or two others. I remember being struck by the optimism which prevailed in high Service circles. The idea was mooted that Hitler would not be strong enough to face the spring campaign, and might collapse even before "Overlord" was launched in the summer. I was so much impressed by the current of opinion that I asked everybody to give his view in succession round the table. All the professional authorities were inclined to think that the German collapse was imminent. The three politicians present took the opposite view. Of course, on these vast matters on which so many lives depend there is always a great deal of guesswork. So much is unknown and immeasurable. Who can tell how weak the enemy may be behind his flaming fronts and brazen mask? At what moment will his will-power break? At what moment will he be beaten down?

*   *   *   *   *

The President had found no time for sightseeing, but I could not bear his leaving without seeing the Sphinx. One day after tea, I said, "You must come now." We motored there forthwith, and examined this wonder of the world from every angle. Roosevelt and I gazed at her for some minutes in silence as the evening shadows fell. She told us nothing and maintained her inscrutable smile. There was no use waiting longer.

On December 7, I bade farewell to my great friend when he flew off from the airfield beyond the Pyramids.

7

In Carthage Ruins

Anzio

Our Air Journey to Tunis — I Have Pneumonia — The Commander-in-Chief in the Mediterranean and in Italy — My Telegram to the President, December 18 — He Agrees with the Appointments — My Wife Arrives from England — A Climax of the War — How to Break the Deadlock in Italy — The Genesis of the Anzio Operation — The British Chiefs of Staff Agree — The Problem of Landing-Craft — Our Meeting on Christmas Day — The Details are Thrashed Out — My Telegram to Chiefs of Staff, December 26 — The Brute Fact of Delaying Fifty-Six Landing-Craft — The Date of "Overlord" — My Report of Our Christmas Conference to the President.

I HAD NOT BEEN AT ALL WELL during this journey and Conference. Soon after I started, I had a temperature. After several days, this was succeeded by a cold and sore throat, which made me keep to my bed most of the time I was in Malta. I arrived voiceless at Teheran, but this did not last long, and I was able to carry on sufficiently. All these symptoms had disappeared when I got back to Cairo. As the Conference drew to its close, I became conscious of being very tired. For instance, I noticed that I no longer dried myself after my bath, but lay on the bed wrapped in my towel till I dried naturally.

A little after midnight on December 11, I and my personal party left in our York machine for Tunis. I had planned to spend one night there at General Eisenhower's villa, and to fly next day to Alexander's and then Montgomery's headquarters

in Italy, where the weather was reported to be absolutely vile
and all advances were fitful.

Morning saw us over the Tunis airfields. We were directed
by a signal not to land where we had been told, and were
shifted to another field some twenty miles away. We all got
out, and they began to unload the luggage. It would be an
hour before motor-cars could come, and then a long drive.
As I sat on my official boxes near the machines I certainly did
feel completely worn out. Now however came a telephone
message from General Eisenhower, who was waiting at the first
airfield, that we had been wrongly transferred and that landing was quite possible there. So we scrambled back into our
York, and in ten minutes were with him, quite close to his
villa. Ike, always the soul of hospitality, had waited two hours
with imperturbable good-humour. I got into his car, and after
we had driven for a little while, I said, "I am afraid I shall
have to stay with you longer than I had planned. I am completely at the end of my tether, and I cannot go on to the front
until I have recovered some strength."

All that day I slept, and the next day came fever and symptoms at the base of my lung which were adjudged to portend
pneumonia. So here I was at this pregnant moment on the
broad of my back amid the ruins of ancient Carthage.

*   *   *   *   *

When the X-ray photographs showed that there was a shadow
on one of my lungs, I found that everything had been diag-
nosed and foreseen by Lord Moran. Dr. Bedford and other
high medical authorities in the Mediterranean and excellent
nurses arrived from all quarters as if by magic. The admirable
M and B, from which I did not suffer any inconvenience, was
used at the earliest moment, and after a week's fever the intruders were repulsed. Although Lord Moran records that he
judged that the issue was at one time in doubt, I did not share
his view. I did not feel so ill in this attack as I had the previous February. The M and B, which I also called Moran
and Bedford, did the work most effectively. There is no doubt

that pneumonia is a very different illness from what it was before this marvellous drug was discovered. I did not at any time relinquish my part in the direction of affairs, and there was not the slightest delay in giving the decisions which were required from me.

Prime Minister to Foreign Secretary   13 Dec. 43

I am caught amid these ancient ruins with a temperature and must wait till I am normal. Future movements uncertain.

Angora must be left under no illusions that failure to comply when request is made on February 15 is the virtual end of the alliance, and that making impossible demands is only another way of saying no.

You should ask the Staffs to report upon the possibilities of the Germans being able to gather enough forces for a further separate invasion of Turkey. I believe this to be absolute rubbish.

Prime Minister to President Roosevelt   15 Dec. 43

Am stranded amid the ruins of Carthage, where you stayed, with fever which has ripened into pneumonia. All your people are doing everything possible, but I do not pretend I am enjoying myself. I hope soon to send you some of the suggestions for the new commands. I hope you had a pleasant voyage and are fit. Love to Harry.

President Roosevelt to Prime Minister   17 Dec. 43

I am distressed about the pneumonia, and both Harry and I plead with you to be good and throw it off rapidly. I have just left the *Iowa* and am on my way up the Potomac. The Bible says you must do just what Moran orders, but at this moment I cannot put my finger on the verse and the chapter. . . . Nothing further seems to be imminent, so do what Sarah says, and give her my love and take it easy.

*   *   *   *   *

It now fell to me, as British Minister of Defence responsible to the War Cabinet, to propose a British Supreme Commander for the Mediterranean. This post we confided to General Wilson, it being also settled that General Alexander should command the whole campaign in Italy, as he had done under General Eisenhower in Tunisia. It was also arranged that General Devers, of the United States Army, should become General Wilson's Deputy in the Mediterranean, and Air Chief Marshal Tedder General Eisenhower's Deputy in "Overlord," and that General Montgomery should actually command the whole cross-Channel invasion force until such time as the Supreme Commander could transfer his Headquarters to France and assume the direct operational control. All this was carried out with the utmost smoothness in perfect agreement by the President and by me, with Cabinet approval, and worked in good comradeship and friendship by all concerned.

I should add that when in December 1944 General Alexander succeeded General Wilson as Supreme Commander in the Mediterranean, I myself proposed, on behalf of His Majesty's Government, that United States General Mark Clark should take command under him of the whole of the forces in Italy, three-quarters of which were British, Imperial, or British-controlled. This he did with marked distinction and success.

The operative telegrams were:

Prime Minister to President Roosevelt   18 Dec. 43

Thank you so much for your telegram. I have hearkened unto the voice of Moran and made good progress, but I am fixed here for another week.

2. Since our last talk on the subject, I have given much thought to the remodelling of the commands, and have had discussions with Eisenhower, Alexander, and Tedder. I have also consulted my colleagues at home, and have today had a long conversation with the C.I.G.S. on his return from a visit to Italy. As a result I am able to place before you the following proposals, which, if you approve them, will, I am satisfied, be generally accepted.

3. I had always thought that Alexander would succeed Eisenhower, but am convinced by the arguments of the C.I.G.S., Eisenhower, and others that it would be impossible for him or Montgomery to act as Supreme Commander and at the same time fight the battles which will take place in Italy after the conquest of Rome. Alexander himself quite saw this.

4. I therefore propose General Wilson as Supreme Commander, *vice* Eisenhower. Under him will be: (*a*) General Commanding, Algiers: a United States officer. We have heard that it might be convenient to you to transfer General Devers from his present post. (*b*) Commander-in-Chief of the Armies in Italy: Alexander. (*c*) General in charge of Operation "Anvil": Clark. We understand that this was what you and General Marshall had in mind. If so, we concur. (*d*) A British major-general in charge of the Yugoslav assistance measures, Tito, Greeks, etc. (*e*) Commander-in-Chief Mid-East, for operational purposes within the Mediterranean theatre, and also in charge of the Turkish operations: Paget (now commanding British Home Forces).

5. The Air Officer Commanding-in-Chief should be an American, appointed by you. Arnold when passing through here spoke of Brereton or Eaker. We would agree to either, but we should miss the latter from the bombing and "Overlord" build-up. Sholto Douglas will be Deputy Air Officer Commanding-in-Chief, and also Commander-in-Chief of all the R.A.F. in the Mediterranean theatre.

6. Political assistance will be provided for the Supreme Commander: (*a*) by Messrs. Murphy and Macmillan, who work hand-in-hand; (*b*) from the French angle by Duff Cooper and Wilson; (*c*) from the Middle Eastern area by the Minister of State or his successor.

7. Bedell Smith will accompany Eisenhower after a few weeks and become his Chief of Staff in England, being replaced here by a British Chief of Staff. We leave it to you to decide whether you would like to have a Deputy Supreme Commander, who would of course be an American.

8. You will understand that I have given most careful consideration to the appointment of Sir Henry Maitland Wilson, and I am satisfied that for the great co-ordination task which will be entrusted to him he has all the qualifications and the necessary vigour. This is also the opinion of the C.I.G.S. When I mentioned this idea to you at Cairo you seemed to like it.

9. Turning to the "Overlord" theatre, I propose to you that Tedder shall be Eisenhower's Deputy Supreme Commander, on account of the great part the air will play in this operation, and this is most agreeable to Eisenhower. The War Cabinet desires that Montgomery should command the first expeditionary group of armies. I feel the Cabinet are right, as Montgomery is a public

hero and will give confidence among our people, not unshared by yours.

10. I beg most earnestly that I may soon have your reply on these proposals, or at least upon the key ones, as the Commander of "Overlord" is urgently required, and I should like to arrange for Wilson to take over from Eisenhower at an early date, and to come to him even sooner in order to settle the many consequential details.

President Roosevelt to Prime Minister 20 Dec. 43

Replying to your telegram of December 18, I am agreeable to an announcement on January 1 of selection of Eisenhower to command "Overlord," Tedder to be Eisenhower's Deputy Supreme Commander, Wilson to relieve Eisenhower as Supreme Commander Mediterranean (this change to be made when Eisenhower reports that conditions in Italy justify the change), Eaker to command Allied Air Force Mediterranean.

2. I prefer to delay announcement of changes in subordinate commands until after the first of the year, because I want to have . opportunity to discuss it with Marshall, who will return to Washington in a few days.

3. I am delighted that you are really so much better, and I wish I could be with you at Marrakesh. I hope you have sent for your brushes.

* * * * *

The days passed in much discomfort. Fever flickered in and out. I lived on my theme of the war, and it was like being transported out of oneself. The doctors tried to keep the work away from my bedside, but I defied them. They all kept on saying, "Don't work, don't worry," to such an extent that I decided to read a novel. I had long ago read Jane Austen's *Sense and Sensibility,* and now I thought I would have *Pride and Prejudice.* Sarah read it to me beautifully from the foot of the bed. I had always thought it would be better than its rival. What calm lives they had, those people! No worries about the French Revolution, or the crashing struggle of the Napoleonic Wars. Only manners controlling natural passion so far as they could, together with cultured explanations of any mischances. All this seemed to go very well with M and B.

One morning Sarah was absent from her chair at the foot of my bed, and I was about to ask for my box of telegrams in the prohibited hours when in she walked with her mother. I had no idea that my wife was flying out from England to join me. She had hurried to the airport to fly in a two-engined Dakota. The weather was bad, but Lord Beaverbrook was vigilant. He got to the airport first, and stopped her flight until a four-engined plane could be procured. (I always think it better to have four engines when flying long distances across the sea.) Now she had arrived after a very rough journey in an unheated plane in midwinter. Jock Colville had escorted her, and was a welcome addition to my hard-pressed personal staff, through whom so much business was being directed. "My love to Clemmie," cabled the President. "I feel relieved that she is with you as your superior officer."

* * * * *

As I lay prostrate, I felt we were at one of the climaxes of the war. The mounting of "Overlord" was the greatest event and duty in the world. But must we sabotage everything we could have in Italy, where the main strength overseas of our country was involved? Were we to leave it a stagnant pool from which we had drawn every fish we wanted? As I saw the problem, the campaign in Italy, in which a million or more of our British, British-controlled, and Allied armies were engaged, was the faithful and indispensable comrade and counterpart to the main cross-Channel operation. Here the American clear-cut, logical, large-scale, mass-production style of thought was formidable. In life people have first to be taught "Concentrate on essentials." This is no doubt the first step out of confusion and fatuity; but it is only the first step. The second stage in war is a general harmony of war effort by making everything fit together, and every scrap of fighting strength plays its full part all the time. I was sure that a vigorous campaign in Italy during the first half of 1944 would be the greatest help to the supreme operation of crossing the Channel, on which all minds were set and all engagements made. But every item which any Staff officer could claim as "essential" or "vital," to use these hard-worked words, had to be argued out as if it carried with it the success or failure of our main purpose. Twenty or a dozen vehicle landing-craft had to be fought for, as if the major issue turned upon them.

The case seemed to me brutally simple. All the ships we had would be used to carry to England everything the United States could produce in arms and men. Surely the enormous forces we could not possibly move by sea from the Italian theatre should play their part. Either they would gain Italy easily and immediately bite upon the German inner front, or they would draw large German forces from the front which we were to attack across the Channel in the last days of May, or the early days of June, as the moon and the tides prescribed.

* * * * *

The deadlock to which our armies in Italy had been brought by the stubborn German resistance on the fifty-mile front from Cassino to the sea had already led General Eisenhower to yearn for an amphibious flanking attack. He had planned to land with one division south of the Tiber and make a dart for Rome, in conjunction with an attack by the main armies. The arrest of these armies and the distance of the landing point from them made everyone feel that more than one division was required. I had of course always been a partisan of the "end run," as the Americans call it, or "cat-claw," which was my term. I had never succeeded in getting this manoeuvre open to sea-power included in any of our Desert advances. In Sicily however General Patton had twice used the command of the sea flank as he advanced along the northern coast of the island with great effect. Both at Carthage and at Marrakesh I was near enough to the scene of action to convene meetings of all the chief commanders.

There was a great deal of professional support. Eisenhower was already committed in principle, though his new appointment to the command of "Overlord" now gave him a different sense of values and a new horizon. Alexander, Deputy Supreme Commander and commanding the armies in Italy, thought the operation right and necessary; Bedell Smith was ardent and helpful in every direction. This was also true of Admiral John Cunningham, who held all the naval cards, and of Air Chief Marshal Tedder. I had therefore a powerful array of Mediterranean authorities. Moreover, I felt sure the British Chiefs of Staff would like the plan, and that with their agreement I could obtain the approval of the War Cabinet. When you cannot give orders, hard and lengthy toils must be faced.

"Overlord" in May was sacrosanct. We had pledged ourselves at Teheran only a month before. Nothing could be considered which prevented our keeping our supreme engagement. In this case troops, air and seapower, presented no obstacles. All turned upon L.S.T.s (Landing-ships, Tanks). This included "Landing-ships, Vehicles," because landing tanks was only a small proportion of their indispensable work. A lengthy correspondence conducted in cipher between me and Whitehall and Washington arose. The military student may some day be interested to read the details of this tense and clear-cut argument, of which only a skeleton is here printed. The L.S.T.s must, in the name of "Overlord," be in England at certain dates. These dates had been calculated with extreme precision, and of course with all the margins for accident which, at every stage, enter into military planning, and would make almost all action impossible if they were not controlled from the top. Everyone claims his margin at every stage, and the sum of the margins is usually "No."

I began my effort on December 19, when the C.I.G.S. arrived at Carthage to see me on his way home from Montgomery's Headquarters in Italy. We had hoped to go there together, but my illness had prevented me. We had a full discussion, and I found that General Brooke had by a separate route of thought arrived at the same conclusion as I had. We agreed on the policy, and also that while I should deal with the commanders on the spot, he would do his best to overcome all difficulties at home. General Brooke then left by air for London. I telegraphed:

Prime Minister to Chiefs of Staff   19 Dec. 43

I am anxiously awaiting a full list of all landing-craft of all types in the Mediterranean now, showing their condition and employment, and especially whether it is true that a large number are absorbed in purely supply work to the prevention of their amphibious duties. There is no doubt that the stagnation of the whole campaign on the Italian Front is becoming scandalous. The C.I.G.S.'s visit confirmed my worst forebodings. The total neglect to provide the amphibious action on the Adriatic side and the failure to strike any similar blow on the west have been disastrous.

None of the landing-craft in the Mediterranean have been put to the slightest use [for assault purposes] for three months, neither coming home in preparation for "Overlord," nor for the Aegean islands, nor in the Italian battle. There are few instances, even in this war, of such valuable forces being so completely wasted.

The Chiefs of Staff had evidently been thinking on the same lines, and, after hearing General Brooke's account, replied on the 22nd.

Chiefs of Staff to Prime Minister   22 Dec. 43

We are in full agreement with you that the present stagnation cannot be allowed to continue. For every reason it is essential that something should be done to speed things up. The solution, as you say, clearly lies in making use of our amphibious power to strike round the enemy's flank and open up the way for a rapid advance on Rome.

After the L.S.T.s are withdrawn for "Overlord" on January 15, General Eisenhower should have at his disposal an amphibious lift sufficient for a little more than one division, and he has a plan to make a landing behind the enemy just south of Rome. The weakness of this plan is that the assault in that strength on the coast cannot be launched until the Fifth Army is within supporting distance of the force to be landed. If the available lift could be increased, however, a stronger force could be landed without waiting for the main army to arrive within immediate supporting distance. Such a landing moreover would have a more far-reaching effect on the whole progress of the campaign, and would be much more likely to open the way for a rapid advance. We think the aim should be to provide a lift for at least two divisions.

We have telegraphed to the Commander-in-Chief Mediterranean
for the information you ask for on landing-craft. We have every
hope that it will be possible to make some economy in this direction, but we must look further afield if we are to give General
Eisenhower the two-divisional lift.

A possible source of supply is the craft already on their way
back from Southeast Asia to the Mediterranean. . . . A small number of craft have also been left in Southeast Asia.

After explaining that the new plan would involve giving up
both the capture of Rhodes and also a minor amphibious operation on the Arakan coast of Burma, they ended:

If you approve the above line of thought, we propose to take
the matter up with the Combined Chiefs of Staff with a view to
action being taken on these lines at once.

* * * * *

This led to a hard scrutiny of our resources. Some landing-
craft for the cancelled operation against the Andamans were
on their way to the Mediterranean across the Indian Ocean.
Others were due to return home for "Overlord." All were in
extreme demand.

I had been reluctant to agree to the abandonment of the
attack on Rhodes we had talked of to President Inönü. A
far greater effort must be made with the Turks, as well as to
expedite the operation and the subsequent return of landing-
craft for "Anvil" (the assault on Southern France). By December 23 however I was becoming resigned to Turkish neutrality,
and I replied from Carthage:

Prime Minister to Chiefs of Staff   23 Dec. 43

You will observe that whereas you are thinking of a decision
in Italy, Ike is looking forward to "Anvil," which is now very
much part of his main interest. I recognise that if the Turks will
not play, we may have to sacrifice the Aegean policy, especially if it
is marked up so high and so slow. I hope however that this decision
will not be taken till after full exploration of the whole scene. I
hope to see Eisenhower today, and Alexander is visiting me. There-

after I shall ask Jumbo [General Wilson] to come here on his way home. I wish to keep all the issues open for the next three or four days. Supposing Turkey jibs and Rhodes is shut out, we must have the big Rome amphibious operation, and also have some clearing up on the Dalmatian coast, especially Argostol, and Corfu. In no case can we sacrifice Rome for the Riviera. We must have both.

Meanwhile, I had had a long talk with Alexander. He demurred to the suggestion that he was not very keen on the Anzio landing. He wanted a two-division lift, and the problem was how this could be supplied. Bedell Smith, who had also arrived, thought he could make up pretty nearly a two-division lift, provided that airborne troops were counted as well. If this were supplied and decision taken on the morrow or the next day, Alexander could strike in the last week of January. The question was, how to find the landing-craft. When I asked Bedell Smith why we should not delay the "Overlord" L.S.T.s, etc., till February 15, he replied he just could not bear asking for a third extension. I had no such compunction.

There were 104 L.S.T.s in the Mediterranean, but most of them were due to return home for "Overlord." By the middle of January, we should have only thirty-six, with another fifteen arriving from the Indian Ocean about that time. To carry two divisions it was said we needed eighty-eight. No more could arrive till April. The only solution was to hold most of those in the Mediterranean for another three weeks. There were good hopes that this could be done without injury to "Overlord," or to the landing in the Riviera.

* * * * *

On the 24th, the Chiefs of Staff sent me a detailed statement of their ideas, and a draft which they proposed to send to their Washington colleagues. They favoured the plan, but feared we should never win American consent.

Their conclusions were:

We ask the Combined Chiefs of Staff to agree: (a) That the remainder of the Andamans assault shipping and craft should be ordered to the Mediterranean. (*b*) That such resources as can reach the Central Mediterranean in time should be employed by the Supreme Allied Commander Mediterranean Theatre for the launching of a two-divisional amphibious assault designed to enable Rome to be captured and the armies to advance to the Pisa-Rimini line, and that instructions to this effect should be issued forthwith. There will be sufficient time for the subsequent withdrawal of these resources for the South of France attack. (*c*) That our negotiations with Turkey should continue on the present basis, but that amphibious operations in the Aegean should be ruled out. (*d*) That Admiral Mountbatten should be informed of these decisions, and instructed to make his final recommendations for operations to be carried out in his theatre with the resources remaining to him.

*   *   *   *   *

I had with me at this tense period from my Defence Office only General Hollis, but he proved a tower of strength. I was also greatly aided by Captain Power, R.N., who was Admiral John Cunningham's Deputy Chief of Staff (Plans). He cleared away a mass of argument which obstructed the decision. He said in his able paper, which the Admiral fully approved:

The L.S.T.s now in the Mediterranean are thoroughly trained. They have all taken part in at least two assault operations, and have done a great deal of additional work on ferrying, continually loading and unloading over beaches, yards, or quays. They are well manned and accustomed to steaming and manoeuvring in close company. They should require no further naval training prior to "Overlord," except that they are unaccustomed to problems of tide and the technique of beaching and unbeaching in tidal waters. Being good seamen, however, they should require but very brief instruction and training before they master the new problem. . . . Mediterranean experience shows that there is no need to marry the L.S.T.s and the troops concerned until eleven days before calling for the operation — three days for initial loading, six days for rehearsal, two days for reloading. . . .

I should estimate that seven days' allowance for tide training would be more than adequate for these well-trained ships.

Total training allowance should therefore be approximately three weeks. . . . They therefore have ample time before "Overlord," except that they cannot all refit at once.

* * * * *

As a result of detailed discussion with the assembled commanders I sent home the following proposals after midnight on the 24th:

Prime Minister to Chiefs of Staff and   25 Dec. 43 (12.30 A.M.)
   First Sea Lord

I have had talks tonight with General Wilson and General Alexander and Air Chief Marshal Tedder and their staffs about Anzio.

We are all agreed that it must be carried out on sufficient scale to ensure success, namely, at least a two-divisional assault. Target date will be about January 20. Assumption is that Rhodes is not on. We feel strongly that the only right course is to delay for not more than one month departure from Mediterranean of all British L.S.Ts now due to leave in January and on February 1 (totalling fifty-six L.S.Ts). The fifteen L.S.T.s from the Bay of Bengal would not arrive in time for Anzio, but would play their part in repayment of "Overlord" a little later. . . .

I wish Chiefs of Staff to give earliest attention to the paper prepared at my request by Captain Power. This sets out the economies in time which might be effected in the preparation of L.S.T.s for "Overlord." All present tonight considered that Captain Power's paper showed a firm grasp of the situation, and his proposals should be capable of achievement. . . .

The Chiefs of Staff were not at first convinced. They mentioned various points of detail; and details were decisive. They also "earnestly hoped" I would agree to their draft note explaining the situation to the Combined Chiefs of Staff. I was sure that we must be agreed among ourselves in all essentials first, and I replied as follows:

Prime Minister to Chiefs of Staff   26 Dec. 43

I have been into the facts most thoroughly with the Admiral and with General Gale and their staffs. There is not the slightest chance of mounting Anzio on a two-division basis unless the whole fifty-six L.S.T.s are held back another three weeks — i.e., until February 5. They know a good deal about training for assault landings in the Mediterranean. Pray let me know the argument as between three weeks and a month, and let me know exactly each day's employment prescribed for vessels on return. . . . You are expected to organise dockyards so as to refit twenty-five a month.

The success of Anzio depends on the strength of the initial landing. If this is two full divisions plus paratroops, it should be decisive, as it cuts the communications of the whole of the enemy forces facing the Fifth Army. The enemy must therefore annihilate the landing force by withdrawals from the Fifth Army Front or immediately retreat. Nothing less than two divisions will serve. Weather uncertainties make it necessary to put them ashore with at least four days' supplies. It is not intended to maintain these divisions for long over the beaches, but rather to bring the battle to a climax in a week or ten days. . . .

It is no use your telegraphing to the Combined Chiefs of Staff until we are in agreement on the one vital matter, namely, the delay of three weeks in the return of the fifty-six L.S.T.s. On this depends the success or ruin of our Italian campaign.

The Chiefs of Staff gave many solid reasons for their anxieties in their reply of December 27, and added, "We feel we should not conceal from you the difficulty we expect with the United States Chiefs of Staff if we tell them frankly the true position as we see it."

*   *   *   *   *

All the morning of Christmas Day our conference at Carthage continued. Eisenhower, Alexander, Bedell Smith, General Wilson, Tedder, Admiral John Cunningham, and other high officers were present. The only one not there was General Mark Clark, of the Fifth Army. This was an oversight which I regret, as it was to his army that the operation was eventually entrusted and he ought to have had the background in his mind. We were all agreed that nothing less than a two-division lift would suffice. At this time I contemplated an assault by two

British divisions from the Eighth Army, in which Montgomery
was about to be succeeded by General Leese. I thought the
amphibious operation involved potential mortal risks to the
landed forces, and I preferred to run them with British troops,
because it was to Britain that I was responsible. Moreover,
the striking force would then have been homogeneous instead of half and half.

Everything turned on landing-craft, which held for some
weeks all our strategy in the tightest ligature. What with the
rigid date prescribed for "Overlord" and the movement, repair,
and refitting of less than a hundred of these small vessels, all
plans were in a straitjacket. The telegrams which passed show
how we escaped, though mauled, from this predicament. But I
must also admit that I was so much occupied in fighting for the
principle that I did not succeed in getting, and indeed did
not dare to demand, the necessary weight and volume for the
"cat-claw." Actually there were enough L.S.T.s for the operation as planned, and in my opinion, if the extravagant demands of the military machine had been reduced, we could,
without prejudice to any other pledge or commitment, have
flung ashore south of the Tiber a still larger force with full
mobility. However, the issue was fought out in terms of
routine Army requirements and the exact dates when L.S.T.s
could be free for "Overlord," making of course all allowances
for their return home in winter Biscay weather, and with the
time-margins for their refits stated at their maximum. If I
had asked for a three-division lift, I should not have got anything. How often in life must one be content with what one
can get! Still, it would be better to do it right.

*   *   *   *   *

The brute fact of delaying the return to England of the
fifty-six L.S.T.s for three weeks had to be faced. Against this
towered up the date of "Overlord" —MAY. The reader will
note in the following telegram the first appearance of JUNE 6.

Prime Minister to Chiefs of Staff   26 Dec. 43

I am proceeding entirely on basis of keeping to the May "Overlord." I am sure this can be done and problem solved by persevering energetically. I may however say in strictest secrecy that both Eisenhower and Montgomery have expressed themselves entirely dissatisfied with what they have heard of the present plan for "Overlord," and I gather they will demand a far larger first flight. I should think it very likely that when they have examined the plan, they will propose a delay. Our contract is "during May," but I do not know whether if responsible commanders required the June moon around June 6, and could show much better prospects then, the extra week might not have to be conceded. Preliminary air bombardment would begin anyhow in May.

Beware therefore that we do not sacrifice our vital task in Italy in order to achieve a date which anyhow may be postponed on other and larger grounds. Eisenhower even spoke of telegraphing himself to Stalin, once he had assumed effective command and was master of the problem, demanding a reasonable measure of delay. I did not lend myself to this at all, as I am fighting the case on the Teheran [agreement] line. All the more do I expect you to help me. Be careful this is kept to yourselves and the three War Cabinet Ministers on Defence Committee, Mr. Attlee, Mr. Eden, and Mr. Lyttelton.

At the close of this decisive Christmas Day Conference at Carthage, I sent the following to the President, and a similar telegram home. I was careful to state the root fact bluntly.

Former Naval Person to President Roosevelt   25 Dec. 43
I held a conference today with Eisenhower, and all his high officers. Report as follows:

General Alexander is prepared to execute the landing at Anzio about January 20 if he can get a lift of two divisions. This should decide the Battle of Rome, and possibly achieve the destruction of a substantial part of enemy's army. To strike with less than two divisions would be to court disaster, having regard to the positions likely to be achieved by that date by Fifth and Eighth Armies.

For this purpose eighty-eight L.S.T.s are required. These can only be obtained by delaying the return home of fifty-six L.S.T.s due to leave the Mediterranean from January 15 onward, sending them home by convoys starting February 5. Nothing less than this will suffice. The fifteen L.S.T.s from India cannot arrive in time, though they would be invaluable to replace casualties and for the building-up of "Anvil."

By various expedients it is believed that the lost three weeks can be recovered and the existing prescribed build-up for "Overlord" maintained. •

Having kept these fifty-six L.S.T.s in the Mediterranean so long, it would seem irrational to remove them for the very week when they can render decisive service. What, also, could be more dangerous than to let the Italian battle stagnate and fester on for another three months? We cannot afford to go forward leaving a vast half-finished job behind us. It therefore seemed to those present that every effort should be made to bring off Anzio on a two-division basis around January 20, and orders have been issued to General Alexander to prepare accordingly. If this opportunity is not grasped we must expect the ruin of the Mediterranean campaign of 1944. I earnestly hope therefore that you may agree to the three weeks' delay in return of the fifty-six landing-craft, and that all the authorities will be instructed to make sure that the May "Overlord" is not prejudiced thereby.

6. I recognise with regret that Rhodes and the Aegean policy must be side-tracked in these higher interests, and it may well be that "Pigstick" [the attack on the Arakan west of Burma] will require to be moderated into "Pigstuck," in order to build up three divisions for the landing in the South of France. This has been most painful to me, but I could not face the Italian stalemate and disaster which will otherwise ensue.

It was at this point, while all hung in suspense, that I flew from Carthage to Marrakesh, bearing my burdens with me.

8

At Marrakesh

Convalescence

L ORD MORAN thought it possible for me to leave Carthage
after Christmas, but insisted that I must have three weeks'
convalescence somewhere. And where else could be better
than the lovely villa at Marrakesh, where President Roosevelt
and I had stayed after Casablanca a year before? All these plans
had been made during the past few days. I was to be the guest
of the United States Army at Marrakesh. It was also thought
that I had been long enough at Carthage to be located. Small
vessels had ceaselessly to patrol the bay in front of the villa in
case some U-boat turned up for a surprise raid. There might
also be a long-range air attack. I had my own protection in a
battalion of the Coldstream Guards. I was too ill, or too busy,
to be consulted about all this, but I saw in my beloved Mar-

rakesh a haven where I could regain my strength. Tedder had planned the flight with great care. The doctors did not want me to fly above six thousand feet, and he had arranged our route through the Atlas Mountains on this basis. I was delighted when the morning of December 27 came and I dressed for the first time again in my uniform. As I was leaving the door, a telegram was put in my hand. The *Scharnhorst* had been sunk by Admiral Fraser in an engagement with the *Duke of York*. I stopped to dictate the following telegram to Stalin:

Prime Minister to Premier Stalin   27 Dec. 43

The Arctic convoys to Russia have brought us luck. Yesterday enemy attempted to intercept with battle-cruiser *Scharnhorst*. Commander-in-Chief Admiral Fraser with the *Duke of York* (35,000-ton battleship) cut off *Scharnhorst's* retreat and after an action sunk her.

2. Am much better, and off to the south for convalescence.

A very cordial reply to this was received a few days later, ending, "I shake your hand firmly."

Outside the villa a magnificent guard of the Coldstream was drawn up. I had not realised how much I had been weakened by my illness. I found it quite a difficulty to walk along the ranks and climb into the motor-car. The flight at six thousand feet had been planned on the weather forecast that the skies would be clear. However, as we sailed on and the uplands of Tunisia began to rise about us, I saw a lot of large fleecy and presently blackish clouds gathering around, and after a couple of hours we were more often in mist than in sunlight. I have always had a great objection to what are called "stuffed clouds" — i.e., clouds with mountains inside them — and flying an intricate route through the various valleys before us in order to keep under six thousand feet seemed to me an unfair proposition for the others in the plane. I therefore sent for the pilot and told him to fly at least two thousand feet above the highest mountain within a hundred miles of his route. Lord Moran agreed. Oxygen was brought by a skilled administrator, specially provided for the journey. We sailed up into the blue. I got along all right and we made a perfect landing at about four o'clock on the Marrakesh airfield. The second plane, which had adhered strictly to its instructions, had a very severe and dangerous flight through the various gorges and passes, many of which were traversed with only fleeting glimpses of the towering mountains. At this low height the weather was by no means good. The plane arrived safely an hour behind us with one of its doors blown off and nearly everybody very sick. I was sorry indeed they should have been put to so much discomfort and risk on my account. They could have flown it all out comfortably under blue skies at twelve or even eleven thousand feet.

Nothing could exceed the comfort, and even luxury, of my new abode, or the kindness of everyone concerned. But one thing rose above all others in my mind — what answer would the President give to my telegram? When I thought of the dull, dead-weight resistance, taking no account of timing and proportion, that I had encountered about all Mediterranean projects, I awaited the answer with deep anxiety. What I asked for was a hazardous enterprise on the Italian coast, and a possible delay of three weeks from May 1 — four if the moon phase was to be observed — in the date of the Channel crossing. I had gained the agreement of the commanders on the spot. The British Chiefs of Staff had always agreed in principle, and were now satisfied in detail. But what would the Americans say to a four weeks' postponement of "Overlord"? However, when one is thoroughly tired out, the blessing of sleep is not usually denied.

*   *   *   *   *

It was with joy, not, I confess, unmingled with surprise, that the next day I received the following:

President Roosevelt to Prime Minister   28 Dec. 43

It is agreed to delay the departure of fifty-six L.S.T.s scheduled for "Overlord" for mounting Anzio on January 20, and on the basis that "Overlord" remains the paramount operation and will be carried out on the date agreed to at Cairo and Teheran. All possible expedients should be undertaken to overcome probable effect on "Overlord" preparation, to which end the other twelve L.S.T.s for "Overlord" should depart as now scheduled and the fifteen L.S.T.s *ex* Andamans arriving in Mediterranean on January 14 should proceed directly to United Kingdom. I agree that Rhodes and the Aegean must be side-tracked and that we cannot give further consideration to launching Rhodes prior to "Anvil" [Riviera]. In view of the Soviet-British-American agreement reached in Teheran, I cannot agree without Stalin's approval to any use of forces or equipment elsewhere that might delay or hazard the success of "Overlord" or "Anvil."

I replied:

Prime Minister to President Roosevelt   28 Dec. 43

I thank God for this fine decision, which engages us once again in wholehearted unity upon a great enterprise.

I have heard from the British Chiefs of Staff that the Admiralty can conform to the conditions provided the releases are made from the Anzio plan of the number which are agreed upon. The Chiefs of Staff will be telegraphing today in full detail to the Combined Chiefs of Staff. Meanwhile, here the word is "Full steam ahead."

After travelling quite unaffected at thirteen thousand feet, I arrived yesterday at our villa, where I am indeed in the lap of luxury, thanks to overflowing American hospitality. Max [Beaverbrook] has just flown in from London. I propose to stay here in the sunshine till I am quite strong again.

Great efforts had indeed been made by the Staffs at home, and especially by the Admiralty, to accomplish the "cat-claw," and I hastened to congratulate them. General Alexander had asked for eighty-eight landing-craft; they promised him all but one. The President's telegram was a marvel. I was sure that I owed it not only to his good will, but to Marshall's balance of mind, to Eisenhower's loyalty to the show he was about to quit, and to Bedell Smith's active, knowledgeable, fact-armed diplomacy.

On the same day Alexander sent us his plan. After conferring with General Mark Clark and General Brian Robertson, Chief Administrative Officer and son of the C.I.G.S. of the First World War, he had decided to use an American and a British division. Armour, paratroops, and Commandos would be on a fifty-fifty basis, and the whole would be under an American corps commander. The attack would go in on January 20. Ten days beforehand he would launch a big offensive against Cassino to draw off the German reserves. The forward plunge of the main armies would follow. I was well content. So far so good.

*   *   *   *   *

I had however another small margin on which to draw. I wired to the Chiefs of Staff:

Prime Minister to Chiefs of Staff   29 Dec. 43

I am fighting the issue [of the date of "Overlord"] entirely on the Teheran basis. This assumed May 20 rather than May 5, which is an altogether new date. Our contract with Stalin would be fulfilled by any date up to May 31. It seems to me from what I have heard from Eisenhower that June 3, which is the corresponding moon phase, would be perfectly permissible, especially if it were asked for by the commanders now nominated for the operation. There is no need to discuss such matters now, but here is something to veer and haul on.

Pray let me have the alternative build-up comparing May 5 with June 3. I repeat this is not to be considered as anything in the nature of a decision for delay, and is not to go to anyone outside our circle.

The Chiefs of Staff replied:

Chiefs of Staff to Prime Minister   29 Dec. 43

To fulfil the conditions of the plan made by existing commanders the "Overlord" assault should take place about May 5. However, this date cannot be regarded as final, and even if delays occur in the return and refitting programme of the L.S.T.s so that all have not joined their assault forces by April 13, this should not rule out a May date for the "Overlord" assault.

The arrangements proposed certainly do not preclude the achievement of a May assault, but the programme is tightly stretched. No violation of the agreement reached at Teheran is however involved, and we do not think it necessary at this stage to consult the Russians.

I commented on this as follows.

Prime Minister to Chiefs of Staff   30 Dec. 43

Our contract would be fulfilled by May 31. In my opinion it would be a *bona fide* execution of it if we fixed June 3, which is the corresponding moon phase to May 5, for the actual assault. It is however better to work to May 5, and thus have a month to spare.

*   *   *   *   *

Now a new point of importance arose.

Prime Minister to Field-Marshal Dill, Washington   3 Jan. 44

Alexander signals as follows: Clark is planning Anzio, and the usual difficulties are coming to light. For example, it appears that we shall not be able to keep 504th American Parachute Brigade, and Eisenhower is reluctant to press for their retention. The British Parachute Brigade is in the line and engaged. I have nothing immediately available to relieve them with, and we cannot afford the delay in getting them out and across to the Naples area. Further, they are not operationally experienced and badly need training.

2. Eisenhower is now with Marshall. Will you appeal to them to let this 504th American Brigade do this one fine and critical job before they come home for "Overlord"? It is so rarely that opportunities for decisive air action by paratroops present themselves, and it seems improvident to take them from the decisive point just when they might render exemplary and outstanding service. They can be sent home immediately afterwards in time for "Overlord," observing that we have already [at home] about double as many parachute and airborne troops for "Overlord" as there are transport aircraft to lift. Let me know what happens.

General Marshall agreed. We shall see later how this sacrifice was wasted.

*   *   *   *   *

I had asked Montgomery to visit me on his way home from Italy to take up his new command in "Overlord." I had offered him this task so full of hazard. Of course, in the absence of special reasons a general should accept any duty to which he is called by national authority. At the same time nothing in the unwritten law obliges enthusiasm. In the Grenadier Guards, with whom I once had the honour to serve, all orders are received with the one word "Sir." However, all kinds of inflections may be given to this monosyllable. I was gratified and also relieved to find that Montgomery was delighted and eager for what I had always regarded as a majestic, inevitable, but terrible task. When he arrived at Marrakesh, we had a two hours' drive out to our picnic at the foot of the Atlas. I had given him early in the morning the plan prepared over so many months by General Morgan and the Anglo-American Joint Staffs in London. After he had read it in summary, he said at once, "This will not do. I must have more in the initial punch." After considerable argument a whole set of arrangements was made in consequence of his opinion, and proved right. Evidently he was a firm believer in the operation, and I was very pleased at this.

The ladies had now come up, and we all lunched by the side of a dazzling stream in fresh air and brilliant sunshine. It was indeed an oasis in the vast desert of human conflict through which we had to toil. Presently I pushed forward into the mountains and our cars zigzagged slowly up the road to a viewpoint which I knew. But the General would have none of this. He got out of the car and walked straight up the hill, "to keep himself in training," as he put it. I warned him not to waste his vigour, considering what was coming. I emphasised the truths that energy of mind does not depend on energy of body; that energy should be exercised and not exhausted; that athletics were one thing and strategy another.

These admonitions were in vain. The General was in the highest spirits; he leaped about the rocks like an antelope, and I felt a strong reassurance that all would be well.

*   *   *   *   *

The New Year opened for me in agreeable correspondence with the President.

Prime Minister (Marrakesh) to President Roosevelt   30 Dec. 43

I have now received from my brother Jack full accounts of the Christmas tree at Chequers.[1] All my grandchildren were there, and a number of other children, and a good time was had by all. Winant, who was present, has promised to write to you about it. Thank you so much for sending me this token. I have also to thank you for the wonderful map case which has arrived from you for me, and which I am longing to see. We are indeed in comfort at this beautiful villa, and I am making good progress. The sun is shining today, but nothing did me the same good as your telegram showing how easily our minds work together on the grimly simple issues of this vast war. Alexander reports he has arranged satisfactory plans with Clark for Anzio. He is using the British 1st and the American 3d Divisions, with paratroops and armour. I am glad of this. It is fitting that we should share equally in suffering, risk, and honour.

I received on the same day congratulations on my recovery from Franco and Tito. So what?

Sarah thanks you for your message and sends her love.

Unhappily the President was himself laid up with influenza.

President Roosevelt to Prime Minister   31 Dec. 43

I am in bed for two or three days with a mild case of the 'flu, which, in a mild form, has become epidemic throughout the country.

I am delighted that you are safely at the villa. I suggest that on New Year's Day you invite the two gentlemen who congratulated you, then lock them in the top of the tower where we saw the

[1] Mr. Roosevelt grew Christmas trees at Hyde Park, and prided himself on this. He had sent me one.

sunset, and tell them you will stay at the bottom to see whether
the black or the red throws the other one over the battlements.

Prime Minister to President Roosevelt   1 Jan. 44

I am so sorry about your influenza. I earnestly hope you will defer
to Dr. McIntyre's advice and show that attitude of submission to
the medical faculty which you have so sedulously enjoined on me.

The villa is perfect. The doctors want me to stay here for the
next three weeks. The weather is bright, though cool. The cook
is a marvel. We go for picnics to the mountains. Last night Eisenhower was with us on his way to you, and I had long talks with
him. Montgomery is here now on his way to England. I think
we have a fine team, and they certainly mean to pull together.

I have not yet been able to arrange the contest in the tower.
The Red is in better training than the Black.

Accept all my best wishes for a New Year which will not only
be marked by triumph but will open wider doors to our future
work together.

Clemmie and Sarah also send their salutations.

*   *   *   *   *

Although the main issue about the landing-craft for Anzio
had been settled, many details of their employment raised
serious discussion.

General Alexander to Prime Minister   4 Jan. 44

I have just returned from conference with General Clark on my
way back from Tunis, and certain factors have come to light which
are causing me grave concern, and I must therefore ask for your
help and assistance. The facts are these. The removal of all but
six of the L.S.T.s after the initial landing will not allow us to put
the two divisions ashore complete with their essential fighting
vehicles. . . . My experience of combined operations is that the
initial assault to get ashore can be effected, but the success of the
operation depends on whether the full fighting strength of the
expedition can be concentrated in time to withstand the inevitable
counterattack. For Anzio two divisions are the minimum force to
put ashore in face of likely German resistance. Yet we are willing
to accept this if the two divisions can be concentrated on land in

strength and in time. . . . We are willing to accept any risks to achieve our object, but if the two divisions get sealed off by the Germans, we obviously cannot leave them there without any support when there will be L.S.T.s somewhere in the Mediterranean sufficient for that purpose. . . . Clark and I are confident that we have a great chance of pulling off something big if given the means with which to do it. The means required are fourteen L.S.T.s for maintenance until such time as the Anzio force and the Fifth Army join hands, and a further ten L.S.T.s for a period of fifteen days from the landing to build up the two divisions in guns, tanks, and other supporting arms to a strength sufficient to fight on level terms with the Germans. Even if this does interfere with preparations for "Anvil" to some extent, surely the prize is worth it.

I therefore summoned the authorities concerned to Marrakesh, and held two conferences on January 7 and 8, attended by Lord Beaverbrook, General Wilson, Admiral John Cunningham, General Alexander, General Devers, General Bedell Smith, and others. Captain Power had just returned from London after clearing up many intricate points about the landing-craft with the Chiefs of Staff, and now with the full support of his admiral, rendered us similar services. I was able to report to the President on the 8th as follows:

Prime Minister to President Roosevelt   8 Jan. 44

A unanimous agreement for action as proposed was reached by the responsible officers of both countries and of all services as a result of our two conferences. Everyone is in good heart and the resources seem sufficient. Every aspect was thrashed out in full detail by sub-committees in the interval between the two conferences. . . . Intention is to land a corps of two divisions for the assault, and to follow up with a mobile striking force based on the elements of a third division to cut enemy's communications.

It should be possible to do this, barring accident, without conflicting with requirements of "Overlord" or "Anvil," and still have sufficiency of landing-craft to maintain the force up till the end of February, weather permitting and God being with us.

General Wilson, who today assumes duty as Supreme Allied

Commander-in-Chief Mediterranean, has issued instructions to subordinate commanders to give effect to the above. He is also informing Combined Chiefs of Staff.

All these calculations were based upon the May (or X) date being maintained for "Overlord," though I myself had always thought that the moon period of June 3 (Y date) would probably be found most suitable, and I was glad to learn from General Eisenhower on his passage through Marrakesh that he was inclining towards this solution, which gave him and Montgomery more time to arrange for the larger forces it was now proposed to use in the first descent. I had telegraphed to the President setting out the whole question, and reminding him of our talks and agreements at Teheran.

Prime Minister to President Roosevelt   6 Jan. 44
Bedell Smith and Devers came through here morning of 5th. Bedell told me that he and Montgomery are convinced that it is better to put in a much heavier and broader "Overlord" than to expand the landing on the Riviera above our pre-Teheran conception, and that he is putting this to Eisenhower and your Chiefs of Staff. I have always expected that when the commanders took the matter into their hands, they would make alterations in the plans, which nevertheless have proved invaluable as a basis for future decisions. As you know, I have always hoped that the initial assault at "Overlord" could be with heavier forces than we have hitherto mentioned.

It also seems to me, from what I heard, very probable that the June moon will be the earliest practicable date. I do not see why we should resist this if the commanders feel they have a better chance then. At Teheran the Chiefs of Staffs' recommendation was June 1 or one day earlier, which you and I agreed to express more agreeably as "during May." In conversation with Uncle Joe, we never mentioned such a date as May 5, or even May 8, but always spoke to him [of] around the 20th. Neither did we at any time dwell upon the exact phase of the operation which should fall on any particular day. If now the June date is accepted as final, I do not feel that we shall in any way have broken faith with him. The operation will anyhow begin in May with feints and softening bombardments, and I do not think U.J. is the kind of man to be unreasonable over forty-eight hours.

On the other hand, the ground will be drier for U.J.'s great operations by June. We shall make a much heavier attack, and with much better chances of success. I am making you suggestions through Leathers for running another Arctic convoy, for which we can provide the escorts if you can provide the ships and cargoes, we having practically finished our quotas.

I do not think it necessary to make any communication to U.J. at the present time, but in a few weeks, after Eisenhower has presented his final conclusions to us, we should no doubt tell him all the story in all its strength, including any modification of "Anvil," with the authority of the responsible commanders behind our statement.

The President answered this important telegram, the facts of which were not in dispute between us, a week later. He had by then also received full reports of the conclusions of our meetings about the Anzio operation, which were all on the basis that the earlier date could be maintained for "Overlord" if desired.

President Roosevelt to Prime Minister   14 Jan. 44

It is my understanding that in Teheran Uncle J. was given a promise that "Overlord" would be launched during May and supported by strongest practicable landing in the South of France at about the same time, and that he agreed to plan for simultaneous Russian attack on Eastern Front.

I do not believe that we should make any decision now to defer the operations, certainly not until the responsible commanders, Eisenhower and Wilson, have had full opportunity to explore all possibilities and make factual reports. In the meantime no communication should be sent to Uncle J. on this subject.

I think the psychology of bringing this thing up at this time would be very bad, in view of the fact that it is only a little over a month since the three of us agreed on the statement in Teheran.

"I am very glad," I replied, on the 16th, "to see that we are in complete agreement."

*   *   *   *   *

Physical weakness oppressed me at Marrakesh following my illness at Carthage. All my painting tackle had been sent out, but I could not face it. I could hardly walk at all. Even tottering from the motor-car to a picnic luncheon in lovely weather amid the foothills of the Atlas was limited to eighty or a hundred yards. I passed eighteen hours out of the twenty-four supine. I never remember such extreme fatigue and weakness in body. On the other hand, every temptation, inducement, exhortation, and to some extent compulsion, to relax and lie down presented itself in the most seductive form. The Taylor villa was a perfect haven, lacking nothing that comfort could require or luxury suggest. I was utterly tired out, and here was the most attractive bed of repose, not only offered by gracious hosts, but enjoined by Lord Moran, the President, and the War Cabinet. However, events continued to offer irresistible distraction.

*　　*　　*　　*　　*

The Polish question which had played so great a part at Teheran, had led me to cable Eden from Carthage.

Prime Minister to Foreign Secretary　　　　　　　　　20 Dec. 43

I think you should now open the Polish frontiers question with the Poles, stating it is at my personal wish, and that I would have done it myself but for my temporary incapacitation. You should show them the formula and the rough line on the map on the eastern side, and the line of the Oder, including the Oppeln district, on the west. This gives them a magnificent piece of country three or four hundred miles across each way, and with over a hundred and fifty miles of seaboard, even on the basis that they do not begin till west of Königsberg. The Poles should understand of course that these are only very broad, tentative suggestions, but that they would be most unwise to let them fall to the ground. Even if they do not get Lvov, I should still advise their acceptance, and that they put themselves in the hands of British and American friends to try to turn this plan into reality. You should put it to them that by taking over and holding firmly the present German territories up to the Oder, they will be rendering a service to

Europe as a whole by making the basis of a friendly policy towards Russia and close association with Czechoslovakia. This would give a chance for the rebirth of the Polish nation brighter than any yet seen.

Once we know that they will accept and endorse these proposals, we will address ourselves to the Russians and endeavour to make matters firm and precise. On the other hand, if they cast it all aside, I do not see how His Majesty's Government can press for anything more for them. The Russian armies may in a few months be crossing the frontiers of pre-war Poland, and it seems of the utmost consequence to have friendly recognition by Russia of the Polish Government and a broad understanding of the post-war frontiers settlement agreed before then. I shall be most interested to hear what their reaction is.

*   *   *   *   *

President Beneš was now on his way from Moscow to London. As these volumes will show, I had a long contact with him. It will be remembered that he had played perhaps a decisive part in warning Stalin of the pro-German conspiracy against him in 1938.[2] At any rate, his relations with the Soviets were of the most friendly and intimate character. I asked him to look in on me at Marrakesh on his way back. His profound knowledge of the Eastern European scene made his views on Poland and on what the Russians would do for Poland most important. For twenty years or more Beneš, as Foreign Secretary or President of Czechoslovakia, had been the faithful ally of France and friend of the Western Powers, while at the same time maintaining a unique association with Stalin. When France and Britain sacrificed Czechoslovakia, and later when on the eve of the war Ribbentrop made his agreement with Molotov, Beneš was a very lonely man. But then, after a lengthy interval, came Hitler's attack on Russia, and all Beneš's common stock with the Soviets came again into full validity. Russia might well have fought Germany about Czechoslovakia in 1938. Anyhow, both were now under the same cruel lash.

It was very pleasant to me to talk in the sunshine and amid the flowers of my Marrakesh abode to this old political as-

2 See Volume I, *The Gathering Storm*, page 288.

sociate and mature European statesman, whom I had first met in 1918, in company with the great Masaryk, the founder of his country and the father of a son who died faithfully in her cause. Beneš was of course at this time optimistic.

I gave the following account of our talk to the President.

Prime Minister to President Roosevelt   6 Jan. 44

Benes has been here, and is very hopeful about the Russian situation. He may be most useful in trying to make the Poles see reason and in reconciling them to the Russians, whose confidence he has long possessed. He brought a new map with pencil marks by U.J. showing the eastern frontier from Königsberg to the Curzon Line, giving the Poles Lomza and Bialystok regions in the north, but not Lemberg [Lvov] at the southern end. For their western frontier he offers the line of the Oder, including the major part of Oppeln. This gives the Poles a fine place to live in, more than three hundred miles square, and with two hundred and fifty miles of seaboard on the Baltic. As soon as I get home, I shall go all out with the Polish Government to close with this or something like it, and, having closed, they must proclaim themselves as ready to accept the duty of guarding the bulwark of the Oder against further German aggression upon Russia, and also they must back the settlement to the limit. This will be their duty to the Powers of Europe, who will twice have rescued them. If I can get this tidied up early in February, a visit from them to you would clinch matters.

The Russians are quite agreeable to Benes having his old pre-Munich frontier back, with a slight military adjustment along the northern crests of the mountains and a little territory to the eastward linking them with Russia.

As this was the last time I ever saw President Beneš, I will record my tribute to him. In all his thought and aims he consistently sustained the main principles on which Western civilisation is founded, and was ever true to the cause of his native land, over which he presided for twenty years. He was a master of administration and diplomacy. He knew how to endure with patience and fortitude long periods of adverse fortune. Where he failed — and it cost him and his country much — was in not taking violent decisions at the supreme

moment. He was too experienced a diplomatist, too astute a
year-to-year politician, to realise the moment and to stake all
on victory or death. Had he told his cannons to fire at Munich
time, the Second World War would have begun under conditions far less favourable to Hitler, who needed many months
to make his army and his armour.

*   *   *   *   *

In spite of the tension with General de Gaulle about
Peyrouton, Boisson, and Flandin, all of whom had been arrested by the Free French authorities in December, I determined to make an effort to renew friendly relations with him
before returning home. On New Year's Day, I asked him to
dine and sleep at the villa on January 3. "This," I said, "would
give us an opportunity of long-needed talks. My wife is with
me here, and if Madame de Gaulle would care to accompany
you, it would give us both much pleasure." The General
evidently thought the notice too short. I ought to have known
that he would not sleep anywhere in North Africa but in a
French official residence. He pleaded the pressure of his other
engagements. So I let it alone. However, having learnt later
that he would arrive in Marrakesh on January 12, I invited
him to luncheon that day, and he accepted. Mr. Duff Cooper
and Lady Diana, Lord Beaverbrook, Mr. Nairn the Consul
and his wife were also our guests. The General arrived in the
best of humour, greeted Mrs. Churchill in English, and spoke
it throughout the meal. To make things equal, I spoke French.
After luncheon the ladies went off to visit the bazaars, and
de Gaulle and I and the other men settled down in the garden
for a long talk. I had a lot of awkward subjects to deal with,
and I thought my speaking French would add a lighter touch
to them. Mr. Nairn, who made a few notes afterwards, records,
"I heard Mr. Churchill say to Mr. Duff Cooper in English in
a very audible whisper, 'I'm doing rather well, aren't I? Now
that the General speaks English so well, he understands my
French perfectly.' Then everyone, General de Gaulle setting
the example, burst out laughing. The Prime Minister con-

tinued in French, but the supersensitive General was completely disarmed and ready to accept Mr. Churchill's comments in a friendly and helpful spirit."

The comments were numerous and serious. Why was he pursuing this vendetta against the French notabilities who had fallen into his power? Did he not realise how much difficulty he made for himself in the United States? How angry the President was with him? How much we all depended on American aid and good will? Why should he complicate his own task by this and all sorts of other needless friction? Why should he always try to offend these powerful Governments, without whose help he could not live? Upon a smaller point, why had he driven General Georges, whom I had specially brought from France to make things easier, off the Committee? At this de Gaulle said he had offered General Georges the Chancellorship of the Legion of Honour. I asked what reply he had received. "I received no reply," he answered. I said I was not surprised. Had he the Chancellorship to bestow? But all ended pleasantly, and the General proposed that I should attend a review he would hold in my honour the next morning, which I agreed to do. And accordingly de Gaulle and I stood on a small platform while quite a large array of French and Moroccan troops marched past for an hour amid the cheers of the inhabitants of the Marrakesh oasis.

*   *   *   *   *

Another question arising out of Teheran raised considerable difficulty. We have seen how Stalin had asked for a share in the Italian Fleet, and the President was under the impression that he himself had mentioned in conversation one-third. The British Chiefs of Staff did not like this, and had always spoken to their Russian colleagues on a different basis. The President was worried about his personal remark "one-third," and set the whole position out to me with great frankness.

President Roosevelt to Prime Minister   9 Jan. 44

As I told you, Harriman requested information on the action we were taking to carry out our commitments to turn over Italian ships to the Soviet by February 1 so that he could discuss the matter with Molotov if he were queried. I told him it was my intention to allocate one-third of the captured Italian ships to the Soviet war effort, beginning February 1, as rapidly as they could be made available.

Harriman then reminded me that Stalin's request at Teheran was a reiteration of the Soviet request originally made at Moscow in October [namely, for one battleship, one cruiser, eight destroyers, and four submarines for North Russia, and forty thousand tons of merchant shipping for the Black Sea], and that no mention was made at Moscow or Teheran of the Russians getting additional ships up to one-third of those captured. Accordingly, Harriman regarded my cable of December 21 as being for his information, and he has not discussed the question of one-third with Molotov.

Harriman also emphasised the very great importance of fulfilling our pledge to yield these ships. For us to fail or to delay would, in his opinion, only arouse suspicion in Stalin and in his associates as to the firmness of other commitments made at Teheran.

On the other hand, the Chiefs of Staff have raised numerous objections to the transfer, based on probable effects that this course would have on pending operations. They fear a loss of Italian naval and military co-operation, and the scuttling or sabotage of valuable ships which we need for "Anvil" and "Overlord." They foresee no material benefit to the Russian war effort at this time, since the warships are presently quite unsuited for Northern waters and the Black Sea is closed to merchant vessels.

The very wise provisions of the modified agreement [negotiated by Admiral Cunningham] give the United Nations the right to make disposition of any or all Italian ships as they may think fit. It is of importance that we should acquire and maintain the confidence of our Ally, and I feel that every practicable effort should be made to arrive at a solution whereby the Italian ships requested by the Soviet be turned over to them, beginning about February 1.

Do you believe it wise to present to Uncle J. the possible effect on "Overlord-Anvil" as expressed by our Staffs, and suggest a delay in assigning Italian ships to him until after the launching of "Overlord-Anvil"? I am particularly desirous of having an expression of your opinion in view of the present British command of the Mediterranean theatre and in order that we may reach a complete agreement as to the action to be taken. It is patently impracticable for either of us to act singly in this matter, but I think you will agree that we must not go back on what we told Uncle J.

This message was not entirely clear. I agreed to the ships mentioned in our agreement of October, but not to the more general terms of "one third." I therefore replied:

Prime Minister to President Roosevelt   9 *Jan.* 44

I entirely agree with you that we must not break faith with Stalin about the ships. I have been for a week in correspondence with Anthony on the subject, and hope to submit a proposal to you for a joint communication from you and me in a day or two.

I was myself in full accord with the Chiefs of Staff on both sides of the Atlantic. I felt that the immediate transfer of these Italian warships, which had so resolutely made their way to Malta and placed themselves in our hands, might have most damaging results to Italian co-operation with the Allies. Throughout the year 1943, my aim had been, not only to make Italy surrender, but to bring her in on our side, with all that that meant to the progress of the war and to the future settlement of Europe. I was therefore prepared to press the War Cabinet and the Admiralty to make a substantial British sacrifice and to supply a number of British ships to the Russians, instead of breaking Italian hearts at this moment, so pregnant, as it seemed to me, with consequences for the future. Various messages passed between us, and I was very glad indeed to find how closely my colleagues at home and the Chiefs of Staff agreed. One could not expect the United States, with the whole burden of war in the Pacific weighing upon them, to make any large contribution. We, on the other hand, had certainly at this time an ample margin of naval power, both in the Mediterranean and, now that the *Scharnhorst* was at the bottom, in home and Arctic waters as well. As soon as I reached an agreement with my friends at home I sent the following proposals to the President:

Prime Minister to President Roosevelt   16 Jan. 44

My recollection is clear that nothing was said at Teheran about "one-third," but that a promise was made to meet the Russian claim put forward at Moscow to have transferred to them one battleship, one cruiser, eight destroyers, four submarines, and forty thousand tons of merchant shipping.

2. On the other hand, the main difficulties raised by the Chiefs of Staff are solid, and I think it very likely that once Stalin is convinced of our intentions and our good faith he will leave us to handle the matter in the smoothest and swiftest way possible.

3. I suggest therefore that we now signal him jointly to the following effect.

(i) . . . The Combined Chiefs of Staff . . . think it would be dangerous to our triple interests actually to carry out any transfer or to say anything about it to the Italians at present. Nevertheless, if after full consideration you desire us to proceed, we will make a secret approach to Badoglio with a view to concluding the necessary arrangements. . . . These would have to be on the lines that Italian ships selected should be sailed to a suitable Allied port, where they would be collected by Russian crews, who would sail into Russian Northern ports which are the only ones now open where any refitting necessary could be undertaken.

(ii) We are however very conscious of the dangers of this course, and have therefore decided to propose the following alternative:

The British battleship *Royal Sovereign* has recently completed refit in the United States. She is fitted with radar for all types of armament. Great Britain has also a cruiser available. His Majesty's Government are willing, for their part, that these vessels should be taken over during February at British ports by Soviet crews and sailed to North Russian ports. You could then make such alterations as you find necessary for Arctic conditions. These vessels would be temporarily transferred on loan to the Soviet Government, and would fly the Soviet flag until, without prejudice to the military operations, the necessary transfer of Italian vessels could be arranged.

(iii) If events should take a favourable turn with Turks and the Straits become open, the vessels would be ready to operate if desired in the Black Sea. We hope you will very carefully consider this alternative, which we think is in every way superior to first proposal.

4. If you could find the cruiser instead of our having to do so, we should be relieved. We cannot do anything about the eight destroyers, but perhaps you may be able to supply this need. Otherwise we must say we have absolutely not got them until after "Overlord" and "Anvil." As to the forty thousand tons of merchant shipping, I should think that with your great supply and vastly improved sinkings you might supply these, but we should be willing to share fifty-fifty.

5. I hope, my dear friend, you will consider all these possibilities and let me know how you feel. In my opinion Stalin will be moved in a favourable manner by this handsome proposal. At any rate, it shows our faith and our good will. I doubt whether, having this alternative before him, he will press for the premature raising of the Italian problem, but we shall have done the right thing.

*   *   *   *   *

This alternative was accepted by the President. The Americans undertook themselves to furnish a cruiser, and the whole matter was presented to Stalin substantially in the form I suggested in a joint telegram from the President and me on January 23. Stalin's reply, when it came later, was as follows:

29 Jan. 44
Premier Stalin to Prime Minister and President Roosevelt

I received on January 23 both your joint messages, signed by you, Mr. Prime Minister, and you, Mr. President, regarding the question of the handing over of Italian shipping for the use of the Soviet Union.

I must say that, after your joint affirmative reply at Teheran to the question which I raised of the handing over to the Soviet Union of Italian shipping by the end of January 1944, I considered this question settled, and the thought never entered my mind of the possibility of any kind of reconsideration of this decision, which was taken and agreed between the three of us. All the more so since, as we agreed at the time, this question was to be completely settled with the Italians. Now I see that this is not so, and that nothing has even been mentioned to the Italians on the subject.

In order however not to complicate this question, which is of such great importance for our common struggle against Germany, the Soviet Government is prepared to accept your proposal regarding the dispatch from British ports to the U.S.S.R. of the battleship *Royal Sovereign* and one cruiser, and regarding the temporary use of these vessels by the Naval High Command of the U.S.S.R. until such time as the appropriate Italian shipping is made available to the Soviet Union. Similarly, we shall be prepared to accept from the U.S.A. and Great Britain forty thousand tons of merchant shipping, which will also be used by us until such time as a similar tonnage of Italian shipping is handed over to us. It is important that there should be no delays now regarding the matter, and that all the shipping indicated should be handed over to us during the month of February.

In your reply however there is no mention of the handing over to the Soviet Union of eight Italian destroyers and four submarines, to the handing over of which to the Soviet Union at the end of January you, Mr. Prime Minister, and you, Mr. President, agreed in Teheran. Meanwhile, for the Soviet Union this very question of destroyers and submarines, without which the handing over of one battleship and one cruiser has no significance, is of capital importance. You understand yourselves that a cruiser and a battleship are powerless without escorting destroyers. Since the whole of Italy's Fleet is under your control, to carry out the decision which was taken at Teheran to hand over for the use of the Soviet Union eight destroyers and four submarines out of that Fleet should present no difficulties. I am agreeable [literally, "I agree"] that, instead of Italian destroyers and submarines, a similar number of American or British destroyers and submarines should be handed over to the Soviet Union for our use. Moreover, the question of the handing over of destroyers and submarines cannot be postponed, but must be settled at one and the same time with the handing over of the battleship and cruiser, as was definitely agreed between us at Teheran.

Eventually the matter was settled as I hoped, although there was a good deal of correspondence, not all of a pleasant character, about it with our Soviet Ally. The *Royal Sovereign* and the American cruiser were handed over as proposed. There was an inevitable delay about the destroyers till after the "Overlord" operation was complete. The Admiralty sweetened this pill by lending Russia four of our modern sub-

marines. As is well known, the Soviets after the war faithfully
returned the ships, and arrangements were made to transfer
vessels from the Italian Fleet in a manner acceptable to all concerned.

*   *   *   *   *

Much as I should have liked, and much as I was pressed, to
recuperate for another fortnight in this delectable asylum, I
determined to be at home before the shock of Anzio occurred.
On January 14, therefore, we all flew in beautiful weather to
Gibraltar, where the *King George V* awaited me. I arrived
early in the afternoon, and repaired again to the Convent.
General Wilson, who had assumed his duties as Supreme Commander of the Mediterranean, and Admiral John Cunningham, the Naval Commander-in-Chief, had both arrived by air
from Algiers, and we had an anxious but hopeful talk about
the momentous operation for which we were all working. On
the 15th, I joined the rest of my party, who were already on
board the *King George V*. She made her way out of Algeciras
Bay wide into the Atlantic, and thence to Plymouth. After a
restful voyage, we were welcomed by the War Cabinet and
Chiefs of Staff, who really seemed quite glad to see me back.
I had been nearly two months away from England, and they
had been through a lot of worry on account both of my illness
and my activities. It was indeed a home-coming, and I felt
deeply grateful to all these trusty friends and fellow-workers.

9

Marshal Tito and Yugoslavia

Mihailovic and Tito — Importance of the Balkan Struggle — The Deakin and Maclean Missions — Growth of Partisan Strength after Italian Surrender — My Telegram to Roosevelt of October 23 — Bitter Quarrels Between Mihailovic and Tito — Three New Factors in Our Policy — Randolph to Join Maclean — Difficult Position of King Peter — My Letter to Tito of January 8, 1944 — His Reply — We Withdraw Our Liaison Officers from Mihailovic — My Account to Parliament of February, 1944 — King Peter Dismisses the Puric Government — My Further Telegrams to Tito.

THE READER must now go back to a fierce and sombre tale, which the main narrative has outstripped. Yugoslavia, since Hitler's invasion and conquest in April 1941, had been the scene of fearful events. The spirited boy King took refuge in England with such of Prince Paul's ministers and others as had defied the German assault. In the mountains there began again the fierce guerrilla with which the Serbs had resisted the Turks for centuries. General Mihailovic was its first and foremost champion, and round him rallied the surviving *élite* of Yugoslavia. In the vortex of world affairs their struggle was hardly noticeable. It belongs to the "unestimated sum of human pain." Mihailovic suffered as a guerrilla leader from the fact that many of his followers were well-known people with relations and friends in Belgrade, and property and recognisable connections elsewhere. The Germans pursued a policy of murderous blackmail. They retaliated for guerrilla activities by

shooting batches of four or five hundred selected people in
Belgrade. Under this pressure Mihailovic drifted gradually
into a posture where some of his commanders made accommodations with the German and Italian troops to be left alone
in certain mountain areas in return for doing little or nothing
against the enemy. Those who have triumphantly withstood
such strains may brand his name, but history, more discriminat-
ing, should not erase it from the scroll of Serbian patriots. By
the autumn of 1941, Serbian resistance to the German terror
had become only a shadow. The national struggle could only
be sustained by the innate valour of the common people. This
however was not lacking.

A wild and furious war for existence against the Germans
broke into flame among the partisans. Among these Tito stood
forth, pre-eminent and soon dominant. Tito, as he called himself, was a Soviet-trained Communist who, until Russia was
invaded by Hitler, and after Yugoslavia had been assailed, had
fomented political strikes along the Dalmatian coast, in accordance with the general Comintern policy. But once he
united in his breast and brain his Communist doctrine with
his burning ardour for his native land in her extreme torment,
he became a leader, with adherents who had little to lose but
their lives, who were ready to die, and if to die to kill. This
confronted the Germans with a problem which could not be
solved by the mass executions of notables or persons of substance. They found themselves confronted by desperate men
who had to be hunted down in their lairs. The partisans under
Tito wrested weapons from German hands. They grew rapidly
in numbers. No reprisals, however bloody, upon hostages or
villages deterred them. For them it was death or freedom. Soon
they began to inflict heavy injury upon the Germans and became masters of wide regions.

It was inevitable that the partisan movement should also
come into savage quarrels with their fellow-countrymen, who
were resisting half-heartedly or making bargains for immunity
with the common foe. The partisans deliberately violated any
agreements made with the enemy by the Cetniks — as the

followers of General Mihailovic were called. The Germans then shot Cetnik hostages and in revenge Cetniks gave the Germans information about the partisans. All this happened sporadically and uncontrollably in these wild mountain regions. It was a tragedy within a tragedy.

*   *   *   *   *

I had followed these events amid other preoccupations so far as was possible. Except for a trickle of supplies dropped from aircraft, we were not able to help. Our headquarters in the Middle East was responsible for all operations in this theatre and maintained a system of agents and liaison officers with the followers of Mihailovic. When in the summer of 1943, we broke into Sicily and Italy, the Balkans and especially Yugoslavia never left my thoughts. Up till this point our missioners had only gone to the bands under Mihailovic, who represented the official resistance to the Germans and the Yugoslav Government in Cairo. In May 1943, we took a new departure. It was decided to send small parties of British officers and non-commissioned officers to establish contact with the Yugoslav partisans, in spite of the fact that cruel strife was proceeding between them and the Cetniks, and that Tito was waging war as a Communist, not only against the German invaders, but against the Serbian Monarchy and Mihailovic. At the end of that month, Captain Deakin, an Oxford don who had helped me for five years before the war in my literary work, was dropped by parachute from Cairo to set up a mission with Tito. Other British missions followed, and by June much evidence had accumulated. The Chiefs of Staff reported on June 6: "It is clear from information available to the War Office that the Cetniks are hopelessly compromised in their relations with the Axis in Herzegovina and Montenegro. During the recent fighting in the latter area, it has been the well-organised partisans rather than the Cetniks who have been holding down the Axis forces."

Towards the end of the month, my attention was drawn to the question of obtaining the best results from local resistance

to the Axis in Yugoslavia. Having called for full information,
I presided at a Chiefs of Staff Conference at Downing Street
on June 23. In the course of the discussion I emphasised the
very great importance of giving all possible support to the
Yugoslav anti-Axis movement, which was containing about
thirty-three Axis divisions in that area. This matter was of
such importance that I directed that the small number of additional aircraft required to increase our aid must be provided,
if necessary at the expense of the bombing of Germany and of
the U-boat war.

On July 7, the eve of our landing in Sicily, I drew General
Alexander's attention to these possibilities.

Prime Minister to General Alexander   7 July 43

I presume you have read about the recent heavy fighting in
Yugoslavia and the widespread sabotage and guerrilla beginning
in Greece. Albania also should be a fertile field. All this has
grown up with no more aid from Britain than the dropping of a
few bundles by parachute. If we can get hold of the mouth of the
Adriatic so as to be able to run even a few ships into Dalmatian
or Greek ports, the whole of the Western Balkans might flare up,
with far-reaching results. All this is however hunting in the next
field.

A fortnight later I elaborated my thought on the essential
connection between the Italian and Balkan theatres in the following important telegram:

Prime Minister to General Alexander   22 July 43

I am going with the Staffs to meet the President before August 15
in Canada. Thus we shall all be on the spot at the time when
Sicily may very likely be cleaned up. . . .

I am sending you by an officer a full account which I have had
prepared of the marvellous resistance put up by the so-called partisan followers of Tito in Bosnia and the powerful cold-blooded
manoeuvres of Mihailovic in Serbia. Besides this, there are the resistances of the guerrillas in Albania and recently in Greece. The
Germans have not only been reinforcing the Balkan peninsula
with divisions, but they have been continually improving the qual-

ity and mobility of these divisions and have been stiffening up the local Italians. The enemy cannot spare these forces, and if Italy collapses the Germans could not bear the weight themselves. Great prizes lie in the Balkan direction.

No objective can compete with the capture of Rome, which in its turn gives a stage later all the advantages hoped for from the Balkan liberation. . . . The fall of Italy, the effect upon the other German satellites, and the subsequent utter loneliness of Germany may conceivably produce decisive results in Europe, especially in view of the vast strength evinced by the Russian armies.

This message is sent to give you my whole mind, which is, I believe, in full harmony with the Chiefs of Staff.

* * * * *

Before leaving for Quebec, I decided to pave the way for further action in the Balkans by appointing a senior officer to lead a larger mission to the partisans in the field, and with the authority to make direct recommendations to me about our future action towards them.

Prime Minister to Foreign Secretary 28 July 43

Mr. Fitzroy Maclean, M.P., is a man of daring character, with Parliamentary status and Foreign Office training. He is to go to Yugoslavia and work with Tito. The idea is that a Brigadier should be sent out to take command later on. In my view we should plump for Maclean and make him the head of any mission now contemplated, and give him a good military staff officer under his authority. What we want is a daring Ambassador-leader with these hardy and hunted guerrillas.

This mission landed in Yugoslavia by parachute in September 1943, to find the situation revolutionised. The news of the Italian surrender had reached Yugoslavia only with the official broadcast announcements. But, in spite of complete absence of any warning by us, Tito took quick and fruitful action. Within a few weeks six Italian divisions had been disarmed by the partisan forces, and another two went over to fight with them against the Germans. With Italian equipment the Yugoslavs were now able to arm eighty thousand more men, and to occupy for the moment most of the Adriatic coastline. There

was now a good chance of strengthening our general position
in the Adriatic in relation to the Italian Front. The Yugoslav
partisan army, now totalling two hundred thousand men, although fighting primarily as guerrillas, was now engaged in
widespread action against the Germans, who continued their
violent reprisals with increasing fury.

One effect of this increased activity in Yugoslavia was to
exacerbate the conflict between Tito and Mihailovic. Tito's
growing military strength raised in an increasingly acute form
the ultimate position of the Yugoslav Monarchy and the exiled
Government. Till the end of the war sincere and prolonged
efforts were made both in London and within Yugoslavia to
reach a working compromise between both sides. I had hoped
that the Russians would use their good offices in this matter.
When Mr. Eden went to Moscow in October 1943, the subject
of Yugoslavia was placed on the Conference agenda. At the
meeting of October 23, he made a frank and fair statement of
our attitude in the hope of securing a common Allied policy
towards Yugoslavia, but the Russians displayed no wish either
to pool information or to discuss a plan of action.

Even after many weeks I saw little prospect of any working
arrangement between the hostile factions in Yugoslavia.

Former Naval Person to President Roosevelt   23 Oct. 43

In spite of the vexatious broils between the followers of Tito
and Mihailovic in Yugoslavia and those that have broken out
between the two sets of Greek guerrillas, the situation in the Balkan
peninsula is grievous for the enemy. . . . We British have about
eighty separate missions under General Wilson's control working
with partisans and patriot bands scattered over these immense
mountainous regions, nine hundred miles by about three hundred
miles in extent. Some of our officers there of Brigadier's rank are
very capable, and have in numerous cases been there for two
years. . . .

The fighting is of the most cruel and bloody character, with
merciless reprisals and executions of hostages by the Huns. But
the enemy also is suffering heavily, and is now consuming not less
than twenty-five German and eight Bulgarian divisions in the

theatre without being able to control more than key points and with increasing difficulty in maintaining railway traffic. We hope soon to compose the Greek quarrels, but the differences between Tito's partisans and Mihailovic's Serbs are very deep-seated.

My gloomy forecast proved true. At the end of November, Tito summoned a political congress of his movement at Jajce, in Bosnia, and not only set up a Provisional Government, "with sole authority to represent the Yugoslav nation," but also formally deprived the Royal Yugoslav Government in Cairo of all its rights. The King was forbidden to return to the country until after the liberation. The partisans had established themselves without question as the leading elements of resistance in Yugoslavia, particularly since the Italian surrender. But it was important that no irrevocable political decisions about the future régime in Yugoslavia should be made in the atmosphere of occupation, civil war, and émigré politics. The tragic figure of Mihailovic had become the major obstacle. We had to maintain close military contact with the partisans, and therefore to persuade the King to dismiss Mihailovic from his post as Minister of War. Early in December, we withdrew official support from Mihailovic and recalled the British missions operating in his territory.

*   *   *   *   *

Yugoslav affairs were considered at the Teheran Conference against this background. Although it was decided by the three Allied Powers to give the maximum support to the partisans, the rôle of Yugoslavia in the war was dismissed by Stalin as of minor importance, and the Russians even disputed our figures of the number of Axis divisions in the Balkans. The Soviet Government however agreed to send a Russian mission to Tito as a result of Mr. Eden's initiative. They also wished to keep contact with Mihailovic.

On my return from Teheran to Cairo, I saw King Peter, and told him about the strength and significance of the partisan movement and that it might be necessary for him to dismiss Mihailovic from his Cabinet. The only hope which the King possessed of returning to his country would be, with our mediation, to reach some provisional arrangement with Tito without delay and before the partisans further extended their hold upon the country. The Russians, too, professed to be willing to work for some kind of compromise. On December 21, the Soviet Ambassador handed the following message to Mr. Eden:

The Soviet Government is aware that at the present time very strained relations exist between Marshal Tito and the National Committee of Liberation of Yugoslavia on the one hand and King Peter and his Government on the other. Mutual attacks and hard accusations on both sides, especially those which have recently taken place, have led to open hostilities, which hamper the cause of the struggle for the liberation of Yugoslavia. The Soviet Government shares the view of the British Government that, in the interests of the fight of the Yugoslavian people against the German invaders, it is necessary to make efforts to find a basis for collaboration between the two sides. The Soviet Government sees the great difficulties standing in the way of the realisation of this task, but it is ready to do everything possible to find a compromise between the two sides, with the purpose of uniting all the forces of the Yugoslavian people in the interests of the common struggle of the Allies.

I received almost unanimous advice as to what course to pursue in this disagreeable situation. Officers who had served with Tito and the commanders of missions to Mihailovic presented similar pictures. The British Ambassador to the Royal Yugoslav Government, Mr. Stevenson, was equally convinced. He telegraphed to the Foreign Office on December 25:

Our policy must be based on three new factors:
The partisans will be the rulers of Yugoslavia. They are of such value to us militarily that we must back them to the full, subordinating political considerations to military. It is extremely doubtful whether we can any longer regard the Monarchy as a unifying element in Yugoslavia.

*   *   *   *   *

This crisis in Yugoslav affairs pressed on me as I lay ill at Marrakesh. Maclean, who had been with me in Cairo, was now due to return to Yugoslavia. He was anxious to have my son with him, and it was arranged that Randolph should join the mission by parachute.

Prime Minister to Foreign Secretary   29 Dec. 43

Randolph, who is now waiting for a drop into Yugoslavia, left behind the following note for me, dated 25th instant. It seems to me sound, and to represent to a large extent your point of view and mine. He will be going in a few days.

"1. Three weeks ago in Cairo Stevenson made no attempt to resist the arguments of Maclean and Deakin that the condition precedent for any useful political action in Yugoslavia was the repudiation of General Mihailovic. Despite the polemics indulged in by both sides, this is as true today as it was three weeks ago, though perhaps, owing to the procrastination of the King, we shall only gain a military and not a political advantage.

"2. Maclean stressed in Cairo that no *quid pro quo* could be obtained for the King by the dismissal of Mihailovic, but that this gesture might create an atmosphere in which the King's fortunes could be advanced. This position has been prejudiced, but is still true, with limitations, today.

"3. Two things are surely therefore required: (i) The immediate repudiation of Mihailovic by His Majesty's Government and if possible by King Peter. (ii) The immediate return to Tito's headquarters of Maclean to try (*a*) to obtain the maximum military advantage from the situation, and (*b*) to explore what advantage may be gained for the King from the new situation that will be created upon the dismissal of Mihailovic."

I added my own views, and a draft reply to Tito.

Prime Minister to Foreign Secretary   30 Dec. 43

There is no possibility now of getting Tito to accept King Peter as a *quid pro quo* for repudiating Mihailovic. Once Mihailovic is gone the King's chances will be greatly improved and we can plead his case at Tito's Headquarters. I thought we were all agreed in Cairo to advise Peter to dismiss Mihailovic before the end of the year. Everything Deakin and Maclean said and all the reports received showed that he had been in active collaboration with the Germans. We shall never bring the parties together till he has been disowned, not only by us, but by the King.

Pray let me know whether I shall send the following message, or whether I shall merely give a friendly acknowledgment, in which latter case I fear we shall have lost a good opportunity of my establishing a personal relationship with this important man.

I do not wish to hawk this private message around to the United States and Stalin, with the inevitable delays involved. Unless you disagree, I propose to send it, as a letter, by air courier to Maclean at Bari, who will deliver it. He and Randolph will be dropping in in a few days. Let me know also the form in which you will repudiate Mihailovic and invite the King to do so. It is, in my opinion, Peter's only chance.

And on January 2:

I have been convinced by the arguments of men I know and trust, that Mihailovic is a millstone tied around the neck of the little King, and he has no chance till he gets rid of him.

The Foreign Secretary agreed, and I now wrote to Tito, who had sent me congratulations on my recovery.

AFRICA: *January* 8, 1944

I thank you very much for your kind message about my health from yourself and the heroic patriot and partisan army of Yugoslavia. From Major Deakin, who is a friend of mine, I learnt all about your valiant efforts. It is my most earnest desire to give you all aid in human power by sea supplies, by air support, and by Commandos helping you in the island fighting. Brigadier Maclean is also a friend of mine, and a colleague in the House of Commons. With him at your Headquarters will soon be serving my son, Major Randolph Churchill, who is also a Member of Parliament.

One supreme object stands before us, namely, to cleanse the soil of Europe from the filthy Nazi-Fascist taint. You may be sure that we British have no desire to dictate the future government of Yugoslavia. At the same time we hope that all will pull together as much as possible for the defeat of the common foe, and afterwards settle the form of government in accordance with the will of the people.

I am resolved that the British Government shall give no further military support to Mihailovic and will only give help to you, and we should be glad if the Royal Yugoslavian Government would dismiss him from their councils. King Peter the Second however escaped as a boy from the treacherous clutches of the Regent Prince Paul, and came to us as the representative of Yugoslavia and as a young prince in distress. It would not be chivalrous or honourable for Great Britain to cast him aside. Nor can we ask him to cut all his existing contacts with his country. I hope therefore that you will understand we shall in any case remain in official relations with him, while at the same time giving you all possible military support. I hope also that there may be an end to polemics on either side, for these only help the Germans.

You may be sure I shall work in the closest contact with my friends Marshal Stalin and President Roosevelt; and I earnestly hope that the Military Mission which the Soviet Government are sending to your Headquarters will work in similar harmony with the Anglo-American Mission under Brigadier Maclean. Please correspond with me through Brigadier Maclean, and let me know anything you think I can do to help, for I will certainly try my best.

Looking forward to the end of your sufferings and to the liberation of all Europe from tyranny . . .

It took nearly a month to get an answer:

Marshal Tito to the Prime Minister [*received February* 3, 1944]
Your Excellency,

Your message brought by Brigadier Maclean is valuable proof that our people have in their superhuman struggle for freedom and independence a true friend and Ally at their side who deeply comprehends our needs and our aspirations. For me personally your message is an honour, for it expresses your high acknowledgment of our struggle and the efforts of our National Liberation Army. I thank you heartily for your photographs from the Teheran Conference, with your dedication. Your Excellency may be sure that we will endeavour to keep your friendship won in a most difficult hour of our people's history, and which is extremely dear to us. The devastation of the country, and the people, exhausted

with suffering, need, and will need in future, the help of our great
Allies not only during the war, but also in peace to enable us to
heal the terrible wounds inflicted on us by the ignoble Fascist invader. It is our wish to fulfil to the utmost our duty as an Ally in
the common military effort against our common enemy. Aid tendered to us by our Allies very much contributes to ease our situation on the battlefield. We also hope, with your help, to obtain
heavy armament (tanks and aircraft), which in the present phase of
the war and owing to the present strength of our National Liberation Army is indispensable to us.

2. I quite understand your engagements towards King Peter II
and his Government, and I will contrive, as far as the interests of
our people permit, to avoid unnecessary politics and not cause
inconvenience to our Allies in this matter. I assure you, however,
your Excellency, that the internal political situation created in this
arduous struggle for liberation is not only a machine for the strivings of individuals or some political group, but it is the irresistible
desire of all patriots, of all those who are fighting and long connected with this struggle, and these are the enormous majority of
the peoples of Yugoslavia. Therefore, the people have set [them-
selves] difficult tasks and we are bound to accomplish them.

3. At the present moment all our efforts turn to one direction,
and that is, (1) assemble all patriotic and honourable elements so
as to render our struggle against the invader as efficient as possible;
(2) to create union and brotherhood of the Yugoslav nations,
which did not exist before this war, and the absence of which
caused the catastrophe in our country; (3) to create conditions for
the establishment of a state in which all nations of Yugoslavia
would feel happy, and that is a truly democratic Yugoslavia, a
federative Yugoslavia. I am convinced that you understand us,
and that we will have your valuable support in these strivings of
our people.

Yours very sincerely,
Tito
Marshal of Yugoslavia

I replied at once:

Prime Minister to Marshal Tito (Yugoslavia)   5 Feb. 44
I am very glad my letter has reached you safely, and I have re-

ceived your message with pleasure. I can understand the position of reserve which you adopt towards King Peter. I have for several months past been in favour of advising him to dismiss Mihailovic and to face the consequent resignation of all his present advisers. I have been deterred from doing this by the argument that I should thus be advising him to cast away his only adherents. You will understand I feel a personal responsibility towards him. I should be obliged if you would let me know whether his dismissal of Mihailovic would pave the way for friendly relations with you and your Movement, and, later on, for his joining you in the field, it being understood that the future question of the Monarchy is reserved until Yugoslavia has been entirely liberated. There is no doubt that a working arrangement between you and the King would consolidate many forces, especially Serbian elements, now estranged, and that it would invest your Government and movement with added authority and provide them with numerous resources. Yugoslavia would then be able to speak with a united voice in the councils of the Allies during this formative period when so much is in flux. I much hope that you will feel able to give me the answer you can see I want.

2. His Britannic Majesty's Government desire to assemble all patriotic and honourable elements so as to render your struggle against the invader as efficient as possible; secondly, to create union and brotherhood of the Yugoslav nations; and, thirdly, to create conditions for a truly democratic and federative Yugoslavia. You will certainly have the support of His Majesty's Government in all this.

3. I have asked the Supreme Allied Commander in the Mediterranean to form immediately an amphibious force of Commandos, supported by air and flotillas, to attack, with your aid, the garrisons which the Germans have left in the islands they have taken along the Dalmatian coast. There is no reason why these garrisons should not be exterminated with forces which will shortly be available. Secondly, we must try to get a through line of communication with you from the sea, even if we have to move it from time to time. This alone will enable tanks and anti-tank guns and other heavy munitions, together with other necessary supplies, to be brought in in the quantities which your armies require. You should talk all this over with Brigadier Maclean, who has my entire confidence and immediate access to me as well as to the Supreme Commander.

Tito replied:

Marshal Tito to Prime Minister   9 Feb. 44

I was obliged to consult the members of the National Committee
of Liberation of Yugoslavia and members of the Anti-Fascist Council of National Liberation on the points raised in your messages.
The analysis of these points led to the following conclusions:

(1) The Anti-Fascist Council of National Liberation of Yugoslavia, as you know, confirmed at their second session on November 29, 1943, that they firmly stand for the Union of Yugoslav
Nations. However, as long as there are two Governments, one in
Yugoslavia and the other in Cairo, there can be no complete
union. Therefore the Government in Cairo must be suppressed,
and with them Draza Mihailovic. That Government must account
to the Government of A.C.N.L.Y. for having squandered enormous
sums of the nation's money.

(2) The National Committee of Liberation of Yugoslavia
should be acknowledged by the Allies as the only Government of
Yugoslavia and King Peter II, in support, should submit to the
laws of A.C.N.L.Y.

(3) If King Peter accepts all these conditions, the Anti-Fascist
Council of National Liberation will not refuse to co-operate with
him on condition that the question of the monarchy in Yugoslavia
be decided after the liberation of Yugoslavia by the free will of the
people.

(4) King Peter II should issue a declaration to the effect that he
has only the interests of his Fatherland at heart, which he wishes
to be free and organised as the people themselves decide after the
war is over by their free will, and until then he will do all in his
power to support the arduous struggle of the peoples of Yugoslavia. . . .

Prime Minister to Marshal Tito   25 Feb. 44

I fully comprehend your difficulties, and I welcome the spirit
in which you approach them. I thank you for understanding mine.
The first step for us is to withdraw our liaison officers safely from
Mihailovic. Orders have been issued accordingly, but may take a
few weeks to fulfil. Meanwhile, can you not assure me that if
King Peter frees himself from Mihailovic and other bad advisers
he will be invited by you to join his countrymen in the field, pro-

vided always that the Yugoslav nations are free to settle their own
Constitution after the war? If I judge this boy aright, he has no
dearer wish than to stand at the side of all those Yugoslavs who
are fighting the common foe, but you can understand that I cannot press him to dismiss Mihailovic, throw over his Government,
and cut off all contact with Serbia before knowing whether he can
count on your support and co-operation.

I have suggested to King Peter that he should return to London
to discuss these matters with me. I hope therefore that you will
on reflection be ready to modify your demands, and thus enable
us both to work for the unification of Yugoslavia against the common enemy. Do not hesitate to make me precise and specific requests. If meanwhile I cannot do all you wish, be sure it is not
from lack of good will to you or your country.

*   *   *   *   *

When I was able to explain all this to Parliament in February 1944, I told the following tale:

Led with great skill, organised on the guerrilla principle, the
partisans were at once elusive and deadly. They were here, they
were there, they were everywhere. Large-scale offensives have been
launched against them by the Germans, but in every case the
partisans, even when surrounded, have escaped, after inflicting
great losses and toil upon the enemy. The partisan movement soon
outstripped in numbers the forces of General Mihailovic. Not only
Croats and Slovenes, but large numbers of Serbians joined with
Marshal Tito, and he has at this moment more than a quarter of
a million men with him, and large quantities of arms taken from
the enemy or from the Italians, and these men are organised into a
considerable number of divisions and corps.

The whole movement has taken shape and form, without losing
the guerrilla quality without which it could not possibly succeed.
Around and within these heroic forces a national and unifying
movement has developed. The Communist element had the honour
of being the beginners, but as the movement increased in strength
and numbers, a modifying and unifying process has taken place
and national conceptions have supervened. In Marshal Tito the
partisans have found an outstanding leader, glorious in the fight

for freedom. Unhappily, perhaps inevitably, these new forces came
into collision with those under General Mihailovic. Their activities
upset his commanders' accommodations with the enemy. He en-
deavoured to repress them, and many tragic fights took place and
bitter feuds sprang up between men of the same race and country,
whose misfortunes were due only to the common foe.

For a long time past I have taken a particular interest in Marshal Tito's movement, and have tried, and am trying, by every
available means to bring him help. A young friend of mine, an
Oxford don, Captain Deakin, now Lieutenant-Colonel Deakin,
D.S.O., entered Yugoslavia by parachute nearly a year ago, and was
for eight months at Marshal Tito's Headquarters. On one occasion
both were wounded by the same bomb. They became friends. Certainly, it is a bond between people, but a bond which, I trust, we
shall not have to institute in our own personal relationships. From
Colonel Deakin's reports we derived a lively picture of the whole
struggle and its personalities.

*   *   *   *   *

For two months longer the political wrangle over Yugoslav
affairs continued in *émigré* circles in London. Each day lost
diminished the chances of a balanced arrangement.

Prime Minister to Foreign Secretary   1 Apr. 44

I consider that the King should be pressed to the utmost limit
to get rid of his present fatal millstone advisers. As you know, I
thought this would have been accomplished before the end of last
year. I do not know what has been gained by all the spinning
out that has gone on. . . . My idea throughout has been that the
King should dissociate himself from Mihailovic, that he should
accept the resignation of the Puric Government or dismiss them,
and that it would not do any great harm if he remained without a
Government for a few weeks. . . . I agree that King Peter should
make a suitable declaration. I fear we must leave things at this
for the time being.

. . . I have seen somewhere that three German divisions have
been recalled out of Yugoslavia to hold down Hungary, and of
course it will be of the greatest importance for Tito's forces to
make contact with the Hungarian partisans and take the fullest

possible advantage of the situation now opening to his northward.

All these developments help us and help Tito, but they certainly do not help the King and his bedraggled Government. Unless he acts promptly, as the sense of your minute indicates, his chances of regaining his throne will, in my opinion, be lost. Since we discussed these matters in Cairo, we have seen the entry of a grandiose Russian Mission to Tito's Headquarters, and there is little doubt that the Russians will drive straight ahead for a Communist Tito-governed Yugoslavia, and will denounce everything done to the contrary as "undemocratic."

I hope therefore you will act most promptly now, draft the King a good declaration, make him dismiss Puric and Company, repudiate all contact with Mihailovic, and make him form a stopgap Government not obnoxious to Tito. Thus we may have a forlorn hope of making a bridge between them in the next five or six weeks. We are not justified in withholding military forces that wish or can be induced to fight with the partisans because of the complexities of Serbian politics.

It was not until nearly the end of May that Mihailovic was dismissed, and a moderate politician, Dr. Subasic, the former Governor of Croatia and member of Dr. Macek's Peasant Party, was asked to form a new administration.

Prime Minister to Marshal Tito (*Yugoslavia*)   17 May 44

This morning, as the result of British advice, King Peter II dismissed M. Puric's administration, which included General Mihailovic as Minister of War. He is now about to form an administration or found a Council of State under the Ban of Croatia (Dr. Ivan Subasic). This of course has the strong approval of His Britannic Majesty's Government.

We do not know what will happen in the Serbian part of Yugoslavia. Mihailovic certainly holds a powerful position locally as Commander-in-Chief, and it does not follow that his ceasing to be Minister of War will rob him of his influence. We cannot predict what he will do. There is also a very large body, amounting perhaps to two hundred thousand, of Serbian peasant proprietary who are anti-German but strongly Serbian, and who naturally hold the views of a peasant's ownership community, contrary to the Karl

Marx theory. My object is that these forces may be made to work with you for a united, independent Yugoslavia, which will expel from the soil of Yugoslavia the filthy Hitlerite murderers and invaders till not one remains.

It is of importance to the common cause and to our relations with you that these changes should be given a fair chance to develop in a favourable way to the main object. I should greatly regret it if you were at all in a hurry to denounce them in public. Crucial events impend in Europe. The battle in Italy goes in our favour. General Wilson assures me of his resolve to aid you to the very utmost. I feel therefore that I have a right to ask you to forbear from any utterances adverse to this new event, at least for a few weeks till we can have exchanged telegrams upon it.

Brigadier Maclean, who is with me now, will be with you in less than three weeks, with all the views he has gathered here, and I hope that at the very least you will await his return.

Meanwhile, I congratulate you once more upon the number of enemy divisions which you are holding gripped on your various fronts. You will realise, Marshal Tito, that the war will soon come to a very high pitch of intensity, and that British, American, and Russian forces will all hurl themselves on the common foe. You must be at your strongest during this climax. While I cannot guarantee a speedy breakdown of the enemy's power, there is certainly a chance of it.

And on the 24th:

Prime Minister to Marshal Tito   24 May 43

The King has sacked Puric and Company, and I think the Ban of Croatia will rally a certain force round him. My idea is that this Government should lie quiet for a bit and let events flow on their course. This, I think, was rather in accord with your idea in the first telegrams we exchanged. I am keeping the Russians and Americans informed of all that goes on between us.

Give my love to Randolph should he come into your sphere. Maclean will be coming back soon. I wish I could come myself, but I am too old and heavy to jump out on a parachute.

Here then we may leave this scene for others not less convulsive but larger.

10

The Anzio Stroke

The Germans Engaged on the Cassino Front — The Anzio Surprise Landing — The Disastrous Pause — Kesselring's Critical Position — Delay at the Beachhead — Renewed Attacks at Cassino — Frustration at Anzio — My Questions to General Wilson of February 6 — My Telegram to Field-Marshal Dill, February 8 — Immense Number of Vehicles in the Beachhead — Disappointment and Casualties — German Effort to Drive Us into the Sea, February 16 — The Deadly Battle Won — Kesselring Accepts Failure, March 1 — My Account to Parliament, February 22, 1944 — Smuts' Message of February 23 — My Reply of February 27 — Important German Forces Diverted from France to Italy.

THE FIRST WEEKS OF JANUARY were spent in intensive preparations for Operation "Shingle," as Anzio was called in our codes, and preliminary operations by the Fifth Army to draw the enemy's attention and reserves away from the beachhead. To that end the Army carried out a series of attacks which, it was hoped, would carry them across the rivers Garigliano and Rapido, while the French Corps on the right swung round to threaten the high ground north of Cassino. Fighting was bitter, for the Germans clearly meant to prevent us from breaking into the Gustav Line, which, with Cassino as its central feature, was the rearmost position of their deep defensive zone. In these rocky mountains a great fortified system had been created, with lavish use of concrete and steel. From their observation posts on the heights the enemy could direct their guns on all movement in the valleys below.

After preliminary attacks in severe winter weather, the Fifth Army opened their main offensive on January 12, with the French Corps making a ten-mile advance on the northern flank. Three days later, the IId United States Corps occupied Monte Trocchio, the last barrier before the river Liri, across which they formed, but could not retain, a bridgehead. Then the Xth British Corps crossed the lower Garigliano, and captured Minturno and the outskirts of Castelforte, but were held in their further attempts to advance northward. Nor could their right wing take San Ambrogio.

All this however had the desired effect on the enemy. It distracted their attention from the approaching threat to their vulnerable seaward flank and caused them to bring up three good divisions from reserve to restore the situation. They attacked the Xth British Corps, but failed to throw it back. By the afternoon of the 21st, the convoys for Anzio were well out to sea, covered by our aircraft. The weather was well suited to a concealed approach. Our heavy attacks on enemy airfields, and especially at Perugia, the German air reconnaissance base, kept many of their aircraft grounded. General Westphal, who was Kesselring's Chief of Staff, gives a vivid picture of the position at German Headquarters during these days:

On January 21, Admiral Canaris, Chief of the German Intelligence, visited Army Group Headquarters, where he was pressed to communicate any information he might have about the enemy intentions in regard to a landing. In particular we wanted to know about the positions of aircraft-carriers, battleships, and landing-craft. Canaris was unable to give any detail, but thought that there was no need to fear a new landing in the near future. This was certainly his view. Not only air reconnaissance, but also the German counter-espionage, was almost completely out of action at this time. A few hours after the departure of Canaris the enemy landed at Anzio.[1]

*   *   *   *   *

It was with tense, but I trust suppressed, excitement that I awaited the outcome of this considerable stroke.

[1] Westphal: *Heer in Fesseln*, page 240.

To Stalin I telegraphed:

Prime Minister to Premier Stalin   21 Jan. 44
We have launched the big attack against the German armies
defending Rome which I told you about at Teheran. The weather
conditions seem favourable. I hope to have good news for you
before long.

Presently I learned that the VIth Corps under the American
General Lucas, had landed on the Anzio beaches at 2 A.M. on
the 22d, the 3d United States Division south of the town and
the 1st British Division north of it. There was very little opposition and practically no casualties. By midnight thirty-six
thousand men and over three thousand vehicles were ashore.
"We appear," signalled Alexander who was on the spot, "to
have got almost complete surprise. I have stressed the importance of strong-hitting mobile patrols being boldly pushed out
to gain contact with the enemy, but so far have not received
reports of their activities."

I was in full agreement with this, and replied: "Thank you
for all your messages. Am very glad you are pegging out claims
rather than digging in beachheads."

                    *   *   *   *   *

But now came disaster, and the ruin in its prime purpose of
the enterprise. General Lucas confined himself to occupying
his beachhead and having equipment and vehicles brought
ashore. General Penney commanding the British 1st Division
was anxious to push inland. His reserve brigade was however
held back with the Corps. Minor probing attacks towards
Cisterna and Campoleone occupied the 22d and 23d. No
general attempt to advance was made by the Commander of
the expedition. By the evening of the 23d, the whole of the
two divisions and their attached troops, including two British
Commandos, the United States Rangers, and parachutists, had
been landed with masses of impedimenta. The defences of the

beachhead were growing, but the opportunity for which great exertions had been made was gone.

Kesselring reacted quickly to his critical situation. The bulk of his reserves were already committed against us on the Cassino front, but he pulled in whatever units were available, and in forty-eight hours the equivalent of about two divisions was assembled to resist our further advance.

The German General Westphal's comments on the way in which this was done are illuminating.

At the moment of the landing south of Rome, apart from certain coastal batteries standing by, there were only two battalions. . . . There was nothing else in the neighbourhood which could be thrown against the enemy on that same day. The road to Rome was open. No one could have stopped a bold advance-guard entering the Holy City. The breath-taking situation continued for the first two days after the landing. It was only then that German counter-measures were effective. What was their nature? In December 1943 the [German] Army Group had issued a comprehensive plan of emergency for the whole of Italy. In it was laid down what troops and columns should move against the possible landing-points, on what roads and times, and what tasks they should undertake. It was only necessary to issue the code-word "Case Richard" to put into effect these prearranged plans. In fact, most of the troops, in spite of icy roads over the Apennines, arrived before schedule. The German High Command helped by sending troops from France, Yugoslavia, and the homeland. . . . The enemy kept surprisingly quiet. They were apparently engaged in building up a bridgehead. It was thus possible to build up a new front opposite them. The command of this sector was taken over by the general headquarters of the Fourteenth Army, up to now based in Northern Italy and under General von Mackensen.[2]

The threat to his flank did not weaken Kesselring's determination to withstand our assaults at Cassino. The German

2 *Heer in Fesseln,* page 242.

intentions were made crystal-clear by an order from Hitler captured on the 24th:

The Gustav Line must be held at all costs for the sake of the political consequences which would follow a completely successful defence. The Fuehrer expects the bitterest struggle for every yard.

He was certainly obeyed.

* * * * *

On the 25th, Alexander reported that the beachhead was reasonably secure. The 3d United States Division was four miles from Cisterna and the British 1st Division two miles from Campoleone, and contact was continuous along the entire front. On the 27th, serious news arrived. Neither place had been taken. The Guards Brigade had beaten off a counterattack of infantry and tanks and had gone forward, but they were still about a mile and a half short of Campoleone, and the Americans were still south of Cisterna. Alexander said that neither he nor General Clark was satisfied with the speed of the advance, and that Clark was going to the beachhead at once. I replied:

Prime Minister to General Alexander   28 Jan. 44
I am glad to learn that Clark is going to visit the beachhead. It would be unpleasant if your troops were sealed off there and the main army could not advance up from the south.

This however was exactly what was going to happen.

* * * * *

Meanwhile, our attacks on the Germans in the Cassino positions continued. The Xth British Corps having drawn to its front most of the enemy reinforcements, it was decided to attack farther north so as to seize the high ground above Cassino and envelop the position from that side. Good progress was made. The IId United States Corps crossed the river Rapido above Cassino town, with the French Corps on their right keeping

abreast of them, and took Monte Castellone and Colle Majola.
Thence they attacked southward against Monastery Hill, but
the Germans had reinforced and held on fanatically. By early
February, the IId Corps had expended its strength. General
Alexander decided that fresh troops would be needed to restore impetus to the assault. He had already ordered a New
Zealand Corps to be formed, under General Freyberg, composed of three divisions brought over from the Eighth Army on
the Adriatic. Indeed, that army, which had attempted to pin
the enemy on their front by offensive action, had had to send no
less than five divisions to sustain the heavy fighting on the west
coast, and for the next few months had to remain on the defensive.

Further severe battles obviously impended on both fronts,
and it was necessary to find more troops. The 3d Polish Car-
pathian Division was due to arrive on the main front at the
beginning of February. General Wilson had ready the 18th
Infantry and the 1st Guards Brigade in North Africa. By January 30, the 1st United States Armoured Division had landed
at Anzio and the 45th United States Division was on its way.
All this had to be done over the difficult beaches or through
the tiny fishing port. "The situation as it now stands," signalled Admiral John Cunningham, "bears little relation to the
lightning thrust by two or three divisions envisaged at Marrakesh, but you may rest assured that no effort will be spared
by the navies to provide the sinews of victory." This promise,
as will be seen, was amply redeemed.

*   *   *   *   *

While the fighting at Cassino was at its zenith, on January
30, the VIth Corps at Anzio made its first attack in strength.
Some ground was gained, but the 3d United States Division
failed to take Cisterna and the 1st British Division, Campoleone. More than four divisions were already ashore in the
beachhead. But the Germans, despite our air action against
their communications, had reinforced quickly and strongly.
Elements of eight divisions faced us in positions which they

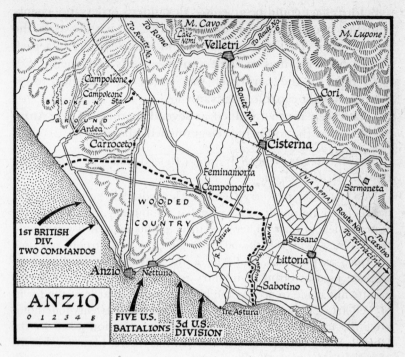

had now had time to fortify. Galling artillery fire harassed the crowded lodgments we had gained and our shipping lying off the beaches suffered damage from air attacks by night. On February 2, Alexander again visited the battle-front, and sent me a full report. German resistance had increased, and was especially strong opposite the 3d United States Division at Cisterna and the 1st British Division at Campoleone. No further offensive was possible until these points were captured. The 3d Division had fought hard for Cisterna during the last two or three days. The men were tired and were still about a mile from the town. A brigade of the 1st Division was holding Campoleone railway station, but they were in a very long and narrow salient and were being shot at "by everything from three sides." Alexander concluded: "We shall presently be in a position to carry out a properly co-ordinated thrust in full strength to achieve our object of cutting the enemy's main line of supply, for which I have ordered plans to be prepared."

Before effect could be given to Alexander's orders, the enemy launched a counter-attack on February 3 which drove in the salient of the 1st British Division and was clearly only a prelude to harder things to come. In the words of General Wilson's report, "the perimeter was sealed off and our forces therein are not capable of advancing."

I had been much troubled at several features of the Anzio operation, as the following telegrams will show:

Prime Minister to General Wilson (Algiers) and   6 Feb. 44
C.-in-C. Mediterranean

I do not want to worry General Alexander in the height of the battle, but I am not at all surprised at the inquiry from the United States Chiefs of Staff. There are three points on which you should touch. First, why was the 504th Regiment of paratroops not used at Anzio as proposed, and why is the existing British Parachute Brigade used as ordinary infantry in the line? Secondly, why was no attempt made to occupy the high ground and at least the towns of Velletri, Campoleone, and Cisterna twelve or twenty-four hours after the unopposed landing? Thirdly, the question asked by the United States Chiefs of Staff: Why has there been no heavily mounted aggressive offensive on the main front to coincide with the withdrawal of troops by the Germans to face the landing?

2. In my early telegrams to General Alexander, I raised all these points in a suggestive form, and particularly deprecated a continuance of the multiplicity of small attacks in battalion, company, and even platoon strength. I repeat however that I do not wish General Alexander's attention to be diverted from the battle, which is at its height, in order to answer questions or write explanations about the past.

General Wilson replied that the 504th Paratroop Regiment was seaborne and not airborne because of a last-minute decision by General Clark. The British paratroops were employed in the line because of infantry shortage. On my second question he said there was no lack of urging from above, and that both Alexander and Clark went to the beachhead during the first forty-eight hours to hasten the offensive. Though General Lucas had achieved surprise, he had failed to take advantage of it. This was due to his "Salerno complex" — that as a prelude to success the first task was to repel the inevitable enemy counter-attack. He did not feel sure of this before the arrival of the 1st United States Armoured Division combat team. The assault, said Wilson, was only geared to function at a slow speed. He also explained the difficulties of forcing the main front on the Rapido River and around Cassino.

General Marshall shared my concern, and I passed this report to Washington with the following comment:

Prime Minister to Field-Marshal Dill (*Washington*)   8 Feb. 44

You should impart this report to General Marshall at your discretion.

. . . My comment is that senior commanders should not "urge," but "order."

All this has been a disappointment to me. Nevertheless, it is a great advantage that the enemy should come in strength and fight in South Italy, thus being drawn far from other battlefields. Moreover, we have a great need to keep continually engaging them, and even a battle of attrition is better than standing by and watching the Russians fight. We should also learn a good many lessons about how not to do it which will be valuable in "Overlord."

*   *   *   *   *

The Admiral had been even better than his word about the landing-craft. I now put a direct question to him:

Prime Minister to Commander-in-Chief Mediterranean   8 Feb. 44

Let me know the number of vehicles landed at Anzio by the seventh and fourteenth days respectively. I should be glad, if it were possible without too much trouble or delay, to distinguish trucks, cannon, and tanks.

The reply was both prompt and startling. By the seventh day, 12,350 vehicles had been landed, including 356 tanks; by the fourteenth day, 21,940 vehicles, including 380 tanks. This represented a total of 315 L.S.T. shipments. It was interesting to notice that, apart from 4000 trucks which went to and fro

in the ships nearly 18,000 vehicles were landed in the Anzio
beachhead by the fourteenth day in order to serve a total force
of 70,000 men, including of course the drivers and those who
did the repair and maintenance of the vehicles.

I replied on February 10:

Prime Minister to Commander-in-Chief Mediterranean   10 Feb. 44
Thank you for information.

How many of our men are driving or looking after eighteen
thousand vehicles in this narrow space? We must have a great
superiority of chauffeurs. I am shocked that the enemy have more
infantry than we. Let me have our latest ration strength in the
bridgehead.

Later the same day, further reports came in. General Wilson
said that the weather had spoilt our air attacks. The 1st British
Division was under severe pressure and had had to give ground
and Alexander was arranging to relieve it.

All this was a great disappointment at home and in the
United States. I did not of course know what orders had been
given to General Lucas, but it is a root principle to push out
and join issue with the enemy, and it would seem that his judgment was against it from the beginning. As I said at the time,
I had hoped that we were hurling a wildcat onto the shore, but
all we had got was a stranded whale. The spectacle of eighteen
thousand vehicles accumulated ashore by the fourteenth day for
only seventy thousand men, or less than four men to a vehicle, including drivers and attendants, though they did not move more
than twelve or fourteen miles, was astonishing. We were apparently still stronger than the Germans in fighting power. The ease
with which they moved their pieces about on the board and the
rapidity with which they adjusted the perilous gaps they had
to make on their southern front was most impressive. It all
seemed to give us very adverse data for "Overlord."

I cabled to Alexander:

Prime Minister to General Alexander   10 Feb. 44
... I have a feeling that you may have hesitated to assert your

authority because you were dealing so largely with Americans and therefore *urged* an advance instead of *ordering* it. You are however quite entitled to give them orders, and I have it from the highest American authorities that it is their wish that their troops should receive direct orders. They say their Army has been framed more on Prussian lines than on the more smooth British lines, and that American commanders expect to receive positive orders, which they will immediately obey. Do not hesitate therefore to give orders just as you would to our own men. The Americans are very good to work with, and quite prepared to take the rough with the smooth.

Alexander replied on February 11:

General Alexander to Prime Minister   11 Feb. 44

The first phase of operations, which started so full of promise, has now just passed, owing to the enemy's ability to concentrate so quickly sufficient force to stabilise what was to him a very serious situation. The battle has now reached the second phase, in which we must now at all costs crush his counter-attacks, and then, with our own forces regrouped, resume offensive to break inland and get astride his communications leading from Rome to the south. This I have every intention of doing. Out of the thirty-five battalions of the VIth Corps casualties are as follows: British, up to February 6 — killed, 285; wounded, 1371; missing, 1048. American, up to February 9 — killed, 597; wounded, 2506; missing, 1116. These losses include those of nine Ranger battalions. Total casualties, 6923. I am very grateful for your kind message at the end of your telegram. I well realise the disappointment to you and all at home. I have every hope and intention of reaching the goal we set out to gain.

*   *   *   *   *

The expected major effort to drive us back into the sea at Anzio opened on February 16, when the enemy employed over four divisions, supported by four hundred and fifty guns, in a direct thrust southward from Campoleone. Hitler's special order of the day was read out to the troops before the attack. He demanded that our beachhead "abscess" be eliminated in three days. The attack fell at an awkward moment, as the 45th United States and 56th British Divisions, transferred from the Cassino front, were just relieving our gallant 1st Division, who soon found themselves in full action again. A deep, dangerous wedge was driven into our line, which was forced back here to the original beachhead. The artillery fire, which had embarrassed all the occupants of the beachhead since they landed, reached a new intensity. All hung in the balance. No further retreat was possible. Even a short advance would have given the enemy the power to use not merely their long-range guns in harassing fire upon the landing-stages and shipping, but to put down a proper field artillery barrage upon all intakes or departures. I had no illusions about the issue. It was life or death.

But fortune, hitherto baffling, rewarded the desperate valour of the British and American armies. Before Hitler's stipulated three days, the German attack was stopped. Then their own salient was counter-attacked in flank and cut out under fire from all our artillery and bombardment by every aircraft we could fly. The fighting was intense, losses on both sides were heavy, but the deadly battle was won.

One more attempt was made by Hitler — for he was the will-power at work — at the end of February. The 3d United States Division, on the eastern flank, was attacked by three German divisions. These were weakened and shaken by their previous failure. The Americans held stubbornly and the attack was broken in a day, when the Germans had suffered more than twenty-five hundred casualties. On March 1, Kesselring accepted his failure. He had frustrated the Anzio expedition. He could not destroy it. I cabled to the President:

Prime Minister to President Roosevelt   1 Mar. 44

I must send you my warmest congratulations on the grand fighting of your troops, particularly the United States 3rd Division in the Anzio beachhead. I am always deeply moved to think of our men fighting side by side in so many fierce battles and of the inspiring additions to our history which these famous episodes will make. Of course I have been very anxious about the beachhead, where we have so little ground to give. The stakes are very

high on both sides now, and the suspense is long-drawn. I feel sure
we shall win both here and at Cassino.

*　　*　　*　　*　　*

On February 22, 1944, I gave a general account of the war
to the House of Commons. In this setting Anzio was presented
in its proportion. I told the story as far as was then possible.

It was certainly no light matter to launch this considerable
army upon the seas — forty thousand or fifty thousand men in the
first instance — with all the uncertainty of winter weather and
all the unknowable strength of enemy fortifications. The operation
itself was a model of combined work. The landing was virtually
unopposed. Subsequent events did not however take the course
which had been hoped or planned. In the upshot we got a great
army ashore, equipped with masses of artillery, tanks, and very
many thousands of vehicles, and our troops moving inland came
into contact with the enemy.

The German reactions to this descent have been remarkable.
Hitler has apparently resolved to defend Rome with the same
obstinacy which he showed at Stalingrad, in Tunisia, and, recently,
in the Dnieper Bend. No fewer than seven extra German divisions
were brought rapidly down from France, Northern Italy, and Yugoslavia, and a determined attempt has been made to destroy the
bridgehead and drive us into the sea. Battles of prolonged and intense fierceness and fury have been fought. At the same time the
American and British Fifth Army to the southward is pressing forward with all its strength. Another battle is raging there.

On broad grounds of strategy, Hitler's decision to send into the
south of Italy as many as eighteen divisions, involving, with their
maintenance troops, probably something like half a million Germans, and to make a large secondary front in Italy, is not unwel-
come to the Allies. We must fight the Germans somewhere, unless
we are to stand still and watch the Russians. This wearing battle
in Italy occupies troops who could not be employed in other greater
operations, and it is an effective prelude to them.

*　　*　　*　　*　　*

General Smuts telegraphed to me next day in terms which
illustrate so well his breadth of vision.

General Smuts to Prime Minister   23 Feb. 44

Your very effective recital of British war effort will greatly impress world public opinion. It gives vast numbers of new facts not generally known, which form the proper pendant to Russia's magnificent effort. It will also counterbalance the one-sided impression given by our propaganda of our own ineffectiveness in Burma and at Anzio in comparison with vast sweep of Russian victories. I myself have not followed our strategy in the Anzio beachhead, which I had thought would link up with the Cassino front with the object of breaking resistance of Germans in the mountains in the south. An isolated pocket has now been created, which is unconnected with enemy's main southern front, and which is itself besieged instead of giving relief to the pressure against us in the south.

The position is once more restored to its right proportions by your emphasis on our vast air effort, which destroys Germany's war effort at its source and prepares for the coming Western Front in the best possible way. But I would not myself give undue publicity to this front, since it may hold unpleasant surprises for us. The retreat of the German armies in the East is not only due to Russian prowess and our attraction of Luftwaffe from that front, but probably also to the Germans withdrawing large strategic reserves to counter our threat in the West. In a theatre where enemy is fully prepared for us, serious delays, if not setbacks, may be met with, and we may have to face grave disappointments. The German plan may be to halt us effectively in the West, and then hasten back to the East to stop the penetration of Russian armies into Germany, which he must mortally fear. If this is not the German plan, I do not understand their strategy of fighting stubbornly against us for every inch of ground in Italy, while letting Russia achieve such successes on the Eastern Front.

Instead of giving undue publicity to our Western Front, our propaganda should for the present be concentrated on our air offensive against Germany. I do believe that this has had even more far-reaching effects than Russian land victories.

If any reserves are called for, remember our now well-trained South African 6th Armoured Division, which is in Egypt. They only need some added transport to give a good account of themselves in a suitable theatre.

To this I replied, expressing views which I hold to this day:

Prime Minister to Field-Marshal Smuts   27 Feb. 44

Thank you for your telegram. During the Conferences at Carthage and at Marrakesh I was able to clear difficulties out of the way and get this big amphibious operation at Anzio soundly organised. My personal efforts did not extend to the conduct of the battle, which of course I left altogether to the commanders, once they were landed safely at the right place, as they were. In all his talks with me, Alexander envisaged that the essence of the battle was the seizure of the Alban Hills with the utmost speed, and to this end I was able to obtain from the United States their 504th Parachute Regiment, although at the time it was under orders to return for "Overlord." But at the last moment General Clark cancelled the use of this regiment, and the American General Lucas, a man of fifty-five, who at Salerno had distinguished himself in command of a corps, seems to have had the idea in his mind that at all costs he must be prepared for a counter-attack. As a result, although directly I learnt the landing was successful, I sent Alexander injunctions that he should peg out claims rather than consolidate bridgeheads, the whole operation became stagnant. Needless to say, the logistic calculations all turned out to be on the overgenerous side and there were very large margins in hand. No one can deny that this was lucky, seeing that plans originally made for 50,000 men are now comfortably supporting 170,000.

Naturally I am very disappointed at what has appeared to be the frittering away of a brilliant opening in which both fortune and design had played their part. I do not in any way however repent of what has been done. As a result the Germans have now transferred into the south of Italy at least eight more divisions, so that in all there are eighteen south of Rome. It is vital to the success of "Overlord" that we keep away from that theatre and hold elsewhere as many German divisions as possible, and hard fighting in Italy throughout the spring will provide for the main operation a perfect prelude and accompaniment.

We had hoped that a big thrust would be launched northwards from the Cassino front to correspond with the landing. This was indeed planned, but it did not take place because apparently it proved immensely difficult to debouch past Cassino up the Liri Valley. Naturally we are striving with might and main to join up the two forces, and at any moment the curtain may go up on the next act of the drama. Truscott, a young American Divisional Commander, whom everyone speaks of most highly, has now superseded Lucas. My confidence in Alexander remains undiminished.

Here at home all goes fairly well, though the little folk are more active. However, their chirrupings will be stilled before long by the thunder of the cannonade.

Most certainly do I look forward to seeing you, and I rejoice that you will be at my side in momentous times.

*   *   *   *   *

Such is the story of the struggle of Anzio; a story of high opportunity and shattered hopes, of skilful inception on our part and swift recovery by the enemy, of valour shared by both. We now know that early in January, the German High Command had intended to transfer five of their best divisions from Italy to Northwest Europe. Kesselring protested that in such an event he could no longer carry out his orders to fight south of Rome and he would have to withdraw. Just as the argument was at its height the Anzio landing took place. The High Command dropped the idea, and instead of the Italian Front contributing forces to Northwest Europe the reverse took place. Hitler was enraged at the failure of his Fourteenth Army to drive the Allies into the sea. After their offensive of February 16, he ordered a selected group of twenty officers of all arms and ranks fighting in Italy to report to him personally about conditions at the front. This was the first and only time that this happened during the war. "He would have done much better," comments General Westphal, "to visit the front himself and been convinced of Allied superiority in planes and guns."

We knew nothing of all these changes of plan at the time, but it proves that the aggressive action of our armies in Italy, and specifically the Anzio stroke, made its full contribution towards the success of "Overlord." We shall see later on the part it played in the liberation of Rome.

11

Italy: Cassino

Mussolini and Ciano — Marshal Badoglio's Harassed Government — Correspondence with President Roosevelt in February — My Statement About Italy in the House of Commons, February 22 — The Monastery at Cassino — The Second Major Attack, February 15 — Deadlock in March — Vesuvius in Eruption — My Telegrams to the President of March 8 and 13 — His Reply Disappoints Me — The Russians Recognise the Badoglio Government — I Report the War Cabinet's View to the President, March 15 — The Campaign in Italy Drags — Alexander's Convincing Explanation, March 20 — Two Months' Delay — Anglo-American Argument About "Overlord," "Anvil," and the Italian Campaign — Views of General Eisenhower and General Wilson — Agreement Reached — My Telegram to General Marshall of April 16 — Italian Politics — The Crown Prince Humbert Becomes Lieutenant-Governor of the Realm — Prelude to the New Allied Offensive in May.

THE BITTERNESS AND CONFUSION of the Italian scene were heightened in the New Year. Mussolini's phantom Republic came under mounting pressure from the Germans. The governing circles round Badoglio in the South were assailed by intrigues in Italy and despised by public opinion in Britain and the United States. Mussolini was the first to react.

When he arrived in Munich after his escape, he found there his daughter Edda and her husband, Count Ciano. These two had fled from Rome at the time of the surrender, and, although Ciano had voted against his father-in-law at the fateful meeting of the Grand Council, he hoped, thanks to the influence of his wife, for a reconciliation. During these days in Munich this in fact happened. This aroused the indignation of Hitler, who had already placed the Ciano family under house arrest on their arrival. The reluctance of the Duce to punish the traitors to Fascism, and particularly Ciano, was perhaps the main reason why Hitler formed such a low opinion of his colleague at this critical time.

It was not until the declining strength of the "Republic of Salo" had fallen far, and the impatience of its German masters had sharpened, that Mussolini agreed to let loose a wave of calculated vengeance. All those leaders of the old Fascist régime who had voted against him in July and who could be caught in German-occupied Italy were brought to trial at the end of 1943, in the mediaeval fortress at Verona. Among them was Ciano. Without exception they received the death sentence. In spite of the entreaties and threats of Edda, the Duce could not relent. In January 1944 the group, which included not only Ciano but also the seventy-eight-year-old Marshal de Bono, a colleague in the march on Rome, were taken out to die a traitor's death — to be shot in the back tied to a chair. They all died bravely.

The end of Ciano was in keeping with all the elements of Renaissance tragedy. Mussolini's submission to Hitler's vengeful demands brought him only shame, and the miserable neo-Fascist Republic dragged on by Lake Garda — a relic of the Broken Axis.

*   *   *   *   *

In the South, Badoglio was continually harassed by the remnants of the opposition to Fascism in its early days and which had sprung up in political groupings since the previous summer. They not only pressed for a broader administration in which they would share, but also sought to destroy the Monarchy, which they declared to be compromised by prolonged acquiescence in Mussolini's rule. There was growing public support for their activities, both in America and in England. In January, a congress of the six Italian parties was held in Bari, and resolutions in this sense were passed.

I therefore telegraphed to the President:

Prime Minister to President Roosevelt 3 Feb. 44

I earnestly hope that the existing régime in Italy will be allowed to function at least until the great battles now being fought by the soldiers of our two countries have resulted in our capture of Rome. I am sure that a disturbance now of such authority as remains in the Italian State and the attempt to create a new authority out of political groups with no real backing will add greatly to our difficulties. Moreover, these groups, when formed into a Government, in order to win credit from the Italian people, would feel it essential to assert Italian interests in a much stronger form than the King and Badoglio dare to do. I feel it would be a great pity if Badoglio threw in his hand, and our reports show that the Italian Navy might be powerfully affected by action against the King. Much British and American blood is flowing, and I plead that military considerations should carry weight.

His reply was reassuring:

President Roosevelt to Prime Minister 11 Feb. 44

I have directed the Department of State to take no action toward effecting any change in the existing Government of Italy at the present time, and until our military situation in the Italian campaign is sufficiently improved to warrant risking the disaffection of those Italians who are now assisting the Allied forces.

I think, though, that you and I should regard this only as a temporary reprieve for the two old gentlemen.

I elaborated my view:

Prime Minister to President Roosevelt 13 Feb. 44

I fully agree we should review the whole scene after we are settled in Rome. We have not got there yet, and Lincoln's birthday celebrations remind me about not crossing the Fox River till you get to it.

The present régime is the lawful Government of Italy, with whom we have concluded an armistice, in consequence of which the Italian Navy came over, and, with some of the Italian Army and Air Force, are fighting on our side. This Italian Government will obey our directions far more than any other that we may laboriously constitute. On the other hand, it has more power over the Fleet, Army officials, etc., than anything else which can be set up out of the worn-out débris of political parties, none of whom have the slightest title by election or prescription. A new Italian Government will have to make its reputation with the Italian people by standing up to us. They will very likely try to wriggle out of the armistice terms. As for being instrumental in handing over without a mutiny part of the Italian Fleet to Russia, I cannot conceive that they would do so, or that if they did their writ would run with the Italian Navy. I hope therefore that when the time comes we shall consult together. I gave strong support to the State Department over Darlan. They seem rueful about that episode now. Looking back upon it, I consider it was right. Several thousand British and American soldiers are alive today because of it, and it got us Dakar at a time when we could ill have spared the large forces needed for its capture. . . .

I have had a letter from Harry. He is an indomitable spirit. I cannot help feeling very anxious about his frail body and another operation. I should always be grateful for any news about him, for I rate him high among the Paladins. I have just heard that his son has been killed in the Marshall Islands battle. As I do not know whether his state of health will have permitted him to receive this news, I am sending him a message through you.

As the President and I were at one on the main issue, I made a statement on Italian political affairs in my speech of February 22 in the House of Commons:

The battle in Italy will be hard and long. I am not yet convinced that any other Government can be formed at the present time in Italy which could command the same obedience from the Italian armed forces. Should we succeed in the present battle and enter Rome, as I trust and believe we shall, we shall be free to discuss the whole Italian political situation, and we shall do so with many advantages that we do not possess at the present time. It is from Rome that a more broadly based Italian Government can best be formed. Whether a Government thus formed will be so helpful to the Allies as the present dispensation I cannot tell. It might of course be a Government which would try to make its position good with the Italian people by resisting, as much as it dared, the demands made on them in the interests of the Allied armies. I should be sorry however to see an unsettling change made at a time when the battle is at its climax, swaying to and fro. When you have to hold a hot coffee-pot, it is better not to break the handle off until you are sure that you will get another equally convenient and serviceable, or at any rate until there is a dish-cloth handy.

The representatives of the various Italian parties who assembled a fortnight ago at Bari are of course eager to become the Government of Italy. They will have no elective authority, and certainly no constitutional authority, until either the present King abdicates himself or his successor invites them to take office. It is by no means certain that they would have any effective authority over the Italian armed forces now fighting with us. Italy lies prostrate under her miseries and disasters. Food is scarce; shipping to bring it is voraciously absorbed by our ever-expanding military operations. I think we have gained this year twelve million tons increase to the Allies, yet the shortage continues, because our great operations absorb every ship as it comes, and the movement of food is difficult.

It would be a mistake to suppose that the kind of political conditions or forces exist in Italy which work so healthily in unbeaten lands, or in countries which have not been shattered by war or stifled by a long period of Fascist rule. We shall see more clearly how to proceed and have more varied resources at our disposal if and when we are in possession of the capital city. The policy therefore which His Majesty's Government have agreed provisionally with the Government of the United States is to win the battle for Rome and take a new view when we are there.

*   *   *   *   *

The second major attack at Cassino began on February 15 with the bombing of the monastery. The height on which the monastery stood surveyed the junction of the rivers Rapido and Liri and was the pivot of the whole German defence. It had already proved itself a formidable, strongly defended obstacle. Its steep sides, swept by fire, were crowned by the famous building which several times in previous wars had been pillaged, destroyed, and rebuilt. There is controversy about whether it should have been destroyed once again. The

monastery did not contain German troops, but the enemy fortifications were hardly separate from the building itself. The
monastery dominated the whole battlefield, and naturally
General Freyberg, the Corps commander concerned, wished
to have it heavily bombarded from the air before he launched
the infantry attack. The Army Commander, General Mark
Clark, unwillingly sought and obtained permission from General Alexander, who accepted the responsibility. On February
15 therefore, after the monks had been given full warning, over
four hundred and fifty tons of bombs were dropped, and heavy
damage was done. The great outer walls and gateway still
stood. The result was not good. The Germans had now every
excuse for making whatever use they could of the rubble of the
ruins, and this gave them even better opportunities for defence
than when the building was intact.

It fell to the 4th Indian Division, which had recently relieved
the Americans on the ridges north of the monastery, to make
the attack. On two successive nights they tried in vain to seize
a knoll that lay between their position and Monastery Hill. On
the night of February 18, a third attempt was made. The fighting was desperate, and all our men who reached the knoll were
killed. Later that night, a brigade by-passed the knoll and
moved directly at the monastery, only to encounter a concealed
ravine heavily mined and covered by enemy machine-guns at
shortest range. Here they lost heavily and were stopped. While
this fierce conflict was raging on the heights above them, the
New Zealand Division succeeded in crossing the river Rapido
just below Cassino town; but they were counter-attacked by
tanks before their bridgehead was secure and forced back again.
The direct attack on Cassino had failed.

At the beginning of March, the weather brought about a
deadlock. Napoleon's fifth element — mud — bogged down
both sides. We could not break the main front at Cassino, and
the Germans had equally failed to drive us into the sea at
Anzio. In numbers there was little to choose between the com-
batants. By now we had twenty divisions in Italy, but both
Americans and French had had very heavy losses. The enemy

had eighteen or nineteen divisions south of Rome, and five more in Northern Italy, but they too were tired and worn.

There could be no hope now of a break-out from the Anzio beachhead and no prospect of an early link-up between our two separated forces until the Cassino front was broken. The prime need therefore was to make the beachhead really firm, to relieve and reinforce the troops, and to pack in stores to withstand a virtual siege and nourish a subsequent sortie. Time was short, since many of the landing-craft had to leave for "Overlord" in the middle of the month. Their move had so far been rightly postponed, but no further delay was possible. The navies put all their strength into the effort, with admirable results. The previous average daily tonnage landed had been three thousand; in the first ten days of March, this was more than doubled. I followed this process with attention.

On March 12, I asked: "What is the ration strength in the bridgehead at present? How many vehicles have been landed there from the beginning? How many days' reserve supplies of food and ammunition have been built up, and what is the basis of this calculation?"

General Alexander replied that the ration strength was 90,200 United States and 35,500 British. Nearly 25,000 vehicles of all kinds had been landed. He gave full details of the supplies of food, ammunition, and petrol. The margins were not large, but improving.

A few days later, Vesuvius was in violent eruption. For several days traffic from the Naples airfields was partially interrupted, but the work in the ports went on. On March 24, a report to the Naval Commander-in-Chief stated: "The Naples group of ports is now discharging at the rate of twelve million tons a year, while Vesuvius is estimated to be doing thirty millions a day. We can but admire this gesture of the Gods."

*   *   *   *   *

While the battles I have described were going on, politics raged around Badoglio. Roosevelt was being clamorously pressed to support major changes in the Italian Government. He suggested that we might yield to the pressure of opinion.

I telegraphed to him:

Prime Minister to President Roosevelt   8 Mar. 44

Your cable causes me concern. It is a departure from your agreement with me of February 11, which you kindly reaffirmed in your [later] cable as "finished business." On the strength of the first assurances I made my statement to Parliament.

My advices do not lead me to believe that any new facts of importance have arisen or that the Allied forces are not capable of maintaining order in the regions they have occupied as the result of the "unconditional surrender" of Italy. It would be a very serious mistake to give way to [local] agitation, especially when accompanied by threats on the part of groups of office-seeking politicians. We should then be liable to set up in Italy an administration which might not command the allegiance of the armed forces, but which would endeavour to make its position with the Italian people by standing up to the Allies. In fact, we should have another but more intractable version of the de Gaullist Committee. Meanwhile, in the midst of a heart-shaking battle we are to get rid of the helpful Government of the King and Badoglio, which is doing its utmost to work its passage and aid us in every way.

I readily admit that the course you recommend would be the more popular and would have at least a transitory success. But I am sure that for the victorious conquerors to have their hands forced in this way by sections of the defeated population would be unfortunate. So also would be the obvious open division between you and me and between our two Governments. I gave you and the State Department loyal and vigorous support over the Darlan affair. Unity of action between our two Governments was never more necessary than at the present time, considering the great battles in which we are engaged and which lie ahead.

His reply on the same day encouraged me to believe that we were in agreement. "It is my strongest wish," he said, "that you and I should continue to work in complete harmony in this matter as in all others. We may differ on timing, but things like that can be worked out, and on the big objectives like self-determination we are as one."

The pressures however continued. The idea of making a bargain with the six Italian Opposition Parties gained support in the Supreme Headquarters at Algiers, and General Wilson telegraphed in this sense to the Combined Chiefs of Staff in Washington and London. This he was entitled to do, as he served both countries. Nevertheless, my views remained unchanged, and my colleagues in the War Cabinet, who saw all that was passing, were in broad agreement with them.

Prime Minister to President Roosevelt   13 Mar. 44

I fear that if we drive out the King and Badoglio at this stage we shall only have complicated the task of the armies. I see that this is also the Soviet view. They are certainly realistic, but of course their aim may be a Communist Italy, and it may suit them to use the King and Badoglio till everything is ready for an extreme solution. I can assure you that this danger is also in my mind. My idea remains that we should try to construct a broadly based Government, taking into account the opinion of the democratic North of Italy and seeking representatives from there. Of course if we cannot get Rome for several months we shall have to act earlier, but without the favourable conditions which will be open to us once we are in possession of the capital. We shall then have much better chances of finding a really representative footing.

The President's reply disappointed me.

President Roosevelt to Prime Minister   13 Mar. 44

I am sorry if earlier messages were not clear. I did not at any time intend to convey to you agreement that we postpone all political decisions until after Rome had been taken. The political situation in Italy has deleveped rapidly since our earlier messages; the military situation has not kept pace. The capture of Rome is still remote and major political decisions must be taken.

I do not like having to use stern measures against our friends in Italy, except for good reason. In the present situation the Commander-in-Chief and his political advisers, both British and American, have recommended that we give immediate support to the programme of the six Opposition Parties. Thus we have, happily for once, our political and military considerations entirely in harmony.

We do not need to intervene beyond informing the Executive Junta of our support of their programme and confirming this to the

King if necessary. The Italians can present the solution to the King and work out the programme among themselves.

I cannot for the life of me understand why we should hesitate any longer in supporting a policy so admirably suited to our common military and political aims. American public opinion would never understand our continued tolerance and apparent support of Victor Emmanuel.

The Russians now complicated the position by sending an official representative to the Badoglio Government without consulting us.

Prime Minister to President Roosevelt   14 Mar. 44

The Russians have announced that they have sent a fully accredited Ambassador to the present Italian Government, with whom we are still technically at war. I do not think it would be wise, without further consideration, to accept the programme of the so-called Six Parties and demand forthwith the abdication of the King and installation of Signor Croce as Lieutenant of the Realm. I will however consult the War Cabinet upon what you justly call "a major political decision." Our war with Italy has lasted since June 1940, and the British Empire has suffered 232,000 casualties in men, as well as our losses in ships. I feel sure that in this matter our view will receive consideration from you. We ought to make every effort to act together. Pray remember that I have committed myself in public and that any divergence will certainly become known.

The War Cabinet considered these messages and I reported their conclusions to the President:

Prime Minister to President Roosevelt   15 Mar. 44

I consulted the War Cabinet this morning on the proposal that the British and American Governments should accept the Six-Party programme without further delay. The War Cabinet asked me to assure you that they agree fully with your wish to establish a more broadly based Government in Italy, and that the future form of government of the Italian people can only be settled by self-determination. They also agree with you that the point to consider is the timing. On this they have no doubt that it would be far better to wait till we are masters of Rome before

parting company with the King and Badoglio, because from Rome
a more representative and solidly based administration can be
constructed than is possible now. They feel that nothing could
be worse for our joint interests and for the future of Italy than
to set up a weak democratic Government which flopped. Even
a settlement reached at Rome could not be final, because it would
be necessary to review it when the northern provinces and great
industrial centres favourable to us and essential to a democratic
solution, like Milan and Turin, have been liberated. They do not
consider that the Six Parties are representative in any true sense
of the Italian democracy or Italian nation, or that they could at the
present time replace the existing Italian Government, which has
loyally and effectively worked in our interests.

In reaching these conclusions the War Cabinet have of course
had before them the telegrams sent by the Allied Commander-in-
Chief [General Wilson] whose views on this subject they do not
share. Meanwhile, we should be quite ready to discuss the suggestions put to the State Department by the Foreign Secretary. It is
also of course recognised that should the capture of Rome be
unduly protracted, say for two or three months, the question of
timing would have to be reviewed.

Finally, they ask me to emphasise the great importance of not
exposing to the world any divergences of view which may exist
between our two Governments, especially in face of the independent action taken by Russia in entering into diplomatic relations with the Badoglio Government without consultation with
other Allies. It would be a great pity if our respective viewpoints
had to be argued out in Parliament and the press, when waiting
a few months may make it possible for all three Governments to
take united action.

This was the end of the matter for the moment.

*   *   *   *   *

Although Anzio was now no longer an anxiety, the campaign
in Italy as a whole had dragged. We had hoped that by this
time the Germans would have been driven north of Rome and
that a substantial part of our armies would have been set free
for a strong landing on the Riviera coast to help the main
cross-Channel invasion. This operation, called "Anvil," had

been agreed in principle at Teheran. It was soon to become a cause of contention between ourselves and our American Allies. The campaign in Italy had obviously to be carried forward a long way before this issue arose, and the immediate need was to break the deadlock on the Cassino front. Preparations for the third battle of Cassino were begun soon after the February failure, but the bad weather delayed it until March 15.

This time Cassino town was the primary objective. After a heavy bombardment, in which nearly a thousand tons of bombs and twelve hundred tons of shells were expended, our infantry advanced. "It seemed to me inconceivable," said Alexander, "that any troops should be left alive after eight hours of such terrific hammering." But they were. The 1st German Parachute Division, probably the toughest fighters in all their army, fought it out amid the heaps of rubble with the New Zealanders and Indians. By nightfall, the greater part of the town was in our hands, while the 4th Indian Division, coming down from the north, made equally good progress and next day were two-thirds of the way up Monastery Hill. Then the battle swung against us. Our tanks could not cross the large craters made by the bombardment and follow up the infantry assault. Nearly two days passed before they could help. The enemy filtered in reinforcements. The weather broke in storm and rain. Our attacks gained ground, but the early success was not repeated, and the enemy were not to be overborne in the slogging match.

I wondered why we did not make flank attacks to dislodge the enemy from positions which had twice already proved so strong.

Prime Minister to General Alexander   20 Mar. 44

I wish you would explain to me why this passage by Cassino, Monastery Hill, etc., all on a front of two or three miles, is the only place which you must keep butting at. About five or six divisions have been worn out going into these jaws. Of course, I do not know the ground or the battle conditions, but, looking at it from afar, it is puzzling why, if the enemy can be held and dominated at this point, no attacks can be made on the flanks. It seems very

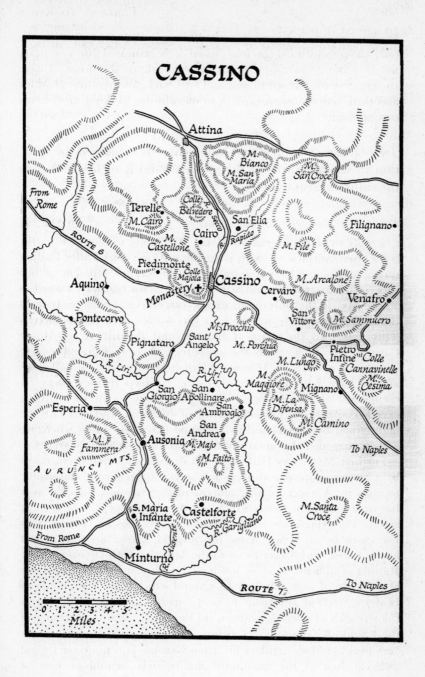

CASSINO

Attina

From Rome

ROUTE 6

M. Bianco
M. San Maria
M. San Croce

Terelle
M. Cairo
Colle Belvedere
R. Secco
Cairo
San'Elia
Filignano
M. Castellone
Rapido
M. Pile

Piedimonte
Colle Majola
Cassino
M. Arcalone
Aquino
Monastery ✝
Cervaro
Venafro

Pontecorvo
San Vittore
M. Sammucro

Pignataro
M. Trocchio
Sant' Angelo
M. Porchia
Pietro Infine
Colle Cannavinelle

R. Liri
R. Liri
M. Lungo
M. Cesima

San Giorgio
San Apollinare
M. Maggiore
Mignano

Esperia
San Ambrogio
M. La Difensa

M. Fammera
San Andrea
M. Camino

Ausonia
M. Majo
To Naples

M. Faito

AURUNCI MTS.

S. Maria Infante
Castelforte
M. Santa Croce

From Rome
R. Ausente
R. Garigliano

Minturno

ROUTE 7
To Naples

0 1 2 3 4 5
Miles

hard to understand why this most strongly defended point is the only passage forward, or why, when it is saturated [in a military sense], ground cannot be gained on one side or the other. I have the greatest confidence in you and will back you up through thick and thin, but do try to explain to me why no flanking movements can be made.

His answer was lucid and convincing. It explained the situation in words written at the moment, and is of high value to the military historian:

General Alexander to Prime Minister   20 Mar. 44

I reply to your telegram of March 20. Along whole main battle-front from Adriatic to south coast there is only Liri Valley leading direct to Rome which is suitable terrain for development of our superiority in artillery and armour. The main highway, known as Route Six, is the only road, except cart-tracks, which leads from the mountains where we are into Liri Valley over Rapido River. This exit into the plain is blocked and dominated by Monte Cassino, on which stands the monastery. Repeated attempts have been made to outflank Monastery Hill from the north, but all these attacks have been unsuccessful, owing to deep ravines, rocky escarpments, and knife-edges, which limit movements to anything except comparatively small parties of infantry, who can only be maintained by porters and to a limited extent by mules where we have managed under great difficulties to make some mule-tracks.

Further, Monastery Hill is cut off almost completely from north by a ravine so steep and deep that so far it has proved impossible to cross it. A wider turning movement is even more difficult, as it has to cross Mount Cairo, which is a precipitous peak now deep in snow. The Americans tried to outflank this Cassino bastion from the south by an attack across the Rapido River, but this, as you know, failed, with heavy losses to the 34th and 36th Divisions. The Rapido is difficult to cross south of Cassino owing to flood-water at this time of year, soft, marshy ground which adds to problems of bridging, lack of any roads to bring up bridging material, and to the strength of enemy's position on far bank. Again, a crossing of the Rapido River south of Cassino, as already proved, comes under very heavy enfilade artillery fire from German gun positions tucked away at foot of the mountains immediately behind or west of

Cassino, and also from foothills of mountains on south of Liri Valley.

Freyberg's attack was designed as a direct assault on this bastion, success depending on crushing enemy resistance by surprise and an overwhelming concentration of fire-power. The plan was to rush Cassino town and then to flow round the east and southern slopes of Monastery Hill and take the bastion by storm from a direction where enemy's artillery could not seriously interfere with our movement. It very nearly succeeded in its initial stages, with negligible losses to us. We got, and still have, two bridges over the Rapido River, one on Highway Six and the other over railway bridge; both are fit for tanks. The Gurkhas got and are still within two hundred to three hundred yards of the monastery. That we have not succeeded in taking our objective within first forty-eight hours may be summarised as follows:

The destruction caused in Cassino to roads and movement by bombing was so terrific that the employment of tanks or any other fighting vehicles has been seriously hampered. The tenacity of these German paratroops is quite remarkable, considering that they were subjected to the whole Mediterranean Air Force plus the better part of eight hundred guns under greatest concentration of fire-power which has ever been put down and lasting for six hours. I doubt if there are any other troops in the world who could have stood up to it and then gone on fighting with the ferocity they have. I am meeting Freyberg and the Army Commanders to-morrow to discuss the situation.

If we call it off, we shall hold on to the two bridges and adjust our positions so as to hold the advantageous key points already gained. The Eighth Army's plan for entering the Liri Valley in force will be undertaken when regrouping is completed. The plan must envisage an attack on a wider front and with greater forces than Freyberg has been able to have for this operation. A little later, when the snow goes off mountains, the rivers drop, and the ground hardens, movement will be possible over terrain which at present is impassable.

Prime Minister to General Alexander   21 Mar. 44

Thank you very much for your full explanation. I hope you will not have to "call it off" when you have gone so far. Surely the enemy is very hard pressed too. Every good wish.

The war weighs very heavy on us all just now.

The struggle in the ruins of Cassino town continued until the 23d, with hard fighting in attacks and counter-attacks. The New Zealanders and the Indians could do no more. We kept hold of a large part of the town, but the Gurkhas had to be withdrawn from their perch high up the Monastery Hill, where supplies could not reach them even by air because of the steep hillside.

* * * * *

In reply to my request General Wilson reported the casualties suffered by the New Zealand Corps during the battle. They totalled: 2d New Zealand Division, 1050; 4th Indian Division, British, 401, Indian, 759, 1160; 78th British Division, 190; grand total, 2400.

This was a heavy price to pay for what might seem small gains. We had however established a firm bridgehead at Cassino over the river Rapido, which, with the deep bulge made by the Xth Corps across the lower Garigliano in January, was of great value when the final, successful battle came. Here and at the Anzio bridgehead we had pinned down in Central Italy nearly twenty good German divisions. Many of them might have gone to France.

Before the Gustav Line could be assaulted again with any hope of success, our troops had to be rested and regrouped. Most of the Eighth Army had to be brought over from the Adriatic side and two armies concentrated for the next battle, the British Eighth on the Cassino front, the American Fifth on the lower Garigliano. For this General Alexander needed nearly two months.

This meant that the Mediterranean could only help the cross-Channel assault in early June, by fighting south of Rome. The United States Chiefs of Staff still strove for a subsidiary landing in Southern France, and for some weeks there was much argument between us about what orders should be given to General Wilson.

* * * * *

The story must here be told of the Anglo-American argument, first as between "Overlord" and "Anvil," and then as
between "Anvil" and the Italian campaign. It will be recalled
that in my talk with Montgomery at Marrakesh on December
31, he said that he must have more in the initial punch across
the Channel, and that on January 6, I telegraphed to the President that Bedell Smith and Montgomery were convinced that
it was better to put in a much heavier and broader "Overlord"
than to expand "Anvil" beyond what we had planned in outline before Teheran.

This was keenly debated at a conference held by General
Eisenhower on January 21, shortly after his arrival in England.
Eisenhower himself firmly believed in the vital importance of
"Anvil" and thought it would be a mistake to impoverish it for
the sake of strengthening "Overlord." As a result of this conference, however, he sent a telegram to the Combined Chiefs
of Staff in Washington, in which he said: " 'Overlord' and 'Anvil'
must be viewed as one whole. If sufficient resources could be
made available, the ideal would be a five divisional 'Overlord,'
and a three divisional 'Anvil.' If insufficient forces are available for this, however, I am driven to the conclusion that we
should adopt a five divisional 'Overlord' and a one divisional
'Anvil,' the latter being maintained as a threat until enemy
weakness justifies its active employment."

On this telegram, the British Chiefs of Staff presented their
own views to Washington, namely: (a) That the first onfall of
"Overlord" should be increased to five divisions, whatever the
cost to "Anvil." (b) That every effort should be made to undertake "Anvil" by using two divisions or more in the assault.
(c) That if these divisions could not be carried, landing-craft
in the Mediterranean should be reduced to the requirements
for a lift of one division.

The American Chiefs of Staff were unable to agree. They
considered that a threat in lieu of an actual operation was inadequate and insisted on a two-divisional assault. On this
telegram I minuted: "Apparently the two-division lift for

'Anvil' is given priority over 'Overlord.' This is directly counter
to the views of Generals Eisenhower and Montgomery."

* * * * *

On February 4, the British Chiefs of Staff, in full consultation with me, sent a lengthy telegram to their American colleagues, in which they emphasised that the paramount
consideration was that "Overlord" should succeed and that the
right solution was to build up "Overlord" to the strength required by the Supreme Commander, and then to allocate to
the Mediterranean whatever additional resources could be
found. They questioned the wisdom of undertaking "Anvil"
at all, in view of the way things were going in Italy, and pointed
out that when "Anvil" first found favour at Teheran we expected that the Germans would withdraw to a line north of
Rome. But now it was clear beyond all doubt that the Germans
intended to resist our advance in Italy to the utmost. They
also pointed out that the distance between the South of France
and the beaches of Normandy was nearly five hundred miles,
and that a diversion could be created from Italy or other points
just as well as through the Rhone Valley. "Anvil" in fact was
too far away to help "Overlord."

On this the United States Chiefs of Staff proposed that the
issue should be decided at a conference between General Eisenhower, who would be their representative, and the British
Chiefs of Staff. To this we readily assented, but several weeks
were to pass before agreement was reached. General Eisenhower was still reluctant to abandon "Anvil," but he was beginning to doubt whether it would still be possible to withdraw
trained divisions from Italy. On March 21, General Wilson was
asked for his opinion. He said he was strongly opposed to
withdrawing troops from Italy until Rome had been captured,
and he advised that "Anvil" should be cancelled and that
we should only land in the South of France if the Germans
cracked.

This turned the scale. The British Chiefs of Staff telegraphed to Washington that it was clear that "Anvil" could

not be carried out on the prescribed date, since it was impossible to withdraw either troops from the battle in Italy or landing-craft from the Anzio bridgehead. The American Chiefs of Staff assented, and agreed that General Wilson should prepare to land in the South of France in July, and also to contain and destroy as many German troops in Italy as possible if it were decided to fight it out there. It was thought that early June would be time enough to decide which plan should be carried out.

That I myself was strongly in favour of maintaining the thrust in Italy can be seen from this telegram:

Prime Minister to General Marshall (Washington)   16 Apr. 44

It is of course very painful to us to forgo the invaluable addition to our landing-craft in the Mediterranean which you so kindly offered under certain conditions and had no doubt great trouble to obtain. What I cannot bear is to agree beforehand to starve a battle or have to break it off just at the moment when success, after long efforts and heavy losses, may be in view. Our forces in Italy are not much larger than those of the enemy. They comprise seven or eight different races, while the enemy is all German. The wet weather has hitherto restricted the full use of our superiority in artillery, in armour, and in the air. Alexander tells me that he strikes out *northeast,* not southeast, from Anzio beachhead shortly after his main thrust across the Rapido. Thus there will not necessarily be a moment when we shall pause and say, "Halt here. Go over to the defensive. All aboard for 'Anvil.'" Nor will there necessarily be an exact moment when the cutting of supplies for the Italian battle for the sake of "Anvil" can be fixed beforehand in imagination. A half-hearted undercurrent sets in with an army which has a divided objective, part to the front and part to the rear. This infects all the rearward services, who cannot help knowing. Remember the terrible bleeding the armies in Italy got when their seven best divisions were taken for "Overlord."

2. Of course, if the battle goes wrong early and we are hung up before other enemy lines of defence and forced to go over to a general defensive, no doubt strong forces could then be spared, but the drain of feeding the bridgehead would continue to press on our landing-craft, and without your Pacific landing-craft there

will be no two-division lift for any amphibious operations, "Anvil" or other.

3. Therefore, it seems to me we must throw our hearts into this battle, for the sake of which so many American and British lives have already been sacrificed, and make it, like "Overlord," an all-out conquer or die. It may well be that by May 31 we shall see many things which are now veiled from us. I regret having to forgo such an hour of choice.

4. Dill tells me that you had expected me to support "Anvil" more vigorously in view of my enthusiasm for it when it was first proposed by you at Teheran. Please do me the justice to remember that the situation is vastly changed. In November, we hoped to take Rome in January, and there were many signs that the enemy was ready to [retire] northward up the Italian peninsula. Instead of this, in spite of our great amphibious expedition, we are stuck where we are, and the enemy has brought down to the battle south of Rome the eight mobile divisions we should have hoped a full-scale "Anvil" would have contained. Thus there has been cause for rejoicing as well as bitter disappointment.

5. The whole of this difficult question only arises out of the absurd shortage of the L.S.T.s. How it is that the plans of two great empires like Britain and the United States should be so much hamstrung and limited by a hundred or two of these particular vessels will never be understood by history. I am deeply concerned at the strong disinclination of the American Government even to keep the manufacture of L.S.T.s at its full height so as to have a sufficient number to give to us to help you in the war against Japan. The absence of these special vessels may limit our whole war effort on your left flank, and I fear we shall be accused unjustly of not doing our best, as we are resolved to do.

The instructions Wilson received reflected my views, and in a telegram to the President on April 24, I said:

Prime Minister to President Roosevelt   24 Nov. 44

I am very glad at what has happened in Italy. It seems to me that we have both succeeded in gaining what we sought. The only thing now lacking is a victory. I had long talks with Alexander when he was here for a few days' consultation. He defended his actions, or inactions, with much force, pointing out the small plurality of his army, its mixed character, there being no fewer than seven separate nationalities against the homogeneous Germans, the vileness of the weather, and the extremely awkward nature of the ground. At latest by May 14, he will attack and push everything in as hard as possible. If this battle were successful, or even raging at full blast, it would fit in very well with other plans.

*   *   *   *   *

Political events in Southern Italy again came to a head. A constitutional compromise was reached whereby the King would hand over his powers to his son, Crown Prince Umberto, as Lieutenant-Governor of the Realm. The fate of the Monarchy would then await a plebiscite after the ultimate victory. The royal decree was signed on April 12, and was to take effect at the moment when the Allies entered Rome. At the end of the month, Badoglio reconstructed his Government to include leading political figures in the South, of whom Croce and Sforza were the most prominent.

*   *   *   *   *

While our armies were preparing to attack, General Wilson used all his air-power to impede and injure the enemy, who like us were using the pause for reorganising and replenishing themselves for further battle. The potent Allied Air joined in attacking enemy land communications in the hope that these could be kept cut and their troops forced to withdraw for lack of supplies. This operation, optimistically called "Strangle," aimed at blocking the three main railway lines from Northern Italy, the principal targets being bridges, viaducts, and other bottlenecks. They tried to starve the Germans out of Central Italy.

The effort lasted more than six weeks, and did great damage. Railway movement was constantly stopped far north of Rome, but it failed to attain all that we hoped. By working their coastal shipping to full capacity, transferring loads to motor transport, and making full use of the hours of darkness, the enemy contrived to maintain themselves. But they could not build enough reserve stocks for protracted and heavy fighting, and in the severe land battles at the end of May they were much weakened. The junction of our separated armies and their capture of Rome took place more rapidly than we had forecast. The German Air Force suffered severely in trying to defend its communications. By early May, it could muster only a bare seven hundred against our thousand combat aircraft.

Here then we may leave the Italian theatre, where much was ripening, for the supreme operation across the Channel.

12

The Mounting Air Offensive

Our Progress in Bomber Expansion — Radar Aids to Target-Finding — The Germans Forced to Turn to Fighter Production — The Americans Join in the Bombing of Axis Europe in 1943 — The Casablanca Directive — British Night Bombing of the Ruhr — The Air Battle at Hamburg — The Onslaught on Berlin — Heavy American Losses at Schweinfurt, October 14, 1943, and Their Sequel — British Losses in the Attack on Nuremberg — American Fortresses at Last Provided with Long-Range Fighters — Increase in the Power of British Bombs — Lord Cherwell's Inquiry — Aluminised Explosives — Effect of Our Air Offensive on German War Economy — Part to be Played by the Allied Air Force in "Overlord" — British War Cabinet's Distress at Heavy French Civilian Casualties — We Accept President Roosevelt's Decision — The Valour and Devotion of British and American Bomber Crews.

BOMBER COMMAND played an ever-growing part in all our war plans, and eventually made a decisive contribution to victory. Some review of its activities is required at this point in the story.

It was not till 1943 that we possessed sufficient and suitable aircraft for striking heavy and continuous blows, and in the same year the bombers of the American Eighth Air Force joined in our strategic air offensive. Ever since 1940, I had encouraged the expansion of our bomber strength. The difficulties were numerous. Production lagged behind forecasts; other theatres of war and the campaign against the U-boats made heavy demands; and when the Americans came into the war their output was of course at first largely diverted to their own needs. Although growth in numbers had been slow, our new four-engined planes carried a far heavier weight of bombs. In the opening months of 1942, the average load per aircraft was 2800 pounds; by the end of that year, it was 4400 pounds; during 1943, it rose to 7500 pounds.

Early in the war, both we and the Germans had found that bombers, even in close formation, could not fight their way in daylight through an efficient fighter defence without overheavy casualties. Like the enemy, we had had to turn to night attacks. We were too confident at first about the accuracy of our bombing, and our attempts in the winter of 1940/41 to destroy German oil plants, paramount but small targets, proved a failure. In the spring of 1941, Bomber Command was called to join in the Battle of the Atlantic, and not till July was the offensive against Germany resumed. The targets now chosen were industrial cities and their railway centres, especially the Ruhr and Hamburg, Bremen, Hanover, Frankfurt, and Stuttgart. However, neither our means nor our methods sufficed. Our losses mounted, and during the winter months we had to reduce our effort. In February 1942, "Gee," the new position-finder already described,[1] was brought into use, and with its help the Ruhr became our primary goal. Under the vigorous leadership of Air Marshal Harris, dramatic results were achieved. His operations included fire-raising attacks on Lübeck and Rostock, the thousand-bomber assault on Cologne in May, and the daylight attack on the submarine Diesel-engine works at Augsburg, when Squadron-Leader Nettleton won the Victoria Cross.

In August, the Pathfinder Force was formed, under Air Commodore Bennett. Radar aids were playing a growing part in navigation and target-finding, and it was a wise measure to entrust the scarce and complicated apparatus to specialists whose duty it was to find the way and point the target to others.

Although accurate night bombing, denied so long, thus came gradually into being, the bomber offensive of 1942 did not

[1] Details of the several devices mentioned in this chapter are given in Volume IV, *The Hinge of Fate*, Book One, Chapter 16, page 280.

lower Germany's war production or civilian morale. The strength of her economy had been underestimated. Productive capacity and labour were drawn extensively from the occupied countries, and German armament production seems to have actually increased. Under the iron discipline imposed by Goebbels, who was in charge of relief measures, civilian morale stood firm, and local disasters were prevented from having a national effect. But the German leaders had become deeply alarmed and were forced onto the defensive in the air. German aircraft production was increasingly devoted to fighters rather than bombers. This was the beginning of defeat for the Luftwaffe, and a turning-point in our struggle for the air supremacy which we gained in 1944, and without which we could not have won the war. Second only in importance to this moral victory over the minds of Hitler and his air commanders was the dangerous Third Air Front created for Germany in the West, to the advantage of the Russians, and of ourselves in the Mediterranean.

Thus we come to the year 1943, when the Americans joined in the bombing of Axis Europe. They had different ideas about method. Whereas we had adopted and were now bringing to efficiency our night-bombing technique, they were convinced that their heavily armed Fortress bombers in close formation could penetrate deeply into Germany by daylight without fighter escort. I was doubtful whether this was a practicable system, and have recorded in a previous volume how at Casablanca I discussed my misgivings with General Eaker, commanding the United States Air Forces in England, and withdrew my opposition.[2] The Casablanca directive, issued to the British and American Bomber Commands in the United Kingdom on February 4, 1943, gave them their task in the following terms:

Your primary object will be the progressive destruction and dislocation of the German military, industrial, and economic system,

[2] Volume IV, *The Hinge of Fate*, Chapter 15, Book Two, "The Casablanca Conference," pages 679–80.

and the undermining of the morale of the German people to a point where their capacity for armed resistance is fatally weakened.

Within that general concept your primary objectives . . . will for the present be in the following priority: (*a*) German submarine yards. (*b*) The German aircraft industry. (*c*) Transportation. (*d*) Oil plants. (*e*) Other targets in enemy war industry.

General Eaker, with the American Eighth Air Force, aimed at destroying six groups of targets by daylight precision bombing. He did not receive the reinforcements for which he had asked, but made many gallant and costly attacks. Air-Marshal Harris, bombing only at night, concentrated from March to July 1943 mainly upon the Ruhr, beginning on the night of March 5/6 with the heavily defended town of Essen. Eight Mosquitoes dropped target indicators, using the blind bombing device of "Oboe"; then twenty-two heavy bombers of the Pathfinder Force further illuminated the target for an intense attack by 392 aircraft. Essen was severely damaged for the first time in the war. As the power and activities of Bomber Command developed, Goebbels became more and more despairing of the outcome, and his diaries bitterly reproach the Luftwaffe for its failure to stop the British bombers. Speer, the most capable German Minister of Production, in an address to Gauleiters in June 1943, referred to the serious losses in production of coal and iron and crankshafts and to the decision to double the anti-aircraft defences of the Ruhr and draft a hundred thousand men for repair duties.

While the British were at last succeeding in wrecking the Ruhr munition centres, the American Fortresses were meeting with serious opposition from German day fighters, and General Eaker soon realised that if his plan was to succeed he must first defeat the German Air Force. In the greatly improved state of the U-boat war, a change in the priorities of targets was accepted by the Combined Chiefs of Staff. In a directive known as "Point-Blank," issued on June 10, 1943, they amended the Casablanca decisions so as to give first emphasis to the attack on the German fighter forces and the German aircraft industry.

On July 24/25, the very heavy British attacks on Hamburg began. Hamburg was beyond the range of "Oboe," and the fullest use was made of the blind-bombing device of H_2S, which was carried in the airplane and did not depend on signals from home. This instrument gave an outline of the main ground features on a screen in the aircraft which resembled a television screen of today. The picture was particularly good where the land was broken up by water, as it is in the dock area of Hamburg. Bomber Command had been gaining experience of H_2S since its first use in January, and for the assault on Hamburg an additional device called "Window," which we had long held in reserve, was used for the first time. As is explained in an earlier volume, this simply consisted of strips of metallised paper dropped by the bombers. A cloud of such strips, tuned to the German wave-length and weighing only a few pounds, looked like an aircraft on the enemy's radar screens, and thus made it very difficult for either their night fighters to be guided to our bombers or for the anti-aircraft guns and searchlights to be aimed at them.

The four attacks against Hamburg from July 24 to August 3 caused greater destruction than had ever been suffered by so large a city in so short a time. The second attack delivered such a concentration of incendiary bombs mixed with high-explosive that there arose a fire tornado which raged through the city with a terrifying howl and defied all human countermeasures. The air battle of Hamburg has been described by many Germans as "the great catastrophe." Speer himself admitted after the war that he had calculated that if similar attacks had been delivered in quick succession against six other major German cities it would have led to a breakdown of war production. Germany was saved from this fate in 1943 partly because H_2S was found to be difficult to use, even for area bombing, if there were no prominent water features within the target, and partly because of the resolute defence put up by Germany's ever-resourceful night fighters.

Our third great air onslaught of 1943 was upon Berlin. It lasted from November 1943 to March 1944. If this great industrial centre could have been paralysed like Hamburg, German war production as well as morale might have been given a mortal blow.

Bomber Command pressed home its attacks with undaunted courage and determination in the face of fearful difficulties. The weather was appalling, and most of the bombing had to rely on the radar eye of H_2S. The night photographs taken by the bombers at the moment of bomb release showed nothing but clouds. The same disappointment befell the daylight flights over Berlin of the Photographic Reconnaissance Unit. We knew from the admissions of Germans themselves that great destruction was being caused, but we could not judge the relative success of our sixteen major attacks by comparing the photographic evidence of each. We had to wait until March 1944 to obtain photographs clear enough for the damage to be assessed. It fell short of what had been achieved at Hamburg.

Meanwhile, the United States Eighth Air Force, in its assault on the enemy's fighter forces and aircraft industry in accordance with the "Point-Blank" directive, was enduring increasing losses at the hands of the German day fighters, which met them with mounting strength and efficiency. The culmination was reached on October 14, 1943. In their attack on the ball-bearing plants at Schweinfurt, which were vital to the German aircraft industry, the Americans had sixty of their large Fortress aircraft destroyed out of 291. It was thereafter accepted that unescorted daylight bombers could not gain air superiority over Germany, and their offensive was suspended until long-range fighters could be produced to cover them in sufficient strength.

Something very like a dispute arose upon whether the British Bomber Command should attack Schweinfurt by their own methods. In the end it was decided that the attack should be made by both air forces in daylight and in darkness. The American Eighth Air Force, aided at last by the long-range fighters for which they had waited a long time, attacked with 266 bombers by daylight on February 24, 1944, and on the same night Bomber Command sent 734 aircraft. Here was a really combined offensive directed towards the common aim.

Unfortunately, the discussion had lasted so long that this tremendous attack was robbed of much of its effectiveness. Warned by the American daylight attack four months earlier, Speer had dispersed the industry.

*   *   *   *   *

Prolonged and obstinate technical argument on the policy of night or day bombing, and generous rivalry in trying out the opposing theories with the utmost sacrifice and heroism by both the British and American Air Forces, reached its climax after the last attack on Berlin. On March 30/31, 1944, out of 795 aircraft dispatched by British Bomber Command against Nuremberg, 94 did not return. This was our heaviest loss in one raid, and caused Bomber Command to re-examine its tactics before launching further deep-penetration attacks by night into Germany. This was proof of the power which the enemy's night-fighter force, strengthened by the best crews from other vital fronts, had developed under our relentless offensive. But by forcing the enemy to concentrate his strength on defending Germany the Western Allies gained the complete air superiority which they needed for the approaching cross-Channel invasion.

*   *   *   *   *

All this time the Americans were intent on bringing their Fortress bombers into action by day as soon as they could be protected by fighters of sufficiently long range to seek out and destroy the enemy fighters in the air or come down and attack them on their airfields. After long delay this vital need was met. First the Thunderbolt, then the Lightning, and finally the Mustang gave them day fighters which had auxiliary fuel tanks and a radius of action which was increased from 475 miles to 850. On February 23, 1944, there began a week of concentrated bomber attacks by day on the German aircraft industry. The American long-range fighters at last mastered the enemy's and the day bombers delivered precision attacks without undue interference or loss.

This was a turning-point in the air war against Germany. From now onward the United States Eighth Air Force was able to bomb targets in Germany by day with high accuracy and ever-increasing freedom. Germany, through her loss of air superiority by day, exposed her vitals to our strategic offensive. The German night fighters, with the cream of their pilots, remained formidable till the end of the war; but this, by lowering the standard of the day fighters, aided the new developments in the American Air Force, and in 1944 daylight air superiority over Germany was gained. By April, new measures of deception and new tactics to confuse the enemy's defences enabled the British to resume their full-scale night offensive against German cities. The United States Eighth Air Force, having got the measure of the enemy's day fighters, was ready to complete this offensive "round the clock." Such was the position at the advent of "Overlord."

*   *   *   *   *

The ever-growing preponderance of our air attack on Germany received an appreciable reinforcement from the new explosive power given to our bombs. This arose as an incident in our anxious discussions in 1943 about the threat of the rockets and the doodlebugs. Those experts who were taking the more gloomy view of our danger made a number of pessimistic assumptions in comparing the effect of our bombs in Germany with the expected effects of rockets in England. German houses, they said, were very much stronger than English houses, so that we might expect twice as many to be destroyed per ton of explosives in England as in Germany. In stating this case, they incidentally took for granted that the enemy bombs were nearly twice as powerful as the British, since the Germans mixed aluminum powder with the high-explosive. Lord Cherwell pointed out this statement to me, and I ordered a searching inquiry to be conducted under his guidance. The results astonished everyone concerned.

Prime Minister to Minister of Production   12 Oct. 43
I recently invited Lord Cherwell to inquire into and report on

the relative efficiency of the high-explosives used by the German and British forces respectively. His preliminary report had shown the undoubted superiority of the German explosive charges.

The Chiefs of Staff strongly recommend that we should change over to aluminised explosives without waiting for the result of further trials. I agree. Pray let me have a report in the course of the next week of what this change will involve.

The question of how this state of affairs has been allowed to arise should be the subject of an inquiry held under the authority of the Minister of Defence. Pray propose three members, with reference. The whole matter is to be kept most secret.

Action was taken accordingly. It appeared that in the early days, when aluminum was scarce, it had been decided to use all the aluminum powder which could be spared for making depth-charges, and that this custom had persisted, although aluminum had now become more plentiful. Orders were immediately given to improve our explosive — in the first place in our heavy bombs — by adding aluminum powder, and their efficiency during the whole latter half of the war was thus increased by about half as much again. I thought these revelations deserved the attention of my colleagues, and sent out the following in February 1944.

ALUMINISED EXPLOSIVES

17 Feb. 44

At the end of September 1943, during discussions about the German long-range rocket, doubts were expressed about the efficiency of our high-explosives as compared with those of the Germans. The Paymaster-General immediately discussed the matter with the Chief of the Air Staff, and the latter proposed to the Chiefs of Staff Committee, who supported his proposals strongly, that urgent action should be taken to establish the true facts, and that if a substantial inferiority was revealed, the competent authorities should be called upon to give an explanation and a proposed remedy.

2. At the suggestion of the Chiefs of Staff Committee, the Paymaster-General undertook the inquiry suggested, and on October 6 submitted a report to the Chiefs of Staff Committee which clearly

established that our explosives were inferior to the Germans' and that an improvement, estimated by various authorities as between 40 per cent and 100 per cent, could be made if aluminised explosives were used instead of the existing types. Lord Cherwell recommended that the most urgent possible preparations to change over should be made without waiting for the result of further trials. With this recommendation the Chiefs of Staff Committee and I agreed, and immediate action was taken to effect the change-over.

3. I also appointed a committee, consisting of Sir Walter Monckton (chairman), Sir Alan Barlow, and Sir Robert Robertson, "to consider the report on the efficiency of our blast bombs, to examine the course of our experimental and development work on this subject during the present war, and to report whether, and if so why, there has been any failure to prosecute research to a successful conclusion or to apply the results of that research in practice."

Briefly, an unfortunate experiment in 1941 gave a misleading result, chiefly owing to the unsatisfactory methods of measuring blast pressures in use at that time. In addition, the impression that in any event no aluminum could be obtained discouraged those in charge from repeating the experiment until midsummer of 1943. It was only when the Paymaster-General's attention was drawn to an alleged superiority of German explosives, as stated above, that the necessary impetus was given to turn the lessons of fresh experiments to account.

4. There is no doubt that the power of aluminised explosives is very much greater than that of the types which were being used earlier, and I have thought it right to bring to the notice of my colleagues the important service rendered by the Paymaster-General in calling attention to a most unsatisfactory state of affairs, which might have continued for some time, with serious detriment to our war effort, unless he had intervened.

This episode shows how useful it is in great organisations to have a roving eye.

*   *   *   *   *

It is difficult to say to what extent German war economy and armament production had so far been damaged by the Anglo-American bomber offensive. Bomber Command's three great area battles of 1943 — the Ruhr, Hamburg, and Berlin

— had created widespread havoc and caused consternation and alarm throughout Germany, and especially in the minds of the German leaders. But they were able to use factories and forced labour from the occupied countries, and under the brilliant control of Speer these were mobilised with extraordinary speed and efficiency. The morale of the people in the bombed cities, though severely shaken, was not allowed to degenerate into a nation-wide panic.

In the reports submitted to Hitler, which must of course be taken with reserve, it was claimed that German armament production was doubled in 1942. Remembering our own loss of output under much less severe bombing, this assertion is difficult to credit. The Germans admitted that production was almost stationary in 1943, and this is evidence of the increasing power of Bomber Command. In the spring of 1944, the Allied strategic bombers were required for "Overlord," and the weight of attack on Germany itself was inevitably reduced. But by now we were the masters in the air. The bitterness of the struggle had thrown a greater strain on the Luftwaffe than it was able to bear. By being forced to concentrate on building fighters, it had lost all power of strategic counter-attack by bombing back at us. Unbalanced and exhausted, it was henceforth unable to defend either itself or Germany from our grievous blows. For our air superiority, which by the end of 1944 was to become air supremacy, full tribute must be paid to the United States Eighth Air Force, once it gained its long range fighters.

*   *   *   *   *

As "Overlord" approached, a momentous question confronted us. What part was the mighty weapon of the air to play in the supreme operation? After prolonged technical controversy among the air authorities of both countries, the plan which prevailed was to destroy German railway communications in France, Belgium, and Western Germany by discharging 66,000 tons of bombs during the three months before D-Day, thus creating a "railway desert" around the German

troops in Normandy. This plan had already entered its early
stages. The principal targets were the repair and maintenance
depots and the locomotives in ninety-three key railway centres
on the many approaches to Normandy. The Tactical Air
Forces assisted in this general plan, and were given in addition
the special task, as D-Day drew near, of destroying bridges and
rolling-stock. I wrote to General Eisenhower on April 3:

Prime Minister to General Eisenhower   3 Apr. 44
    The Cabinet today took rather a grave and on the whole an
adverse view of the proposal to bomb so many French railway
centres, in view of the fact that scores of thousands of French
civilians, men, women, and children, would lose their lives or be
injured. Considering that they are all our friends, this might be
held to be an act of very great severity, bringing much hatred on
the Allied Air Forces. It was decided that the Defence Committee
should consider the matter during this week, and that thereafter
the Foreign Office should address the State Department and I should
myself send a personal telegram to the President.
    The argument for concentration on these particular targets is
very nicely balanced on military grounds.

    General Eisenhower replied on the 5th:

General Eisenhower to Prime Minister   5 Apr. 44
    We must never forget that one of the fundamental factors leading
to the decision for undertaking "Overlord" was the conviction that
our overpowering Air Force would make feasible an operation
which might otherwise be considered extremely hazardous, if not
foolhardy. . . . The weight of the argument that has been brought
against the bombing of transportation centres in occupied territories
is heavy indeed. But I and my military advisers have become convinced that the bombing of these centres will increase our chances
for success in the critical battle. . . . I personally believe that estimates of probable casualties have been grossly exaggerated.

                    *   *   *   *

    As the air offensive against the railways developed, the losses
of French and Belgian civilians, though far less than the prior
estimates, caused the British War Cabinet distress and anxiety.

Prime Minister to President Roosevelt   7 May 44

The War Cabinet have been much concerned during the last three weeks about the number of Frenchmen killed in the raids on the railway centres in France. We have had numerous Staff meetings with our own officers, and I have discussed the matter with General Eisenhower and Bedell Smith. There were and are great differences of opinion in the two Air Forces — not between them, but criss-cross — about the efficacy of the "railway plan" as a short-term project. In the end, Eisenhower, Tedder, Bedell Smith, and Portal all declare themselves converted. I am personally by no means convinced that this is the best way to use our Air Forces in the preliminary period, and still think that the German Air Force should be the main target. . . .

2. When this project was first put forward a loss of eighty thousand French civilian casualties, including injured, say twenty thousand killed, was mentioned. The War Cabinet could not view this figure without grave dismay on account of the apparently ruthless use of the Air Forces, particularly of the Royal Air Force, on whom the brunt of this kind of work necessarily falls, and the reproaches that would be made upon the inaccuracy of night bombing. The results of the first, say, three-sevenths of the bombing, have however shown that the casualties to French civil life are very much less than was expected by the commanders. . . .

3. I am satisfied that all possible care will be taken to minimise this slaughter of friendly civilian life. Nevertheless, the War Cabinet share my apprehensions of the bad effect which will be produced upon the French civilian population by these slaughters, all taking place so long before "Overlord" D-Day. They may easily bring about a great revolution in French feeling towards their approaching United States and British liberators. They may leave a legacy of hate behind them. It may well be that the French losses will grow heavier on and after D-Day, but in the heat of battle, when British and United States troops will probably be losing at a much higher rate, a new proportion establishes itself in men's minds. It is the intervening period that causes me most anxiety. . . .

4. The Cabinet ask me to invite you to consider the matter from the highest political standpoint and to give us your opinion as a matter between Governments. It must be remembered, on the one hand, that this slaughter is among a friendly people who have committed no crimes against us, and not among the German foe,

with all their record of cruelty and ruthlessness. On the other hand, we naturally feel the hazardous nature of Operation "Overlord" and are in deadly earnest about making it a success. I have been careful in stating this case to you to use only the most moderate terms, but I ought to let you know that the War Cabinet is unanimous in its anxiety about these French slaughters, even reduced as they have been, and also in its doubts as to whether almost as good military results could not be produced by other methods. Whatever is settled between us, we are quite willing to share responsibilities with you.

The President replied on the 11th:

President Roosevelt to Prime Minister   11 Apr. 44

I share fully with you your distress at the loss of life among the French population incident to our air preparations for "Overlord."

I share also with you a satisfaction that every possible care is being and will be taken to minimise civilian casualties. No possibility of alleviating adverse French opinion should be overlooked, always provided that there is no reduction of our effectiveness against the enemy at this crucial time.

However regrettable the attendant loss of civilian lives is, I am not prepared to impose from this distance any restriction on military action by the responsible commanders that in their opinion might militate against the success of "Overlord" or cause additional loss of life to our Allied forces of invasion.

This was decisive. Meanwhile, the rate of the casualties to French civilians continued to be less than had been feared. The sealing-off of the Normandy battlefield from reinforcement by rail may well have been the greatest direct contribution that the bomber forces could make to "Overlord." The price was paid.

*   *   *   *   *

This chapter has been dominated by technical matters. The British and United States rival themes of air attack by night or day have been shown under the hard test of results. The improvements in our explosives and the intricacies of radar and all its variants have been presented, I trust, in a form intelligible to the lay reader. But it would be wrong to end without paying our tribute of respect and admiration to the officers and men who fought and died in this fearful battle of the air, the like of which had never before been known, or even with any precision imagined. The moral tests to which the crew of a bomber were subjected reached the limits of human valour and sacrifice. Here chance was carried to its most extreme and violent degree above all else. There was a rule that no one should go on more than thirty raids without a break. But many who entered on their last dozen wild adventures felt that the odds against them were increasing. How can one be lucky thirty times running in a world of averages and machinery? Detective-Constable McSweeney, one of the Scotland Yard officers who looked after me in the early days of the war, was determined to fight in a bomber. I saw him several times during his training and his fighting. One day, gay and jaunty as ever but with a thoughtful look, he said, "My next will be my twenty-ninth." It was his last. Not only our hearts and admiration, but our minds in strong comprehension of these ordeals must go out to these heroic men whose duty to their country and their cause sustained them in superhuman trials.

I have mentioned facts like "the Americans had 60 of their large Fortress aircraft destroyed out of 291," and on another occasion "out of 795 aircraft dispatched by British Bomber Command against Nuremberg 94 did not return." The American Fortresses carried a crew of ten men, and the British night bombers seven. Here we have each time six or seven hundred of these skilled, highly trained warriors lost in an hour. This was indeed ordeal by fire. In the British and American bombing of Germany and Italy during the war, the casualties were over a hundred and forty thousand, and in the period with which this chapter deals there were more British and American aircrew casualties than there were killed and wounded in the great operation of crossing the Channel. These heroes never flinched or failed. It is to their devotion that in no small measure we owe our victory. Let us give them our salute.

13

The Greek Torment

T
HE GREEKS rival the Jews in being the most politically minded race in the world. No matter how forlorn their circumstances or how grave the peril to their country, they are always divided into many parties, with many leaders who fight among themselves with desperate vigour. It has been well said that wherever there are three Jews it will be found that there are two Prime Ministers and one leader of the Opposition. The same is true of this other famous ancient race, whose stormy and endless struggle for life stretches back to the fountain springs of human thought. No other two races have set such a mark upon the world. Both have shown a capacity for survival, in spite of unending perils and sufferings from ex-

532

ternal oppressors, matched only by their own ceaseless feuds, quarrels, and convulsions. The passage of several thousand years sees no change in their characteristics and no diminution of their trials or their vitality. They have survived in spite of all that the world could do against them, and all they could do against themselves, and each of them from angles so different has left us the inheritance of its genius and wisdom. No two cities have counted more with mankind than Athens and Jerusalem. Their messages in religion, philosophy, and art have been the main guiding lights of modern faith and culture. Centuries of foreign rule and indescribable, endless oppression leave them still living, active communities and forces in the modern world, quarrelling among themselves with insatiable vivacity. Personally I have always been on the side of both, and believed in their invincible power to survive internal strife and the world tides threatening their extinction.

*   *   *   *   *

After the withdrawal of the Allies in April 1941, Greece was occupied by the Axis Powers. The collapse of the Army and the retirement of the King and his Government into exile revived the bitter controversies of Greek politics. Both in the country and in Greek circles abroad there was hard criticism of the Monarchy, which had sanctioned the dictatorship of General Metaxas, and thereby directly associated itself with the régime which had now been defeated. When King George II left Crete in May 1941, he took with him a Government which was mainly Royalist, headed by M. Tsouderos. Their long journey by Cairo and South Africa to London provided ample time for political discussion among Greek communities abroad. The Constitution had been suspended in 1936, and the debate upon the future régime when Greece should finally be liberated had to be conducted among refugees on Allied soil.

I had long realised the importance of this issue, and in October 1941, addressed a letter to the Greek Prime Minister, congratulating him on his first broadcast from London to occupied Greece, and expressing my gratification that Greece had been declared to be a democratic country under a constitutional Monarchy. The King himself broadcast in the New Year to his country on the same lines. If a united nation was to rise out of the war, it was essential that links should be maintained between the exiles and Greek opinion at home.

During the first winter of Axis occupation, Greece suffered severely from famine, partially relieved by Red Cross shipments, and also from the exhaustion of the fighting which had ended in the destruction of her army. But at the time of the surrender, arms were hidden in the mountains, and in sporadic fashion, and on a minor scale, resistance to the enemy was planned. In the towns of Central Greece, starvation provided plenty of recruits. In April 1942, the body calling itself the National Liberation Front (known by its initials in Greek as E.A.M.), which had come into being in the previous autumn, announced the formation of the People's Liberation Army (E.L.A.S.). Small fighting groups were recruited during the following year, particularly in Central and Northern Greece, while in Epirus and the mountains of the northwest remnants of the Greek Army and local mountaineers gathered round the person of Colonel Napoleon Zervas. The E.A.M.-E.L.A.S. organisation was dominated by a hard core of Communist leaders The adherents of Zervas, originally Republican in sympathy, became as time passed exclusively anti-Communist. Around these two centres Greek resistance to the Germans gathered. Neither of them had any direct contact with the Greek Government in London, nor any sympathy for its position.

On the eve of Alamein, we decided to attack the German supply lines leading down through Greece to the Piraeus, the port of Athens and an important base on the German route to North Africa. In the autumn of 1942, the first British Military Mission, under Lieutenant-Colonel Myers, was accordingly dropped by parachute into Greece and made contact with the guerrillas. With their aid a vital viaduct on the main Athens railway line was destroyed. Simultaneously, brilliant and daring sabotage operations were carried out by Greek agents against Axis shipping in the Piraeus. The success of these operations encouraged Middle East Headquarters to send more British parties with supplies of explosives and arms. Thus direct contact with occupied Greece was established.

During the spring of 1943, the British missions were strengthened. We had an added motive for stimulating activities in this area as a cover for our pending operations in Sicily. Special efforts were made to convince the enemy that, following on their defeat in Tunisia, the Allies were planning a major landing on Greek soil. Combined Anglo-Greek parties blew another railway bridge on the main Athens line, and other sabotage operations were successful. The result was that two German divisions were moved into Greece which might have been used in Sicily. This however was the last direct military contribution which the Greek guerrillas made to the war, and henceforward the scene was dominated by the struggle to gain political power at the end of hostilities.

Political quarrels hampered guerrilla warfare, and we soon found ourselves in a complicated and disagreeable situation. It was becoming clear that there were three divergent elements: E.L.A.S., now numbering twenty thousand men, and predominantly under Communist control; the Zervas bands, known as E.D.E.S., totalling five thousand; and the Royalist politicians, grouped in Cairo or in London round the King, to whom we had a special obligation as the head of a state which had fought as our Ally in 1941. All now thought that the Allies would probably win the war, and the struggle among them for political power began in earnest to the advantage of the common foe. In March 1943, a group of prominent politicians in Athens signed a manifesto enjoining the King not to return after the war until a plebiscite had been held. It was important that the King should make clear where he stood. On July 4, therefore, he made a conciliatory broadcast to the Greek people promising that a General Election would be held as soon as the country was liberated and that the Greek Government abroad would resign when it arrived in Athens in order that a broadly based administration could be formed. But opinion inside Greece sought more immediate action. Shortly afterwards, a minor

mutiny took place in the small Greek forces which we had
assembled in the Middle East, where E.A.M. propaganda was
now spreading. In August, a delegation of six leaders from the
main resistance groups in Greece was brought to Cairo, and
they too urged that a plebiscite should be held before the King
returned, and that three places in the exiled Government
should be held by politicians inside Greece. Neither the King
nor his Prime Minister would agree.

While I was in Quebec, I had received the following message
from King George II about these developments:

King of Greece (Cairo) to Prime Minister and   19 Aug. 43
President Roosevelt

On July 4, I declared to my people that after their liberation
they will be invited to determine by means of free election the
form of their Government.

I am now suddenly faced by the most curious situation, of the
unexpected arrival of certain individuals from Greece who are
supposed to represent various guerrilla bands; in addition, a representative of certain old political parties, who wish to press me
to declare that I should return only after a plebiscite which would
decide the form of the future régime. . . . In these circumstances
I would much appreciate your advice as to the policy which would
at this time best serve the cause of Greece and the United Nations.

My present personal inclination is to continue the policy agreed
between us before I left England. I feel very strongly that I should
return to Greece with my troops, even if I left my country after a
short period to work for its national interests among our Allies,
should subsequent developments make it politic for me to do so.

I had minuted on this:

Prime Minister to Foreign Secretary   19 Aug. 43

If substantial British forces take part in the liberation of Greece,
the King should go back with the Anglo-Greek Army. This is much
the more probable alternative. If however the Greeks are strong
enough to drive out the Germans themselves, we shall have a good
deal less to say in the matter. It follows that the King should
demand equal Royalist representation with the Republicans now
proposed. In any case he would make a great mistake to agree in

any way to remain outside Greece while the fighting for the liberation is going on and while conditions preclude the holding of a peaceful plebiscite.

Smuts, who followed Greek fortunes attentively, also sent a prescient comment:

General Smuts to Prime Minister 20 Aug. 43

There appears to be strong suspicion that British Intelligence agents who brought Greek patriots and other party representatives to Cairo are anti-Royalist, and that patriot representatives even have Communist leanings. King George has always been strongly pro-Ally, and sacrificed much for Allied cause, and we have every good reason to stand by him in this crisis. It seems to me sound policy that you should once more make it quite clear to the Greek Government that the United Kingdom Government stands by the King, at least until such time as Greek people, under proper conditions of public tranquillity, are able to decide on their future régime. A plebiscite or General Election on the régime immediately on the Allied occupation of Greece should be ruled out as likely to lead to civil strife, if not to civil war, in the existing bitterness of feeling. Allied administration under military occupation should be continued until public opinion has settled down and safe conditions of public tranquillity have been established. During this interim period of Allied administration, King George and the Royal Family might well return to Greece to lend their moral support and authority to the Allied administration.

I very much fear that, in the inflamed conditions of public feeling, not only in Greece but also in other Balkan countries, chaos may ensue after the Allied occupation unless a strong hand is kept on the local situation. With politics let loose among those peoples, we may have a wave of disorder and wholesale Communism set going all over those parts of Europe. This may even be the danger in Italy, but certainly in Greece and the Balkans. It should therefore be made plain at this stage that we mean to maintain public order and authority under Allied control until the situation is safe for local self-determination. The Greek situation brings matters to a head, and you may now consider it proper to raise this matter with the President, as a very important question of future policy is involved. The Bolshevisation of a broken and ruined Europe remains a definite possibility, to be guarded against by supply of food and work and interim Allied control.

*   *   *   *   *

The Italian surrender in September 1943 affected the whole balance of forces in Greece. E.L.A.S. was able to acquire most of the Italian equipment, including the weapons of an entire division, and thus gained military supremacy. The danger of · a Communist *coup d'état* in the event of German withdrawal, which now became a practical possibility, needed careful attention. On September 29, I sent a minute to the Chiefs of Staff:

Prime Minister to General Ismay,   29 Sept. 43
for C.O.S. Committee

I am in full agreement with the Foreign Secretary in this essentially political question. Should the Germans evacuate Greece, we must certainly be able to send five thousand British troops with armoured cars and Bren gun carriers into Athens. They need have no transport or artillery. The Greek troops in Egypt would accompany them. Their duty would be to give support at the centre to the restored lawful Greek Government. The Greeks would not know how many were coming behind them. There may be some bickering between the Greek guerrilla bands, but great respect will be paid to the British, more especially as the saving of the country from famine depends entirely on our exertions in the early months of liberation. The troops need not be organised to contend with more than rioting in the capital or incursion into the capital from the countryside. . . . Once a stable Government is set up, we should take our departure.

This was the first suggestion that we might be forced to intervene in Greek internal affairs at the moment of liberation.

The pace of events now increased as E.L.A.S. developed its plans to take over political power as soon as the Germans withdrew and before an ordered constitutional Government could be established. During the winter there was little activity against the enemy. In October, E.L.A.S. forces attacked E.D.E.S. (Zervas), and the British Headquarters in Cairo suspended all shipments of arms to the former. Every effort was made by our missions on the spot to limit and bring to an end the civil war which had now broken out in the ruined and occupied country.

*   *   *   *   *

The decisions of the conferences in Cairo and in Teheran indirectly affected the position in Greece. There would never be a major Allied landing there, nor was it likely that any considerable British forces would follow a German retreat. The arrangements to prevent anarchy had therefore to be considered. The one figure presented to us above party rancour was Damaskinos, Archbishop of Athens. While in Cairo, Mr. Eden had impressed on the King the advantages of a temporary regency. At the same time we hoped by sending the Greek Brigade in the Middle East to fight in Italy to raise the prestige of the exiled Government, and also to have loyal troops to send into Western Greece if need be.

The King would not agree to a regency and returned to London. By now E.A.M., with its military component E.L.A.S., had formed a state within a state in the mountains of Central and Northern Greece. In February 1944, British officers succeeded in establishing an uneasy truce between E.L.A.S. and E.D.E.S. But the Soviet armies were now on the borders of Rumania. The chances of a German evacuation of the Balkans increased, and with them the possibilities of a return of the Royal Government, with British support. Assuming that both these events might take place in April, the E.A.M. leaders decided to act.

On March 26, a Political Committee of National Liberation was set up in the mountains, and the news broadcast to the world. This was a direct challenge to the future authority of the Tsouderos Government. An alternative Communist-controlled administration was thus formed as a rallying-point for all Greeks. This was the signal for trouble in the Greek armed forces in the Middle East and in Greek Government circles abroad. On March 31, a group of officers from the Army, Navy, and Air Force called on Tsouderos in Cairo to demand his resignation. Matters had now come to a head, but the Greek King in London did not appreciate their urgency. Mr. Leeper, our Ambassador to the Greek Government located in Cairo, telegraphed on April 6:

I feel I must express myself with some bluntness. The King of

Greece is playing with fire. He is endangering not only the interests of the Monarchy but those of his country by not realising in time the rapid trend of events. . . . E.A.M. have realised the danger to them of a united front between politicians in Athens and the Greek Government in Cairo. They have realised that the outcome of an agreement would be the reinforcement of the Government here and the end of their experiment to set up a separate Government in the mountains. They have therefore used the interval to strike at the Greek Government by subverting the Greek forces. Their agitation has had some success, and within the next few days it may have more. M. Tsouderos finds himself in a dilemma. He had secured a good basis of collaboration with his colleagues as a result of messages of support from the Archbishop and politicians in Athens, but this agreement was based on his being able to induce the King to sign a constitutional act appointing the Archbishop as regent. Some weeks have now passed, during which time M. Tsouderos has received no final reply from the King, but merely a preliminary view from him of a negative character. This he concealed from his colleagues in order to avoid an explosion. . . . The situation could have been held but for recent E.A.M. agitation in the Army.

Later in the day M. Tsouderos resigned and recommended M. Venizelos, the Minister of Marine in his Government, as his successor. On April 4, disorders broke out in the Greek Army, the 1st Brigade of which I was hoping could take part in the Italian campaign. On the 5th, the office of the Greek Provost-Marshal in Cairo was occupied by a hundred mutineers, who had to be surrounded by British troops and Egyptian police and were removed without trouble in lorries to an isolation camp. At Alexandria, a leader of the Greek seamen's union had barricaded himself in his house with thirty supporters, and was defying the police. Five ships of the Royal Hellenic Navy declared themselves in favour of a republic and demanded the resignation of every member of the existing Government. All the members of the Greek Government tendered their resignations to the King, but agreed to remain in office pending acceptance.

*   *   *   *   *

I was at this time in charge of the Foreign Office, owing to Mr. Eden's absence. I thus had all the threads directly in my hands. I had sent the following to the Supreme Allied Commander in the Mediterranean:

Prime Minister to General Wilson;   5 Apr. 44
repeated to General Alexander

It is now more than three months since we agreed that a Greek brigade, if necessary without its vehicular equipment, should be sent from Egypt to Italy to take part in the Allied offensive. I am told that one company has already got there, and that the others will be there during the month. Why is there all this delay and difficulty in moving this handful of men? They are very liable in Egypt to be contaminated by revolutionary and Communist elements there. Satan finds some mischief still for idle hands to do. Now do please try to get them shipped off out of Egypt as soon as possible and assembled in some suitable town in Southern Italy. I feel this small matter, which has large political significance, ought not to have hung fire so long.

I also sent the following message to M. Tsouderos on April 6: "I was much shocked to hear of your resignation, which seems to leave Greece forlorn at a moment of peril for her national life. The King, whom I have just seen, tells me he has not accepted your resignation. He is coming out to Alexandria next week. Surely you can await his arrival."

The situation in the Greek Army and Navy had by now further deteriorated, and Venizelos announced that he could no longer accept office. M. Tsouderos replied on April 7: "I shall remain at my post, as the laws of Greece require and as you desire, until this present crisis has found lawful solution. If the King waits until he returns to Egypt before he resolves this crisis, I fear that by that time there may be no longer any opportunity of resolving it."

Mr. Leeper telegraphed to the Foreign Office on April 7:

"What is happening here among the Greeks is nothing less than a revolution.

"It is under such conditions that a makeshift Greek Government in exile, suffering from all the weakness which that im-

542 TEHERAN TO ROME

plies, has been trying to cope with the situation. It has failed
completely, but has been handicapped by being able to make
no legal change without the sanction of the King at a distance. . . ."

Our Ambassador hoped however that the situation could be
settled in Cairo without the King's presence. "The King of
Greece's return here at present would certainly provoke fresh
trouble. Tsouderos and all his colleagues are strongly of this
opinion. He would find himself isolated and unable to do anything, and would be a grave embarrassment to us." He asked
the Foreign Office to do everything in their power to stop his
return. "In the circumstances in which we are living here at
the moment, the advice of people on the spot should, I submit,
be accepted. My views are shared by everybody here."

*   *   *   *   *

The King of Greece came to luncheon with me in London
on this day. I showed him the Ambassador's telegram without
comment. He said he would go to Cairo at once. I thought he
was quite right.

Prime Minister to Mr. Leeper   7 Apr. 44

I have discussed the situation with the King. He is resolved to
return to Cairo, leaving by air Sunday evening, and notwithstanding your telegram (which I have shown the King) I consider he is
right to do so. If, as you say, what is happening in Cairo is a
Greek revolution, I cannot advise him to stay away and allow
the issue to be decided in his absence. . . . All local Greek politicians and agitators should at the same time be warned that we
shall not hesitate to take adequate measures of security to prevent
agitation and demonstrations which might threaten law and order
in Egypt and the position and authority of the King and the Greek
Government. . . . You should inform M. Tsouderos that I count
on him to remain at his post until the present crisis has found a
lawful solution. . . .

This is an occasion for you to show those qualities of im-
perturbability and command which are associated with the British
Diplomatic Service.

And the next day I added:

Prime Minister to Mr. Leeper 8 Apr. 44

Weather permitting, the King will leave Sunday night. Meanwhile, it is M. Tsouderos' duty to stand to his post. Of course, if he can get M. Sophocles Venizelos to stay with him, all the better. When the King arrives, the British Security Service must ensure his personal safety. He may require a few days to make up his mind, and must on no account be hustled. I am asking the military commanders to move the Greek Brigade as fast as possible to Italy. They will of course weed out recalcitrant elements. In the same way the Admiral is expected to preserve the discipline of all ships under his command, using no more force than is necessary.

For you yourself there is a great opportunity. You should stick to the line I have marked out and not be worried about the consequences. You speak of living on the lid of a volcano. Wherever else do you expect to live in times like these? Please however be careful to follow very exactly the instructions you are receiving from me, namely, first in priority, order and discipline to be maintained in the armed forces; secondly, the safety of the King's person to be ensured; thirdly, every effort to be made to induce Tsouderos to hold office till the King returns and has had time to look around; fourthly, try to get Venizelos to remain with Tsouderos; fifthly, celebrate Easter Sunday in a manner pious and becoming.

*   *   *   *   *

On April 8, a Greek destroyer refused to obey orders to proceed to sea unless a Government was formed which would include E.A.M. representatives. The mutinous Greek Brigade had taken up defensive positions round their camp, and trouble was expected in the small Greek Air Force units as well. I was forced to give up my hopes of getting the Greek Brigade sent to Italy. Later, I telegraphed to General Paget, who commanded the British forces in Egypt:

Prime Minister to General Paget 8 Apr. 44

A mutinous brigade threatening its officers should certainly be surrounded and forced to surrender by stoppage of all supplies. Why do you leave out water? Will this not bring the desired result quicker? Obviously, these troops should be disarmed. I agree that the hope of getting them to Italy may have to be abandoned. Keep me fully informed of plans for disarming. We cannot tolerate political revolutions carried out by foreign military formations for which we are ultimately responsible. In all cases large numbers of British troops should be used so as to overawe, and thus minimise bloodshed.

I also sent Mr. Leeper a full statement of our policy for use with the Greeks.

Prime Minister to Mr. Leeper   9 Apr. 44

Our relations are definitely established with the lawfully constituted Greek Government headed by the King, who is the ally of Britain and cannot be discarded to suit a momentary surge of appetite among ambitious *émigré* nonentities. Neither can Greece find constitutional expression in particular sets of guerrillas, in many cases indistinguishable from banditti, who are masquerading as the saviours of their country while living on the local villagers. If necessary, I shall denounce these elements and tendencies publicly in order to emphasise the love Great Britain has for Greece, whose sufferings she shared in a small measure, being, alas, not then armed as we are now. Our only desire and interest is to see Greece a glorious, free nation in the Eastern Mediterranean, the honoured friend and ally of the victorious Powers. Let all therefore work for this objective, and make it quite clear that any failure in good conduct will not be overlooked.

I had been working very hard to arrange the movement of the Greek Brigade into Italy. Here they might still take part in the entry into Rome which is to be expected during the summer. This brigade, the 1st Greek Brigade, representatives of the army which had beaten back the Italian invader and were only felled by the treacherous and brutal intervention of the German hordes, had and still has the chance of raising the name of Greece high in the world. It is a lamentable fact that they should have signallised this opportunity by an undignified, even squalid, exhibition of indiscipline, which many will attribute to an unworthy fear of being sent to the front.

In the same way the Greek Navy, which is full of daring seamen and is playing a worthy part upholding its country's good name, should not suddenly have tried to meddle with politics and presume to dictate a constitution to the Greek people. I believe that both of these two forces can be brought back to a high sense of national honour and duty if courageous leadership is forthcoming, backed by overwhelming force in reserve.

All the time I have been planning to place Greece back high in the counsels of the victorious nations. Witness how we have included them in the Italian Advisory Council and tried to send a brigade to take part in the impending victories in Italy. Greeks who are in safety in Egypt under our protection, equipped with our vessels or armed with our weapons or otherwise in security under the military authority of the British Commander-in-Chief Middle East, will place themselves in an abject and shameful position before all history if they allow their domestic feuds to mar their performance of the solemn duties to their country of which they have become the heirs. They may easily, by selfish, excitable behaviour, reduce Greece to a country without expression either at home or abroad, and their names will be stained as long as history is written.

The King is the servant of his people. He makes no claim to rule them. He submits himself freely to the judgment of the people as soon as normal conditions are restored. He places himself and his Royal House entirely at the disposition of the Greek nation. Once the German invader has been driven out, Greece can be a republic or a monarchy, entirely as the people wish. Why then cannot the Greeks keep their hatreds for the common enemy, who has wrought them such cruel injuries and would obliterate them as a free people, were it not for the resolute exertions of the Great Allies?

* * * * *

General Paget now reported to me that, as the 1st Greek Brigade had mutinied against its officers and refused to hand in its arms under specific orders from him, he proposed to take direct action to carry out such orders. I telegraphed on April 9: "These small-scale events are developing rapidly, and I fully concur with the action you are taking. . . . *You will have achieved success if you bring the brigade under control without bloodshed. But brought under control it must be. Count on my support.*"

The Greek Brigade was now surrounded by superior British forces. Its strength was forty-five hundred men, with over fifty guns, which were all deployed in defensive positions against us. On April 12, I sent further directions to Mr. Leeper and all others concerned:

Prime Minister to Mr. Leeper (Cairo)   12 Apr. 44

There can be no question of making terms with mutineers about political matters. They must return to their duty unconditionally. They must submit to be disarmed unconditionally. It would be a great pity to give any assurances about the non-punishment of ringleaders. . . . The question of clemency would rest with the King. Let me know how this stands before taking any decisive action.

And further:

Prime Minister to Mr. Leeper   14 Apr. 44
and all Principals concerned (Cairo)

Surely you should let lack of supplies work its part both in the camp and the harbour before resorting to firing. You should use the weapon of blockade to the full and defend yourselves against attempts to break out. Do not worry too much about the external effects. Do not show yourself overeager to parley. Simply keep them rounded up by artillery and superior force and let hunger play its part. On no account accept any assistance from American or Russian sources, otherwise than as specially enjoined by me. You have ample force at your disposal and plenty of time. It is much more important that the [mutineers] should be reduced to proper discipline than that any particular Greek Government should be set up. It would even be harmful if a brigade and a flotilla had been permitted to meddle in political issues.

My latest information reports that the situation of the Greek Brigade shows signs of improving and that they have finished their rations. You should take full advantage of these tendencies and keep me informed.

And the next day:

Prime Minister to Mr. Leeper   15 Apr. 44

Do not be influenced by possible anti-British sentiment among the local Greeks. It would be a great mistake to end this grave business up in a pleasant kiss all round. That might come later as an act of clemency from the King and his new Government. We have got to get these men into our hands disarmed, without conditions, and I trust without bloodshed.

* * * * *

Meanwhile, the King had arrived in Cairo, and on April 12 had issued a proclamation stating that a representative Government composed largely of Greeks from within Greece would be formed. The next day Venizelos took office in succession to Tsouderos, and steps were taken in secret to bring out representatives from metropolitan Greece.

I now reported the whole position to President Roosevelt, who was sympathetic to my view and to King George of Greece.

Prime Minister to President Roosevelt   16 Apr. 44

The outbreak in the Greek Army and Navy followed closely on the establishment in the mountains of Greece of the Political Committee sponsored by E.A.M., and there is little doubt that the extremist elements, who have long been working to subvert the allegiance of the Greek forces to their legitimate King and Government, seized on this as a Heaven-sent opportunity for open and violent action. The dissident elements are undoubtedly opposed to the King and in favour of a republic, but throughout the disturbances there have been almost no direct attacks on the King's personal position, and the only specific demand put forward is that the Greek Government should take immediate and effective steps to recognise and associate with themselves the Political Committee in Greece.

This crisis came at a particularly unfortunate moment, since M. Tsouderos had already sent an invitation to a number of moderate politicians in Athens urging them to come to Cairo to join the Government. He had also invited representatives of E.A.M., the Communist-controlled organisation which has created and now dominates the Political Committee. Tsouderos was thus doing everything in his power to create a truly representative Greek Government.

In this programme he had the support of his colleagues, and they appear to have had no hand in provoking the disturbances in the Greek forces. But they were extremely jealous of Tsouderos' position, and used the trouble in the Greek Army, which was at first on a small scale, to get rid of him. Feeling that he had lost control of the situation, Tsouderos resigned and proposed Venizelos for the Premiership. The trouble in the Greek Army rapidly spread to the Navy, and assumed the proportions of a full-scale mutiny in both forces. The politicians in Cairo realised that the matter had gone beyond one of personal rivalries or ambitions, and their only thought was to find some candidate for the Premiership sufficiently notorious for his Left Wing views to be acceptable to the mutinous element in the forces.

The King of Greece was reluctant to accept a new Government whose composition was in effect dictated by the mutineers. He considered that order in the Greek armed forces must be restored before any lawful reconstruction of the Government could be undertaken. I entirely agreed with him, and instructed our Ambassador to the Greek Government to do his utmost to induce the Greek Ministers to remain at their posts until the King could get back to Cairo and take stock of the situation. This, I am glad to say, they agreed to do. I also gave instructions to the military authorities in the Middle East to deal firmly with indiscipline in the Greek forces under their command. Order in the Greek Army and Navy has not been completely reestablished, but the dissident elements are being isolated, and once the ringleaders are under arrest the mutiny should rapidly subside.

The King of Greece has now reached Cairo, and, after studying the position for himself, has formed a Government under M. Venizelos.

The President sent me the following most helpful message:

President Roosevelt to Prime Minister   18 Apr. 44

Thank you for the information regarding recent difficulties encountered in Greek participation in our Allied effort.

I join with you in a hope that your line of action toward the problem may succeed in bringing the Greeks back into the Allied camp and to a participation against the barbarians that will be worthy of traditions established by the heroes of Greek history. Frankly, as one whose family and who personally has contributed by personal help to Greek independence for over a century, I am unhappy over the present situation, and hope that Greeks everywhere will set aside pettiness and regain their sense of proportion. Let every Greek think of their glorious past and show a personal unselfishness which is so necessary now. You can quote me if you want to in the above sense.

Prime Minister to President Roosevelt   18 Apr. 44

Thank you so much. I have told our people to make use of your
message to the King and his new Ministers, and to read it to the
mutinous brigade and recalcitrant ships. It may have a most salu-
tary effect.

*   *   *   *   *

As matters reached a climax at Alexandria, I telegraphed to
the Naval Commander-in-Chief:

17 Apr. 44

You should leave the senior member of the *Averoff*[1] in no doubt
that his guarantee that the use of firearms will be avoided will not
be reciprocated by us. We shall fire on mutineers whenever it is
necessary. No officers or sailors of the Greek Navy have the slightest
right to meddle in the formation of the new Government. Their
duty is to obey the orders they receive from the Greek Government
recognised by the Great Allies.

The mutiny in the Greek Brigade was also approaching a
crisis.

Prime Minister to General Paget   22 Apr. 44

If you find it necessary to open fire on the mutineers' camp you
should consider whether you might not start with a few ranging
shots directed on their batteries which are aiming at you. If they
make no reply, after an appropriate interval let them have a
stiffer dose, and at the same time tell them the weight of fire which
you are ready to direct on them if they persist. We are prepared
to use the utmost force, but let us avoid slaughter if possible. It
is proposed that the onus should lie to the account of the British
rather than of the slender, tottering Greek Government.

I received by return the following reply:

General Paget to Prime Minister   23 Apr. 44

My plan is in line with your suggestions. In order to get close
observation of their camp, we must first capture two Greek posts
on high ground. This will be done, by infantry only, just before

[1] The Greek cruiser.

dawn. When it is light, we will lay a smoke-screen over their camp for ten minutes. Then there will be a pause for the smoke to clear away, after which leaflets will be dropped. They will state that there will be a further smoke-screen for half an hour, under cover of which all who wish should leave camp and come over to our lines. If mutineers are still holding out after this, a few shells will be fired at one of their batteries, followed by a further pause to allow for surrender. We shall continue this process until all their guns are knocked out. If the mutineers still will not surrender, it will be necessary to make an infantry assault on the camp under covering fire from artillery and tanks; but tanks will be used in sniping rôle and will not advance into the camp, as the mutineers are known to be well supplied with anti-tank weapons. They are undoubtedly now very short of food, but they have managed to get some from the local Arabs. It has not proved possible to invest the camp closely enough to stop this.

On the evening of the same day, the mutinous Greek ships were boarded by loyal Greek sailors, and with about fifty casualties the mutineers were collected and sent ashore. General Paget now hoped to obtain the surender of the Greek Brigade by parley and without bloodshed. The handling of the affair was completely successful, and I was able to inform President Roosevelt the next day that British troops had occupied key positions on the ridge overlooking the Greek camp after slight opposition. There were no Greek casualties, but one British officer was killed. The Greek Brigade surrendered and laid down its arms, and was evacuated to a prisoner-of-war cage, where the ringleaders were arrested. The naval mutineers had surrendered unconditionally twenty-four hours earlier.

To General Paget I said: "I congratulate you on the satisfactory outcome of your firm and well-devised action."

The President shared my relief:

President Roosevelt to Prime Minister   26 Apr. 44

I am very pleased indeed by your success in handling the Greek naval and military mutiny. I will hope for a similar success in your efforts with the Egyptian political problem. Our prospects of assisting "Overlord" by vigorous action in Italy do look much

better with a fixed date upon which we may exert all our pressure
against the enemy. In view of our postponement of "Anvil," a real
success in Italy now seems essential.

Everything goes well here in my vacation residence. The doctor
agrees with me that I am better.

*   *   *   *   *

We had also kept the Russians informed of these events, both
by messages to Molotov and through the Soviet Embassy in
Cairo. The Soviet Government confined itself to criticism of
our actions, and when on May 5 a formal request to Russia for
co-operation in Greek affairs was made in Moscow, the reply
was that it would be improper to join in any public pronounce-
ments on political matters in Greece.

*   *   *   *   *

With the end of the mutiny, the question of the formation
of a Greek Government became acute. It was not felt that
Venizelos was suitable for this task, and the leader of the Greek
Social Democratic Party, Papandreou, who had been specially
brought out of Greece, took office on April 26. The following
day he issued a proclamation which was to form the agenda for
a conference of all parties, including leaders from the Greek
mountains. These delegates met at a mountain resort in the
Lebanon on May 17, where it was agreed, after a fierce debate
lasting three days, to set up an administration in Cairo in which
all groups would be represented under the Premiership of
Papandreou, while in the mountains of Greece a united military organisation would continue to struggle against the Germans. This arrangement held promise for the future.

On May 24 came the announcement of the new Greek Government. I reported these events to the House of Commons
on the same day:

After prolonged discussion complete unity was reached at the
Lebanon Conference, and all parties will be represented in the
new Government, which will devote itself to what is after all the
only purpose worthy of consideration, namely, the formation of a

National Army in which all the guerrilla bands will be incorporated, and the driving, with this army, of the enemy from the
country, or, better still, destroying him where he stands.

On Monday there was published in the newspapers the very
agreeable letter which I received from the leaders of the [Greek]
Communists and the extreme Left Wing Party. There is published
today in the papers the letter I have received from M. Papandreou
expressing the hopes which he has for the future of his Government, and thanks for the assistance we have given in getting round
these troubles — what I call the diseases of defeat, which Greece
has now a chance of shaking off. I believe that the present situation — I hope and pray that it may be so — indicates that a new
and fair start will come to Greece in her struggle to cleanse her
native soil from the foreign invader. I have therefore to report
to the House that a very marked and beneficial change has occurred in the situation in Greece, which is more than I could say
when I last spoke upon this subject.

Thus this dangerous episode, which, although on a small
scale compared with the vast movement of the war, might have
been the cause of endless discussion detrimental to our affairs,
came to a satisfactory conclusion. I have recorded it in detail
because of the very direct personal responsibility which I assumed. I circulated all my telegrams to the War Cabinet as
they were sent, and my colleagues in no way hampered my freedom of action. It was certainly an achievement that our military commanders were able, by overwhelming force, firmness,
and patience, to quell these political mutinies among such
fiery troops without bloodshed, except for the loss of a single
British officer, Major J. R. Copeland, of the 2d Battalion Rifle
Brigade, who certainly did not die in vain.

The difficulties and struggles which lay before us all in this
nerve-centre of Europe and the world will be recounted in their
proper place. I consider however that, taken by and large, my
policy was vindicated by events; and this is true not only of
the period of the war, but up to the present time of writing.

14

Burma and Beyond

A Retrospect — The United States and Australian Advance in the Pacific — General MacArthur's Four-Hundred-Mile Leap — His Attack on Salamaua, 1943 — Rabaul By-Passed — Admiral Nimitz's Attack on the Gilbert Islands — Admiral Spruance's Attack on Tarawa — A Year of Immense Advance Against Japan — The American Airlift over the Hump — Our Divergence of View — The President's Telegram of February 25 — Successful Opening of the Burma Campaign of 1944 — Japanese Offensive Against India — Wingate's Brilliant Counter-Stroke — He is Killed — The Japanese Attack on Imphal Begins — Defence of Kohima — The Climax of the Battle — All Depends on the Air — General Stilwell Captures Myitkyina — The Struggle Around Imphal — Defeat of the Japanese Advance on India.

T HE READER must now be asked to hark back nearly a year in order that a summary may be presented to him of the war against Japan in the Pacific, which was at this time the main effort of the United States and of the Commonwealth of Australia.

By the latter half of 1943, the Japanese had lost the eastern end of New Guinea. Before he could attack the Philippines, General MacArthur had first to reoccupy all its northern shore. Part of the 41st United States Division worked their way towards Salamaua, and at the end of June other troops landed near it from the sea. They were joined by the 3d Australian Division from Wau, and began their attack on Salamaua. It was purposely deliberate, so as to draw reinforcements from

Lae, the next major objective. The attack on Lae began on
September 4, 1943, when the 9th Australian Division, of Alamein fame, landed on the coast ten miles east of the town.
Next day American parachutists dropped on Nadzab, in the
Markham Valley, and, with the help of Australian pioneers,
rapidly made an airfield. The 7th Australian Division flew
in, and immediately advanced. Attacked from two sides, Lae
was taken on September 16. Salamaua had fallen a few days
before, and Finschhafen fell on October 2. All were fiercely
defended. The Markham Valley, running northwest from Lae,
had many potential airfields, and the 7th Australian Division,
swift to exploit success, occupied its length in a series of airborne assaults. All the operations were well conceived and
skilfully executed, and the co-operation of all three fighting
Services was brought to a high pitch.

The Australian capture of Finschhafen was followed by fierce
Japanese counter-attacks, and there was much fighting during
the last fortnight of October. By mid-November, the 5th Aus-

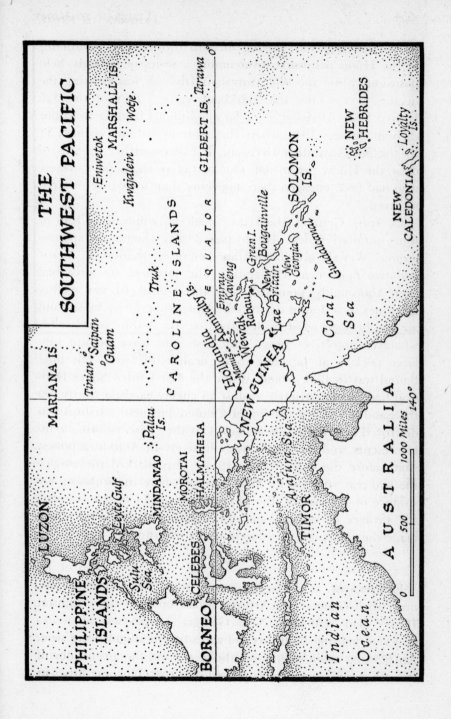

THE
SOUTHWEST PACIFIC

tralian Division was moving forward through the mountains of the Huon peninsula, overcoming a series of strongly held positions, while the 9th Australian Division was clearing the heights overlooking the Markham Valley. Part of the 32d United States Division made an amphibious landing at Saidor early in January 1944, where they were joined on February 11 by the 5th Australian Division. It had taken five months to clear the Huon peninsula. Out of twelve thousand Japanese who had been engaged there not more than forty-two hundred survived.

In April, General MacArthur made an amphibious leap of four hundred miles. He by-passed fifty thousand Japanese around Wewak, and landed an American division at Aitape and two more near Hollandia. The Japanese air force had been thoroughly pounded, and three hundred and eighty machines were found destroyed. Allied superiority by sea and air was henceforward so decisive that MacArthur could select whatever objectives suited him best, and leave behind him large pockets of Japanese to be dealt with later. His final bound was to Biak Island, where the 41st United States Division had a fierce struggle against an enemy garrison nearly ten thousand strong. A convoy of a dozen Japanese warships was destroyed or crippled by air attack as they tried to bring reinforcements, and the island was effectively in American possession before the end of June 1944. This marked the end of the two-year struggle in New Guinea, where the stubborn resistance of the enemy, the physical difficulties of the country, the ravages of disease, and the absence of communications made the campaign as arduous as any in history.

*   *   *   *   *

Farther east, at the beginning of July 1943, and simultaneously with General MacArthur's attack on Salamaua, Admiral Halsey had struck in New Georgia. After several weeks of severe fighting both this and the adjacent islands were won. Air fighting again dominated the scene, and the ascendancy of the American airmen soon proved decisive. Japanese losses in

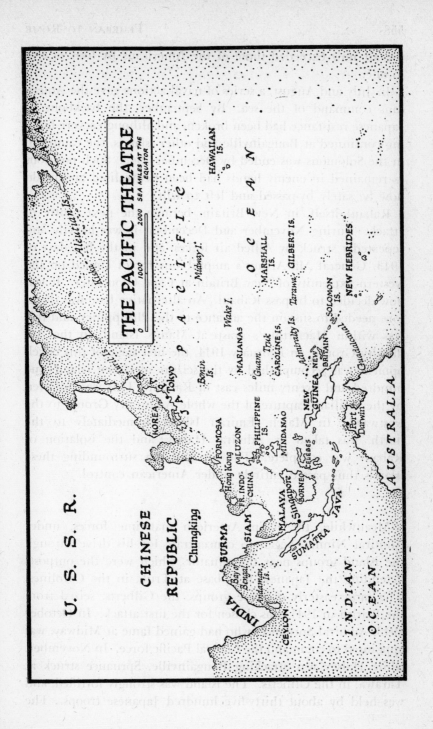

THE PACIFIC THEATRE

0   1000   2000   SEA MILES AT THE
                    EQUATOR

the air now exceeded those of the Americans by four or five to one.

In July and August, a series of naval actions gave the Americans command of the sea. By September, the backbone of Japanese resistance had been broken, and although severe fighting continued at Bougainville and other islands, the campaign in the Solomons was ended by December 1943. Such positions as remained in enemy hands had been neutralised and could now be safely by-passed and left to wilt.

Rabaul itself, in New Britain, became the next centre of attack. During November and December, it was heavily and repeatedly struck by Allied air forces, and in the last days of 1943, General MacArthur's amphibious forces landed on the western extremity of New Britain at Cape Gloucester. It was now decided to by-pass Rabaul. An alternative base was therefore needed to sustain the advance to the Philippines, and this was within MacArthur's grasp at Manus Island, in the Admiralty Group. In February 1944, the first stage of this envelopment was accomplished by the seizure of Green Island, one hundred and twenty miles east of Rabaul. This was followed by the brilliant capture of the whole Admiralty Group, to the westward. In March, Emirau Island, immediately to the north, was taken by Admiral Halsey, and the isolation of Rabaul was complete. The air and sea surrounding these islands thus passed entirely under American control.

*　　*　　*　　*　　*

Meanwhile, the main American maritime forces, under Admiral Nimitz, began to concentrate for his drive through the island groups near the equator, which were the outposts defending the Japanese fleet base at Truk, in the Carolines. The most easterly of these groups, the Gilberts, seized from the British in 1941, was chosen for the first attack. In October 1943, Admiral Spruance, who had gained fame at Midway, was appointed to command the Central Pacific force. In November, while Halsey was attacking Bougainville, Spruance struck at Tarawa, in the Gilberts. The island was strongly fortified, and was held by about thirty-five hundred Japanese troops. The landing by the 2d Marine Division was bitterly contested, in spite of heavy preliminary air attacks. After four fierce days, in which casualties were heavy, the island was captured.

With Tarawa eliminated, the way was clear for attack on the Marshall Group, to the north and west of the Gilberts. In February 1944, they were the object of amphibious operations on the greatest scale yet attempted in the Pacific, and by the end of the month the Americans were victorious. Without pause, Spruance began the next phase of his advance, the softening by air attack of Japanese defences in the Carolines and Marianas. The flexibility of seaborne attack in an ocean area is the most remarkable feature of these operations. While we in Europe were making our final preparations for "Overlord" with immense concentration of force in the narrow waters of the Channel, Spruance's carriers were ranging over huge areas, striking at islands in the Marianas, Palau, and Carolines, deep within the Japanese defensive perimeter, and at the same time helping MacArthur in his attack on Hollandia. On the eve of "Overlord," Japan's strength was everywhere on the wane; her defence system in the Central Pacific had been breached at many points and was ripe for disruption.

Summing up these operations in the Southwest Pacific, General Marshall could report that in a little over twelve months the Allies had "pushed 1300 miles closer to the heart of the Japanese Empire, cutting off more than 135,000 enemy troops beyond hope of rescue."

*   *   *   *   *

The curtain must now rise on a widely different scene in Southeast Asia. For more than eighteen months the Japanese had been masters of a vast defensive arc covering their early conquests. This stretched from the jungle-covered mountains of Northern and Western Burma, where our British and Indian troops were at close grips with them, across the sea to the Andamans and the great Dutch dependencies of Sumatra and Java, and thence in an easterly bend along the string of lesser islands to New Guinea.

The Americans had established a bomber force in China

which was doing good work against the enemy's sea communications between the mainland and the Philippines. They wanted to extend this effort by basing long-range aircraft in China to attack Japan itself. The Burma Road was cut, and they were carrying all supplies for them and the Chinese armies by air over the southern spurs of the Himalayas, which they called "the Hump."

This was a stupendous task. I had always advocated air aid to China and the improvement of the air route and protection of the airfields, but I hoped this might be done by forces essentially airborne and air-sustained on the Wingate model, but on a larger scale. The wish of the Americans to succour China, not only by an ever-increasing air-lift, but also by land, led to heavy demands upon Britain and the Indian Empire. They pressed as a matter of the highest urgency and importance the making of a motor road from their great air starting-point at Ledo through five hundred miles of jungles and mountains into Chinese territory. Only one narrow-gauge, single-line railway ran through Assam to Ledo. It was already in constant use for many other needs, including the supply of the troops who held the frontier positions; but in order to build the road to China, the Americans wanted us to reconquer Northern Burma first and quickly.

*   *   *   *   *

Certainly we favoured keeping China in the war and operating air forces from her territory, but a sense of proportion and the study of alternatives were needed. I disliked intensely the prospect of a large-scale campaign in Northern Burma. One could not choose a worse place for fighting the Japanese. Making a road from Ledo to China was also an immense, laborious task, unlikely to be finished until the need for it had passed. Even if it were done in time to replenish the Chinese armies while they were still engaged, it would make little difference to their fighting capacity. The need to strengthen the American air bases in China would also, in our view, diminish as Allied advances in the Pacific and from Australia gained us

airfields closer to Japan. On both counts therefore we argued
that the enormous expenditure of man-power and material
would not be worth while. But we never succeeded in deflect-
ing the Americans from their purpose. Their national psychology is such that the bigger the Idea, the more wholeheartedly
and obstinately do they throw themselves into making it a
success. It is an admirable characteristic, provided the Idea is
good.

We of course wanted to recapture Burma, but we did not
want to have to do it by land advances from slender communications and across the most forbidding fighting country imag-
inable. The south of Burma, with its port of Rangoon, was
far more valuable than the north. But all of it was remote from
Japan, and for our forces to become side-tracked and entangled
there would deny us our rightful share in a Far Eastern victory. I wished, on the contrary, to contain the Japanese in
Burma, and break into or through the great arc of islands
forming the outer fringe of the Dutch East Indies. Our whole
British-Indian Imperial Front would thus advance across the
Bay of Bengal into close contact with the enemy, by using
amphibious power at every stage. This divergence of opinions,
albeit honestly held and frankly discussed, and with decisions
loyally executed, continued. It is against this permanent background of geography, limited resources, and clash of policies
that the story of the campaign should be read.

*   *   *   *   *

The Washington standpoint was clearly set forth to me by
the President.

President Roosevelt to Prime Minister   25 Feb. 44
My Chiefs of Staff are agreed that the primary intermediate objective of our advance across the Pacific lies in the Formosa-China
coast-Luzon area. The success of recent operations in the Gilberts
and Marshalls indicates that we can accelerate our movements
westward. There appears to be a possibility that we can reach the
Formosa-China-Luzon area before the summer of 1945. From the
time we enter this vital zone until we gain a firm lodgment in this

area, it is essential that our operations be supported by the maximum air power that can be brought to bear. This necessitates the greatest expansion possible of the air strength based on China.

I have always advocated the development of China as a base for the support of our Pacific advances, and now that the war has taken a greater turn in our favour, time is all too short to provide the support we should have from that direction.

It is mandatory therefore that we make every effort to increase the flow of supplies into China. This can only be done by increasing the air tonnage or by opening a road through Burma.

Our occupation of Myitkyina will enable us immediately to increase the air-lift to China by providing an intermediate air-transport base as well as by increasing the protection of the air route.

General Stilwell is confident that his Chinese-American Force can seize Myitkyina by the end of this dry season, and once there, can hold it, provided Mountbatten's 4th Corps from Imphal secure the Shwebo Monywa area. I realise this imposes a most difficult task, but I feel that with your energetic encouragement Mountbatten's commanders are capable of overcoming the many difficulties involved.

The continued build-up of Japanese strength in Burma requires us to undertake the most aggressive action within our power to retain the initiative and prevent them from launching an offensive that may carry them over the borders into India. . . . I most urgently hope therefore that you back to the maximum a vigorous and immediate campaign in Upper Burma.

*   *   *   *   *

The campaign had been opened in December, when General Stilwell, with two Chinese divisions, organised and trained by himself in India, crossed the watershed from Ledo into the jungles below the main mountain ranges.[1] He was opposed by the renowned Japanese 18th Division, but forged ahead steadily, and by early January had penetrated forty miles, while the road-makers toiled behind him. In the south, the British XVth Corps, under General Christison, began their advance down the Arakan coast on January 19. At the same time the Allied air forces redoubled their efforts, and, with the aid of

1 See map, "Burma."

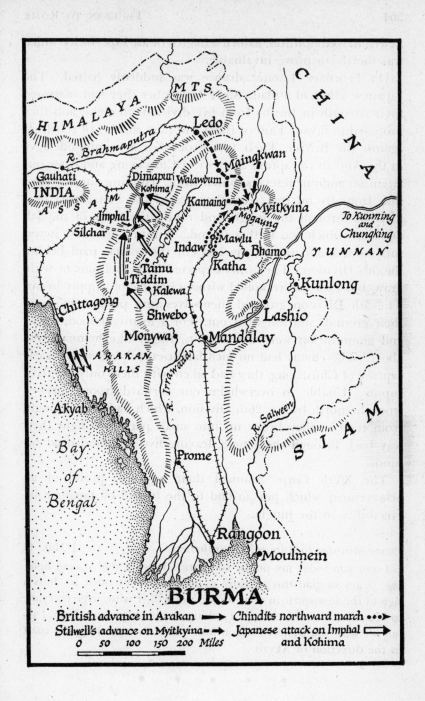

BURMA

British advance in Arakan ➡
Stilwell's advance on Myitkyina ⇢
Chindits northward march ••••➤
Japanese attack on Imphal and Kohima ⟹

0   50   100   150   200 Miles

newly arrived Spitfires, gained a degree of air superiority which
was shortly to prove invaluable.

On February 4, our advance was suddenly halted. The
Japanese also had a plan. Since November they had increased
their strength in Burma from five divisions to eight, and they
proposed to invade Eastern India and raise the flag of rebellion
against the British. Their first stroke was a counter-offensive
in the Arakan to capture the port of Chittagong and draw our
attention and our reserves to that front. Holding our 5th Division frontally on the coast, they passed the better part of a
division through the jungle and round the flank of the 7th
Division, which was farther inland. Within a few days it was
surrounded, and the enemy had cut the coastal road behind
the 5th Division. They fully expected both divisions to withdraw, but they had reckoned without one factor, supply by air.
The 5th Division grouped themselves into perimeters, stood
their ground, and fought it out. For a fortnight food, water,
and ammunition were delivered to them, like manna, from
above. The enemy had no such facilities; relying on the early
capture of Chittagong, they had taken with them only ten days'
supply. Unable to overwhelm our forward troops, pressed
from the north by our 26th Division, which had been brought
from reserve, they broke up into small parties to fight their
way back through the jungle, leaving five thousand dead behind.

The XVth Corps resumed their advance, proud of an
achievement which put an end to the legend of Japanese in-
vincibility in the jungle.

Prime Minister to Admiral Mountbatten   1 Mar. 44

I sent you today my public congratulations on the Arakan fighting. I am so glad this measure of success has attended it. It is a
sign of the new spirit in your forces, and will, I trust, urge everyone
to keep closer to the enemy. Looking at the maps from here, I do
not see why you should not continue your advance along the coast
in the direction of Akyab

*   *   *   *   *

In early March, there were sure signs that the enemy were
also preparing an attack on the central front against Imphal,
thereby forestalling our own projected advance to the Chind-
win. The now famous Chindit [2] operation was a part of our
offensive plan. Although it was clear that the Japanese would
get their blow in first, it was decided that Wingate's brigades
should carry on with their task. This was principally to cut
the enemy's communications near Indaw, thereby dislocating
their supply system, and notably that of the Japanese 18th
Division, with whom Stilwell was at close grips. The enemy
would moreover be forced to detach troops to deal with the
menace behind his fighting front. One Chindit brigade, the
16th British, had already started on February 5 from Ledo.
They marched across four hundred and fifty miles of mountain
and jungle and were supplied solely from the air.

On March 5, sustained by an American "Air Commando"
of two hundred and fifty machines, the fly-in of the 77th and
111th Brigades, British and Gurkha troops, began. After assembly at their rallying-points, they set out upon their task and
cut the railway north of Indaw.

I sent a full account of all this to the President.

Prime Minister to President Roosevelt   14 Mar. 44

I feel you will be interested to hear about the flying-in of two
of Wingate's Long-Range Penetration Brigades. Landing-strips in
two areas were selected from which the brigades could advance
westward, primarily to interrupt the Japanese lines of communication, and so assist the American-Chinese operations taking place
farther north. The strips were a hundred miles inside enemy territory and two hundred and sixty-six miles from the transport base.

The first landings were made by gliders, whose occupants then
prepared the strips to receive transport aircraft. Between March 6
and March 11 seventy-five hundred men, with all their gear and
with mules, were successfully landed. The only losses were a number of the gliders, and some of these should be repairable. The
brigades have now started their advance, but a small holding party
has been left at one of the strips to receive a flight of Spitfires and a

2 "Chindit," the familiar name for Wingate's Long-Range Penetration Force.

squadron of Hurricane fighter-bombers which were to fly in to protect the base and provide air support.

The only serious mishap occurred on the first night. One of the strips in the northern area was found to have been obstructed by the Japanese, and the surface of the remaining strip was much worse than was expected, causing crashes which blocked the strip and prevented further landings that night. A few of the gliders had to be turned back in the air, and failed to reach our territory. Another strip was immediately prepared in this area, and was ready for landing two days later. The total of killed, wounded, and missing is at most one hundred and forty-five.

The operation appears to have been a complete surprise for the Japanese. There has been no enemy air action against the strips in the northern area, and the one in the south was only bombed on March 10 after our men had left it. As it happened, the enemy were concentrating aircraft at airfields in the Mandalay area as part of their own plans. In consequence the strong air forces we had collected to protect the landings had a very good bag, and in two days destroyed sixty-one enemy aircraft for the loss of only three of our own.

We are all very well pleased that Wingate's venture has started so well, and the success of this flying-in operation augurs well for the future. Your men have played an important part both in the transport squadrons and in the supporting air operations.

"I am thrilled," replied Roosevelt the next day, "by the news of our success under Wingate. If you wire him, please give him my hearty good wishes. May the good work go on. This marks an epic achievement for the airborne troops, not forgetting the mules."

Wingate did not live long to enjoy this first success or to reap its fruits. On March 24, to my great distress, he was killed in the air. He insisted on starting. The facts are unknown. Probably the pilot lost his way in thick weather. The aircraft crashed into a hillside, and when a rescue party arrived none were alive. With him a bright flame was extinguished.

*   *   *   *   *

On March 8, three Japanese divisions began their expected

attack on our central front. General Scoones withdrew his
IVth Corps, also of three divisions, to the Imphal plateau, so
as to fight concentrated on more open ground. If the enemy
cut the road to the railhead at Dimapur, he would have to
depend upon the air until the battle was won. The Japanese
repeated the hazardous plan they had used with misfortune
in the Arakan. They counted on capturing our stores at Imphal to feed themselves. They also intended to cut, not only
the road to Dimapur, but also the railway, and thus sever the
supply route maintaining Stilwell's force and the United States
air-lift to China. Important issues were therefore at stake.

The key lay again in transport aircraft. Mountbatten's resources, though considerable, were not nearly enough. He
sought to borrow a hundred United States aircraft from the
"Hump" traffic to win the battle. This was a hard requirement
to make or to procure. In the anxious weeks that followed, I
gave him my strongest support. "Chiefs of Staff and I," I told
him, "are backing you up to the full. I have telegraphed to
the President. In my view nothing matters but the battle. Be
sure you win."

By the end of March, the Japanese had cut the road to Dimapur and were pressing hard on the fringes of the Imphal plain
from three sides. The fourth quadrant of the circle was barred
by jungle-covered mountains. Two brigades of the 5th Indian
Division were flown into Imphal from the Arakan, where operations were halted, and the 7th Indian Division was flown into
Dimapur. Thither by rail came the headquarters of the
XXXIIId Corps, under General Stopford, the 2d British Division, an independent Indian brigade, and also the last remaining brigade of Wingate's force.

At Kohima, a roadside village among the hills, the Japanese
northern attack was held. Here the garrison consisted of a
battalion of the Royal West Kent, a Gurkha battalion, and a
battalion of the Assam Regiment, with every man, and even
convalescents from the hospital, who could bear arms. They
were attacked on April 4 by the Japanese 31st Division, slowly
forced back into diminishing area, and finally onto a single

hill. They had no supplies except what was dropped on them
by parachutes. Attacked on every side, they held on stead-
fastly, supported by bombing and cannon-fire from the air,
until they were relieved on the 20th by the leading brigade of
the 2d Division which fought its way up from Dimapur. Four
thousand Japanese were killed. The valiant defence of
Kohima against enormous odds was a fine episode.

*   *   *   *   *

We had the command of the air, but we depended upon
having enough transport planes. The climax came in May.
Sixty thousand British and Indian soldiers, with all their modern equipment, were confined in a circle on the Imphal plain.
I could feel the stress amid all other business. On the principle, "Nothing matters but the battle," I used my authority.

Prime Minister to Admiral Mountbatten   4 May 44
    Let nothing go from the battle that you need for victory. I will
not accept denial of this from any quarter, and will back you to the
full.

Prime Minister to General Ismay, for C.O.S. Committee   9 May 44
    The gap must be filled at all costs, either by delaying the de-
parture of the seventy-nine transport aircraft to the Mediterranean,
or by drawing twenty plus fifty-nine from the Hump, or by a combination of both. We cannot on any account throw away this battle.
I am quite willing to telegraph to the President pointing out to him
the disastrous consequences to his own plans for helping China
which would follow the casting away of this battle.

Prime Minister to General Ismay and General Hollis,   14 May 44
for C.O.S. Committee
    Whatever happens, Admiral Mountbatten is not to send away
the seventy-nine aircraft to the Mediterranean except as they are
replaced in his command by suitable American aircraft either from
United States or the Hump. His argument seems to me unanswerable.
    I have not been given any sufficient reasons to show that General
Alexander's battle will be hampered if the date of the arrival of
these aircraft in the Mediterranean is postponed. General Wilson

has already an overwhelming superiority in the air, and these aircraft are not needed so much for the battle as for amphibious operations following its success, whereas they are vital to the operations proceeding in Burma.

General Hollis should therefore prepare me a short note which I will discuss with him at midnight tonight. Meanwhile, this minute should be brought to the attention of the Chiefs of Staff. I am determined that Mountbatten's battle shall not be ruined by the folly of flying a hundred and fifty aircraft five thousand miles in opposite directions, and I will appeal to the President tomorrow unless I am satisfied that the needs are met.

*   *   *   *   *

Meanwhile, on the northern front Stilwell was making good progress towards the line Mogaung-Myitkyina, against the stubborn resistance of the Japanese 18th Division. He was anxious about his eastern flank, where their 56th Division, along the Chinese frontier, might turn upon him. President Roosevelt persuaded Chiang Kai-shek to send Stilwell another Chinese division, but it was not till April 21 that the Generalissimo agreed to order his troops in Yunnan to advance into Burma. On May 10, four Chinese divisions crossed the Salween at and above Kunlong, thus worrying the Japanese flank.

The Chindits, operating on the enemy communications, had been reinforced in early April by two more brigades, so that five were now in action. They worked northward up the railway, preventing the passage of reinforcements and destroying dumps as they went. But Wingate was no more. The Japanese withdrew nothing from the Imphal front and only one battalion from Stilwell's. They brought their 53d Division from Malaya and tried, without success, to quell the nuisance.

On May 17, Stilwell sprung a surprise both on the Japanese and ourselves by capturing the airfield at Myitkyina by a swift advance of General Merrill's United States brigade. Reinforcements were flown in to assault the town, but the Japanese held it obstinately till early August. At the end of May, Mogaung, Stilwell's other main objective, was invested by the leading Chindit brigade, the 77th, and finally fell to them on June 26. These successes were largely due to Stilwell's leadership, energy, and pertinacity; but his troops were exhausted by their efforts and many had to be withdrawn.

*   *   *   *   *

Around Imphal the situation was still at full strain. Our Air Force was dominant, but the monsoon was hindering the air-supply, on which our success depended. All our four divisions were slowly pushing outward from their encirclement. Along the Kohima road the relieving force and the besieged were fighting their way towards each other. It was a race against time. We marked their progress with tense feelings.

Prime Minister to Admiral Mountbatten   22 June 44

The Chiefs of Staff have expressed anxiety about the situation in Imphal, particularly in respect of reserves of supplies and ammunition. You are absolutely entitled to ask for all aircraft necessary to maintain the situation, whether they come from the Hump or any other source. The Hump must be considered the current reserve, and should be drawn upon whenever necessary. The Americans have by a brilliant feat of arms landed us in Myitkyina, but neither Myitkyina nor Imphal can be held without drawing on the Hump. If you fail to make your demands in good time, invoking me if necessary to help from here, it will be no good complaining afterwards if it is not a success. Keep your hand close on the job, which seems to me both serious and critical. Every good wish.

The finale came while this message was on the way. I quote Admiral Mountbatten's report:

In the third week in June, the situation was critical, and it seemed possible, after all the efforts of the previous two months, that early in July the IV Corps would finally run out of reserves. But on June 22, with a week and a half in hand, the 2d British and 5th Indian Divisions met at a point twenty-nine miles north of Imphal and the road to the plain was open. On the same day the convoys began to roll in.

Mountbatten was justified in adding, "The Japanese bid for India was virtually over, and ahead lay the prospect of the first major British victory in Burma."

15

Strategy Against Japan

The Choice Before Us — My Minute of January 24, 1944 — Arrival of Admiral Mountbatten's Mission — The New Plan — United States Objections — Mountbatten's Mission at Washington — The Main Japanese Fleet Moves to Singapore — Prevention of Amphibious Operations — We No Longer Command the Bay of Bengal — My Telegram to President Roosevelt of March 10 — The President's Reply — I Give a Ruling to the Chiefs of Staff, March 20 — The Decision Accepted.

WHILE THE FIERCE AND CRITICAL FIGHTING by land and air described in the last chapter was raging in Burma and the Pacific, the whole future policy of the conduct of the war against Japan was being hotly debated among ourselves in London, among the Americans in Washington, and between London and Washington. I have already mentioned the report of the Combined Chiefs of Staff at the Cairo Conference on the long-term policy in the Pacific, and the British share in it, and how this had been initialled by the President and me without our being able in the pressure of events to study it, or discuss it together or with our advisers. It was only when at Marrakesh I received a request to transmit a dispatch on the subject to the Dominions that I became aware how far the British Chiefs of Staff had developed their opinions. I found myself immediately in disagreement, and thus arose the only considerable difference which I and the War Cabinet had with our trusted military colleagues.

Briefly, the following choice lay before us: Should we send

571

our naval forces and any troops or air-power we could spare or transport to act with the left flank of the United States forces in the Southwest Pacific, basing ourselves upon Australia? Our Chiefs of Staff thought we should, and they had had no difficulty in reaching agreement with their American comrades in Cairo. On the other hand, I and my colleagues held that we should advance eastward to the Malay Peninsula and the Dutch islands, using India as our base. The Chiefs of Staff contended that, whereas Mountbatten could not carry out amphibious operations on a major scale until six months after a German defeat, their Pacific reinforcement plan, to which they suggested we were committed, could be begun much sooner.

As soon as I got home, I convened a meeting of the Defence Committee, where the whole subject was for the first time effectively examined and thrashed out between us.

A few days later I wrote the following minute:

Prime Minister to General Ismay, for C.O.S. Committee   24 Jan. 44

All my Ministerial colleagues who were present at the meeting on the 19th have spoken to me about the projects then expounded by the Planners in a strongly adverse sense. I myself am not in agreement with these plans, and the issue will have to be debated as between Governments. It must also be remembered that this plan is entirely different from that expounded to us by General MacArthur's Chief of Staff, so that evidently there is a great difference of opinion even among the Americans themselves upon it.

2. No one would object to sending the handful of ships proposed to work with the American Fleet in any June operation they may have in view, and of course we should always be ready to build up a fleet in the Pacific. But no plan of war in these theatres could be considered satisfactory which provided no outlet in 1944/45, before Hitler is defeated, for the very large air and military forces we have standing in India and around the Bay of Bengal.

3. For these forces, the only effectual operation is Sumatra ["Culverin"]. I have long been convinced that this is the most practical manner of drawing off very large numbers of Japanese aircraft, and possibly of troops, or, in the alternative, of regaining important territory and securing bases from which we may strike equally at Singapore, at Bangkok, in the Malacca Straits, and along

the Japanese communications with Burma. My colleagues agree with me in thinking that it is upon this that we should concentrate our efforts, making it clear to the Americans that if we help them in the Pacific, as we shall do, we shall expect them to assist us with a proper supply of landing-craft in time to attack Sumatra in October, November, or December. This they can perfectly well do from the immense new construction of L.S.T.s which will be continuous throughout the year. . . .

4. We must await the arrival of the officers whom Admiral Mountbatten is sending to go into the matter fully with them, and we cannot send any telegrams to the Dominions until we have at least formed our own view.

In mid-February 1944, Mountbatten's Mission arrived, headed by his able American Deputy Chief of Staff, General Wedemeyer. Mountbatten did not believe the American project for a through road from Northern Assam to China could be completed for two-way traffic before June 1946. He therefore advised dropping it and expanding the existing air route instead. If this were done he would not have to recapture so large a part of Northern Burma. With the resources thus released, he wished to penetrate the enemy perimeter of Malaya and the Dutch East Indies, and push rapidly northeastward from base to base along the Asiatic coast. This would open better communication with China by sea, and would be a direct help to the American advances on Japan from the Central Pacific and New Guinea. Sumatra would have to be captured first, and he proposed to do this as soon as amphibious resources were released from Northwest Europe. "Culverin" was thus revived.

This strategy was however opposed to the recommendations which the Combined Chiefs of Staff had agreed upon at Cairo. It raised our differences about long-term policy in an immediate and practical form. Having long been an advocate of the Sumatra enterprise, I liked Mountbatten's new plan. I still believed that the size of the forces considered necessary for Sumatra was excessive, but nevertheless there would be a surplus over the needs of the Burma land campaign, as proposed by Mountbatten, and I was against sending them to play a minor part in MacArthur's operations. In this I was fully supported by the Foreign Office, who thought that the British rôle in the Far East should not be a mere minor contribution to the Americans; this was not likely to appeal to the British people. Moreover, the peoples of Asia were little interested in the Pacific islands as compared with the wide regions which meant most to them. In contrast, the strategy advocated by Southeast Asia Command would have immediate psychological and political effects which would hasten the defeat of Japan.

I was quite sure that American minds would move in a different direction. I was not therefore surprised at a passage in President Roosevelt's telegram to me of February 25, 1944:

I am gravely concerned over the recent trends in strategy that favour an operation toward Sumatra and Malaya in the future rather than to face the immediate obstacles that confront us in Burma. I fail to see how an operation against Sumatra and Malaya, requiring tremendous resources and forces, can possibly be mounted until after the conclusion of the war in Europe. Lucrative as a successful "Culverin" might be, there appears much more to be gained by employing all the resources we now have available in an all-out drive into Upper Burma so that we can build up our air strength in China and ensure the essential support for our westward advance to the Formosa-China-Luzon area.

This did not augur well for the success of Wedemeyer's Mission. They presented themselves in Washington in March to the American Chiefs of Staff. They were not the first in the field. Admiral Mountbatten's Commanders-in-Chief had fully supported his plans, but not so his Deputy, the American General Stilwell. This was understandable, as Stilwell combined the office of Deputy with several others, notably that of Chief of Staff to Chiang Kai-shek. It was not a good arrangement on the part of the Americans, but we had had no option but to consent. Stilwell favoured every measure which might conceivably aid China, and believed that supply by road could begin sooner than Southeast-Asia Command expected. He was entitled to urge his views on Admiral Mountbatten, and when they were not accepted, to represent them with Mountbatten's consent to his superiors in Washington. But he also permitted himself, without Mountbatten's knowledge, to send a mission to Washington to state his case there.

The American Chiefs of Staff had recently decided that though General MacArthur's advance towards the Philippines should continue, the main attack should be made by Admiral Nimitz from the Central Pacific against Formosa. They therefore thought the strategic value of liberating Malaya and the Dutch East Indies would be small and tardy. They saw no need for any attack on Sumatra. Their hearts were still set on flying more supplies to China over the "Hump" and building the Burma Road. They also had a new plan for basing long-range bombers in China to attack Japan, which would need more to supply tonnage than they had so far required. Wedemeyer marshalled the arguments for Mountbatten's proposals with great skill, but he failed to convince his auditors and masters.

*   *   *   *   *

However, at this very time an unexpected event of the first importance occurred. The main Japanese Fleet, including seven battleships, moved from the Central Pacific to Singapore. Their purpose was uncertain. Probably it was chiefly to station them nearer to the oil supplies of the Dutch East Indies; but they might break into the Bay of Bengal. This possibility put a stop for the time being to "Culverin" or other amphibious adventures in Indian waters. We no longer had even local naval superiority. I immediately recognised this unpleasant fact.

Prime Minister to General Ismay, for C.O.S. Committee   7 Mar. 44

The plan for Sumatra was made on the assumption that no considerable detachment would be made from the Japanese main fleet. This was of course pure assumption based on what it would be reasonable for the enemy to do, and there never could be any guarantee that the enemy would not do unreasonable things. However, at that time the Japanese were believed to be concerned in defending Truk and Rabaul and other outposts against the United

States, and in holding themselves in readiness for the possibilities of a fleet action. They have now abandoned any such intentions, if they had them, and, falling back from their outpost line, are able to make defensive dispositions of their fleet which includes the stationing of a strong force at Singapore. While that fleet is there, it is evident that we could not do Sumatra, or anything like it, unless our own naval forces were built up to the point where we should welcome a fleet action. It is very much for the advantage of the United States that the Japanese should be held at Singapore. The longer they are there, the greater the opportunities for Admiral Nimitz to act with freedom and advance with rapidity. How long the Japanese can afford to remain at Singapore depends upon the progress of the American advance. It seems quite certain they will have to reunite their fleet and, having reunited it, will have again to contemplate the idea of a general engagement for the sake of the Philippines or nearer home. The probabilities of their coming back to Singapore, should they leave it, can only be assessed in relation to the situation prevailing at the time. The longer we can detain them in their present position at Singapore, the greater the help we can give the United States. This will be achieved by continued preparations for large amphibious attacks the moment they are forced by the United States main advance to reunite their fleet and withdraw into the Pacific.

2. Make sure this minute is put before the Joint Planners.

Meanwhile, our discussions with our Chiefs of Staff were long and sometimes tense. The policy of helping General MacArthur or Admiral Nimitz depended on what size of force could be based on Australia, and whether on the east or north and west coasts. We had insufficient information, and further investigation was admittedly needed. It would obviously be a very great strain on our shipping. In March, we seemed to have reached a deadlock among ourselves at home. The Chiefs of Staff felt that the Americans were expecting us to send a fleet to the Pacific for operations which might occur in June. I therefore thought it necessary to clear up this point with the President and also to inform him of the whole position.

Prime Minister to President Roosevelt   10 Mar. 44

In the Final Report of the Cairo Conference, the Combined

Chiefs of Staff reported that they had "approved in principle as a basis for further investigation and preparation" an over-all plan for the defeat of Japan. This plan contemplated the dispatch to the Pacific of a detachment of the British Fleet which was provisionally scheduled to become operational in the Pacific in June 1944. Although you and I both initialled the Final Report, neither of us had had the opportunity of going into these matters personally as we were concerned with affairs of more immediate urgency. Since then the War Cabinet and Chiefs of Staff have been "investigating," and we have not so far reached united conclusions. Meanwhile, the Japanese Fleet has arrived at Singapore, which constitutes in my mind a new major fact.

2. After the surrender of the Italian Fleet in September 1943, I was very keen on sending a detachment of our Fleet as quickly as possible to the Pacific, but when I opened this to Admiral King, he explained to me how very strong the United States Navy was already in those waters compared with the Japanese, and I formed the impression that he did not need us very much. I have also seen several telegrams from our naval representatives in Washington which tend to confirm the above impression. On the other hand, I am told that Admiral King has informed the First Sea Lord that he would like to have our detachment, provided it did not arrive until August or September, when its logistic requirements could more easily be met. I am, in the upshot, left in doubt about whether we are really needed this year.

3. Accordingly, I should be very grateful if you could let me know whether there is any specific American operation in the Pacific, (a) before the end of 1944 or (b) before the summer of 1945, which would be hindered or prevented by the absence of a British Fleet detachment.

4. On the other hand, the movement of the Japanese Fleet to Singapore, which coincided *inter alia* with their knowledge of the movement of our battleship squadron into the Indian Ocean, seems to show their sensitiveness about the Andamans, Nicobars, and Sumatra. It would surely be an advantage to you if, by keeping up the threat in the Bay of Bengal, we could detain the Japanese Fleet or a large portion of it at Singapore, and thus secure you a clear field in the Pacific to enable your by-passing process and advance to develop at full speed.

5. General Wedemeyer is able to unfold all Mountbatten's plans

in the Indian theatre and the Bay of Bengal. They certainly seem to fit in with the kind of requests which Chiang Kai-shek was making, which you favoured but which we were unable to make good before the monsoon on account of the Mediterranean and "Overlord" operations. I am personally still of opinion that amphibious action across the Bay of Bengal will enable all our forces and establishments in India to play their highest part in the next eighteen months in the war against Japan. We are examining now the logistics in detail and, *prima facie,* it seems that we could attack with two or three times the strength the islands across the Bay of Bengal and thereafter the Malay peninsula than we could by prolonging our communications about nine thousand miles round the south of Australia and operating from the Pacific side and on your southern flank. There is also the objection of dividing our Fleet and our effort between the Pacific and Indian Oceans and throwing out of gear so many of our existing establishments from Calcutta to Ceylon and way back in the Suez Canal zone.

6. Before however reaching any final conclusions in my mind about this matter, I should like to know what answer you would give to the question I posed in paragraph 3, namely, would your Pacific operations be hindered if, for the present at any rate and while the Japanese Fleet is at Singapore, we kept our centre of gravity in the Indian Ocean and the Bay of Bengal and planned amphibious operations there as resources come to hand.

The President's reply to my direct question was conclusive.

President Roosevelt to Prime Minister   13 Mar. 44

(a) There will be no specific operation in the Pacific during 1944 that would be adversely affected by the absence of a British Fleet detachment. (b) It is not at the present time possible to anticipate with sufficient accuracy future developments in the Pacific to be certain that a British Fleet detachment will not be needed there during the year of 1945, but it does not now appear that such a reinforcement will be needed before the summer of 1945.

In consideration of recent enemy dispositions, it is my personal opinion that unless we have unexpected bad luck in the Pacific your naval force will be of more value to our common effort by remaining in the Indian Ocean.

All of the above estimates are of course based on current conditions and are therefore subject to change if the circumstances change.

* * * * *

Thus fortified upon the distressing controversy in which I and my Cabinet colleagues were engaged with the Chiefs of Staff, I felt it my duty to give a ruling. In this case I addressed myself to each of the Chiefs of Staff personally and not collectively to them as a Committee.

Prime Minister to First Sea Lord, C.I.G.S. and C.A.S.   20 Mar. 44

I have addressed the attached minute to each of the Chiefs of Staff personally.

My question and the President's reply are directed . . . solely to the point as to whether there is any obligation to the American authorities that we send a detachment of the British Fleet to the Pacific before the summer of 1945, and whether their operations would be hampered if we stood out. We now know that there is no obligation and that their operations will not be hampered, also that they will not in any case require our assistance (barring some catastrophe) before the summer of 1945. We are therefore free to consider the matter among ourselves and from the point of view of British interests only.

. . . .

3. The serious nature of the present position has been brought home to me by the reluctance of the Chiefs of Staff to meet with their American counterparts for fear of revealing to the United States their differences from me and my Cabinet colleagues. The Ministers on the Defence Committee are convinced, and I am sure that the War Cabinet would agree if the matter were brought before them, that it is in the interest of Britain to pursue what may be termed the "Bay of Bengal Strategy," at any rate for the next twelve months. I therefore feel it my duty, as Prime Minister and Minister of Defence, to give the following rulings:

   (*a*) Unless unforeseen events occur, the Indian theatre and the Bay of Bengal will remain, until the summer of 1945, the centre of gravity for the British and Imperial war effort against Japan.

(*b*) All preparations will be made for amphibious action across the Bay of Bengal against the Malay peninsula and the various island outposts by which it is defended, the ultimate objective being the reconquest of Singapore.

(*c*) A powerful British Fleet will be built up based on Ceylon, Adu Atoll, and East Indian ports, under the shield of our strong shore-based aircraft. The fleet train for this Eastern Fleet must be developed as fast as possible, subject to the priority needs of "Overlord" and the Mediterranean, and the necessary feeding of this country on its present rations.

(*d*) The plans of Southeast Asia Command for amphibious action across the Bay of Bengal should be examined, corrected, and improved with the desire of engaging the enemy as closely and as soon as possible.

(*e*) The Reconnaissance Mission to Australia should be sent as soon as I have approved the personnel. They should report promptly upon the existing facilities in Australia and on the re-captured islands to the north of it, and propose measures for carrying the Eastern Fleet and its fleet train, with any additions that may be required, into the Southwest Pacific and basing it on Australian ports should we at any time wish to adopt that policy.

4. I should be very ready to discuss the above rulings with the Chiefs of Staff in order that we may be clear in our minds as to the line we are going to take in discussions with our American friends. Meanwhile, with this difference on long-term plans settled, we may bend ourselves to the tremendous and urgent tasks which are now so near and in which we shall have need of all our comradeship and mutual confidence.

These rulings were accepted. Nevertheless, in a scene melting and reshaping so rapidly, I preferred to keep the options open. If the Bay of Bengal were excluded by the pressure of the main Japanese Fleet, means might be found to support General MacArthur's advance by operations on his flank. This plan became known in our circle as the "middle strategy." It aimed at forming a British and Australian task force of all arms under the over-all control of General MacArthur, to assist in the liberation of the East Indies, and at the same time to outflank Singapore from the south. This did not mature.

Happily, the course of events soon changed fundamentally the conditions which prevailed or could be foreshadowed at the Cairo Conference or in the months which followed, and anyhow the war with Japan ended in a manner and at a date which no one dreamed of at the time of the discussions I have described.

16

Preparations for "Overlord"

Hard Memories — The Cross-Channel Plan — The Commanders — The Increased Weight of the Assault — The Mulberry Harbours — Plan for Airborne Attack — Waterproofing of Vehicles — Fire Plans of the Naval Bombardment — My Telegram to General Marshall, March 11 — Training the Troops in Amphibious Operations — D-Day and H-Hour — Final Dispositions and First Objectives — The Navy's Task — The Air Offensive — Deception Devices — The Germans Misled — All Southern England One Vast Camp.

THOUGHT ARISING FROM FACTUAL EXPERIENCE may be a bridle or a spur. The reader of these volumes will be aware that, while I was always willing to join with the United States in a direct assault across the Channel on the German sea-front in France, I was not convinced that this was the only way of winning the war, and I knew that it would be a very heavy and hazardous adventure. The fearful price we had had to pay in human life and blood for the great offensives of the First World War was graven in my mind. Memories of the Somme and Passchendaele and many lesser frontal attacks upon the Germans were not to be blotted out by time or reflection. It still seemed to me, after a quarter of a century, that fortifications of concrete and steel armed with modern fire-power, and fully manned by trained, resolute men, could only be overcome by surprise in time or place by turning their flanks, or by some new and mechanical device like the tank. Superiority of bombardment, terrific as it may be, was no final answer. The defenders could easily have ready other lines behind their first, and the intervening ground which the artillery could conquer would become impassable crater-fields. These were the fruits of knowledge which the French and British had bought so dearly from 1915 to 1917.

Since then new factors had appeared, but they did not all tell the same way. The fire-power of the defence had vastly increased. The development of minefields both on land and in the sea was enormous. On the other hand, we, the attackers, held air supremacy, and could land large numbers of paratroops behind the enemy's front, and above all block and paralyse the communications by which he could bring reinforcements for a counter-attack.

Throughout the summer months of 1943, General Morgan and his Allied inter-Service Staff had laboured at the plan. In a previous chapter I have described how it was presented to me during my voyage to Quebec for the "Quadrant" Conference. There the scheme was generally approved, but there was one feature of it which requires comment. The size and scope of the first assault on the Normandy beaches was necessarily limited by the numbers of landing-craft available. General Morgan's instructions were to plan an assault by three divisions, with two divisions as an immediate follow-up. He accordingly proposed to land the three divisions on the coast between Caen and Carentan. He would have liked to land part of the force north of Carentan, nearer to Cherbourg, but he thought it unwise to divide so small a force. The estuary of the river Vire at Carentan was marshy and it would have been difficult for the two wings of the attack to keep in touch. No doubt he was right. I would certainly have preferred a stronger attack on a broader front, but at that time, ten months before the event, we could not be sure of having enough landing-craft.

It was the absence of important harbours in all this stretch of coast which had impelled Mountbatten's Staff to propose the synthetic harbours. The decisions at Quebec confirmed the need and clarified the issues. I kept in touch with the development of this project, which was pressed forward by a committee of experts and Service representatives, summoned

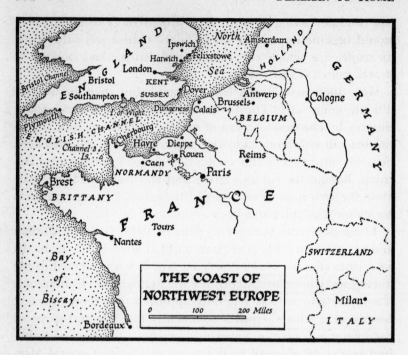

THE COAST OF
NORTHWEST EUROPE

0   100   200 Miles

by Brigadier Bruce White of the War Office, himself an eminent civil engineer. It was a tremendous undertaking, and high credit is due to many, not least to Major-General Sir Harold Wernher, whose task it was to co-ordinate the many interests concerned.

Here too should be mentioned "Pluto," the submarine pipelines which carried petrol from the Isle of Wight to Normandy and later from Dungeness to Calais. This idea and many others owed much to Mountbatten's Staff. Space forbids description of the many contrivances devised to overcome the formidable obstacles and minefields guarding the beaches. Some were fitted to our tanks to protect their crews; others served the landing-craft. All these matters aroused my personal interest, and, when it seemed necessary, my intervention.

*　　*　　*　　*　　*

General Morgan and his Staff were well content with the

approval given at Quebec to their proposals. The troops could now begin their training and their special equipment could be made. For this Morgan had been given powers greater than a Staff officer usually wields.

The discussions which led to the appointment of General Eisenhower to the Supreme Command and of General Montgomery to command the expeditionary army have already been related. Eisenhower's Deputy was Air Chief Marshal Tedder. Air-Marshal Leigh-Mallory was appointed to the Air and Admiral Ramsay to the Naval Command. General Eisenhower brought with him General Bedell Smith as his Chief of Staff, to whom General Morgan was appointed Deputy.

Eisenhower and Montgomery disagreed with one important feature of General Morgan's proposals. They wanted an assault in greater strength and on a wider front, so as to gain quickly a good-sized bridgehead in which to build up their forces for the break-out. Also it was important to capture the docks at Cherbourg earlier than had been planned. They wanted a first assault by five divisions instead of three. Of course, this was perfectly right. But where were the extra landing-craft? Southeast Asia had already been stripped. There were sufficient in the Mediterranean to carry two divisions, but these were needed for "Anvil," the seaborne assault on Southern France which was to take place at the same time as "Overlord" and draw German troops away from the North. If "Anvil" were to be reduced, it would be too weak to be helpful. It was not until March that General Eisenhower, in conference with the British Chiefs of Staff, made his final decision. The American Chiefs of Staff had agreed that he should speak for them. Having recently come from the Mediterranean, he knew all about "Anvil," and now as Supreme Commander of "Overlord" he could best judge the needs of both. It was agreed to take the ships of one division from "Anvil" and to use them for "Overlord." The ships for a second division could be found by postponing "Overlord" till the June moon period. The output of new landing-craft in that month would fill the gap. As for the additional troops and fighting ships required, Britain and the

United States would each contribute one division to bring the total up to five. The United States also agreed to provide naval support for their extra division. Thus the naval forces allocated to the operation were roughly eighty per cent British and twenty per cent American. Planning now went ahead on this revised and greatly improved foundation.

*   *   *   *   *

As soon as I returned from Marrakesh, I busied myself with the many technical matters of the "Overlord" preparations. Across the Channel the whole front bristled with obstacles; defences had been built and manned. The enemy expected us, but did they know *where* or *when* or *how?* They had no flanks that could be turned, at any rate within the range of our fighter air-cover. Ships were more vulnerable than ever to shore batteries which could aim by radar. Once our troops were landed, they still had to be supplied and the enemy's air and tank counter-attacks beaten off. I never ceased to search for means to overcome the perils which lay before us.

Prime Minister to General Ismay and   23 Jan. 44
Sir Edward Bridges

In view of the many repercussions which "Overlord" preparations will make on our life, and in order to keep the whole matter under constant survey, I propose to set up a weekly committee, over which I will preside myself. This committee will be a substitute for the Anti-U-boat Warfare Committee, which can now be put on a two-monthly basis.

Pray let me have your suggestions for the personnel of this new committee.

*   *   *   *   *

The "Mulberry" harbours, I now heard, were meeting with difficulties. I therefore summoned a conference on January 24. It was intended to plant a breakwater ("Gooseberry") in each divisional assault area. This now meant a total of five "Gooseberries," two of which would in due course be absorbed into the "Mulberries." On the suggestion of Admiral Tennant, who was in charge of the operational side of the "Mulberry" plan, it was agreed that all the "Gooseberries" should be composed of blockships, although this meant using many more vessels. Moving under their own power, they could quickly reach the scene and be sunk in the right place, thus providing a certain amount of shelter almost at once. All could be laid in four or five days. The "Phoenix" concrete caissons to complete the "Mulberries" would be towed over by instalments, but this would take at least fourteen days. There was a shortage of tugs, and I gave instructions for a census. The Admiralty needed eight thousand yards of blockships. Nearly all were provided by using seventy old merchant ships and four obsolete warships. As the British were building most of the "Mulberries," I thought we could reasonably expect the Americans to help with the blockships. At my suggestion they did so, contributing nearly half. For the rest, the twenty-three "Whale" floating pier units were progressing well, but the steel "Bombardons," for the outer breakwaters, were meeting technical troubles which the Admiralty had to solve.

* * * * *

The plans for airborne attack seemed to me to deserve special attention and support.

Prime Minister to General Ismay, for C.O.S. Committee 28 Jan. 44

I am not at all satisfied with the provision that, on existing plans, is being made for the carriage of airborne troops for "Overlord." There are four airborne divisions available, but I am told that there are only sufficient aircraft to lift one of these divisions. This is not on account of lack of production, but because the date by which everything must be ready has been set at March 15. The production of Stirlings and Albemarles between March 15 and May 15 will be a hundred and ten aircraft — seventy Stirlings and forty Albemarles. All these should be available for the battle. I have also asked you to examine how many aircraft can be made available from Coastal Command. It is clear to me that if strenuous effort is made much more ample resources could be secured for General Eisenhower.

2. General Eisenhower should be asked to state the maximum

airborne forces he desires to launch simultaneously at the opening
of "Overlord." At the same time I should be glad to receive a
statement of what we are giving him under present plans. I will
preside at a meeting next week to review the position and see how
we can meet General Eisenhower's requirements.

*   *   *   *   *

The appointment of the commanders gave a fresh impetus.
"D.D." tanks which could swim ashore had already been successfully used in the Mediterranean, and would certainly be
wanted again. There was also a process of "waterproofing"
ordinary tracked and wheeled vehicles to enable them to drive
ashore under their own power through several feet of water.
But, as usual, the Army's demands for vehicles of all kinds
seemed wildly extravagant.

Prime Minister to Minister of Production and   25 Jan. 44
Minister of Supply

Pray let me have the report upon the possibilities of producing
three hundred D.D. tanks by the end of April.

2. What is the position of waterproofing material?

3. I understand that General Montgomery has given a list of
some of his priorities to the Ministry of Supply. Let me see this
list, with comments upon the possibility of meeting his wishes.

Prime Minister to General Montgomery   31 Jan. 44

You spoke to me about waterproofing materials, and every effort
is being made to produce what is necessary. Surely however the
whole two hundred thousand vehicles with their one hundred
varieties, each of which is a separate proposition, do not require to
be waterproofed. Many of these vehicles will not come in till three
or four months after the landing has begun, and we hope that by that
time the troops will not have to wade ashore. It is very necessary
that selective processes and refinements should play their part in
the preparations for "Overlord" at this stage in the war, when one
need can usually be met only at the expense of another. I know
you will bear this in mind.

2. I am most anxious that you should have, if possible, a two-
division lift for your airborne force. This would be helped if a
firm date could be fixed. The Air Ministry and Ministry of Aircraft

Production have been given target dates — for instance, March 15 as the date for providing certain aircraft, such as Albemarles, etc., of which one hundred and eighty are to be available. If however without prejudice to the above a two-months later date were acceptable, then in this batch alone, instead of one hundred and eighty there would be two hundred and seventy by May 15. I cannot doubt that similar expansions could be obtained in the case of many other requisites. I am well aware of the arguments about training, but it is the crews and not the machines which need training. If highly skilled crews can be obtained (from, say, the Fleet Air Arm), they can practise on the existing stock of machines so as to have a redundancy of troops to be taken, up till zero hour, over the outflow of machines. Talk to me about this when we meet.

I was most interested in the fire plan of the opening bombardment, particularly its naval aspect.

Prime Minister to First Sea Lord   20 Feb. 44

As you will remember, I have several times stressed in my minutes to the Chiefs of Staff the great importance of a bombarding squadron or fleet in Operation "Overlord." Once the air shield has been established, the power of the warships is liberated. High-velocity guns are particularly suited for the smashing of concrete pillboxes. You have told me of the arrangements that you are making, and I consider they should be pressed to the fullest possible extreme.

2. I had a talk yesterday with Admiral Cooke [U.S.N.], who showed me photographs of the Kwajalein attack in the Marshalls. He also stressed the great value of short-range bombardment, at, say, two thousand yards. The beaches in our case will not be convenient for that, I presume. Nevertheless, the greater the power that can be brought to bear the better. Here is the time to use the *Ramillies* class; and, as I have said, men can be taken off other ships in order to work up a bombardment for the actual event of the landing, after which they can return to their duties.

3. I propose to have a Defence Committee meeting on Monday week, February 28, to discuss this aspect of "Overlord." Meanwhile, I shall be glad to have a paper from you.

In the event naval bombarding forces included six battleships, two large monitors, and twenty-two cruisers, besides large numbers of destroyers and smaller vessels. Two-thirds of these were British.

* * * * *

I was anxious that General Marshall should realise the efforts I was making to sustain the plan he had so long desired. I accordingly telegraphed:

Prime Minister to General Marshall (Washington)   11 Mar. 44

Since I got home from Marrakesh I have looked carefully into the following aspects of "Overlord," namely: (i) "Mulberry" and all connected with it; (ii) airborne assault lift, including method of glider attack; (iii) inshore bombarding squadrons; and (iv) Air Command arrangements.

I have presided at a series of meetings at which either Ike or Bedell has been present, and I am satisfied that everything is going on well. Ike and Bedell will probably tell you they are well pleased. I am hardening very much on this operation as the time approaches, *in the sense of wishing to strike if humanly possible, even if the limiting conditions we laid down at Moscow are not exactly fulfilled.*[1] I hope a chance may come for us to have a talk before long. Every good wish.

* * * * *

Once the size of the expedition had been determined, it was possible to go ahead with intensive training. Not the least of our difficulties was to find enough room. A broad partition was arranged between British and American forces, whereby the British occupied the southeastern and the Americans the southwestern parts of England. The inhabitants of coastal areas accepted all the inconveniences in good part. One British division with its naval counterpart did all its earlier training in the Moray Firth area in Scotland. The winter storms prepared them for the rough-and-tumble of D-Day.

The theory and practice of amphibious operations had long been established by the Combined Operations Staff, under

[1] Author's italics.

Admiral Mountbatten, who had been succeeded by General Laycock. It had now to be taught to all concerned, in addition to the thorough general training needed for modern warfare. This of course had long been going on in Britain and America in exercises great and small with live ammunition. Many officers and men entered into battle for the first time, but all bore themselves like seasoned troops.

Lessons from previous large-scale exercises, and of course from our hard experience at Dieppe, were applied in final rehearsals by all three Services, which culminated in early May. All this activity did not pass unnoticed by the enemy. We did not object, and special pains were taken that they should be remarked by watchers in the Pas de Calais, where we wanted the Germans to believe we were coming.

Our plans had to be altered and kept up to date as fresh information came in about the enemy. We knew the general layout of his troops and his principal defences, the gun positions, the strong points and entrenchments along the coast, but after Rommel took command in late January, great additions and refinements began to appear. In particular we had to discover any new types of obstacle that might be installed, and contrive the antidote.

Constant air reconnaissance kept us informed of what was going on across the Channel. And of course there were other ways of finding out. Many trips were made by parties in small craft to resolve some doubtful point, to take soundings inshore, to examine new obstacles, or to test the slope and nature of a beach. All this had to be done in darkness, with silent approach, stealthy reconnaissance, and timely withdrawal.

* * * * *.

An intricate decision was the choice of D-Day and "H-Hour," the moment at which the leading assault craft should hit the beach. From this many other timings had to be worked backwards. It was agreed to approach the enemy coast by moonlight, because this would help both our ships and our airborne troops. A short period of daylight before H-Hour was also needed to give order to the deployment of the small craft and accuracy to the covering bombardment. But if the interval between first light and H-Hour was too long, the enemy would have more time to recover from their surprise and fire on our troops in the act of landing.

Then there were the tides. If we landed at high tide, the underwater obstacles would obstruct the approach; if at low tide, the troops would have far to go across the exposed beaches. Many other factors had to be considered, and it was finally decided to land about three hours before high water. But this was not all. The tides varied by forty minutes between the eastern and western beaches, and there was a submerged reef in one of the British sectors. Each sector had to have a different "H-Hour," which varied from one place to another by as much as eighty-five minutes.

Only on three days in each lunar month were all the desired conditions fulfilled. The first three-day period after May 31, General Eisenhower's target date, was June 5, 6, and 7. Thus was June 5 chosen. If the weather were not propitious on any of those three days, the whole operation would have to be postponed at least a fortnight — indeed, a whole month if we waited for the moon.

*   *   *   *   *

By April our plans were taking final shape. The Second British Army, under General Dempsey, was to land three divisions on beaches north and northwest of Caen. One airborne division was to be dropped, a few hours before, northeast of Caen to capture the bridges over the lower Orne and protect the eastern flank. On the British right, the First United States Army, under General Omar Bradley, was to land one division on the coast east of the Vire estuary and one division north of it. The latter would be aided by a previous drop of two airborne divisions a few miles inland. Each army had one division in ships for immediate reinforcement.

The first objectives of the attack included Caen, Bayeux, Isigny, and Carentan. When these were gained, the Americans

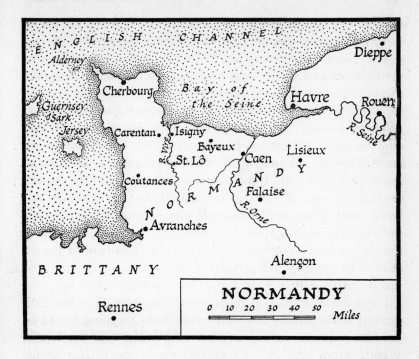

ENGLISH   CHANNEL
Alderney
Dieppe
Cherbourg
Bay of the Seine
Havre
Rouen
Guernsey
dSark
Jersey   Carentan
Isigny
Bayeux
Lisieux
R. Wre
St. Lô   Caen
Coutances
N   O   R   M   A   N   D   Y
Falaise
R. Orne
N
Avranches
Alençon
BRITTANY

NORMANDY

Rennes
0   10   20   30   40   50
Miles

would advance across the Cotentin peninsula, and also drive northward to capture Cherbourg. The British would protect the American flank from counter-attack from the east, gaining ground south and southeast of Caen where we could create airfields and use our armour. It was hoped to reach the line Falaise-Avranches three weeks after the landing, and, with the strong reinforcements by that time ashore, to break out eastward towards Paris, northeastward towards the Seine, and westward to capture the Brittany ports.

These plans depended on our ability to maintain a rapid build-up over the beaches. To co-ordinate all the intricate shipping movements a special organisation was established at the Supreme Commander's Headquarters at Portsmouth, with subordinate inter-Service bodies at the embarkation ports. This enabled the commanders on the far shore to control the flow of supplies to their beaches. A similar organisation controlled supplies from the air. The nourishing and expanding of the numerous organisations on the beaches of France was a prime feature. They would soon be as busy as a major port.

The Navy's task would be to carry the Army safely across the Channel and support the landing with all available means; thereafter to ensure the timely arrival of reinforcements and supplies, despite all the hazards of the sea and the enemy. Admiral Ramsay commanded two Task Forces, one British and the other American. The Eastern Task Force, under Admiral Vian, would control all naval operations in the British sector. Admiral Kirk, U.S.N., operated similarly for the American First Army. These two commands contained five assault forces, each carrying the fighting elements of a division and each having its own specialised craft to give close support to the troops in the landings. Here was the hard core of the attack. Surrounding and protecting the assault forces would be the powerful Allied Navies and Air Forces.

From the embarkation ports, stretching from Felixstowe on the east to the Bristol Channel on the west, shipping would be brought coastwise in convoy to a rendezvous near the Isle of Wight. From here the vast armada would sail to Normandy. Because of the great congestion in our southern ports and to help our deception plans, the heavy naval bombarding forces would assemble in the Clyde and at Belfast.

Mines were the chief danger during the approach, although U-boats and light surface craft would also present a threat, and minesweeping was of vital concern. A mine barrier extended across our line of approach, and we could not tell what more the enemy might do at the last moment in the assault area itself. Ten separate channels through the barrier must be swept for the assault convoys, and thereafter the whole area must be searched. Twenty-nine flotillas of minesweepers were assembled, amounting to about three hundred and fifty craft.

The mighty offensive, assigned to Bomber Command and described in an earlier chapter, had already been in progress for many weeks. The Allied Tactical Air Forces, under Air Chief-Marshal Leigh-Mallory, not only helped the heavy bombers to destroy enemy communications and isolate the battle area, but also had to defeat the enemy's air force before the battle began on land. German airfields and installations were attacked for three weeks before D-Day in growing weight of bombardment, while fighter sweeps tempted the reluctant enemy to battle. For the assault itself the initial task was to protect our naval forces and convoys from attack by sea or air; then to neutralise the enemy's radar installations, and, while joining in the joint bombardment plan, additionally to provide fighter cover over the anchorages and beaches. Three airborne divisions were to be delivered safely and in darkness onto their objectives, together with a number of special parties to stir and encourage the seething Resistance Movement.

* * * * *

The bombardment to cover the first landing was a prime factor. Before D-Day preliminary air attacks had been delivered on many coastal batteries, not merely those covering the invasion beaches, but, for the sake of deception, all along the French shore. On the night before D-Day, a great force of British heavy bombers would attack the ten most important batteries that might oppose the landings. At dawn their place was to be taken by medium bombers and ships' gunfire, directed by spotting aircraft. About half an hour after first light, the full weight of the United States heavy and medium bombers would fall upon the enemy defences. A great variety of guns and rockets mounted in naval assault craft would join in a crescendo of fire.

* * * * *

Of course, we had not only to plan for what we were really going to do. The enemy was bound to know that a great invasion was being prepared; we had to conceal the place and time of attack and make him think we were landing somewhere else and at a different moment. This alone involved an immense amount of thought and action. Coastal areas were banned to visitors; censorship was tightened; letters after a certain date were held back from delivery; foreign embassies were forbidden to send cipher telegrams and even their diplomatic bags were delayed.

Our major deception was to pretend that we were coming across the Straits of Dover. It would not be proper even now to describe all the methods employed to mislead the enemy, but the obvious ones of simulated concentrations of troops in Kent and Sussex, of fleets of dummy ships collected in the Cinque Ports, of landing exercises on the near-by beaches, of increased wireless activity, were all used. More reconnaissances were made at or over the places we were *not* going to than at the places we were. The final result was admirable. The German High Command firmly believed the evidence we obligingly put at their disposal. Rundstedt, the Commander-in-Chief on the Western Front, was convinced that the Pas de Calais was our objective.

* * * * *

The concentration of the assaulting forces — 176,000 men, 20,000 vehicles, and many thousand tons of stores, all to be shipped in the first two days — was in itself an enormous task. It was handled principally by the War Office and the railway authorities, and with great success. From their normal stations all over Britain the troops were brought to the southern counties, into areas stretching from Ipswich round to Cornwall and the Bristol Channel. The three airborne divisions, which were to drop on Normandy before the sea assault, were assembled close to the airfields whence they would set out. From their concentration areas in rear troops were brought forward for embarkation in assigned priority to camps in marshalling areas near the coast. At the marshalling camps they were divided up into detachments corresponding to the ship- or boat-loads in which they would be embarked. Here every man received his orders. Once briefed, none were permitted to leave camp. The camps themselves were situated near to the embarkation points. These were ports or "hards" — i.e., stretches of beach concreted to allow of easy embarkation on smaller craft. Here they were to be met by the naval ships.

It seemed most improbable that all this movement by sea and land would escape the attention of the enemy. There were many tempting targets for their Air, and full precautions were taken. Nearly seven thousand guns and rockets and over a thousand balloons protected the great masses of men and vehicles. But there was no sign of the Luftwaffe. How different things were four years before! The Home Guard, who had so patiently waited for a worth-while job all those years, now found it. Not only were they manning sections of anti-aircraft and coast defences, but they also took over many routine and security duties, thus releasing other soldiers for battle.

All Southern England thus became a vast military camp, filled with men trained, instructed, and eager to come to grips with the Germans across the water.

17

Rome

May 11—June 9

The Regrouping of the Allied Armies — Alexander's Great Offensive Begins, May 11 — General Juin Takes Ausonia — The Poles Capture the Cassino Monastery — General Advance of the Allies — My Telegram to Alexander of May 17 and His Reply — The Climax Approaches — The Canadian Corps in the Liri Valley — The Anzio Army under General Truscott Advances to the Alban Hills and Valmontone — Stubborn German Resistance — Alexander's Telegram of May 30 and My Reply — Valmontone Captured by the Americans, June 2 — The War Cabinet Send Congratulations to All — The Allied Entry into Rome, June 5 — My Telegram to Stalin of June 5 — Magnificent Achievements of the Russian Armies — German Retreat Along the Whole Eastern Front — Hitler Faces Impending Doom on Three Fronts.

T HE REGROUPING OF OUR FORCES in Italy was undertaken in great secrecy. Everything possible was done to conceal the movements from the enemy and to mislead him. By the time they were completed, General Clark, of the Fifth Army, had over seven divisions, four of them French, on the front from the sea to the river Liri; thence the Eighth Army, now under General Leese, continued the line through Cassino into the mountains with the equivalent of nearly twelve. Six divisions had been packed into the Anzio beachhead ready to sally forth at the best moment; the equivalent of only three remained in the Adriatic sector. In all the Allies mustered over twenty-eight divisions.

Opposed to them were twenty-three German divisions, but

our deception arrangements, which included the threat of a
landing at Civitavecchia, the seaport of Rome, had puzzled
Kesselring so well that they were widely spread. Between
Cassino and the sea, where our main blows were to fall, there
were only four divisions, and reserves were scattered and at a
distance. Our attack came unexpectedly. The Germans were
carrying out reliefs opposite the British front, and one of their
Army Commanders had planned to go on leave.

In the morning of May 11, Alexander and I exchanged
telegrams.

Prime Minister to General Alexander   11 May 44

All our thoughts and hopes are with you in what I trust and
believe will be a decisive battle, fought to a finish, and having for
its object the destruction and ruin of the armed force of the enemy
south of Rome.

General Alexander to Prime Minister   11 May 44

All our plans and preparations are now complete and everything
is ready. We have every hope and every intention of achieving our
object, namely, the destruction of the enemy south of Rome. We
expect extremely heavy and bitter fighting, and we are ready for it.
I shall signal you our private code-word when the attack starts.

The great offensive began at eleven that night, when the
artillery of both our armies, two thousand guns, opened a violent fire, reinforced at dawn by the full weight of the Tactical
Air Force. North of Cassino, the Polish Corps tried to sur-
round the monastery on the ridges that had been the scene of
our previous failures, but they were held and thrown back.
The British XIIIth Corps, with the 4th British and 8th Indian
Divisions leading, succeeded in forming small bridgeheads
over the Rapido River, but had to fight hard to hold them.
On the Fifth Army front the French soon advanced to Monte
Faito, but on the seaward flank the IId United States Corps
ran into stiff opposition and struggled for every yard of ground.
After thirty-six hours of heavy fighting, the enemy began to
weaken. The French Corps took Monte Majo, and General

Juin pushed his motorised division swiftly up the river
Garigliano to capture San Ambrogio and San Apollinare, thus
clearing all the west bank of the river. The XIIIth Corps
bit more deeply into the strong enemy defences across
the Rapido, and on May 14, with the 78th Division coming up
to reinforce, began to make good progress. The French thrust
forward again up the Ausente Valley and took Ausonia, and
General Juin launched his Goums [1] across the trackless mountains westward from Ausonia. The American Corps succeeded
in capturing Santa Maria Infante, for which they 'had been
fighting for so long. The two German divisions, which on
this flank had had to support the attack of six divisions of
the Fifth Army, had suffered crippling losses, and all the German right flank south of the Liri was breaking.

Despite the collapse of their seaward flank, the enemy north
of the Liri hung on desperately to the last elements of the
Gustav Line. But gradually they were overborne. On the 15th,
the XIIIth Corps reached the Cassino-Pignataro road, and
General Leese brought up the Canadian Corps to be ready to
exploit his success. Next day the 78th Division broke through
the defences in a northwesterly drive which reached Route 6,
and on the 17th the Poles attacked north of the monastery.
This time they succeeded, and occupied the ridges northwest
of it which overlooked the highway.

On the morning of May 18, Cassino town was finally cleared
by the 4th British Division, and the Poles triumphantly hoisted
their red and white standard over the ruins of the monastery.
Although they were not the first to enter it, they greatly distinguished themselves in this their first major engagement in
Italy. Later, under their thrustful General Anders, himself a
survivor from Russian imprisonment, they were to win many
laurels during the long advance to the river Po. The XIIIth
Corps had also advanced all along their front, reaching the
outskirts of Aquino, with the Canadian Corps driving forward
to the south of them. On the other bank of the Liri, the

[1] Goums: native Moroccan troops, under French officers and N.C.O.s, highly
skilled in mountain warfare. They numbered about 12,000.

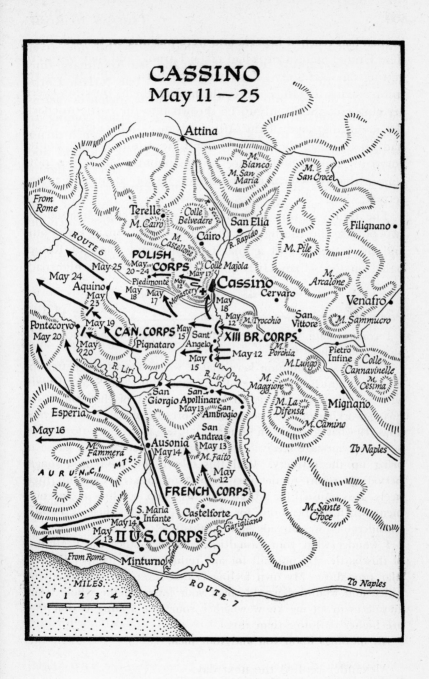

CASSINO
May 11 — 25

Attina

M.¹ Bianco
M. San Maria

M. San Croce

From Rome

ROUTE 6

Terelle
M. Cairo

Colle Belvedere

Cairo

San Elia

Filignano

M. Castellone

M. Rapido

M. Pile

POLISH CORPS
May 20-24

Colle Majola

M. Arcalone

Venafro

May 25

Piedimonte

May 12

Cassino

Cervaro

May 24

Aquino
May 23

May 18

May 17

Monastery

May 18

M. Sammucro

Pontecorvo
May 20

May 19

May 20

CAN. CORPS

Pignataro

May 15

Sant' Angelo

M. Trocchio

San Vittore

M. Porchia

Pietro Infine

Colle Cannavinelle

M. Cesima

May 12

XIII BR. CORPS

R. Liri

May 15

R. Liri

San Giorgio

San Apollinare
May 13

San Ambrogio

M. Maggiore

M. La Difensa

M. Lungo

Mignano

Esperia

San Andrea
May 13

M. Camino

May 16

M. Fammera

Ausonia
May 14

M. Faito

May 12

To Naples

A U R U N C I   M T S.

FRENCH CORPS

S. Maria Infante
May 14

Castelforte

M. Sante Croce

May 13

II U.S. CORPS

R. Garigliano

From Rome

Minturno

MILES
0 1 2 3 4 5

R O U T E   7

To Naples

French had reached Esperia and were pushing on towards Pico.
The United States Corps had taken Formia, and they too were
getting on splendidly. Kesselring had been sending down reinforcements as fast as he could muster them, but they were
arriving piecemeal, only to be thrown into the battle to check
the mounting flood of the Allied advance. The Eighth Army
had yet to break the Adolf Hitler Line, running from Pontecorvo to Aquino and thence to Piedimonte, but it was now
certain that the Germans would soon be forced into a general
retreat.

The minds of our commanders were therefore focused on
two points: the timing and direction of the Anzio break-out,
and the possibility of a final German stand south of Rome,
based on the Alban Hills and Valmontone on the highroad.

                    *   *   *   *   *

Prime Minister to General Alexander   17 May 44

I congratulate you wholeheartedly on the fine advance made
along your whole front.

There is some opinion here that it would have been better for
the Anzio punch to have been let off first. But C.I.G.S. and I agree
with you that it is better to keep the threat of the compressed
spring working on the enemy in the present phase. Let me know
however what you have in mind.

In your message received this morning you speak of a pause to
bring up the artillery. Will this take a few days or a longer
period? It seems to me very important to keep close on their
heels. It is unusual for a beaten army to stop at a line of entrench-
ment which has been dug for them in rear unless there is another
considerable force already holding this line.

I wonder what your casualties have been since the beginning
of this battle. Do not call for any returns which hamper the regular procedure. My own feeling is that seven or eight thousand
killed and wounded would cover your losses on the whole front.
It suffices to let me know whether your own feeling is that they
are higher or lower than this.

All blessings upon you and your men.

Alexander replied the next day:

General Alexander to Prime Minister   18 May 44

Many thanks for your congratulations, which we all greatly appreciated.

2. I weighed very carefully the pros and cons of an Anzio break-out, and among many factors two influenced me most. First, the enemy's reserves in that area were too strong, with 90th Division and 26th Division, and I wanted to draw them away first. As you know, 90th Division has been drawn down to main battle area, and part of 26th Division has also been moved. Secondly, the German expected Anzio to be the major thrust, and to gain surprise I did what he did not expect. I have ordered 36th United States Division to start moving into bridgehead tonight. I am trying to dribble them in unseen. When right moment comes, the Americans will punch out to get astride enemy's communications to Rome. If successful, this may well prove decisive.

3. The intention is not only to keep up the present pressure on the main battle-front, but to step it up. I have ordered Eighth Army to use the utmost energy to break through the Adolf Hitler Line in the Liri Valley before the Germans have time to settle down in it. I have also directed that Poles press on at once to Piedimonte, so as to turn this line from north. And I have directed that French Corps, after reaching Pico, should turn north and come in behind enemy facing Eighth Army. If these manoeuvres are successful, it will go a long way toward destroying right wing of German Tenth Army. If we get held up in front of the Adolf Hitler Line and are unable to turn it from north or south, a full-scale mounted attack will be necessary to break it; in which case the heavier artillery will have to be moved forward, and this will take several days. But you may be sure that there will be no unnecessary delay. The Germans are very quick to regain their balance, and I have no intention of allowing them to do so.

4. My latest information on casualties is as follows: Eighth Army, 6000; Fifth Army, 7000; total, 13,000.

5. Capture of Cassino means a great deal to me and both my armies. Apart from its Foreign Office value, it seems to me to have great propaganda possibilities.

General Wilson, who had gone to the front from Algiers, also reported:

General Wilson to Prime Minister   18 May 44

Battle continues to progress satisfactorily. I visited Poles today. They are elated at their hard-won success at Monte Cassino, where fighting was very severe.

2. Eighth Army and Americans have resources to maintain impetus of attack, but those of Juin's corps uncertain after eight more days of hard fighting, at present rate of casualties. I discussed this with de Gaulle today at Juin's Headquarters. He has agreed to send from North Africa one armoured and one infantry regiment at once, and to follow this up with further reinforcements as soon as they have been trained in American weapons.

*   *   *   *   *

The Eighth Army found that probing attacks on the Adolf Hitler Line in the Liri Valley gave no results, for although the defenders had been hurriedly thrown into them they were resolute men and the defences themselves were formidable. A set-piece assault was necessary, which could not be launched until May 23, but in the meantime the French had taken Pico after a stiff fight, and the United States IId Corps were in Fondi. The Germans had good cause to be anxious for their southern flank.

Prime Minister to General Alexander   23 May 44

Your battle seems to be approaching its climax, and all thoughts here are with you. Owing to the enemy pivoting backwards on his left, the advances of the French and the Americans are naturally filling the headlines. Your well-deserved message to the Poles also gained them great prominence.

At Cabinet yesterday some queries were made as to whether the part played by the British troops was receiving proportionate notice. They have been up against the stiffest and most unyielding parts of the line. We do not want anything said that is not justified, but reading the current press one might well doubt if we were making any serious contribution. I know of course what the facts are, but the public may be upset. Could you therefore bring them a little more into the communiqués, presuming of course you think that such mentions are deserved?

It fell to the Canadian Corps to make the main attack in the

Liri Valley. By noon of the 24th, they had made a clear break-through, and their Armoured Division pierced towards Ce-prano. Next day the Germans were in full retreat and hotly pursued on the whole of the Eighth Army front.

*   *   *   *   *

General Alexander had decided that the punch from the Anzio beachhead should be simultaneous with the break-through of the Eighth Army. The American General Truscott now struck his blow against Cisterna with two divisions of his army, still called the VIth Corps. Cisterna was captured on the 25th after two days of stiff fighting, and on the same day the beachhead forces gained contact with the leading troops of the United States IId Corps, which had captured and thrust for-ward from Terracina. At long last all our forces were re-united, and we began to reap the harvest from our winter sowing at Anzio.

General Alexander to Prime Minister   24 May 44
Herewith some interesting and pleasant facts. My usual daily report to C.I.G.S. follows through normal channels.

The Gustav Line, which the enemy has been preparing all win-ter, and which was guarded by Rapido River, was penetrated by both armies in the initial assault, and the enemy was driven out of it in first week of battle. Cassino, which was an almost impreg-nable fortress, was turned by a brilliant pincers movement, which ended by isolating it from the battlefield.

The much-vaunted Adolf Hitler Line, fortified by wire, mines, and concrete and steel pillboxes, has been smashed on the front of Eighth Army.

The beachhead enabled us to position a strong force on the German rear flanks, which is now in operation to complete another larger pincers manoeuvre. The deepest penetration up to date is a distance of thirty-eight miles as the crow flies.

In the Anzio sector the Americans have advanced four thousand yards through heavily prepared fixed defences, and have sur-rounded Cisterna.

We have taken over ten thousand prisoners, and killed and wounded a large number of the enemy, of which figures are not yet

available. Owing to extent of battlefield and rate of advance, it has
not been possible yet to check the material captured, but it includes
not less than a hundred guns of various types and a great deal of
ammunition and other equipment. Much mechanical transport has
been destroyed and damaged by our air forces, who claim at least
a hundred vehicles destroyed today.

Of German divisions that have been engaged, the 71st and 94th
Infantry Divisions have been destroyed as fighting formations. The
1st Parachute Division, 90th Panzer Grenadier Division, and 15th
Panzer Grenadier Division have lost the greater part of their effective strength. Heavy losses have been inflicted on 26th Panzer, 29th
Panzer Grenadier Division, 715th and 362d Infantry Divisions;
576th Regiment, 305th and 131st Regiments, 44th Division, have
also been practically wiped out. All enemy reserves, including a
division which was believed to have been north of Rome, have
been drawn into the battle, and there are strong indications that
the Hermann Goering Division, which was in O.K.W. Reserve, is
on its way south to try to stem the tide, though this cannot be
referred to in public, as this division has not yet been identified in
the fighting.

Co-operation between the two armies and Allied Air Forces has
been quite excellent. British, American, French, Canadian, New
Zealand, Indian, and Polish troops have all been engaged in fighting. British troops have played a conspicuous part in very bitter
fighting, especially for the crossings over the Rapido River and in
turning Cassino from the south. I will see that they have their
share of publicity in the communiqués. British and American Air
Forces have combined in both the close and more distant support
of both armies. Allied naval forces are co-operating by bombardment and by the movement of troops and stores by sea. It is, and
will continue to be, in every sense an Allied battle.

Finally, we have freed five hundred square miles of Italy from
the grip of the German aggressor in under a fortnight.

*   *   *   *   *

General Truscott quickly took advantage of the breach he
had made at Cisterna. Under General Clark's orders, he dispatched three divisions, one of them armoured, to Velletri and
the Alban Hills; but only one, the 3d United States Division,
towards Valmontone, where they would cut the most impor-

tant escape route of the enemy farther south. This was not in accord with Alexander's instructions, which put Valmontone as the primary objective.

Prime Minister to General Alexander   28 May 44

We are all delighted to hear your good news. At this distance it seems much more important to cut their line of retreat than anything else. I am sure you will have carefully considered moving more armour by the Appian Way up to the northernmost spearhead directed against the Valmontone-Frosinone road. A cop is much more important than Rome, which would anyhow come as its consequence. The cop is the one thing that matters.

Prime Minister to General Alexander   28 May 44

Further to my telegram [above], I have been looking through the tank strength as we get it from various sources. C.I.G.S. furnishes me with figures showing that you have at least twenty-five hundred serviceable. Surely one-half of these could be used, and indeed used up, in making a scythe movement cutting off the enemy's retreat.

I am going to send you and your armies a public message in a few days, and will back you up whatever happens, but I should feel myself wanting in comradeship if I did not let you know that the glory of this battle, already great, will be measured, not by the capture of Rome or the juncture with the bridgehead, but by the number of German divisions cut off. I am sure you will have revolved all this in your mind, and perhaps you have already acted in this way. Nevertheless, I feel I ought to tell you that it is the cop that counts.

But the Hermann Goering Division and elements of others, delayed though they were by damaging attacks from the air, got to Valmontone first. The single American division sent by General Clark was stopped short of it and the escape road remained open. That was very unfortunate.

The enemy in the South were in full retreat, and the Allied Air did its utmost to impede movement and break up concentrations. Obstinate rearguards frequently checked our pursuing forces, and their retirement did not degenerate into a rout. The IId United States Corps moved on Priverno, the

French to Ceccano, while the Canadian Corps and British XIIIth Corps advanced up the valley to Frosinone and the Xth Corps up the road to Avezzano. The three American divisions dispatched from the Anzio breach towards Velletri and the Alban Hills, later reinforced by a fourth, the 36th, had met very stiff resistance, and for three days could make no ground. They got ready to renew the attack on Valmontone, which Kesselring had been reinforcing with any troops he could find that were fit to fight. However, a brilliant stroke by the 36th United States Division must have disconcerted him. They had been fighting hard at the southwest corner of the Alban Hills. On the night of May 30, they found that the Germans had left a commanding height unguarded. Their infantry moved forward in close columns, and occupied their key points. Within twenty-four hours the whole 36th Division was firmly established and the last German defence line south of Rome penetrated.

General Alexander to Prime Minister   30 May 44

Thank you for your telegram.

Our serviceable tank strength is about two thousand.

You will see in my Operation Order that my aim is to destroy German Army in the field.

Except for the use of roads through Rome, battle formations are not to go into the city. Further, I am considering the advisability of only mentioning the capture of Rome in my military communiqué among inhabited localities taken by my armies in their stride from day to day. I shall appreciate your advice in this matter.

You will have heard of fresh enemy divisions which are on their way here. I hope our tap will not be turned off too soon, as it was before, and prevent us from gaining full fruits of our present advantageous position.

Prime Minister to General Alexander   31 May 44

I entirely agree with your operational intention, and trust you will execute it.

The capture of Rome is a vast, world-wide event, and should not be minimised. I hope that British as well as Americans will enter the city simultaneously. I would not lump it in with other towns taken on the same day. Nevertheless, as you rightly state, the destruction of the German Army in the field gives us Rome and the rest thrown in.

How lucky it was that we stood up to our United States Chiefs of Staff friends and refused to deny you the full exploitation of this battle! I will support you in obtaining the first priority in everything you need to achieve this glorious victory. I am sure the American Chiefs of Staff would now feel this was a bad moment to pull out of the battle or in any way weaken its force for the sake of other operations of an amphibious character, which may very soon take their place in the van of our ideas.

All good luck.

*   *   *   *   *

The success of the 36th United States Division did not bear immediate fruit. The enemy hung on desperately both in the Alban Hills and at Valmontone, although the retreat of most of their army had now been deflected northward towards Avezzano and Arsoli, where they were hunted by the Xth and

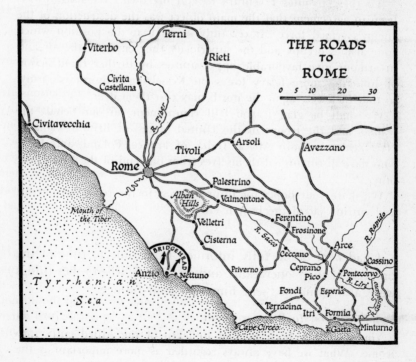

XIIIth British Corps and the aircraft of the Tactical Air Force. Unhappily, the mountainous country stopped us from using our great strength in armour, which otherwise could have been employed to much advantage.

On June 2, the IId United States Corps captured Valmontone and drove westward. That night German resistance broke, and next day the VIth United States Corps in the Alban Hills, with the British 1st and 5th Divisions on its left, pressed on towards Rome. The IId American Corps led them by a short head. They found the bridges mostly intact, and at 7.15 P.M. on June 4 the head of their 88th Division entered the Piazza Venezia, in the heart of the capital.

On June 9, I sent the congratulations of the War Cabinet to all concerned, and also the following personal telegram to Alexander:

Prime Minister to General Alexander   9 June 44

To these tributes I venture to add my own. We have always been in agreement that the main object was the destruction of the enemy's armed force. It certainly seems that the position which your armies occupy and the superiority they enjoy in the air and in armour give favourable opportunities by further rapid action of inflicting more heavy losses on Kesselring's disordered army, so that their retreat to the north may cost them dear.

We shall be glad if you will compliment on our behalf the leaders and the troops of the United States, of Britain, Canada, New Zealand, South Africa, India, of France, Poland, and Italy, who have distinguished themselves from one end of the line to the other.

We share your hopes for future success in the relentless pursuit and cutting off of the beaten enemy.

*   *   *   *   *

I had kept Stalin fully informed from time to time of the progress of these operations, and on June 5, when other things were also going on, sent him our good tidings.

Prime Minister to Premier Stalin   5 June 44

You will have been pleased to learn of the Allied entry into Rome. What we have always regarded as more important is the cutting-off of as many enemy divisions as possible. General Alexander is now ordering strong armoured forces northward on Terni, which should largely complete the cutting-off of all the divisions which were sent by Hitler to fight south of Rome. Although the amphibious landing at Anzio and Nettuno did not immediately fructify as I had hoped when it was planned, it was a correct strategic move, and brought its reward in the end. First, it drew ten divisions from the following places: one from France, one from Hungary, four from Yugoslavia and Istria, one from Denmark, and three from North Italy. Secondly, it brought on a defensive battle for us in which, though we lost about twenty-five thousand men, the Germans were repulsed and much of the fighting strength of their divisions broken, with a loss of about thirty thousand men. Finally, the Anzio landing has made possible the kind of movement for which it was originally planned, only on a far larger scale. General Alexander is concentrating every effort now on entrapping the divisions south of Rome. Several have retreated into the mountains, leaving a great deal of their heavy weapons behind, but we hope for a very good round-up of prisoners and material. As soon as this is over, we shall decide how best to use our armies in Italy to support the main adventure. Poles, British, Free French, and Americans have all broken or beaten in frontal attack the German troops opposite them, and there are various important options which will soon have to be considered.

2. I have just returned from two days at Eisenhower's Headquarters watching the troops embark [for Normandy]. The difficulties of getting proper weather conditions are very great, especially as we have to consider the fullest employment of the air, naval, and ground forces in relation to tides, waves, fog, and cloud. With great regret General Eisenhower was forced to postpone for one night, but the weather forecast has undergone a most favourable change and tonight we go. We are using five thousand ships, and have available eleven thousand fully mounted aircraft.

From many quarters came messages of warm congratulation. I even got a pat from the Bear.

Marshal Stalin to Prime Minister   5 June 44

I congratulate you on the great victory of the Allied Anglo-American forces — the taking of Rome. This news has been greeted in the Soviet Union with great satisfaction.

*   *   *   *   *

Stalin had cause to be in a good mood, for things were going well with him. The scale of the Russian struggle far exceeded the operations with which my account has hitherto been concerned, and formed of course the foundation upon which the British and American Armies approached the climax of the war. The Russians had given their enemy little time to recover from their severe reverses of the early winter of 1943. In mid-January their attacks on the hundred-and-twenty-mile front from Lake Ilmen to Leningrad had pierced the defences in front of the city. Farther south, by the end of February, the Germans had been driven back to the shores of Lake Peipus. Leningrad was freed once and for all, and the Russians stood on the borders of the Baltic States.

Successful Russian attacks west of Kiev had forced the Germans back towards the old Polish frontier. The whole southern front was aflame and the German line deeply penetrated at many points. One great pocket of surrounded Germans was left behind at Kersun, from which few escaped.

Throughout March the Russians pressed their advantage all along the line and in the air. From Gomel to the Black Sea the invaders were in full retreat, which did not end until they had been thrust across the Dniester, back into Rumania and Poland. Then the spring thaw brought them a short respite. In the Crimea however operations were still possible. After three days' fighting, the Russians broke through the Perekop Neck on April 11, joined hands with others that had crossed at Kerch, and set about destroying the Seventeenth German Army and regaining Sebastopol.

The situation of Hitler's armies at the end of May was forlorn. His two hundred divisions on the Eastern Front could not hope to withstand the Russian flood when it was again released. Everywhere he was faced with imminent disaster. Now was the time for him to decide how to regroup his forces, where they should withdraw and where hold. But instead his orders were for them all to stand and fight it out. There was to be no withdrawal, anywhere. The German armies were thus condemned to be broken on all three fronts.

THE FRONT IN RUSSIA

January – June 1944

Front Jan. 1, 1944 ----

Front June 1, 1944 ∘∘∘∘∘∘

FINLAND

Lake Ladoga

Baltic Sea

● Leningrad

Lake Ilmen

Lake Peipus

ESTHONIA

LATVIA

● Velikie Luki

● Moscow

● Vitebsk

● Viazma

LITHUANIA

● Smolensk

● Vilna

● Mogilev

● Bryansk

● Minsk

● Orel

POLAND

Pinsk

PRIPET MARSHES

● Gomel

● Kursk

● Bielgorod

● Korosten

● Kiev

● Pereyaslav

● Kharkov

U K R A I N E

R. Donetz

Lemberg

● Jitomir

Kersun

● Kremenchug

R. Dnieper

● Dniepropetrovsk

● Tarnopol

R. Bug

Krivoi Rog

Taganrog

SLOVAKIA

Cernowitz

R. Dniester

● Nikopol

Rostov

● Jassy

● Odessa

Perekop

Sea of Azov

● Kerch

RUMANIA

CRIMEA

R. Pruth

● Sevastopol

Black Sea

MILES

0   100   200

18

On the Eve

O**N MONDAY, MAY 15,** three weeks before D-Day, we held
a final conference in London at Montgomery's Headquarters in St. Paul's School. The King, Field-Marshal Smuts,
the British Chiefs of Staff, the Commanders of the expedition,
and many of their principal Staff officers were present. On the
stage was a map of the Normandy beaches and the immediate
hinterland, set at a slope so that the audience could see it
clearly, and so constructed that the high officers explaining
the plan of operations could walk about and point out the
landmarks.

General Eisenhower opened the proceedings, and the forenoon session closed with an address by His Majesty. I, too, spoke and in the course of my remarks I said, "I am hardening on this operation." General Eisenhower in his book [1] has taken this to mean that in the past I had been against the cross-Channel operation, but this is not correct. If the reader will look back to Chapter 16, page 590, he will see that I wrote these very words to General Marshall on March 11, and explained that I used them "in the sense of wishing to strike if humanly possible, even if the limiting conditions we laid down are not exactly fulfilled." Montgomery then took the stage and made an impressive speech.

He was followed by several Naval, Army, and Air Commanders, and also by the Principal Administrative Officer, who dwelt upon the elaborate preparations that had been made for the administration of the force when it got ashore. The amount of paraphernalia sounded staggering, and reminded me of Admiral Andrew Cunningham's story of the dental chairs being landed at Algiers in the first flight of Operation "Torch." I was told, for example, that two thousand officers and clerks were being taken across the sea to keep records, and I was given the following statement, which showed that twenty days after the landing — D+20 — there would be one vehicle ashore for every 4.77 men. Each vehicle required a driver and its share of maintenance staff.

	U.S.		BRITISH		TOTAL	
	Vehicles	Personnel	Vehicles	Personnel	Vehicles	Personnel
D + 20	96,000	452,000	93,000	450,000	189,000	902,000
D + 60	197,000	903,000	168,000	800,000	365,000	1,703,000

Plus replacement of casualties.

Although these figures included fighting vehicles, such as guns, armoured cars, and tanks, I remembered too well the swarm in the Anzio beachhead, and after reflection I asked Ismay to write to Montgomery and express my concern about

[1] *Crusade in Europe*, page 245.

what seemed to me an excess of motor-cars and non-fighting vehicles of all kinds. This he did, and we arranged to discuss it when I visited the General's Headquarters on Friday, May 19. This interview has been misrepresented. Montgomery is said to have led me into his study and advised me not to speak to his Staff, and to have threatened to resign if I insisted on altering the loading plans at the eleventh hour, and I am alleged to have given way, and, after telling his officers that I was not allowed to talk to them, to have walked out. It may be well therefore to state what actually happened.

When I arrived for dinner, Montgomery asked to speak to me alone, and I went into his room. I do not remember the actual course of the conversation, but no doubt he explained the difficulties of altering the loading scale at this stage, seventeen days before D-Day. I am sure however that at no time, either in this conversation or in any other of the many I had with him during the war, did he threaten to resign, and that nothing in the nature of a confrontation with his Staff took place. I should not have accepted such behaviour. After our talk we went to dinner, at which only eight or nine persons, mostly the General's personal staff, were present. All our proceedings were of a most friendly character, and when that night the General asked me to put something for him in his private book, as I had done before other great battles, I wrote the following, which has already been published elsewhere: "On the verge of the greatest adventure with which these pages have dealt, I record my confidence that all will be well, and that the organisation and equipment of the Army will be worthy of the valour of the soldiers and the genius of their chief."

I may add however that I still consider that the proportion of transport vehicles to fighting men in the early phase of the cross-Channel invasion was too high and that the operation suffered both in risk and execution from this fact.

*   *   *   *   *

Another project was close to my heart. Our aim was to liberate France, and it seemed both desirable and fitting that a

French division should be landed early in the operation and the French people told that their troops were fighting once more on the soil of France. The 2d French Armoured Division, commanded by General Leclerc, had had a long and distinguished career in North Africa, and as early as March 10, I had told de Gaulle that I hoped they would be with us in the main battle. Since then the matter had been much probed by the Chiefs of Staff. Eisenhower was glad to have the division, and General Wilson did not plan to use it in the attack on the Riviera. The problem was how to get it home and properly mounted in time. The troops could be shifted easily enough, but there was little room in home-coming ships for their equipment and their vehicles. After correspondence between the British and United States Chiefs of Staff and Allied Headquarters in Algiers, much had been transported in the landing-ships which were sailing back from the Mediterranean. But on April 4, the Chiefs of Staff reported that they would still be short of about two thousand vehicles. To give them British ones would seriously complicate Eisenhower's problems of maintenance, and a few days later his Headquarters declared that no American ones could be provided either from the United Kingdom or the United States. This meant that the division would not be able to fight until long after the landing, all for the lack of comparatively few vehicles out of the immense numbers to be employed. Mr. Eden shared my disappointment, and on May 2, I made a personal appeal by letter to General Eisenhower.

Prime Minister to General Eisenhower   2 May 44

Please provide from your vast masses of transport the few vehicles required for the Leclerc division, which may give real significance to French re-entry into France. Let me remind you of the figures of Anzio — viz., 125,000 men with 23,000 vehicles, all so painfully landed to carry them, and they only got twelve miles.

Forgive me for making this appeal, which I know you will weigh carefully and probe deeply before rejecting.

His answer was reassuring.

General Eisenhower to Prime Minister   10 May 44

I have gone very carefully into the transportation status of the Leclerc division, and members of my Staff have conferred with General Leclerc on the same subject.

I find that about eighteen hundred vehicles of the division, including nearly all the track and armoured vehicles, have already arrived here, or will arrive by May 15. Approximately twenty-four hundred vehicles remain to be shipped, and on the present schedule all but four hundred of these vehicles should be in England by June 12, the remainder reaching here by June 22. General Leclerc says that he now has adequate material for training, and he is being assisted by the American Third Army, to which he is attached. His general supply situation is good, and the minor deficiencies which remain after his vehicles arrive, including provision for maintenance, will be met from American sources. I believe that the shipping and equipment schedule of the division will ensure their being properly provided prior to their entry into combat.

Thus all was arranged, and the march which had begun at Lake Chad ended through Paris at Berchtesgaden.

*   *   *   *   *

As D-Day approached, the tension grew. There was still no sign that the enemy had penetrated our secrets. He had scored a minor success at the end of April by sinking two American L.S.T.s which had been taking part in an exercise, but apparently he did not connect this with our invasion plans. We observed some reinforcement of light naval forces at Cherbourg and Havre during May, and there was more mine-laying activity in the Channel, but in general he remained quiescent, awaiting a definite lead regarding our intentions.

Events now began to move swiftly and smoothly to the climax. After the conference on May 15, His Majesty had visited each of the assault forces at their ports of assembly. On May 28, subordinate commanders were informed that D-Day would be June 5. From this moment all personnel committed to the assault were "sealed" in their ships or at their camps and assembly points ashore. All mail was impounded and private messages of all kinds forbidden except in case of personal emergency. On June 1, Admiral Ramsay assumed control of operations in the Channel, the functions of the naval Commanders-in-Chief in the home ports being subordinated to his requirements.

I thought it would not be wrong for me to watch the preliminary bombardment in this historic battle from one of our cruiser squadrons, and I asked Admiral Ramsay to make a plan. He arranged for me to embark in H.M.S. *Belfast,* in the late afternoon of the day before D-Day. She would call in at Weymouth Bay on her passage from the Clyde, and would then rejoin her squadron at full speed. She was one of the bombarding ships attached to the centre British force, and I would spend the night in her and watch the dawn attack. I was then to make a short tour of the beaches, with due regard to the unswept mine areas, and come back in a destroyer which would have completed her bombardment and was to return to England for more ammunition.

Admiral Ramsay felt it his duty however to tell the Supreme Commander of what was in the air. Eisenhower protested against my running such risks. As Supreme Commander he could not bear the responsibility. I sent him word, as he has described, that while we accepted him as Supreme Commander of the British forces involved, which in the case of the Navy were four to one compared with those of the United States, we did not in any way admit his right to regulate the complements of the British ships in the Royal Navy. He accepted this undoubted fact, but dwelt on the addition this would impose upon his anxieties. This appeared to be both out of proportion to the scale of events and to our relations. I too had responsibilities, and felt I must be my own judge of my movements. The matter was settled accordingly.

However, a complication occurred which I have His Majesty's permission to recount. When I attended my weekly luncheon with the King on the Tuesday before D-Day (May 30), His

Majesty asked me where I intended to be on D-Day. I replied that I proposed to witness the bombardment from one of the cruiser squadrons. His Majesty immediately said he would like to come too. He had not been under fire except in air raids since the Battle of Jutland, and eagerly welcomed the prospect of renewing the experiences of his youth. I thought about this carefully, and was not unwilling to submit the matter to the Cabinet. It was agreed to discuss the matter with Admiral Ramsay first.

Meanwhile, the King came to the conclusion that neither he nor I ought to go. He was greatly disappointed, and wrote me the following letter:

BUCKINGHAM PALACE
May 31, 1944

My dear Winston,

I have been thinking a great deal of our conversation yesterday, and I have come to the conclusion that it would not be right for either you or I to be where we planned to be on D-Day. I don't think I need emphasise what it would mean to me personally, and to the whole Allied cause, if at this juncture a chance bomb, torpedo, or even a mine, should remove you from the scene; equally a change of Sovereign at this moment would be a serious matter for the country and Empire. We should both, I know, love to be there, but in all seriousness I would ask you to reconsider your plan. Our presence, I feel, would be an embarrassment to those responsible for fighting the ship or ships in which we were, despite anything we might say to them.

So, as I said, I have very reluctantly come to the conclusion that the right thing to do is what normally falls to those at the top on such occasions, namely, to remain at home and wait. I hope very much that you will see it in this light too. The anxiety of these coming days would be very greatly increased for me if I thought that, in addition to everything else, there was a risk, however remote, of my losing your help and guidance.

Believe me,
Yours very sincerely,
GEORGE R.I.

And later:

BUCKINGHAM PALACE
May 31, 1944

My dear Winston,

I hope you will not send me a reply to my letter, as I shall be seeing you tomorrow afternoon, when you can then give me your reactions to it before we see Ramsay.

I am,

Yours very sincerely,

GEORGE R.I.

*   *   *   *   *

At 3.15 P.M. on June 1, the King, with Sir Alan Lascelles in attendance, came to the Map Room at the Annexe, where I with Admiral Ramsay awaited him. The Admiral, who did not then know that there was any idea of the King coming, explained what the *Belfast* would do on the morning of D-Day. It was clear from what he said that those on board the ship would run considerable risks, and also would see very little of the battle. The Admiral was then asked to withdraw for a few minutes, during which it was decided to ask his opinion on the advisability of His Majesty also going to sea in the *Belfast*. The Admiral immediately made it clear that he was not in favour of this. I then said that I should feel obliged to ask the Cabinet and to disclose the Admiral's opinion about the risk, and I said I was sure they would not recommend His Majesty to go. Ramsay then departed. The King said that if it was not right for him to go, neither was it right for me. I replied I was going as Minister of Defence in the exercise of my duty. Sir Alan Lascelles, who the King remarked was "wearing a very long face," said that "His Majesty's anxieties would be increased if he heard his Prime Minister was at the bottom of the English Channel." I replied that that was all arranged for, and that moreover I considered the risk negligible. Sir Alan said that he had always understood that no Minister of the Crown could leave the country without the

Sovereign's permission. I answered that this did not apply, as I should be in one of His Majesty's ships. Lascelles said the ship would be well outside territorial waters. The King then returned to Buckingham Palace.

*   *   *   *   *

On the morning of Friday, June 2, I set out in my train for our siding by Eisenhower's Headquarters near Portsmouth, with Field-Marshal Smuts, Mr. Ernest Bevin, General Ismay, and my personal Staff. Just before we started, a further letter arrived from the King.

BUCKINGHAM PALACE
June 2, 1944

My dear Winston,

I want to make one more appeal to you not to go to sea on D-Day. Please consider my own position. I am a younger man than you, I am a sailor, and as King I am the head of all these Services. There is nothing I would like better than to go to sea, but I have agreed to stay at home; is it fair that you should then do exactly what I should have liked to do myself? You said yesterday afternoon that it would be a fine thing for the King to lead his troops into battle, as in old days; if the King cannot do this, it does not seem to me right that his Prime Minister should take his place.

Then there is your own position. You will see very little, you will run a considerable risk, you will be inaccessible at a critical time, when vital decisions might have to be taken, and however unobtrusive you may be your mere presence on board is bound to be a very heavy additional responsibility to the Admiral and Captain. As I said in my previous letter, your being there would add immeasurably to my anxieties, and your going without consulting your colleagues in the Cabinet would put them in a very difficult position, which they would justifiably resent.

I ask you most earnestly to consider the whole question again, and not let your personal wishes, which I very well understand, lead you to depart from your own high standard of duty to the State.

Believe me,
Your very sincere friend,

GEORGE R.I.

Meanwhile, my train lay just outside Southampton, and we were soon connected by telephone with Eisenhower's Headquarters. That afternoon we paid him a visit. His tents and caravans were very well concealed in a wood nearby. His Majesty was concerned at not having had a reply from me to his letter. At 11.30 P.M. in response to inquiries I spoke to Lascelles at Windsor Castle on the scrambler telephone and said that I had cancelled my arrangements in deference to His Majesty's desire. I wrote the following letter in the small hours of the morning and sent it at once by dispatch-rider to Windsor:

June 3, 1944

Sir,

I must excuse myself for not having answered Your Majesty's letter earlier. It caught me just as I was leaving by the train, and I have been in constant movement ever since. I had a dispatch-rider standing by in order to take it to you tonight.

Sir, I cannot really feel that the first paragraph of your letter takes sufficient account of the fact that there is absolutely no comparison in the British Constitution between a Sovereign and a subject. If Your Majesty had gone, as you desire, on board one of your ships in this bombarding action, it would have required the Cabinet approval beforehand, and I am very much inclined to think, as I told you, that the Cabinet would have advised most strongly against Your Majesty going.

On the other hand, as Prime Minister and Minister of Defence, I ought to be allowed to go where I consider it necessary to the discharge of my duty, and I do not admit that the Cabinet have any right to put restrictions on my freedom of movement. I rely on my own judgment, invoked in many serious matters, as to what are the proper limits of risk which a person who discharges my duties is entitled to run. I must most earnestly ask Your Majesty that no principle shall be laid down which inhibits my freedom of movement when I judge it necessary to acquaint myself with conditions in the various theatres of war. Since Your Majesty does me the honour to be so much concerned about my personal safety on this occasion, I must defer to Your Majesty's wishes, and indeed commands. It is a great comfort to me to know that they arise from Your Majesty's desire to continue me in your service. Though

I regret that I cannot go, I am deeply grateful to Your Majesty
for the motives which have guided Your Majesty in respect of
Your Majesty's humble and devoted servant and subject,

                                        WINSTON S. CHURCHILL

I may add that the cruiser squadron concerned was, as I had
justly estimated, not exposed to any undue danger. In fact, it
did not sustain a single casualty. I should not have referred
to this matter if it had not been publicised in a friendly but
unwittingly inaccurate form by General Eisenhower.

I may here set down the view I have formed over many years
on this sort of thing. A man who has to play an effective part
in taking, with the highest responsibility, grave and terrible
decisions of war may need the refreshment of adventure. He
may need also the comfort that when sending so many others
to their death he may share in a small way their risks. His
field of personal interest, and consequently his forces of action,
are stimulated by direct contact with the event. As a result of
what I saw and learned in the First World War, I was convinced that generals and other high commanders should try
from time to time to see the conditions and aspect of the
battle-scene themselves. I had seen many grievous errors made
through the silly theory that valuable lives should not be en-
dangered. No one was more careful of his personal safety than
I was, but I thought my view and theme of the war were
sufficiently important and authoritative to entitle me to full
freedom of judgment as to how I discharged my task in such a
personal matter.

                    *   *   *   *   *

The weather now began to cause anxiety. A fine spell was
giving way to unsettled conditions, and from June 1 onward a
Commanders' meeting was held twice daily to study the
weather reports. At their first meeting, poor conditions were
predicted for D-Day, with low clouds. This was of prime importance to the Air Forces, affecting both the bombing and
the airborne landings. That same evening, the first warships
sailed from the Clyde, as well as two midget submarines from

Portsmouth, whose duty was to mark the assault areas. June 3 brought little encouragement. A rising westerly wind was whipping up a moderate sea; there was heavy cloud and a lowering cloud base. Predictions for June 5 were gloomy.

That afternoon I drove down to Portsmouth with Mr. Bevin and Field-Marshal Smuts and saw a large number of troops embarking for Normandy. We visited the Heaquarters ship of the 50th Division, and then cruised down the Solent in a launch, boarding one ship after another.

On the way back, we stopped at General Eisenhower's camp and wished him luck. We got back to the train in time for a very late dinner. While it was in progress, Ismay was called to the telephone by Bedell Smith, who told him that the weather was getting worse and that the operation would probably have to be postponed for twenty-four hours. General Eisenhower would wait until the early hours of June 4 before making a definite decision. Meanwhile, units of the great armada would continue to put to sea according to programme.

Ismay came back and reported the bleak news. Those who had seen the array in the Solent felt that the movement was now as impossible to stop as an avalanche. We were haunted by the knowledge that if the bad weather continued and the postponement had to be prolonged beyond June 7 we could not again get the necessary combination of moon and tide for at least another fortnight. Meanwhile the troops had all been briefed. They clearly could not be kept on board these tiny ships indefinitely. How was a leakage to be prevented?

But the anxiety that everyone felt was in no way apparent at the dinner-table in the train. Field-Marshal Smuts was at his most entertaining pitch. He told the story of the Boer surrender at Vereeniging in 1902 — how he had impressed on his colleagues that it was no use fighting on and that they must throw themselves on the mercy of the British. He had been assailed as a coward and a defeatist by his own friends, and he had spent the most difficult hour of his life. In the end however he had won through, had gone to Vereeniging, and peace was made. The Field-Marshal then went on to speak about his experiences at the outbreak of the Second World War, when he had to cross the floor of the House and fight his own Prime Minister, who wished to remain neutral.

We went to bed at about half-past one. Ismay told me that he would wait up to hear the result of the morning conference. As there was nothing I could do about it, I said that I was not to be woken to hear the result. At 4.15 A.M. Eisenhower again met his Commanders, and heard from the weather experts the ominous report, sky overcast, cloud ceiling low, strong south-westerly wind, with rain and moderate sea. The forecast for the 5th was even worse. Reluctantly he ordered a postpone-ment of the attack for twenty-four hours, and the whole vast array was put into reverse in accordance with a carefully pre-pared plan. All convoys at sea turned about and small craft sought shelter in convenient anchorages. Only one large con-voy, comprising a hundred and thirty-eight small vessels, failed to receive the message, but this too was overtaken and turned round without arousing the suspicions of the enemy. It was a hard day for the thousands of men cooped up in landing-craft all round the coast. The Americans, who came from the West Country ports, had the greatest distance to go and suf-fered most.

At about five o'clock that morning, Bedell Smith again tele-phoned Ismay confirming the postponement, and Ismay went to bed. Half an hour later, I woke up and sent for him. He told me the news. He says I made no comment.

*   *   *   *   *

The early post brought me a letter from the President, written a fortnight before and withheld for delivery till the fateful moment came. Alas, I cannot find it. F.D.R. expressed in the most kindly terms his feelings about our joint work and comradeship, and his hopes and longings for our success. I cabled a grateful but somewhat discursive reply.

Prime Minister to President Roosevelt   4 June 44

I was so glad to get your charming letter of May 20. Our friend-ship is my greatest stand-by amid the ever-increasing complications of this exacting war. Averell brought me a good account of your physical health, and I have sustained from many quarters impressions that your political health is also greatly improved. I am here near Ike's Headquarters in my train. His main preoccupation is the weather. There are wonderful sights to see with all these thousands of vessels.

De Gaulle's Committee by a large majority decided that he should accept my invitation to come here. He hummed and hawed, but Massigli and several others threatened to resign if he did not do so. We expect him on D minus 1. If he arrives, Eisenhower will see him for half an hour and explain to him the position exclusively in its military aspect. I shall return to London during the night of D-Day. I do not expect that very much can be done with de Gaulle, but I still hope the word "leadership," which I am told you approved in Hull's speech, may prove serviceable. I do not expect we shall get more than a certain number of miles from the beaches, and probably what we get will be a depopulated area wearing the aspect of a battlefield. This I can explain to de Gaulle safely here when he arrives. I will also deliver him your friendly message to come over to see you. I shall keep you constantly informed.

I see some of your newspapers are upset at my references in the House of Commons to Spain. This is very unfair, as all I have done is to repeat my declaration of October 1940. I only mentioned Franco's name to show how silly it was to identify Spain with him or him with Spain by means of caricatures. I do not care about Franco, but I do not wish to have the Iberian Peninsula hostile to the British after the war. I do not know how I can depend on a de Gaullist France. Germany would have to be held down by main force, and we have a twenty-years alliance with Russia. You must remember that we are very near to all this pleasant outlook.

We should not be able to agree here in attacking countries which have not molested us because we dislike their totalitarian form of government. I do not know whether there is more freedom in Stalin's Russia than in Franco's Spain. I have no intention to seek a quarrel with either.

After D-Day, ought not you and I to send a short message to Stalin, which can be published? Perhaps it would be well to wait till we are definitely established over the other side.

We this month have the all-time high record for the U-boat war
— only four ships of all the United Nations, amounting to about
twenty thousand tons, sunk. In addition, we have four U-boats
sunk for every ship of ours and a tremendous plurality of enemy
ships sunk by our own combined fleets.

I am so glad Alex has not belied your support and impressions
of him. How magnificently your troops have fought. I hear that
relations are admirable between our armies in every rank there,
and here certainly it is an absolute brotherhood. I am looking forward to seeing your Chiefs of Staff. I have been delighted to
receive increasingly good news about Harry. I earnestly hope that
this will be maintained. I am deeply grieved that you cannot come
before that very distant [October] date. Let me know if I can help
matters by a journey.

Presently Mr. Eden arrived with General de Gaulle, who
had just flown in from Algiers. I told de Gaulle that I had
asked him to come because of the forthcoming operation. I
could not do this by telegraph, and I felt that the history of our
two countries required that the liberation of France must not
be undertaken by the British and Americans without the
French being informed. I had intended to invite him a little
before D-Day, but the weather had forced us to postpone the
assault for twenty-four hours, and it might even be later. This
was a grave fact. Thirty-five divisions and four thousand ships
had been assembled in the ports and camps and a hundred and
fifty thousand troops had been embarked for the first wave of the
attack. Many of these had to be kept in conditions of extreme
discomfort in small craft. Eleven thousand planes were ready,
of which eight thousand would go into action, provided the
weather was all right. I then went on to say how much we
regretted the bombing of the French railways, with its loss of
French life, but we had fewer infantry than the Germans, and
it was the only way we could stop them bringing up overpowering reinforcements while we built up our front.

The General was bristling. He asked for an absolutely free
right to telegraph to Algiers in his own cipher. As the recognised head of a great empire, he said it was impossible to deny

him free right of communication. I asked him for an assurance that he would not impart any military information about the forthcoming assault to any of his colleagues, except those actually at our meeting. De Gaulle said that he must be free to keep in touch with Algiers about operations in Italy, and I explained that I was only talking about "Overlord." I then unfolded to him our plan. After he had thanked me for this, I asked him if he would send a public message to France as soon as the armada had actually sailed. Queen Wilhelmina, King Haakon of Norway, and rulers of other countries which the enemy expected us to attack had agreed to do so, and I hoped he would do the same. He said he would.

Mr. Eden now intervened in the conversation, saying that the great operation impending had taken all our thoughts, but after it was launched it might be useful to discuss certain political questions. I explained that I had been in correspondence with the President for some time, and that while he had begun by wanting the General to visit the United States, he did not seem so anxious about it now. This was perhaps because of the way General Giraud had been treated. The President had arranged with Giraud for the French forces to be equipped, and now Giraud was dismissed. To this, de Gaulle replied that he thought it was better at this moment to be in England rather than Washington. I warned him that "liberated France" might for some time only consist of a few people under fire, and both Eden and I strongly urged him to visit Mr. Roosevelt soon. De Gaulle said that he was quite willing to do this, and had so told the President, but he was anxious about who was to administer liberated France. This should have been arranged long ago, last September.

This remark made me speak bluntly.. The United States and Great Britain were willing to risk the lives of scores of thousands of men to liberate France. Whether de Gaulle went to Washington or not was his own affair, but if there was a split between the National Committee of Liberation and the United States, we should almost certainly side with the Americans. About the administration of liberated French soil, if

General de Gaulle wanted us to ask the President to give him
the title-deeds of France the answer was "No." If he wanted us
to ask the President to agree that the Committee was the principal body with whom he should deal in France, the answer was
"Yes." De Gaulle replied that he quite understood that if the
United States and France disagreed, Britain would side with
the United States. With this ungracious remark the interview
ended.

In a little while I took de Gaulle to Eisenhower's Headquarters in the woodland, where he was most ceremoniously
received. Ike and Bedell Smith vied with one another in their
courtesy. Presently Ike took him to their map tent, and for
twenty minutes imparted to him the whole story of what was
about to happen. We then returned to my train. I had expected that de Gaulle would dine with us and come back to
London by this, the swiftest and most convenient route, but he
drew himself up and stated that he preferred to motor with his
French officers separately.

*   *   *   *   *

The hours dragged slowly by until, at 9.15 on the evening of June 4, another fateful conference opened at Eisenhower's battle headquarters. Conditions were bad, typical of
December rather than June, but the weather experts gave
some promise of a temporary improvement on the morning of
the 6th. After this, they predicted a return of rough weather
for an indefinite period. Faced with the desperate alternatives
of accepting the immediate risks or of postponing the attack
for at least a fortnight, General Eisenhower, with the advice
of his Commanders, boldly, and as it proved wisely, chose to go
ahead with the operation, subject to final confirmation early
on the following morning. At 4 A.M. on June 5, the die was
irrevocably cast: the invasion would be launched on June 6.

In retrospect this decision rightly evokes admiration. It was
amply justified by events, and was largely responsible for gaining us the precious advantage of surprise. We now know
that the German meteorological officers informed their High

Command that invasion on the 5th or 6th of June would not be possible owing to stormy weather, which might last for several days. The fact that such a complex series of movements could be accomplished without detection by a wary and determined enemy is a remarkable tribute to the work of the Allied Air Forces and the excellence of our deception plans.

*   *   *   *   *

All day on June 5, the convoys bearing the spearhead of the invasion converged on the rendezvous south of the Isle of Wight. Thence, in an endless stream, led by the minesweepers on a wide front and protected on all sides by the might of the Allied Navies and Air Forces, the greatest armada that ever left our shores set out for the coast of France. The rough conditions at sea were a severe trial to troops on the eve of battle, particularly in the terrible discomfort of the smaller craft. Yet, in spite of all, the vast movement was carried through with almost the precision of a parade, and, although not wholly without loss, such casualties and delays as did occur, mostly to small craft in tow, had no appreciable effect on events.

Round all our coasts the network of defence was keyed to the highest pitch of activity. The Home Fleet was alert against any move by German surface ships, while air patrols watched the enemy coast from Norway to the Channel. Far out at sea, in the Western Approaches and in the Bay of Biscay, aircraft of Coastal Command, in great strength, supported by flotillas of destroyers, kept watch for possible enemy reactions. Our Intelligence told us that over fifty U-boats were concentrated in the French Biscay ports ready to intervene when the moment came. The hour was now striking.

*   *   *   *   *

Here, then, we reach what the Western Powers may justly regard as the supreme climax of the war. Nor, though the road might be long and hard, could we doubt that decisive victory would be gained. Africa was cleared. India had been defended from invasion. Japan, overstrained and disillusioned, was recoiling on her home land. All danger to Australia and New Zealand had passed away. Italy was fighting on our side. The Russian armies had driven the German invaders from their country. All the gains Hitler had acquired so swiftly from the Soviets three years before had vanished with staggering losses of men and equipment. The Crimea had been cleared. The Polish frontiers had been reached. Rumania and Bulgaria were desperately seeking to escape the vengeance of their Eastern conquerors. Russia's new offensive timed with our Continental landing was about to break. While I sat in my chair in the Map Room of the Annexe, the thrilling news of the capture of Rome arrived. The immense cross-Channel enterprise for the liberation of France had begun. All the ships were at sea. We had the mastery of the oceans and of the air.

The Hitler tyranny was doomed. Here, then, we might pause in thankfulness and take hope, not only for victory on all fronts and in all three elements, but also for a safe and happy future for tormented mankind.

END OF BOOK TWO

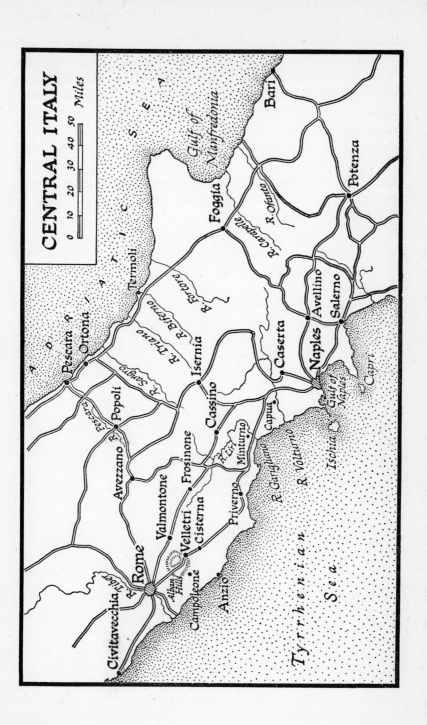

CENTRAL ITALY

0 10 20 30 40 50 Miles

A D R I A T I C S E A

Gulf of Manfredonia

Bari

Potenza

Foggia

R. Ofanto

R. Carapelle

Avellino

Salerno

Naples

Caserta

Capri

Gulf of Naples

Ischia

Termoli

Ortona

Pescara R.

Popoli

Avezzano

R. Fortore

R. Biferno

R. Trigno

R. Sangro

Isernia

Cassino

Frosinone

R. Liri

Minturno

Priverno

R. Garigliano

Capua

R. Volturno

Valmontone

Velletri

Cisterna

Rome

Alban Hills

R. Tiber

Civitavecchia

Campoleone

Anzio

Tyrrhenian Sea

★

Appendices

Contents

★

★

Book one

Appendix A, Book One

LIST OF ABBREVIATIONS

A.A. GUNS.	Anti-aircraft guns, or ack-ack guns
A.D.G.B.	Air Defence of Great Britain
A.F.V.s	Armoured fighting vehicles
A.T. RIFLES	Anti-tank rifles
A.T.S.	(Women's) Auxiliary Territorial Service
C.A.S.	Chief of the Air Staff
C.I.G.S.	Chief of the Imperial General Staff
C.-in-C.	Commander-in-Chief
C.O.S.	Chiefs of Staff
D.N.C.	Director of Naval Construction
F.O.	Foreign Office
G.H.Q.	General Headquarters
G.O.C.	General Officer Commanding
H.M.G.	His Majesty's Government
M.A.P.	Ministry of Aircraft Production
M.E.W.	Ministry of Economic Warfare
M.O.I.	Ministry of Information
M. OF L.	Ministry of Labour
M. OF S.	Ministry of Supply
P.M.	Prime Minister
V.C.A.S.	Vice-Chief of the Air Staff
V.C.I.G.S.	Vice-Chief of the Imperial General Staff
V.C.N.S.	Vice-Chief of the Naval Staff
W.A.A.F.	Women's Auxiliary Air Force
W.R.N.S.	Women's Royal Naval Service ("Wrens")

Appendix B, Book One

LIST OF CODE–NAMES

ACCOLADE: Operations in the Aegean.

ADMIRAL Q: President Roosevelt.

ANAKIM: Recapture of Burma.

ANVIL: Allied landings in the South of France, 1944.

AVALANCHE: Amphibious assault on Naples (Salerno).

BAYTOWN: Attack across the Straits of Messina.

BOMBARDON: Steel outer breakwater used in artificial harbours.

BUCCANEER: Operation against the Andaman Islands.

COLONEL WARDEN: The Prime Minister.

CULVERIN: Operations against Northern Sumatra.

EUREKA: The Teheran Conference, 1943.

GEE: Radar aid to bomber navigation.

GOOSEBERRY: Breakwater used in artificial harbours.

HABAKKUK: Floating seadrome made of ice.

HERCULES: The Capture of Rhodes.

HUSKY: The Capture of Sicily.

JUPITER: Operations in Northern Norway.

LILO: Breakwater used in artificial harbours.

MULBERRY: Artificial harbour.

OBOE: Blind-bombing device.

OLEANDER: Akyab.

OVERLORD: The Liberation of France in 1944.

PENITENT: Operations against the Dalmatian coast.

PHOENIX: Concrete caisson used in artificial harbours.

PIGSTICK: Landings behind the Japanese positions south of Mayu peninsula, on the Arakan coast of Burma.

PLOUGH FORCE: Special Combined Operations Force.

PLUTO: Oil pipe-line across the English Channel.

QUADRANT: The Quebec Conference, 1943.

ROUND-UP: Plan for liberation of France in 1943.

SATURN: Establishment of an Allied force in Turkey in 1943.

SEXTANT: The Cairo Conference, 1943.

SHINGLE: Amphibious operation south of Rome at Anzio.

SLEDGEHAMMER: Plan for attack on Brest or Cherbourg in 1942.

STRANGLE: Air attack on railway lines in Northern Italy.

TENTACLE: Floating airfield, constructed mainly of concrete.

TORCH: Allied invasion of French North Africa in 1942.
TRIDENT: The Washington Conference, 1943.
TUBE ALLOYS: Atomb bomb research.
WHALE: Floating pier used in artificial harbours.
WINDOW: Tinfoil strips used to confuse German radar.
ZIP: Signal used by Commanders-in-Chief to denote the start of an operation.

Appendix C, Book One

PRIME MINISTER'S PERSONAL MINUTES AND TELEGRAMS

June–October, 1943

JUNE

Prime Minister to Minister of War Transport and First Sea Lord   6 June 43

I should be obliged if you would let me have a note on the ships that have passed through the Mediterranean in the different convoys, the character of the cargoes, and what stores have been carried for the British Red Cross to Russia. Let me also know what is proposed in the future.

Prime Minister to Secretary of State for Air and   8 June 43
Minister of Home Security

Please let me have a report setting out what is being done to protect our reservoirs from attacks like those we have made recently in Germany. [On the Mohne Dam.]

POST–WAR CIVIL AVIATION
A PRELIMINARY NOTE

Prime Minister to Lord Cherwell   10 June 43

My ideas about post-war civil aviation are based on the principle of "a fair field and no favour." All the airports of the world should be open to the through traffic of all nations (except the guilty nations) on the payment of reasonable expenses for maintenance and service. No country would however have *the right* to operate an air company, state or private, inside the territory of another. If possible no subsidies should be paid by any Governments. If the traffic proved unremunerative, the necessary support should be given on a schedule agreed by the countries concerned, and in part on the basis of air mail contracts. Subject to the above, any company or corporation, state or individual would be free to operate throughout the world.

2. After the war it is proposed that a world organisation responsible for maintaining peace should be set up. Air-power resulting from civil aviation would necessarily be subject to the control of this body. A sub-committee of the world council or sub-committees of the Continental councils (if any) would regulate disputes and supervise or control quasi-military developments and

644

implications. Subject to this, nations would be encouraged and afforded all facilities to render the best service from the point of view of safety, comfort, and speed of which they were capable.

3. The difficulty of getting agreement among the Dominions at this stage should not prevent the formulation of British policy after consultation with them. At the same time it is of the utmost importance and urgency to ascertain the views and wishes of the United States. Everything will be much easier if agreement is reached with them. . . .

Prime Minister to Major Morton 11 June 43

What is the truth about the tales I hear of application by various bodies for the leading captured generals to visit some of our education centres and generally to be taken about the country to see things? There was an idea, for instance, that [the Italian] General Jesse should visit Eton. I should be opposed to any of this nonsense. These generals are not to be moved out of their places of internment without my being informed beforehand in each case.

Prime Minister to Sir Edward Bridges 13 June 43

Please draft for me a further warning to all Ministers, high officials, Parliamentary Private Secretaries, etc., about speaking with extreme caution and reticence to foreign [neutral] diplomatic representatives in this country. Although these are very often quite friendly and sincerely wish us to win the war, they do not hesitate to magnify their own positions with their Governments by reporting anything they can pick up, and the Governments may trade this to the enemy in return for other items. Only those who have the duty and authority, either general or special, to impart information should discuss war matters with them or in their presence.

2. Even general war matters and items appearing in the newspapers should not be discussed, because confirmation of these is obtained by these foreigners when they come into contact with persons who have secret knowledge. Lunches and dinners of an informal character with members of the diplomatic staffs should be avoided. You should be consulted in any particular case, and you have my authority to advise. Personal intimacy with foreigners should be reduced to a minimum.

Prime Minister to First Lord 13 June 43

Admiral Cunningham expressed the opinion to me that our light naval craft could have achieved even more in the Mediterranean if the engines of the motor torpedo boats had been more reliable. Let me have a report on this, and let me know whether this is a local problem connected with the maintenance of these craft or whether there is a basic weakness in the design.

Prime Minister to Foreign Secretary and Minister of Information 13 June 43

I have read the report on German morale in Tunisia. It is hardly possible to pay a higher tribute to the fighting qualities of the German soldier, and the introduction of words like "brutish" in no way detracts from the formidable impression this account gives. Their "extraordinary stupidity" certainly does not extend to the use of their arms or to their seizing of tactical opportunities.

Prime Minister to General Ismay and Sir Edward Bridges   15 June 43

Will you please make the following terminology effective in all British official correspondence:

For "aeroplane" the word *"aircraft"* should be used; for "aerodrome" either *"airfield"* or *"airport."* The expression "airdrome" should not be used by us.

It is a good thing to have a rule and stick to it.

Prime Minister to Minister of Aircraft Production [Sir Stafford Cripps]   15 June 43

I am very pleased to see that you are keeping so well up to your programme. You are quite right about the harm that is done by overcalling the hand. Promises which cannot be fulfilled lead to a large waste of effort by the Air Ministry in training, buildings, etc., quite apart from the effect on your own factories.

What I am not quite clear about is your labour situation. I note that you have received a very much smaller quota than was allocated to you. Had you discounted this when you made the programme, or does the fact that you could fulfil it mean that efficiency has increased beyond your expectations? These matters will all have to be considered most carefully in view of the constantly increasing labour stringency. You certainly seem to have received a smaller fraction than any other department so far.

I approve of your list of aircraft with special priorities. As you say, anything that can be done to exceed the programme would be particularly valuable for these types.

I am very pleased that you are pushing ahead with new types of fighters. I am particularly interested in the jet-propelled type of aircraft, of which you showed me a model the other day. Please report progress from time to time, and let me know when we may expect these machines to become available for operations.

Prime Minister to Director of Military Intelligence   15 June 43

What is your present most detailed estimate of the strength in Sicily? First, the Germans: we know the strength in detail of the division which is forming. It is under seven thousand. What oddments are there, including air grounds-men? What reinforcements have reached them, or are on the way?

Secondly, give me an analysis of the Italians there. There was a story about eighty-four battalions for coastal garrison purposes; also, another estimate said seven or eight divisions. How are they divided? The easy surrender of the fifteen thousand men on Pantelleria and the four or five thousand on Lampedusa shows the temper of these Italian masses.

Prime Minister to Chief of the Air Staff   16 June 43

The air forces in Egypt, etc., are very large indeed. Pray let me know how they are to play their part in the next few months. They seem to be doing very little at present. What state of preparation have the plans for reinforcing Turkey reached? What proportion of the air forces in Egypt, etc., are employed in helping in Sicily? We cannot afford to have any part of the Air Force standing idle.

Prime Minister to General Ismay   17 June 43

I am strongly of the opinion that wound stripes should be issued as in the last war. Pray bring this to the notice of the three departments. The War Office are of course the principal party concerned. I wish to make a submission to the King by Monday. The matter must have been previously considered. Let me have any papers on the subject. There must be no further delay in this, on account of the "Purple Hearts" which the Americans are giving to their own soldiers and are distressed not to give to ours.

2. The second question is the issue of chevrons for every year of service abroad, which I think also would be greatly appreciated by the soldiers.

Prime Minister to General Ismay, for C.O.S. Committee   17 June 43

I am anxious about deception plans for Sicily, and therefore asked last night for a special report. The newspapers all seem to be pointing to Sicily, and, to judge by the maps and cartoons that are published in so many organs here, and, I have no doubt, in the United States, this objective would seem to be proclaimed and common property.

2. Safety lies in multiplication and confusion of objectives. A helpful note seems to have been struck this morning in some papers in saying that we have sufficient forces to attack several objectives at once. This should be stressed. Mr. Bracken is seeing the press representatives this afternoon. Also, surely Greece requires some prominence?

Prime Minister to General Ismay, for C.O.S. Committee   18 June 43

Why cannot we fit some of these Fijian Commandos into the Burma fighting or elsewhere?

Prime Minister to Chief of the Air Staff   19 June 43

I quite understand the relief given to Takoradi by the new route through Casablanca, and by the opening of the Mediterranean. Indeed, the time has come to consider economies of personnel on the Takoradi route, and I shall be glad to receive your proposals to this end.

Prime Minister to Secretary of State for India   20 June 43

I entirely agree with the Deputy Prime Minister that the pay of the Indian

Army should be increased. Broadly speaking, I should make a twenty-five per cent reduction in the numbers and spread the saving over the pay of the rest.

Prime Minister to Lord President of the Council   20 June 43

Would it not be well to instruct the Minister of Works and Buildings to use his compulsory powers for land acquisition and to build these three thousand cottages [for agricultural labourers] exactly as if they were airfields or war factories, and to fit them in as best possible with the necessary war requirements, assigning them a reasonable priority? To ask local authorities all over the country, unarmed with the necessary powers, to get a move on in respect of this handful of cottages and to make their way through the inevitable correspondence with all the public departments engaged in war activities would lead to an immense amount of futile effort. It seems to me that everybody is being disturbed and that we are becoming involved in discredit through this comparatively small job. Broadly speaking, my view is, either do it or don't do it.

Prime Minister to Brigadier Jacob   22 June 43

Please make out the table about the coast defences of Tripoli, showing the contrast between the pre-war estimates and what was actually found. Naturally, as the war progressed, we learnt through frequent contacts more about the defence armaments of Tripoli. We shall now however be attacking a number of new places with which we have not been in contact, and for these the inflated pre-war estimates may exercise an undue influence. This was the whole point of my inquiry.

Prime Minister to C.I.G.S.   25 June 43

What is the position about the increased proportion of rifle strength in an infantry battalion? It was agreed that it should be increased by thirty-six, and I hoped that it might be by seventy-two.

Prime Minister to Lord Chancellor   25 June 43

What is the position of the King's elder daughter? At what age does she become officially of age, (a) while still the Heir-Apparent, and (b) should she succeed?

Surely if the King and Queen leave the country, Princess Elizabeth, having reached the age of eighteen years, ought to be a member of a Council of State? It may be that after the war the King and Queen will make a progress through their Dominions, and in that case it would certainly be desirable that the future Queen should have every opportunity of acquiring experience in affairs.

Prime Minister to Secretary of State for War   26 June 43

I am glad to see that large receipts of .300 ball ammunition are expected by the end of July. In view of these, and having regard to the existing stocks, it should be possible to make extra issues to the Home Guard for training at once, so as to take advantage of the remaining summer months.

Prime Minister to Chiefs of Staff Committee 30 June 43

I note that ninety-five per cent of the Army and R.A.F. vehicles shipped in May to theatres other than North Africa were boxed. This is most satisfactory, and a considerable contribution to the war effort.

I trust you will aim at a similarly high standard in the remaining theatres. Every month gained in getting adequate assembly plant running is a real saving.

Prime Minister to Minister of Production and 30 June 43
President of the Board of Trade

I am still anxious about the leather position. Are you satisfied that there will not be a run on the shops when the new ration books become valid? Cannot anything be done to ease the shoe repair position?

In view of the seriousness of the civilian situation, could any relief be obtained from the Services, either in boots or in leather? I note that stocks of boots for the two and a half million men in the Army are higher than civilian stocks for fourteen million men.

What are you doing about the long-term outlook? Would it not be desirable to work out with the Americans a picture of world supply and demand over, say, the next twelve months?

Prime Minister to C.I.G.S. 30 June 43

I understand that seventy-five cargo ships are said to be required to carry the equipment of the British troops who will return from North Africa in the winter. This presumably means that they will bring back most of their vehicles with them.

As we are still sending out considerable numbers of vehicles to North Africa, could we not make a saving of shipping in both directions if the returning divisions left most of their vehicles in Africa and were given new ones in England.

JULY

Prime Minister to General Ismay, for C.O.S. Committee 2 July 43

The North African Headquarters seem to be getting more than ever "sicklied o'er with the pale cast of thought." It is quite right for Planning Staffs to explore mentally all possible hypotheses, but happily human affairs are simpler than that.

2. We must first fight the battle which is in the hands of Alexander and Montgomery. Supposing that all goes well, or that there is even a collapse, the next step will show itself quite clearly. If, on the other hand, we do not succeed in Sicily, no question of the next step arises.

3. We cannot allow the Americans to prevent our powerful armies from having full employment. Their Staffs seem now to be wriggling away to [the idea of] Sardinia. We must stiffen them all up and allow no weakness. I trust the Chiefs of Staff will once again prevent through the Combined Chiefs of Staff this weak shuffling away from the issue.

4. Above all we must preserve to ourselves the full power to judge and launch once we know what Sicily tastes like.

5. I should be very glad to discuss this with you today at 3 P.M. I do not like the present attitude. Strong guidance must be given.

MAN-POWER

Prime Minister to Lord Cherwell   3 July 43

Please divide the subject into seven or eight main claimants — Army, Navy, Air, Ministry of Aircraft Production, etc. How many did they have, and what did they ask for in the January review? What did they get, and how many have they got now? How many more are they asking for now?

It is on this table that I propose to work.

Let me have it tonight.

Prime Minister to Lord President of the Council and Sir Edward Bridges   3 July 43

What is the exact situation now about these cottages for agricultural la- bourers? Who is in charge of building them, and when are they going to get built? The Minister of Works and Buildings led me to understand that he has the whole matter in his hands now. Is this so?

Prime Minister to Lord President of the Council   5 July 43

You may remember my note last December about the increase in short-term sickness, shown in figures compiled by the Government Actuary.

It is disquieting to find that the rising trend has continued during the winter. The addition, thus revealed, to the numbers normally kept away from work by sickness is quite an appreciable fraction of our total labour force; and the effect on the war effort is the same if a large proportion of them are war-weary rather than genuinely ill.

Prime Minister to Secretary of State for Air and Chief of the Air Staff   5 July 43

In view of all the assurances given about the comparative impotence of enemy bombing, I am of the opinion that the time has come to review the question of the black-out so far as night work in industrial establishments is concerned.

The need for saving labour in every direction in order to speed up the aircraft programme makes it indispensable that night work is not hampered by black- out restrictions.

I should like an assurance that the Air Ministry is not insisting on any restrictions of this character which hamper production.

Prime Minister to Secretary of State for War   5 July 43

I am glad to note that your requirements of crude rubber are no higher than in 1942, and that the Army is helping to conserve our supplies of vital raw materials. Since the number of Army vehicles will be greater this year, the result is satisfactory.

Prime Minister to Minister of Economic Warfare   5 July 43

I do not view the situation in France as you do, and I do not agree with your sweeping generalisations, taken from much too narrow a base. If the [French] Liberation Committee so conduct themselves as to win the confidence of the British and United States Governments, we could no doubt transfer to them the responsibility of financing the resistance movements in France. It is however the Committee, and not General de Gaulle, with whom we should work. We are now endeavouring to build up the collective and impersonal strength of the Committee and to elevate the civilian influences as much as possible.

Prime Minister to Sir Edward Bridges   11 July 43

I am very much interested in the question of Basic English. The widespread use of this would be a gain to us far more durable and fruitful than the annexation of great provinces. It would also fit in with my ideas of closer union with the United States by making it even more worth while to belong to the English-speaking club.

2. I propose to raise this tomorrow at the Cabinet with a view to setting up a committee of Ministers to examine the matter, and, if the result is favourable, to advise how best to proceed. The Minister of Information, the Colonial Secretary, the President of the Board of Education, and perhaps Mr. Law, representing the Foreign Office, would all seem suitable.

3. I contemplate that the B.B.C. should teach Basic English every day as part of their propaganda, and generally make a big push to propagate this method of interchange of thought.

4. Let me know your ideas about the committee, and put the matter on the agenda for tomorrow.

Prime Minister to Foreign Secretary   11 July 43

About King Peter's marriage, we should recur to first principles. The whole tradition of military Europe has been in favour of "*les noces de guerre*," and nothing could be more natural and nothing could be more becoming than that a young king should marry a highly suitable princess on the eve of his departure for the war. Thus he has a chance of perpetuating his dynasty, and anyhow of giving effect to those primary instincts to which the humblest of human beings have a right.

2. Against this we have some tale, which I disbelieve of a martial race, that the Serb principle is that no one must get married in wartime. *Prima facie* this

would seem to condone extra-marital relations. Then a bundle of Ministers that has been flung out of Yugoslavia are rolling over each other to obtain the shadow offices of an *émigré* Government. Some are in favour of the marriage, some are not. The King and the Princess are strongly in favour of it, and in my view in this tangle they are the only ones whose opinions should weigh with us.

3. The Foreign Office should discard eighteenth-century politics and take a simple and straightforward view. Let us tell the King and tell his Ministers we think the marriage should take place, and if the King is worthy of his hazardous throne we may leave the rest to him.

4. I may add that I am prepared to go into action in the House of Commons or on any democratic platform in Great Britain or the United States on the principles set forth above; and I think the Cabinet ought to have a chance of expressing its own views. We might be back in the refinements of Louis XIV instead of the lusty squalor of the twentieth century. Are we not fighting this war for liberty and democracy? My advice to the King, if you wish me to see him, will be to go to the nearest Registry Office and take a chance. So what?

AIRCRAFT FOR AUSTRALIA

Prime Minister to Secretary of State for Air and Chief of the Air Staff   12 July 43

It is of high importance for the future of the British Commonwealth and Empire that we should be represented in the defence of Australia and the war in the Pacific. From this point of view the single squadron of the Royal Air Force which we have sent has played a part out of all proportion to the size of the unit. The fact that Australia has over here eighty-one hundred Australian air crews, including some of their very best airmen, and the share they have taken in the Empire Training Scheme, certainly leaves us heavily in their debt so far as the air is concerned.

2. It is not merely a question of Spitfires or other fighter aircraft, but of British squadrons capable of doing full justice to the Royal Air Force. I should therefore like to send three Spitfire fighter squadrons to Australia during the present year, and persuade the Americans to give us the fighter aircraft they would otherwise have sent to Australia. I have little doubt that I can explain all this quite satisfactorily to the President. You will note however that I am not proposing to mount Australian airmen on British machines, but to send complete British units. I note from my last return that you have nine hundred and forty-five more fighter pilots on effective strength than fighter machines serviceable, and therefore it seems to me that forty or fifty could easily be spared out of these. It is my duty to preserve good will between the Mother Country and this vast continent of Australia, inhabited by six million people of our race and tongue.

3. Pray let me have your comments and proposals.

(*Action this day.*)
Prime Minister to General Ismay, for C.O.S. Committee   13 July 43

The time has come to bring the Polish troops from Persia into the Mediterranean theatre. Politically this is highly desirable, as the men wish to fight, and once engaged will worry less about their own affairs, which are tragic. The whole corps should move from Persia to Port Said and Alexandria. The intention is to use them in Italy.

2. We have five months in hand to use all our strength against Italy. Let me have a list of the British-controlled [Allied] troops available which are not yet committed to the Sicilian battle and are capable of active field operations.

Prime Minister to First Sea Lord   13 July 43

I am shocked to see the destruction of the *Duchess of York* convoy. Will you let me have a copy of the signal from the C.-in-C. Mediterranean about ten days ago, warning us of the "intolerable" (I think that was the word) dangers of the air attack on this route too near the Spanish coast? The loss of these large ships will spoil our monthly record, which anyhow is burdened with operational casualties. Pray let me know what will be done to avoid this form of air attack in the future. Surely it is worth while going farther out beyond the range of Focke-Wulfs.

2. I see that *Port Fairy* was damaged west of Cape St. Vincent. Where did the aircraft come from, and how far out was she? If the enemy could reach her why could not Gibraltar air give her protection?

Prime Minister to Sir Edward Bridges   14 July 43

The Public Relations Officers are becoming a scandal, and the whole system requires searching scrutiny and drastic pruning. Pray advise me how to proceed. A small Cabinet committee with a suitable reference would seem to be indicated.

(*Action this day.*)
Prime Minister to Secretary of State for War and C.I.G.S.   16 July 43

I learn with great concern from C.I.G.S. that our 1st Armoured Division, a unit of exceptional quality and experience, on which years of training have been lavished, is now being used to guard prisoners of war. As an emergency measure for (say) a month this might be tolerated. It must now immediately be brought to an end. Rifle-armed formations, not incorporated in divisional units, to the number of at least ten thousand, must be sent to North Africa either from this country or the Delta to guard prisoners. Lord Leathers should regard the shipping for any from this country on a high priority.

2. At the earliest moment the 1st Armoured Division is to be reconstituted with its vehicles and brought up to full strength. The necessary training to restore its efficiency cannot be delayed. Let me have a programme and time-table. I understand that C.I.G.S. has already protested to General Eisenhower. Let me know exactly what happened, and what the answer was.

3. Are there any more units in this condition? Let me have a list of all divisional and separate brigade formations (*a*) in Northwest Africa and (*b*) in the Middle East, stating the condition of each and the task on which it is employed. What is the state of the South African Division? What has happened to the 201st Guards Brigade? Where is the 7th Armoured Division? Where is the 4th Indian Division? Is the New Zealand Division progressing to schedule? What stage has been reached in the movement of the Polish Division to Syria? How far are these divisions complete and equipped?

Prime Minister to Chief of the Air Staff   16 July 43

I still do not understand why it is necessary to have 2946 crews on effective strength [in Fighter Command] in order to man 1732 serviceable aircraft, or indeed a total initial equipment of 1966.

See how different are the figures of Bomber Command, who are far more heavily engaged than the fighters, and who have only 1353 crews to an initial establishment of 1072 aircraft, and only 1095 crews operational for 1039 aircraft serviceable.

The losses in Fighter Command are not comparable to those endured by the bombers, and yet it has this enormous surplus of crews. How far does this personnel surplus extend into the ground staff?

Prime Minister to Lord President of the Council   17 July 43

I have promised Lord Winterton a further communication about the building of the agricultural cottages. I now feel however that as I should like him to have a fuller explanation of the position than could conveniently be contained in a letter it would be helpful if you could see Lord Winterton yourself.[1]

(*Action this day.*)
Prime Minister to C.I.G.S.   19 July 43

I do not feel very comfortable about the strength of the Dover garrison, which I visited on Saturday. There is only one battalion in Dover, and another at St. Margaret's Bay. These can be reinforced by a brigade after some hours. There are of course plenty of troops farther back.

2. There is of course no question of invasion, but when I asked General Swayne what would happen if three or four thousand Storm Troopers of the Commando type came across one night, he was not able to give me a very reassuring answer. He said they would certainly get ashore, but would be turned out afterwards, and he also emphasised the shortness of the warning that would be received. This is not good enough. Dover is so near that perhaps half an hour is all the notice you would get by radar. I do not think the Germans are likely to try, but it would be a tremendous score if they did have possession of part of Dover for even three or four hours. It would produce

[1] See minute of July 3 to Lord President of the Council.

an effect on public opinion ten times as bad as the *Scharnhorst* and *Gneisenau* incident.

3. I should be much against locking up too many troops even at this point on the coast, but it seems to me we have gone to the other extreme and are exposing ourselves to what might be a most vexatious affront. In my opinion, at least another brigade should be actually in the coast defences or the strong points, and available for immediate action should a landing be attempted. We should all look very silly if some of our valuable guns were blown up.

Pray go into this matter anew.

Prime Minister to Secretary of State for War and   19 July 43
Minister of Information

In difficult cases about releases from military service it is important that the rules should not be broken or relaxed. Nevertheless, the Secretary of State has a discretionary power, where the public service may be advantaged, to make exceptions in respect of high-class personnel whose contributions to the war effort may be greater in their civilian employment. In using this discretion he would naturally have regard to the fact that only a very small part of the Army is engaged in actual fighting, and that many transferences from civil life to the Army merely involve a change of non-combatant jobs.

2. It is the duty of Ministers to settle such matters by personal arrangement, and not to let them come to a point where either departmental antagonisms arise on small points or I am called upon to intervene.

Prime Minister to Minister of Information   19 July 43

I saw again yesterday the two American Army films *Divide and Conquer* and *The Battle of Britain*. I think they are the best propaganda yet seen in this country. Moreover, they teach people about what happened in 1940, which few realised completely at the time and which is already beginning to fade in memory. I consider that these films should have the widest possible showing. Is there any difficulty in our picture houses taking them? What terms, broadly, would you arrange with them? If there is any monopolistic refusal, do not hesitate to come to me. I would ask for legislation if necessary.

2. Where are the other four films? Two have certainly been mentioned by name. I wish to see them. Why is there this long delay? Are the film companies making underground resistance? Please let me have a report on these second two films. What is holding them up?

3. As you know, I am willing to make a short statement introducing the films and praising the attitude of the Americans. But I wish to see the other two films first. I take much interest in this business, and I hope you will press it forward strongly.

Prime Minister to Chief of the Air Staff   21 July 43

I am disposed to sanction this proposal of the Secretary for Petroleum. You know I attach the greatest importance to the creation of a sufficiency of landing grounds specially adapted to meet fog conditions. I hope this is fully realised.

Prime Minister to First Lord   23 July 43

I think it is rather a pregnant fact that out of forty-five thousand officers and ratings [in the Fleet Air Arm], of which over four thousand are officers, only thirty should have been killed, missing, or have been taken prisoners during the three months ending April 30. I am very glad of course that they have not suffered, but the whole question of the scale of the Fleet Air Arm is raised by this clear proof of how very rarely it is brought into contact with the enemy. When such immense demands are made upon us by the Fleet Air Arm in respect of men and machines, one is bound, however ungrateful the task may seem, to scrutinise its actual employment against the enemy. I am sure it is not the fault of the officers and men that they have not had more opportunity, and it may be the period in question was exceptional. We cannot however keep such a large mass of high-class personnel of the highest fighting quality in a condition of non-activity so far as actual contact with the enemy is concerned.

Pray give this matter your careful consideration, because I shall be returning to it in the near future.

Prime Minister to General Ismay, for C.O.S. Committee   24 July 43

See now how all these difficulties [in Burma] are mounting up, and what a vast expenditure of force is required for these trumpery gains. All the commanders on the spot seem to be competing with one another to magnify their demands and the obstacles they have to overcome.

2. All this shows how necessary it is to decide on a commander. I still consider he should be a determined and competent soldier, in the prime of life and with the latest experience in the field. General Oliver Leese is, I believe, the right man, and as soon as the fighting in Sicily is over he should come back to this country for consultation. I consider Wingate should command the army against Burma. He is a man of genius and audacity, and has rightly been discerned by all eyes as a figure quite above the ordinary level. The expression "the Clive of Burma" has already gained currency. There is no doubt that in the welter of inefficiency and lassitude which has characterised our operations on the Indian front, this man, his force and his achievements, stand out, and no mere question of seniority must obstruct the advance of real personalities to their proper stations in war. He too should come home for discussion here at an early date.

Prime Minister to General Ismay, for C.O.S. Committee   25 July 43

See the various telegrams about the ill-treatment of our people in North Russia. The only way to deal with this kind of thing is for ostentatious preparations to be made to withdraw the whole of our personnel without saying anything to the Russian authorities. Let a plan be made for this. As soon as the local Russians see that we are off, they will report to Moscow, and will of course realise that the departure of our personnel means the end of the Arctic convoys. If anything will bring them to their senses, this will. If not, anyway we had better be out of it, as it only causes friction. Experience has taught me that it is not worth while arguing with Soviet people. One simply has to confront them with the new fact and await their reactions.

Prime Minister to C.I.G.S. 25 July 43

I am obliged to you for reviewing the strength of the Dover garrison. I had not taken into consideration the important forces mentioned by you. Are you sure that all these, especially the Royal Navy and Royal Air Force, are organised for immediate action at the shortest notice? Of course, it could only be by night.

The possibility I had in mind was a smash-and-grab raid by about two thousand Storm Troopers brought across in fast motor-boats. Provided you are satisfied that there is no danger of this, that the cliffs are unscalable and that the landing points and defences are adequately garrisoned, I am content.[2]

Prime Minister to General Ismay, for C.O.S. Committee 26 July 43

It is vital and urgent to appoint a young, competent soldier, well trained in war, to become Supreme Commander [in the Burma theatre], and to re-examine the whole problem of the war on this front so as to infuse vigour and audacity into the operations.

2. I know the Chiefs of Staff fully realise what a foolish thing it now looks to go and concentrate precious resources from the Mediterranean in order to attack the one speck of land in the whole of this theatre, namely, Akyab, which the enemy are making a kind of Gibraltar and are capable of reinforcing up to an entire Japanese division. For this petty purpose, now rightly stripped of its consequential attempt upon Rangoon, we are to utilise the whole amphibious resources available in the Bay of Bengal for the whole of the year 1944. Even Ramree is to be left over until after the 1944 monsoon. A more silly way of waging war by a nation possessing overwhelming sea-power and air-power can hardly be conceived, and I should certainly not be prepared to take responsibility for such a waste of effort and above all of time.

3. The proper course for the campaign of 1944 is as follows: (*a*) Maximum air aid to China, improvement of the air route and protection of the airfields. (*b*) Maximum pressure by operations similar to those conducted by General Wingate in Assam, and, wherever [else] contact can be made on land, with the Japanese forces. (*c*) The far-flung amphibious operation hitherto called "Second Anakim," which can be launched in regions where fighting is not interrupted by the monsoon season and where our naval and air powers can be brought into the fullest play. It is on this that the most urgent and intense study should now be concentrated by the Staffs.

[2] See minute of July 19 to C.I.G.S.

4. The matter must now be brought up before the Defence Committee, in order that their views in principle may be ascertained before our conference at Quebec.

Prime Minister to President of the Board of Trade   26 July 43

I am told that in spite of contributions from civilian supplies there is at present a shortage of playing cards for use by the forces and workers in industry. The importance of providing amusement for the forces in their leisure hours and in long periods of waiting and monotony in out-of-the-way places, and for the sailors penned up in their ships for months together, cannot be overstated. Nothing is more handy, more portable, or more capable of prolonged usage than a pack of cards.

Let me have a report on this subject, and show me how you can remedy this deficiency. It ought to mean only a microscopic drain on our resources to make a few hundred thousand packs.

Prime Minister to Secretary of State for War (to see) and C.I.G.S.   26 July 43

I am willing not to send a personal telegram to Eisenhower on the state of the 1st Armoured Division in order that he may not think you were pressing me to do so. However, I can only agree to this if prompt and drastic action is taken, for I am determined that this fine unit shall be immediately brought to the highest state of efficiency and equipment. We shall need it all the more if large distances have to be covered rapidly in Italy, and especially if our front broadens out into the northern part of Italy and the valley of the Po.

2. Will you therefore inform General Eisenhower that I am deeply concerned in this matter, and procure a prompt and satisfactory settlement with him.

3. Will you also give me a programme of the re-equipment of the division, and thereafter let me have reports fortnightly on the progress made towards its becoming in all ways fit for action.[3]

Prime Minister to Minister of Agriculture   30 July 43

I shall be much obliged if you will give me a brief report on the harvest, both hay and corn.

Prime Minister to Colonel Price   31 July 43

I do not consider that the date 1948 should now be mentioned as the hypothetical date for the ending of the war with Japan. This matter can be discussed between us during our conference at Quebec and on the way to it. Obviously the long-term projects of the Admiralty must be before us at the time of taking any such decisions.

Prime Minister to Minister of Aircraft Production   31 July 43

I am concerned that you hold out such slender hopes of our getting jet-

[3] See minute of July 16 to Secretary of State for War.

propelled aircraft soon. I have heard that there is considerable diffusion of effort, and that even the air-frames, which should not present any difficulty, are apt to be behindhand.

Would it not be a good thing to examine the numerous engines which it seems are under development and to concentrate our efforts on the two or three [types] which we may hope to get into production quickly? There are numerous reports of German jet-propelled aircraft, and we cannot afford to be left behind.

AUGUST

Prime Minister to President of the Board of Trade   1 Aug. 43

Thank you for your note about shortages of playing cards.[4] What happened to the 1,950,000 produced over and above the 1,300,000 issued in the last twelve months?

2. As to the future twelve months, the demands appear to be well under 2,000,000 packs, against which you propose to make 2,250,000 packs. I should be very willing to support you in getting the twenty more workers and hundred tons of paper necessary to make an additional million, but first I must know what has happened to the 1,950,000 surplus in the last twelve months, and, secondly, what is the reserve you consider necessary to have "in hand for emergency." The important thing is to have the cards freely forthcoming when called for, and although the soldiers should have priority civilian workers need them too.

Prime Minister to First Sea Lord   1 Aug. 43

I have suggested to the President that we issue from Hyde Park during our conference at Quebec our monthly statement about the anti-U-boat warfare. This will mean it will come out on the 13th or 14th, instead of on the 10th.

2. I am anxious to strike a strong and heavy blow this time on German hopes, and I should like to press the President to agree to the following items: (*a*) In the first half of 1942, 1.6 ships. In the second half of 1942, .8 of a ship. In the first half of 1943 .4 of a ship. (*b*) In the ninety-two days of May, June, and July, eighty-seven, or whatever is the figure, U-boats are known to have been destroyed in addition to the many which have been damaged. (*c*) The losses of Allied merchant shipping all over the world were greater in July than in June, which was a record month, but they are substantially less than the average of, say, the period January 1942 to June 1943, inclusive, or January 1943 to June 1943, inclusive, whichever you like. The operational losses in the capture of Sicily do not exceed, say, seventy thousand tons. (*d*) During the present year — that is, to the end of July — the new ships completed by the United States, Great Britain, and Canada exceeded all sinkings in the shipping

---

[4] See minute of July 26 to President of the Board of Trade.

of the United Nations by upwards of, say, three million tons — i.e., the nearest million under the true figure.

Pray let these points be considered before we leave, so that I can discuss the whole matter with the President.

P.S. — How many of them were sunk by the British?

Prime Minister to General Ismay   2 Aug. 43

Make sure that no code-names are approved without my seeing them first.

Prime Minister to C.I.G.S.   2 Aug. 43

Eisenhower's telegram about relief of the 1st Armoured Division from garrison duties.

Please let me know what can be done, consulting Lord Leathers about shipping, to meet the further requirements of guards for prisoners of war.[5]

2. I do not understand why it was necessary to strip all other armoured units in the Middle East in order to provide the very limited armoured forces taking part in "Husky." Let me have a report showing the exact number of tanks held by each of the various units in Africa, and also the last tank report, which showed, I think, nearly three thousand tanks in possession of Middle East Command.

3. We should not hesitate to take Shermans from a British armoured division in this country to send out at once by special ships in order to get the 1st Armoured Division rapidly re-equipped.

4. Let me also have a return showing the number of tanks available in Great Britain, and the number expected from America and from supply in the next three months.

Prime Minister to C.I.G.S.   2 Aug. 43

I am counting on you to make sure that these prime units of our Army which we have had so much trouble and delay in making are not melted down into slush by uncomprehending hands.[6]

We are getting a mass of tanks of all kinds in the Middle East, and also at the same time a litter of bits and pieces of personnel, where once stood perfectly organised veteran armoured divisions and brigades.

Nothing must stand in the way of rehabilitation.

Prime Minister to Lord President of the Council   2 Aug. 43

I am much obliged to you for all the trouble you have taken, and I welcome the further inquiries you are to make into the Army Bureau of Current Affairs.

Every effort should be used to prevent extra time, money, and military personnel being absorbed in these activities, which, although admirable in themselves, must not be allowed unduly to cumber the military machine and

---

[5] See minutes of July 16 and 26.
[6] See previous minute.

increase the heavy disproportion of non-combatant services. Above all, no man fit to fight should be drawn into this organisation, and the utmost vigilance must be used to correct the tendency of all such bodies to magnify themselves and their numbers.

Prime Minister to Minister of Aircraft Production   3 Aug. 43

The fall in engine production is very painful. I quite realise that it is the holiday season, but the fall in new production seems to have been much greater this year than last.

Prime Minister to Deputy Prime Minister   6 Aug. 43

Your committee on Air Force establishments should certainly probe the enormous surpluses of crews compared with serviceable aircraft in the fighter squadrons.[7] 3038 crews are maintained to man 1725 aircraft. The reason given is that they have to be standing about waiting to take off at any moment, but this reason is good only over certain areas and under certain conditions. The fighter aircraft have not had heavy losses since the Battle of Britain, and it looks to me as if substantial economies could be made here. One wonders whether everything is on a similarly lavish scale. Bomber Command, although in far more continuous heavy action, work on a much smaller margin. Coastal Command are however remarkably well supplied with surplus crews. Here however the need to have as many aircraft as possible out on the long patrols is paramount, and may be only satisfiable by practical duplication of crews. This, I repeat, does not apply to fighter aircraft.

2. Another point which requires searching is the accumulation of Hurricanes and Spitfires at Takoradi. In the latest return, dated July 30, there are 183, of which 43 are Spitfires. Considering that this route is falling into abeyance on account of a much better route becoming open through the Mediterranean, we should scrutinise narrowly the personnel employed on the route, as well as this habit of keeping a mass of invaluable aircraft additional to all Middle East reserves in the tank at Takoradi.

Prime Minister to Foreign Secretary   6 Aug. 43

I do not think that the Russians have any anxieties about the rearmament of Turkey on its present scale. The Russians' preponderance of strength is so great that the trifling improvements we are making in the Turkish forces need not, and I believe will not, disturb them.

2. No doubt they would be annoyed by Turkey complicating the situation in the Balkans without doing anything effective to help Russia defeat Germany.

3. Obviously however the Russians will not remain contented with the present state of the Straits, and I do not suppose they have forgotten that we offered them Constantinople in the earlier part of the late war. Turkey's greatest safety lies in the active association with the United Nations. As you

[7] See minute of July 16 to Chief of the Air Staff.

know, the time may come very soon when we shall ask her to admit our air squadrons and certain other forces to protect them in order to bomb Ploesti and gradually secure the control of the Straits and the Black Sea. There is not much basis of real conversation with Russia about Turkey till we know what line Turkey takes.

Prime Minister to General Ismay   8 Aug. 43

I have crossed out on the attached paper many unsuitable names. Operations in which large numbers of men may lose their lives ought not to be described by code-words which imply a boastful and overconfident sentiment, such as "Triumphant," or, conversely, which are calculated to invest the plan with an air of despondency, such as "Woebetide," "Massacre," "Jumble," "Trouble," "Fidget," "Flimsy," "Pathetic," and "Jaundice." They ought not to be names of a frivolous character, such as "Bunnyhug," "Billingsgate," "Apéritif," and "Ballyhoo." They should not be ordinary words often used in other connections, such as "Flood," "Smooth," "Sudden," "Supreme," "Fullforce," and "Fullspeed." Names of living people — Ministers or Commanders — should be avoided; e.g., "Bracken."

2. After all, the world is wide, and intelligent thought will readily supply an unlimited number of well-sounding names which do not suggest the character of the operation or disparage it in any way and do not enable some widow or mother to say that her son was killed in an operation called "Bunnyhug" or "Ballyhoo."

3. Proper names are good in this field. The heroes of antiquity, figures from Greek and Roman mythology, the constellations and stars, famous racehorses, names of British and American war heroes, could be used, provided they fall within the rules above. There are no doubt many other themes that could be suggested.

4. Care should be taken in all this process. An efficient and a successful administration manifests itself equally in small as in great matters.

Prime Minister to General Ismay, for C.O.S. Committee   10 Aug. 43

Please see this telegram.[8] There is no objection to the employment of Commandos, which are in fact regular troops of the highest order and the only ones we are likely to be able to spare for the Balkans this year. Fully accredited British military or diplomatic officers can of course accompany the Commandos to negotiate any surrender that may be asked for. The Middle East Commanders-in-Chief must not be encouraged to take conventional reactionary views.

Prime Minister to Minister of Production and Minister of Supply   11 Aug. 43

I am shocked at the appallingly low output of thirty-nine tanks for the week

[8] From Middle East Defence Committee, deprecating the employment of Commandos in the Dodecanese, etc., as the Italians and Germans were unlikely to surrender to them.

ending July 31. I do not feel that the explanation of summer holidays is sufficient, and I shall be glad if you will let me have a full report. How does this figure compare with forecasts, and are your forecasts being realised, especially in the modern type of tanks? I shall require to be fully convinced on this matter, which has an important bearing on our policy regarding acceptance of American tanks.

Prime Minister to Foreign Secretary   14 Aug. 43

All this is quite true, but it might better have been left unsaid. The displacement of Ribbentrop by von Papen would be a milestone of importance, and would probably lead to further disintegration in the Nazi machine. There is no need for us to discourage this process by continually uttering the slogan "Unconditional Surrender." As long as we do not have to commit ourselves to dealing with any particular new figure or new Government, our advantage is clear. We certainly do not want, if we can help it, to get them all fused together in a solid desperate block for whom there is no hope. I am sure you will agree with me that a gradual break-up in Germany must mean a weakening of their resistance, and consequently the saving of hundreds of thousands of British and American lives.

Prime Minister to First Sea Lord   15 Aug. 43

I hope you will consider whether it is not possible to arrest the traffic in the Cape area by turning your ships into Simonstown and Kilindini until the anti-U-boat reinforcements now on the way have arrived. I have asked Lord Leathers to give me the proportion of ships sunk to the total sailed. Nineteen is, however, a very heavy loss on a small and severely rationed traffic.

SEPTEMBER

Prime Minister (Washington) to Sir Ronald Campbell   13 Sept. 43

I have drafted the following message, as you desire, for our Consuls in the Middle West.

Before sending it out, you should consult Mr. Harry Hopkins privately as to whether he thinks it would be a suitable intervention for me to make.

"British Consuls in the Middle West should let everyone there know how much we in Britain admire and value the tremendous war effort made by so many of these States, which, though a thousand miles from the sea, are making their weight tell on all the battle-fronts and hastening the triumph of the good cause.

"I wish indeed I could have come to some of these great cities to express myself our British thanks for the splendid exertions which are being made."

CIVIL AVIATION

Prime Minister to President Roosevelt   13 Sept. 43

I have told our Government that you made no objection when I said that we intended to hold a preliminary Commonwealth meeting in London or Canada, and that this would be only to focus our own British Commonwealth ideas for subsequent discussion with the United States Government.

2. I said that, about the proposed International Conference, you thought it might wait till the matter had been discussed at the forthcoming tripartite Anglo-Soviet-American meetings.

3. I mentioned that your preliminary view comprised the following: (i) There should be private ownership. (ii) Key points should be available for international use on a reciprocal basis. (iii) Internal traffic should be reserved to internal companies. (iv) Government support may be required on an international basis for certain non-paying routes.

Prime Minister to Lord President of the Council   16 Sept. 43

The Italians have not been able to comply with the conditions specified in General Eisenhower's broadcast of July 29, and in my view we may therefore consider our hands free in the matter. We should proceed with all arrangements now made for the further importation of Italian prisoners. Where are the great mass that we have taken? Over 250,000 were captured by General Wavell alone. It would be rather difficult to move to England men taken after the Armistice, who in many cases have done their best to help us or have not resisted at all, but we have these larger pools to draw on, and work in the United Kingdom is more important than in India or South Africa. There should be a certain amount of return shipping from India. The War Office should supply the exact location of all Italian prisoners belonging to us, wherever they may be.

2. An arrangement could no doubt be made with the Badoglio Government, whom we have many ways of helping, in respect of further supplies of Italian labour. As a result of an arrangement with the Italian Government by which we get more labour, I see no reason why the status of Italian prisoners now in Great Britain should not be modified and they be placed on the basis of civilian Pioneer Corps internees, or something like that. I certainly look forward to getting 100,000 more Italians into England for work purposes during 1944.

Prime Minister to First Lord and V.C.N.S.   26 Sept. 43

What is being done to equip our submarines with an acoustic torpedo for their own defence when submerged and attacked by enemy anti-submarine craft?

Prime Minister to Minister of Food and Minister of War Transport   27 Sept. 43

I think we should certainly use some of the shipping space in vessels returning from North Africa for bringing over oranges and lemons from the Mediterranean area to this country. Pray consult together and let me have a note setting out what is being done and what is possible.

Prime Minister to First Lord 27 Sept. 43

Please see that Lord Cherwell is kept informed about the German glider bomb, and also about the foxing devices, so that he can keep me in touch with all developments.

Prime Minister to Minister of War Transport 29 Sept. 43

It is indispensable to diminish the queues for the buses and provide a better service for workers returning home, especially in the London area. This is certainly possible in view of the greatly improved oil position. Pray make proposals for immediate action in good time before the winter comes. You should aim at a twenty-five per cent increase in the evening services. War efficiency is lost when people are tired out before they get home.

Prime Minister to C.I.G.S. 30 Sept. 43

Let me have a short return of the present garrison at Cyprus. They ought to be able to find seven or eight thousand men in case the opportunity comes for an unopposed re-entry into Greece. There would be no question of occupying the country, but only giving a political support to a lawful restored Government.

Prime Minister to President of the Board of Trade and 30 Sept. 43
Minister of Food

It seems clear that there may be a world shortage of many important foodstuffs after the liberation of Europe. I am anxious lest we should be committed to any estimates of relief requirements, which might prejudice our own supplies, before the Cabinet has had an opportunity of discussing the whole question.

Pray let me have a note on this as soon as possible.

OCTOBER

Prime Minister to Admiral Mountbatten, and to 2 Oct. 43
General Ismay, for C.O.S. Committee

It seems to me that this draft Order of the Day would be a very good text for Admiral Mountbatten to use when visiting detachments of his forces. I deprecate however at this stage any general publication of such a document. The only consequence of it will be to draw more Japanese to this theatre. I cannot too strongly emphasise the importance of damping down all publicity about this theatre for at least three months. If it is communicated to any portion of the troops, the strictest censorship should be used to prevent it being printed either in the Indian or world press. I shall myself by referring to the southeast Asia theatre when I next speak in the House of Commons, in terms like these: "The climatic conditions, the famine and the floods, have greatly set back all possibilities in this theatre. The new Commander-in-Chief will require to survey the whole situation on the spot and to visit many parts of the great regions with which he is concerned. Further prolonged periods of training are necessary for the troops. It would be very foolish to base expectations of large-scale action upon the fact that a new Commander-in-Chief has been appointed and that the Command is undergoing a very complete reorganisation."

This is much the best way to get through these next three or four months. It need in no way prevent the animation of the Army by visits of Admiral Mountbatten to the various widely separated centres of the Command or his infusing into all officers and men the sense of great days coming. The opposite impression should however be given to the world public and to the enemy.

> "The sower went forth sowing,
> The seed in secret slept
> Through months of faith and patience,
> Till out the red blade leapt."

Basic English

Prime Minister to Secretary of State for India   3 Oct. 43

I was shocked to find on my return to this country that the Cabinet Committee appointed on July 12, 1943, had never once met. You volunteered to undertake this task, and I certainly thought you would be admirably qualified for it. Pray let me have a report of your progress up to date.

I have received a letter from Mr. Ogden suggesting that a special investigator should be sent to spend a week with him to learn all about Basic English, and I think it would be very wise to accept this invitation, so that your committee can be advised on details at an early date. The matter has become of great importance, as Premier Stalin is also interested. If you feel the pressure of your other duties is too heavy on you, I will myself take on the duty of presiding over the Committee, but I hope you will be able to relieve me of this.[9]

Prime Minister to First Lord   4 Oct. 43

I should be obliged if you would let Lord Cherwell make me a short report on acoustic homing torpedoes, as he will be able to explain them to me very briefly.

Prime Minister to Minister of War Transport   4 Oct. 43

Surely we ought to get hold of this 24,000-ton ship [Italian merchant ship *Saturnia*] and put her on the Atlantic route at the earliest moment for the build-up for "Overlord," etc.

[9] See minute of July 11 to Sir Edward Bridges.

Prime Minister to Minister of Labour and National Service   6 Oct. 43

I am glad to see you have managed to get 17,800 new workers into Ministry of Aircraft Production's labour force in August, apart from increases in the additional work done for M.A.P. in other factories. If you can keep up this excellent rate, we should achieve the target set on July 23 by the end of the year.

Prime Minister to Chief of the Air Staff   6 Oct. 43

Recent evidence shows that the Germans are working hard on jet-propelled aircraft, and accentuates the need for the utmost pressure to be put on their development here.

Prime Minister to Foreign Secretary   6 Oct. 43

It should be remembered that the reason why we sheered off making this agreement about the western frontiers of Russia and substituted the Twenty Years Treaty was the perfectly clear menace of very considerable division of opinion in the House of Commons. I know of no reason for supposing that this same opposition might not manifest itself again, perhaps in an even stronger form. The opponents would have the advantage of invoking very large principles against us.

At a Peace Conference the position can be viewed as a whole, and adjustments in one direction balanced by those in another. There is therefore the greatest need to reserve territorial questions for the general settlement. This is even more true of the United States position, especially in an election year. It would be well therefore to have the American attitude clearly deployed before we adopt a new position in advance of the Twenty Years Treaty.

2. I think we should do everything in our power to persuade the Poles to agree with the Russians about their eastern frontier, in return for gains in East Prussia and Silesia. We could certainly promise to use our influence in this respect.

Fog Dispersal

Prime Minister to Chief of the Air Staff   7 Oct. 43

Lord Cherwell tells me he had seen the installation working at Graveley, although not in fog, and that he was much impressed by it. Although it burns several tons of oil per minute, this will probably be improved. If the installations allow us to operate on nights which have hitherto been barred because there is a risk of fog, a lot will be gained even if the burners never have to be turned on. And of course the saving of bombers, if and when fog occurs, is worth many tons of oil, of which we now happily have a good stock.

I hope that the rate of progress with the installations will be maintained and that all eight will be operational by December.

Prime Minister to Foreign Secretary and Minister of War Transport 7 Oct. 43

What is this report from Washington so widely quoted in today's newspapers, on the Allied shipping position, stating that at least 2,500,000 Americans can be sent over here before Christmas and that the invasion of the Continent can be advanced by at least six months? This nonsense is said to emanate from the Senate Sub-Committee on War Mobilisation.

I shall certainly be asked questions about this when the House meets.

Prime Minister to Secretary of State for War and C.I.G.S.   11 Oct. 43

Confusion is caused by the attempt to calculate Allied and enemy strength in "divisions." The word "division" is no common standard. For instance, the establishment of a German standard division is 20,000. The average standard strength on the Russian Front is probably not more than 7000 or 8000. We had a case the other day of a German division of no more than 1800 infantry and eighteen guns. What is the establishment and strength of the Russian divisions opposite to them? Let me have a list of the German divisions south of Rome, showing their estimated battle strength. What are the estimated battle strengths of all British divisions in Italy and in North Africa in men and guns, including anti-tank and anti-aircraft? What is the believed strength of the United States divisions in Italy and in Africa? What is the strength of each British division in the Expeditionary Force — i.e., the number of men who will actually go overseas as a unit?

It is said that a British division with its share of corps troops and L. of C. is 42,000, yet when they are moved abroad 15,000 seems to be the maximum. I have been told that the United States divisions being built up for "Overlord" have an over-all strength of 51,000. How many of these per division will actually proceed overseas?

2. A report showing the effective strengths of all divisions in the West should be prepared, and I should like to have this return kept up to date every month, according to the best information or estimates possible.

3. Let me have the best analysis you can make of the British forces in Italy, showing the number of divisions and their battle strengths, and also, separately, the ration strength of the British army now landed in Italy.

Prime Minister to Minister of War Transport   11 Oct. 43

Let me have a report on bus queues in London and other great cities, and what measures you are taking to reduce them.

Prime Minister to Minister of Production   12 Oct. 43

I recently invited Lord Cherwell to inquire into and report on the relative efficiency of the high explosives used by the German and British forces respectively. A copy of his preliminary report is attached.

The Chiefs of Staff strongly recommend that we should change over to aluminised explosives without waiting for the result of further trials. I agree. Pray let me have a report of what this change will involve in the course of the next week.

The question of how this state of affairs has been allowed to arise should be the subject of an inquiry held under the authority of the Minister of Defence. Pray propose three members, with reference. The whole matter is to be kept most secret.

Prime Minister to Foreign Office,   13 Oct. 43
Lord President of the Council, and Chancellor of the Exchequer

Field-Marshal Smuts tells me that he has about 80,000 Italian prisoners in South Africa, and that he would be very glad to let us have a large number of them — he mentioned up to 40,000 — for work in the United Kingdom.

This seems to me very important, and should be considered.[10]

Prime Minister to Brigadier Jacob   16 Oct. 43

Let me have the most detailed analysis possible, without undue delay, of the base troops [in Egypt], amounting to 241,000. What are they the base of now the war has moved away from the Middle East and the armies remain based on Northwest Africa to a large extent? It seems to me that this figure of 241,000 men, including 116,000 British, requires most searching examination, and I propose that a special committee shall be appointed on that subject. Let me first of all however have the facts immediately available.

BUS QUEUES

Prime Minister to Minister of War Transport   16 Oct. 43

I am glad you are taking steps to improve the position. In the London Passenger Transport Board region about five and a half million bus journeys are made daily. An extra minute wasted per journey every day is equivalent to 10,000 persons working a nine-hour day over the year in this area alone.[11]

Prime Minister to Brigadier Hollis, for C.O.S. Committee   24 Oct. 43

This paper about directives to Supreme Commanders looks very simple from a distance and appeals to the American sense of logic. However, in practice it is found not sufficient for a Government to give a general a directive to beat the enemy, and wait to see what happens. The matter is much more complicated. The general may well be below the level of his task, and has often been found so. A definite measure of guidance and control is required from the Staffs and from the high Government authorities. It would not be in accordance with the British view that any such element should be ruled out.

Prime Minister to Home Secretary   24 Oct. 43

Once we are sure that we have a plan for Food, Work, and Homes ready in case Hitler collapses, it will be quite possible to refine it.

[10] See minute of September 16 to the Lord President of the Council.
[11] See minutes of September 29 and October 11.

Prime Minister to First Lord   24 Oct. 43

I do not consider you have any right to strike off these forty vessels from the escort and fleet destroyer strength. They may, if you will, be left unmanned in material reserve and only brought out in case of serious emergency.

It is quite impossible for us to take up so much of the war effort of the country in building up such enormous new programmes if you do not make full use of your material. Considering that you are now building destroyers which take two years to build, we must consider whether these older ones cannot be repaired and kept going. This failure, coupled with the immense demands for aircraft-carriers, causes me a great deal of concern now that the Italian Fleet and the German Navy are practically extinct. Future naval programmes must be subjected to a very strict scrutiny, not only by me but by the War Cabinet.

Prime Minister to Brigadier Hollis   27 Oct. 43

Why has it been decided to abandon the rubber Lilo? Let me have photographs showing the cruciform Lilo, and explain how it produces the desired effect. It seems to me that a complete change of plan has been made.

What is the difference between this concrete and steel structure and ordinary breakwaters? What time would it take to put down? How many ships would it require to carry, and so on?

It would be a pity to spoil a promising plan by magnifying the demands on material and labour to an excessive degree.

Prime Minister to Chancellor of the Duchy of Lancaster   27 Oct. 43

I am not in favour of the appointment to high military rank of, or of the wearing of uniform by, civilians holding civilian or quasi-civilian posts unless this is clearly necessary to the successful performance of their duties. In this light, pray inquire into the principles adopted in the Security Service for gazetting its officers to commissions and as regards their wearing uniform. Let me have a short report.

Prime Minister to Brigadier Hollis   31 Oct. 43

Let me have a return showing the present development of the British forces for "Overlord"; also a statement of what formations will be left here at home apart from the above.

Appendix D, Book One

PLANS FOR THE TRANSITION PERIOD

At their meeting on October 21, the War Cabinet approved generally the line of approach set out in my memorandum of October 19,[1] and I undertook to circulate a further note setting out the procedure for ensuring the completion of plans for the transition period.

I

2. The first step is to obtain a list of all the action which has to be taken, the schemes which must be prepared, and the administrative arrangements which must be planned and organised in advance, so that when hostilities with Germany cease, the country as a whole will find that the new emergency has been foreseen and the necessary preliminary action has been taken.

3. For this purpose each department is called upon to submit to the Secretary of the War Cabinet, not later than November 10, a schedule showing all the action which they will have to take and the measures required, (a) in the period immediately after hostilities with Germany end; (b) so far as can reasonably be foreseen during the rest of the transition period, which may be taken as a working basis as two years from the defeat of Germany.

4. The returns should cover all matters for which each department is primarily responsible. There are however numerous questions of common concern to many departments which have been remitted for examination to special organisations or committees. In these cases returns should be submitted by the head of the organisation or the chairman of the committee concerned.

5. The returns should include the following particulars: (a) The state of preparedness of the schemes — i.e., whether they are ready now or how long they will take to complete. (b) Points of principle on which decisions are necessary before further work can be carried out. (c) Whether legislation by statute, Order in Council, or Defence Regulation is called for, whether such legislation has been prepared, and whether it needs to be enacted before the defeat of Germany.

6. An important part of the plan will be a careful survey of the whole field of legislation (including Defence Regulations and other subordinate legislation) to determine which war-time powers must be retained and which can be dispensed with in the transitional period.

II

7. The second stage will be for a general survey to be framed showing the whole range of preparations for the transition period. At this stage we must

---

[1] See Book One, Chapter 9, pages 170–71.

make sure that there are no gaps or contradictions between the different parts of the plan. I will myself supervise this process.

8. While the transition from peace to war differs in many respects from the transition from war to peace, and War Book procedure is not altogether appropriate, it will probably be convenient that all departments should have a copy of this survey to assist them in understanding how their preparations fit in with the general scheme.

An officer of high rank should be designated in each department who should be personally responsible for seeing that the schedule of the preparations for which his department is primarily responsible is kept continuously up to date.

III

9. The third stage will be to make sure that the whole scheme is brought to a state of readiness and is so maintained. It may be found, in the first instance, that preparatory action on a number of important matters is being delayed because decisions have not been reached on points of principle. I propose, when the general plan has been drawn up, to preside over a series of meetings at which the various parts will be reviewed, and decisions thereafter obtained from the War Cabinet on any matters which hamper the progress of preparations.

Appendix E, Book One

MONTHLY TOTALS OF SHIPPING LOSSES, BRITISH, ALLIED, AND NEUTRAL, BY ENEMY ACTION

Month	British		Allied		Neutral		Total	
	No. of Ships	Gross Tons	No. of Ships	Gross Tons	No. of Ships	Gross Tons	No. of Ships	Gross Tons
Jan. 1943	19	98,096	24	143,358	7	19,905	50	261,359
Feb.	29	166,947	39	232,235	5	3,880	73	403,062
March	62	384,914	53	303,284	5	5,191	120	693,389
April	33	194,252	27	137,081	4	13,347	64	344,680
May	31	146,496	26	151,299	1	1,633	58	299,428
June	12	44,975	13	75,854	3	2,996	28	123,825
July	30	187,759	26	166,231	5	11,408	61	365,398
Aug.	14	62,900	9	56,578	2	323	25	119,801
Sept.	12	60,541	15	94,010	2	1,868	29	156,419
Oct.	11	57,565	17	81,631	1	665	29	139,861
Nov.	15	61,593	12	82,696	2	102	29	144,391
Dec.	10	55,611	21	112,913	—	—	31	168,524
Totals...	278	1,521,649	282	1,637,170	37	61,318	597	3,220,137
Jan. 1944	16	67,112	9	62,115	1	1,408	26	130,635
Feb.	12	63,411	8	53,244	3	200	23	116,855
March	10	49,637	14	104,964	1	3,359	25	157,960
April	3	21,439	10	60,933	—	—	13	82,372
May	5	27,297	—	—	—	—	5	27,297
Totals...	46	228,896	41	281,256	5	4,967	92	515,119

Appendix F, Book One[1]

SUMMARY OF ORDER OF BATTLE, GERMAN AND ITALIAN DIVISIONS, SEPTEMBER 8, 1943 [2]

ITALIAN DIVISIONS

Divisions marked with a star are recorded as being weak or of low category

	Italian	*German*
North Italy	5 infantry *5 infantry	6⅓ infantry 2 motor and armoured
Central Italy	3 infantry 2 motor and armoured *2 infantry	2 motor and armoured
South Italy	3 infantry *1 infantry	2 infantry 4 motor and armoured
Sardinia	4 infantry	1
South France	4 infantry (under relief by German troops, strength unknown, from Rundstedt's Command)	
Corsica	2 infantry	⅓ infantry 2 motor and armoured
Slovenia, Croatia, Dalmatia	8 infantry	9 infantry 6 brigades (Croat Alpine troops)
Herzegovina, Montenegro	6 infantry	2 infantry 1 motor and armoured 2 brigades (Croat Alpine troops)

[1] See Book One, Chapter 8.
[2] From General Francesco Rossi, *Come arrivammo all' armistizio.*

Albania	5 infantry 1 motor	Nil (but a call on 2 German and 2 Bulgarian Divisions in Serbia and Macedonia)
Greece	7 infantry	6 infantry 1 armoured
Crete	1 infantry	1 infantry
Aegean	2 infantry	1 infantry with A.F.V.s

Totals:	Italian	German
Italian mainland	21 divisions (of which 8 are weak or of low category)	16⅓
"Overseas"	36	24⅓
Grand Total:	61 divisions (of which 8 are weak or of low category)	40⅔ divisions

German Dispositions in Detail

Army Group — Rommel

North Italy   *Area*

24th Armoured Division   Parma — Bologna
Hitler S.S. Armoured Division
44th Infantry Division   Alto Adige
One Infantry Brigade
71st Infantry Division   Tarvisio — Piedicolle — Postumia
65th Infantry Division   Sestri Levante — Val Taro —
76th Infantry Division   Pontremoli — Apuania
94th Infantry Division
305th Infantry Division

German Southern Command — Kesselring

Central Italy

3d Panzer Group Motor and Armoured   Lake Bolsena — Viterbo
2d Panzer Group Parachute

South Italy

15th Infantry Division   Formia
Goering Armoured Division   Naples
16th Armoured Division   Salerno

1st Parachute Division   Puglia Basilicata
26th Armoured Division   Calabria
29th Panzer Group Motor Division   Calabria

Sardinia

90th Infantry Motor Division

Corsica

One brigade, "Reich Fuehrer," Motor and Armoured

German Southeast Command — Lohr

Slovenia, Croatia, Dalmatia

114th Infantry Division   Bihac
373d (German–Croat) Infantry Division
187th Infantry Division   Sava
369th (German–Croat) Infantry Division
173d Infantry Division
Two (?) Infantry Divisions   Zagreb
One S.S. Division
One (Croat) Mountain Division   Various
Six (Croat) Mountain Brigades

Herzegovina, Montenegro

Prinz Eugen S.S. Motor and Armoured
  Division   Mostar
118th (? 108th) Infantry Division   Prijepolie Plevlja
297th Infantry Division   Ibar Valley
Two (Croat) Mountain Brigades   Various

Greece

One Mountain Division   Janina
One L. of C. Division   Salonica
One Infantry Division   Larissa
104th Infantry Division   Agrinion
11th Infantry Division   Piraeus
117th Infantry Division   Peloponnese
One Armoured Division

Crete

22d Infantry Division

Rhodes

55th Motor and Armoured Division

★

BOOK TWO

Appendix A, Book Two

THE RELEASE OF THE MOSLEYS
CONSTITUTIONAL ISSUES

WHILE WE WERE IN CONFERENCE at Cairo and Teheran, a domestic issue of Constitutional importance which had been before us since the beginning of October came to a head. It is recounted here in order not to break the general narrative.

Prime Minister to Home Secretary   6 Oct. 43

Let me know what is the report of the Medical Commissioners upon Sir Oswald Mosley's state of health. I have received privately some rather serious medical reports about him, but they are of course unofficial.

Mr. Morrison's reports confirmed this information, and he decided to release Sir Oswald and his wife. I was sure this would raise controversy.

Prime Minister to Home Secretary   21 Nov. 43

I expect you will be questioned about the release of the Mosleys. No doubt the pith of your case is health and humanity. You might however consider whether you should not unfold as a background the great principle of *habeas corpus* and trial by jury, which are the supreme protection invented by the British people for ordinary individuals against the State. The power of the Executive to cast a man into prison without formulating any charge known to the law, and particularly to deny him judgment by his peers for an indefinite period, is in the highest degree odious, and is the foundation of all totalitarian Governments, whether Nazi or Communist. It is only when extreme danger to the State can be pleaded that this power may be temporarily assumed by the Executive, and even so its working must be interpreted with the utmost vigilance by a Free Parliament. As the danger passes, persons so imprisoned, against whom there is no charge which courts and juries would accept, should be released, as you have been steadily doing, until hardly any are left. Extraordinary powers assumed by the Executive with the consent of Parliament in emergencies should be yielded up when and as the emergency declines. Nothing can be more abhorrent to democracy than to imprison a person or keep him in prison because he is unpopular. This is really the test of civilisation.

Differences arose between Ministers on the step the Home Secretary proposed to take. I assured him of my full support, though I should have preferred to deal with the question as a whole, rather than in a particular case.

Prime Minister (Cairo) to Home Secretary   25 Nov. 43

I am convinced 18B should be completely abolished, as the national emergency no longer justifies abrogation of individual rights of *habeas corpus* and trial by jury on definite charges. I doubt very much whether any serious resistance would be made to this. There are of course a number of totalitarian-minded people who like to keep their political opponents in prison on *lettres de cachet*, but I do not think they constitute a majority. I have already on more than one occasion expressed in Parliament my distaste for these exceptional powers, and my hope that success and security would enable us to dispense with them. However, as these views conflict with the line you have adopted I shall not press them at this stage.

Any unpopularity you have incurred through correct and humane exercise of your functions will be repaid in a few months by public respect.

Prime Minister (Cairo) to Deputy Prime Minister and   25 Nov. 43
Home Secretary

In case there is a debate on an amendment to the Address to terminate 18B, I would strongly counsel the line that we very much regret having to be responsible for such powers, which we fully admit are contrary to the whole spirit of British public life and British history. These powers were conferred on us by Parliament because of the dire peril of the State, and we have to administer them in accordance with the principles of humanity, but all the time we desire to give back these powers from the Executive to Parliament. The fact that we have gained great victories and are in a much safer position makes the Government the more desirous of parting with exceptional powers. The time has not yet come when these can be fully dispensed with, but we can look forward to that day.

2. On no account should we lend any countenance to the totalitarian idea of the right of the Executive to lock up its political opponents or unpopular people. The door should be kept open for the full restoration of the fundamental British rights of *habeas corpus* and trial by jury on charges known to the law. I must warn you that departure from these broad principles because the Home Office have a few people they like to keep under control by exceptional means may become a source of very grave difference between us and the totalitarian-minded folk. In such a quarrel I am sure I could carry the majority in the House of Commons and the mass of the nation. Anyhow, I would try. It seems to me you have a perfectly good line in deploring the fact that such powers are thrust on you and in proclaiming your resolve to use them with the utmost circumspection and humanity. Do not quit the heights.

Mr. Attlee now reported to me that the Cabinet had decided to support the Home Secretary in releasing the Mosleys from prison. There was, I learned, considerable Parliamentary agitation against this step.

Prime Minister (Teheran) to Home Secretary   29 Nov. 43

Considering you are supported by the Cabinet, and by me as Prime Minister, you have no choice whatever but to fight the matter through, and you will no doubt be supported in any direct issue by a very large majority.

2. There is no hurry about the general question of 18B. I certainly recommend however that you express your distaste for such powers and your regret that dangers of the country have forced you to assume them, and your earnest desire to return to normal. This is a becoming attitude in a democratic Minister.

Mr. Morrison showed firmness and courage in resisting the storm that threatened him, and, as is often the case, it dispersed. People who are not prepared to do unpopular things and to defy clamour are not fit to be Ministers in times of stress.

Prime Minister (Teheran) to Home Secretary   2 Dec. 43

I congratulate you on the strong support given to you by the House of Commons. Your courageous and humane discharge of your most difficult and disagreeable functions will gain its reward in the respect of the British nation.

Appendix B, Book Two

PRIME MINISTER'S PERSONAL MINUTES AND TELEGRAMS

November 1943–*May* 1944

NOVEMBER

Prime Minister to C.I.G.S. 1 Nov. 43

Thank you for your information, which still however leaves me mystified on various points. I entirely agree that we must have a "yardstick," and that is exactly what I am in search of. A yardstick is a common measure, and it is just by this test that the use of the word "division," which may mean a German 20,000 or a Russian 15,000 or a British and American 42,000, so lamentably fails.

2. Please let me have the best analysis the Intelligence Department can make of a gross British and a full German division,[1] showing of what elements the additional British 22,000 consists. . . .

4. Let us take the 5th British Infantry Division, which has newly arrived in Italy, as an example. It has 18,480 men on its strength. Where are the other 23,000-odd? When do they come into Italy? What proportion of these 23,000 are combatant troops in the sense of taking their places in the fighting line at some time or other?

5. Could I also have a list of the corps and army formations in Italy, with their estimated ration strength attached? Of course, I quite understand these estimates may not be exactly up to date.

6. In the British Expeditionary Force what part is played by the Polish Armoured Division, which I see has no fewer than 400 tanks? It does not appear to be included either in the Twenty-First Army Group or the Home Field Army. Are there any other units of this kind? What happens to all the army tank brigades, of which there are eight on my latest return? It is absolutely necessary for me to form an opinion on these matters.

7. My impression is that the Germans get about 12,000 men who actually fight out of divisions of 20,000 gross, and we get about 15,000 or 16,000 out of divisions of 42,000. If so, the result is not very encouraging, considering that the Germans fight at least as well as we do and move over great distances with much rapidity. On the other hand, the British corps and army commanders have larger proportions of artillery, engineers, signals, etc., in their

---

[1] See minute of October 11 to Secretary of State for War, Appendix C, Book One.

hands than the Germans, and can therefore support their divisions more powerfully as circumstances require.

8. As far as possible, when giving me returns, pray let me have ration strength, number of battalions, number of tanks, and number of guns. I take a grave view of the increasing sedentary and non-combatant tail which we are acquiring. For an operation like "Overlord," where every man has to have his place in the boat and be fed over beaches, the most thorough analysis must be made of the rearward services, especially in the opening phases. I hope to find time shortly to go into this in some detail at the Defence Committee or Staff meeting.

Prime Minister to First Lord   1 Nov. 43

I am at first sight wholly in favour of your view about the light fleet carriers and I shall be glad to discuss the matter with you and the First Sea Lord and Controller some time this week. I cannot see that there is any need for such great numbers in 1945 and 1946.

2. The whole question of our naval strength must however now be raised. The Admiralty are demanding 288,000 more men for the Fleet in 1944 and 71,000 for the shipyards, total about 360,000. This is at a time when the man-power shortage enforces heavy cuts on every form of national war activity. The question arises, why does the Admiralty require more men in 1944 than in 1943, observing that the new facts are: (*a*) The decisive defeat of the U-boats, largely through the air assistance. (*b*) The surrender of the Italian Fleet. (*c*) The accession of the *Richelieu* and many lesser French units to active service. (*d*) The establishment by the United States of two-to-one strength over the Japanese in the Pacific. (*e*) The immobilisation for a good many months to come of the *Tirpitz*, the only hostile capital unit in the Western world (unless the new German carrier is ready).

3. One would expect that in view of these immense new facts it would be possible to make very sensible reductions even in the existing personnel of the Navy and to lay up old vessels in care and maintenance without hesitation as new ones come out. It is for Cabinet consideration whether a very large pro-gramme of laying up old vessels and also of slowing down or suspending the more distant units now under construction should not be adopted. All this would be in answer to the question, why should you ask for so much more when your opponents' force is so much less and your Allies' so much stronger? The Admiralty would not render the best service to the country at this crisis if it kept in commission a single vessel that was not needed against the enemy.

4. With regard to the forty-odd destroyers which it is proposed to lay up, I think the right course would be to keep them all in care and maintenance after refitting them and to slow down or suspend the long-range fleet destroyers, which we shall not get for two years.

5. Let me now have a list of all warships which you propose to keep in commission in 1944, compared with those which existed at the time when Italy

and Germany were both our enemies, say January 1, 1941, together with their complements. The destroyers and smaller craft may be stated in categories with the complements aggregated. Let me have the estimate as it stood at January 1, 1941, as it stands today, and as you propose it for January 1, 1945, distinguishing between afloat and ashore and including the Fleet Air Arm.

6. I note that the United States have definitely diminished their programme of anti-U-boat craft in order to develop landing-craft. Hitherto I have perpetually pressed for the ceaseless construction of anti-U-boat vessels as each slip became vacant, but our growing numbers, and many signs of weakness in the enemy's production and in the morale of their crews, require that the whole of this section should be reviewed.

Prime Minister to Minister of Aircraft Production   6 Nov. 43

I am impressed by the large number of man-hours which your minute of October 27 shows to be consumed in modifications to service aircraft. I hope the modifications are confined to those strictly necessary to improve the fighting value of our aircraft.

Looking at the tables attached to your minute, the disquieting fact emerges that we have no really heavy bomber under development. The Vickers Windsor will not really be much larger — though we must trust it will be better — than the improved Lancaster, which will be coming into production at the end of next year. In the meanwhile the Americans have the Boeing B-29 already in production, with an all-up weight of 120,000 pounds, stated to carry nine tons of bombs with a range of 3000 miles. I understand they also have projected a six-engine aircraft, the B-36, with an all-up weight of over 250,000 pounds, designed to carry a load of over thirty tons with a range of 4600 miles. Ought we not to be looking forward to making aircraft of similar performance?

Prime Minister to Secretary of State for War and C.I.G.S.   6 Nov. 43

As I understand it, the plan is that on D-Day the Americans will have fifteen divisions in "Overlord" and we twelve. Now it seems to me a great pity that we cannot make our quota equal, or if possible one better. So much depends upon the interpretation given to the word "division." [2] I should like to be able to tell them [the Americans], "We will match you man for man and gun for gun on the battle-front," and also that we have made extra exertions for this. In this way we should maintain our right to be effectively consulted in operations which are of such capital consequence.

2. For the above purpose I would run considerable risks with what is left in the Island. If necessary the Home Guard could be largely mobilised during the period when all the Regular troops have left the country, and the resulting decline in the factory munitions output accepted.

3. We have carried the recent trouble about the Italian campaign entirely by mentioning that we had preponderance on the battle-front. We ought to

[2] See minutes of October 11 and November 1.

have at least equality in this other most critical task. Moreover, the announce-ment of the fact that we had lifted [i.e., increased] our contribution would sweeten all the discussions which are now proceeding, and might well enable us to secure any necessary retardation of D-Day. Pray think this over and let us talk together.

Prime Minister to the Lord President of the Council   11 Nov. 43

I hope that out of the present surplus of grain you will manage to do a little more for the domestic poultry-keeper. He can usually provide or collect scrap to balance the grain, so that we get more eggs for a given amount than if it were handed to the commercial producer. It costs no labour, and the extra eggs are not an undue reward for the enterprise and initiative of the owner. Moreover, it gives him an interest and something to talk about. The present miserably small allowance of one ration per ration card frequently does not allow enough hens to be kept in a small household to justify putting up the poultry run, etc. I feel sure that if it were increased, a good many more people would produce their own eggs, and thus save shipping and labour.

Prime Minister to the President of the Board of Education   11 Nov. 43

Thank you for your report of September 16 about the use of the cinema in schools. I have read it with interest, and I am glad to know that you are giving your personal attention to this matter.

2. There must be a number of children whose talents would remain un-developed, or at any rate underdeveloped, if the written and spoken word was not supplemented by visual aids of this kind. In addition, really good films should benefit all school-children. The films produced might possibly fall into two main categories: (*a*) films designed to fit in with and illustrate the ordinary curriculum; and (*b*) films to show children the proud inheritance to which they are the heirs, and of which they will become in time the guardians.

3. You will not expect me to enter into any commitment on the financial side. The additional costs of the educational proposals shown in the appendix to your White Paper are considerable, and no doubt this particular aspect will be assessed in relation to the various other parts of your programme. I note however that in Germany a fee used to be charged to the parents to finance the provision of films and projectors. I am not clear how this would fit in with your proposals, more especially if the film becomes a part of the regular curricu-lum at which the children's attendance is compulsory, but if there were volun-tary shows presumably some form of charge could be made. Perhaps you would kindly develop this point for me in rather more detail.

Prime Minister to General Ismay, for C.O.S. Committee   16 Nov. 43

The reasons which led us to supply a more substantial garrison to the Falkland Islands were serious, and I should like to know in what way they have been altered by the course of events before any reduction is authorised. It would be a pity if a Japanese cruiser took over these islands, including the new defences which we are to leave unmanned. This is not a likely contingency, but it exists nonetheless. What would you propose to do with the fifteen hundred men? What regiments do they belong to?

Prime Minister to First Sea Lord, and to General Ismay,   21 Nov. 43
for C.O.S. Committee

The centre point of my thought is the capture of Rome at the beginning of January and the capture of Rhodes at the end. The former is already provided for. For the latter two requisites are necessary: first, a declaration of war by Turkey and the use of the Turkish bases; second, a good British division to be landed at the first wave, to be backed up and followed by the 10th Indian as the second wave. Landing ships and craft will be required therefore on the scale of a division. These divisions need not be fully equipped with transport, etc., on account of the small distances over which they have to operate and the fact that the eight thousand Germans will be pinned down to key points. How much landing-craft will be needed? Where can it be obtained? The First Sea Lord has in mind that some landing-ships now in Southeast Asia Command should come to the Mediterranean for this job and then return in time for "Culverin" [Sumatra] or any other operation there.

2. If it be true that Admiral Mountbatten has abandoned "Culverin," there really cannot be much hurry. The capture of the Andamans is a trivial prize compared with Rhodes, and also it can be undertaken at any time later in the year. In addition to the capture of Rhodes and all that follows from it, the surrender or destruction of eight or nine thousand Germans will give us three times the [German] prisoners we have so far taken during all our operations in Italy.

DECEMBER

Prime Minister to Secretary of State for War   13 Dec. 43

While in the Middle East my attention was drawn by the 4th Hussars to Army Council Instruction 1408, published on November 26, about the wearing of unauthorised headdresses. According to this, authorised headdress for all units of the Royal Armoured Corps (except 11th Hussars) is described as "black beret to be worn both with battle-dress and with service-dress," although permission is given for officers to wear service-dress caps if in their possession until replacement becomes necessary.

2. The 4th Hussars are concerned lest after the war this ruling will continue and they, like the Tank Corps, will have no hat they can wear except the black beret.

3. As Colonel of the regiment, I should like to be able to assure them that, so far as the 4th Hussars are concerned, this is only a wartime measure, and that when supplies are more plentiful they will once more be allowed to purchase and wear service-dress caps.

4. I should like this assurance to be given. Pray let me know your views.

JANUARY

Prime Minister (Marrakesh) to Secretary of State for War   7 Jan. 44

We should make every effort to ease the lot of the Home Guard, whose duties are more exhausting than those of any form of civil defence. Most of the men are now proficient and should not be compelled to attend parades merely to complete forty-eight hours of duty a month. Anti-aircraft Home Guard are credited with twelve hours for each night's duty, whether there is an Alert or not, but the ordinary Home Guard's parades are in the evenings and every week-end. Many of these men have had little free time for more than three years, and compulsory parades with fines, sometimes ending in imprisonment, for non-attendance can cause considerable industrial unrest.

At this stage in the war Home Guard hours of duty should be officially reduced and not left to the discretion of the unit commander. Guards and strenuous exercises should be cut to a minimum, and parades for those holding proficiency badges limited to weapon maintenance.

RADIO PROXIMITY FUSE

Prime Minister to First Lord and First Sea Lord   10 Jan. 44

Are you content with the situation in which the American Navy will have a good supply of fuses, even for four-inch guns, by the spring, whereas we shall have no such facilities during the war? I consider this point is a serious one and should be faced by the Admiralty.

2. Is there any possibility of our obtaining an allocation from the United States, or are you satisfied that our methods are good enough?

Prime Minister to General Ismay, for C.O.S. Committee   17 Jan. 44

This report [by the Joint Intelligence Staff on Japanese intentions in the Southeast Asia area] confirms the view I have held for some time that the danger of invasion of India by Japan has passed. During the next few months the Eastern Fleet will come into being, and will soon grow to a strength superior to any detachment which it would be worth while for the Japanese to make, having regard to the preoccupations in the Pacific. The air defence of India has also become very strong.

2. All the above brings me again to the conclusion that there ought to be a continuous reduction in the vast mass of low-grade troops now maintained under arms in India. Nearly two million men are on our pay-lists and ration strength, apart from the British troops in the country and on the frontier. The Viceroy and General Auchinleck should be instructed to reduce the numbers by at least half a million during the course of the present year. In this process, which will no doubt largely take place by uncompensated wastage, the greatest care should be taken to improve the quality of the remaining units and to rely as much as possible upon the martial races. An effort should be made to get back to the high efficiency and standard of the pre-war Indian

troops. The officers and skilled personnel from the disbanded battalions should be concentrated on these units, thus increasing the officer, and particularly the white officer, cadre. The standards of recruiting should everywhere be stiffened, and the intake reduced to the limits of the really trustworthy fighting recruits.

3. Meanwhile I should like to have a financial statement from the India Office showing the cost of the military establishments in India (exclusive of British troops) for every year since the outbreak of war, together with the average bearing of man-power.

Prime Minister to General Ismay   19 Jan. 44

It would seem to be about time that the circular sent to generals and other high commanders about making speeches should be renewed. Let me see the text of it. There seem to have been a lot of speeches and interviews lately.

Prime Minister to General Ismay, for C.O.S. Committee   19 Jan. 44

We ought to assert domination of the Dalmatian coast. It is within easy reach of our commanding Air Force in Italy. We have large naval superiority. After "Anzio" is over it ought to be easy to organise a circus of, say, two thousand Commando men and a dozen or so light tanks, and go round and clean up every single island the Germans have occupied, killing or capturing their garrisons. A plan should be made for this which we could consider and then present to the Supreme Commander for his consideration.

Pray let work be begun upon this at once. We are letting the whole of this Dalmatian coast be sealed off from us by an enemy who has neither the command of the air nor the sea. How can he garrison the islands in any strength to resist a concentrated attack?

Prime Minister to Dominions Secretary   23 Jan. 44

I have always wanted the New Zealand Division to take part in the Battle of Rome, more as a symbol than because we cannot find other troops. This they are now very likely to do. It would be a pity for them to quit the European scene.

I should prefer to let the numbers of the division fall until they became a brigade group. Even so they could be called a division and some other brigade be attached to them. I like to have them there, and they will be proud of it in future years.

I should not ask Mr. Fraser to run into any serious difficulties about the return of particular individuals.

Prime Minister to General Ismay   25 Jan. 44

General Montgomery speaks of his need to have ten Commando units for "Overlord" and has only seven. Pray let me know whether this request could be met. What arrangements have been made for bringing home some of the specialised personnel for teaching purposes of the 2d Special Air Service Regiment? It is not intended to bring the regiment home, but I agreed that some of the special personnel should come as instructors.

Prime Minister to General Ismay, for C.O.S. Committee   25 Jan. 44

I have now read this paper about "British Strategic Needs in the Levant States." The Chiefs of Staff seem to assume that partition [of Palestine] will arouse Jewish resentment. It is, on the contrary, the White Paper policy that arouses the Jewish resentment. The opposition to partition will come from the Arabs, and any violence by the Arabs will be countered by the Jews. It must be remembered that Lord Wavell has stated that, left to themselves, the Jews would beat the Arabs. There cannot therefore be any great danger in our joining with the Jews to enforce the kind of proposals about partition which are set forth in the Ministerial paper. I therefore cannot accept in any way the requirements for internal security set out in the table, which proceeds upon the assumption that both the Jews and the Arabs would join together to fight us. Obviously we shall not proceed with any plan of partition which the Jews do not support.

Prime Minister to Dominions Secretary   25 Jan. 44

It is to my mind very unwise to make plans on the basis of Hitler being defeated in 1944. The possibility of his gaining a victory in France cannot be excluded. The hazards of battle are very great. The reserves of the enemy are capable of being thrown from point to point with great facility. All my information from the interior of Germany goes to show that Hitler and his Government are still in the fullest control, and that there is no sign of revolt as a result of the bombings. In all our contacts with the German troops, such as we see in Italy, their quality, discipline, and skill are apparent.

Prime Minister to Secretary of State for War and C.I.G.S.   25 Jan. 44

I do not approve of the title "Allied Central Mediterranean Force," and it should not have been made public without my having been previously consulted.

2. An army which will amount to upwards of twenty divisions should not be described as a "Force." The activities of this army are not coextensive with the Central Mediterranean. For instance, Malta and Tunis are both in the Central Mediterranean; likewise Corsica and Sardinia. Furthermore, Yugoslavia, which is specially reserved to the Supreme Commander, is not — except possibly for purely operational purposes — placed under General Alexander. The title is therefore from every point of view a misnomer.

3. The appointment which I offered General Alexander and which he accepted was "Commander of the Allied Armies in Italy." This follows the precedent of the last war, when "British Expeditionary Force" was changed as the armies grew to "British Armies in France and Flanders." The change

should therefore be made, and a convenient moment to do so would be when the Battle of Rome has decided itself, assuming the decision is satisfactory.

Prime Minister to General Montgomery   27 Jan. 44

Herewith is an interim answer from the Minister of Production about D.D. tanks. It does not look too bad.

2. I shall have a further report presently about waterproofing material. Two hundred thousand vehicles seem a vast outfit to attach to an army which, at thirty divisions of 20,000 men apiece, would only have 600,000 men, of whom less than three-quarters would actually fight. As each vehicle takes at least a man and a half to drive and look after, here are 300,000 men already absorbed. One hopes there will be enough infantry with rifles and bayonets to protect this great mass of vehicles from falling into the hands of the enemy.

Prime Minister to Major-General Hollis   28 Jan. 44

It would not be a good thing for the main headquarters in the Mediterranean to be set up in Italy. General Wilson's sphere comprises the entire North African front, and he should not be located in any one particular area. General Alexander should have the command in Italy without being overshadowed by the presence of the Supreme Commander's Headquarters. I do not feel enough effort has been made to overcome the difficulties of a move [of these Headquarters] to the Tunis area. Has Malta been investigated? If nothing else will serve, it would be better for him to remain at Algiers, after conducting a proper purge of the excessive officers who have accumulated there.

Prime Minister to Home Secretary   30 Jan. 44

Your minute to me of January 24 about the employment of Communists on secret Government work.

I agree that the existence of the panel must be a secret. All members should be specially warned. Final decision whether action is to be taken against a Communist sympathiser must rest with the department employing him, whose Ministerial head is responsible to Parliament.

There are three degrees of responsibility in this business.

M.I.5 is responsible for the evidence produced before the panel. The panel is responsible for weighing that evidence and deciding whether to proceed with the department concerned. The department is responsible for deciding what action to take, if any.

I agree that the panel should include a senior representative of the Treasury experienced in handling staff questions, but am against compelling the panel to include a representative of the interested department. If the panel rejects a case it would be unfair that a member of the suspect's department should know it had ever been brought up. The chairman of the panel should have discretion to co-opt a member of the interested department according to circumstances.

Prime Minister to Foreign Secretary   30 Jan. 44

I think Sir Owen O'Malley should be asked very secretly to express his opinion on the Katyn Wood inquiry. How does the argument about the length of time the birch trees had grown over the graves fit in with this new tale? Did anybody look at the birch trees?

Prime Minister to First Lord and First Sea Lord   31 Jan. 44

I am willing that four of the fast improved carriers should be included in the forthcoming Admiralty programme; but I consider that the first two should have a considerable lead over the second two, in order that advantage may be taken of any possible improvements noticeable during construction. I also consider that the four battleships sanctioned by Parliament but not proceeded with during the war, namely, *Lion*, *Temeraire*, *Conqueror*, and *Thunderer*, should also remain in the naval programme, it being understood that no work is done upon them other than designing. Efforts should be made to finish *Vanguard* by the summer of '45. Let me know what is involved in this.

2. I wonder whether you are not ordering far more warships than we can even lay down during the war. In 1943, 888,000 tons displacement were ordered, only 402,000 tons laid down, and 337,000 tons were completed. Thus, unless ships are laid down much faster than in 1943, it would take two and a quarter years even to lay down last year's orders. Hitherto we have been having at least two programmes a year, with the result that you have an immense amount of sanctioned shipbuilding, far more than you can possibly carry out or digest. It is not in the interest of the Navy to present such an aspect to critical eyes. This should certainly govern the whole of the new programme, and I do not think any vessel should be included in it which either obstructs the completion of a similar vessel already ordered or cannot itself be laid down during the calendar year 1944 — or, if you will, the financial year 1944–45.

3. We spoke of the War Fleet against Japan in 1945. I consider we should have the four *King George V's*, the *Renown*, *Nelson*, *Queen Elizabeth*, and *Warspite*, in all eight battleships, together with as many armoured carriers and auxiliary carriers as have come to hand, the above being supported as necessary by cruiser squadrons and flotillas. A programme for developing the Fleet Train [3] stage by stage should be submitted. I hope the *Vanguard* will be able to join during the autumn. The question of fitting the *Littorios* for this service should also be considered. Let me know what it involves in time, labour, and money.

4. I agree that in June 1944 we should furnish the contingent you have already prepared, provided always that the United States desire it. Above all, we must be careful not to prejudice the operation "Culverin" [Sumatra], which is the only means of bringing the large military and air forces we have around the Bay of Bengal into effective action against the enemy in 1944–45. The disposition of the Fleet between the Bay of Bengal and the Pacific must provide for the

[3] An organisation for supplying the Fleet with fuel, stores, etc.

execution of "Culverin" if other difficulties are surmounted and unless unexpected developments occur.

5. We must ask the United States Chiefs of Staff to lend us a proper supply of landing-craft for November or December at "Culverin," and in view of the help we are to give them with the Fleet they should not deny these to us. This matter however awaits the arrival of Admiral Mountbatten's officers.

6. For the post-war Fleet we should aim at survivors of the four *King George V's*, one modernised *Nelson*, *Vanguard*, four sixteen-inch battleships, which will be kept on our lists and proceeded with as may be possible, and we should claim the two *Littorios*, a potential total of twelve battleships. This of course depends upon whether the battleship is not rendered obsolete by new inventions. So far this has certainly not been the case. On the contrary, the U-boat danger to battleships has been largely mastered and the air menace to them is under much better control than ever before. I hold strongly that we have an overwhelming claim on the *Littorios* because of the preponderance of our efforts in the Mediterranean and the fact that we have sacrificed new construction of heavy ships to the immediate needs of the war. Perhaps you will let me have your sketch of a post-war Fleet — say, in 1947 — balanced on this sort of scale, in order that I may consider the whole picture more maturely.

7. I approve the policy of using the *Warspite*, and I hope also the *Rodney*, as part of our bombarding fleet for "Overlord." What other vessels have you available for this purpose? I presume measures are being taken to provide the proper gunnery complements, training of the latest kind, and the necessary spotters, and that there is no lack of ammunition, both anti-personnel and for destroying concrete defences. Under the air shield the bombarding squadrons should have great scope.

8. I will send you my comments on your man-power proposals later. I should think you now have at least one hundred thousand men in the training establishments, harbour services, and bases, men in transit, etc., on which you can draw during the next two years before trenching upon our limited pools. This will require a very sensible reduction of the training establishments and plants.

FEBRUARY

Prime Minister to General Ismay, for C.O.S. Committee   2 Feb. 44

All experience shows that once a great offensive has been launched, quiescence and comparative unpreparedness prevail on other parts of the front not affected. The battle draws everything into itself, and there are moments when gains of priceless value in other quarters can be gathered cheaply or perhaps for nothing.

2. Pray have the following examined with the utmost secrecy: (*a*) During March, April, and May move the 1st and 6th British Armoured and the 6th South African Armoured Divisions into Morocco. Cover would be perhaps local unrest, or anyhow reinforcements for "Overlord." (*b*) On D plus say

twenty or thirty, when everyone is all out, bring these divisions to Bordeaux with a minimum of landing-craft after seizing the place by *coup de main*. This should be possible, as the air would all have been drawn into the northward. A force of this character let loose in the south and centre of France would instantly arouse widespread revolt and would be of measureless assistance to the main battle.

3. Examine also the possibilities of the move overland quietly of these troops to Morocco, embarkation in great secrecy, and a [sea] move by a wide curve to the point of attack.

4. The above is without prejudice to "Anvil," in which none of these forces would be involved.

5. Should the operation, which may be called ' Caliph," prosper, a follow-up by the United States with infantry divisions brought directly across the Atlantic to the new base could be arranged.

6. Arising from the above, how many ships would be wanted to convey the three armoured divisions? How many landing-craft would be required for, say, five thousand Commandos to make sure of the entries (it is of course intended to land the divisions at regular quays)? How could the shipping be found and brought to Casablanca without attracting undue notice? How long would the embarkation, the voyage, and, if all went well, the disembarkation take? A carrier force would have to be provided to cover the landing, but this should not be difficult if by then we have got shore bases established in the north. It is silly to go on as we are, butting at only one place, without trying to reap the immense opportunities which will be open almost everywhere else.

Prime Minister to Dominions Secretary   2 Feb. 44

I could have a special Cabinet meeting on Friday, if desired, to consider the presence in Dublin of Axis diplomatic missions. Otherwise it can be brought up on Monday at the full meeting.

2. Much more dangerous even than the information betrayed about the movements of Anglo-American troop convoys is what will certainly be passing in a stream about our preparations for "Overlord." If the German and Japanese Ministers remain at their posts in Dublin, it may be necessary on military grounds to sever all contacts between Ireland and the Continent in the near future for a period of months. At present anyone can get in an Irish ship to Spain and give the latest news he has picked up in England about British and American preparations. Even if complete severance by sea were instituted, it would not prevent the German Ambassador from sending a wireless warning of zero, even though that was the last he was able to send.

3. I am preparing a telegram for President Roosevelt, bringing to his notice some of these dangers, which I think very grave; and I am asking also that it should be considered by the C.O.S. Committee.

Prime Minister to Foreign Secretary   5 Feb. 44

Your minute about raising certain legations to the status of embassies.

I must say I think Cuba has as good a claim as some of the other places —
"*la perla de las Antillas*." Great offence will be given if all the others have it
and this large, rich, beautiful island, the home of the cigar, is denied. Surely
Cuba has much more claim than Venezuela. You will make a bitter enemy if
you leave them out, and after a bit you will be forced to give them what you
have given to the others.

Prime Minister to General Ismay   7 Feb. 44

Where is the report on "Caliph"? You should also tell the Planners, if they
have not finished their work, that the assembly area of Morocco should be used
for at least three French divisions to follow up the inroad of the British armour
at "Caliph."

Prime Minister to Sir Edward Bridges   12 Feb. 44

I have no intention of moving from the Cabinet War Room until after we
have had at least one blitz which is altogether out of relation to anything we
have previously experienced. I do not think the new forms of bombardment
make any difference to this. You should provide reasonable accommodation
for the Lord Privy Seal. The other Ministers' rooms can stay as at present.

Prime Minister to Sir Edward Bridges   19 Feb. 44

The principle enunciated in Lord Selborne's note about housing in the
transitional period after the war seems to me unanswerable. To peg land
prices at the 1939 level without relation to any alteration in the value of money
would be a confiscatory act applied only to one class of property. Provision
must be inserted in any legislation that the value shall be the same as it was
in 1939 — i.e., the same in real value.

Prime Minister to General Ismay, for C.O.S. Committee   19 Feb. 44

The object of "Plough" Force was to operate in Norway during the snow
period, and much depended in essence upon small tanks being carried by
aircraft in which the men could fight and move and, to some extent, find
shelter. Since then "Plough" has been taken for ordinary duties as Commandos. How far has the flying-tank principle been made effective? What
are the numbers of the "Plough" Force? Whereabouts in Italy is it actually
at the present moment? How has it acquitted itself?

2. I do not myself think it wise to rule out "Jupiter" finally from the operations of this war. We ought of course to have liberated Norway during the
campaign of 1943, but our American Allies would probably not have consented
to such strategy, and it would not have been possible to obtain the necessary
support here. In the event of "Overlord" not being successful or Hitler
accumulating forces there quite beyond our power to tackle, it would perhaps
be necessary to adopt the flanking movements both in Norway and from
Turkey and the Aegean in the winter of 1944–45. In view of such contingencies

I am reluctant to liquidate this force. It could surely meanwhile be employed in the Balkans or in exterminating the German garrisons in the islands off the Dalmatian coast.

3. Pray let me have your views upon the above.

Prime Minister to Home Secretary   22 Feb. 44

It would be a great mistake to have a national day of prayer for "Overlord." In my view there is no need for another day of prayer or thanksgiving at the present time.

Prime Minister to Foreign Secretary   25 Feb. 44

We "invade" all countries with whom we are at war.

2. We "enter" all subjugated Allied lands we wish to "liberate."

3. With regard to a country like Italy, with whose Government we have signed an armistice, we "invaded" in the first instance, but, in view of the Italian co-operation, we must consider all further advances by us in Italy to be in the nature of "liberation."

Prime Minister to Foreign Secretary   27 Feb. 44

I entirely agree that we should pay out of hand all civil claims against members of the United States forces over the five-thousand-dollar limit which the Americans are apparently constitutionally unable to settle.

2. The remedy for the reckless driving which is causing so much trouble is a conversation between me and Eisenhower. I am sure that if the case is put to him, he will exercise a controlling and effective authority. At any rate, we ought to try this first.

3. Surely it is not necessary to make all this long statement in Parliament, which seems to me to be likely to cause a lot of ill-feeling in the United States; and I was not aware that you were subjected to much pressure in the House on this matter. I should greatly prefer to let Eisenhower put his screw on and see what happens, meanwhile confining your statement to the fact that we will pay the claims over five thousand dollars pending further discussion by His Majesty's Government with that of the United States.

Prime Minister to General Ismay and General Pile   28 Feb. 44

There is no doubt that the blast effect of the new German bombs has increased. In these circumstances, and indeed on general grounds, would it not be well to provide, so far as possible, slit trenches and blast or splinter cover for anti-aircraft personnel not on duty during the air raids? Each raid is likely to be short on account of the enemy's reliance on "Window," and the anti-aircraft personnel, a large proportion of whom are women, should be directed to use the slit trenches when not otherwise employed during the raids. In most cases the batteries should be able to do the bulk of the work themselves if materials are provided. Where outside assistance is required, priority should be given to the most exposed positions.

MARCH

Prime Minister to Minister of Aircraft Production 1 Mar. 44

My congratulations upon the output of aircraft for February, and upon beating the programme. Pray convey to all those who have achieved or exceeded their programme my best thanks.

Prime Minister to President Roosevelt 2 Mar. 44

Here is a suggested item for your draft of our monthly anti-U-boat war statement, provided later information about sinkings in February 1944 does not considerably increase the figure shown below: "February 1944 was the best month since the United States entered the war. The total sinkings of all Allied shipping in February by enemy action only were less than one-fifth of the sinkings in February 1943, and less than one-ninth of the sinkings in February 1942." The figures in British notation are: February 1944, 70,000 tons; February 1943, 378,000; February 1942, 659,500. We have a very good haul of U-boats too.

Prime Minister to Minister of Home Security 2 Mar. 44

Thank you for the analysis of the returns of the civilian respirator inspections which you sent to me. I see that about nine out of every ten people have a serviceable mask. This seems an adequate insurance against the risk of the enemy's starting gas warfare at a period when we are dropping more than thirty times the tonnage of bombs on Germany that she is dropping on us.

Prime Minister to Sir Alan Lascelles 4 Mar. 44

You should see the Home Secretary's minute about a national day of prayer for "Overlord." I think there are serious dangers in drawing attention to the coming shock in this way, especially as no one can know when it is going to be. We have to be very much on our guard against unduly depressing the troops.

Prime Minister to Minister of Aircraft Production 5 Mar. 44

I am informed that American aircraft are now being produced without paint, and that, apart from economies in time and material, as much as twenty miles an hour may thus be added to the speed of certain types. Pray let me know whether it is intended to adopt a similar policy with regard to British aircraft.

Prime Minister to Minister of Supply 7 Mar. 44

Just off the main road between Amersham and Uxbridge, at a place called Chalfont St. Giles, there is a rubbish heap or salvage dump where for the last three years work has been going on. I pass it every time I go to Chequers. Are tins and metal objects being recovered from what was a dump in past years, or are they being thrown down there together with other rubbish? Is it being sifted or extended? It is impossible to see as one passes. The one thing that is evident is that the work is endless, and apparently makes no progress.

Prime Minister to Lord Portal   7 Mar. 44

Just below the Foreign Office, on the grass opposite St. James's Park lake, there is a very untidy sack with holes in it and sand leaking out, a sandbag structure, and some kind of obstacle formerly used as a practice ground by the local Home Guard. It does not seem to have been used for a very long time. Such a conspicuous place ought not to look untidy, unless there is some real need which can be satisfied in no other way.

Prime Minister to Chancellor of the Exchequer,   7 Mar. 44
First Lord of the Admiralty, Secretary of State for War, and
Secretary of State for Air

I understand that you are considering the best means of making minor improvements in the allowances of the Forces. I am quite firm about changes in basic pay. But the war has now been going on a long time, and this, together with the arrival of large numbers of better-paid American Service personnel, does justify some concession to our own forces. Without having gone into the matter deeply, I consider that it would not be unreasonable if the concessions made involved an additional expenditure at the rate of £20,000,000 per annum. Furthermore, I think that special consideration should be given to married personnel, and in this category especially to the lowest-paid classes.

I should be glad if you would take the above into account in framing your proposals, which you will no doubt submit to me.

Prime Minister to Secretary of State for War   8 Mar. 44
(Minister of War Transport to see)

Except for combat landings we cannot afford to ship vehicles on wheels.

I understand there were about two hundred thousand Army vehicles of all types in the Mediterranean area on December 31, and some one thousand have been shipped from the United Kingdom and North America in January. Is not this shipment equivalent to about four months' wastage at the September-December rate?

With this large stock in hand, would it not be possible to stop shipment of vehicles going in the next three or four months, when shipping space will be so urgently needed for other purposes?

Prime Minister to President Roosevelt   9 Mar. 44

Gold and dollar holdings in the United States.

You will remember that we discussed the dollar balances in Cairo on December 8, and that I gave a memorandum to Harry. I certainly understood that you felt we ought not to be treated worse than France or Russia in these matters. France has at least two billions, and no overseas liabilities against them. So has Russia. These dollar balances are not, as your telegram might suggest, a particular part of our assets which is available in the United States, but our total reserves. Against these reserves we have incurred for the common cause liabilities of at least ten billions on the other side of the account.

2. Since our talk Lord Halifax met Mr. Hull and Mr. Morgenthau as recently as January 8, when the matters mentioned in the first paragraph of your telegram under reply were discussed. Lord Halifax reported to us that Mr. Morgenthau stated to him that it was not at present intended to reduce our dollar balances in any other way, and in reliance on this personal assurance to Lord Halifax we agreed to the exclusion of the politically difficult items from Lend-Lease.

3. Will you allow me to say that the suggestion of reducing our dollar balances, which constitute our sole liquid reserve, to one billion dollars would really not be consistent either with equal treatment of Allies or with any conception of equal sacrifice or pooling of resources? We have not shirked our duty or indulged in an easy way of living. We have already spent practically all our convertible foreign investments in the struggle. We alone of the Allies will emerge from the war with great overseas war debts. I do not know what would happen if we were now asked to disperse our last liquid reserves required to meet pressing needs, or how I could put my case to Parliament without it affecting public sentiment in the most painful manner, and that at a time when British and American blood will be flowing in broad and equal streams and when the shortening of the war even by a month would far exceed the sums under consideration.

4. I venture to put these arguments before you in order that you may be fully armed with our case, for my confidence in your sense of justice, and, I may add, in that of the American people, is unshakable.

5. But see also my immediately following.

Prime Minister to President Roosevelt   9 Mar. 44

Further to my telegram, I have laid before you our case about dollar balances in its full strength, but I have wondered whether you might be meaning only that we should search for some arrangement to enable us to put a portion of our balance less conspicuously in the limelight. If this is so, and if you desire it, we will go into this very carefully with Stettinius when he visits us.

2. Since we received your telegram we now learn that Mr. Crowley on March 8 promised to give Congress the amount of our dollar balances now and at the outbreak of war. This raises serious dangers. I am confident in the justice of our case if it could be stated as a whole, and of course if the matter becomes public property we shall have to justify ourselves in public. The disclosure of the vast debit balance which is growing up against us outside the United States would certainly have most injurious effects upon our sterling position, and consequently upon the whole strength of the Allies at this period.

We therefore ask that there shall be no disclosure; if this is not possible, that the disclosure shall be in strict confidence, and also that the substance of our case should be stated to the body to whom the disclosure is made.

Prime Minister to Minister of Supply 9 Mar. 44

I am told that the demand for the new insecticide, D.D.T., is urgent and increasing. Pray let me know what output is to be expected, whether this is completely adequate, and, if not, whether anything can be done to expand and accelerate it. It is most important, especially for the Southeast Asia Command, that ample supplies should be made available at the earliest possible moment.

Please try to get a move on on a large scale.

Prime Minister to President Roosevelt 10 Mar. 44

I am sending you today by courier an inscription I have had drawn up for Harry about his boy who was killed. It would be very kind of you to have it sent him wherever he is recuperating. How does his operation stand now?

Prime Minister to General Giraud (Algiers) 10 Mar. 44

Pray accept my profound sympathy with you in the death of your daughter, who was captured in Tunisia and carried off into Germany with her four children.

Prime Minister to Mr. Duff Cooper (Algiers) 10 Mar. 44

You may let General de Gaulle know privately that I am much in favour of the Leclerc division fighting with us in the main battle here, and from my talks with General Eisenhower I gather he has the same view. I am therefore working in this sense to overcome the difficulties of transportation, etc., and am pretty confident I shall succeed.

Prime Minister to First Lord and First Sea Lord 11 Mar. 44

Let me have a short report on the character and quality of the U-boat prisoners now being taken, compared with any other significant period of the war.

Prime Minister to Foreign Secretary 11 Mar. 44

It seems to me a pity to move Mallet from Stockholm at this critical time I always deprecate military men being moved from employments or commands where they have gained a great mass of special information and are pursuing a definite theme, because of promotion in ordinary Service routine. In wartime the convenience of the State ranks above the careers of individuals. An Ambassador has to be given time to take root. The first year he is probably not much use. The second he begins to function effectively. He is nearly always brought away in the third. Mallet must be in the midst of all this Stockholm tangle. I am most anxious that Sweden shall eventually come into the war, which I think there is quite a chance of her doing.

Prime Minister to C.I.G.S.   13 Mar. 44

What is all this about, and what are these troops that are taking part and have lost thirty lives in these vigorous manoeuvres?[4]   Surely these forces should be brought into battle somewhere or other instead of losing their lives in exercises. How many are engaged?

Prime Minister to Lord President, Chancellor of the Exchequer,   14 Mar. 44
Minister of Works and Buildings, and Minister of Health

General Bedell Smith mentioned to me yesterday the very high and extortionate prices now being charged to American officers over here for flats and small houses. A medium-sized flat, he said, was twenty-eight pounds a week, and the small house that he occupied was thirty-five pounds a week. There is no reason why the Americans should not pay a fair and equitable price for accommodation, which they are quite willing to do, but I do not think extortion or profiteering should be allowed.

I am not certain who deals with this, but would you very kindly give it your attention and let me know, first, about the facts, and, secondly, whether there is any remedy.

Prime Minister to C.A.S. and General Ismay   18 Mar. 44

What air authority in Italy was responsible for ordering low-level machine-gunning attacks on civilians in the streets? I can quite understand bombing the marshalling yards in Rome, but I trust it was not a British airman who committed the offence here described.

Let me have a special report.

Prime Minister to President Roosevelt   19 Mar. 44

We have followed Gray's[5] lead in Ireland, and it is early days to start reassuring de Valera. There is not much sense in a doctor telling a patient that the medicine he has just prescribed for his nerve troubles is only coloured water. I think it would be much better to keep them guessing for a while.

2. I do not propose to stop the necessary trade between Britain and Ireland or to prevent anything going into Ireland. I do propose to stop ships going from Ireland to Spain and Portugal and other foreign ports until "Overlord" is launched. One must remember that a ship may start out in one direction and turn off in another. There is no difficulty in stopping ships. The above also applies to outward-bound airplanes, which we shall try to stop by every means in our power. The object of these measures is not spite against the Irish, but preservation of British and American soldiers' lives and against our plans being

---

[4] Military exercises in Transjordan.
[5] The United States representative in Dublin.

betrayed by emissaries sent by sea or air from the German Minister in Dublin. Since the beginning of 1943 only nineteen Irish ships have left Irish ports, some several times, so the evil is not very great. We are also cutting off telephones and restricting communications to the utmost, and also stopping the Anglo-Irish air line from running. I repeat, all our actions will be taken from motives of self-preservation and none from those of spite.

3. If however the Irish retaliate by doing something which in no way helps them but merely annoys us, such as stopping the Foynes airport facilities, I, should feel free to retaliate on their cross-Channel trade. They would have opened a new chapter and economic measures of retaliation would be considered. I would tell you about these before we took them.

4. It seems to me that so far from allaying alarm in de Valera's circles we should let fear work its healthy process. Thereby we shall get behind the scenes a continued stiffening-up of the Irish measures to prevent leakages which even now are not so bad.

5. I gather that the State Department will probably not disagree with the above, for Mr. Hull says in his message: "I am inclined to believe however that for the time being at least we should not make any statement to the press or commit ourselves to the Irish Government that we have no intention of instituting economic sanctions." And I hope this may also be your view.

Prime Minister to General Ismay, for C.O.S. Committee   19 Mar. 44

The difference between a Chief of Staff and a Commander-in-Chief in the field is more apparent than real. Both are office workers. Both may make periodical trips to the front. Both are subject to air raids. Indeed, in many cases the similarity might be extended to Army Group Commanders, and even to Army Commanders. The modern conditions under which the military art is practised nowadays are not at all similar to those of former generations. There is therefore no reason why General Marshall should not receive the Soviet military decoration.

Prime Minister to First Lord and First Sea Lord   19 Mar. 44

This is a serious disaster. Who were the 1055 drowned? Were they troops outward or homeward bound? British or American?

How is it that in a convoy of this kind more could not be rescued? [6]

Prime Minister to Director of Military Intelligence   19 Mar. 44

Why must you write "intensive" here? "Intense" is the right word. You should read Fowler's *Modern English Usage* on the use of the two words.

---

[6] The British transport *Khedive Ismail*, proceeding in convoy from East Africa to Ceylon, was torpedoed by a Japanese U-boat near Addu Atoll on February 12 and sank in two minutes. She carried 1947 passengers including British, American, and African troops and members of the Women's Services. The U-boat was sunk soon afterwards by British destroyers.

Prime Minister to Foreign Secretary   19 Mar. 44

It seems to me most improvident in time of war to take a man away from a post where he has gained great influence and knowledge and to send him to some entirely different atmosphere where he has to begin all over again. I gather you now propose to move two Ambassadors. Surely we are in an extraordinary period in our lives and history, and procuring the highest service for the public during this crisis should be our only aim.

All the great Ambassadors who have exercised influence have remained long at their posts. Maisky was here for about ten years. Monsieur de Staël, whom I remember as a boy, was a tradition. Several [Portuguese Ambassador] was here, I think, for fifteen years or more. I could quote many other examples.

The departmental view is no doubt opposed to long tenures and the doctrine of "Buggins's turn" is very powerful. I agreed to your moving Sir Noel Charles from Rio because of the very great need there is in Italy for a competent diplomatist. You have yourself told me how many regrets this move has caused in Brazil. I certainly did not expect it would lead to a kind of "general post" among the Ambassadors, each moving into a field about which he knows nothing, and I should greatly deplore this. In my opinion, and I speak from long experience, the natural term of an Ambassador's mission should be six years, unless he is guilty of incompetence or divergence from the Government's policy, when, of course, he cannot be recalled too soon.

Prime Minister to Leader of the House and   29 Mar. 44
Secretary of State for War

It seems to me that the Army annual bill should be the occasion for making the following amendments in our present practice: (*a*) It should be made clear that every reasonable facility will be given for serving officers and men of all ranks to be adopted as candidates for constituencies either for by-elections or general elections. (*b*) No serving officers or men of any party, other than Members of Parliament, must take part in political demonstrations or in political agitation. They may attend meetings, but they must not appear on public platforms during the period of their service. (*c*) In the event of a by-election occurring involving a Service candidate, he should be given leave from the issue of his address or other formal opening of his candidature till the declaration of the poll, after which his rights as a Member of Parliament are valid. (*d*) The regulation against Regular officers not being eligible to stand for constituencies must be deemed henceforward to have lapsed till the end of the war, during which period Regulars and "hostilities-only" men will be treated equally. (*e*) Members of Parliament serving with the forces must be free to speak in any constituency and not merely in their own. Will you please concert this together and arrange with the Admiralty and Air Ministry, who must conform.

April

Prime Minister to Mr. Geoffrey Lloyd, Secretary for Petroleum   1 Apr. 44

I was most interested to hear of the successful use of the fog-dispersal equipment at Fiskerton on March 18, when it increased the visibility from two hundred yards to one thousand five hundred yards and enabled five bombers to land safely. I am delighted to know that this equipment is giving so good an account of itself. It is a fine reward to you and your department that your labours have already resulted in the saving of valuable lives and equipment. You have my full support in further developing this project.

Prime Minister to Lord Cherwell   1 Apr. 44

Pray let me have the figures of our casualties since the beginning of the campaign on the Italian mainland analysed, first of all in relation to the numbers of fighting troops engaged in the theatre, then in relation to the proportions of killed and wounded to missing. It must be remembered that "missing" includes prisoners who give themselves up. The lower the proportion of missing the more creditable.

Prime Minister to General Ismay,   2 Apr. 44
for Chiefs of Staff and Vice-Chiefs of Staff

By all means dispose of the anti-aircraft defences in the United Kingdom as may be necessary to sustain the "Overlord" ports. You are answerable that reasonable, though reduced, security is provided elsewhere. It is quite understood that the British public will take their share of anything that is going.

Prime Minister to General Ismay, for Chiefs of Staff   2 Apr. 44

I should think we have such good supplies of poison gas now that there could be a definite reduction in the personnel employed by forty per cent, including the ten per cent already accomplished — i.e., thirty per cent more. Let me have your views after consulting with the Ministry of Supply.

Prime Minister to Secretary of State for War and   2 Apr. 44
Secretary of State for Air

I hear that the new insecticide D.D.T. has proved extremely successful. As it takes some time to produce, it would be well to make sure the demands stated to the Ministry of Supply will really meet all your needs, especially in the Asiatic theatre.

Pray let me know what the position is.[7]

Prime Minister to Deputy Prime Minister   2 Apr. 44

I am sure Bedell Smith would not have mentioned the matter to me if the charges were not excessive. Twenty-eight pounds a week for a medium-sized

[7] See minute of March 9 to Minister of Supply.

flat and thirty-five pounds a week for a small house seem outside the bounds of reason. Perhaps these few cases could be examined by Lord Portal himself. Anyhow, if he got into touch with General Bedell Smith, I should have done my bit.[8]

Prime Minister to Minister of Food   2 Apr. 44

Good. You will gain much credit by stamping on these little trashy prosecutions [against a baker], and also by purging the regulations from petty, meticulous, arrogant officialism, which tends to affect the reputation of a great and successful department.

Prime Minister to Minister of Works   2 Apr. 44

I agree with all your comments on my paper about Emergency Housing. Pray let me have my print amended to suit them, and then submit the proof in print.

In addition we must have a better word than "prefabricated." Why not "ready-made"?

Prime Minister to Home Secretary   3 Apr. 44

Let me have a report on why the Witchcraft Act, 1735, was used in a modern court of justice.

What was the cost of this trial to the State? — observing that witnesses were brought from Portsmouth and maintained here in this crowded London for a fortnight, and the Recorder kept busy with all this obsolete tomfoolery, to the detriment of necessary work in the courts.

Prime Minister to General Montgomery   4 Apr. 44

You spoke to me the other night about the 6th Guards Army Tank Brigade. I have given a good deal of thought to this matter, which I am prepared to discuss with you as well as with the War Office at any time. Meanwhile I have said no action to destroy this brigade is to be taken.

Prime Minister to Secretary of State for War and C.I.G.S.   4 Apr. 44

There is the 6th Guards Army Tank Brigade, equipped with the latest Churchills. For over two years these men have been trained together with one object and purpose. It seems to me a disastrous procedure to disband them now and fling the men into the general pool, either of any particular armoured division or of the Foot Guards or infantry of the Line. No action should be taken on this point until it has been thoroughly discussed between us.

2. I had an idea, which I should like examined, of letting the two brigades of the Guards Armoured Division and the 6th Guards Army Tank Brigade, three brigades in all, go into action together, and fold up as casualties occur to

[8] See minute of March 14.

men and vehicles until they come down to the ordinary divisional strength. Thus we should have more punch at the outset and fold up out of the carefully prepared material, instead of dissipating a portion of this material and destroying all the unities that have been so laboriously evolved. I trust I may have your help in this.

Prime Minister to Secretary of State for War and C.I.G.S. 9 Apr. 44
(General Montgomery to see)

I have carefully considered the points you put to me. Instead of melting down the Guards, why do we not keep them up at the expense of the Line? The Russians are doing this; they make Guards divisions on a very large scale. The Germans also gear upwards; for instance, creating Panzer Grenadier divisions which actually cost them fewer men than infantry divisions, and calling a lot of determined youngsters, gathered largely from the airfields, "paratroops." There is no doubt these special terms raise *esprit de corps*. No one doubts that the performances of the Guards fully justify the prestige which attaches to them.

2. Therefore, I wish that the Guards should draw upon the Line and that the existing Guards formation shall be maintained, not only from Guards recruits, but where necessary from Line recruits. This does not affect the pooling of the two brigades in Italy, for which I have already given approval.

3. Subject to the above writing-up of the Guards at the expense of the Line: (a) I agree to the running-down of the six lower establishment divisions and the reorganisation of the residues into two cadre divisions. (b) I do not agree to the abolition of the 6th Guards Tank Brigade.[9] (c) I agree to the dispersal of the headquarters and divisional troops of the 10th Armoured Division, retaining the Armoured Brigade of this division. (d) The largest possible block of the R.A.F. Regiment should be scraped off the airfields and incorporated in the general pool of infantry of the Army. Some may be fitted direct into the reinforcements of the Guards. At least twenty-five thousand men should be extracted from the Royal Air Force Regiment.

Prime Minister to Minister of State and Sir Alexander Cadogan 13 Apr. 44

You will remember that we are purging all our secret establishments of Communists because we know they owe no allegiance to us or to our cause and will always betray secrets to the Soviet, even while we are working together. The fact of the two Communists being on the French Committee requires extremely careful treatment of the question of imparting secret information to them.

Prime Minister to Secretary of State for Air and 18 Apr. 44
Secretary of State for War

The serious reductions which we now have to face in the formations of the

[9] See minutes of April 4.

Army make it necessary to examine all possible means of economy. I do not think we can afford to continue to maintain a special body of troops purely for the defence of airfields. The R.A.F. Regiment was established at a time when invasion of this country was likely, and when our life depended upon the security of our fighter airfields. Since then it has been reduced, but the time has now come to consider whether the greater part of it should not be taken to reinforce the field formations of the Army. Pray examine this proposal in consultation. The largest possible block of the R.A.F. Regiment should be incorporated in the general pool of infantry of the Army. I consider that at least twenty-five thousand men should be so transferred.[10]

2. The matter is urgent, so I should like to have your definite proposals as soon as possible.

Prime Minister to Secretary of State for War and C.I.G.S.   19 Apr. 44

I think we ought to do something for Martel.[11] You cannot blame him for his ill success in Russia. They treat all our people like dogs. Martel fought a good fight with his tanks about Armentières in France. He gave a very far-sighted account of the Russian Army when he visited it two years before the war. I do not agree with him in some ways about tanks, but I am sure he is an officer of exceptional quality. It should certainly be possible to find him a job. Let me know what you will do.

"Unconditional Surrender"

Prime Minister to Sir Alexander Cadogan   19 Apr. 44

I have pointed out to the Cabinet that the actual terms contemplated for Germany are not of a character to reassure them at all, if stated in detail. Both President Roosevelt and Marshal Stalin at Teheran wished to cut Germany into smaller pieces than I had in mind. Stalin spoke of very large mass executions of over fifty thousand of the Staffs and military experts. Whether he was joking or not could not be ascertained. The atmosphere was jovial, but also grim. He certainly said that he would require four million German males to work for an indefinite period to rebuild Russia. We have promised the Poles that they shall have compensation both in East Prussia and, if they like, up to the line of the Oder. There are a lot of other terms implying the German ruin and indefinite prevention of their rising again as an armed Power. . . .

On the other hand, they know that "unconditional surrender" was interpreted in a very favourable manner in the case of the Italians, and we see now what the Rumanians are offered if they will come over.

Prime Minister to Foreign Secretary and Sir Alexander Cadogan   23 Apr. 44

Our supreme object is that the Russians should declare war on the Japanese as soon as possible. You will remember Stalin's declaration at Teheran. From

[10] See minute of April 9.
[11] Lieutenant-General Sir Giffard Martel.

this point of view it is difficult to see why an agreement which shows the Russians' eagerness to prevent the breaking of the Russo-Japanese Neutrality Pact of April 1941 is "good" for us. The mere fact that the Japanese are prepared to make substantial sacrifices for it shows what they think about it, and that they hope to delay a Russian breach. This is very natural on their part. Why is it "good" for us?

2. The Japanese motives are clear, but as to the Russian motives, personally I thought the business looked rather suspicious. They are cashing in on the fact that Britain and the United States are at war with Japan, which causes Japan embarrassment. They are getting their own quarrels with Japan settled. This will put them in a better position to drive a hard bargain with us when Hitler is defeated before they embark upon hostilities with Japan. It may of course be part of a deception scheme to lull the Japanese into a false sense of security. Personally I do not like it.

Prime Minister to Foreign Secretary   29 Apr. 44

I agree with your minute [on negotiations with Germany about food relief for occupied countries]. There can be no question at present of interfering with the sink-at-sight zones, which have been increasingly established by the Admiralty to facilitate operations.

2. There is no question of our approaching the Swiss or any other Government on a policy we do not accept.

3. It should be made clear that in any relief of Europe we shall certainly subject our population to any levels of rationing or dieting for which the United States sets an example.

Prime Minister to First Lord and First Sea Lord   29 Apr. 44

Admiral James Somerville has added new claims to our confidence by his brilliant attack at Sabang while the main Japanese Fleet was at Singapore. Why do we want to make a change here at all?

It seems to me he knows the theatre, has right ideas about it, and is capable of daring action. Does he want to go to Washington and give up his fighting command?

Prime Minister to Minister of Food   29 Apr. 44

None of the papers you have sent me touch the question of the excessive demands of the United States for meat. I consented to delay putting the facts before the President because you said you would raise the matter. So far as I can make out, your Ministry take the line that provided the Americans meet our requirements then we should agree to their demands from Australia and New Zealand. But it is surely necessary for the Governments concerned, including our own, to be satisfied about the scale of provision.

2. Invaluable meat is being wasted, and at the same time the Americans are complaining that the Australians and New Zealanders are withdrawing men

from the front, while the Australians blithely retort that they have all come back to grow meat for the American Army.

Unless your reply to me is of a satisfactory character I shall have to telegraph to the President. I ought to have done it weeks ago.

Prime Minister to Lord Cherwell   30 Apr. 44

Before I approve the Admiralty's paper [on the German acoustic torpedo ("Gnat")] let me know whether there is anything in the following idea:

Fire a mechanism from a depth-charge projector, which would be called a "Squawker." This might either lie (floating or submerged) where it fell, and "squawk," or it might be given a motion likely to intercept a "Gnat." There seems to be no reason why fifteen or twenty of these, fired at the right time and on a reasonable judgment of the enemy's attack, might not attract him.

Alternatively, "Squawkers" might circle round our own ships at moments of danger. They would do them no harm if they hit them, but they might cover their tails very effectively.

Is there anything in this?

May

Prime Minister to Foreign Secretary, and to   1 May 44
General Hollis for C.O.S. Committee

I am all for getting the Brazilian division into Italy as soon as possible. Every effort should be made, subject to battle exigencies, to bring this [division] into Italy. There should be no talk of a token force. The above also applies to the air squadron.

Prime Minister to Foreign Secretary   4 May 44

A paper should be drafted for the Cabinet, and possibly for the Imperial Conference, setting forth shortly — for that is essential — the brute issues between us and the Soviet Government which are developing in Italy, in Rumania, in Bulgaria, in Yugoslavia, and above all in Greece. It ought to be possible to get this on one page.

Broadly speaking, the issue is, Are we going to acquiesce in the Communisation of the Balkans and perhaps of Italy? Mr. Curtin touched upon this today, and I am of opinion on the whole that we ought to come to a definite conclusion about it, and that if our conclusion is that we resist the Communist infusion and invasion, we should put it to them pretty plainly at the best moment that military events permit. We should of course have to consult the United States first.

Prime Minister to Foreign Secretary   4 May 44

Pray consider whether it might not be wise for us to recall our Ambassador from Moscow for consultation. We should like to have a talk to him. It would make a good gap with the Russians at the present time. Averell Harriman has already departed for the United States.

2. Let me know how you feel about this. I am not very clear on it myself, but evidently we are approaching a showdown with the Russians about their Communist intrigues in Italy, Yugoslavia, and Greece, and I do not think they would like very much a period in which they had neither a British nor an American Ambassador in Moscow. I must say I think their attitude becomes more difficult every day. I hope you have had a talk with Harriman. Take some opportunity of telling me about all this.

Prime Minister to General Ismay 7 May 44

I do not like press conferences, even off the record, on the eve of an important battle. Once zero hour has struck, the principles desired by General Alexander should be inculcated upon the press, who should be allowed to mingle in the fighting. I have recently been perturbed at reported statements from Naples, one in the *Corriere*, explaining that we are about to attack. Is it really necessary to tell the enemy this? Of course, he may possibly think we are such fools that it is an obvious blind, but this is a dangerous chance to take.

Prime Minister to General Hollis 7 May 44

I certainly expressed myself strongly against these military missions to Algiers, from what I heard about them at the Gibraltar Conference, and I greatly regret that they should have piled themselves up and ensconced themselves at Algiers where they are not needed in any way, but only add to the horribly bloated staffs which are lurking there, most of them away from all participation in the war. I certainly wish this matter to be taken up with a view to recalling and putting to some useful work these highly paid and no doubt highly skilled and experienced officers. The best thing would be to form a Sacred Legion of about one thousand Staff officers and let them set an example to the troops in leading some particularly desperate attack. Anyhow, the missions should be liquidated.

Prime Minister to Director of Military Intelligence 7 May 44

Please let me have the best return possible of killed, wounded, and prisoners in Italy, by nationalities, including Germans, together with the ratio in all cases as far as possible between (a) killed and missing and (b) killed, wounded, and missing. We seem to have lost 38,000 in killed, missing, and prisoners of war; whereas we have taken about 35,000 prisoners of war, to which should perhaps be added 20,000 killed, making a total missing and killed of, say, 55,000 Germans to our over-all figure of 38,000, of whom 19,000 were killed. This is upon the fronts of armies where the enemy is on the whole considerably the smaller. It seems to me that very satisfactory figures might emerge from this final calculation, even though on the whole fronts our ratio of killed to missing is less satisfactory than the Americans'.

Prime Minister to Foreign Secretary 7 May 44

I am puzzled at the procedure which Ambassador Clark Kerr uses in Moscow.

Apparently he takes every telegram and delivers it personally to Molotov or Stalin, whichever he can get at, and waits sometimes for several days if these potentates are away or do not choose to give audience. Now there are some telegrams which certainly he should deliver himself, but should not others be sent by an officer and be presented? I wish you would let me know what is the proper usage about all this. It seems to me that it would be much better, for instance when we send a very stiff message, not to have our man waiting about to be bulldozed and afterwards sometimes offer deprecatory observations which weaken the force of what it has been decided to say.

Prime Minister to Lord Privy Seal   7 May 44

I feel sure you cannot have looked into the extraordinary consequences of our coming out of this war owing India a bigger debt, after having defended her, than we owed to the United States at the end of the last war. Your note does not seem at all to take into consideration these frightful consequences.

Prime Minister to First Lord of the Admiralty   10 May 44

Thank you for your report of April 5 about the "Gnat." It occurred to me that if fifteen or twenty noise-makers (which might be called "Squawkers") could be fired overboard from a depth-charge or other projector at the right time they might attract and distract the "Gnats." This would have the great advantage of avoiding any towing gear and the other demerits of "Foxers."

I am glad to learn that you are thinking and working on these lines, and I hope you will be able to get these "Squawkers" into operation soon.[12]

Prime Minister to Lord Portal   14 May 44

It is now some months since I begged you to have some more samples made of your prefabricated house.[13] I hear that each one takes about six weeks' labour to prepare, and that in addition to the house at the Tate Gallery another has been constructed and is on its way to Scotland for exhibition, and two others are shortly to be built, with all the improvements. I am very glad to hear of this, although it is less than I had hoped. You must give your house a chance to be seen by working women and people of all classes. Please see that the ones you are making are pressed on.

Prime Minister to Secretary of State for Air   20 May 44

You have been asked to supply twenty-five thousand men from the R.A.F. Regiment, which was built up in quite different circumstances from those which now exist. These men are vitally needed for the support of the Army in the forthcoming battle. I was willing to go into this in detail with you at an early date, but as I have to make a speech in the House on Wednesday of this

[12] See minute of April 30 to Lord Cherwell.
[13] See minute of April 2 to Minister of Works.

week I could not find the time beforehand. Meanwhile I have asked that you supply two thousand good men for the upkeep of the Guards. They will be much better employed there than loafing around overcrowded airfields warding off dangers which have ceased to threaten. I must ask you to comply with this request. Otherwise it will be necessary to bring the matter before the War Cabinet on Tuesday next at a special meeting, for immediate decision. I must make it clear that this is without prejudice to the further demands that will be made upon you by a committee which will be set up for the purpose of extracting the necessary men.

2. The Army have already had a very considerable comb-out from their anti-aircraft regiments of men suitable for infantry, and it is quite wrong at the present stage in the war to retain many of the first-class men in the R.A.F. Regiment in a purely passive rôle.

3. There is of course no difficulty in effecting the transfer. This was clearly shown when both the Army and the R.A.F. transferred men to the Navy at the end of last year, when there was an urgent need for landing-craft crews. I have little doubt that many would volunteer, but everyone well understands in these days that men must be directed to where their services can best be used in the common task.

4. I therefore ask you to help me by carrying out my request for the two thousand men. Time is short and the need urgent.[14]

Prime Minister to C.I.G.S.   21 May 44

Why are we told that the 1st Polish Armoured Division cannot function because there are not sufficient rear administrative units available to maintain it? Surely a reasonable effort at adjustment could be made to enable this fine division to strengthen our already too slender forces on the Continent. Pray let me have an account of the deficiencies.

Prime Minister to Minister of Production   21 May 44

Thank you for your minute of May 11 about penicillin. By all means try to get as large an allocation from America as you can, but do not let anything stand in the way of increasing our output here. It does not seem as if we shall produce much this year.

Prime Minister to Mr. Sandys   21 May 44

You might read this report [from General O'Connor, about the armour protection and escape arrangements of the Cromwell tank], and make any remarks you like about it tomorrow in writing. I had rather gathered the idea that the difficulty about the lower man escaping would become extreme if the cordite or the petrol in the compartment above him caught fire. Perhaps you can reassure me on this.

[14] Two thousand men were transferred in June 1944.

Prime Minister to Foreign Secretary   22 May 44

It is said about Foreign Office minutes that if you read the odd paragraph numbers and the even paragraph numbers in series you get both sides of the case fully stated. Why would it not be sufficient to say, both to the United States and Russia, "We are not in favour of giving Italy Allied status at this stage"?

2. I have read this telegram through, and it states very well all the arguments for and against every course, with a highly questionable and unexpected conclusion that "a partial peace treaty should be arranged with Italy as soon as conditions permit." It may well be that even when all the Governments meet together there will be no peace treaty after the fall of Hitler, but only a prolonged armistice.

3. I am sure you would find that a shorter, simple indication of our position would carry more weight and would be more likely to reach the highest quarters. Pray speak to me about this, especially if you do not like my comments.

Prime Minister to Foreign Secretary, Minister of War Transport,   23 May 44
Minister of Production, and Minister of Food

All this matter [reduction of imports on account of "Overlord"] is left between Lord Leathers and General Eisenhower, but I have said that I would sacrifice five hundred thousand tons additional imports into this country for the next four months, provided that the United States guarantee this amount shall be made up in the two or three months following. Twenty-four millions a year is our absolute minimum.

Prime Minister to Foreign Secretary   23 May 44

I saw in one of the papers that Russia was about to recognise the provisional Government of France. I approved of your telegram to Sir A. Clark Kerr. This has not perhaps reached Stalin, but the matter is very important, because I am determined not to sever myself from the President on this and be found lining up with Russia against him. It would be very bad if we had to say that Russia did not consult us on this matter and that we are now in consultation with the United States. But even that would be better than a line-up by Britain and Russia against the President. In fact, I would have nothing to do with it on this subject. Russia has no right to take this step without consultation with her two Allies, who are doing all the fighting in the West.

Prime Minister to General Ismay, for C.O.S. Committee   25 May 44

Obviously garrisons must be provided by the British Empire for redeemed territories. The problem will become insoluble if it is to be expressed in the usual jargon of divisions. Once the enemy has been driven out, battalions and armoured car companies, with occasional assignments of artillery and tanks, all fitted to the particular districts concerned, are all that is needed. There must be a mass of troops in India who could be drawn upon for this.

2. A division is a kind of athletic entity, capable of the highest operations of war   It has nothing whatever to do with the particular static or mobile police forces which are required to hold down doubtful countries. These should always have a large admixture of local people, and they have never got to consider the question of bringing seventy guns into action at one time.

Prime Minister to Foreign Secretary   25 May 44

As I see it, the Big Three or Big Four will be the trustees or steering committee of the whole body in respect of the use of force to prevent war; but I think much larger bodies, and possibly functional bodies, would deal with the economic side. You should make it clear that we have no idea of three or four Great Powers ruling the world. On the contrary, their victory will entitle them to serve the world in the supreme respect of preventing the outbreak of more wars. We should certainly not be prepared ourselves to submit to an economic, financial, and monetary system laid down, by, say, Russia, or the United States with her fagot-vote China.

The Supreme World Council or Executive is not to rule the nations. It is only to prevent them tearing each other in pieces. I feel I could argue this very strongly from the point of view of derogation of national sovereignties.

Prime Minister to Minister of Food   26 May 44

I am glad to hear of all you say about better rations, and think what you are doing very wise. Try to cut out petty annoyances, whether in the hotels, the little shops, or the private lives of ordinary people. Nothing should be done for spite's sake. The great work of rationing in this country, which has given so much confidence and absence of class feeling, should not be prejudiced by little trumpery regulations which when enforced make hard cases. Let me have some of your ideas on this.

Prime Minister to Foreign Secretary   27 May 44

It is a great pity, when an important message agreed upon between us has been sent to Stalin from me, that it should not be delivered as fast as possible. There would always be an opportunity for the Ambassador to give a warning if he thought it would do extreme harm, and in exceptional cases he might use his discretion. But the idea that the message should be left hanging about in Moscow for four, five, or six days to find time for Stalin to see him, or until he returns from the front, cannot be necessary. An officer in uniform should be given facilities to deliver the message as a letter.

Sometimes misunderstandings arise because one sends a message and waits a long time for an answer. After it comes, one finds it is quite a nice answer, but meanwhile one has been thinking the worse of the silence. Nothing should stand in the way of prompt communication.[15]

[15] See minute of May 7 to Foreign Secretary.

Prime Minister to C.I.G.S.   27 May 44

Please do not on any account let the Polish Division be kept out of the battle-front. Not only is it a magnificent fighting force, but its exploits will help to keep alive the soul of Poland, on which much turns in the future. Could I kindly have a list of the rearward services which it lacks, showing the number of vehicles, officers, personnel, etc.?

P.S. General Bedell Smith says he can help in getting some drafts for this division by flying them from Africa and the United States.[16]

Prime Minister to Minister of Aircraft Production   27 May 44

Many congratulations on the record flight of 506 miles per hour set up by De Haviland's jet aircraft. Please pass this on to those concerned.

I am a little perturbed to hear that you are proposing to centralise jet-propulsion development in your new Government company. There is a great deal to be said for encouraging overlapping in research and development rather than putting all the eggs in one basket. I quite appreciate that the many delays in jet-propulsion development may have led you to consider that some new organisation is required, but I wonder whether it is wise to remove work on jet-propulsion from Farnborough, where I understand much solid work has been done, and where it is so easy for engine and aircraft development to proceed hand in hand.[17]

Prime Minister to Minister of Fuel and Power   27 May 44

I hope you will put a stop to nonsense like this. [Report in the *Yorkshire Post* that a householder was fined one pound, with two guineas costs, for having borrowed coal from a neighbour.] Nothing makes departments so unpopular as these acts of petty bureaucratic folly which come to light from time to time, and are, I fear, only typical of a vast amount of silly wrongdoing by small officials or committees.

You should make an example of the people concerned with this.

Prime Minister to First Lord and First Sea Lord   28 May 44

Do not hesitate to be blunt with these Russians when they become unduly truculent. This is better done by manner and attitude than by actual words, which can be reported, and also by neglect of certain civilities to the superior people when they have been intolerably offensive. They should certainly be given a feeling that we are not afraid of them.

2. On the other hand, any ceremonial they may wish in regard to the handing over of the vessels [British warships in lieu of Italian] should be staged with the utmost formality and made a public success. I am certainly not going to communicate with Marshal Stalin about any of this. It is for the Russians to show gratitude rather than for us to show deference. All friendly relations

[16] See minute of May 21 to C.I.G.S.
[17] See minutes of July 31 and October 6, 1943.

between the junior officers should be cultivated. Not one word of thanks has ever been expressed to us for this transfer of ships. We have borne the brunt of meeting their requests for shipping. There are all sorts of ways of making people feel that you resent their insults.

3. If however their conduct improves, you should neglect nothing which will encourage this amendment.

Prime Minister to Deputy Supreme Commander,   29 May 44
Allied Expeditionary Force

Thank you for your minute of May 11 about Mailly-le-Camp [German tank training depot]. There is no doubt that the attack on this compact target was a great success. It would seem right, as we urged, to continue to give a high priority to operations of this sort, which contribute directly towards the disorganisation of the German armies and involve no French casualties.

Have you exceeded the ten thousand limit [of French civilian casualties]?

Prime Minister to First Lord   29 May 44

The reason why this Communist newspaper has not been allowed to send war correspondents to operational theatres or to occasions where security has to be maintained is because Communists do not hesitate to betray any British or American secrets they may find to the Communist Party, no doubt for transmission to Russia. In this case any betrayal they may make to their masters will not do any harm. They should however be told that the Russian Government have stipulated that not a word is to get out about these ships until they have safely made their way to Russia. They will certainly obey this injunction once it is proved to them. Their treason and their loyalties only work on single tracks. In these circumstances I approve of their being invited, after having been made acquainted with the fact that the Russians have stipulated that the secret is to be kept till the ships are safely in Russian hands.

Appendix C, Book Two

MINISTERIAL APPOINTMENTS

June 1943–*June* 1944

(Members of the War Cabinet are shown in italics)

Prime Minister and First Lord of the Treasury, Minister of Defence	*Mr. Winston S. Churchill*
Admiralty, First Lord of the	Mr. A. V. Alexander
Agriculture and Fisheries, Minister of	Mr. R. S. Hudson
Air, Secretary of State for	Sir Archibald Sinclair
Aircraft Production, Minister of	Sir Stafford Cripps
Burma, Secretary of State for	Mr. L. S. Amery
Chancellor of the Duchy of Lancaster	(*a*) Mr. A. Duff Cooper
	(*b*) Mr. Ernest Brown (appointed November 17, 1943)
Chancellor of the Exchequer (Treasury)	(*a*) Sir Kingsley Wood
	(*b*) *Sir John Anderson* (appointed September 28, 1943)
Colonies, Secretary of State for the	Colonel Oliver Stanley
Dominion Affairs, Secretary of State for	(*a*) *Mr. Clement Attlee*
	(*b*) Viscount Cranborne (appointed September 28, 1943)
Economic Warfare, Minister of	The Earl of Selborne
Education, President of the Board of	Mr. R. A. Butler (By the Education Act, 1944, the title of the office was changed to "Minister of Education")
Food, Minister of	(*a*) Lord Woolton
	(*b*) Colonel J. J. Llewellin (appointed November 12, 1943)
Foreign Affairs, Secretary of State for	*Mr. Anthony Eden*
Fuel and Power, Minister of	Major G. Lloyd George
Health, Minister of	(*a*) Mr. Ernest Brown
	(*b*) Mr. H. U. Willink (appointed November 17, 1943)
Home Department, Secretary of State for the	*Mr. Herbert Morrison*
India, Secretary of State for	Mr. L. S. Amery
Information, Minister of	Mr. Brendan Bracken
Labour and National Service, Minister of	*Mr. Ernest Bevin*
Law Officers:	
Attorney-General	Sir Donald Somervell
Lord Advocate	Mr. J. S. C. Reid
Solicitor-General	Sir David Maxwell Fyfe
Solicitor-General for Scotland	Sir David King Murray
Lord Chancellor	Viscount Simon

716

Lord President of the Council	(a) *Sir John Anderson*
	(b) *Mr. Clement Attlee*
	(appointed September 28, 1943)
Lord Privy Seal	(a) Viscount Cranborne
	(b) Lord Beaverbrook
	(appointed September 28, 1943)
Minister of State	Mr. R. K. Law
	(appointed September 25, 1943)
Minister without Portfolio	Sir William Jowitt
Paymaster-General	Lord Cherwell
Pensions, Minister of	Sir Walter Womersley
Postmaster-General	Captain H. F. C. Crookshank
Production, Minister of	*Mr. Oliver Lyttelton*
Reconstruction, Minister of	*Lord Woolton*
	(appointed November 12, 1943)
Scotland, Secretary of State for	Mr. Thomas Johnston
Supply, Minister of	Sir Andrew Duncan
Town and Country Planning, Minister of	Mr. W. S. Morrison
	(appointed February 5, 1943)
Trade, President of the Board of	Mr. Hugh Dalton
War, Secretary of State for	Sir James Grigg
War Transport, Minister of	Lord Leathers
Works, Minister of	Lord Portal
Ministers Overseas:	
Middle East, Minister of State Resident in the	(a) *Mr. R. G. Casey*
	(until December 23, 1943)
	(b) Lord Moyne
	(appointed January 29, 1944)
	(c) Sir Edward Grigg
	(appointed November 22, 1944)
Washington, Minister Resident for Supply in	(a) Colonel J. J. Llewellin
	(b) Mr. Ben Smith
	(appointed November 12, 1943)
Allied Force Headquarters, Mediterranean Command, Minister Resident at	Mr. Harold Macmillan
West Africa, Minister Resident in	Viscount Swinton
Middle East, Deputy Minister of State Resident in the	Lord Moyne
	(until January 29, 1944, when office lapsed)
House of Lords, Leader of the	Viscount Cranborne
House of Commons, Leader of the	*Mr. Anthony Eden*

★

INDEX

INDEX

746   INDEX

Simeto River, 34

Simon, Viscount, Lord Chancellor, minute to, 648

Sinclair, Sir Archibald, Secretary of State for Air, minutes to, 644, 650, 652, 697, 703, 705–06, 710–11

Singapore, 575–76, 577–78

Ski-sites, so-called, in Northern France, 236, 239

Slessor, Sir John, Air-Marshal, appointed Chief of Coastal Air Command, 6–7

Smith, General Walter Bedell (U.S.), Secretary, Combined Chiefs of Staff, and Chief of Staff to Eisenhower, 105, 106, 424, 428, 431, 434, 441, 448, 511, 529, 585, 625, 626, 630; opens negotiations with Badoglio's emissary at Lisbon, 105–06; meeting with Castellano in Sicily, 108–09; signs Italian Armistice terms, 111

Smolensk, 260

Smuts, General J. C., Prime Minister of the Union of South Africa, message to, on Mediterranean, from Churchill, 35–36; exchanges with Churchill on conduct of war, 126–31, 491–94; his reminiscences of Vereeniging, 625–26

Solomon Islands, retrospect of sea and air fights around, 20–21; campaign of '43–'44, 556–58

Somerville, Admiral Sir James, Churchill's minute as to, 707

South Dakota, U.S.S., damaged, 18

Southeast Asia Command, proposals as to forming, 77–78; decisions at Quebec regarding, 86. *See also* Mountbatten

Southern France, diversionary attack on, plans for. *See* "Anvil"

Spaatz, Major-General Carl, Commander of U.S. Army Air Force, 27

Spears, Sir Edward, H.M. Minister to Syria and Lebanon, 185

Speer, Dr., German Minister of Munitions, 230, 520, 521, 523, 527

Spruance, Raymond A., Admiral (U.S.N.), Commander of forces at taking of Marshall Islands, 558, 559

"Squawker" mechanism, 708, 710

Stalin, Marshal Joseph, congratulates Roosevelt and Churchill on Naples landing, 144; note to Churchill on winter convoys and British personnel in North Russia, 267–69; on meeting of heads of three Governments, 277–78; to Churchill and Roosevelt rejecting Fairbanks as place of meeting and agreeing to Foreign Ministers' Conference, 279–80; proposes Moscow for Foreign Ministers' Conference, Persia for personal meeting between heads of three Governments, 281; on arrangements at "Cairo Three" (Teheran), 307; informs Churchill Molotov cannot go to Cairo, 320; statement of, on joining war against Japan, 349; on Russian Front and European operations, 349–50; on the Mediterranean, 351; addresses questions to Churchill on military plans in Europe, 353–56; views on Turkey's entrance into war, 355; strongly favours invading Southern France to help "Overlord," 356; conversation with Churchill on Germany and the post-war world, 359–61; on the Polish question, 361–62; expresses views on China and "Four Policemen" theory, 363; receives Stalingrad Sword of Honour from Churchill, 363–64; at second plenary session, on importance of selecting Commander for "Overlord," 365–66; declaration on Soviet attitude to Bulgaria in event of Turkish entry into the war, 368; attitude of, on "Overlord," 369–71, 373; is host at dinner, 373–74; direct personal interview with Churchill, 376–81; raises at luncheon of "Three Only" question of warm-water ports for Russia, 381; revision of Treaty of Sèvres, 381; agreeable to Staffs collaborating on